T0236336

Lecture Notes in Computer Science   9879

Commenced Publication in 1973
Founding and Former Series Editors:
Gerhard Goos, Juris Hartmanis, and Jan van Leeuwen

Editorial Board

David Hutchison
  Lancaster University, Lancaster, UK
Takeo Kanade
  Carnegie Mellon University, Pittsburgh, PA, USA
Josef Kittler
  University of Surrey, Guildford, UK
Jon M. Kleinberg
  Cornell University, Ithaca, NY, USA
Friedemann Mattern
  ETH Zurich, Zurich, Switzerland
John C. Mitchell
  Stanford University, Stanford, CA, USA
Moni Naor
  Weizmann Institute of Science, Rehovot, Israel
C. Pandu Rangan
  Indian Institute of Technology, Madras, India
Bernhard Steffen
  TU Dortmund University, Dortmund, Germany
Demetri Terzopoulos
  University of California, Los Angeles, CA, USA
Doug Tygar
  University of California, Berkeley, CA, USA
Gerhard Weikum
  Max Planck Institute for Informatics, Saarbrücken, Germany

More information about this series at http://www.springer.com/series/7410

Ioannis Askoxylakis · Sotiris Ioannidis
Sokratis Katsikas · Catherine Meadows (Eds.)

Computer Security – ESORICS 2016

21st European Symposium on Research in Computer Security
Heraklion, Greece, September 26–30, 2016
Proceedings, Part II

 Springer

Editors

Ioannis Askoxylakis
Institute of Computer Science
Foundation for Research and
  Technology - Hellas
Heraklion
Greece

Sotiris Ioannidis
Institute of Computer Science
Foundation for Research and
  Technology - Hellas
Heraklion
Greece

Sokratis Katsikas
Norwegian University of Science and
  Technology
Gjøvik
Norway

Catherine Meadows
Naval Research Laboratory
Washington, DC
USA

ISSN 0302-9743   ISSN 1611-3349 (electronic)
Lecture Notes in Computer Science
ISBN 978-3-319-45740-6   ISBN 978-3-319-45741-3 (eBook)
DOI 10.1007/978-3-319-45741-3

Library of Congress Control Number: 2016950583

LNCS Sublibrary: SL4 – Security and Cryptology

© Springer International Publishing Switzerland 2016
This work is subject to copyright. All rights are reserved by the Publisher, whether the whole or part of the material is concerned, specifically the rights of translation, reprinting, reuse of illustrations, recitation, broadcasting, reproduction on microfilms or in any other physical way, and transmission or information storage and retrieval, electronic adaptation, computer software, or by similar or dissimilar methodology now known or hereafter developed.
The use of general descriptive names, registered names, trademarks, service marks, etc. in this publication does not imply, even in the absence of a specific statement, that such names are exempt from the relevant protective laws and regulations and therefore free for general use.
The publisher, the authors and the editors are safe to assume that the advice and information in this book are believed to be true and accurate at the date of publication. Neither the publisher nor the authors or the editors give a warranty, express or implied, with respect to the material contained herein or for any errors or omissions that may have been made.

Printed on acid-free paper

This Springer imprint is published by Springer Nature
The registered company is Springer International Publishing AG Switzerland

Preface

This volume contains papers selected for presentation and publication at the 21st European Symposium on Research in Computer Security, ESORICS, held September 26–30, in Heraklion, Greece.

Out of 285 submissions from 40 countries, the conference accepted 60 papers, resulting in an acceptance rate of 21 %. These papers cover a wide range of topics in security and privacy, including data protection, systems security, network security, access control, authentication, and security in such emerging areas as cloud computing, cyber-physical systems, and the Internet of Things. The papers were reviewed and then discussed online by a 105-member Program Committee, along with 313 external reviewers.

ESORICS 2016 would not have been possible without the contributions of the many volunteers who devoted their time and energy to make this happen. We would like to thank the Program Committee and the external reviewers for their hard work in evaluating the papers. We would also like to thank the ESORICS Steering Committee and its Chair Pierangela Samarati; the Publicity Chairs, Manolis Stamatogiannakis and Youki Kadobayashi; the Local Arrangement Committee, Nikolaos Petroulakis, Andreas Miaoudakis, and Panos Chatziadam, for arranging the beautiful location in Crete; the workshop chair, Javier Lopez, and all workshop co-chairs, who organized workshops co-located with ESORICS. We also give thanks to the many institutions for their support of ESORICS: the Horizon 2020 projects SHARCS and Virtuwind, the Hellenic Authority for Communication Security and Privacy (ADAE), the European Agency for Network and Information Security (ENISA), Huawei Technologies Co., Bournemouth University, and the CIPSEC project.

Finally, we would like to give our thanks to the authors who submitted their papers to ESORICS. They, more than anyone else, are what makes this conference possible.

Welcome to ESORICS 2016!

July 2016

Ioannis Askoxylakis
Sotiris Ioannidis
Sokratis Katsikas
Catherine Meadows

Organization

General Chairs

Ioannis Askoxylakis   Hellenic Authority for Communication Security
and Privacy (ADAE) & FORTH, Greece
Sotiris Ioannidis   FORTH, Greece

Program Chairs

Sokratis K. Katsikas   Norwegian University of Science and Technology,
Norway
Catherine Meadows   Naval Research Laboratory, USA

Workshops Chair

Javier Lopez   University of Malaga, Spain

Program Committee

Gail-Joon Ahn	Arizona State University, USA
Magnus Almgren	Chalmers University of Technology, Sweden
Manos Antonakakis	Georgia Institute of Technology, USA
Alessandro Armando	DIBRIS - University of Genoa, Italy
Michael Backes	Saarland University and Max Planck Institute for Software Systems, Germany
Giampaolo Bella	Università degli studi di Catania, Italy
Carlo Blundo	Università degli Studi di Salerno, Italy
Stefan Brunthaler	SBA Research, Austria
Rainer Böhme	University of Innsbruck, Austria
Christian Cachin	IBM Research - Zurich, Switzerland
Liqun Chen	Hewlett Packard Labs, UK
Tom Chothia	University of Birmingham, UK
Sherman S.M. Chow	Chinese University of Hong Kong, Hong Kong
Cas Cremers	University of Oxford, UK
Frédéric Cuppens	Telecom Bretagne, France
Nora Cuppens-Boulahia	Telecom Bretagne, France
Mads Dam	KTH, Sweden
Sabrina De Capitani di Vimercati	Università degli Studi di Milano, Italy
Hervé Debar	Télécom SudParis, France
Roberto Di Pietro	Bell Labs, France

Josep Domingo-Ferrer	Universitat Rovira i Virgili, Spain
Pavlos Efraimidis	Democritus University of Thrace, Greece
Hannes Federrath	University of Hamburg, Germany
Bao Feng	Huawei, China
Simone Fischer-Hübner	Karlstad University, Sweden
Riccardo Focardi	Università Ca' Foscari, Italy
Simon Foley	University College Cork, Ireland
Sara Foresti	Università degli Studi di Milano, Italy
Katrin Franke	Norwegian University of Science and Technology, Norway
Felix Freiling	Friedrich-Alexander-Universität Erlangen-Nürnberg, Germany
Dieter Gollmann	Hamburg University of Technology, Germany
Dimitris Gritzalis	Athens University of Economics and Business, Greece
Stefanos Gritzalis	University of the Aegean, Greece
Joshua Guttman	Worcester Polytechnic Institute & MITRE, USA
Gerhard Hancke	City University of Hong Kong, China
Marit Hansen	Unabhängiges Landeszentrum für Datenschutz Schleswig-Holstein, Germany
Feng Hao	Newcastle University, UK
Xinyi Huang	Fujian Normal University, China
Michael Huth	Imperial College London, UK
Aaron D. Jaggard	U.S. Naval Research Laboratory, USA
Sushil Jajodia	George Mason University, USA
Vasilios Katos	Bournemouth University, UK
Dogan Kesdogan	Universität Regensburg, Germany
Kwangjo Kim	Korea Advanced Institute of Science and Technology-KAIST, South Korea
Steve Kremer	Inria Nancy - Grand Est, France
Ralf Küsters	University of Trier, Germany
Junzuo Lai	Singapore Management University, Singapore
Costas Lambrinoudakis	University of Piraeus, Greece
Peeter Laud	Cybernetica AS, Estonia
Adam J. Lee	University of Pittsburgh, USA
Ninghui Li	Purdue University, USA
Yingjiu Li	Singapore Management University, Singapore
Antonio Lioy	Politecnico di Torino, Italy
Peng Liu	The Pennsylvania State University, USA
Javier Lopez	University of Malaga, Spain
Pratyusa K. Manadhata	Hewlett-Packard Laboratories, USA
Luigi V. Mancini	Università di Roma "La Sapienza", Italy
Heiko Mantel	TU Darmstadt, Germany
Olivier Markowitch	Université Libre de Bruxelles (ULB), Belgium
Fabio Martinelli	IIT-CNR, Italy
Antonio Maña	University of Malaga, Spain
John Mitchell	Stanford University, USA

Aikaterini Mitrokotsa	Chalmers University of Technology, Sweden
Refik Molva	EURECOM, France
Charles Morisset	Newcastle University, UK
Flemming Nielson	Technical University of Denmark, Denmark
Rolf Oppliger	eSECURITY Technologies, Switzerland
Stefano Paraboschi	Università di Bergamo, Italy
Dusko Pavlovic	University of Hawaii, USA
Roberto Perdisci	University of Georgia, USA
Olivier Pereira	Université catholique de Louvain, Belgium
Günther Pernul	Universität Regensburg, Germany
Wolter Pieters	Delft University of Technology, The Netherlands
Michalis Polychronakis	Stony Brook University, USA
Joachim Posegga	University of Passau, Germany
Kui Ren	State University of New York at Buffalo, USA
Mark Ryan	University of Birmingham, UK
Peter Y.A. Ryan	University of Luxembourg, Luxembourg
Andrei Sabelfeld	Chalmers University of Technology, Sweden
Rei Safavi-Naini	University of Calgary, Canada
Pierangela Samarati	Università degli Studi di Milano, Italy
Ravi Sandhu	University of Texas at San Antonio, USA
Ralf Sasse	ETH Zürich, Switzerland
Nitesh Saxena	University of Alabama at Birmingham, USA
Andreas Schaad	Huawei European Research Center, Germany
Steve Schneider	University of Surrey, UK
Joerg Schwenk	Ruhr-Universität Bochum, Germany
Basit Shafiq	Lahore University of Management Sciences, Pakistan
Ben Smyth	Huawei, France
Einar Snekkenes	Norwegian University of Science and Technology, Norway
Willy Susilo	University of Wollongong, Australia
Krzysztof Szczypiorski	Warsaw University of Technology, Poland
A Min Tjoa	Vienna University of Technology, Austria
Aggeliki Tsohou	Ionian University, Greece
Jaideep Vaidya	Rutgers University, USA
Vijay Varadharajan	Macquarie University, Australia
Luca Viganò	King's College London, UK
Michael Waidner	Fraunhofer SIT and TU Darmstadt, Germany
Cong Wang	City University of Hong Kong, China
Edgar Weippl	SBA Research, Austria
Christos Xenakis	University of Piraeus, Greece
Meng Yu	University of Texas at San Antonio, USA
Ben Zhao	University of California at Santa Barbara, USA
Jianying Zhou	Institute for Infocomm Research, Singapore
Sencun Zhu	The Pennsylvania State University, USA

Additional Reviewers

Ahmed, Tahmina
Akand, Mamun
Ali, Mohammed
Aliberti, Giulio
Aminanto, Muhamad Erza
Anagnostopoulos, Marios
Anand, S. Abhishek
Asghari, Hadi
Asif, Hafiz
Axelsson, Stefan
Bacis, Enrico
Balliu, Musard
Bardas, Alexandru G.
Batten, Ian
Baumann, Christoph
Bayou, Lyes
Bello, Luciano
Berrang, Pascal
Bhatt, Sandeep
Biswas, Bhaskar
Blanco-Justicia, Alberto
Bruni, Alessandro
Bugiel, Sven
Calzavara, Stefano
Carbone, Roberto
Carmichael, Peter
Cha, Sang Gil
Chang, Bing
Chen, Ping
Chen, Rongmao
Cheng, Yuan
Choi, Rakyong
Chu, Cheng Kang
Chu, Cheng-Kang
Ciampi, Michele
Cianfriglia, Marco
Clarke, Dylan
Cohn-Gordon, Katriel
Coletta, Alessio
Costa, Gabriele
Costantino, Gianpiero
Cuvelier, Edouard

Dai, Ting
Davies, Philip
De Gaspari, Fabio
De Meo, Federico
Dehnel-Wild, Martin
Denzel, Michael
Dimitriadis, Antonios
Djoko, Judicael
Dreier, Jannik
Drogkaris, Prokopios
Drosatos, George
Elkhiyaoui, Kaoutar
Emms, Martin
Engelke, Toralf
Espes, David
Fahl, Sascha
Farràs, Oriol
Fett, Daniel
Fuchs, Ludwig
Garratt, Luke
Garrison, William
Gay, Richard
Geneiatakis, Dimitris
Georgiopoulou,
    Zafeiroula
Giannetsos, Thanassis
Giustolisi, Rosario
Gottschlich, Wolfram
Grohmann, Bjoern
Guan, Le
Guanciale, Roberto
Guarnieri, Marco
Gupta, Maanak
Gyftopoulos, Sotirios
Hallberg, Sven M.
Hallgren, Per
Han, Jinguang
Hassan, Sabri
Haupert, Vincent
He, Yongzhong
Hedin, Daniel
Henricksen, Matt

Hitaj, Briland
Horst, Matthias
Hu, Wenhui
Huang, Heqing
Huang, Qiong
Hummer, Matthias
Iliadis, John
Imran-Daud, Malik
Iovino, Vincenzo
Iwaya Horn, Leonardo
Jackson, Dennis
Jager, Tibor
Jarecki, Stanislaw
Jasser, Stefanie
Jiang, Hemin
Journault, Anthony
Kamm, Liina
Kandias, Miltos
Karegar, Farzaneh
Karopoulos, George
Koshutanski, Hristo
Koutsiamanis,
    Remous Aris
Krishnan, Ram
Kuchta, Veronika
Kunz, Michael
Kywe, Su Mon
Köhler, Olaf Markus
Lai, Russell W.F.
Lancrenon, Jean
Laube, Stefan
Lauer, Sebastian
Leichter, Carl
Lerman, Liran
Li, Depeng
Li, Yan
Li, Yuping
Lim, Hoon Wei
Lindemann, Jens
Lindner, Andreas
Liu, Jianghua
Liu, Naiwei

Liu, Ximing
Liu, Xing
Luhn, Sebastian
Lyvas, Christos
Ma, Jinhua
Magkos, Emmanouil
Magri, Bernardo
Manoharan, Praveen
Manulis, Mark
Marktscheffel, Tobias
Martinovic, Ivan
Marwah, Manish
Marx, Matthias
McCorry, Patrick
Mehrnezhad, Maryam
Meng, Weizhi
Merlo, Alessio
Meyer, Maxime
Min, Byungho
Moataz, Tarik
Mogire, Nancy
Mohamed, Manar
Mohammadi, Esfandiar
Montoya, Lorena
Moore, Nicholas
Mowbray, Miranda
Mueller, Johannes
Mykoniati, Maria
Mylonas, Alexios
Möser, Malte
Müller, Tilo
Müller, Tobias
Nelson, Mark
Nemati, Hamed
Neupane, Ajaya
Nguyen, Binh
Nuñez, David
Ntantogian, Christoforos
Önen, Melek
Pagnin, Elena
Palmieri, Paolo
Panico, Agostino
Pankova, Alisa
Park, Jaehong
Parra Rodriguez, Juan D.
Parra-Arnau, Javier

Peroli, Michele
Peters, Thomas
Petrovic, Slobodan
Pham, Vinh
Pitropakis, Nikolaos
Pridöhl, Henning
Puchta, Alexander
Pulls, Tobias
Quaglia, Elizabeth
Radomirovic, Sasa
Rafnsson, Willard
Ranise, Silvio
Rao, Prasad
Reif, Sebastian
Reinecke, Philipp
Rekleitis, Evangelos
Ren, Chuangang
Reuben, Jenni
Rial, Alfredo
Ribeiro De Mello,
    Emerson
Ribes-González, Jordi
Ricci, Sara
Richthammer, Hartmut
Rios, Ruben
Rizomiliotis, Panagiotis
Rocchetto, Marco
Rochet, Florentin
Roenne, Peter
Roth, Christian
Rothstein Morris, Eric
Ruan, Na
Salas, Julián
Saracino, Andrea
Schmitz, Guido
Schranz, Oliver
Schreckling, Daniel
Schöttle, Pascal
Seidel, Peter-Michael
Sgandurra, Daniele
Shafienejad, Masoumeh
Shah, Ankit
Shahandashti, Siamak
Sharifian, Setareh
Sheikhalishahi, Mina
Shi, Jie

Shirvanian, Maliheh
Shojaie, Bahareh
Shrestha, Babins
Shrestha, Prakash
Shulman, Haya
Sideri, Maria
Siim, Sander
Sjösten, Alexander
Soria-Comas, Jordi
Sorniotti, Alessandro
Sprick, Barbara
Squarcina, Marco
Stamatelatos, Giorgos
Stamatiou, Yannis
Staudemeyer, Ralf C.
Stergiopoulos, George
Stüttgen, Johannes
Su, Dong
Sy, Erik
Sänger, Johannes
Taheri, Somayeh
Tasch, Markus
Tasidou, Aimilia
Teheri, Somayeh
Teixeira, André
Tempesta, Mauro
Thoma, Cory
Thompson, Matthew
Truderung, Tomasz
Tsalis, Nikolaos
Tsoumas, Bill
Tupakula, Udaya
Verderame, Luca
Virvilis, Nick
Vrakas, Nikos
Walter, Marie-Therese
Wang, Bolun
Wang, Gang
Wang, Guilin
Wang, Ruoyu
Weber, Alexandra
Weber, Michael
Wei, Zhuo
Williams, David
Wolff, Marcus
Wu, Shuang

Wu, Wei
Wundram, Martin
Wüchner, Tobias
Xiao, Gaoyao
Xing, Xinyu
Xu, Jia
Xu, Ke
Yahia, Muzamil
Yaich, Reda

Yang, Guomin
Yang, Weining
Yautsiukhin, Artsiom
Yerukhimovich, Arkady
Yfantopoulos, Nikos
Yu, Jiangshan
Yu, Xingjie
Yuen, Tsz Hon
Zang, Wanyu

Zavatteri, Matteo
Zerkane, Salaheddine
Zhang, Liang Feng
Zhang, Weiquan
Zhao, Yongjun
Zhou, Lan
Zimmer, Ephraim

Contents – Part II

Attacks

Attribute-Based Cryptography

Contents – Part I

Detection and Monitoring

Cryptography for Cloud Computing

Operating Systems Security

Information Flow

Software Security

Leakage Management and Obfuscation

Towards Efficient Evaluation of a Time-Driven Cache Attack on Modern Processors

Andreas Zankl[1]($\boxtimes$), Katja Miller[1], Johann Heyszl[1], and Georg Sigl[2]

[1] Fraunhofer Research Institution AISEC, Munich, Germany
{andreas.zankl,katja.miller,johann.heyszl}@aisec.fraunhofer.de
[2] Technische Universität München, Munich, Germany
sigl@tum.de

Abstract. Software implementations of block ciphers are widely used to perform critical operations such as disk encryption or TLS traffic protection. To speed up cipher execution, many implementations rely on pre-computed lookup tables, which makes them vulnerable to cache-timing attacks on modern processors. For *time-driven* attacks, the overall execution time of a cipher is sufficient to recover the secret key. Testing cryptographic software on actual hardware is consequently essential for vulnerability and risk assessment. In this work, we investigate the efficient and robust evaluation of cryptographic software on modern processors under a time-driven attack. Using a practical case study, we discuss necessary adaptations to the original attack and identify promising new micro-architectural side-channels for it. To leverage the leakage of multiple side-channels, we propose a simple, heuristic way to combine their corresponding attacks. As an additional benefit, combined attacks simplify a comprehensive evaluation of cryptographic software across multiple different processors. We finally formulate practical evaluation suggestions based on the results of our case study.

Keywords: ARM · New side-channels · Efficient evaluation · Vulnerability testing · Exploiting performance events · Rank estimation · AES

1 Introduction

Block ciphers are commonly used to protect bulk data. Their implementations provide high throughput and consequently focus on fast execution time. In software, processing steps can be saved by using pre-computed lookup tables. The transformation tables of AES are a prominent example of this speed-up technique. The disadvantage of lookup tables is that if they are accessed depending on a secret (e.g. a key), they can introduce a timing side-channel when the software is executed on a processor with cache. In the past, this gave rise to the field of cache attacks. In literature, cache attacks are typically split into three groups: access-driven, trace-driven, or time-driven. Access-driven cache attacks allow a spy program to precisely learn the part of the processor cache (e.g. which cache line) that was accessed by a victim program [18]. In trace-driven cache attacks,

© Springer International Publishing Switzerland 2016
I. Askoxylakis et al. (Eds.): ESORICS 2016, Part II, LNCS 9879, pp. 3–19, 2016.
DOI: 10.1007/978-3-319-45741-3_1

the spy is able to observe the results of a sequence of cache requests issued by the victim (e.g. hit, miss, miss, ...) [1]. For time-driven cache attacks, the spy requires only the overall time the victim needs to complete a cipher run [6–8].

In this work we focus on the time-driven cache attack proposed by Bernstein in 2005 [6], because it is a well-studied attack with minimalistic assumptions about the hardware under attack. It has been applied in settings ranging from mobile phones [14,15] and embedded systems [22,23] to virtual machines used in cloud computing [2]. As the attack relies on execution time measurements, the resolution and quality of the timing source is crucial to the success of the attack. In the original publication [6], time is measured with a hardware-based clock cycle counter. Similarly, Spreitzer and Plos [15], Spreitzer and Gérard [14], and Weiß et al. [22,23] successfully use the cycle count register of ARM Cortex-A8/-A9 processors in the attack. Atici et al. [5] use a level 1 (L1) data cache (D-cache) miss counter on various x86 processors in an adaptation of Bernstein's attack targeted at the last round of AES. In other work, Tiri et al. [17] use an L1 cache miss counter to verify their analytical model for time-driven cache attacks on multiple not further specified processors. Uhsadel et al. [19] investigate the L1/L2 D-cache miss counters as well as a clock cycle counter on x86 processors and apply them in the time-driven cache attack proposed by Bonneau and Mironov [8]. These publications show that so-called hardware performance events like clock cycles and cache misses are valuable side-channels for time-driven cache attacks. As a consequence, these performance events are also critical in an evaluation context, because they allow to construct a worst-case attack scenario. The more an implementation is resistant against attacks using high resolution performance events, the better it withstands less powerful attacker models that are more likely in practice. In addition, the better the side-channel source, the fewer measurements are required to identify leaks in the implementation.

Because of these benefits, we investigate hardware performance events known from literature and new events that have not yet been analyzed in the context of Bernstein's attack. For a fair comparison of the events, the original attack needs to be adapted, because it does not reliably determine the remaining entropy of the secret key after the attack. We therefore extend it with a recent key rank estimation algorithm. To further improve evaluation efficiency and robustness, we propose a new and heuristic way of combining multiple attacks. The combination of attacks is strongly advisable given that all of the performance events in our tests leak information about the secret key. Combined attacks thereby help to construct an improved worst-case test scenario, as they leverage the leakage of multiple performance events while filtering out noisy or poor-quality ones. Given that not all events leak equally on every processor, combined attacks can be used as a global measure to simplify testing across multiple different processors. For our case study, we use the modified attack by Bernstein to test a vulnerable AES implementation taken from the OpenSSL library on an ARM Cortex-A9 processor. Based on the results, we provide practical evaluation suggestions. To the best of our knowledge, our work is the first that discusses Bernstein's cache attack exclusively in an evaluation context and provides efficient ways to determine the vulnerability of a software component to the attack.

The rest of the paper is organized as follows. Background information about the time-driven cache attack by Bernstein is provided in Sect. 2. The application of key rank estimation and its benefits to the attack are discussed in Sect. 3. Our proposal for attack combination is given in Sect. 4. The selection of hardware performance events is discussed in Sect. 5. We shortly present our measurement setup in Sect. 6 before we discuss the results of our case study in Sect. 7. Based on the results, we provide practical suggestions in Sect. 8 before we finally conclude in Sect. 9. Further details about the AES implementation under attack are given in Appendix A.

2   Bernstein's Time-Driven Cache Attack

In 2005, Bernstein [6] proposed a profiled time-driven cache attack and successfully applied it to the T-table-based AES implementation that is part of the OpenSSL library v0.9.7a. The attack is embedded in a client-server scenario, with the client being the spy and the server being the victim. The attack itself consists of four phases: the *learn phase*, the *attack phase*, the *correlation phase*, and the *brute-force key search phase*.[1]

The *learn phase* is the profiling phase of the attack. The spy knows the secret key $\mathbf{k}$ and sends a set of plaintexts to the victim. The responses of the victim contain the overall encryption times. By randomly choosing the inputs and keeping track of the corresponding processing times, the spy creates a cache profile of the lookup tables under the known key $\mathbf{k}$. This is possible, because the lookup indices in the first round of AES are given by the XOR of plaintext and initial key: $\mathbf{p} \oplus \mathbf{k}$. The cache profile is written as matrix $\mathbf{CP_k}[b][v]$ with one row for each input byte in the plaintext (indexed by b) and one column for each byte value (indexed by v). For AES, $\mathbf{CP}$ has the shape 16×256. Every timing measurement is added b times to $\mathbf{CP}$, while the plaintext is used to index the matrix. The input byte positions determine the row, the input byte values specify the column. After all measurements have been added, the average timing is computed for each matrix element and subtracted by the total average of all timings. After sufficient timing observations, the cache profile contains information about which input bytes and values cause longer or shorter processing times. Since the key $\mathbf{k}$ is known in this phase, the cache profile indicates which parts of the lookup tables are cached and which are not cached on average in the first round of AES. In the original work, the known key $\mathbf{k}$ is set to zero and the key length is 128 bits. In the *attack phase*, an unknown key $\tilde{\mathbf{k}}$ is used by the victim. The spy again sends a set of plaintexts, keeps track of the processing times and creates a second cache profile $\mathbf{CP_{\tilde{k}}}[b][v]$, now for the unknown key.

In the *correlation phase*, the spy permutes the profile of the attack phase and correlates it with the one from the learn phase. Permutation is done by accessing the attack profile with indices that are XOR'ed with a possible key hypothesis

---

[1] Naming convention borrowed from the work by Neve et al. [13].

h: $\mathbf{CP}_{\tilde{k}}[b][v \oplus h]$, $h \in \{0, \dots, 255\}$. The correlation is then calculated for each row in the profiles. The profile of the learn phase will be similar to the profile of the attack phase, if permuted by the correct key hypothesis h_c: $\mathbf{CP}_k[b][v] \approx \mathbf{CP}_{\tilde{k}}[b][v \oplus h_c]$. In this case the correlation will peak. The underlying assumption is that in the first round of AES the same parts of the lookup tables are cached or not cached. This causes both profiles to capture the same cache state and allows the correlation phase to compare them. The correlation values for each key byte b and each hypothesis value h are then entered in the correlation matrix $\mathbf{C}[b][h]$. The final step in this phase eliminates hypotheses with low correlation using a variance-based threshold decision. A *brute-force key search phase* is added to assemble key candidates from all left-over hypotheses and to test them against a known plaintext-ciphertext pair. For this step, the attack code iterates over the most likely key candidates and stops when the correct key has been found.

The original attack by Bernstein has a success rate limit that is determined by the cache line size of the target processor and the lookup table entry size of the cipher implementation. If multiple table entries fit on one cache line, they all exhibit the same timing behavior when accessed by the processor. This causes the values of each input byte to form groups with similar timing values in the cache profiles. The number of values per group, which equals the number of table entries per cache line, is denoted as L in this paper. For each hypothesis of a group, the correlation phase generates similar correlation values. As a consequence, a single hypothesis becomes indistinguishable from other members of its group and all of them have to be tested in the brute-force step. This introduces a minimum brute-force effort that cannot be reduced further with the original attack. More information about Bernstein's attack including the success rate limit can be obtained from the work by Neve et al. [13].

3   Key Rank Estimation in Bernstein's Attack

Instead of using the threshold decision in the correlation phase to eliminate unlikely key byte hypotheses, we implement a key rank estimation algorithm, which ranks the correct key against all other key candidates. The rank of the correct key represents the true brute-force effort an attacker would have to spend to recover it. Key rank estimation is necessary during evaluation, because the original threshold decision might eliminate the correct key byte hypothesis from each list. This can happen, if there is little statistical information for one key byte in the measurements. If a correct hypothesis is eliminated, the brute-force step cannot recover the key and fails. In this case there is no resulting brute-force effort that can be evaluated or compared to other attacks. As a consequence, attacks that are marginally successful will hardly ever show useful results. In an evaluation, this must be avoided, because the attack effort is required to determine the current level of security. Especially for testing an implementation on multiple different systems and comparing the results obtained from them, the attack effort must always be available.

In literature, the adverse impact of the threshold decision is noted by Spreitzer and Gérard [14], who rank key candidates instead of eliminating hypotheses with the threshold. In their work they discuss the key rank techniques proposed by Veyrat-Charvillon et al. [20,21]. In contrast, we implement the key rank estimation algorithm proposed by Glowacz et al. [10], because it has an improved time and memory efficiency and scales better to larger key sizes. Since the algorithm expects probabilities instead of correlations, two transformation steps have to be done. First, we calculate Pearson's correlation coefficient instead of taking the original values from the correlation phase. This is necessary, because the original values are not bound to the interval $[-1, 1]$. With the standard formula for Pearson's correlation coefficient we obtain

$$\mathbf{C}'[b][h] = \frac{\sum_{j=0}^{255} \mathbf{CP_k}[b][j] \cdot \mathbf{CP_{\tilde{k}}}[b][j \oplus h]}{\sqrt{\sum_{j=0}^{255} \mathbf{CP_k}[b][j]^2} \cdot \sqrt{\sum_{j=0}^{255} \mathbf{CP_{\tilde{k}}}[b][j \oplus h]^2}}. \tag{1}$$

$\mathbf{C}'[b][h]$ denotes the new correlation matrix with key byte position b and key byte hypothesis h. The second step is to convert the correlation coefficients to probabilities. Using the formula proposed by Gérard and Standaert [11] we obtain

$$\mathbf{P}[b][h] = normalize \left(e^{2 \cdot \mathbf{C}'[b][h]} \right), \tag{2}$$

which is a simplified Bayesian extension of the correlation coefficient distribution approximated with Fisher's transform. $\mathbf{P}[b][h]$ denotes the final probability matrix, which is the input to the key rank estimator. The function $normalize$ scales all values such that each row b in $\mathbf{P}$ sums up to 1. The output of the estimation algorithm is the estimated rank r of the secret key that is limited by an upper (u) and a lower (l) estimation bound, all given in $\log_2$. An attacker would face an estimated brute-force effort of 2^r, but at least 2^l and at most 2^u, to recover the secret key. For a precise estimation, the bound tightness ($u - l$) must be kept small. We choose the estimation precision such that ($u - l$) $\leq$ 1.07 for all estimations in our experiments. As this is sufficiently small for our discussions, we only refer to the estimated key rank r (or the $\log_2$ thereof) in subsequent sections.

4   Proposal for Attack Combination

In the original work by Bernstein, multiple attacks are combined by assigning weights to leftover key byte hypotheses depending on the lengths of the lists they are on. This approach does not work with key rank estimation, because key byte hypotheses are not removed from their lists anymore. We therefore propose a new method for attack combination using the multiplication and normalization step discussed by Mather et al. [12]. To illustrate our method we start with M separate attacks. First, their probability matrices $\mathbf{P_m}[b][h]$, $m \in \{0, ..., M - 1\}$ are calculated as previously explained. Combining two attacks n and $n + 1$ is done by multiplying the probability matrices $\mathbf{P_m}$ element-wise and normalizing the rows of the resulting matrix $\mathbf{P_{Comb}}$ such that they again sum up to 1. The multiplication and normalization step is defined as

$$\mathbf{P_{Comb}}[b][h] = normalize \left(\mathbf{P_n}[b][h] \cdot \mathbf{P_{n+1}}[b][h] \right). \tag{3}$$

This step affects probabilities differently based on their values. In theory, an attack with no information about a key byte will yield a uniform probability distribution for all 256 hypotheses values. All probabilities in one row of $\mathbf{P}$ will have the value $\frac{1}{256}$. To illustrate the combination effects, assume an attack m_0 was given with a probability for the correct hypothesis $p_{h_c} > \frac{1}{256}$. If this attack is combined with an attack m_1 with a uniform probability distribution, the combined attack will exhibit the identical probability values as m_0. If attack m_1 contains a probability $p_{h_c} > \frac{1}{256}$, then after the normalization step the combined attack exhibits a p_{h_c} that is higher than the maximum of m_0 and m_1. This is desirable, because the correct hypothesis is easier to find in the brute-force search. If attack m_1 contains a probability $p_{h_c} < \frac{1}{256}$, the combined attack exhibits a p_{h_c} that is smaller than the one in m_0. This should be avoided, as it increases the brute-force effort. Naturally, it is best to combine only those attacks that improve the probabilities of the correct hypotheses. If all "bad" attacks would yield a uniform probability distribution and all "good" attacks would exhibit a $p_{h_c} > \frac{1}{256}$, combination can be done by simply multiplying and normalizing all available probability matrices. Our practical experiments, however, show that bad attacks often have a slight non-uniform probability distribution with $p_{h_c} < \frac{1}{256}$. Including them in the combination would degrade the combined attack.

We thus propose a heuristic filter approach that excludes bad attacks from the combination. In the first step, all M attacks are ranked according to the sum of their L highest probabilities for a given key byte b. The reason why the L highest probabilities are taken into account is that on a processor where L lookup table entries fit on one cache line, good attacks arrange the hypotheses of one key byte into groups of size L. All hypotheses within a group have almost equal probabilities and are indistinguishable in the rest of the attack. Bad attacks do not exhibit this behavior in our experiments and are thus less likely to get a high rank, if the first L probabilities are considered. More details about the value L in Bernstein's original attack are provided in Sect. 2. Given the ranking of all M attacks, we start with attack m_{1st} that has the largest sum and combine it with attack m_{2nd} that has the second largest sum. We decide to keep the combination, if the probabilities of the L most likely hypotheses from attack m_{1st} increase in the combined attack. Otherwise, the combination is discarded and attack m_{1st} is combined with m_{3rd}. This step is repeated until all available attacks are processed. After the filter and combination step, the combined probabilities for key byte b are stored in matrix $\mathbf{P_{Comb}}[b][h]$, which is eventually used to estimate the key rank of the combined attack.

This method assumes that the best out of M available attacks (the one with the largest sum) is always a good one. This is consistent with our experiments, where good attacks have a higher deviation from the uniform distribution than bad attacks. In addition, considering L probabilities at once makes the filter step more robust against bad attacks. The combination step helps to achieve a better overall attack, which is desirable when evaluating software in a worst-case scenario. The advantage of our heuristic approach is that it allows to automatically combine multiple attacks by only providing the value L, which is easily derived from the cache line size of the processor and the lookup table entry size of the tested implementation. The simplicity of our approach is based on the observations about "good" and "bad" attacks, its effectiveness is shown by our practical experiments.

5   Performance Events on ARM Processors

Performance events provide detailed insight into the micro-architecture of a processor while it is working on a task. They are typically needed for debugging and performance evaluations on real hardware. Because of the fine granularity with which a processor can be observed, performance events can be powerful side-channels for the profiled cache attack by Bernstein. Previous literature illustrated that clock cycle and cache miss events allow to successfully perform the attack. Since these events are only a small subset of performance events that are typically available, we propose a more comprehensive study.

Table 1. Selection of performance events and corresponding descriptions according to the ARM manuals [3,4].

	ID	Lit.	Description
ARMv7-A/R	03_h	√	Level 1 D-cache refill
	04_h	-	Level 1 D-cache access
	05_h	-	Level 1 data TLB refill
	06_h	-	Load instructions
	11_h	√	CPU cycles
	CCNT	√	Clock cycle counter
Cortex-A9	50_h	-	Coherent linefill miss
	61_h	-	D-cache stall cycles
	65_h	-	D-cache eviction requests
	72_h	-	Load/store instructions
	85_h	-	Data micro TLB stall cycles

Table 2. Selection of ARMv7-A/R processor cores and available hardware counters.

Core	#
Cortex-A5	2
Cortex-A7/8	4
Cortex-A9/15/17	6
Cortex-R4/5	3
Cortex-R7	8

Our target platform is an ARM Cortex-A9 processor, which belongs to the ARMv7-A/R architecture family. The ARMv7-A/R reference manual [4] defines hardware performance events that can be measured on all compliant processors. The ARM Cortex-A9 MPCore reference manual [3] specifies events that are additionally available on the Cortex-A9. Each event is identified by an event ID and can be counted by one of the hardware counters present on every processor core. Table 1 shows the two selections of performance events we analyze in our case study. The first set of events is common to all ARMv7-A/R compliant processors, the second one is specific to the ARM Cortex-A9. The events are displayed with their event IDs and descriptions as found in the reference manuals. All events previously used in literature in the context of Bernstein's attack are labeled with $\sqrt{}$ in the table, illustrating that most events are used for the first time.

Measuring multiple performance events in parallel is possible but limited by the number of hardware counters available. Table 2 shows a selection of current ARMv7-A/R processor cores and the number of available hardware counters taken from the corresponding MPCore reference manuals. Each counter can be configured to capture a specific event. The counter is then enabled and continuously counts occurrences of the configured hardware event. Configuration and access to the counter values is realized through registers of the co-processor 15. By default, this is only allowed from privileged (e.g. kernel) code. As the goal of our work is an efficient evaluation and not an improved attack, this poses no limitation. The subsequent paragraphs in this section discuss the selection of performance events in more detail. They are organized in categories *clock cycles*, *cache*, *TLB*, and *memory access*.

Clock Cycles. The clock cycle event labeled CCNT is counted by the register called PMCCNTR, which does not occupy any of the available hardware counters. The event is known from literature and for the purpose of comparison, we include it in our event selection. In addition, the clock cycle event can also be measured through event ID 11_h. We analyze it in our experiments to compare it to the CCNT.

Cache. Cache miss events have also been investigated in Bernstein's attack. To provide a link to previous literature, we analyze level 1 data cache misses (03_h). In addition, we include events that have a close relation to L1 D-cache misses. Those events are cache requests that miss coherently in all processor cores (50_h), clock cycles the processor core is stalled because of a pending request from a cache miss (61_h), and the number of cache eviction requests that are caused by cache misses (65_h). All of them are likely to show similar key-dependent variations as those expected for L1 D-cache miss events.

TLB. Similar to the processor cache, the translation lookaside buffer (TLB) is also involved in fetching data from main memory. It is used by the memory management unit to speed up translations of virtual addresses. Since TLBs are buffers with limited size, lookups can result in hits or misses. On the ARM Cortex-A9, the *micro* TLB is a first level TLB that is separated into instruction and data part. The *main* TLB is a unified second level TLB, which catches the misses in the underlying micro TLBs. Because of the similarities to the processor cache, we include TLB-related events in our experiments. In particular, we measure misses in the data micro or main TLB (05_h) and stall cycles caused by misses in the data micro TLB (85_h).

Memory Access. Based only on the ARM reference manuals, it is difficult to conclude whether some events are applicable to the selected cache attack. Either not enough information is provided in the event descriptions or events are by definition counted approximately rather than precisely or the final counting behavior is defined by the processor implementation itself. Because of these uncertainties, we analyze memory read and write operations causing accesses to at least the L1 data or unified cache (04_h) as well as the number of load respectively load and store instructions (06_h and 72_h). Note that the tested AES software performs a constant number of memory accesses as discussed in Appendix A.

6   Measurement Setup

For our practical case study, we implement a client-server setup as proposed in the original attack by Bernstein. The client, or spy, establishes a network connection to the victim, which is running on a Linux server system (kernel v3.19.0) featuring an ARM Cortex-A9 quad-core processor. The measurements are performed with enabled L1 and L2 caches, program flow prediction, cache pre-fetcher and cache critical word first filling. We choose a full Linux operating system and leave all hardware acceleration features enabled to provide a realistic setting for our evaluation.

Direct access to the performance monitoring registers of the co-processor 15 is by default only allowed from kernel mode. User space access can either be enabled in the PMUSERENR register or realized by exposing the performance counter subsystem of the kernel with the perf tool set. While perf enables convenient user access to all the events tested in this work, using it adds another potential source of measurement noise. We avoid this by enabling direct user access in the PMUSERENR register with a custom system call. This has to be done once and gets reset when the system is powered off. As we conduct our experiments in an evaluation rather than an attack context, such low-level control over the target system is given.

As some of the measured performance events occur in core-private caches or TLBs, we force the victim program to run on one specific processor core. This is done with the taskset program from the Linux utilities. Restricting the victim to one core is no disadvantage but even beneficial. Letting the victim program float between processor cores adds noise to the measured performance events, which (1) prolongs the measurement phase until a stable attack success rate is achieved and (2) is no worst-case attack scenario that we aim to establish for this evaluation. During the measurements, the target system is idling and the victim program is competing for resources with itself and the system processes that run in the background. The AES-128 implementation under attack is written in ARM assembly, uses a 1 kiB lookup table, and executes a constant and key-value-independent number of instructions during encryption. More details about the implementation are given in Appendix A.

For every attack we take two sets of $30 \cdot 10^6$ ($\approx 2^{24.84}$) measurements, one for the learn phase and one for the attack phase. In the learn phase, we use a zero key, in the attack phase we use a random one. The attack is then performed with additional key rank estimation. For each of the selected performance events, we repeat this process 33 times in order to achieve a reasonable statistical significance for our practical experiments. We choose 33 repetitions to keep the measurement effort manageable. In the last step, the estimated key ranks of all 33 attacks are averaged for each event to form the final key ranks presented in the next section.

7   Discussion of Practical Results

Table 3 shows the attack results for the performance events in our case study. The left side of the table displays event IDs, coverage in previous literature, and descriptions. The right side of the table shows the average estimated key ranks in $\log_2$ that are achieved using the corresponding performance events. The combination ARMv7 combines attacks from all tested ARMv7-A/R compliant events according to our method proposed in Sect. 4. The combination ALL combines all available attacks and additionally includes the events specific to the ARM Cortex-A9.

The first and most interesting observation from Table 3 is that all analyzed performance events reduce the entropy of the secret key. The average key ranks range between 2^{120} and 2^{51}. This is a significantly lower effort compared to searching for a full-entropy 128-bit key with an expected average key rank of 2^{127}. The best attacks with the current event selection are based on events 11_h and CCNT, which both count clock cycles. A further reduction of key entropy is only achieved by combining multiple attacks. The key ranks of the combinations ARMv7 and ALL fall below those of the CCNT by 2^2 and 2^3, respectively. Although these improvements might seem moderate, they show that our proposed combination and filter method indeed excludes poor-quality side-channels and constructively combines the available leakage to improve the overall result. Events with poor attack results, such as 03_h, 50_h, and 65_h, do not degrade the ARMv7 and ALL combinations. Instead, the available side-channels improve the already good attack results retrieved from the CCNT measurements. The improvement is more significant, if fewer measurements are available to the attack. This is illustrated in Fig. 1, which shows the attack results over an increasing number of measurements.

Every plot in the figure shows the average estimated key ranks in $\log_2$ as the y-coordinate and the number of measurements as the x-coordinate. Note that the plots end at $15 \cdot 10^6$ measurements to better illustrate the early attack stages, in which fewer measurements are available. In this phase the combined attacks

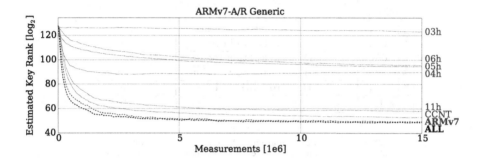

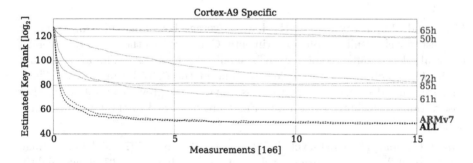

Fig. 1. Estimated key ranks over an increasing number of measurements. Top plot shows results for ARMv7-A/R events, bottom plot shows ranks for Cortex-A9 events. Combined attacks `ARMv7` and `ALL` are plotted with dashed lines and marked with bold labels.

Table 3. Estimated key ranks achieved with the selected performance events.

Performance Events			Estimated Key Ranks
ID	Lit.	Description	[$\log_2$]
ARMv7-A/R 03$_h$	$\checkmark$	L1 D-cache refill	119
04$_h$	-	L1 D-cache access	90
05$_h$	-	L1 D-TLB refill	91
06$_h$	-	Load instructions	93
11$_h$	$\checkmark$	CPU cycles	57
CCNT	$\checkmark$	Clock cycle counter	51
ARMv7	-	-	49
Cortex-A9 50$_h$	-	Coherent linefill miss	116
61$_h$	-	D-cache stall cycles	67
65$_h$	-	D-cache eviction requests	120
72$_h$	-	Load/store instructions	76
85$_h$	-	D-micro TLB stall cycles	83
ALL	-	-	48

Notes:

ARMv7 .... Combination of ARMv7-A/R compliant events
ALL ..... Combination of all events measured on the Cortex-A9

ARMv7 and ALL clearly exhibit the lowest average key ranks and consequently the best attack results in our experiments. Compared to the CCNT, the average key rank of the ARMv7 combination is smaller by up to 2^{11}. The average rank of the ALL combination falls below the one of the CCNT by up to 2^{16}. These improvements decrease with more measurements, as previously noted. Further observations from both Table 3 and Fig. 1 are discussed in the following paragraphs.

Clock Cycles. The clock-cycle-based events 11$_h$ and CCNT yield low average key ranks of 2^{57} and 2^{51}, respectively. We assume that the CCNT shows slightly better results, because once enabled, it is accessible with only one read request to the co-processor 15. All other events are counted such that their corresponding hardware counter has to be selected first in order to read its current value. This additional request to the co-processor 15 adds noise to the measurements, but is necessary if multiple events are counted in parallel. Because of its superior attack results and because it does not occupy any of the limited hardware counters in the processor, the PMCCNTR register is clearly recommended to measure the clock cycle event on our target system.

Cache. Among the cache-miss-related performance events, the D-cache stall cycles (61$_h$) yield the best attack result with an average key rank of 2^{67}. In contrast, cache misses, coherent linefill misses, and data eviction requests (03$_h$, 50$_h$, and 65$_h$) do not exhibit average key ranks below 2^{116}. One possible explanation is that stall cycles incorporate additional and more fine-grained key-dependent variations that are not reflected in the total number of cache misses or eviction requests counted by the other events.

TLB. The results of the TLB refill and TLB stall cycle events (05_h and 85_h) show that translation lookaside buffers offer a potent side-channel source for the implemented attack. These events perform superior to most cache-miss-related events on our target system. With an average key rank of 2^{83} compared to 2^{91}, the D-micro TLB stall cycles yield better results than the L1 D-TLB refills. We assume that the stall cycles again contain more exploitable information and that less noise in the micro TLB renders their results more successful.

Memory Access. The attacks based on L1 D-cache accesses as well as load and store instructions (04_h, 06_h, and 72_h) are successful, which is counter-intuitive given that the number of memory accesses in the tested AES implementation is constant and independent of the key value. This suggests that these events incorporate key-dependent variations such that the attack is able to reduce the secret key entropy. Since detailed information about the implementation of these events is not publicly available, further investigations are necessary to identify the source of their leakage.

Combined Attacks. The additional, Cortex-A9 specific events added to the ALL combination improve the average key rank of the ARMv7 combination by at most 2^9. This maximum difference is shown in Fig. 1 before the attacks reach the $5 \cdot 10^6$ measurements mark. When more measurements are added, the improvement becomes approximately 2^1, as illustrated in Table 3. Given our event selection, this shows that good results can already be obtained using generic ARMv7-A/R events. On the other hand, combinations of platform-specific events not analyzed in this work may still be able to outperform ARMv7-A/R generic combinations.

8   Practical Evaluation Suggestions

Our case study shows that hardware performance events offer a promising pool of side-channels that can be exploited in the profiled cache attack by Bernstein. For a fair and complete assessment of the leakage contained in the events, key rank estimation has proven to be a useful tool. Although it adds complexity, determining the attack effort is unreliable in practice with the original approach. To control the computational cost, one can adapt the estimation bound tightness to one's specific requirements.

Within our selection of performance events, each one allows to reduce the entropy of the secret key. Among these events, clock cycles provide the best results on our ARM Cortex-A9 test system. If minimum measurement and post-processing effort are required, the evaluation can be limited to the CCNT. It is a high-resolution side-channel source that is available on all ARMv7-A/R compliant processor cores. It consequently allows to compare the leakage behavior of multiple systems in a simple way. However, further studies are necessary to verify that it also performs best on other ARM-Cortex-based systems. For now, we strongly recommend to consider more than just the clock cycle event.

Since attacking multiple performance events increases the measurement and post-processing effort, a minimum selection of events with maximum leakage is desirable. The lack of detailed information in the public ARM manuals and the uncertainty of how a processor actually counts certain events show that an optimal choice of performance events is not trivial to make. According to our case study, the ARMv7-A/R compliant performance events provide good results on the selected test system. Their combination is only slightly inferior compared to the combination of all tested events, including those specific to the ARM Cortex-A9. To maintain platform independence, we recommend to limit the tested events to ARMv7-A/R compliant ones. If fewer hardware counters are available on the processor under test, the results displayed in Table 3 and Fig. 1 can be a starting point for reducing the number of measured events. In order to compare the leakage behavior of multiple processors, we suggest to combine the attacks of each system with our proposed method. The resulting combinations represent robust overall attacks, regardless of which specific event leaks the most information on each processor. This allows to get a comprehensive view of the vulnerability of a cipher implementation on a range of different systems.

9   Conclusion

In this work, we studied the evaluation of a block cipher implementation on a modern processor with the profiled time-driven cache attack proposed by Bernstein. The application of key rank estimation as well as the combination of multiple attacks are generic extensions that might also be of interest in other cache attack work. In our case study, we identified new micro-architectural side-channels on our ARM-based test system that can successfully be exploited in Bernstein's attack. Since performance counters are not only available on ARM systems, we assume that new side-channels can also be found on other modern (e.g. x86) processors. As all tested events in the case study leak information about the secret key, the practical results strongly suggest that even more performance events might be exploitable than those analyzed both in literature and in our work. Together with the fact that the counting behavior of certain events is not properly documented and is even defined by the final processor implementation, a comprehensive study of performance events across multiple processors is a promising direction for future work. Furthermore, it is an open question whether a more effective filter approach exists that better separates good and bad attacks in the combination step. Eventually, these directions may lead to an optimal choice of events needed to evaluate the profiled cache attack by Bernstein with maximum efficiency.

Acknowledgements. This work was funded by the German Federal Ministry of Education and Research (BMBF) in the project SIBASE through grant number 01IS13020C.

A   AES T-table Implementation

The profiled time-driven cache attack by Bernstein targets a software implementation of AES that uses so-called transformation tables. These T-tables are proposed by Daemon and Rijmen [9] to speed up AES in software. The tables reduce a round of AES to 16 table lookups and 16 XOR operations with 4-byte operands. The encryption process uses four $1\,kiB$ T-tables $\mathbf{T}_{0..3}$ for all rounds except the initial and the last one, which lacks the MixColumns transformation. Encryption using T-tables is illustrated in Eq. 4. Note that it does not define the initial state, $\mathbf{s}^{(0)}$, and the final one, $\mathbf{s}^{(R)}$, because of their different treatment in the cipher. The cipher state in round $r \in \{1, ..., R-1\}$, $R \in \{10, 12, 14\}$ is given as $\mathbf{s}^{(r)}_{i..i+3}$ whereas the round key is given as $\mathbf{k}^{(r)}_{i..i+3}$, with $(i..i+3)$ denoting a consecutive 4-byte chunk of the state and the round key, respectively. The initial state $\mathbf{s}^{(0)}$ is a simple XOR operation between the plaintext $\mathbf{p}$ and the initial key $\mathbf{k}^{(0)}$, $\mathbf{s}^{(0)} = \mathbf{p} \oplus \mathbf{k}^{(0)}$.

$$
\begin{aligned}
\mathbf{s}^{(r)}_{0..3} &= \mathbf{T}_0[\mathbf{s}^{(r-1)}_0] \oplus \mathbf{T}_1[\mathbf{s}^{(r-1)}_5] \oplus \mathbf{T}_2[\mathbf{s}^{(r-1)}_{10}] \oplus \mathbf{T}_3[\mathbf{s}^{(r-1)}_{15}] \oplus \mathbf{k}^{(r)}_{0..3} \\
\mathbf{s}^{(r)}_{4..7} &= \mathbf{T}_0[\mathbf{s}^{(r-1)}_4] \oplus \mathbf{T}_1[\mathbf{s}^{(r-1)}_9] \oplus \mathbf{T}_2[\mathbf{s}^{(r-1)}_{14}] \oplus \mathbf{T}_3[\mathbf{s}^{(r-1)}_3] \oplus \mathbf{k}^{(r)}_{4..7} \\
\mathbf{s}^{(r)}_{8..11} &= \mathbf{T}_0[\mathbf{s}^{(r-1)}_8] \oplus \mathbf{T}_1[\mathbf{s}^{(r-1)}_{13}] \oplus \mathbf{T}_2[\mathbf{s}^{(r-1)}_2] \oplus \mathbf{T}_3[\mathbf{s}^{(r-1)}_7] \oplus \mathbf{k}^{(r)}_{8..11} \\
\mathbf{s}^{(r)}_{12..15} &= \mathbf{T}_0[\mathbf{s}^{(r-1)}_{12}] \oplus \mathbf{T}_1[\mathbf{s}^{(r-1)}_1] \oplus \mathbf{T}_2[\mathbf{s}^{(r-1)}_6] \oplus \mathbf{T}_3[\mathbf{s}^{(r-1)}_{11}] \oplus \mathbf{k}^{(r)}_{12..15}
\end{aligned}
\tag{4}
$$

In order to reduce the storage space required by the T-table implementation, three of the T-tables can be exchanged for 12 extra rotations per round of AES. This is because each entry of a T-table is the byte-wise rotation of the same entry of any other table. The rotation factor remains constant for each table. Hence, we can rewrite Eq. 4 as follows, assuming $\mathbf{T} = \mathbf{T}_0$ is the only table available. The function $ror(v,n)$ rotates the 4-byte value v by n number of bytes cyclically to the right.

$$
\begin{aligned}
\mathbf{s}^{(r)}_{0..3} &= \mathbf{T}[\mathbf{s}^{(r-1)}_0] \oplus ror(\mathbf{T}[\mathbf{s}^{(r-1)}_5], 1) \oplus ror(\mathbf{T}[\mathbf{s}^{(r-1)}_{10}], 2) \oplus ror(\mathbf{T}[\mathbf{s}^{(r-1)}_{15}], 3) \oplus \mathbf{k}^{(r)}_{0..3} \\
\mathbf{s}^{(r)}_{4..7} &= \mathbf{T}[\mathbf{s}^{(r-1)}_4] \oplus ror(\mathbf{T}[\mathbf{s}^{(r-1)}_9], 1) \oplus ror(\mathbf{T}[\mathbf{s}^{(r-1)}_{14}], 2) \oplus ror(\mathbf{T}[\mathbf{s}^{(r-1)}_3], 3) \oplus \mathbf{k}^{(r)}_{4..7} \\
\mathbf{s}^{(r)}_{8..11} &= \mathbf{T}[\mathbf{s}^{(r-1)}_8] \oplus ror(\mathbf{T}[\mathbf{s}^{(r-1)}_{13}], 1) \oplus ror(\mathbf{T}[\mathbf{s}^{(r-1)}_2], 2) \oplus ror(\mathbf{T}[\mathbf{s}^{(r-1)}_7], 3) \oplus \mathbf{k}^{(r)}_{8..11} \\
\mathbf{s}^{(r)}_{12..15} &= \mathbf{T}[\mathbf{s}^{(r-1)}_{12}] \oplus ror(\mathbf{T}[\mathbf{s}^{(r-1)}_1], 1) \oplus ror(\mathbf{T}[\mathbf{s}^{(r-1)}_6], 2) \oplus ror(\mathbf{T}[\mathbf{s}^{(r-1)}_{11}], 3) \oplus \mathbf{k}^{(r)}_{12..15}
\end{aligned}
\tag{5}
$$

In our experiments we test a $1\,kiB$ T-table implementation of AES that follows Eq. 5. It is part of the OpenSSL software library v1.0.2 and written in ARM assembly. The code is located under crypto/aes/asm/aes-armv4.pl in the GitHub repository of the library [16]. As suggested by the equation, the chosen implementation uses a constant and key-value-independent number of instructions. The only conditional branch in the code is used to realize the AES encryption loop. For each plaintext that is encrypted with AES-128, the processor performs 144 T-table lookups with ldr instructions and 16 S-box lookups with ldrb instructions, which are needed in the last encryption round. As it is common to many T-table-based implementations of AES, the secret key is leaked only through the table lookups themselves, because it is used to compute the indices of the tables.

References

1. Acııçmez, O., Koç, Ç.K.: Trace-driven cache attacks on AES (Short Paper). In: Ning, P., Qing, S., Li, N. (eds.) ICICS 2006. LNCS, vol. 4307, pp. 112–121. Springer, Heidelberg (2006)
2. Apecechea, G.I., Inci, M.S., Eisenbarth, T., Sunar, B.: Fine grain Cross-VM attacks on Xen and VMware are possible! Cryptology ePrint Archive, Report 2014/248 (2014). http://eprint.iacr.org/
3. ARM: ARM Cortex-A9 MPCore Technical Reference Manual, June 2012. Revision r4p1
4. ARM: ARM Architecture Reference Manual ARMv7-A and ARMv7-R Edition, May 2014. Revision C.c
5. Atici, A., Yilmaz, C., Savas, E.: An approach for isolating the sources of information leakage exploited in cache-based side-channel attacks. In: 2013 IEEE 7th International Conference on Software Security and Reliability-Companion (SERE-C), pp. 74–83, June 2013
6. Bernstein, D.J.: Cache-timing attacks on AES. Tech. rep., The University of Illinois at Chicago (2005). http://cr.yp.to/antiforgery/cachetiming-20050414.pdf
7. Bogdanov, A., Eisenbarth, T., Paar, C., Wienecke, M.: Differential cache-collision timing attacks on AES with applications to embedded CPUs. In: Pieprzyk, J. (ed.) CT-RSA 2010. LNCS, vol. 5985, pp. 235–251. Springer, Heidelberg (2010)
8. Bonneau, J., Mironov, I.: Cache-collision timing attacks against AES. In: Goubin, L., Matsui, M. (eds.) CHES 2006. LNCS, vol. 4249, pp. 201–215. Springer, Heidelberg (2006)
9. Daemen, J., Rijmen, V.: The Design of Rijndael. Springer-Verlag New York Inc., Secaucus (2002)
10. Glowacz, C., Grosso, V., Poussier, R., Schueth, J., Standaert, F.X.: Simpler and more efficient rank estimation for side-channel security assessment. Cryptology ePrint Archive, Report 2014/920 (2014). http://eprint.iacr.org/
11. Gérard, B., Standaert, F.-X.: Unified and optimized linear collision attacks and their application in a non-profiled setting. In: Prouff, E., Schaumont, P. (eds.) CHES 2012. LNCS, vol. 7428, pp. 175–192. Springer, Heidelberg (2012)
12. Mather, L., Oswald, E., Whitnall, C.: Multi-target DPA attacks: pushing DPA beyond the limits of a desktop computer. In: Sarkar, P., Iwata, T. (eds.) ASIACRYPT 2014. LNCS, vol. 8873, pp. 243–261. Springer, Heidelberg (2014)
13. Neve, M., Seifert, J.P., Wang, Z.: A refined look at bernstein's aes side-channel analysis. In: Proceedings of the 2006 ACM Symposium on Information, Computer and Communications Security, ASIACCS 2006, pp. 369–369. ACM, New York (2006)
14. Spreitzer, R., Gérard, B.: Towards more practical time-driven cache attacks. In: Naccache, D., Sauveron, D. (eds.) WISTP 2014. LNCS, vol. 8501, pp. 24–39. Springer, Heidelberg (2014)
15. Spreitzer, R., Plos, T.: On the applicability of time-driven cache attacks on mobile devices. In: Lopez, J., Huang, X., Sandhu, R. (eds.) NSS 2013. LNCS, vol. 7873, pp. 656–662. Springer, Heidelberg (2013)

16. The OpenSSL Project: OpenSSL (2015). https://github.com/openssl/openssl
17. Tiri, K., Acıiçmez, O., Neve, M., Andersen, F.: An analytical model for time-driven cache attacks. In: Biryukov, A. (ed.) FSE 2007. LNCS, vol. 4593, pp. 399–413. Springer, Heidelberg (2007)
18. Tromer, E., Osvik, D.A., Shamir, A.: Efficient cache attacks on aes, and countermeasures. J. Cryptology **23**(2), 37–71 (2010)
19. Uhsadel, L., Georges, A., Verbauwhede, I.: Exploiting hardware performance counters. In: 5th Workshop on Fault Diagnosis and Tolerance in Cryptography, FDTC 2008, pp. 59–67, August 2008
20. Veyrat-Charvillon, N., Gérard, B., Renauld, M., Standaert, F.-X.: An optimal key enumeration algorithm and its application to side-channel attacks. In: Knudsen, L.R., Wu, H. (eds.) SAC 2012. LNCS, vol. 7707, pp. 390–406. Springer, Heidelberg (2013)
21. Veyrat-Charvillon, N., Gérard, B., Standaert, F.-X.: Security evaluations beyond computing power. In: Johansson, T., Nguyen, P.Q. (eds.) EUROCRYPT 2013. LNCS, vol. 7881, pp. 126–141. Springer, Heidelberg (2013)
22. Weiß, M., Heinz, B., Stumpf, F.: A cache timing attack on AES in virtualization environments. In: Keromytis, A.D. (ed.) FC 2012. LNCS, vol. 7397, pp. 314–328. Springer, Heidelberg (2012)
23. Weiß, M., Weggenmann, B., August, M., Sigl, G.: On cache timing attacks considering multi-core aspects in virtualized embedded systems. In: Yung, M., Zhu, L., Yang, Y. (eds.) INTRUST 2014. LNCS, vol. 9473, pp. 151–167. Springer, Switzerland (2014)

More Practical and Secure History-Independent Hash Tables

Michael T. Goodrich[1], Evgenios M. Kornaropoulos[2(✉)],
Michael Mitzenmacher[3], and Roberto Tamassia[2]

[1] Department of Computer Science, University of California, Irvine, USA
goodrich@acm.org
[2] Department of Computer Science, Brown University, Providence, USA
{evgenios,rt}@cs.brown.edu
[3] School of Engineering and Applied Science, Harvard University, Cambridge, USA
michaelm@eecs.harvard.edu

Abstract. Direct-recording electronic (DRE) voting systems have been
used in several countries including United States, India, and the
Netherlands to name a few. A common flaw that was discovered by
the security researchers was that the votes were stored sequentially
according to the time they were cast, which allows an attacker to
break the anonymity of the voters. Subsequent research pointed out
the connection between vote storage and the privacy property *history-independence*. In a weakly history-independent data structure, every possible sequence of operations consistent with the current set of items is
equally likely to have occurred. In a strongly history-independent data
structure, items must be stored in a canonical way, i.e., for any set of
items, there is only one possible memory representation. Strong history-
independence implies weak history-independence but considerably constrains the design choices of the data structures. In this work, we present
and analyze an efficient hash table data structure that simultaneously
achieves the following properties:

- It is based on the classic *linear probing* collision-handling scheme.
- It is *weakly history-independent*.
- It is secure against *collision-timing attacks*. That is, we consider adversaries that can measure the time for an update operation, but cannot
  observe data values, and we show that those adversaries cannot learn
  information about the items in the table.
- All operations are *significantly faster in practice* (almost 2x faster for
  high load factors) than those of the commonly used strongly history-
  independent linear probing method proposed by Blelloch and Golovin
  (FOCS'07), which is not secure against collision-timing attacks.

To our knowledge, our hash table construction is the first data structure
that combines history-independence and protection against a form of
timing attacks.

Keywords: Hash table · History-independence · Timing attack · Vote
storage

© Springer International Publishing Switzerland 2016
I. Askoxylakis et al. (Eds.): ESORICS 2016, Part II, LNCS 9879, pp. 20–38, 2016.
DOI: 10.1007/978-3-319-45741-3_2

1   Introduction

Hashing is a classic technique [21] for implementing a dynamic dictionary of key-value items supporting the following operations:

- insert(k, v): Insert item[1] (k, v).
- find(k): Return the value with key equal to k, or null if none exists.
- delete(k): Delete the item with key equal to k.

The are many applications of such a data structure and it is well-known that hashing can achieve $O(1)$ expected-time performance for each operation (e.g., see [16]). In such a scheme, the items are stored in an array, T, according to a mapping derived from a hash function, hash$(\cdot)$, such that the item (k, v) is ideally stored in the cell $T[\text{hash}(k)]$. If multiple items map to the same cell, then we say that a *collision* has occurred, and we need some way of resolving the collision. One of the classic collision resolution methods is *linear probing* [21]. In this scheme, one simply incrementally searches the next cells in the array, $T[\text{hash}(k) + 1]$, $T[\text{hash}(k) + 2]$, and so on, modulo the size of T, until one finds an empty cell. Linear probing achieves $O(1)$ expected time performance if the ratio of the number of occupied cells to the total number of cells, which is known as the *load factor*, is a constant strictly less than 1 (e.g., see [16,21]). Although this is a classic hashing scheme, its use is nevertheless ubiquitous in computing today, including many instances where security and privacy are essential. Thus, we are interested in this paper in hash table schemes that can provide measurable protections against various security and privacy attacks.

History-Independence. The property of *history-independence* was introduced by Naor and Teague [29] by extending a related structural obliviousness property by Micciancio [25]. The goal of history-independence is to design a data structure so that an adversary who examines the computer memory will only discover the current contents of the data structure but will not learn anything about the sequence of operations that led to the current state of the data structure. History-independence comes in two flavors [29]—in *weakly history-independence* (WHI), the adversary can examine the memory only once, whereas in *strongly history-independence* (SHI), the adversary may examine the memory multiple times. Several history-independent data structures have been proposed. Blelloch and Golovin [7] present a SHI hash table based on linear probing. The work of Naor *et al.* [28] presents a SHI Cuckoo Table that performs insertions and deletions in $O(\log n)$ time, with high probability, where n is the current number of elements in the table. Buchbinder *et al.* [8] show time complexity separation between the weak and the strong notions of history-independent data structure. Our focus in this paper is on the WHI framework, as we feel it is has a more realistic risk scenario. Moreover, by a lower bound due to Hartline *et al.* [18], in order for a data structure to be SHI, it *must have* a canonical memory representation, which is a fairly restrictive requirement that seems to conflict with protections against the next type of attack that we consider in this paper.

---

[1] We assume that keys are unique, but all of our results extend to the setting where insertion of an already allocated key with a new value replaces the current value.

Vote Storage. The DRE AccuVote-TS voting machine was used by 10 % of the voters in the 2006 US general election. Security flaws were found both in the software [22] and the hardware [12] of the device. For example, Kohno *et al.* [22] found that each vote is written sequentially to the file that stores the votes, which can break the anonymity of the system. An attacker with some side-channel information can link the ballot to a voter based on the order that the votes are stored. The same privacy flaw was also found in the Indian Electronic Voting Machines that have been used for national elections of India since 2004. The work by Wolchok *et al.* [33] reports that votes are stored in the order cast. Later work recognized the connection of the above privacy issue with the notion of history-independence and suggested the use of strongly history-independent data structures [6,26,27]. In fact, in March 2015 the United States Election Assistance Committee approved the next generation of Voluntary Voting System Guidelines where they specify that ballot images *must be recorded in a randomized order* by the DRE for the election (Sect. 2.4.4.2 in [1]). Given that the voting machines are examined usually after the election process, i.e. post-election audits [2,31], the notion of weak history-independence seems to be more appropriate than the stronger notion of strong history-independence.

Memory Attacks. Beyond voting machines, there are other cases where an adversary can obtain access to a snapshot of the working memory and weak history-independence can be usefully applied. A direct memory access attack, or DMA attack, is an attack where the adversary with physical access to the machine bypasses all security measures of the operating system and directly accesses the memory via the high-speed expansion ports. Tools such as "Inception" [24] mount a DMA attack over PCI interfaces and acquire a complete image of the working memory. Cold boot attacks [17] allow the attacker to dump the image of the memory to an external medium, which can even identify and reconstruct the cryptographic keys from the acquired image and thus overcome disk encryption. In application scenarios such as ballot storage [26] or hospital admission management [4] such leakage might violate desired privacy.

Other History-Independent Systems. Bajaj and Sion proposed a history-independent file system named HIFS [3] that provides history-independence across both file system and disk layers of the storage stack. We note here that HIFS deploys the SHI hash table from [7], which is significantly slower than our WHI construction. A direct substitution, followed by some minor changes, would significantly speed up their design while maintaining suitable privacy guarantees for many applications. Unfortunately, the history-independence of HIFS [3] is not guaranteed for flash storage devices. The reason is that the block placement algorithms in flash storage devices are managed internally (in a non-history-independent manner) in order to maximize performance and lifetime of the storage. To remedy that, Chen and Sion proposed history-independent schemes that are tailored for flash-based block devices [10]. Another system, Ficklebase [4], suggests the use of history-independent data structures within a relational database architecture for the underlying database storage engine in order to avoid unwanted recovery of deleted information through forensic analysis.

Timing Attacks. Another type of attack that can cause a data structure to leak information is a *timing attack*. In such a side-channel attack, an adversary does not get direct access to the memory layout of a data structure or to the operands of the executed operation, but he can nevertheless precisely time the execution of data structure operations. Such attacks typically come in two forms—in the first form, an attacker passively observes the timing of data structure operations performed by others, and in the second form, he is allowed to directly interact with the data structure, e.g., to form malicious inputs that cause errors or significant time delays that can reveal information put into the data structure by others.

In the first type of attack, the eavesdropping adversary gains knowledge about the private data using the duration of an abstract-data-type operation of the data structure. An example of such a real-world attack is presented in [13], where an attacker can measure the execution time of an insertion in a B-tree in order to detect a node split. Using this split detection information, the attacker can recover values from the database table that is under attack. As a means to formally characterize such attacks, Lipton and Naughton [23] define a *clocked adversary* to be an eavesdropping attacker who can accurately time operations of a data structure and who succeeds if he can distinguish whether the system is in a state s_1 or state s_2 given just the timing information.

For the second type of timing attack, an adversary utilizes the predictable time performance of known data structure implementations to mount an active attack. For example, Crosby and Wallach [11] introduce *algorithmic complexity attacks*, where an adversary provides inputs to a data structure so as to trigger its worst case performance. In addition, Bethea and Reiter [5] introduce *timing-unpredictability*, which is used to quantify the uncertainty of an attacker about the time performance of future operations.

Our Results. In Sect. 3, we present and analyze the first efficient hash table data structure that defends against the above information leakage attacks. Our construction, denoted as WHI, achieves the following properties:

- It is *weakly history-independent*.
- It is secure against *collision-timing attacks* (see Definition 3 below).
- Operations find, insert and delete are significantly *faster in practice* than the strongly history-independent linear probing scheme of [7].

In Table 1, we qualitatively compare our WHI scheme to several previous linear-probing hashing schemes that achieve some degree of history-independence or defend against collision-timing attacks, noting that none of them achieves protection against both types of attacks. We review these other schemes in Sect. 4 and we provide the results of experimental comparisons in Sect. 5.

Table 1. Privacy properties of hashing with linear probing

	History-Independence		Secure Against Collision-Timing Attacks
	Strong HI	Weak HI	
First-Come-First-Served (FCFS)	-	-	✓
Last-Come-First-Served (LCFS) [30]	-	-	✓
Robin Hood, Tie-Break w. FCFS/LCFS [9]	-	-	✓
Robin Hood, Tie-Break w. Key Sort	✓	✓	-
Blelloch & Golovin [7]	✓	✓	-
WHI (This work)	-	✓	✓

2   Security Model

2.1   History-Independence

An *Abstract Data Type* (ADT) is a mathematical model of a data structure that describes the type of the data stored, the operations that can be performed on the data as well as the parameters of each operation. In this work, a data structure is associated with a set of items that is also called the *logical state of an ADT*, or simply *state*. An ADT *operation* deterministically transforms the state of the data structure. A *sequence of operations S* is an ordered list of ADT operations of the data structure as defined by the corresponding ADT. A *memory representation of an ADT*, or simply a *representation*, is a mapping of the state of the data structure into the memory. In general, there can be multiple memory representations for a given state. An implementation of a data structure is a function $F : M \times O \to M$, where M is the set of all possible memory representations and O is the set of all possible ADT operations.

Following the terminology of Hartline *et al.* [18], let a and b denote the memory representation of states A and B respectively. Let S be a sequence of operations then by $A \xrightarrow{S} B$ we indicate that the sequence of operations S takes state A to state B. Let also $\Pr[a \xrightarrow{S} b]$ denote the probability that starting from memory representation a of state A, the sequence of operations S run by the corresponding implementation yields memory representation b of state B. The initially empty memory representation is denoted as $\oslash$.

Definition 1 (Hartline *et al.* [18]). *A data structure is **weakly history-independent** if, for any two sequences of operations S_1 and S_2 that take the data structure from the initialization to state A, the distribution over the memory after sequence S_1 is performed is identical to the distribution after sequence S_2 is performed. That is:*

$$(\oslash \xrightarrow{S_1} A) \wedge (\oslash \xrightarrow{S_2} A) \Rightarrow \forall a \in A, \Pr[\oslash \xrightarrow{S_1} a] = \Pr[\oslash \xrightarrow{S_2} a].$$

Definition 2 (Hartline *et al.* [18]). *A data structure is **strongly history-independent** if, for any two (possibly empty) sequences of operations S_1 and S_2 that take a data structure from state A to state B, the distribution over the memory representations of B after sequence S_1 is performed on representation a is identical to the distribution after sequence S_2 is performed on representation a. That is:*

$$(A \xrightarrow{S_1} B) \wedge (A \xrightarrow{S_2} B) \Rightarrow \forall a \in A, \forall b \in B, \Pr[a \xrightarrow{S_1} b] = \Pr[a \xrightarrow{S_2} b].$$

2.2 Collision-Timing Attack

For an adversary with timing capabilities, the duration of an insert/delete operation in a hash table can reveal significant information. In our motivating scenario for this security notion, the attacker cannot read the data transferred in the communication channel between the user and the cloud provider (i.e., the encrypted channel) but he can accurately time the interaction between the two entities. We model the desired security property by introducing a game where the adversary picks two input items that collide in the hash table, the cloud provider inserts/deletes only one of them. The goal of the adversary is to distinguish which of the two items was processed relying solely only the execution time of the operation. We consider a hash table secure against collision-timing attacks if the adversary succeeds in the above game with negligible probability.

Our model only deals with the timing of colliding items. In order not to leak whether a collision occurs, one would have to deploy a hash table for which the execution time is *not affected by collisions*. Notice that it is particularly challenging to decouple the time performance of a hash table from the occurrence of collisions. One may think that in order not to leak whether collision occurs it is enough to have constant worst-case time performance for updates. This is not necessarily true since there can be maintenance actions in the hash table, that take constant time but reveal whether a collision took place.

Finding Colliding Items. As shown in the work of Lipton and Naughton [23], there is a straightforward process for an adversary to generate a pair of colliding items, i.e., a collision-discovery attack, even if the hash function is not known. As a first step, we describe a process from [23] that checks whether two items collide. Let t_0 be the time it takes to insert item u_0 to an empty hash table, similarly let t_1 be the time it takes to insert u_1 to an empty table. Now we insert u_1 in a hash table that already contains u_0 and check whether the time for insertion is larger[2] than t_1, if yes then the items u_0, u_1 collide. In order to find which pair of items to test for a collision, we can simply generate $\Omega(\sqrt{m})$ random items, where m is the table size. Indeed, assuming that the hash function distributes the items

---

[2] In the work of [23] the authors define a clocked adversary that has access to a clock that is accurate to within ϵ and can discover the difference between two measurements t_0 and t_1 with $O(\epsilon/|t_1 - t_0|)$ repetitions of the corresponding operations. For the ease of exposition we assume that our measurements are always accurate (i.e. $\epsilon = 0$) therefore no repetitions are required.

to the m bins uniformly at random, we can use the birthday-paradox and show that within this set of items there is a pair of colliding items with probability roughly $1/2$. Given that collision-discovery attacks for hash tables are difficult to avoid in practice, we focus on preventing information leakage from the eviction strategy, i.e., a collision-timing attack.

Security Definition. We indicate with λ the security parameter and with Op an update operation of the hash table, $Op \in \{\text{insert}, \text{delete}\}$. We indicate with $a \in A$ a memory representation of the state A of the hash table and with u_0, u_1 two items from the universe of input keys, K. With the term HT we denote an implementation of the hash table that has access to a source of randomness, e.g., a pseudorandom generator G. A memory representation is called *admissible* with respect to the implementation HT and the hash function hash(), if it can be reached with non-zero probability. We define an *evidence of admissibility* of a, denoted as evd_a, a pair consisting of (1) a sequence of operations S_a and (2) a random tape rnd_a such that if S_a is applied to an empty hash table using rnd_a when necessary, then the hash table reaches memory representation a. We use a game-based definition to describe the security of our setup. The game is denoted with $\text{PRV-CTA}_{HT}^{\mathcal{A}}(\lambda)$ and is shown in Fig. 1, where CTA stands for collision-timing attack. The game begins with an algorithm run by adversary $\mathcal{A}$. When $\mathcal{A}$ finishes executing, the game performs further steps with $\mathcal{A}$'s output to produce the challenge for $\mathcal{A}$. The adversary processes the challenge and outputs a bit, which is returned by the game.

$\text{PRV-CTA}_{HT}^{\mathcal{A}}(\lambda)$:
1. $(a, \text{hash}, evd_a, Op, u_0, u_1) \leftarrow \mathcal{A}(1^{\lambda})$, where $\text{hash}(u_0) = \text{hash}(u_1)$
2. **if** evd_a is not an evidence of admissibility of a **return** 0
3. Initialize the implementation HT with memory representation a and $G(\lambda)$
4. Choose at random a bit $b \in \{0, 1\}$
5. Execute operation Op according to HT with input argument u_b and record the execution time in t_b
6. $b' \leftarrow \mathcal{A}(t_b)$
7. **return** $(b = b')$

Fig. 1. Indistinguishability game for the security of a hash table against collision-timing attacks.

Indistinguishability game PRV-CTA assumes a powerful adversary that is allowed to choose the memory representation of the hash table, i.e. the state, the allocation of the items to the cells of the table as well as its hash function hash(). We denote as advantage of $\mathcal{A}$ the quantity $2 \cdot \Pr\left(\text{PRV-CTA}_{HT}^{\mathcal{A}}(\lambda) = 1\right) - 1$.

Definition 3. *Let λ be the security parameter and let HT be an implementation of a hash table. We say that implementation HT is secure against collision-timing attacks if for all PPT adversaries $\mathcal{A}$, the advantage $\mathcal{A}$ in game PRV-$CTA_{HT}^{\mathcal{A}}(\lambda)$ is negligible.*

3   Weakly History-Independent Linear Probing

In this section, we describe a weakly history-independent dictionary that is based on an open addressing hash table. For the proofs see the full version [15]. Let T be a hash table of size m and let K be the universe of keys. We hash the set of keys $U \subseteq K$ into T using hash function hash() and handle collisions with linear probing. In the following, the symbol $\perp$ indicates an empty cell and arithmetic over cell indices is modulo m. A *cluster* of T is a maximal contiguous sequence of nonempty cells of T.

Profile of a Set. Following the terminology of [20], we define the following sets and values for a cell i of T:

- H_i: set of items of U that hash to cell $T[i]$, of size $h_i = |H_i|$;
- P_i: set of items of U that probed cell $T[i]$, of size $p_i = |P_i|$.

The above quantities are a function of the set U and of hash(), but for succinctness we do not denote that explicitly. Clearly, we have $H_i \subseteq P_i$. Also, if $p_i \geq 1$, then exactly one of the items in P_i ends up in cell $T[i]$ while the remaining $p_i - 1$ items probe the next cell $T[i + 1]$. This observation yields the following recurrence relation (same relation as in [20] but different notation):

$$P_{i+1} = H_{i+1} \cup (P_i - \{v_i\}) \qquad \text{and} \qquad p_{i+1} = h_{i+1} + max(p_i - 1, 0), \qquad (1)$$

where v_i indicates the item allocated in $T[i]$. Sequence $(p_0, \ldots, p_{m-1})$ is called the *profile* of set U. Note that set P_i depends on both the performed sequence of operations and on the eviction strategy between colliding items. In contrast, the profile of U does not depend on the eviction strategy [20], since it only counts the number of items that probed a cell. Using the above fact one can easily show that the profile is also independent of the order in the sequence of operations.

Intuition. In our insertion algorithm, we use a randomized eviction strategy. Suppose $p_i \geq 1$ items have probed the i-th cell so far. When a new item u probes the i-th cell, it evicts the current item with probability $1/(p_i + 1)$. Hence, each cell is a reservoir sample [32] of size 1, so that every item probing that cell has an equal likelihood of being stored there.

We show that this technique gives a weakly history-independent insertion process. The challenge is that, to delete an item u from a cell i, we must construct a memory representation that is consistent with u never having been inserted. Note that algorithm find(u) simply performs a linear forward scan starting from hash(u) until we either find u or an empty cell.

3.1   Insertion

We use an auxiliary table, $P[]$, to keep track of the profile, where $P[i] = p_i$. All entries in $P[]$ are initially set to 0. We assume that the hash table can access random values on the fly as we need them by means of method getRand(s), which returns a random integer in the range $\{1, \ldots, s\}$.

Analysis. Let T be a hash table with linear probing where insertions are performed with Algorithm 1. As defined before, a memory representation is called admissible if it can be reached with non-zero probability.

Algorithm 1. WHI.insert(u)

Input : an item u to be inserted
1 $i \leftarrow \mathsf{hash}(u)$
2 **while** $T[i] \neq \bot$ **do**
3 $\quad P[i] \leftarrow P[i] + 1$
$\quad$ // Item u is stored in $T[i]$ with probability $1/p_i$
4 $\quad r \leftarrow \mathsf{getRand}(P[i])$
5 $\quad$ **if** $r = 1$ **then**
6 $\quad\quad |$ Swap the content of $T[i]$ and u
7 $\quad$ **end**
8 $\quad i \leftarrow i + 1$
9 **end**
10 $P[i] \leftarrow 1$
11 $T[i] \leftarrow u$

Lemma 1. *Let U be a set of items and let R be the random variable over the set of admissible representations of U in table T. Let S be a sequence of insert operations, according to Algorithm 1, that insert the items of U. Then the probability that R takes value ρ given that we follow S is given by:*

$$\Pr(R = \rho) = \prod_{j=0}^{m-1} \frac{1}{max(p_j, 1)}.$$

The next lemma follows immediately from Lemma 1.

Lemma 2. *A hash table with linear probing where only insertions are performed, according to Algorithm 1, is weakly history-independent.*

We note here that since the notion of history-independence was originally formed under an information-theoretic security framework, for consistency with previous work, our lemmas above assume the availability of true randomness.

It is straightforward to relax both strong and weak history-independence definitions to a semantically secure framework and extend our results accordingly. In this case, denoting with λ the security parameter, getRand would be derived from the output of a cryptographic pseudorandom generator with security parameter λ [14] to which the hash table, but not the adversary, has oracle access. In practice, we implement getRand by means of the secure hardware random number generator provided by modern microprocessors.

3.2   Deletion

To delete an item u from the hash table we must change the memory representation, with the right probability, so that it is as though u was never inserted.

Algorithm. The deletion method is shown in Algorithms 2–3. Given that item u is allocated in cell $T[i]$ and that it hashes to cell $\mathsf{hash}(u)$ we have to: (1) decrease by one the values of $P[\mathsf{hash}(u)], P[\mathsf{hash}(u) + 1], \ldots, P[i]$ and (2) cover the gap at $T[i]$ by picking an item uniformly at random among the items that probed $T[i]$. The above two steps are repeated, in case we create an additional gap by covering the first one.

Algorithm 2. WHI.delete(u)

Input : an item u to be deleted
1 $i \leftarrow \mathsf{hash}(u)$
2 **while** $T[i] \neq \perp$ **do**
      // Reverse the effect of u on table P
3     $P[i] \leftarrow P[i] - 1$
4   **if** $T[i] = u$ **then**
5        $T[i] \leftarrow \perp$
         // Fill the gap at cell $T[i]$
6   CoverGap(i)
7   **return**
8   **end**
9     $i \leftarrow i + 1$
10 **end**

Algorithm 3. CoverGap

Input : the index i_g of the gap in T
1 **if** $P[i_g] = 0$ **then**
2 | **return**
3 **end**
   // There are p_{i_g} items that probed $T[i_g]$. Cover with the
   rightmost.
4 $cnt \leftarrow P[i_g]$
5 $i \leftarrow i_g + 1$
6 **while** $T[i] \neq \perp$ **do**
7     $P[i] \leftarrow P[i] - 1$
8   **if** *the item in $T[i]$ probed cell $T[i_g]$* **then**
9        $cnt \leftarrow cnt - 1$
10   **if** $cnt = 0$ **then**
            // Cover the gap at $T[i_g]$, recurse for the new gap at
            $T[i]$
11          $T[i_g] \leftarrow T[i]$
12          $T[i] \leftarrow \perp$
13   CoverGap(i)
14   **return**
15   **end**
16   **end**
17    $i \leftarrow i + 1$
18 **end**

An interesting question is how to pick an item to cover the gap. One approach is to scan the cells from $T[i+1]$ until the end of the cluster and choose one of the items of P_i uniformly at random. The above randomized approach is correct but requires additional randomness and can potentially lead to a significant number of moves between the allocated items. Our technique takes advantage of the fact that in an admissible memory representation of U, the relative order of the items that probed $T[i]$ is a random permutation. Therefore, by picking the item of $T[i]$ placed furthest from $T[i]$ in the cluster, the "rightmost" item or else the p_i-th eligible item to cover the gap, is equivalent to sampling uniformly at random among the items of set P_i. Besides maintaining the weak history-independence of our construction, the benefit of this technique is twofold in terms of performance. By recursively choosing items as far to the right as possible from the gap we *reduce the number of moves* between the allocated items, and we *do not require any randomness* for the deletion process. In Algorithm 2, we locate and delete the item u; an action that creates a gap. Let $T[i_g]$ be the cell where u was allocated before the deletion. Algorithm 3 covers the gap in $T[i_g]$ with the rightmost item that probed cell $T[i_g]$.

Line 8 of Algorithm 3 checks whether the item in cell $T[i]$ probed cell $T[i_g]$ on its way to cell $T[i]$. This can be implemented as follows, if the distance of the hashed location $\mathsf{hash}(T[i])$ from the start of the cluster is less than or equal to the distance of cell $T[i_g]$ from the start of the cluster, then the item in $T[i]$ probed cell $T[i_g]$.

Analysis. We build our WHI proof based on two lemmas. Given a sequence of insertions S, we first prove that the relative order of H_i in the resulting memory representation is a random permutation. Using this, we prove the more general statement that the relative order of P_i in the resulting memory representation is a random permutation. Thus, by picking the rightmost item of P_i in the memory representation, we cover the gap with a randomly chosen item from P_i. Finally, by recursively covering the gaps in this manner, we create the same probability distribution over the memory representation as if the deleted item was never inserted.

Lemma 3. *Let U be a set of items, let π_1, π_2 be two permutations of $H_i \subseteq U$ and let S be a sequence of insertions of U according to Algorithm 1. For a location i in the hash table, let R_i be the random variable that represents the relative order of set H_i associated with cell $T[i]$ in the resulting memory representation ρ. Then, by inserting the items of U into T according to S, we have:*

$$\Pr(R_i = \pi_1) = \Pr(R_i = \pi_2)$$

Lemma 4. *Let U be a set of items, let π_1, π_2 be two permutations of $P_i \subseteq U$ and let S be a sequence of insertions of U according to Algorithm 1. For a location i in the hash table, let R'_i be the random variable that represents the relative order of set P_i associated with cell $T[i]$ in the resulting memory representation ρ. Then, by inserting the items of U into T according to S, we have:*

$$\Pr(R'_i = \pi_1) = \Pr(R'_i = \pi_2)$$

The next theorem summarizes the history-independence of our construction.

Theorem 1. *The linear probing hash table implementation described by Algorithms 1, 2 and 3 is a weakly history-independent data structure that performs searches, insertions and deletions in $O(1)$ expected time.*

3.3   Protection Against Collision-Timing Attacks

Section 2.2 gives the definition of security against collision-timing attacks for the case of general hash table implementation. We consider now the case where the hash table follows a linear probing approach.

When using linear probing, the execution time of a find, insert, or delete operation of the hash table depends on two factors, (1) whether the input item collides with an item that is already in the hash table and (2) on the eviction strategy in case there is a collision. The work of Lipton *et al.* [23] addresses the first timing factor for hash tables with chaining as well as for hash tables with open addressing. The authors propose attacking strategies that only use the execution time to discover if two given items collide in a hash table as well as a method to generate a pair of colliding items for a given hash table. In the same spirit, the adversary of PRV-CTA chooses two items that hash to the same cell. In case the items were allowed to hash to different cells, then it would be trivial for the adversary to win game PRV-CTA. Specifically, it would be enough for the adversary to pick a memory representation in which u_0 hashes to an empty cell while u_1 hashes to the beginning of a long cluster of consecutive items. Thus we turn our attention to the second timing factor, that is on the eviction policy.

Due to the nature of linear probing, the insertion/deletion process will probe the same cells regardless of whether u_0 or u_1 is chosen in PRV-CTA. Therefore, what can potentially make a hash table insecure with respect to PRV-CTA is the eviction policy. Hash tables that are secure according to Definition 3 should follow an eviction policy that is *oblivious to the value of the items*. The SHI linear probing scheme proposed in [7] is *not* secure against collision-timing attacks since a priority function that takes the values of the two items as an input (See [29] for a thorough treatment of the subject) is necessary to decide which item to evict.

We note here that the definition of security against collision-timing attacks is formed under a semantically-secure framework, thus we use the notion of a cryptographic PRNG G with a given security parameter λ in our analysis.

Theorem 2. *Let WHI be the implementation of a hash table where the insertion and deletion methods follow Algorithms 1, 2 and 3. If G is a pseudorandom number generator then the implementation WHI is secure against collision-timing attacks according to Definition 3.*

3.4   Analysis of Individual Displacement

In a hash table with linear probing, the *individual displacement* of an item is the distance between (a) the location where the item hashes to and (b) the location where the item is placed.

In this section, we derive the asymptotic performance of the individual displacement in the case of our WHI linear probing variation. In case the individual displacement is large the algorithm find has to scan a large number of cells in order to locate the requested item which slows down the performance of the operation. We note that the techniques we use are standard but the analysis appears novel. In particular, we focus on the distribution of the individual displacement in the case $n/m \to \alpha$ for $0 < \alpha < 1$. We note that the total displacement is independent of the insertion policy (as long as the policy falls within the standard class of policies; see e.g. [20]); hence the average displacement is the same for all policies, but the distribution of displacements is not. Our starting point is the Eq. (1): $p_{i+1} = h_{i+1} + max(h_i - 1, 0)$. Given a table with load α, it is helpful to start by obtaining a distribution on the entries of the profile. That is, let η_k be the fraction of bins with a count of k in the asymptotic regime as the number of bins grows to infinity. Thus, we have $\eta_k = \#\{i : p_i = k\}/m$.

Asymptotically, we can use the standard Poissonization approach of letting the h_i be distributed as independent Poisson random variables with parameter α. In this case, the p_i form a simple Markov chain, and we can consider its stationary distribution; this gives us the asymptotic distribution for η_k. In particular, a cell i has $p_i = 0$ only if the previous cell has $p_{i-1} = 0$ or $p_{i-1} = 1$ and no items hash to i, hence, $\eta_0 = (\eta_0 + \eta_1)\Pr(h_i = 0) \Rightarrow \eta_0 = (\eta_0 + \eta_1)e^{-\alpha}$.

More generally, for $k \geq 1$, we find

$$\eta_{k+1} = \eta_k \frac{1 - e^{-\alpha}\alpha}{e^{-\alpha}} - \eta_0 \frac{\alpha^k}{k!} - \sum_{l=1}^{k-1} \eta_l \frac{\alpha^{k-l+1}}{(k-l+1)!}. \tag{2}$$

From these equations, we can numerically derive the distribution using the fact that $\sum_{k=0}^{n} \eta_k = 1$. For the individual displacement, we work with a random item u, and compute the limiting distribution of its displacement. Let X_q be a random variable that takes value 0 with probability $1/q$ and value 1 otherwise. Let also Z_k be the random variable that takes as a value the displacement of u given that $p_{\mathsf{hash}(u)} = k$. For a given $k \geq 1$ we have the following recursive function:

$$Z_k = X_k \left(1 + \sum_{j=0}^{n-k+1} Z_{k-1+j} e^{-\alpha} \frac{\alpha^j}{j!} \right). \tag{3}$$

That is, with probability $1/k$ there is no displacement because u is stored in the cell it hashed to; otherwise, 1 is added to the displacement and it moves to the next cell, which has Z_{k-1+j} items that probed it, where j is the number of items that hash to that cell.

As Z_k is conditioned on the event that for cell $\mathsf{hash}(u)$ we have that $p_{\mathsf{hash}(u)} = k$, the displacement of u is a random variable D_u given by:

$$D_u = \sum_{k=0}^{n-1} Z_{k+1} \eta_k \tag{4}$$

Using Eqs. (2) and (3) one can numerically derive the distribution of the individual displacement of u for a fixed α. In Sect. 5 we show the sample variance of the individual displacement for various load factors and compare it to the variance of other linear probing schemes.

4   Previous Linear Probing Schemes

The standard linear probing scheme is a first-come-first-served (FCFS) policy, since previously allocated items do not move during an insertion. Poblete and Munro [30] propose a last-come-first-served (LCFS) policy, where an incoming item has higher priority than those previously allocated. These two policies are easily seen not to be weakly history-independent, since the resulting memory representation clearly depends on the order of updates.

Consider, instead, an alternative scheme inspired by the well-known Fisher-Yates random shuffling algorithm. That is, in the case of collision occurring in the insertion of an item, u, place the item u in the first available cell found by linear probing under the FCFS rule. Then swap u with a uniformly randomly chosen item from range of cells $T[\mathsf{hash}(u)]$ to the last cell of the cluster (wrapping around the beginning of T if needed). Let us call this eviction technique, "Random-Swap" it is easy to see that this variation is not weakly history-independent either.

In Robin Hood hashing [9], when we probe an occupied cell $T[i]$ during the insertion of an item u, we swap u into $T[i]$ if u is further from its desired cell than the current occupant (and we then probe $T[i+1]$ for the remaining item). Ties occur when u and $T[i]$ are equidistant from their desired cell. Different tie-breaking techniques give different security properties to the resulting construction. If we break ties based on the arrival time ("Robin Hood, Tie-Break w. FCFS/LCFS" in Table 1) then the scheme is secure against collision-timing attacks since the evictions do not depend on the value but it is not history-independent. Suppose, instead, that we break ties fairly, by randomly choosing between the two items with probability $1/2$, to split the "arrow" in half, using the Robin Hood metaphor. One might think that this fair-split strategy allows Robin Hood hashing to be weakly history-independent, but that is not the case.

Lemma 5. *FCFS, LCFS, Random-Swap, Robin Hood where ties break with FCFS, Robin Hood where ties break with LCFS, and Robin Hood where ties break with fair-split are (1) secure against collision-timing attacks but (2) not weakly history-independent, even in an insertion-only scenario.*

If we follow a Robin Hood hashing and break ties by choosing the larger/ smaller value ("Robin Hood, Tie-Break w. Key Sort" in Table 1, also addressed as "age-rules" in [29]), then the scheme becomes strongly history-independent but it is not secure against collision-timing attacks. Note that one has to design a new appropriate deletion process that respects the SHI property of the above RH variation, in this work we only consider the insertion process of this scheme (see Sect. 5). Finally the strongly history-independent linear probing technique from [7] is also not secure against collision-timing attacks.

Lemma 6. *Robin Hood hashing where ties break with key-sort as well as the SHI scheme of [7] are (1) strongly history-independent but (2) not secure against collision-timing attacks.*

The above observations are summarized in Table 1. The proposed linear probing scheme of this work is the first that satisfies both privacy properties.

5   Evaluation

We have implemented the strongly history independent linear probing scheme of [7], denoted as SHI, and our WHI linear probing scheme in C++ and conducted experiments to compare the performance of the two history independent techniques. The values in the (key, value) pairs consist of 10-character strings. All experiments were performed in the same machine running OSX 10.10.5 with Quad Core 2.6 GHz Intel Core i7 processor and 8 GB RAM. We used Intel's on-chip hardware random generator, instruction RdRand, that is available in "Ivy Bridge" processors [19].

Method find. The first set of experiments, depicted in Fig. 2, addresses the performance of method find. We focus on the displacement, i.e., the distance of an item from its hashed location, which affects the performance of find. For completeness, we also show the results for Robin-Hood hashing, which is known to minimize the variance of the displacements among all linear probing algorithms. We use a table of size $m = 10^7$ and we initialize the data structures

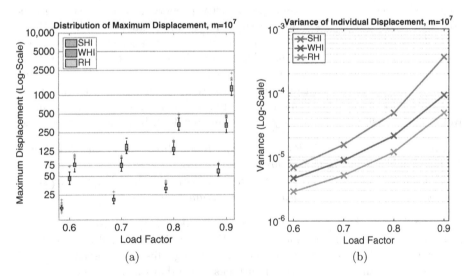

(a)   (b)

Fig. 2. Comparison of the displacement of items in Robin Hood (where ties-break with FCFS), SHI [7] and WHI (our scheme). The plot summarize results from experiments run 100 times on a table of size $m = 10^7$ with varying load factors: (a) maximum displacement; (b) variance of individual displacement.

up to load factors $\alpha = 0.6, 0.7, 0.8$, 0.9 by inserting the same set of unique randomly generated items in the same randomly chosen order to all hash tables. After the initialization, we record the displacement of each item and compute the sample variance and the maximum displacement. The above process was repeated for 100 distinct initializations. The box-plot of the maximum displacement, Fig. 2(a), shows that the average maximum displacement of WHI is much smaller than that of SHI. As another data point, in a similar experiment with a table of size $m = 10^7$, for load $\alpha = 0.9$ the maximum recorded displacement for WHI is 476 whereas for SHI it is 2228. Finally, in the plot of Fig. 2(b) shows that the variance of the individual displacement for WHI is much lower than that for SHI.

Methods insert and delete. The second set of experiments, depicted in Fig. 3, addresses the performance of methods insert and delete. In this experiment we use a table of size $m = 10^5$ and initialize the data structures up to a fixed load factor, i.e. $\alpha = 0.6 - 0.9$ by inserting the same set of unique randomly generated items in the same randomly chosen order. After the initialization we perform 10^3 find calls that take as an input a randomly chosen item among those that are already in the table in order to warm-up the cache. Then we perform an insertion (resp. deletion) of a randomly generated (resp. chosen) item and record the number of cycles executed by the method. We obtain the number of cycles as the difference between processor time stamps by means of instruction rdtsc. The above process

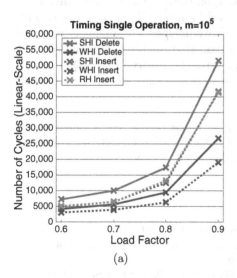
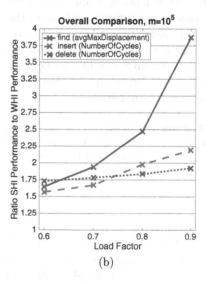

(a)   (b)

Fig. 3. Comparison of methods insert and delete in Robin Hood (where ties-break with FCFS), SHI [7] and WHI (our scheme). Plot (a) summarizes the experiments conducted 10^3 times on a table of size $m = 10^5$ with varying load factors. In each experiment, we measured the number of CPU cycles executed by a single call of method insert or delete. Plot (b) depicts the ratio between the performance of SHI to WHI.

was repeated 10^3 times for various values of α. Figure 3(a) presents the sample mean of the number of cycles, showing that our WHI scheme is significantly faster than SHI. For comparison, we also include the performance of the variation of Robin Hood linear probing where ties break in a FCFS fashion. This variation gives the fastest insertion process over all Robin Hood variations since we don't move items in case of a tie.

Overall Comparison. As an overall comparison Fig. 3(b) shows the ratio of SHI's performance to WHI's performance for each of the above operations. Each line represents an operation (i.e. find, insert, delete) and each data point of the line represents the ratio of SHI performance (in terms of average maximum displacement or number of cycles) to WHI's performance. It is clear that the average maximum displacement of WHI is significantly smaller compared to SHI, which translates to a faster worst-case time performance for find method. Specifically, the average maximum displacement of an item for the SHI eviction strategy is almost 4 times higher than the average maximum displacement of WHI, for high load factors. As for the update operations, WHI performs almost 2x faster than SHI for high load factors.

6   Conclusion and Discussion

In this paper, we have presented a linear probing hashing scheme that is weakly history-independent and secure against collision-timing attacks. According to our evaluation, all three methods of the proposed hash table (find, insert, delete) are much faster than those of the strongly history-independent analogue proposed by Blelloch and Golovin [7]. Our results suggest that weakly history-independent data structures can be more efficient than strongly history-independent ones in real-world privacy-preserving applications such as ballot storage and hospital admissions management.

Acknowledgments. This work was supported in part by the U.S. National Science Foundation under grants CCF–1535795, CCF–1320231, CNS–1228485, CNS–1228598, and CNS–1228639, and by the Kanellakis Fellowship at Brown University.

References

1. Voluntary Voting System Guidelines, Ver. 1.1, vol. 1. Technical report, United States Election Assistance Commission (2015). www.eac.gov/assets/1/Documents/VVSG.1.1.VOL.1.FINAL.pdf
2. Aslam, J.A., Popa, R.A., Rivest, R.L.: On auditing elections when precincts have different sizes. In: Proceedings of the USENIX EVT (2008)
3. Bajaj, S., Sion, R.: Ficklebase: looking into the future to erase the past. In: Proceedings of 29th IEEE ICDE, pp. 86–97 (2013)
4. Bajaj, S., Sion, R.: HIFS: history independence for file systems. In: Proceedings of 20th ACM CCS, pp. 1285–1296 (2013)

5. Bethea, D., Reiter, M.K.: Data structures with unpredictable timing. In: Backes, M., Ning, P. (eds.) ESORICS 2009. LNCS, vol. 5789, pp. 456–471. Springer, Heidelberg (2009)
6. Bethencourt, J., Boneh, D., Waters, B.: Cryptographic methods for storing ballots on a voting machine. In: Proceedings of 14th NDSS, pp. 209–222 (2007)
7. Blelloch, G.E., Golovin, D.: Strongly history-independent hashing with applications. In Proceedings of 48th IEEE FOCS, pp. 272–282 (2007)
8. Buchbinder, N., Petrank, E.: Lower and upper bounds on obtaining history independence. Inf. Comput. 204(2), 291–337 (2006)
9. Celis, P., Per-Ake Larson, J., Munro, I.: Robin hood hashing. In: Proceedings of 26th IEEE FOCS, pp. 281–288 (1985)
10. Chen, B., Sion, R.: Hiflash: a history independent flash device. CoRR, abs/1511.05180 (2015)
11. Crosby, S.A., Wallach, D.S.: Denial of service via algorithmic complexity attacks. In: Proceedings of 12th USENIX Security Symposium (2003)
12. Feldman, A.J., Alex Halderman, J., Felten, E.W.: Security analysis of the Diebold AccuVote-TS voting machine. In: Proceedings of the USENIX EVT (2007)
13. Futoransky, A., Saura, D., Waissbein, A.: Timing attacks for recovering private entries from database engines. In: BlackHat USA (2007)
14. Goldreich, O.: The Foundations of Cryptography, Basic Techniques, vol. 1. Cambridge University Press, Cambridge (2001)
15. Goodrich, M.T., Kornaropoulos, E.M., Mitzenmacher, M., Tamassia, R.: More practical and secure history-independent hash tables. Cryptology ePrint Archive, Report 2016/134 (2016). http://eprint.iacr.org/2016/134
16. Goodrich, M.T., Tamassia, R.: Algorithm Design and Applications, 1st edn. Wiley (2014). ISBN:1118335910, 9781118335918
17. Alex Halderman, J., Schoen, S.D., Heninger, N., Clarkson, W., Paul, W., Calandrino, J.A., Feldman, A.J., Appelbaum, J., Felten, E.W.: Lest we remember: cold boot attacks on encryption keys. In: Proceedings of 17th USENIX Security Symposium, pp. 45–60 (2008)
18. Hartline, J.D., Hong, E.S., Mohr, A.E., Pentney, W.R., Rocke, E.: Characterizing history independent data structures. Algorithmica 42(1), 57–74 (2005)
19. Hofemeier, G.: Intel Digital Random Number Generator (DRNG) software implementation guide. Technical report (2012)
20. Janson, S.: Individual displacements for linear probing hashing with different insertion policies. ACM Trans. Algorithms 1, 177–213 (2005)
21. Knuth, D.E.: The Art of Computer Programming: Sorting and Searching, vol. 3, 2nd edn. Pearson (1998)
22. Kohno, T., Stubblefield, A., Rubin, A.D., Wallach, D.S.: Analysis of an electronic voting system. In: Proceedings of 25th IEEE S&P, pp. 27–40 (2004)
23. Lipton, R.J., Naughton, J.F.: Clocked adversaries for hashing. Algorithmica 9(3), 239–252 (1993)
24. Maartmann-Moe, C.: Inception: a physical memory manipulation and hacking tool exploiting PCI-based DMA
25. Micciancio, D.: Oblivious data structures: applications to cryptography. In: Proceedings of 29th ACM STOC, pp. 456–464 (1997)
26. Molnar, D., Kohno, T., Sastry, N., Wagner, D.: Tamper-evident, history-independent, subliminal-free data structures on PROM storage-or-how to store ballots on a voting machine. In: Proceedings of IEEE S&P, pp. 365–370 (2006)

27. Moran, T., Naor, M., Segev, G.: Deterministic history-independent strategies for storing information on write-once memories. In: Arge, L., Cachin, C., Jurdziński, T., Tarlecki, A. (eds.) ICALP 2007. LNCS, vol. 4596, pp. 303–315. Springer, Heidelberg (2007)
28. Naor, M., Segev, G., Wieder, U.: History-independent cuckoo hashing. In: Aceto, L., Damgård, I., Goldberg, L.A., Halldórsson, M.M., Ingólfsdóttir, A., Walukiewicz, I. (eds.) ICALP 2008, Part II. LNCS, vol. 5126, pp. 631–642. Springer, Heidelberg (2008)
29. Naor, M., Teague, V.: Anti-presistence: history independent data structures. In: Proceedings of 33rd ACM STOC, pp. 492–501 (2001)
30. Poblete, P.V., Munro, J.I.: Last-come-first-served hashing. J. Algorithms 10(2), 228–248 (1989)
31. Rivest, R.L., Shen, E.: A Bayesian method for auditing elections. In: Proceedings of USENIX EVT/WOTE (2012)
32. Vitter, J.S.: Random sampling with a reservoir. ACM Trans. Math. Softw. 11(1), 37–57 (1985)
33. Wolchok, S., Wustrow, E., Halderman, J.A., Prasad, H.K., Kankipati, A., Sakhamuri, S.K., Yagati, V., Gonggrijp, R.: Security analysis of India's electronic voting machines. In: Proceedings of 17th ACM CCS, pp. 1–14 (2010)

On Manufacturing Resilient Opaque Constructs
Against Static Analysis

Brendan Sheridan and Micah Sherr[✉]

Georgetown University, Washington DC 20057, USA
msherr@cs.georgetown.edu

Abstract. Opaque constructs have developed into a commonly used primitive in obfuscation, watermarking, and tamper-proofing schemes. However, most prior work has based the resilience of these primitives on a poorly defined reduction to a known $\mathcal{NP}$-complete problem. There has been little scrutiny of the adversarial model and little discussion of how to generate instances that are always hard. In this paper, we offer what we believe to be the first complete algorithm for generating *resilient* opaque constructs against static analysis. We base their resilience on the complexity of 3SAT instances with cn clauses for $c = 6$ and n distinct variables. We draw on existing theoretical bounds to show that these instances always require exponential time to defeat under formal notions of resolution complexity.

This paper also explores in-depth the security of opaque constructs in real-world settings. We argue that the common theoretical model used in prior work (as well as our resilient opaque construction scheme) is too optimistic. It does not offer practical obfuscation against an adversary who tolerates some small false positive rate. We offer a heuristic-based attack to demonstrate this issue. Our results suggest that opaque constructs should be viewed with a high degree of skepticism until they can be proven secure under more useful theoretical models.

1 Introduction

Code obfuscation is the process of transforming source or machine code such that the original functionality is maintained, but is hard to discern from inspection of the transformed code. Traditionally, obfuscation was employed to confuse a human reader with the goal of preventing reverse-engineering or hiding certain functionality. This adversarial setting spawned an ecosystem of sophisticated automated obfuscation, and conversely, increasingly sophisticated de-obfuscation and analysis techniques. Currently, an effective obfuscation scheme must not only make the code unreadable, but also difficult to analyze for both targeted and generalized adversarial analysis.

Opaque predicates [9] were introduced to formalize the notion that an effective obfuscation scheme must be able to conceal at least one bit of information from an adversary. Informally, the runtime value of the opaque predicate should be known a priori by the obfuscater based on asymmetric information involved

© Springer International Publishing Switzerland 2016
I. Askoxylakis et al. (Eds.): ESORICS 2016, Part II, LNCS 9879, pp. 39–58, 2016.
DOI: 10.1007/978-3-319-45741-3_3

in its creation, but difficult for an adversary to determine without that same information. This primitive allows an obfuscation scheme to naturally obscure the control flow of a program by simply inserting opaque predicates into conditional branch tests. Since the obfuscater can predict the runtime value of the predicate, they can structure the program branching accordingly whereas an adversary must consider both possible values and their associated control flow. This same primitive has similarly been used in software watermarking [20], the embedding of information that can later be used to identify the original author via public key cryptography, as well as tamper-proofing, the goal of obfuscation such that modifying the functionality is difficult [7].

Unfortunately, while these primitives have seen heavy use, their theoretical basis is very weak. Most commonly, they base their hardness on a reduction to a $\mathcal{NP}$-complete problem. This is an unfortunately common fallacy because these problems are only known to be hard in the worst case. Moreover, since these problems are being artificially generated, there is no inherent guarantee that any of them will be hard in practice. There is an extensive line of work originating from the study of satisfiability problems in artificial intelligence (AI) which suggests that natural choices for generation algorithms actually produce instances that can be solved in polynomial time on average [5, 10, 24]. However, this line of work has also established that it is possible to construct instances that are always hard with careful parameter selection. We seek to formally apply this line of work to the obfuscation context in order to strengthen the theoretical basis of opaque constructs.

Using opaque predicates to construct an actual obfuscation scheme is largely beyond the scope of this work. To simplify discussion and establish context, we primarily focus on formalizing and extending the work of Moser et al. [19] on obfuscation in the context of static analysis. The authors offer an impressive engineering contribution, fully implementing their x86 binary rewriting scheme and defeating state-of-the-art semantics-aware malware detectors with reasonable overhead. However, they claim their scheme is provably hard to analyze for any static code analyzer based only on an informal reduction from their obfuscation primitive to a 3-satisfiability problem (3SAT) [17]. We believe this assertion to be accurate, but seek to formalize it by more narrowly defining static analysis, giving an algorithm for picking appropriate 3SAT instances, and explicitly proving the reduction as well as the original theorem. In the Appendix, we also examine alternative problems on which to base the primitive, but it is currently unclear if any candidate is a fundamentally better choice than 3SAT due to open problems in cryptography and complexity.

While our main focus is the theoretical strength of the obfuscation primitive, we also offer extensions to the overall obfuscation scheme. Notably, we will show how the ability to obfuscate a single bit, consistent with the original obfuscation primitive, can be generalized to securely and efficiently encrypt the data section. This technique systematically defeats problems the original authors encountered when testing against commercial, regular expression based, malware detectors.

As a second major contribution, we offer a critique of this model and explore its efficacy in the real-world. We present a *heuristic* attack against an obfuscation scheme employing our resilient predicates. Analyzing its effectiveness and efficiency, we find that targeted heuristic approaches can defeat the theoretically resilient construct with high probability. Our results reveal weaknesses in the commonly used model for opaque constructs and suggest the need for increased skepticism over the use of opaque constructs in obfuscation schemes.

2 Problem and Definitions

Code obfuscation is applicable in a wide variety of contexts. To simplify discussion, we adopt the use-case of Moser et al. [19]. The authors were interested in exploring the limits of static analysis for malware detection, where malware is simply defined as malicious code. The obfuscator is given a piece of (presumably malicious) machine code and must transform the program using opaque constructs such that its functionality remains the same and its runtime performance is not drastically altered. The transformed code should be difficult to identify as the original code. The static adversary, in turn, seeks to identify the obfuscated code given only the original code. For our purposes, it is unnecessary to restrict the behavior of the adversary. However, most prior work first seeks to remove binary obfuscation from the program to allow disassembly, then uses semantic analysis to identify known malicious functionality. Figure 1 gives a graphical representation of this use-case.

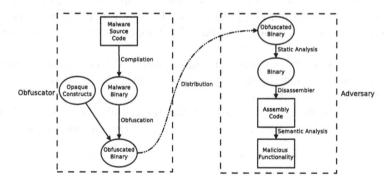

Fig. 1. Malware detection use-case where the obfuscator seeks to hide the malicious nature of the program using opaque constructs and the static adversary seeks to find malicious functionality.

It should be noted that this overall problem more generally falls under black-box obfuscation and the general case is suspected to be impossible for formal hardness guarantees [2]. Our problem is, more simply, to generate resilient opaque primitives. More specifically, it is to generate opaque constructs in polynomial time that can be evaluated in linear time but are resilient with exponential resolution complexity.

Definition 1. *A construct is said be **opaque** at point p in a program if its value q is known at obfuscation time with exponentially high probability (w.h.p). We denote an **opaque predicate** P_p^q and an **opaque variable** V_p^q, and we drop the subscript of both when the execution point is obvious from context.*

This definition slightly weakens the original definition from Collberg et al. [9] for convenience purposes. The original contains no notion of probability. However, we show that the probability of one of our constructs failing is exponentially small with respect to n, so it should not be a concern in practice. We discuss the issue in more detail in Appendix A. We also discuss how obfuscation schemes should avoid compounding this probability in Sect. 4. We concern ourselves only with constant opaque constructs, i.e., those for which q is independent of p. However, prior work has shown how to construct dynamic opaque predicates based on several constant opaque predicates [9,19].

Definition 2. *Given a program, P, an obfuscation transformation, $\mathcal{T}$, and a positive scalar-valued complexity measuring function, E, the **potency** of $\mathcal{T}$ measures the complexity increase in the result program, P'. Formally, the potency of $\mathcal{T}$ on the program P, $\mathcal{T}_{pot}(P)$, is given by $\mathcal{T}_{pot}(P) \equiv E(P')/E(P) - 1$.*

Abstractly, the potency of an obfuscation transformation measures how complex or unreadable the resulting program is compared to the original. By convention, E increases with the logical complexity of the input program so an obfuscator should seek to maximize potency. However, the concrete definition is dependent on E. It is natural to draw on various software engineering metrics to measure readability and complexity, but they are often context dependent and subjective, with no de facto standard. Collberg et al. [8] give a taxonomy of potential choices.

Fortunately, since we are primarily interested in the obfuscation primitive itself rather than any motivating obfuscation scheme, it suffices to assume that the inclusion of the primitive increases the complexity of the resulting program, $E(P')$. For ease of discussion, we assume that the primitive is used as a branch condition and the goal of the deobfuscator is to remove unreachable branches.

Definition 3. *The **resilience** of an opaque predicate is formally the time and space required by an automatic deobfuscater to effectively reduce the potency of an obfuscation transformation, $\mathcal{T}$.*

To distinguish our model from the more relaxed approximation-based methods for static analysis commonly employed in software verification research, we offer a more restricted definition of static analysis. However, we note that prior research in this context makes no such distinction.

Definition 4. *We define **complete static analysis** as any algorithm which takes program code as input and enumerates all possible execution paths of the given code unless it can prove via resolution strategy that a branch will never be taken.*

This definition is consistent with the traditional notion of a complete static analyzer, that is, one which returns no false-positives. We have only augmented it to include a notion of computational complexity that is dependent on resolution complexity. This is, to our knowledge, the most appropriate and formal notion of complexity available.

One might argue that a more appropriate goal is resilience against a **sound static analyzer**, that is, one which sacrifices false-positives but does not allow false-negatives (it is easy to see that soundness and completeness are competing goals since an analysis that is both sound and complete would cover the halting problem). In fact, we argue in Sect. 5 that the requirement of complete static analysis is unrealistic.

Unfortunately, it is difficult to formalize the notion of sound static analysis in this context. Any such notion would likely also be contingent on stealth (since detecting obfuscation is reasonable grounds to flag a program), and we argue informally that stealth is most likely unachievable.

Importantly, our definition is consistent with the prior work in this context, which assumes the analyzer must cover all possible execution paths unless it can prove a path will never be taken [4,19].

Definition 5. *A **resolution strategy** is any algorithm that proves unsatisfiability via resolution reduction. We call the size of the resulting proof the **resolution complexity**.*

Our assumption that resolution complexity is representative of computational complexity is common in AI research and consistent with prior work on random 3SAT hardness [5,10,24]. We are unaware of any more formal lower-bounds for the complexity of artificially generated $\mathcal{NP}$-complete instances.

Definition 6. *3-satifiability or **3SAT** is the boolean satisfiability problem, given a boolean expression in the form $\bigwedge_{i=1}^{m}(X_{i,1} \bigvee X_{i,2} \bigvee X_{i,3})$ and assignment of n boolean variables and their negation to the m clauses, $X_{i,j} \in \{x_1, x_2, ..., x_n, \overline{x_1}, \overline{x_2}, ..., \overline{x_n}\}$, of determining if the expression is satisfiable for some truth value assignment of each variable. It is known to be $\mathcal{NP}$-complete in the number of the variables [17]. By convention, we say that $m = c \times n$ so we can refer to the ratio of clauses to variables, or **density**, as c.*

For simplicity in our analysis, we also adopt the notion of a random 3SAT problem consistent with the works by Kamath et al. [16] and Chvátal and Szemerédi [5].

Definition 7. *A **random 3SAT** problem is defined by the random distribution used to create it. Each clause is chosen independently by choosing three distinct variables uniformly at random and independently negating each with probability $1/2$; the variables are then assigned to $X_{i,1}, X_{i,2},$ and $X_{i,3}$ accordingly.*

3 Generating Opaque Constructs

This section gives our first main contribution: algorithms for constructing theoretically strong opaque constructs and proofs of their resilience against complete static analysis. To start, we must first outline the intended usage of an opaque predicate instance. Algorithm 1 shows the intended inclusion of an opaque predicate in an obfuscation scheme. The 3SAT instance is naturally encoded into a boolean statement that is evaluated at runtime. Each variable in the statement is set randomly at runtime during the call to evaluate. For an opaque predicate, P^f, the obfuscater knows w.h.p. that this branch will never be followed. However, the adversary cannot discount the possibility without proving the statement's unsatisfiability. This formulation is taken directly from Moser et al. [19].

Algorithm 1. Runtime evaluation of opaque predicate

```
/* index variables and their inverses                              */
S[] ← [x₁, x₂, ..., xₙ, x̄₁, x̄₂, ..., x̄ₙ]
/* input X_{i,j}: constructed predicate                            */
satisfied ← evaluate(S, X_{i,j})
...
if (satisfied) then
  └ branch

Function evaluate(S, X_{i,j})
  │ Input: S− index variables
  │ Input: X_{i,j} − opaque predicate
  │ Output: satisfied− boolean indicating if predicate was satisfied
  │ /* assign boolean values randomly                              */
  │ for i in 0..n − 1 do
  │   │ S[i] ← rand(true, false)
  │   └ S[n + i] ← ¬V[i]
  │ /* record satisfaction in predicate                            */
  │ satisfied ← true
  │ for i in 0..X_{i,j}-1 do
  │   │ if ¬S[X_{i,1}] ∧ ¬S[X_{i,2}] ∧ ¬S[X_{i,3}] then
  │   │   └ satisfied ← false
  │ return satisfied
```

Lemma 1. *The runtime evaluation indicated by Algorithm 1 takes $O(n)$ time given a predicate with $O(n)$ clauses.*

Proof. The algorithm performs two loops with a constant number of operations in each body. This first is over n explicitly and the second is over the number of clauses which we have specified is $O(n)$. The entire algorithm therefore runs in $O(n)$.

Algorithm 2 gives our method for producing opaque predicates. Special attention should be paid to the choice of density $c = 6$. Maintaining the appropriate ratio of clauses to variables allows us to directly apply known resolution complexity bounds. Moser et al. did not explicitly specify their algorithm for predicate generation, but we can reasonably assume they did not maintain this ratio because they discuss changing the number of clauses in their performance section without any mention of the number of variables.

We show that our formulation is efficient, correct, and resilient.

Algorithm 2. 3SAT based method for generating strong opaque predicates

---

Function *generate_predicate(n)*
    Input: $n-$ number of 3SAT variables
    Output: $X_{i,j}-$ 2D array of variable assignments for each variable(j) in each
        clasue(i)
    `/* maintain minimum clause/variable ratio                    */`
    `num_clauses` $\leftarrow n \times 6$
    `/* randomly set each clause                                   */`
    for i **in** *0..num_clauses-1* **do**
        `/* chose boolean indices at random                        */`
        choose x_1, x_2, and x_3 from 0..n-1
        `/* negate each with Pr=1/2                                 */`
        for j **in** *1..3* **do**
            if *rand(true, false)* **then**
                $X_{i,j} \leftarrow x_i$
            else
                $X_{i,j} \leftarrow x_i + n$
    return $X_{i,j}$

Lemma 2. *Algorithm 2 generates a valid opaque predicate, P^f, and runs in $O(n)$.*

Proof. The algorithm enumerates each clause in the expression and explicitly constructs it based on Definition 7. We can therefore say that it is a valid random 3SAT instance by construction. A valid opaque predicate P^f must also evaluate to false w.h.p. By construction, every set of variable assignments has uniform probability of satisfying a random 3SAT instance. Therefore, w.l.o.g. consider the specific assignment of true to each variable, $\{x_1 = ... = x_n = true\}$. The probability of a randomly chosen clause being satisfied by this assignment is the probability that at least one of the chosen variables is not negated, $1 - (1/2)^3 = 7/8$. Since all clauses are constructed independently, the probability of all clauses being satisfied is thus $(7/8)^{cn}$. Given our choice of $c = 6$, $(7/8)^{6n} \approx (1/2)^{1.16n}$ for any positive integer n, so the probability of the predicate being satisfied at runtime clearly grows exponentially small with respect to n.

Since our algorithm merely enumerates each clause, making a constant number of random decisions for each, we can conclude that it runs in $O(m)$. We have explicitly set $m = 6n$ so it runs in $O(m) = O(n)$.

Lemma 3. *Any complete static analysis of the opaque predicate controlled branch from Algorithm 1 must consider both execution paths unless it can prove that the boolean statement is unsatisfiable and will never be followed.*

Proof. This follows directly from our definition of complete static analysis. We require that a complete static analysis algorithm consider all possible execution paths. Unless the adversary can prove that the boolean statement will never evaluate to false, it must consider the possibility that the branch will be followed and include it in their analysis.

Lemma 4. *Opaque predicates generated by Algorithm 2 are resilient with exponential resolution complexity.*

Proof. From Definition 2, resilience is the time and space required to remove a predicate from the static analysis. Lemma 3 states that a branch cannot be eliminated without proving that the opaque predicate always evaluates to false. Therefore the problem of reducing branching complexity is equivalent to proving the unsatisfiability of our opaque predicate construction and the associated random 3SAT instance with $c > 6$. Here, we can draw on a lower bound from Chvátal and Szemerédi [5]. The authors proved that, for every choice of positive integers c and k such that $k \geq 3$ and $c2^{-k} \geq 0.7$, the unsatisfiability resolution proof for a randomly chosen family of cn clauses of size k over n variables generates at least $(1 + \epsilon)^n$ clauses. Since we are working with 3SAT, $k = 3$ and this theorem applies for $c \geq 5.6$. We have deliberately chosen $c = 6$ corresponding to $\lceil 5.6 \rceil$ so that this result can be applied directly. Because any resolution proof of our predicates requires at least exponential space, we can say that they are resilient with exponential resolution complexity.

Next, we show how to use our opaque predicates to trivially generate opaque variables of arbitrary constant length and a given value, q. Note that q is not somehow encoded in the variable itself, but rather passed into the runtime evaluation. This may seem counterintuitive because our overall goal is to hide information from the adversary and the information is clearly human readable in this form. However, preventing things like human readability is the responsibility of the overall obfuscation scheme. Here, it suffices to provide the promised resilience against complete static analysis and trust that the calling obfuscation scheme uses the primitive appropriately. This is consistent with our abstract interpretation of potency from Sect. 2. We do show that these variables exhibit the same resilience and correctness guarantees as our predicates.

Lemma 5. *Algorithm 3 generates valid opaque variables, V^q and runs in $O(n)$ given a constant bit-length l.*

Algorithm 3. Generating opaque variables from opaque predicates

---

Function $generate\_variable(n, l)$
   Input: $l-$ desired bit-length
   Input: $n-$ number of 3SAT variables
   Output: $V-$ array of opaque predicates
   `/* generate predicate for each bit`   `*/`
   for i *in* $0..l\text{-}1$ **do**
      $V[i] \leftarrow$ generate_predicate(n)
   return V

Function $evaluate\_variable(q, l, V)$
   Input: $q-$ desired variable value
   Input: $l-$ bit-length of variable
   Input: $V-$ opaque variable
   Output: $Q-$ evaluated value of variable
   `/* bool array to represent bits of `q `*/`
   $Q[]$
   for i *in* $0..l\text{-}1$ **do**
      $Q[i] \leftarrow$evaluate_predicate$(V[i]) \oplus q[i]$
   return Q

Proof. Each bit of q is simply xor'ed with the evaluation of an opaque predicate; thus, it suffices to show that none of these predicates are satisfied w.h.p. Lemma 2 gives us that the probability of any single predicate being satisfied by a random assignment is $(7/8)^{6n}$. Therefore the probability that any of these predicates are satisfied is $\sum_{i=1}^{l} \left(\frac{7}{8}\right)^{6n} \approx l \cdot 2^{-1.16n}$, which clearly still grows exponentially small w.r.t. n.

The methods simply perform l different instances of generate_predicate and evaluate_predicate respectively. Lemmas 1 and 2 state that these both run in $O(n)$. We have required that l is constant so both methods run in $O(n)$.

Lemma 6. *Opaque variables generated by Algorithm 3 are resilient with exponential resolution complexity.*

Proof. Here, our measure of potency is the possible 2^l possible values of V^q that a static adversary must consider. Clearly, since each bit of V can take the value 0 or 1 based on the result of the xor with an opaque predicate, the adversary cannot reduce the potency of the variable without defeating one of the opaque predicates. We have from Lemma 4 that each predicate is resilient with exponential resolution complexity so we can say that these opaque variables also have exponential resolution complexity.

4   Obfuscation Scheme Extensions

We next offer a simple extension to the original obfuscation scheme given by Moser et al. [19]. We also discuss how one might intelligently scale the number of variables, n, and the density, c, based on the desired properties of the overall obfuscation scheme.

4.1 Encrypting Data Against Complete Static Analysis

One notable shortcoming of the original obfuscation scheme is that it is potentially vulnerable to the simple data section pattern matching used by commercial virus scanners. Opaque variables cannot be readily used to hide data patterns from a heuristic-based adversary and the linear space increase associated with using an opaque variable for the entire data section is unappealing in practice.

Moser et al. contend that this is a non-issue because an obfuscater can simply encrypt the data section using a unique key stored in the binary, unpacking the data accordingly at runtime. We argue that this is inconsistent with their goal of defeating static analysis. Given a secret key naïvely stored in the binary as well as a known or unobfuscated encryption algorithm, even a static adversary can simply decrypt the data section before applying a pattern matching strategy. However, to defeat a static adversary, it suffices to hide the secret key with an opaque variable. Algorithm 4 gives a straightforward key generation algorithm based on this intuition. The key can be used in any stateless symmetric encryption scheme, $\mathcal{SE} = (\mathcal{K}, \mathcal{E}, \mathcal{D})$, such as CTR-C with AES [14]. The actual cryptography is interchangeable and the resilience of the scheme derives simply from the resilience of our opaque variables shown in Lemma 6.

Algorithm 4. $\mathcal{K}-$ Opaque key generation

Function *generate_key(n)*

    Input: $n-$ number of 3SAT variables

    Output: $K-$ opaque cryptographic key

    $K \leftarrow_\$ \mathbb{Z}_p$

    $V \leftarrow$ generate_variable$(n, |K|)$

    $K \leftarrow$ evaluate_variable$(K, |K|, V)$

    return K

Lemma 7. *Algorithm 4 takes $O(n)$ time to generate a constant-length opaque key from a cryptographic key of the same length. The resulting key has exponential resolution complexity.*

Proof. We assume here that an appropriate constant-length key is supplied or is trivial to select. We have from Lemma 5 that generate_variable and evaluate_variable both run in $O(n)$ given a constant bit length variable. generate_key simply applies both to the constant length cryptographic key so it must also run in $O(n)$.

We also have from Lemma 6 that the resulting variable (in this case the key) is a valid opaque construct with exponential resolution complexity.

4.2   Choosing Opaque Construct Parameters

There are several tradeoffs arising from our opaque construct generation algorithms that can be controlled via the number of 3SAT variables, n, and the ratio of clauses to variables, c.

First, we can exponentially increase the resilience of our constructs by increasing n. This comes at a linear $O(n)$ cost in the size of the transformed code, the runtime of the generation algorithm, and the runtime of the opaque evaluation.

The second is a very subtle property of random 3SAT refutation. Although we are guaranteed exponential resolution complexity for any positive integer $c \geq 5.6$ and increasing c decreases the probability that our construct will ever be incorrectly evaluated, there is a hidden drawback to allowing c to be much larger than 6. In practice, large values of c make the resulting 3SAT instance very over-constrained and easier to resolve. For example, Crawford and Auton [11] showed experimentally that the growth rate of their algorithm was approximately $2^{n/17}$ for $c = 4.3$ compared to only $2^{n/57}$ for $c = 10$. Selman et al. [24] later showed this is due to a monotonically decreasing behavior in the search space above the critical point of roughly $c = 4.3$. As such, we feel it is wise to choose c as close to the theoretically proven lower bound as possible.

4.3   Compounding Effects

There is an error probability compounding effect resulting from the use of multiple opaque constructs. Since an error in any single construct affects the overall correctness of the transformed code, one should consider the probability of any single construct failing when bounding the error probability of their obfuscation scheme. Fortunately, this probability can be calculated explicitly as in Lemma 5 and the scaling is very favorable. It suffices to choose n sufficiently large to exercise the exponential scaling.

5   Heuristic Attacks

Given the strong formal guarantees described in the previous sections, we next take a different tack and explore the efficacy of opaque constructs in practice. That is, we ask a more fundamental question: are these theoretical constructs actually useful?

A major weakness of the formal model considered by Moser et al. [19] and adopted by us in the proceeding sections is that it envisions an unrealistic adversary. Malware detectors (unlike compilers) are typically uninterested in precisely proving that a transformation is safe. They intentionally tolerate some small false positive rate, sacrificing completeness for soundness.

Such detectors often employ heuristic strategies against which our construction would not be provably resilient. In what follows, we highlight this potential problem by offering an effective attack against the predicates we previously proved were resilient with exponential resolution complexity against complete static analysis.

We start by giving a heuristic based algorithm designed to correctly identify predicates generated by Algorithm 2 in polynomial time. We show that, assuming our heuristic can correctly identify instances of random 3SAT, we can identify our generated opaque predicates with perfect recall in polynomial time. We also show that the probability of incorrectly identifying a satisfiable predicate as opaque is bounded by a small constant, making the chance that we change the functionality of the program similarly small.

Algorithm 5 gives our heuristic-based detection strategy. First, the algorithm tests to see if the predicate is controlled by a random 3SAT instance: we naïvely verify that the predicate is a 3SAT instance and we also test whether the observed literals follow the expected uniform distribution; the details of which of are discussed in Sect. 5.1. If either test fails, we abandon analysis of the predicate since our generation algorithm only produces random 3SAT instances.

If the predicate has been determined to be a random 3SAT instance, the algorithm then tests the estimated value of c to determine if $\tilde{c} > 6$. If so, the tester can be extremely confident that the branch will never be followed because we know that random 3SAT instances with sufficient values of c are unsatisfiable w.h.p. Thus, the branch can be safely removed without altering the program's functionality.

Algorithm 5. Heuristic method for defeating opaque predicates generated by Algorithm 2

Function *check_predicate(s)*
　　Input: s−boolean formula controlling branch
　　/* check if 3SAT instance   */
　　for *each clause in s* **do**
　　　　if *variables* $\neq$ 3 **then**
　　　　　　└ **return**

　　/* check for uniform distribution using χ^2-test for uniformity */
　　if χ^2_*test(s)* > *uniformity_threshold* **then**
　　　　└ **return**
　　/* count the unique variables in s */
　　$\tilde{n}$ ←count(s)
　　/* check estimated value of c */
　　$\tilde{c}$ ←clauses$(s)/\tilde{n}$
　　if $\tilde{c} < 6$ **then**
　　　　└ **return**
　　/* if all tests pass, assume opaque   */
　　remove(branch(s))
　　remove(s)

Lemma 8. *Algorithm 5 runs in polynomial time.*

Proof. The algorithm simply steps once through a series of tests and each test runs in polynomial time so the algorithm as a whole must also run in polynomial time.

Next, we would like to account for the potential skew in the observed value of $\tilde{n}$, and consequently skew in the estimated value of c, $\tilde{c}$. Since the attack sees only the generated predicate, it can potentially underestimate the actual number of variables in the generating distribution. Formally,

Definition 8. *We consider the result of Algorithm 5 to be a **true-positive** if the true value of $c = 6$ and the branch and predicate are appropriately removed.*

Given this definition, we can actually show that an opaque predicate will always be correctly identified.

Lemma 9. *The recall of Algorithm 5 is exactly 1, i.e. $TPR = 1$.*

Proof. By Definition 8, a false-negative can only occur when $c = 6$. By construction, the predicate and branch are only removed when $\tilde{c} < 6$. Since, also by construction, $\tilde{c} = cn / \tilde{n}$, they are removed when $\tilde{n} \leq n$. Clearly, we will never observe more than n variables because there are only n variables in the distribution. Thus, our algorithm can never mistakenly reject an opaque predicate generated by Algorithm 2 provided that it successfully passed the uniformity test.

We would also like to show that the possibility of incorrectly identifying a satisfiable predicate as opaque is appropriately small. To do so, we use the Satisfiability Threshold Conjecture for random 3SAT. It states that there exists a single density, c, such that generated instances with density $\leq c$ are satisfiable whereas generated instances with density $> c$ are unsatisfiable w.h.p. The best known upper bound for this conjecture is $c = 4.51$ [3] so we will conservatively consider the probability that a given predicate with $c = 4.51$ is determined to be opaque and incorrectly removed. We do not distinguish between our generated opaque predicates and predicates that coincidentally have $c > 4.51$ because, regardless, it is safe to remove a predicate and branch that will never be satisfied.

Lemma 10. *The probability that Algorithm 5 removes a satisfiable branch is guaranteed to be small, i.e., $P\{c \leq 4.51\} < 5.33 \times 10^{-6}$.*

Proof. From Algorithm 5, we remove a predicate when the estimated value of c, $\tilde{c} \geq 6$. We have assumed that $c = 4.51$ and $\tilde{c}$ is calculated with $\tilde{c} = cn / \tilde{n}$ so we would like to bound the probability that $\tilde{n} / n \leq 4.51 / 6$. Let Y be an indicator variable for the absence of the i-th variable from the generating distribution in the predicate. We can say that $\tilde{n} = n - \sum Y$, so we would like to bound the probability that $\sum Y \geq .25n$. Applying Markov's inequality gives us a very loose but sufficient bound, i.e.

$$Y_i = \begin{cases} 1 & \text{if } x_i \text{ does not appear} \\ 0 & \text{otherwise} \end{cases} \implies P\left\{\sum Y \geq .25n\right\} \leq \frac{E(\sum Y)}{.25n}$$

and we can calculate $E\left(\sum Y\right)$ directly by linearity of expectation. The probability that a particular variable, x_i, is left out of every clause is

$$P\{Y_i = 1\} = \left(\frac{n-3}{n}\right)^{cn} \implies E\left(\sum Y\right) = n\left(\frac{n-3}{n}\right)^{cn}$$

Substituting in, we are left with a monotonically increasing function for $n \geq 3$,

$$P\left\{\sum Y \geq .25n\right\} \leq 4\left(\frac{n-3}{n}\right)^{4.51n} < 5.33 \times 10^{-6}$$

5.1 Distribution Testing

The testing of the distribution is, theoretically, the weak-point of this detection strategy. However, we will argue that it is reasonable to assume its effectiveness in practice. We first address the non-adversarial setting. That is, we assume all input boolean formulas are generated via some random distribution and we need only distinguish between uniform and non-uniform distributions. This is a standard use-case for a χ^2-test and fairly trivial given a sufficiently large sample.

In Fig. 2, we compare average p-values as a function of n to truncated normal distributions with increasing variance. Although there is some skew due to the sampling without replacement in random 3SAT generation, we see, as expected, that there is a very drastic fall-off in all the non-uniform distributions.

To ensure a sufficiently large sample, it suffices to remove 3SAT instances that can be solved in small constant time. For example, we found experimentally that, given $c = 6$, we could consistently solve instances with $n < 58$ in under a minute using eight processors and a simple 3SAT solver. In contrast, all the distributions we tested had already suitably diverged by $n = 10$.

One could make this classification problem arbitrarily hard by using a generating distribution that more closely approximates uniformity. However, the resulting misclassified 3SAT instances effectively approximate the frequency distribution of a random 3SAT instance. Since proofs for the unsatisfiable threshold primarily rely on the frequency distribution, they should be fairly insensitive to such instances. We leave formally bounding this insensitivity as a future research direction.

5.2 Potential Defenses

Of course, the assumption that all input instances are randomly generated is arguably optimistic. A simple defense against this heuristic attack might entail inserting artificially generated formulas that resemble random 3SAT but are known to be satisfiable. In the AI context, this could be considered the problem of generating hard satisfiable instances in the over-constrained region. Our context adds the additional constraint that these instances cannot be too tightly

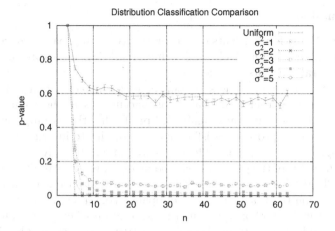

Fig. 2. Mean p-values for uniform distribution and truncated normal distributions with different variance values as a function of n, c=6. Error bars show standard error of the sample size r, std-dev/$\sqrt{r}$.

clustered (otherwise they can be identified and removed heuristically). We argue that there is no such known method.[1]

Finding satisfiable random 3SAT instances in the over-constrained region by brute-force is intractable since candidates are unsatisfiable with exponentially high probability. As such, it is typical to start with some truth assignment and select only clauses which satisfy the truth assignment. The resulting instances are called **planted 3SAT**.

Unfortunately, this skews the distribution of variables and their negation (since the form that agrees with the truth assignment is more likely to appear in viable clauses). Even in the general form, where the frequency distribution used to select clauses is allowed to vary arbitrarily, there are known algorithms for solving planted 3SAT in polynomial time w.h.p [6]. Moreover, experimental results show that all satisfiable instances in the over-constrained region are tightly clustered, suggesting that they could be easily solved even if they were not generated with a planted assignment.

Since there are no known algorithms that meet the resulting satisfiable 3SAT generation criteria and any such algorithm would represent a considerable breakthrough in AI community, we conjecture that any such defense against a targeted heuristic attack is infeasible.

---

[1] Moser et al. [19] mention this strategy as part of a proposed heuristic-based defense, but they offered no specific construction scheme so we cannot make a direct comparison.

5.3 Discussion

In summary, Algorithm 5 defeats our theoretically strong opaque construct generation algorithm by iteratively and w.h.p. removing unsatisfiable branches, effectively "unraveling" its opaqueness.

We suspect the effectiveness of our heuristic attack against a provably resilient opaque construct is indicative of inaccuracies in the commonly used assumptions for modeling static analysis. Specifically, the assumption that the static analyzer must prove unsatisfiability of a predicate in order to remove it is too strong. In practice, it is sufficient, and computationally much easier, to determine the value of the predicate with some high probability. This issue seems fundamentally at odds with the correctness of a constant opaque predicate, which calls into question the practical utility of opaque constructs for obfuscation.

We conjecture that all opaque construct generation schemes are vulnerable to similar targeted heuristic attacks because generating instances of a hard problem with known solutions naturally limits the instances to some subset of the problem space with measurable properties. Recent experimental results, which we discuss next in Sect. 6, seem to support this conjecture.

6 Related Work

The concept of an opaque predicate was first introduced by Collberg et al. [9]. However, in addition to resilience and cost, the authors also design their obfuscation scheme around a poorly defined stealth metric. Consequently, they base their main primitive on the hardness of precise flow-sensitive alias analysis. More specifically, their scheme builds a set of complex dynamic structures with a set of implicit invariants. The invariants are known a priori but difficult to verify statically so they can be tested at runtime as an opaque predicate. Precise flow-sensitive alias analysis is known to be undecidable in general [23], but this formulation is only known to be $\mathcal{NP}$-hard in the worst case [15]. They argue informally that this is not dissimilar to data structures kept by real applications, achieving stealth. However, it is unclear how to scale this scheme since each opaque predicate requires an invariant. They offer a second scheme based on the potential interleaving of parallel regions, but it suffers from the same faults in addition to being architecture specific and potentially indeterminate on a loaded operating system. In contrast, we seek to achieve a scalable scheme that is proven to be $\mathcal{NP}$-complete in the average case. We have also abandoned the stealth metric because we suspect it is unachievable even against static analysis.

Unfortunately, the feasibility of stealth remains an open question, largely dependent on its formalization. Probably the most intuitive definition is that an obfuscated function should behave as a "virtual black box", meaning that an adversary cannot compute anything with the obfuscated function that they could not compute with oracle access to the same function. This definition implicitly includes both resilience and stealth, but was shown to be impossible in general [2]. The result is not necessarily applicable to obfuscation primitives which can be specialized functions lending themselves to obfuscation, but it does imply that there is no clever way to apply said primitives to achieve the virtual black box property for an arbitrary application. This work partially motivates our conservative focus on opaque predicates themselves as well as resilience only against static analysis. However, our work is only tangentially related since we intentionally avoid the impossible general case.

Heuristic-based approaches to stealthy opaque predicates have produced an academic arms race. Most continue to base their resiliency on pointer alias analysis, but offer no formal definition of stealth [7,13,20,22]. These techniques remain vulnerable to targeted detection [12], and were recently shown to be detectable in general with dynamic analysis by Ming et al. [18]. We diverge from this line of work by abandoning the goal of stealth and focusing on resilience against static analysis, giving us arguably weaker properties, but ones that can be formally proven.

There are several notable exceptions to the trend of using pointer alias analysis as a basis for resilience. Ogiso et al. [21] and later Borello and Mé [4] both base their hardness on the related problem of inter-procedural analysis. Or, more specifically, the problem of determining if there exists an execution path such that a given function pointer points to a given function at a given point of the program. This formulation naturally reduces to 3SAT, making the problem $\mathcal{NP}$-complete and analysis of the entire program $\mathcal{NP}$-hard. Unfortunately, the inter-procedural focus does not lend itself to a scalable self-contained obfuscation primitive, nor is this formulation known to be $\mathcal{NP}$-complete in the average case. Our approach seeks to guarantee both of these properties. It is most similar to the work of Moser et al. [19], who similarly base their hardness on 3SAT but make the encoding explicit and self-contained. We seek mainly to improve on their theoretical contribution by proving that a deliberate 3SAT instance selection algorithm produces opaque predicates that are $\mathcal{NP}$-complete in the average case.

7   Conclusions

Opaque constructs are a commonly employed primitive in obfuscation, watermarking, and tamper-proofing schemes. However, their theoretical basis has historically been very weak. We have proven the resilience and correctness of random 3SAT based opaque constructs under formal notions of resolution complexity and complete static analysis. However, in doing so we have revealed some weaknesses in the commonly used model and potentially opaque constructs as an obfuscation primitive in general. We suggest that future research apply more skepticism to the use of opaque constructs in obfuscation schemes since their theoretical basis remains dubious.

Acknowledgments. We are grateful for the helpful comments and suggestions from the anonymous reviewers. This work is partially funded from National Science Foundation (NSF) grants CNS-1445967, CNS-1527401, and CNS-1149832. Any opinions, findings, and conclusions or recommendations expressed herein are those of the authors and do not necessarily reflect the views of the NSF.

Appendix

A   Alternative Sources of Hardness

Random 3SAT may seem like a strange source of hardness given that our goal is simply to hide information from the static analyzer. However, the information must be known at runtime and the obfuscator cannot use traditional means to store a key without also making it available to the static analyzer. Therefore, more traditional means of encryption are inapplicable in this setting. Below, we briefly describe the relative merits and drawbacks of some alternate choices:

Integer factorization: As the basis of most modern cryptography, integer factorization was naturally one of our first considerations. Unfortunately, we found no natural way to incorporate the problem into an opaque predicate. We conjecture that trap-door functions in general are unsuitable because the opaque construct still needs to be evaluated at runtime without adding any additional knowledge to the system.

Primality testing: Collberg et al. [9] mention primality testing as a possible basis for opaque predicates The strategy being to pick a prime during obfuscation and have the runtime evaluation try to evenly divide the prime by a random number. Naturally, an adversary cannot guarantee the division will fail without proving that the number is prime. Unfortunately, it has since been proven that primality testing can always be done in polynomial time [1], making it too weak to serve as a hardness basis.

One-way functions: A one-way function is more natural than a trap-door function since we can apply it to a chosen input during obfuscation and compare that result to the result of a random input evaluated at runtime. However, if the generating value is included in the set of possible runtime inputs, there is at least one potential collision. Typically, the resulting correctness bound is weaker than our 3SAT based construction.

Flow-sensitive alias analysis: Alias analysis is the basis primarily employed by Collberg et al. [9]. It has the arguable advantage of naturally resembling normal code. This would make it a better candidate for meeting some formal notion of "stealth". However, since no one has proposed a usable metric of stealth and recent impossibility results suggest it is not obtainable, we do not feel stealth is an appropriate goal. Alias analysis also has the advantage of provable correctness but it comes at the cost of scalability since it's unclear how to generate an arbitrary number of the deliberately crafted invariants used to guarantee correctness.

Race conditions: Another possible basis briefly mentioned by Collberg et al. [8] takes advantage of concurrency and the intractability of precise race detection. Intuitively, an attacker might be able to insert a data race into a concurrent program and be fairly confident of the outcome on a particular platform. Static analysis, in contrast would not be able to reliably find the data race, let alone determine its outcome. This has (often unintentionally) been a source of hardness in reverse engineering programs for the purpose of porting them to a different platform. Unfortunately, this basis would require that the original program be concurrent and might violate correctness on platforms other than the particular one targeted. Even ignoring these problems, scaling would be problematic because its unclear how to reliably generate appropriate data races in general.

Random 3SAT: The main advantage of using random 3SAT for our hardness basis was the large body of existing work from the AI context on satisfiability and provably hard instance generation [3,5,10,24]. Resolution complexity is an arguably weak hardness conjecture because it states only that actually proving satisfiability is hard. As we showed in Sect. 5, a less restricted adversary can still make a very accurate guess. However, our assumptions were consistent with prior work and we failed to find any stronger hardness conjectures that were applicable in this context.

References

1. Agrawal, M., Kayal, N., Saxena, N.: PRIMES is in P. Ann. Math. **2**, 781–793 (2002)
2. Barak, B., Goldreich, O., Impagliazzo, R., Rudich, S., Sahai, A., Vadhan, S.P., Yang, K.: On the (im)possibility of obfuscating programs. J. ACM **59**(2), 6 (2012)
3. Biere, A., Biere, A., Heule, M., van Maaren, H., Walsh, T.: Handbook of Satisfiability. Frontiers in Artificial Intelligence and Applications, vol. 185. IOS Press, Swansea (2009)
4. Borello, J.-M., Mé, L.: Code obfuscation techniques for metamorphic viruses. J. Comput. Virol. **4**(3), 211–220 (2008)
5. Chvátal, V., Szemerédi, E.: Many hard examples for resolution. J. ACM **35**(4), 759–768 (1988)
6. Coja-Oghlan, A., Krivelevich, M., Vilenchik, D.: Why almost all satisfiable k-CNF formulas are easy. In: 2007 Conference on Analysis of Algorithms, AofA 2007, pp. 95–108. Discrete Mathematics and Theoretical Computer Science (2007)
7. Collberg, C., Thomborson, C.: Watermarking, tamper-proofing, and obfuscation - tools for software protection. Trans. Softw. Eng. **28**(8), 735–746 (2002)
8. Collberg, C., Thomborson, C., Low, D.: A taxonomy of obfuscating transformations (1997)
9. Collberg, C., Thomborson, C., Low, D.: Manufacturing cheap, resilient, and stealthy opaque constructs. In: ACM POPL. ACM (1998)
10. Cook, S.A., Mitchell, D.G.: Finding hard instances of the satisfiability problem: a survey, pp. 1–17. American Mathematical Society (1997)
11. Crawford, J.M., Auton, L.D.: Experimental results on the crossover point in random 3-SAT. Artif. Intell. **81**(1–2), 31–57 (1996)
12. Preda, M.D., Madou, M., De Bosschere, K., Giacobazzi, R.: Opaque predicates detection by abstract interpretation. In: Johnson, M., Vene, V. (eds.) AMAST 2006. LNCS, vol. 4019, pp. 81–95. Springer, Heidelberg (2006)
13. Darwish, S., Guirguis, S., Zalat, M.: Stealthy code obfuscation technique for software security. In: International Conference on Computer Engineering and Systems (ICCES), pp. 93–99 (2010)
14. Goldwasser, S., Bellare, M.: Lecture notes on cryptography (2001)

15. Horwitz, S.: Precise flow-insensitive may-alias analysis is NP-hard. ACM Trans. Program. Lang. Syst. **19**(1), 1–6 (1997)
16. Kamath, A., Motwani, R., Palem, K., Spirakis, P.: Tail bounds for occupancy and the satisfiability threshold conjecture. In: FOCS (1994)
17. Karp, R.M.: Reducibility among combinatorial problems. In: Miller, R.E., Thatcher, J.W., Bohlinger, J.D. (eds.) Complexity of Computer Computations. The IBM Research Symposia Series, pp. 85–103. Springer, New York (1972)
18. Ming, J., Xu, D., Wang, L., Wu, D.: Loop: Logic-oriented opaque predicate detection in obfuscated binary code. In: CCS (2015)
19. Moser, A., Kruegel, C., Kirda, E.: Limits of static analysis for malware detection. In: Computer Security Applications Conference (ACSAC), pp. 421–430 (2007)
20. Myles, G., Collberg, C.: Software watermarking via opaque predicates: Implementation, analysis, and attacks. Electron. Commer. Res. **6**(2), 155–171 (2006)
21. Ogiso, T., Sakabe, Y., Soshi, M., Miyaji, A.: Software obfuscation on a theoretical basis and its implementation. IEICE Trans. Fundam. Electron. Commun. Comput. Sci. **86**(1), 176–186 (2003)
22. Preda, M., Giacobazzi, R.: Control code obfuscation by abstract interpretation. In: Software Engineering and Formal Methods (SEFM), pp. 301–310 (2005)
23. Ramalingam, G.: The undecidability of aliasing. ACM Trans. Program. Lang. Syst. **16**(5), 1467–1471 (1994)
24. Selman, B., Mitchell, D.G., Levesque, H.J.: Generating hard satisfiability problems. Artif. Intell. **81**(1–2), 17–29 (1996)

Secure Multiparty Computation

Robust Password-Protected Secret Sharing

Michel Abdalla, Mario Cornejo$^{(\boxtimes)}$, Anca Nitulescu, and David Pointcheval

ENS, CNRS, INRIA, and PSL Research University, Paris, France
{michel.abdalla,mario.cornejo,anca.nitulescu,david.pointcheval}@ens.fr

Abstract. *Password-protected secret sharing* (PPSS) schemes allow a user to publicly share its high-entropy secret across different servers and to later recover it by interacting with some of these servers using only his password without requiring *any* authenticated data. In particular, this secret will remain safe as long as not too many servers get corrupted. However, servers are not always reliable and the communication can be altered. To address this issue, a *robust* PPSS should additionally guarantee that a user can recover his secret as long as enough servers provide correct answers, and these are received without alteration. In this paper, we propose new robust PPSS schemes which are significantly more efficient than the existing ones. Our contributions are two-fold: First, we propose a generic technique to build a *Robust Gap Threshold Secret Sharing Scheme* (RGTSSS) from some threshold secret sharing schemes. In the PPSS construction, this allows us to drop the verifiable property of *Oblivious Pseudorandom Functions* (OPRF); Then, we use this new approach to design two new robust PPSS schemes that are quite efficient, from two OPRFs. They are proven in the random-oracle model, just because our RGTSSS construction requires random non-malleable fingerprints, which is provided by an ideal hash function.

Keywords: Password-Protected Secret Sharing · Robust Gap Threshold Secret Sharing Scheme · Oblivious Pseudorandom Functions

1 Introduction

Nowadays, cloud storage is quite popular with zettabytes of data spread all over the world. Even if providers give some backup guarantees, they cannot always prevent compromises, and so the data are subject to leakage, with possibly huge consequences if the data are sensitive (financial, economic, medical, etc.). Clearly, the provider can encrypt the data before storing them, but this is not an end-to-end protection for the user: the provider itself has access to the data. For better security, the user should encrypt the data before sending them to the cloud. But this leads to a key management issue: Users have to remember their secret keys!

Humans cannot remember large secret keys, but just low-entropy passwords (and not too many). Such a password is definitely not enough to deterministically derive a symmetric encryption key, since a simple offline dictionary attack would allow the recovery. On the other hand, there are techniques using passwords that

© Springer International Publishing Switzerland 2016
I. Askoxylakis et al. (Eds.): ESORICS 2016, Part II, LNCS 9879, pp. 61–79, 2016.
DOI: 10.1007/978-3-319-45741-3_4

are not vulnerable to such offline dictionary attacks, like *password authenticated key exchange* (PAKE) [7]. For these PAKE protocols, the best attacks require the adversary to be online, and to make the exhaustive search by interacting with the honest parties, hence the idea to combine PAKE with secret sharing, in order to achieve the best of the two worlds. This allows the recovery of a high-entropy symmetric key by interacting with several servers while just using a low-entropy password [18, 22], without relying on any authenticated data, where the best attacks are online dictionary attacks.

Password-Protected Secret Sharing. A (t, n)-*password-protected secret sharing* (PPSS) is a protocol that allows a user to reconstruct a high-entropy secret from a single (human-memorable) password, by communicating with at least $t + 1$ honest servers (among n possible ones).

This framework formalized in [2] first defines a secure *initialization* phase where the secret is processed together with the password, and some server information, in order to distribute the secret among n independent servers. Only public information (to enable the later reconstruction) is eventually stored on each server. We however stress that this public information does not have to be authentic for the later security. Then, during the *reconstruction* phase, the user can recover his secret by interacting with any subset of $t + 1$ honest servers using just his password. If the public information has been altered, the knowledge of the password will be enough to detect it. However, in [2] they prove their scheme secure in the random-oracle model assuming an additional PKI. Whereas this assumption of a safe PKI makes sense during the initialization phase, which can be run in a safe environment, it is not reasonable to make this assumption for the reconstruction phase, which will be executed many times on various weak devices.

A PPSS protocol satisfies the following properties: (i) the user can retrieve the data by executing the reconstruction protocol with the same password as the one used in the initialization phase and it is guaranteed to succeed as long as at least $t + 1$ honest servers are available. (ii) An attacker who controls up to t servers cannot learn any information about the secret other than doing an online dictionary attack with another server. Two additional properties have been defined: *Soundness* and *Robustness*. The first guarantees that even if the adversary compromises all the servers, and provides consistent but fake public information, it cannot make the user reconstruct and accept a secret different from the one originally stored by the user. On the other hand, robustness guarantees the recovery of the secret as long as the user communicates without disruptions with at least $t + 1$ honest servers.

We stress that the adversary can control all the communication network by blocking, delaying, altering, or duplicating any flow. As such, no server is trusted, and no PKI is assumed either, since the only authenticated data we allow is a short password that the user can remember.

Contributions. Our PPSS protocol follows the methodology from [23]: it is based on the use of *pseudorandom functions* (PRFs) evaluated on the password to mask the shares of the secret. These evaluations are performed, in an oblivious way, with servers that own the PRF keys, hence the so-called *oblivious pseudorandom functions* (OPRFs).

Our main contribution is the efficient realization of the robustness in only one round of communication with each server, possibly in a concurrent way. We also avoid any complex zero-knowledge proof. This comes from the fact that we do not need to distinguish between correct and incorrect shares at each individual evaluation with a server as in [23]. Compared to the later solution with ZK proofs given in [24], our scheme needs only a single global check at the very end, during the secret reconstruction, which significantly reduces the communication costs.

Actually, we propose a new efficient method to convert some Secret Sharing Schemes into (t_ℓ, t_r, n)-*Robust Gap Threshold Secret Sharing Schemes* (RGTSSS) that guarantees to efficiently identify the correct values (and reconstruct the secret) if at least t_r shares are correct. However, if at most $t_\ell - 1$ shares are correct, the protocol *leaks* no information about which shares are correct. Our construction is more general and with similar efficiency than using error-correcting code such as Reed-Solomon [27]. Such a (t_ℓ, t_r, n)-RGTSSS allows constructing a sound and robust PPSS scheme: If the number of correct servers' answers is above the threshold t_r, the user can efficiently identify the valid ones and reconstruct the secret. If the number of answers is strictly below another threshold t_ℓ, no information about the secret is leaked. It is indeed important that not too few correct shares can be detected as correct as this could result in offline dictionary attacks. For instance, in the case where shares could be individually checked, a dishonest server could easily mount an offline dictionary attack. With our new primitive, even $t_\ell - 1$ corrupted servers cannot perform an offline dictionary attack as they would still need to interact with at least one additional server. The main difference to [23] is in the way to achieve robustness: We ask a bit more from the secret sharing scheme, but much less from the OPRF, allowing more efficient constructions for the latter, which highly improves on the global efficiency.

While similar to [24] in terms of server interaction efficiency for the PRF evaluation, our technique takes advantage of the RGTSSS to optimize the secret reconstruction. The scheme proposed by [24] has one significant drawback: the client is supposed to specify the exact set of servers involved in the secret recovery from the beginning, which may lead to frequent failures as the servers may misbehave. Moreover, in case of such a failure, the user is unable to detect the cheating servers. To overcome this drawback when a large number of servers are involved in the protocol, our approach makes use of the *robustness* feature of the secret sharing scheme to ensure the recovery of the secret and the detection of dishonest servers.

We propose two efficient OPRF constructions: The first one is based on the One-More Gap Diffie-Hellman assumption and its efficiency is quite similar to the one in [24]. Secondly, we introduce a new oblivious evaluation of the Naor-Reingold PRF [25], based on the sole DDH assumption.

For this new construction, we compare very favorably to other oblivious evaluations of the Naor-Reingold PRF: our protocol simply uses ElGamal encryption [17] in prime order groups with simple zero-knowledge proofs, whereas for example the scheme in [23] has to work in composite order groups with Paillier encryption [26] and more complex zero-knowledge proofs.

By combining these building bricks, we eventually reach efficient PPSS schemes that satisfy *Soundness* and *Robustness* properties. The two proposed solutions are eventually proven in the *Random-Oracle Model* (ROM) [4], as our RGTSSS construction requires random non-malleable fingerprints. This can be achieved by using a hash function that is modeled as a random oracle [4].

Related Work. A *threshold secret sharing scheme* allows a user to distribute a secret among different participants preventing a sole party breaking the security or obstructing the reconstruction. This idea was introduced by Shamir [28] and Blakey [9]. This concept was later generalized by using two thresholds, a *upper* and a *lower* one to set the size of the sets to reconstruct and to preserve privacy respectively. In Shamir's secret sharing scheme, the privacy threshold is defined as t and the reconstruction threshold as $t + 1$. When this gap is higher, then the secret sharing scheme is called *ramp* scheme. Ramp schemes to achieve a robust secret sharing scheme have been extensively studied, we refer the reader to [8,14]. While this is well-known that the Shamir secret sharing scheme can be made robust using Reed-Solomon error correcting codes, our approach is more general with similar efficiency.

The first formal definition of *Password Protected Secret Sharing* was introduced by Bagherzandi *et al.* [2]. They proved their scheme secure in the random-oracle model assuming an additional PKI. Moreover, if an adversary is able to obtain the keypair of one server, the adversary can perform an offline attack. Later, Camenisch *et al.* [12] introduce a protocol of password-authenticated secret sharing that also assumes a PKI and only two servers. Both protocols contradict the requirement to be *password-only*, since they assume additional authenticated data. Whereas this assumption of a safe PKI makes sense during the initialization phase, which can be run in a safe environment, it is not reasonable to make this assumption for the reconstruction phase, which will be executed many times on various weak devices. Later, Camenisch *et al.* [10] introduce a (t, n)-PPSS (called TPASS, for Threshold Password-Authenticated Secret Sharing) in the Universal Composability (UC) framework [13] that is password-only during the reconstruction phase. However, in this protocol all servers jointly validate if the password matches or not. Yi *et al.* [29] propose a more efficient TPASS based on distributing the password, a secret and a digest of the secret. Nevertheless, in the recovering protocol, at least t servers execute a broadcasting protocol to generate and return the ElGamal encryptions of both the secret and the digest. Then the users verify it matches.

Camenisch *et al.* [11] present a very lightweight protocol with a similar construction to our work, yet with differences. Since this protocol does not rely on robust secret sharing scheme nor zero-knowledge, it is not possible to identify which shares are valid. Then, if in the end the validation fails, the protocol must restart with a different set of servers contradicting the requirement of *robustness* and leading to a possible Denial-of-Service (DoS) attack.

Jarecki *et al.* [23] have been the first to design a PPSS scheme that is both *password-only* during the reconstruction phase and *robust*, to avoid easy DoS attacks. It makes use of a *Verifiable Oblivious Pseudorandom Function* (VOPRF) that assures robustness by providing computation guarantees from the servers: the user actually knows which server has tried to cheat, or which communication links have been altered. Recently, the work [24] improves the performance of this password-only PPSS on the cost of dropping the robustness property. Their protocol is relaxing the verifiable property of the OPRF, giving up the ability to discard incorrect computations during interactions with servers. This can be a good alternative for a small number n of servers, the only setting that allows checking in a reasonable time different subsets of servers until finding a non-corrupted one.

2 Security Model

In order to analyze the security of PPSS protocols, we first provide a formal description of the security model. This is a game-based security definition, in the same vein as [5,6] for key distribution schemes and [3] for password-authenticated key exchange. It adapts the PPSS definition from [2] and the security model from [23]. We define security in terms of a *key derivation mechanism* or indistinguishability of the actual secret from a random one, as in [23], since our goal is to later use the secret as a symmetric key. In particular, we do not want to rely on a PKI or any authenticated public values, hence our model description is similar to security models for PAKE.

2.1 Password-Protected Secret Sharing

Participants and Parameters. We assume a fixed set of participants involved in the protocol, each of which is either a user or a server. The set of all participants is the union of the nonempty disjoint and finite sets, User ∪ Server.

Each user $U \in$ User holds two threshold values t_ℓ and t_r, where t_r is the number of shares required to *recover* the secret and t_ℓ is the number of shares that start *leaking* some information about the secret, as well as some password pw chosen independently and uniformly from a dictionary $\mathcal{D}$ of cardinality $\#\mathcal{D}$.

Each server $S \in$ Server holds a secret key sk, and possibly an associated public key pk. However we stress that even if there is a public key pk, authenticity cannot be assumed *a priori* during the reconstruction phase since users will just have to remember their passwords and nothing else that would be required to authenticate additional data.

Initialization. The goal of the user U is to generate a key K so that he later can recover it with the help of t_r servers among n available servers, just using his password. He thus runs an initialization protocol with n servers, using their public keys, his password and some random coins. He ends up with a random key K and some additional information PInfo: nobody else than U has any information about K, however PInfo can be made public.

Secret Reconstruction. While the initialization phase assumes that all the servers are honest, the public keys are authentic, and the data are not modified during the communication, for the reconstruction phase, the adversary controls the network and can forward, alter, delay, replay, or delete any message. The adversary can also provide fake public data: nothing is authenticated anymore!

Anyway, just using his password, the user U should be able to recover K, with the help of the servers, in a verifiable/robust way, even if some information in PInfo is not guaranteed to be correct.

Each participant (either user or server) can run several executions of the protocol, possibly concurrently, we thus denote an instance i of player P as P^i. Each instance may be activated once only: the adversary is given oracle accesses to interact with all the user's and server's instances that are stateful interactive polynomial-time Turing machines.

2.2 The Adversarial Model

During the reconstruction phase, the adversary is given total control of the network. It is thus given access to the following oracles:

- Execute($U^i, \{S_k^{j_k}\}$): This query models a passive attack. This makes an instance U^i to interact with several instances of servers $\{S_k^{j_k}\}$ as they would do during the reconstruction protocol. The adversary gets the entire transcript;
- Send(P^i, m): This query models an active attack. This sends a message m to the instance P^i. A specific message Start_k^j to a user's instance U^i makes it initiate a communication with the server's instance S_k^j.

The security goal is to guarantee the privacy of the secret key K reconstructed by the user. This is usually modeled by an indistinguishability game, with access to a Test-query, where b is a global secret random bit:

- Test(U^i): This query characterizes the indistinguishability of the key K computed by instance U^i. If this instance has not yet completed the reconstruction, the answer is UNDEFINED; if the reconstruction failed, the answer is $\perp$; otherwise, the answer is either the real reconstructed value if $b = 1$ or a random one (always the same for user U, but independent of the real one) if $b = 0$.

The adversary eventually outputs its guess b' for the bit b. One can note that in the random case ($b = 0$), which models the ideal executions, a user U always terminates with the same key, or fails. This means that the adversary should not be able to make him accept a different key.

In addition to control the network and the communications, the adversary can corrupt servers, and get back their secret keys, due to, e.g., a poorly-administered server, compromise of a host computer, or cryptanalysis. This is modeled by the Corrupt-query:

- Corrupt(S_k): This outputs the secret key sk_k of the server S_k.

2.3   Semantic Security

Definition. Once the initialization phase is completed for many users, with random passwords uniformly and independently drawn from a dictionary $\mathcal{D}$, the security game models the indistinguishably of the secret keys, a.k.a. *semantic security*, the adversary can ask as many oracle queries (Execute, Send, Test, and Corrupt), as it wants, in any order it wants, in order to guess the bit b: it outputs its guess b'. We measure the quality of an adversary $\mathcal{A}$ by its advantage

$$\mathsf{Adv}(\mathcal{A}) = \Pr[b' = 1 | b = 1] - \Pr[b' = 1 | b = 0] = 2 \times \Pr[b' = b] - 1.$$

Trivial Attacks. Two kinds of "on-line dictionary attacks" are unavoidable:

- if the adversary guesses the correct password, it will be able to reconstruct the actual secret K after q_c corruption queries and $t_r - q_c$ interactions with honest servers. Even after just $t_\ell - q_c$ interactions, it may come up with t_ℓ shares, which may leak some information about the actual secret key: it thereafter asks for an Execute-query, and tests the instance involved in this session, to distinguish the real case from the random case. Its success probability is however upper-bounded by $q_s/(t_\ell - q_c) \times 1/\#\mathcal{D}$, where q_s is the number of server instances involved during the attack, q_c the number of Corrupt-queries, and $\#\mathcal{D}$ the size of the password dictionary.
- whereas the initialization phase was assumed to be done with authentic server public keys, for the reconstruction phase, the adversary can send totally fake public keys in PInfo that it generated itself from a randomly chosen password pw. It thus also knows the secret keys and can simulate the view of the user by emulating all the servers. If the password guess was correct, the user should successfully terminate, whereas a wrong guess would lead to inconsistent information. Its success probability is therefore upper-bounded by $q_u/\#\mathcal{D}$, where q_u is the number of user instances involved in the attack.

2.4   Secure PPSS

As a consequence, we will say a (t_r, n)-PPSS scheme is (t_ℓ, ε, t)-secure if for any adversary $\mathcal{A}$, running within time t, asking at most $q_c < t_\ell$ Corrupt-queries and invoking at most q_u user instances and q_s server instances,

$$\mathsf{Adv}(\mathcal{A}) \leq \frac{1}{\#\mathcal{D}} \times \left(\frac{q_s}{t_\ell - q_c} + q_u \right) + \varepsilon.$$

In [23], they proposed such a protocol that achieves the optimal t_ℓ-security, for $t_\ell = t_r$, but at the cost of verifiable oblivious pseudorandom functions. Our goal is to build much more efficient protocols, possibly with a larger gap between t_ℓ and t_r.

Correctness. To be viable, a password-protected secret sharing must guarantee that at least t_r honest servers should allow the user that plays with his password pw to recover his secret K.

Soundness. As guaranteed by our security model, when a user terminates with a key K', this is the correct key K in almost all the cases, unless the adversary guesses the password. More precisely, when playing with the correct password pw, the user should end up with $K' \in \{K, \bot\}$:

$$\Pr[K' \notin \{\bot, K\}] \leq \frac{1}{\#\mathcal{D}} \times \left(\frac{q_s}{t_\ell - q_c} + q_u \right) + \varepsilon.$$

Robustness. While one cannot avoid Denial-of-Service (DoS) attacks, since the adversary can simply block any communication, an important property, already required by [23], is the so-called *robustness*: even if the adversary alters many messages, as soon as t_r communications with servers are unmodified the user can *efficiently* recover its secret.

The general issue with robustness is that when the user has interacted with n servers but only t_r shares are valid, the cost of trying all the t_r-subsets is exponential! In [23], they addressed this issue by making some inner protocols secure against malicious servers, with additional zero-knowledge proofs of honest behavior, but this is at a high communication cost. Our goal is to provide this property at a much lower cost.

3   High-Level Description

We review the well-known computational assumptions and the classical building blocks in the full version [1]. Our general construction follows the one from [23], with first an initialization phase and then a reconstruction phase.

Each server S_i owns a key-pair $(\mathsf{sk}_i, \mathsf{pk}_i)$ that defines a PRF F_i, with public parameters defined by pk_i and a secret key defined by sk_i. For a password $\mathsf{pw} \in \mathcal{D}$, the user asks for an oblivious evaluation of $\pi_i = F_i(\mathsf{pw})$ to n servers, where $\Pi = (\mathsf{pk}_i)_i$ is the tuple of the public keys of the involved servers. The secret key K is then split into shares $(s_1, \ldots, s_n)$ and some extra public information PInfo, specific to the user, is derived from it and distributed to all servers. This information allows the user to later recover his secret, in a robust way.

We stress that, during this initialization phase, $(\mathsf{pk}_i)_i$ are all the true public keys, and $(\pi_i)_i$ are the correct evaluations of the PRFs. However, during the reconstruction phase, the values provided by the servers are sent through an insecure channel and they might be altered by the adversary: the user interacts with at least t_r servers, that provide him PInfo, and help him to compute each $\pi_i = F_i(\mathsf{pw})$ in an oblivious way. We assume that the user received the same value PInfo from at least t_r servers, and then the user keeps the majority value. Using PInfo and enough evaluations π_i, the user can extract enough shares among $(s_1, \ldots, s_n)$ and reconstruct a value K. He can then verify whether this is the expected secret key, from the majority PInfo which is however not considered authentic. We can note that there are two crucial tools for this generic construction:

- a pseudorandom function F that can be evaluated in an oblivious way: the server input is the secret key sk and the user input is the password pw, and the user only gets the output $F_{\mathsf{sk}}(\mathsf{pw})$, but none of the players learn any additional information about the other player's input;
- a (t_ℓ, t_r, n)-threshold secret sharing scheme that allows to share a secret among n players so that any subset of t_r shares allows efficient reconstruction of the secret, while $t_\ell - 1$ shares do not leak any information.

An additional non-malleable commitment scheme [16] will provide the soundness, by limiting the ability for an adversary to present a modified PInfo, whereas it controls all the communications.

However, in order to achieve the robustness to the PPSS protocol, we need to make sure that when t_r communications with the servers are unmodified, the user can reconstruct the secret: either one can detect alterations of the communications during the oblivious evaluations of the PRF, which is the approach followed by [23] with *Verifiable Oblivious PRFs* (VOPRFs), or one can efficiently reconstruct a secret from any set of shares that contains at least t_r valid shares, which is our approach with *Robust Gap Threshold Secret Sharing Scheme*.

4 A Robust Gap Threshold Secret Sharing Scheme

Our technique can generically apply to most threshold secret sharing schemes, with two algorithms ShareGen and Reconstruct that respectively share a secret into n parts and reconstruct it from t_r shares (while no information leaks from $t_r - 1$ shares, which look independent random elements). One can for example use the classical Shamir's secret sharing scheme [28] to which we will add this new robustness feature, at the cost of having a threshold gap secret sharing scheme that is enough to get a robust PPSS scheme (for details about secret sharing schemes see the full version [1]).

4.1 Intuition

The valid shares are denoted $(s_1, \ldots, s_n)$ and the fingerprints of these shares $(\sigma_1, \ldots, \sigma_n)$. At the same time of the share distribution, the product $\mathcal{S}$ of all fingerprints modulo an integer N is published. In order to reconstruct the secret, having received m candidate shares, one computes its fingerprints $(\tau_1, \ldots, \tau_m)$

and the product of them $T = \prod \tau_i$. The ratio $T/S \bmod N$ will cancel out the fingerprints of all the correct share values leading to the ratio $T'/S' \bmod N$, where S' is the product of the fingerprints of the valid shares that the receiver does not have in the list of candidates and T' the product of the fingerprints of the candidates that are invalid. From S', one could easily check for every candidate, whether it is in this product or not, and therefore identify which candidate is correct or not.

Of course, S' has to be computed with good precision to allow the last verification, but not too much in order to avoid individual checks or any unnecessary leakage of information. The computations are thus performed modulo N, for a well-chosen value.

4.2   Description

We now explain how one can detect the valid shares when the fingerprints are either correct or random.

Initialization. We assume we have a set of n initial values $(s_1, \ldots, s_n)$, and their k-bit string fingerprints $(\sigma_1, \ldots, \sigma_n)$. As fingerprint function we use a hash function $F : \{0,1\}^* \to \{0,1\}^k$ modeled as a random oracle.

In the following, we will be given a set of m candidate shares, whose fingerprints are $(\tau_1, \ldots, \tau_m)$: these fingerprints are either correct (the same as in the list $(\sigma_1, \ldots, \sigma_n)$ or random for incorrect candidate shares). From this set of candidate shares, if at least t_r are correct, we want to efficiently identify the correct values (to *recover* the secret in a threshold secret sharing scheme, hence the r-subscript in t_r). However, if at most $t_\ell - 1$ are correct, the protocol should not leak any information about which candidates are valid and which are not (hence the ℓ-subscript in t_ℓ, the number of shares that start *leaking* information).

From the initial set $(\sigma_1, \ldots, \sigma_n)$ of size n and the threshold t_r, one chooses a prime number N such that $2^{2k(n-t_r)+1} < N \leq 2^{2k(n-t_r)+2}$, computes the product $S = \prod_{i=1}^n \sigma_i \bmod N$, and publishes $\mathsf{SSInfo} = (S, N)$.

Reconstruction. Given the $\mathsf{SSInfo} = (S, N)$ and fingerprints $(\tau_1, \ldots, \tau_m)$ of the $m \leq n$ candidates, which are either correct (at least t_r of them) or random (all the other ones), one computes the ratio $\gamma = \prod_{i=1}^m \tau_i/S \bmod N$, which can be written as $\gamma = T'/S' \bmod N$, where T' is the product of the fingerprints of the invalid candidates and S' the product of the fingerprints of the values that are not in the list of the candidates, both over the integers. Then, we know that $T' < 2^{k(m-t_r)} \leq 2^{k(n-t_r)}$ and $S' < 2^{k(n-t_r)}$.

Unfortunately, using the following result from [19], we can only recover the irreducible fraction T''/S'' of γ, where all the small common factors of T'/S' were canceled out, with $T'' \leq T' < 2^{k(n-t_r)}$ and $S'' \leq S' < 2^{k(n-t_r)}$, under appropriate conditions.

Theorem 1 (Numerical Rational Number Reconstruction). *Let $z = \frac{x}{y} \bmod N$ such that $-X \leq x \leq X$ and $0 < y \leq Y$. If N is relatively prime to y and $2XY < N$ then the solution is unique and it is possible to recover x and y efficiently by using two-dimensional lattice theory.*

Considering $X = 2^{k(n-t_r)} - 1$ and $Y = 2^{k(n-t_r)} - 1$, we indeed have $2XY \leq 2(2^{k(n-t_r)} - 1)(2^{k(n-t_r)} - 1) < N$ and $X > 0$, $Y > 0$, hence we can efficiently recover $\mathcal{T}''$ and $\mathcal{S}''$ from γ. Now, if τ_i is the fingerprint of a valid share, it should be canceled out in $\mathcal{T}'$, but there might still be some small factors in common between τ_i and $\mathcal{T}''$ (we assume that the size of the common part is less than half of the size of τ_i). On the other hand, if τ_i is the fingerprint of a random invalid share, it should not be completely canceled out in $\mathcal{T}'$. However, there is still a chance that some small factors have been canceled out, leading to $\mathcal{T}''$ in the irreducible form (we assume that less than half of it cancels). Hence, our decision algorithm is the following one: we denote t_i the bit size of $|\gcd(\mathcal{T}'', \tau_i)|$; if $t_i \geq k/2$, this is an invalid share, otherwise this is a valid share.

In Fig. 1, we present experimental results that validate this decision algorithm for 128-bit fingerprints. It clearly shows that for a valid τ_i, t_i is a small number (half of them equal to 1) and for an invalid τ_i, t_i is a large number (44 % of them is equal to 2^k). We have computed 2^{21} times the value of $\gcd(\mathcal{T}'', \tau_i)$ and in case of Fig. 1a, the highest bit size of t_i is 35 (much less than 64). On the other hand, in Fig. 1b the least value is 96 (much more than 64). A more fine analysis can be found in the full version [1].

Information Leakage. On the opposite, we would like to evaluate the information leaked by $\mathcal{S}$ when there are at most $t_\ell - 1$ valid values. More precisely, given $\mathcal{S}$, is it possible to distinguish $t_\ell - 1$ valid values for the shares from $t_\ell - 1$ random values? We focus on a t_r-threshold secret sharing scheme, for a k-bit secret and k-bit shares. Then, the entropy of the tuple $(\sigma_1, \ldots, \sigma_n)$ is $k(t_r - 1)$. Since $\mathcal{S}$ reveals the product of the k-bit fingerprints modulo N, with $N < 2^{2k(n-t_r)+2}$, the remaining entropy on the shares is at least $k(t_r - 1) - 2k(n - t_r) - 2 = k(3t_r - 2n - 1) - 2$. If this is greater than $k(t_\ell - 1)$, no one can distinguish $t_\ell - 1$ random values from $t_\ell - 1$ correct values for the shares:

(a) $\gcd(\mathcal{T}'', \tau_i)$-bitlength for valid τ_i.   (b) $\gcd(\mathcal{T}'', \tau_i)$-bitlength for invalid τ_i.

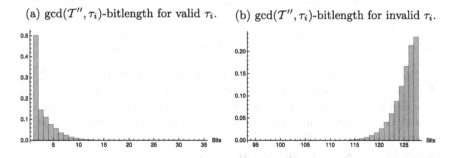

Fig. 1. Length in bits of $\gcd(\mathcal{T}'', \tau_i)$ for a fingerprint of size 128-bits and 32 shares

we thus need $k(3t_r - 2n - 1) - 2 \geq k(t_\ell - 1)$. When $k > 2$, this essentially means $t_\ell \leq 3t_r - 2n$: by choosing $t_\ell = 3t_r - 2n$, we are safe. For example, one can take $t_r = \lceil 3n/4 \rceil$ and $t_\ell = \lfloor n/4 \rfloor$. And the same argument, with $2k$-bit secret and shares but still k-bit fingerprints, leads to $t_r = \lceil 2n/3 \rceil$ and $t_\ell = \lfloor n/3 \rfloor$, which makes sense for a 256-bit secret key and 128-bit fingerprints.

5 Our Password-Protected Secret Sharing Protocols

Thanks to our new (t_ℓ, t_r, n)-RGTSSS, we do not need to use a VOPRF, as in [23], which is at the cost of complex zero-knowledge proofs. We can now describe our general structure of PPSS protocol, using an OPRF as black-box. We thereafter provide two instantiations, with two appropriate OPRFs, in the same vein as the ones proposed in [23], using similar computational assumptions (see the full version [1]):

- the first OPRF relies on the CDH evaluation, similar to the protocol 2HashDH, but without NIZKs. The PPSS construction is then quite similar to [24].
- the second OPRF is an oblivious evaluation of the Naor-Reingold PRF [25]. Then, in the PPSS, the gain of the zero-knowledge proofs by the server is quite significant.

5.1 General Description

As already presented in the high-level description, our protocols are in two phases: the initialization phase which is assumed to be executed in a safe environment and the reconstruction phase during which the password only is considered correct, while all the other inputs can be faked by the adversary.

Initialization. We assume that each server S_i owns a key pair $(\mathsf{sk}_i, \mathsf{pk}_i)$ that defines a PRF F_i, with public parameters defined by pk_i and a secret key defined by sk_i, that admits an OPRF protocol to allow a user with input m to evaluate $F_i(m)$ without leaking any information on m to the server.

We additionally use a (t_ℓ, t_r, n)-robust gap threshold secret sharing scheme and a non-malleable commitment scheme (see the full version [1]). Since we already are in the random-oracle model for the PRF, we can implement the commitment scheme with a simple second-preimage-resistant hash function H_{Com}, which allows a better efficiency. The user U first chooses a secret password pw:

1. the user interacts with n servers to obliviously evaluate $\pi_i = F_i(\mathsf{pw})$, and $\Pi = (\mathsf{pk}_i)_i$ is the tuple of the public keys of the involved servers;
2. for a random value $R = K\|r$, where K is the random secret key the user wants to reconstruct and r some random coins for the commitment. The user generates $(s_1, \ldots, s_n, \mathsf{SSInfo}) \leftarrow \mathsf{ShareGen}(R)$, so that any subset of t_r shares among $\{s_1, \ldots, s_n\}$ can efficiently recover R;
3. then, the user builds $\sigma_i = \pi_i \oplus s_i$, for $i = 1, \ldots, n$, and sets $\Sigma = (\sigma_i)_i$;

4. the user generates $\mathsf{Com} = H_{\mathsf{Com}}(\mathsf{pw}, \Pi, \Sigma, \mathsf{SSInfo}, K; r)$. We denote by $\mathsf{PInfo} = (\Pi, \Sigma, \mathsf{SSInfo}, \mathsf{Com})$ the public information that the user will need later to recover his secret K;
5. the user thus gives PInfo to all the servers.

We stress that during this initialization phase, all the values of Π are the real public keys and $(\pi_i)_i$ are the correct evaluations of the PRFs. On the opposite, during the reconstruction phase, all the values in PInfo will be provided by the servers, but through the adversary, who might alter them.

Reconstruction. For the reconstruction, the user interacts with at least t_r servers, that provide him $\mathsf{PInfo} = (\Pi, \Sigma, \mathsf{SSInfo}, \mathsf{Com})$, and help him to compute $\pi_i = F_i(\mathsf{pw})$ for several values of i, using pk_i from Π. No information is trusted anymore, and so the reconstruction phase perform several verifications:

1. the user first limits the oblivious evaluations of $\pi_i = F_i(\mathsf{pw})$ to the servers that sent the same majority tuple $\mathsf{PInfo} = (\Pi, \Sigma, \mathsf{SSInfo}, \mathsf{Com})$. If the number of such servers is less than t_r, one aborts with $K \leftarrow \perp$;
2. for all these π_i (or similarly, all the i he kept), the user computes $s_i = \sigma_i \oplus \pi_i$, using σ_i from Σ (from PInfo);
3. using these $\{s_i\}$ with at least t_r correct shares, and SSInfo (from PInfo), with RGTSSS, the user reconstructs the shared secret R (or aborts with $K \leftarrow \perp$ if the reconstruction fails);
4. the user parses the secret R as $K\|r$, and checks, from PInfo, whether $\mathsf{Com} = H_{\mathsf{Com}}(\mathsf{pw}, \Pi, \Sigma, \mathsf{SSInfo}, K; r)$;
5. if the verification succeeds, K is the expected secret key, otherwise the user aborts with $K \leftarrow \perp$.

5.2   Protocol I: One-More-Gap-Diffie-Hellman-Based PRF

Our first instantiation is based on CDH-like assumptions in the random-oracle model. The arithmetic is in a finite cyclic group $\mathbb{G} = \langle g \rangle$ of prime order q. We need a full-domain hash function H_1 onto $\mathbb{G}$, and another hash function H_2 onto $\{0,1\}^{\ell_2}$. The commitment scheme uses a simple hash function $H_{\mathsf{Com}} = H_3$ onto $\{0,1\}^{\ell_3}$.

For a private key $\mathsf{sk} = x \in \mathbb{Z}_q$, we consider the pseudorandom function $F_x(m) = H_2(m, g^x, H_1(m)^x)$, for any bitstring $m \in \{0,1\}^*$, where the public key is $\mathsf{pk} = y = g^x$. In the full version [1], we prove this is indeed a PRF, as already shown in [23].

In addition, it admits an oblivious evaluation, that does not leak any information, thanks to the three simulators $\mathcal{S}im$, $\mathcal{S}im_U$ and $\mathcal{S}im_S$, as presented in Fig. 2: $\mathcal{S}im$ simulates an honest transcript, $\mathcal{S}im_U$ simulates an honest user interacting with a malicious server, and $\mathcal{S}im_S$ simulates an honest server with a malicious user. These simulators will be used by our simulator in the full security proof. They generate perfectly indistinguishable views to the adversary, but they require $\mathsf{CDH}_g(y, \cdot)$ and $\mathsf{DDH}_g(y, \cdot, \cdot)$ evaluation, and thus oracle access when the secret keys are not known. Since the indistinguishability of the PRF relies on the $\mathsf{CDH}_g(y, \cdot)$ assumption, the overall security relies on the One-More Gap Diffie-Hellman (OMGDH) assumption (see the full version [1]) as shown in the last step of the proof.

User		Server
m	$\mathsf{pk} = y = g^x$	$\mathsf{sk} = x$
$\alpha \xleftarrow{\$} \mathbb{Z}_q^*, \; A \leftarrow H_1(m)^\alpha$	$\xrightarrow{\quad A \quad}$	
If $B = 1$, then abort	$\xleftarrow{\quad B \quad}$	$B \leftarrow A^x$
$C \leftarrow B^{1/\alpha}, \; R \leftarrow H_2(m, y, C)$		

Sim		Sim_U		Sim_S
$\alpha \xleftarrow{\$} \mathbb{Z}_q^*$		$A \xleftarrow{\$} \mathbb{G} \xrightarrow{\; A \;}$	$\xrightarrow{\; A \;}$	
$A \leftarrow g^\alpha \xrightarrow{\quad A \quad}$		$\xleftarrow{\; B \;}$	$\xleftarrow{\; B \;}$	$B \leftarrow \mathsf{CDH}_g(y, A)$
$\xleftarrow{\quad B \quad} \quad B \leftarrow y^\alpha$		$\neg\mathsf{DDH}_g(y, A, B)$ $\implies \text{fail}$		

Fig. 2. Secure oblivious evaluation of the PRF based on OMGDH

Theorem 2. *For any adversary $\mathcal{A}$, against the Protocol I, that corrupts no more than q_c servers, involves at most q_s instances of the servers, q_u instances of the user, and asks at most q_1, q_2, q_3 queries to H_1, H_2, H_3, respectively*

$$\mathsf{Adv}(\mathcal{A}) \leq \left(q_u + \frac{4q_s}{n - 4q_c} \right) \times \frac{1}{\#\mathcal{D}} + \varepsilon.$$

where $\varepsilon = n \times \mathsf{Succ}^{\mathsf{omgdh}}(q_1, q_s, t, n \cdot q_u + q_2) + (q_3^2 + 2) \cdot 2^{-\ell_3}/4.$

Security Proof. The complete and detailed proof of the Theorem is given in the full version [1]. The rough idea is the following: in the real attack game, we focus on a unique user, against a static adversary (the corrupted servers are known right after the initialization, and before any reconstruction attempt). All the parameters are honestly generated, the simulator knows the secret informations to answers the queries, and two random keys K_0 (random) and K_1 (real), as well as a bit b, are selected randomly to answer Test-queries. In the final game, we simulate all the answers to the adversary without using a password. A random value will be chosen at the very end of the simulation and used as a password in order to decide if some bad events should have occurred, which will immediately upper-bound the advantage of the adversary.

We first modify the way Execute-queries are answered, using Sim that perfectly simulates honest transcripts user-servers, and we set user's key to K_1.

Then, we deal with Send-queries to the honest user, trying to exclude the cases of a fake public information PInfo' (sent by the majority of servers): first, we do as before if the commitment Com' in PInfo' is different from the expected value C generated during the initialization, but eventually we set $K \leftarrow \perp$. This would just make a difference for the adversary if Com' indeed contains the good password pw, which is defined as the event PWinC. This event PWinC can be evaluated using the list of queries asked to H_3. Then, a similar argument applies when a wrong PInfo' is sent, but with a correct Com, under the binding propriety of the commitment H_3.

Once we have fixed this, and we trust the public values, we can use $\mathcal{S}im_U$, that perfectly simulates a flow A from the user to a server, and can decide on the honest behavior of the servers. Then $\mathcal{S}im_U$ accepts with $K \leftarrow K_1$ in the honest case or aborts with $K \leftarrow \perp$ otherwise. Hence, we remark that we answer Send-queries without calling the H_1 or H_2 oracles, but just using K_1, and no secret sharing reconstruction is used anymore.

Next step is to replace all the shares in the initialization phase by random and independent values. We know that until the adversary does not get more than $t_\ell = n/4$ of these shares, it cannot detect whether they are random or correct. We define the event PWinF to be the bad event, where the adversary has enough evaluations of the PRF to notice the change. Again, our simulator is able to decide the event PWinF by checking whether pw has been queried with the right inputs to H_2, and how many times. We eventually replace the hash value Com in the initialization phase by a random Com.

One can note that, in the end, the password pw is not used anymore during the simulation, but just to determine whether the events PWinC or PWinF happened. In addition, K_1 does not appear anymore during the initialization phase, hence cannot make any difference between K_0 and K_1: $\mathsf{Succ}_{\mathcal{A}} = 1/2$ in the last game. As a consequence, $\mathsf{Adv}(\mathcal{A}) \leq \Pr[\mathsf{PWinC}] + \Pr[\mathsf{PWinF}] + \varepsilon$, where ε comes from the collisions or guesses in the random oracles. To evaluate the two events PWinC or PWinF to happen, we choose a random password pw at the very end only: $\Pr[\mathsf{PWinC}]$ is clearly upper-bounded by $q_u/\#\mathcal{D}$, since q_u is the maximal number of fake commitment attempts containing the right pw that can be different from the expected ones; PWinF means that the adversary managed to get $n/4 - q_c$ evaluations of the PRFs under the chosen pw, since it can evaluate on its own the values under the q_c corrupted servers. But unless the adversary gets more evaluations than the number q_s of queries asked to the servers (which can be proven under the OMGDH assumption), the number of bad passwords (for which the knows at least $n/4 - q_c$ evaluations of the PRFs) is less than $q_s/(n/4 - q_c)$. So the probability that the chosen pw is such a bad password is less than $q_s/(n/4 - q_c) \times 1/\#\mathcal{D}$.

5.3   Protocol II: DDH-Based PRF

Our second instantiation makes use of the Naor and Reingold [25] pseudorandom function. We consider the group $\mathbb{G} = \langle g \rangle$ of prime order q that is a safe prime: $q = 2s + 1$. In the multiplicative group of scalar $\mathbb{Z}_q^*$, we consider the cyclic group

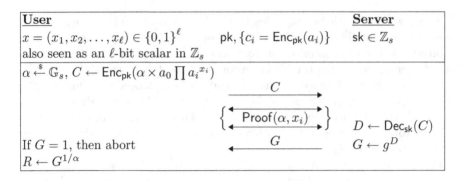

Fig. 3. Secure oblivious evaluation of the NR-PRF

$\mathbb{G}_s$ of order s (this is the group of elements in $\mathbb{Z}_q^*$ with Jacobi symbol equals to $+1$). In both groups, the DDH assumption can be made.

The PRF key is a tuple $a = (a_0, a_1, \ldots, a_\ell) \overset{\$}{\leftarrow} (\mathbb{G}_s \backslash \{1\})^{\ell+1}$, and $F_a(x) = g^{a_0 \prod a_i^{x_i}}$, where $x = (x_1, x_2, \ldots, x_\ell) \in \{0, 1\}^\ell$. This function has been proven to be a PRF under the DDH assumption [25] on ℓ-bit inputs. It also admits a simple oblivious evaluation (just the messages C and G from Fig. 3), using a multiplicatively homomorphic encryption scheme in $\mathbb{G}_s$, such as ElGamal for $(\mathsf{Enc_{pk}}, \mathsf{Dec_{sk}})$, which allows the computation of C from x, α, and the ciphertexts $\{c_i\}_i$. Unfortunately, without additional proofs, this is not secure against malicious users, since it works only for honest inputs $x \in \{0, 1\}^\ell$. Hence the more involved protocol presented in Fig. 3 that makes use of a zero-knowledge proof of knowledge of $(x_i)_i \in \{0, 1\}^\ell$ and $\alpha \in \mathbb{G}_s$. This can be efficiently done under the sole DDH assumption. Whereas our oblivious evaluation of the PRF is in the standard model, overall, the PPSS protocol based on this OPRF is in the random-oracle model as it makes use of the RGTSSS. As a consequence, one could replace the interactive ZK proofs by NIZK proofs "à la Schnorr". This would reduce the number of flows to only 2. The full proof of our protocol II (including the DDH-based OPRF) can be found in the full version [1].

6   Comparisons

We can assume that PInfo is stored in the Cloud, it does not need to be sent by each server, then the global communication is linear in n. More precisely, our first protocol is quite similar to the one from [24]. Of course, we did not provide any security result in the UC framework [13], but our ultimate goal was the same as [23]: an efficient robust password-protected secret sharing scheme, in a BPR-like security model [3]. To this aim, there is no reason to use UC-secure building blocks, but tailored primitives.

Our algebraic OPRF structure is more efficient than the one in [20], since their construction makes use of Oblivious Transfers (OT) and expensive public-key operations. In the online setting, this kind of protocols are almost infeasible, as the number of desired OTs is not known in advance while our zero-knowledge proofs are much simpler to use. Given the work of Ishai *et al.* [21], a better efficiency can be achieved, considering each OT evaluation at the cost of a private-key operation. In our case, the main cost in communication is that of a single zero-knowledge proof.

Our second protocol, based on this oblivious evaluation and with an additionally CRS turns out to be much more efficient than the one from [23]. Even if it uses the same Naor-Reingold PRF, the oblivious evaluation is much more efficient and relies on the DDH assumption only. Our full construction only makes use of ElGamal and Cramer-Shoup encryption schemes, and no Paillier's encryption [26] nor Cramer-Shoup signature [15] that require both stronger assumptions, such as the strong-RSA assumption and the decisional composite residuosity assumption, and much larger parameters, which lead to huge communication load. The main reason comes from the relaxation on the OPRF: since we do not need verifiability of server's computations, it does not have to make any zero-knowledge proof, which allows us to use a much more efficient OPRF.

Acknowledgments. We are grateful to Stanislaw Jarecki for his valuable comments on this work. This work was supported in part by the European Research Council under the European Community's Seventh Framework Programme (FP7/2007-2013 Grant Agreement no. 339563 – CryptoCloud).

References

1. Abdalla, M., Cornejo, M., Nitulescu, A., Pointcheval, D.: Robust password-protected secret sharing. Cryptology ePrint Archive, Report 2016/123 (2016). http://eprint.iacr.org/2016/123
2. Bagherzandi, A., Jarecki, S., Saxena, N., Lu, Y.: Password-protected secret sharing. In: Chen, Y., Danezis, G., Shmatikov, V. (eds.) ACM CCS 2011, pp. 433–444. ACM Press, October 2011
3. Bellare, M., Pointcheval, D., Rogaway, P.: Authenticated key exchange secure against dictionary attacks. In: Preneel, B. (ed.) EUROCRYPT 2000. LNCS, vol. 1807, pp. 139–155. Springer, Heidelberg (2000)
4. Bellare, M., Rogaway, P.: Random oracles are practical: a paradigm for designing efficient protocols. In: Ashby, V. (ed.) ACM CCS 1993, pp. 62–73. ACM Press, November 1993
5. Bellare, M., Rogaway, P.: Entity authentication and key distribution. In: Stinson, D.R. (ed.) CRYPTO 1993. LNCS, vol. 773, pp. 232–249. Springer, Heidelberg (1994)
6. Bellare, M., Rogaway, P.: Provably secure session key distribution: the three party case. In: 27th ACM STOC, pp. 57–66. ACM Press, May/June 1995
7. Bellovin, S.M., Merritt, M.: Encrypted key exchange: password-based protocols secure against dictionary attacks. In: 1992 IEEE Symposium on Security and Privacy, pp. 72–84. IEEE Computer Society Press, May 1992
8. Bishop, A., Pastro, V., Rajaraman, R., Wichs, D.: Essentially optimal robust secret sharing with maximal corruptions. Cryptology ePrint Archive, Report 2015/1032 (2015). http://eprint.iacr.org/2015/1032

9. Blakley, G.R.: Safeguarding cryptographic keys. In: Proceedings of AFIPS 1979 National Computer Conference, vol. 48, pp. 313–317 (1979)
10. Camenisch, J., Lehmann, A., Lysyanskaya, A., Neven, G.: Memento: how to reconstruct your secrets from a single password in a hostile environment. In: Garay, J.A., Gennaro, R. (eds.) CRYPTO 2014, Part II. LNCS, vol. 8617, pp. 256–275. Springer, Heidelberg (2014)
11. Camenisch, J., Lehmann, A., Neven, G.: Optimal distributed password verification. In: Ray, I., Li, N., Kruegel, C. (eds.) ACM CCS 2015, pp. 182–194. ACM Press, October 2015
12. Camenisch, J., Lysyanskaya, A., Neven, G.: Practical yet universally composable two-server password-authenticated secret sharing. In: Yu, T., Danezis, G., Gligor, V.D. (eds.) ACM CCS 2012, pp. 525–536. ACM Press, October 2012
13. Canetti, R.: Universally composable security: a new paradigm for cryptographic protocols. In: 42nd FOCS, pp. 136–145. IEEE Computer Society Press, October 2001
14. Cheraghchi, M.: Nearly optimal robust secret sharing. Cryptology ePrint Archive, Report 2015/951 (2015). http://eprint.iacr.org/2015/951
15. Cramer, R., Shoup, V.: Signature schemes based on the strong RSA assumption. In: ACM CCS 1999, pp. 46–51. ACM Press, November 1999
16. Di Crescenzo, G., Ishai, Y., Ostrovsky, R.: Non-interactive and non-malleable commitment. In: 30th ACM STOC, pp. 141–150. ACM Press, May 1998
17. ElGamal, T.: A public key cryptosystem and a signature scheme based on discrete logarithms. IEEE Trans. Inf. Theory 31, 469–472 (1985)
18. Ford, W., Kaliski Jr., B.S.: Server-assisted generation of a strong secret from a password. In: Proceedings of the 9th IEEE International Workshops on Enabling Technologies: Infrastructure for Collaborative Enterprises, pp. 176–180. IEEE Computer Society, Washington, DC (2000)
19. Fouque, P.-A., Stern, J., Wackers, J.-G.: CryptoComputing with rationals. In: Blaze, M. (ed.) FC 2002. LNCS, vol. 2357, pp. 136–146. Springer, Heidelberg (2003)
20. Freedman, M.J., Ishai, Y., Pinkas, B., Reingold, O.: Keyword search and oblivious pseudorandom functions. In: Kilian, J. (ed.) TCC 2005. LNCS, vol. 3378, pp. 303–324. Springer, Heidelberg (2005)
21. Ishai, Y., Kilian, J., Nissim, K., Petrank, E.: Extending oblivious transfers efficiently. In: Boneh, D. (ed.) CRYPTO 2003. LNCS, vol. 2729, pp. 145–161. Springer, Heidelberg (2003)
22. Jablon, D.P.: Password authentication using multiple servers. In: Naccache, D. (ed.) CT-RSA 2001. LNCS, vol. 2020, pp. 344–360. Springer, Heidelberg (2001)
23. Jarecki, S., Kiayias, A., Krawczyk, H.: Round-optimal password-protected secret sharing and T-PAKE in the password-only model. In: Sarkar, P., Iwata, T. (eds.) ASIACRYPT 2014, Part II. LNCS, vol. 8874, pp. 233–253. Springer, Heidelberg (2014)
24. Jarecki, S., Kiayias, A., Krawczyk, H., Xu, J.: Highly-Efficient and Composable Password-Protected Secret Sharing. Cryptology ePrint Archive, Report 2016/144 (2016). http://eprint.iacr.org/
25. Naor, M., Reingold, O.: Number-theoretic constructions of efficient pseudo-random functions. In: 38th FOCS, pp. 458–467. IEEE Computer Society Press, October 1997
26. Paillier, P.: Public-key cryptosystems based on composite degree residuosity classes. In: Stern, J. (ed.) EUROCRYPT 1999. LNCS, vol. 1592, pp. 223–238. Springer, Heidelberg (1999)

27. Reed, I.S., Solomon, G.: Polynomial codes over certain finite fields. J. Soc. Ind. Appl. Math. **8**(2), 300–304 (1960)
28. Shamir, A.: How to share a secret. Commun. Assoc. Comput. Mach. **22**(11), 612–613 (1979)
29. Yi, X., Hao, F., Chen, L., Liu, J.K.: Practical threshold password-authenticated secret sharing protocol. In: Pernul, G., Ryan, P.Y.A., Weippl, E. (eds.) ESORICS. LNCS, vol. 9326, pp. 347–365. Springer, Heidelberg (2015). doi:10.1007/978-3-319-24174-6_18

Compiling Low Depth Circuits for Practical Secure Computation

Niklas Buescher[1(✉)], Andreas Holzer[2], Alina Weber[1],
and Stefan Katzenbeisser[1]

[1] Technische Universität Darmstadt, Darmstadt, Germany
buescher@seceng.informatik.tu-darmstadt.de
[2] University of Toronto, Toronto, Canada

Abstract. With the rise of practical Secure Multi-party Computation
(MPC) protocols, compilers have been developed that create Boolean
or Arithmetic circuits for MPC from functionality descriptions in a
high-level language. Previous compilers focused on the creation of size-
minimal circuits. However, many MPC protocols, such as GMW and
SPDZ, have a round complexity that is dependent on the circuit's depth.
When deploying these protocols in real world network settings, with network latencies in the range of tens or hundreds of milliseconds, the round
complexity quickly becomes a significant performance bottleneck.

In this work, we present ShallowCC, a compiler extension that creates depth minimized Boolean circuits from ANSI-C. We first introduce
novel optimized building blocks that are up to 50 % shallower than previous constructions. Second, we present multiple high- and low-level depth
minimization techniques and implement these in the existing CBMC-
GC compiler. Our experiments show significant depth reductions over
hand-optimized constructions (for some applications up to 2.5×), while
maintaining a circuit size that is competitive with size-minimizing compilers. Evaluating exemplary functionalities in a GMW framework, we
show that depth reductions lead to significant speed-ups in any real-
world network setting. For an exemplary biometric matching application
we report a 400× speed-up in comparison with a circuit generated from
a size-minimizing compiler.

1 Introduction

In the thirty years since Yao's seminal paper [33], Secure Multiparty Computation (MPC) has transitioned from purely theoretic construction to a practical
tool. In MPC, two or more parties jointly evaluate a function over their inputs in
such a way that each party keeps its input hidden from the other parties. Thus,
MPC provides a generic way to construct Privacy-Enhancing Technologies, which
protect sensitive data during processing steps in untrusted environments. In the
last decade, many new protocols and optimizations made MPC practical for various applications. Nevertheless, MPC is still multiple orders of magnitude slower
than classic computation.

© Springer International Publishing Switzerland 2016
I. Askoxylakis et al. (Eds.): ESORICS 2016, Part II, LNCS 9879, pp. 80–98, 2016.
DOI: 10.1007/978-3-319-45741-3_5

The performance of most MPC protocols usually depends on the complexity of either a Boolean or an Arithmetic circuit representing the functionality to be computed. Unfortunately, the manual construction of efficient circuits is a complex, error-prone, and time-consuming task. Therefore, multiple compilers, for example CBMC-GC [17], Frigate [26], KSS [22], or the SecreC Compiler [4], have been developed that compile a functionality described in a high-level language into circuits satisfying the requirements of MPC protocols.

The creation of circuits from a high-level functionality shares similarities with hardware synthesis. Yet, hardware synthesis tools differ in two factors. First, no layout or space considerations have to be made when designing circuits for MPC. Second, the costs for different types of gates differ significantly. For example, in classic logic synthesis, Boolean NAND gates are favored over XOR gates due to their placement costs. However, in many MPC protocols the evaluation costs of all non-linear gates (e.g., AND, NAND and OR) are equivalent to each other, while the evaluation of linear gates (e.g., XOR) is essentially free [14]. Therefore, previous works on MPC compilers mainly focussed on producing circuits with a minimal number of non-linear gates.

Nevertheless, many practically relevant MPC protocols, such as BGW [3], GMW [14], Sharemind [4], SPDZ [9] and TinyOT [28] have a round complexity that is proportional to the circuit depth. Hence, for these MPC protocols it is crucial to also consider the circuit depth as a major optimization goal, because every layer in the circuit increases the protocol's runtime by the round trip time (RTT) between the computing parties. This is of special importance, as latency is the only computational resource that has reached its physical boundary. (For computational power and bandwidth, parallel resources can always be added.) Thus, asymptotically it is much more vital to minimize the depth of circuits, rather than speeding-up the computational efficiency. To illustrate these thoughts, the performance of a state-of-the-art implementation of the GMW protocol [14], such as ABY [11], shows that more than 10 million non-linear gates per second can be computed on a single core of a commodity CPU. At the same time, the network latency between Asia and Europe[1] is in the range of a hundred milliseconds. In this setting, the evaluation time of any circuit with less than 100,000 parallel gates per circuit level will increase by at least one order of magnitude. Therefore, it is worthwhile to investigate optimization and compilation techniques for the automatic creation of low depth Boolean circuits.

Even though this work focusses on depth-minimized Boolean circuits, MPC protocols using Arithmetic circuits or FHE schemes can also profit from the ideas presented here, as they require Boolean circuits for all control flow operations. Moreover, we note that a shallower and broader circuit allows for better parallelization in MPC protocols with constant round complexity, for example in Parallel Yao's Garbled Circuits [6].

---

[1] Even though, MPC is often benchmarked in a LAN setting, the WAN setting is the more natural deployment model of MPC.

Contribution. In this work, we present *ShallowCC*, a compiler that takes ANSI-C as input and automatically generates low depth Boolean circuits, optimized for MPC protocols that favor a minimal number of non-linear gates. Our approach for the generation of depth minimized circuits is threefold. First, we present and investigate minimization techniques that operate on the source code level. This involves the detection of sequential reductions, which can be regrouped in a tree based manner. We refer to reductions as the aggregation of multiple programming variables into a single result variable, e.g., minima computation over an array. We also present techniques to detect consecutive arithmetic operations, which can be instantiated more efficiently by a dedicated circuit rather than a composition of multiple individual arithmetic building blocks. Second, we present depth and size optimized constructions of major building blocks, e.g., adder and multiplexer, required for the synthesis of larger circuits. These hand-optimized building blocks have a depth that is significantly smaller than depth-minimized blocks presented in recent works [10,30]. An overview of significant improvements is given in Table 1. Third, we adapt multiple low level optimization methods that minimize circuit depth on the gate level. Finally, we contribute an implementation of our ideas as an extension to the open-source CBMC-GC compiler.

Table 1. *Depth of Building Blocks.* Comparison of the depth of the here presented building blocks with the previously known best constructions.

Operation	Previous work [30]	This work
n-bit Addition	$2\log_2(n) + 1$	$\log_2(n) + 1$
n-bit Multiplication	$3\log_2(n) + 4$	$2\log_2(n) + 3$
m:1 Multiplexer	$\log_2(m)$	$\lceil \log_2(\lceil \log_2(m+1) \rceil) \rceil$

Comparing with the hand optimized computations, e.g., computation of the Manhattan distance [10], we report depth reductions between 30 % and 60 %. Comparing with previous compilers, we report circuits, e.g., a privacy preserving biometric matching functionality, that are up 400 times shallower. Evaluating the depth minimized circuits with the GMW protocol [14], we observe speed-ups of the online protocol run time that are proportional to the depth savings, even for RRTs below 10ms. For example, we observe a speed-up of 400 times for the aforementioned biometric matching functionality.

Outline. Next, we discuss related work. An introduction into circuit design is given in Sect. 3. In Sect. 4 we present ShallowCC and its minimization techniques. An evaluation of ShallowCC is given in Sect. 5.

2   Related Work

Along with the early development of practical frameworks for MPC, circuit compilers have been developed, mainly because the manual creation of circuits for privacy preserving applications requires expertise in hardware synthesis and can be an error prone task with circuits scaling to billions of gates. Here, we first discuss compilers for the creation of Boolean circuits mainly tailored towards Yao's Garbled Circuits, before discussing compilers for arithmetic circuits. Moreover, an overview of optimized circuit libraries is given.

Boolean circuit compilers. The development of compilers for MPC started with the Fairplay framework by Malkhi et al. [25]. Fairplay compiles a domain specific hardware description language (SFDL) into a gate list for the use in Yao's Garbled Circuits. Henecka et al. [16] presented the TASTY compiler with a domain specific language (DSL) that supports basic data types and arithmetic operations to allow the efficient combination of Garbled Circuits with additively homomorphic encryption. The PAL compiler by Mood et al. [27] also relies on Fairplay's SFDL input format, but aims at low-memory devices as the compilation target. The KSS compiler by Kreuter et al. [22] is the first compiler that shows scalability up to a billion of gates. KSS compiles circuits from a domain specific hardware language and employs advanced optimization methods, e.g., constant propagation or dead gate elimination. ObliVM by Liu et al. [23] is a framework for Java that enables the automatized combination of oblivious data structures with MPC. Songhori et al. [31] presented Tiny Garble, which uses commercial hardware synthesis tools to compile circuits from VHDL. One the one hand, this approach allows to use a broad range of existing functionalities in hardware synthesis, but also shows the least degree of abstraction, by requiring the developer to have experience in hardware design. Zahur and Evans [35] presented a compilation approach, named Obliv-C, that compiles a DSL into executable C code, thus, combining compiler and execution environment. Very recently, Mood et al. [26] presented the Frigate compiler, which aims at very fast and extensively tested compilation of another DSL.

The CBMC-GC compiler by Holzer et al. [17] is the first compiler that creates Boolean circuits for MPC from ANSI-C. CBMC-GC utilizes the Bounded Model Checker CBMC, originally used for the verification of C code, to reliably compile a large subset of C to circuits. ParCC, presented by Buescher et al. [6], is a source-to-source compiler, which extends CBMC-GC by the capability to compile parallel circuits. The PCF compiler by Kreuter et al. [21] is compiles C using the intermediate representation of the portable LCC compiler.

Mood et al. [26] give an overview on many of the aforementioned compilers and benchmark their performance. The authors indicate limited robustness of many existing compilers, as most have been developed for research purposes. We observe that all compilers apply various optimization methods, yet all aim at the creation of size and not depth minimal circuits.

Arithmetic circuit compilers. Multiple compilers that aim at the creation of circuits for use in secret sharing based MPC have been developed. Early compilers are the FairplayMP compiler by Ben-David et al. [2] and the VIFF compiler by Damgard et al. [8], which both compile a DSL. The Sharemind framework by

Bogdanov et al. [4] is nowadays the most advanced compiler for MPC. It compiles a DSL, implements a broad range of functionalities and supports multiple MPC protocols during runtime. The Picco compiler by Zhang et al. [36] compiles ANSI-C into interpretable arithmetic circuits, yet has not been open sourced.

Optimized circuit libraries. Kolesnikov and Schneider [19,20] presented first size optimized low-level building blocks, e.g., adder and multiplexer, for their use in Yao's Garbled Circuits. Zahur and Evans [34] presented optimized circuit structures for more advanced building blocks, such as stacks and queues. Schneider and Zohner [30] identified the need of low depth circuits for a fair comparison between GMW und Yao's Garbled Circuits and presented multiple depth minimized building blocks. Most recently, Demmler et al. [10] presented a library of low depth circuits exported from a commercial hardware synthesis tool. In this work, we compare our results with these hand optimized circuits.

3   Preliminaries in Digital Circuit Design for MPC

Digital circuit design, also known as logic synthesis, deals with the construction and optimization of digital circuits. Common optimization goals are the reduction of the placement costs and the signal delay under several physical constraints. In circuit design for MPC, however, many of the classical design criteria (e.g., signal amplification) can be omitted, because the created circuits are evaluated 'virtually' in software. In this work, we investigate the creation of Boolean circuits based on gates with two input wires, as these provide the most general circuit description. In the following paragraphs, we describe the used notation, as well as some basic concepts applied in logic synthesis.

Notation. We use s^{nX} to notate the total number of non-linear gates of a circuit, also referred to as size, and d^{nX} to denote the circuit's depth in the number of non-linear gates. Furthermore, we denote bit strings in capital letters, e.g. X, and denote their negation with $\overline{X}$. We refer to single bit at position i within a bit string with X_i. The Least-Significant Bit (LSB) is X_0. Moreover, we denote the Boolean XOR gate with $\oplus$, AND with $\cdot$ and OR with $+$. When useful, we abbreviate the AND gate $A \cdot B$ with AB.

Half- and Full-Adder. Arithmetic building blocks are constructed of smaller building blocks, namely Half-Adders (HA) and Full-Adders (FA). A Half-Adder is a combinatorial circuit that takes two bits A and B and computes their sum $S = A \oplus B$ and carry bit $C_{out} = A \cdot B$. A Full-Adder allows an additional carry-in bit C_{in} as input. The sum is computed by XOR-ing all inputs $S = A \oplus B \oplus C_{in}$, the carry-out bit can be computed by $C_{out} = (A \oplus C_{in})(B \oplus C_{in}) \oplus C_{in}$ [20]. Both, the HA and FA have size $s^{nX} = 1$ and depth $d^{nX} = 1$.

Carry-Save Adder. In the early 1960s [12], Carry-Save Addition was introduced to compute the sum of k numbers in logarithmic depth. The main component of a Carry-Save Addition is the 3:2 Carry-Save Adder (CSA). A 3:2 CSA reduces the sum of three numbers $A + B + C$ to the sum of two numbers $X + Y$ in small constant depth [29]. A CSA for three n-bit values A, B and C can be instantiated by n parallel FAs. This instantiation has a depth of one and allows to compute the partial sums X and Y for k numbers with depth $d_{CSA}^{nX}(k) = \lceil \log_2(k) - 1 \rceil$ [30].

Parallel Prefix Circuit. A parallel prefix circuit is used in depth minimizing adders and computes n outputs $O_1, \ldots, O_n$ from n inputs $X_1, \ldots, X_n$ for an arbitrary associative two-input operator $\circ$ as follows [15]:

$$O_1 = X_1, \quad O_2 = X_1 \circ X_2, \quad \ldots, \quad O_n = X_1 \circ X_2 \cdots \circ X_n.$$

All outputs can then be computed with at most logarithmic depth when applying the operator $\circ$ in a tree structure over all inputs, e.g., $O_4 = (X_1 \circ X_2) \circ (X_3 \circ X_4)$.

Two's complement. The two's complement is the common representation of signed numbers in hardware. In the two's complement, negative numbers are represented by flipping all bits and adding one. In the following sections, we assume a two's complement representation, when referring to negative numbers.

4 Creation of Low Depth Circuits

In this section, we present the design of our compiler extension ShallowCC as well as multiple depth minimization techniques. ShallowCC is built on top of CBMC-GC, which, even though being the first compiler for ANSI-C, creates circuits that are still competitive in size [26]. CBMC-GC is open sourced, well documented and shows great reliability due to is origin in model checking. Moreover, it implements powerful minimization techniques on the gate level that make it an optimal candidate to implement the ideas presented in this section.

ShallowCC follows CBMC-GC's compilation approach and adopts them for depth minimization as illustrated in Fig. 1. Adaptations and extensions are marked in gray. The compiler reads ANSI-C code with a special naming convention for input arguments and output variables (see [17] for code examples). First,

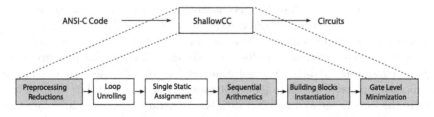

Fig. 1. ShallowCC's compilation chain from ANSI-C to Boolean circuits.

```
unsigned max_abs(int a[], unsigned len) {
  unsigned i, max = abs(a[0]);
  for(i = 1; i < len; i++)
    if(abs(a[i]) > max)
      max = abs(a[i]);
  return max;
}
```

Listing 1. Exemplary function that computes the maximum norm.

the code is preprocessed to detect and transform reduction statements on the source code level (see Sect. 4.1). In the second and third step all bounded loops and recursions are unrolled using symbolic execution and the resulting code is transformed into Single Static Assignment (SSA) form. In the fourth step, the SSA form is used to detect and annotate successive composition of arithmetic statements (see Sect. 4.1). Afterwards, all statements are instantiated with hand-optimized building blocks (see Sect. 4.2), before a final gate-level minimization takes place (see Sect. 4.3).

4.1   Code Level Minimization Techniques

In the following paragraphs we discuss two techniques that operate on the source code level to decrease the circuit depth.

Reduction Statements. We refer to a reduction as the compression of multiple programming variables into a single result variable, e.g., the sum of an array. Consider the code example in Listing 1. This code computes the maximum norm of a vector. It iterates over an integer array, computes the absolute value of every element and then reduces all elements to a single value, namely their maximum. A straight forward translation of the maximum computation leads to a circuit consisting of len − 1 sequentially aligned comparators and multiplexers, as illustrated in Fig. 2a. However, the same functionality can be implemented with logarithmic depth when using a tree structure, as illustrated in Fig. 2b. Thus, when optimizing circuits for depth, it is worthwhile to rewrite sequential reductions. To relieve the programmer from this task, ShallowCC automatically replaces sequential reductions found in loop statements by tree-based reductions.

Since detecting reductions in loop statements is a common task in automatized parallelization, we adapt the recent work on parallel circuits by Buescher and Katzenbeisser [6]. The authors use the parallelization framework Par4all [1] to detect parallelism on source code level. As a side product, Par4all also identifies and annotates sequential reductions. We extend the techniques presented in [6] to parse these reduction annotations and to rewrite the code during the preprocessing phase with *clang* (source-to-source compilation). For this, we first identify the loop range and reduced variable to instantiate a code template that computes the reduction in a tree structure. This optimization improves the depth of reductions over m elements from $O(m)$ to $O(\log m)$. To give an example, for a minimum computation of a 32-bit integer array with 100 elements, we observe a depth reduction from 592 to 42 non-linear gates, cf. Sect. 5.3.

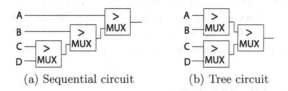

(a) Sequential circuit   (b) Tree circuit

Fig. 2. Maximimum search circuit, consisting of comparators and multiplexers.

Carry-Save Networks (CSNs). CSNs are efficient circuit constructions for multiple successive arithmetic operations that outperform their individual composition in size and depth. Consider the following lines of code as an example:

```
unsigned a, b, c, d;
unsigned t = a + b;
unsigned sum = t + c + d;
```

A straight forward compilation, as in CBMC-GC, leads to a circuit consisting of three binary adders: sum = ADD(ADD(ADD(a,b), c), d). However, if it is possible to identify that a sum of four independent operands is computed, a CSA with four inputs can be initiated instead: sum = CSA(a,b,c,d). This reduces the circuit's depth in this example from 18 to 7 non-linear gates.

Detecting these operations on the gate level is feasible, for example with the help of pattern matching, yet impractically costly considering that circuits reach sizes in the range of billions of gates. Therefore, ShallowCC aims at detecting these successive statements before their translation to the gate level. We do this by utilizing the capabilities of the bounded model checker CBMC [7] that ShallowCC is built upon. CBMC compiles C code into the SSA form, where each variable is written only once. The SSA form allows efficient data flow analyses and as such, also the search for successive arithmetic operations. Our detection algorithm consists of two parts. First, a breadth-first search from output to input variables is initiated. Whenever an arithmetic assignment is found, a second backtracking algorithm is initiated to identify all preceding (possibly nested) arithmetic operations. This second algorithm stops whenever a guarded or non-arithmetic statement is found. Once all preceding inputs are identified, the initial assignment can be replaced by a CSN. After every replacement, the search algorithm continues its search towards the input variables. We note that this greedy replacement approach is depth minimizing, yet not necessarily size optimal, since intermediate results in nested statements may be computed multiple times. A trade-off between size and depth is possible by only instantiating CSNs for non-nested arithmetic statements.

Quantifying the improvements, assuming that the addition of two numbers requires a circuit of depth d_{Add}^{nX}, we observe that by sequential composition $m > 2$

numbers can be added with depth $(m - 1) \cdot d_{Add}^{nX}$. When using a tree-based structure the same sum can be computed with a depth of $\lceil \log_2(m) \rceil \cdot d_{Add}^{nX}$. However, when using a CSA, m numbers can be added with a depth of only $\lceil \log_2(m) - 1 \rceil + d_{Add}^{nX}$. Furthermore, multiplications and additions can be merged in a single CSN, as every multiplication internally consists of additions of partial products, cf. Sect. 4.2. For the exemplary computation of a 5×5 matrix multiplication, we observe an improvement in depth of more than 60%, cf. Sect. 5.3.

4.2 Optimized Building Blocks

Optimized building blocks are an essential part when designing complex circuits. They facilitate efficient compilation, as they can be highly optimized once and subsequently instantiated at practically no cost during compilation. In the following paragraphs, we present new depth and size optimized building blocks constructed from Boolean gates for basic arithmetic and control flow operations.

Adder. An n-bit *adder* takes two bit strings A and B of length n, representing two (signed) integers, as input and returns their sum as an output bit string S of length $n+1$. The standard adder is the Ripple Carry Adder (RCA) that consists of a successive composition of n FAs. This leads to a linear circuit size and depth $s_{RCA}^{nX} = d_{RCA}^{nX} = O(n)$. Parallel Prefix Adders (PPAs) are widely used in logic synthesis to achieve faster addition under size trade-offs by using a tree based prefix network with logarithmic depth. PPAs have been investigated for their use in MPC [10,30]. Surprisingly, and to the best of our knowledge, none of these constructions challenged the textbook design of PPAs, which never considered the 'free' XOR cost model. In the full version of this paper[2], we prove that it is possible to replace one of the two non-linear gates by an XOR gate in every layer of the a PPA. Applying this design to the Sklansky adder, which shows the least depths of all PPAs (see taxonomy of Harris [15]), we achieve a construction with a depth of $d_{Sk}^{nX}(n) = \lceil \log_2(n) \rceil + 1$ and a size of $s_{Sk}^{nX} = n\lceil \log_2(n) \rceil$ for an input bit length of n and output bit length of $n+1$. In Table 2 a depth and size comparison of the standard Ripple-Carry adder, the Ladner-Fischer adder, as proposed in [30], the here optimized Sklansky adder, and an alternative to the Sklansky adder, namely the Brent-Kung adder [15] is given for different bit-widths. We observe that the RCA provides the least size and the Sklansky adder the least depth. The Brent-Kung adder provides a trade-off between size and depth. Both of our optimized constructions significantly outperform the previous best known depth-minimized construction in size and depth.

Subtractor. A subtractor can be implemented with one additional non-linear gate by using the two's complement representation $a - b = a + \bar{b} + 1$, with $\bar{b}$ being the negated binary representation [19]. The addition of negative numbers in the Two's complement is equivalent to an addition of positive numbers. Hence, the subtractor profits to the same degree from the optimized addition.

---

[2] Full version available at http://www.seceng.de/people/buescher/.

Table 2. *Adders.* Comparison of circuit size s^{nX} and depth d^{nX} of the standard RCA, the previously best known depth-optimized adder [30] and our newly optimized Brent-Kung and Sklansky adder.

	depth d^{nX}				size s^{nX}			
Bit-width	n	16	32	64	n	16	32	64
Ripple-Carry	$n-1$	15	31	63	$n-1$	15	31	63
Ladner-Fischer [10, 30]	$2\lceil \log(n)\rceil + 1$	9	11	13	$1.25n\lceil \log(n)\rceil + 2n$	113	241	577
Brent-Kung-opt	$2\lceil \log(n)\rceil - 1$	7	9	11	$3n$	48	96	192
Sklansky-opt	$\lceil \log(n)\rceil + 1$	5	6	7	$n\lceil \log(n)\rceil$	64	160	384

Multiplier. A multiplier takes two input strings of length n as input and returns their product in form of an output bit string of length $2n$. The standard approach for multipliers is the 'school' method. Here n partial products of length n are computed and then added. This approach leads to a quadratic size $s^{nX}_{MUL,s} = 2n^2 - n$ and linear depth $d^{nX}_{MUL,s} = 2n - 1$, cf. [30].

A faster addition of the partial products can be achieved when using Carry-Save Adders (CSAs, cf. Sect. 3). Such a tree based multiplier consists of three steps: First, the computation of all $n \times n$ partial products, then their aggregation in a tree structure using CSAs, before the final sum is computed using a two-input adder. The first step is computed with a constant depth of $d^{nX}_{PP} = 1$, as only one single AND gate is required. For the last step, two bit strings of length $2n - 1$ have to be added. Using our Sklansky adder, this addition can be realized in $d^{nX}_{Sk}(n) = \lceil \log_2(2n-1)\rceil + 1$. The second phase allows many different designs, as the CSAs can arbitrarily be composed. The fastest composition is the Wallace tree [32], which leads to a depth of $d^{nX}_{CSA}(n) = \log_2(n)$ for MPC. Combing all three steps, a multiplication can be realized with a depth of $d^{nX}_{Wa}(n) = d^{nX}_{PP} + d_{CSA}(n) + d^{nX}_{Sk}(2n - 1) = 2\log_2 n + 3$.

In Table 3 we present a comparison of the multipliers discussed above with the depth optimized one presented in [30]. Compared with this implementation, we are able reduce the depth by at least a third for any bit-width.

Table 3. *Multipliers.* Comparison of circuit depth d and size s of the school method, the multiplier given in [30] and our optimized Wallace construction.

	depth d^{nX}				size s^{nX}			
Bit-width	n	16	32	64	n	16	32	64
Standard	$2n-1$	45	93	189	$n^2 - n$	496	2016	8128
MulCSA [30]	$3\lceil \log_2(n)\rceil + 4$	16	19	22	$\approx 2n^2 + 1.25n\log_2(n)$	578	2218	8610
Wallace-opt	$2\lceil \log_2(n)\rceil + 3$	11	13	15	$\approx 2n^2 + n\log_2(n)$	512	2058	8226

Multiplexer. A multiplexer (MUX) is the most important building block for the control and data flow of any MPC application. MUXs are used to represent conditionals and dynamic array access. A 2:1 n-bit MUX consists of two input bit strings D^0 and D^1 of length n and a control input bit C. The control input decides which of the two input bit strings is propagated to the output bit string O of the same bit length. Kolesnikov and Schneider [20] presented a construction of a 2:1 MUX that only requires one single non-linear gate for every pair of input bits by computing the output as $O = (D^0 \oplus D^1)C \oplus D^0$. This leads to a circuit size of $s_{MUX}^{nX}(n) = n$ and depth of $d_{MUX}^{nX}(n) = 1$. A 2:1 MUX can be extended to a m:1 MUX that selects between m input strings $D^0, D^1, \ldots, D^m$ using $\log_2(m)$ control bits $C{=}C_0, C_1, \ldots C_{\log(m)}$ by tree based composition of 2:1 MUXs leading to a circuit of size $s_{MUX\_tree}^{nX}(m, n) = (m - 1) \cdot s_{MUX}^{nX}(n)$ with logarithmic depth $d_{MUX\_tree}^{nX}(m, n) = \log_2(m)$ [30].

We propose a further depth reduction by a logarithmic factor when constructing the multiplexer in disjunctive normal form (DNF) over all combinations of choices. Every conjunction of the DNF encodes a single choice together with the associated data wire. For MPC, this construction leads to a very low depth, because the disjunctive ORs can be replaced by XORs, as all choices are mutually exclusive. For example, a 4:1 MUX is constructed by:

$$O = D^0 \overline{C_0 C_1} \oplus D^1 \overline{C_0} C_1 \oplus D^2 C_0 \overline{C_1} \oplus D^3 C_0 C_1.$$

Thus, the depth of a m:1 MUX can be reduced to the depth of one conjunction $d_{MUX\_DNFd}^{nX}(m, n) = \lceil \log_2(\lceil \log_2(m) \rceil + 1) \rceil$. Unfortunately, a naïve implementation of a n-bit m:1 MUX$_{DNFd}$, as described above, increases the size to $s_{MUX\_DNFd}^{nX}(m, n) = mn \cdot \log(m)$. Since this size increase can be quite significant for larger m, we propose a second construction, referred to as MUX$_{DNFs}$. The idea is first to compute every choice conjunction, before AND-gating them with the data inputs, leading to a depth of $d_{MUX\_DNFs}^{nX}(m, n) = \lceil \log_2(\lceil \log_2(m) \rceil) \rceil + 1$. Now, every conjunction can be computed size efficiently, by avoiding the duplicated computations of choice combinations, e.g., the choices $C_0 C_1 C_2$ and $\overline{C_0} C_1 C_2$ require both the computation of $C_1 C_2$, which can be merged. This reduces the size to:

$$s_{MUX\_DNFs}^{nX}(m, n) = m + \frac{m}{2^0} + \frac{m}{2^1} + \cdots + \frac{m}{2^{m-2}} + mn < 2m + mn.$$

In Table 4 a comparison of the three MUXs is given for a different number of inputs m and a typical bit-width of 32 bits. In summary, we improved the depth of MUXs by a logarithmic factor with a moderate increase in size.

4.3 Gate Level Minimization Techniques

Minimizing the circuit on the gate level is the last step in ShallowCC's compilation chain. We first give a high level description of CBMC-GC's optimization flow, before discussing the adaptations made for ShallowCC.

Table 4. *Multiplexers.* Exemplary comparison of circuit depth d and size s a of $m{:}1$ multiplexers for a different number of inputs m of bit-width $n = 32$.

Input choices	depth d^{nX}				size s^{nX}			
	m	8	128	1024	m	8	128	1024
MUX_{Tree}	$\lceil \log(m) \rceil$	3	7	10	$(m-1) \cdot n$	244	4,064	31,968
MUX_{DNFd}	$\lceil \log_2(\lceil \log_2(m) + 1 \rceil) \rceil$	2	3	4	$mn \cdot \lceil \log(m) \rceil$	768	28,672	320,000
MUX_{DNFs}	$\lceil \log_2(\lceil \log_2(m) \rceil) \rceil + 1$	3	4	5	$2m + mn$	272	1,088	34,000

Finding a minimal circuit for a given functionality is known to be Σ_2^P complete [5]. Therefore, CBMC-GC follows an heuristic approach when minimizing circuits: First, structural hashing is applied to identify and remove duplicated sub circuits. Then, a fixed-point optimization algorithm is initiated (the algorithm runs until no further improvements are made), which itself consists of two alternating phases. In the first phase, a template based circuit rewriting is executed, which applies Boolean theorems to reduce the circuit size. For example, the Idempotent law $X + X = X$ forms a template, namely an OR gate with the same inputs can safely be removed. In the second phase SAT sweeping is applied, which identifies unused gates with the help of a SAT solver. For ShallowCC, we left the structural hashing and SAT sweeping unmodified, as both help to reduce the circuit complexity. Instead, we adapt the template based rewriting phase.

The circuit rewriting in CBMC-GC only considers patterns that are size decreasing and have a depth of at most two binary gates. For depth reduction, as required in ShallowCC, however, it is useful to also consider deeper circuit structures, as well as patterns that are size preserving but depth decreasing. For example, sequential structures, $X = A + (B + (C + (D + E)))$ can be replaced by tree based structures $X = ((A + B) + C) + (D + E)$ with no change in circuit size. Therefore, in ShallowCC we extend the rewriting phase by several depth minimizing patterns, which are not necessarily size decreasing. In total 21 patterns changed, resulting in more than 70 patterns that are searched for (see full version of this paper for a list of example patterns). Furthermore, we extend the formerly fixed-depth pattern matching algorithm by a recursive search to deeper sequential structures, as in the example above. To apply the new patterns in an efficient manner, we modify CBMC-GC's fixed point algorithm such that the algorithm only terminates if no further size *and* depth improvements are made or a user defined time limit is reached. Moreover, for performance reasons, the rewriting first only applies fixed depth patterns, before applying the search for deeper sequential structures.

Quantifying the improvements of individual patterns is almost impossible. This is because the heuristic approach commonly allows multiple patterns to be applied at the same time and every replacement has an influence on future applicability of further patterns. Nevertheless, the whole set of patterns that we identified is very effective, as circuits before and after gate level minimization differ up to a factor of $20\times$ in depth, cf. Sect. 5.3.

5   Evaluation

The evaluation of ShallowCC in split in three parts. First, we compare ShallowCC with existing depth and size minimized circuits from recent works. Then, we exemplarily evaluate the different optimization techniques of ShallowCC to illustrate their effectiveness. Finally, we show that the depth minimized circuits, even under size trade-offs, significantly reduce the online time of the GMW protocol for different network configurations. We begin with a discussion of the benchmarked functionalities.

5.1   Functionalities

For comparison purposes, we focus on functionalities that have been used before to benchmark MPC. The evaluated functionalities include basic building blocks as well as more complex applications, such as biometric matching.

Arithmetic building blocks and floating point operations. Due to their importance in almost every computational problem, we benchmark arithmetic building blocks individually. For multiplication we follow the example of [26] and distinguish results for output bit strings of length n and of length $2n$ (overflow free) for n-bit input strings. Floating point calculations are necessary for all applications where numerical precision is required, e.g., privacy preserving statistics. We abstain from implementing hand-optimizing floating point circuits, but instead rely on ShallowCC's capabilities to compile a IEEE-754 compliment software floating point implementation written in C.

Distances. Various distances are used in privacy preserving protocols. The *Hamming* distance between two bit strings is the number of pairwise differences in every bit position. Due to its application in biometrics, the Hamming distance has often been used for benchmarking MPC compilers, e.g., [17,22,26,31]. The Hamming distance can be parametrized by the bit length of the input strings. The *Manhattan* distance $dist_M = |x_1 - x_2| + |y_1 - y_2|$ between to points $a = (x_1, y_1)$ and $b = (x_2, y_2)$ is the distance along a two dimensional space, when only allowing horizontal or vertical moves. The *Euclidian* distance between two points is defined as $dist_E = \sqrt{(x_1 - x_2)^2 + (y_1 - y_2)^2}$. Due to the complexity of the square root function, it is common in MPC to benchmark the squared Euclidian distance [30].

Matrix-vector/matrix multiplication. Algebraic operations such a matrix multiplications are building blocks for many privacy-preserving applications and have repeatedly been used before to benchmark MPC [10,17,21]. Being a purely arithmetic task, its a good showcase to illustrate the automatic translation of arithmetic operations into CSNs with very low depth.

Oblivious arrays. Oblivious data structures are a major building block for the implementation of privacy preserving algorithms. The most general data structure is the oblivious array that hides the accessed index. Here, we only benchmark the array read operation, as its circuit is more complex and thus, interesting than the write operation [18].

Biometric matching. In biometric matching a party matches one biometric sample against the other's party database of biometric templates. Example scenarios are face-recognition or fingerprint-matching [13]. One of the main concepts is the computation of a distance, e.g., Euclidean, between the sample and all database entries. Once all distances have been computed, the minimal distance determines the best match. For the following experiments, we fix the dimension of a sample to $d = 4$, as it has been used before in MPC benchmarking [6,11].

5.2   Circuit Comparison

We implemented all the aforementioned functionalities in C and compiled them with ShallowCC on an Intel Xeon E5-2620-v2 CPU with a minimization time limit of 10 min. To illustrate the used sources codes, we refer the reader to the full version of this paper. The resulting circuit dimensions for different parameters and bit-widths are given in Table 5. Furthermore, the circuit size, when compiled with the size minimizing Frigate compiler and CBMC-GC v0.93 is given, as well as a comparison with the depth-minimized circuit constructions of [10,30]. The results for Frigate, [10,30] are taken from the publications.

Comparing the depth of the circuits compiled by ShallowCC with the hand minimized circuits of [10,30] we observe a depth reduction at least 30 % for most functionalities. The only exception are the floating point operations, which do not reach the same depth as given in [10]. This is because floating point operations mostly consist of bit operations, which can significantly be hand optimized on a gate level, but are hard to optimize when complied from a high-level implementation in C. When comparing circuit sizes, we observe that ShallowCC is compiling circuits that are competitive in size to the circuits compiled from the size minimizing compilers. A negative exception is the addition, which shows a significant trade off between depth and size. However, the instantiation of CSNs allows ShallowCC to compensate these trade-offs in applications with multiple additions, e.g., the matrix multiplication. In Sect. 5.4 we analyze these trade-offs in more detail. In summary, ShallowCC is compiling ANSI-C code to Boolean circuits that outperform hand crafted circuits in depth, with moderate increases in size.

5.3   Evaluation of the Optimizations Techniques

In Table 6 an evaluation of the different optimization techniques for various example functionalities is given. For every functionality the same source code is compiled twice, once with the specified optimization technique enabled and once without. Obviously, not all optimizations apply to all functionalities, therefore, we only investigate a selection of functionalities that profit from the different optimization

Table 5. Comparison of circuit size s^{nX} and depth d^{nX} compiled by the size minimizing Frigate [26], CBMC-GC v0.93 [17] compiler, the best, manually depth minimized circuits given in [10,30] and the circuits compiled by ShallowCC. Improvements are computed in comparison with the previous work [10,30]. The '-' indicates that no results were given. Marked in bold face are cases with significant depth reductions.

Circuit	n	size minimized Frigate s^{nX}	CBMC-GC s^{nX}	d^{nX}	depth minimized Prev. [10,30] s^{nX}	d^{nX}	ShallowCC s^{nX}	d^{nX}	improv d^{nX}
Building Blocks									
Add $n \to n$	32	31	31	31	232	11	159	**5**	**54 %**
Sub $n \to n$	32	31	61	31	232	11	159	**5**	**54 %**
Mul $n \to 2n$	32	2,082	4,600	67	2,218	19	2,520	**15**	**21 %**
Mul $n \to n$	64	4,035	4,782	67	-	-	4,350	**16**	-
Arithmetics									
Div	32	1,437	2,787	1,087	7,079	207	5,030	**192**	**7 %**
Matrix 5x5	32	128,252	127,225	42	-	-	128,225	**17**	-
FloatAdd	32	-	2,289	164	1,820	59	2,437	62	-5 %
FloatMul	32	-	3,499	134	3,016	47	3,833	54	-14 %
Distances									
Hamming-160	1	719	371	9	-	-	281	**7**	-
Hamming-1600	1	4,691	7,521	31	-	-	1,021	**12**	-
2D-Euclidian	16	-	826	47	1,171	29	1,343	**19**	**34 %**
2D-Euclidian	32	-	3,210	95	3,605	34	5,244	**23**	**32 %**
2D-Manhatten	16	-	187	31	296	19	275	**13**	**31 %**
2D-Manhatten	32	-	395	63	741	23	689	**16**	**30 %**
Privacy Preserving Protocols									
BioMatch-32	16	-	88,385	1,101	-	-	90,616	**55**	-
BioMatch-1024	16	-	2.9M	35,821	-	-	2.9M	**90**	-
Ob.Array-32	8	-	803	66	248	5	538	**3**	**40 %**
Ob.Array-1024	32	-	100,251	2,055	32,736	10	65,844	**4**	**60 %**

techniques. The CSN detection shows its strengths for arithmetic functionalities. For example, the 5x5 matrix multiplication shows a depth reduction of 60 %, when optimizations are enabled. This is because the computation of a single vector element can be grouped into one CSN. The detection of reductions is a very specific optimization, yet, when applicable, the depth saving can be significant. When computing the minima of 100 integers, a depth reduction of 92 % is visible. Note that in this test the circuit size itself is unchanged, as only the order of multiplexers is changed. Gate level minimization is the most important optimization technique for all functionalities, which do not use all bits available in every program variable. In

Table 6. Comparison of circuit dimensions when compiled by ShallowCC with different optimization techniques enabled or disabled.

Circuit	n	w/o optimization		w/ optimization		Improvement	
		size s^{nX}	depth d^{nX}	size s^{nX}	depth d^{nX}	size s^{nX}	depth d^{nX}
Optimization: Carry-Save Networks CSNs							
Matrix 5x5	32	143,850	42	128,225	17	11 %	60 %
4D-EuclidianDst	16	2,993	40	2,459	20	18 %	50 %
Optimization: Reduction							
Minima-100	16	5,742	594	5,742	42	0 %	92 %
BioMatch-1024	16	2,9M	7,181	2,9M	90	0 %	98 %
Optimization: Gate level minimization							
Hamming-160	1	5,389	77	281	7	95 %	88 %
FloatAdd	32	10,054	194	2,431	74	75 %	61 %

these cases constant propagation applies, which leads to significant reductions in size and depth, as exemplary shown for the floating point addition and computation of the Hamming distance. In general, when applicable, the optimization methods significantly improve the compiled circuits of ShallowCC.

5.4 Protocol Runtime

To show that depth minimization improves the online time of MPC protocols, we evaluate a selection of circuits in the ABY framework [11]. ABY provides a state-of-the-art two-party implementation of the GMW protocol [14] secure in the semi-honest model. We extended the ABY framework by an adapter to parse ShallowCC's circuit format. For our experiments, we connected two machines, which are equipped with an AMD FX 8350 CPU and 16 GB of RAM, running Ubuntu 15.10 over a 1 Gbit ethernet connection in a LAN. To simulate different network environments we made used of the Linux network emulator *netem*.

In this experiment the *online* protocol runtimes of size and depth minimized circuits for different RTTs are compared. We omit timings of the pre-processing *setup* phase, as this pre-computation can take place independently of the evaluated circuits and with any degree of parallelism. We ran this experiment for different RTTs, starting with zero delay up to a simulated RTT of 80 ms.

The first functionality that we investigate is the biometric matching application with a database of 1024 entries. Here, we compare the circuits generated by CBMC-GC and ShallowCC. The resulting circuit dimensions are given in Table 5. The results, which are averaged over 10 runs, are given in Fig. 3a. We observe speed-ups of ShallowCC's circuit over CBMC-GC's circuit of a factor between 2 and 400, when increasing the RTT from ∼1 ms to 80 ms. A further comparison of size and depth optimized circuits is given in the full version of this paper.

The second functionality that we evaluate is the array read (MUX), which allows to analyze a size-depth trade-off. We compiled the read access to an array

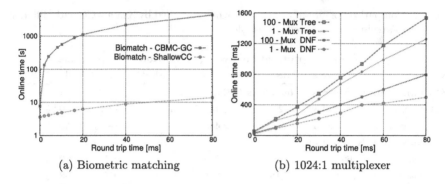

Fig. 3. GMW protocol runtime of depth and size minimized functionalities. (a) compares the BioMatch functionality compiled with CBMC-GC and ShallowCC. (b) compares the depth-minimzed DNF and size-minimzed tree 1024:1 multiplexer, for a single and parallel execution. The resulting run times are plotted for different RTTs. We observe that the depth optimized circuits significantly outperform the size optimized circuits for any $RTT > 1$ ms.

with $1024\times$ 32 bit integers. We compare the tree based MUX, as proposed in [30] with depth $d^{nX} = 10$ and size $s^{nX} = 32,736$ with our depth optimized MUX_{DNFd}, which has a depth of $d^{nX} = 4$ and size $s^{nX} = 65,844$ after gate level minimization. Each circuit is evaluated with ABY individually, as well as 100 times in parallel. This allows to also investigate whether single instruction multiple data (SIMD) parallelism, which is favored in GMW [11], has a significant influence on the results. The resulting online runtimes for both circuits are illustrated in Fig. 3b. All data points are averaged over 100 runs. We observe that for almost every network configuration beyond 1 ms RTT, the depth optimized circuits outperform their size optimized counterparts by a factor of two. The reason for the factor of two is, that the GMW protocol requires one communication round for the input sharing as well as one round for the output sharing, which leads to 6 communication rounds in total for the MUX_{DNFd} and 12 rounds for the tree MUX. Moreover, we observe that here applied data parallelism shows no significant effect on the speed-up gained through depth reduction.

In conclusion, the experiments support our introductory statement that depth minimization is of uttermost importance to gain further speed-ups in round-based MPC.

6   Conclusion

In this work we presented ShallowCC, the first depth-minimizing compiler that compiles a high-level language to Boolean circuits for MPC. We proposed and implemented multiple optimization techniques and presented newly optimized building blocks. ShallowCC is capable of compiling circuits that are up to 2.5 times shallower than hand optimized circuits and up to 400 times shallower than circuits compiled from size optimizing compilers, while still maintaining a competitive circuit size.

We note that ShallowCC is currently missing the support of an interpreted or mixed-mode language, which allows the efficient evaluation of very large applications. However, we are convinced that the combination of a mixed-mode interpreter, e.g., [21,24,26,35], with ShallowCC is mostly an engineering task rather than a research challenge and therefore leave it for future work.

Acknowledgments. This work has been co-funded by the DFG as part of project S5 within the CRC 1119 CROSSING, by the DFG as part of project A.1 within the RTG 2050 "Privacy and Trust for Mobile User", and by an Erwin Schrödinger Fellowship (Austrian Science Fund (FWF): J3696-N26).

References

1. Amini, M., Creusillet, B., Even, S., Keryell, R., Goubier, O., Guelton, S., McMahon, J.O., Pasquier, F.-X., Péan, G., Villalon, P.: Par4All: from convex array regions to heterogeneous computing. In: Workshop on Polyhedral Compilation Techniques (2012)
2. Ben-David, A., Nisan, N., Pinkas, B.: Fairplaymp: a system for secure multi-party computation. In: ACM CCS (2008)
3. Ben-Or, M., Goldwasser, S., Wigderson, A.: Completeness theorems for non-cryptographic fault-tolerant distributed computation. In: ACM STOC (1988)
4. Bogdanov, D., Laur, S., Willemson, J.: Sharemind: a framework for fast privacy-preserving computations. In: Jajodia, S., Lopez, J. (eds.) ESORICS 2008. LNCS, vol. 5283, pp. 192–206. Springer, Heidelberg (2008)
5. Buchfuhrer, D., Umans, C.: The complexity of boolean formula minimization. J. Comput. System Sci. **77**, 1 (2011)
6. Büscher, N., Katzenbeisser, S.: Faster secure computation through automatic parallelization. In: USENIX Security (2015)
7. Clarke, E., Kroning, D., Lerda, F.: A tool for checking ANSI-C programs. In: Jensen, K., Podelski, A. (eds.) TACAS 2004. LNCS, vol. 2988, pp. 168–176. Springer, Heidelberg (2004)
8. Damgård, I., Geisler, M., Krøigaard, M., Nielsen, J.B.: Asynchronous multiparty computation: theory and implementation. In: Jarecki, S., Tsudik, G. (eds.) PKC 2009. LNCS, vol. 5443, pp. 160–179. Springer, Heidelberg (2009)
9. Damgård, I., Pastro, V., Smart, N., Zakarias, S.: Multiparty computation from somewhat homomorphic encryption. In: Safavi-Naini, R., Canetti, R. (eds.) CRYPTO 2012. LNCS, vol. 7417, pp. 643–662. Springer, Heidelberg (2012)
10. Demmler, D., Dessouky, G., Koushanfar, F., Sadeghi, A., Schneider, T., Zeitouni, S.: Automated synthesis of optimized circuits for secure computation. In: ACM CCS (2015)
11. Demmler, D., Schneider, T., Zohner, M.: ABY - a framework for efficient mixed-protocol secure two-party computation. In: NDSS (2015)
12. Earle, J.: Latched carry-save adder. IBM Techn. Discl. Bull. **7**(10), 909–910 (1965)
13. Erkin, Z., Franz, M., Guajardo, J., Katzenbeisser, S., Lagendijk, I., Toft, T.: Privacy-preserving face recognition. In: Goldberg, I., Atallah, M.J. (eds.) PETS 2009. LNCS, vol. 5672, pp. 235–253. Springer, Heidelberg (2009)
14. Goldreich, O., Micali, S., Wigderson, A.: How to play any mental game. In: ACM STOC (1987)
15. Harris, D.: A taxonomy of parallel prefix networks. In: IEEE ASILOMAR (2003)

16. Henecka, W., Kögl, S., Sadeghi, A., Schneider, T., Wehrenberg, I.: TASTY: tool for automating secure two-party computations. In: ACM CCS (2010)
17. Holzer, A., Franz, M., Katzenbeisser, S., Veith, H.: Secure two-party computations in ANSI C. In: ACM CCS (2012)
18. Keller, M., Scholl, P.: Efficient, oblivious data structures for MPC. In: Sarkar, P., Iwata, T. (eds.) ASIACRYPT 2014, Part II. LNCS, vol. 8874, pp. 506–525. Springer, Heidelberg (2014)
19. Kolesnikov, V., Sadeghi, A.-R., Schneider, T.: Improved garbled circuit building blocks and applications to auctions and computing minima. In: Garay, J.A., Miyaji, A., Otsuka, A. (eds.) CANS 2009. LNCS, vol. 5888, pp. 1–20. Springer, Heidelberg (2009)
20. Kolesnikov, V., Schneider, T.: Improved garbled circuit: free XOR gates and applications. In: Aceto, L., Damgård, I., Goldberg, L.A., Halldórsson, M.M., Ingólfsdóttir, A., Walukiewicz, I. (eds.) ICALP 2008, Part II. LNCS, vol. 5126, pp. 486–498. Springer, Heidelberg (2008)
21. Kreuter, B., Shelat, A., Mood, B., Butler, K.: PCF: A portable circuit format for scalable two-party secure computation. In: USENIX Security (2013)
22. Kreuter, B., Shelat, A., Shen, C.: Billion-gate secure computation with malicious adversaries. In: USENIX Security (2012)
23. Liu, C., Huang, Y., Shi, E., Katz, J., Hicks, M.W.: Automating efficient ram-model secure computation. In: IEEE S&P (2014)
24. Liu, C., Wang, X.S., Nayak, K., Huang, Y., Shi, E.: Oblivm: a programming framework for secure computation. In: IEEE S&P (2015)
25. Malkhi, D., Nisan, N., Pinkas, B., Sella, Y.: Fairplay - secure two-party computation system. In: USENIX Security (2004)
26. Mood, B., Gupta, D., Carter, H., Butler, K., Traynor, P.: Frigate: a validated, extensible, and efficient compiler and interpreter for secure computation. In: IEEE European Symposium on Security and Privacy (2016)
27. Mood, B., Letaw, L., Butler, K.: Memory-efficient garbled circuit generation for mobile devices. In: Keromytis, A.D. (ed.) FC 2012. LNCS, vol. 7397, pp. 254–268. Springer, Heidelberg (2012)
28. Nielsen, J.B., Nordholt, P.S., Orlandi, C., Burra, S.S.: A new approach to practical active-secure two-party computation. In: Safavi-Naini, R., Canetti, R. (eds.) CRYPTO 2012. LNCS, vol. 7417, pp. 681–700. Springer, Heidelberg (2012)
29. Paterson, M.S., Pippenger, N., Zwick, U.: Optimal carry save networks
30. Schneider, T., Zohner, M.: GMW vs. Yao? efficient secure two-party computation with low depth circuits. In: Sadeghi, A.-R. (ed.) FC 2013. LNCS, vol. 7859, pp. 275–292. Springer, Heidelberg (2013)
31. Songhori, E.M., Hussain, S.U., Sadeghi, A., Schneider, T., Koushanfar, F.: Tinygarble: Highly compressed and scalable sequential garbled circuits. In: IEEE S&P (2015)
32. Wallace, C.S.: A suggestion for a fast multiplier. IEEE Trans. Electron. Comput. 13(1), 14–17 (1964)
33. Yao, AC.-C.: Protocols for secure computations (Extended Abstract). In: Annual Symposium on Foundations of Computer Science, FOCS 1982 (1982)
34. Zahur, S., Evans, D.: Circuit structures for improving efficiency of security and privacy tools. In: IEEE S&P (2013)
35. Zahur, S., Evans, D.: Obliv-c: a language for extensible data-oblivious computation. IACR Cryptology ePrint Archive 2015 (2015)
36. Zhang, Y., Steele, A., Blanton, M.: PICCO: a general-purpose compiler for private distributed computation. In: ACM CCS (2013)

Secure Computation of MIPS Machine Code

Xiao Wang[1]([⊠]), S. Dov Gordon[2], Allen McIntosh[3], and Jonathan Katz[1]

[1] University of Maryland, College Park, USA
{wangxiao,jkatz}@cs.umd.edu
[2] George Mason University, Fairfax, USA
gordon@gmu.edu
[3] Applied Communication Sciences, Basking Ridge, USA
amcintosh@appcomsci.com

Abstract. Existing systems for secure computation require programmers to express the program to be securely computed as a *circuit*, or in a *domain-specific language* that can be compiled to a form suitable for applying known protocols. We propose a new system that can securely execute *native MIPS code* with no special annotations. Our system allows programmers to use a language of their choice to express their programs, together with any off-the-shelf compiler to MIPS; it can be used for secure computation of "legacy" MIPS code as well.

Our system uses oblivious RAM for fetching instructions and performing load/store operations in memory, and garbled universal circuits for the execution of a MIPS CPU in each instruction step. We also explore various optimizations based on an offline analysis of the MIPS code to be executed, in order to minimize the overhead of executing each instruction while still maintaining security.

1 Introduction

Systems for secure two-party computation allow two parties, each with their own private input, to evaluate an agreed-upon program on their inputs while revealing nothing other than the result of the computation. This notion originated in the early 1980s [25], and until recently was primarily of theoretical interest, with research focusing entirely on the design and analysis of low-level cryptographic protocols. The situation changed in 2004 with the introduction of Fairplay [18], which provided the first implementation of a protocol for secure two-party computation in the semi-honest setting. Since then, there has been a flurry of activity implementing two-party protocols with improved security and/or efficiency [1,4,9–11,13–17,19,20,26].

Many (though not all) of these implementations provide an *end-to-end system* that, in principle, allows non-cryptographers to write programs that can automatically be compiled to some intermediate representation (e.g., a boolean circuit) suitable for use by back-end protocols that can securely execute programs expressed in that representation. In practice, however, such systems have several drawbacks. First of all, the user cannot write the program in a language of their

© Springer International Publishing Switzerland 2016
I. Askoxylakis et al. (Eds.): ESORICS 2016, Part II, LNCS 9879, pp. 99–117, 2016.
DOI: 10.1007/978-3-319-45741-3_6

choice; just as there is no programming language that is best for every application, there is no domain-specific language for secure computation that is best for every purpose. Second, existing domain-specific languages [10,16,17,20,26] can be hard to learn and use, or are simply limited in terms of expressiveness. For example, Secure Computation API (SCAPI) [4] does not provide a high-level language to specify the function to compute. Sharemind [2] fails to support conditional statements branching on private variables according to the user manual. Obliv-C [26], an extension of C, requires the programmer to use special annotations along with an extended set of keywords for secret values and branching statements. Even if the language is a subset of a standard language (such as ANSI C [10]), the programmer must still be aware of limitations and which features of the language to avoid; moreover, legacy code will not be supported. Finally, compilers from high-level languages to boolean circuit representations (or other suitable representations) can be slow; as discussed in detail in Sect. 5.1, some previous compilers [13,14] require more than 2000 s just to compile a program for matrix multiplication of dimension 16 into a circuit representation, not even including any cryptographic operations. Furthermore, most compilers requires recompiling the program when the input size changes.

Motivated by these drawbacks, we explore in this work the design of a system for secure execution, in the semi-honest setting, of *native MIPS machine code*. That is, the input program to our system—i.e., the program to be securely computed—is expressed in MIPS machine code, and our system securely executes this code. We accomplish this via an emulator that securely executes each instruction of a MIPS program; the emulator uses oblivious RAM [7] for fetching the next instruction as well as for performing load/store operations in memory, and relies on a universal garbled circuit for executing each instruction. Our system addresses all the problems mentioned earlier:

- Programmers can write their programs in a language of their choice, and compile them using any compiler of their choice, so long as they end up with MIPS machine code. Legacy MIPS code is also supported.
- Because our system does not require compilation from a domain-specific language to some suitable intermediate representation, such as boolean circuits, we can use fast, off-the-shelf compilers and enjoy the benefits of all the optimizations such compilers already have. The number of instructions we securely execute is identical to the number of instructions executed when running the native MIPS code (though, of course, our emulator introduces overhead for each instruction executed).

Our code is open sourced online[1].

Our primary goal was simply to develop a system supporting secure execution of native MIPS code. In fact, though, because of the way our system works—namely, via secure emulation of each instruction—we also gain the benefits of working in the RAM model of computation (rather than in a boolean-circuit model), as in some previous work [8,16,17]. In particular, the total work required

---

[1] https://github.com/wangxiao1254/Secure-Computation-of-MIPS-Machine-Code.

for secure computation of a program using our system is proportional (modulo polylogarithmic factors) to the actual number of instructions executed in an insecure run of that same program on the same inputs; this is not true when using a circuit-based representation, for which all possible program paths must be computed even if they are eventually discarded. Working in the RAM model even allows for computation time sublinear in the input length [8] (in an amortized sense); we show an example of this in Sect. 5.3.

Performance. Our goal is generality, usability, and portability; we expressly were **not** aiming to develop a yet-more-efficient implementation of secure computation. Nevertheless, for our approach to be viable it must be competitive with existing systems. We describe a number of optimizations that rely on an offline analysis of the (insecure) program to be executed; these can be done before the parties' inputs are known and before execution of any protocol between them begins. We view these optimizations as one of the main contributions of our work, as they improve the performance by as much as a factor of 30× on some programs, bringing our system to the point where it is feasible. In fact, for certain applications we are only ∼25 % slower than ObliVM [17] (see Sect. 5.3).

Trade-off between efficiency and usability. Our work explores part of the spectrum between *efficiency* and *usability* for secure-computation systems. Most work in this area has concentrated on the former, focusing on optimizing the back-end protocol, implementation aspects, or improved compilation time. Here, we are expressly interested in maximizing usability, envisioning, e.g., a non-expert user maintaining a large code base, perhaps written in several languages, who occasionally wishes to run some of this code securely. Such a user might gladly sacrifice run-time efficiency in order to avoid re-writing their code in the domain-specific language of the moment. To support this level of generality, the only feasible approach is to securely compute on a low-level language. One goal of our work is to explore how much efficiency must be sacrificed in order to achieve this level of generality.

Related and concurrent works. Songhori et al. [21] explored using hardware-optimization techniques to reduce the size of boolean circuits and demonstrated a circuit containing MIPS-I instructions. However, the goal of their work was different: they aim to minimize the size of a single universal circuit for private function evaluation (PFE), while we aim to optimize the emulation of an entire public MIPS program. In particular, they do not investigate optimizations to accelerate execution of the program, something that is a key contribution of our work. Fletcher et al. [5] designed an interpreter based on the Turing machines, using static analysis on the program to improve the efficiency. Their levelization technique shares some similarities to some of our techniques. However their system does not support general RAM computation, therefore is simpler than our setting.

Concurrently, Keller [12] recently built a system that executes C code over the SPDZ protocol. Their high level idea is similar to our *basic system*: using a universal circuit for ALU and ORAM for memory access. However, they didn't explore how to use static analysis to further accelerate the system, as in our *optimized system* described in Sect. 4.

2 Preliminaries

We briefly describe some background relevant to our work.

Secure computation and garbled circuits. Protocols for two-party computation allow two parties, each with their own private input, to compute some agreed-upon function on their inputs while revealing nothing to either party other than the result of the computation. In this paper we exclusively focus on the semi-honest model, where both parties are assumed to execute the protocol correctly, but each may try to infer additional information about the other party's input based on their own view of the protocol transcript.

Our emulator uses as a building block Yao's garbled-circuit protocol [25] for secure two-party computation, which assumes the function to be computed is represented as a boolean circuit. At a high level, the protocol works as follows: one party, acting as a *garbled-circuit generator*, associates two random cryptographic keys with each wire in the circuit. One of these keys will represent the value 0 on that wire, and the other will represent the value 1. The circuit generator also computes a garbled table for each gate of the circuit; the garbled table for a gate g allows a party who knows the keys associated with bits b_L, b_R on the left and right input wires, respectively, to compute the key associated with the bit $g(b_L, b_R)$ on the output wire. The collection of garbled gates constitutes the garbled circuit for the original function. The circuit generator sends the garbled circuit to the other party (the *circuit evaluator*) along with one key for each input wire corresponding to its own input. The circuit evaluator obtains one key for each input wire corresponding to *its* input using oblivious transfer. Given one key per input wire, the circuit evaluator can "evaluate" the garbled circuit and compute a single key per output wire.

If the circuit generator reveals the mapping from the keys on each output wire to the bits they represent, then the circuit evaluator can learn the actual output of the original function. However, it is also possible for the circuit generator to use the output wires from one garbled circuit as input wires to a subsequent garbled circuit (for some subsequent computation being done), in which case there is no need for this decoding to take place. In fact, this results in a form of "secret sharing" that we use in our protocol; namely, the sharing of a bit b will consist of values (w^0, w^1) held by one party, while the other party holds w^b.

Oblivious RAM (ORAM). Oblivious RAM [7] allows a "client" to read/write an array of data stored on a "server," while hiding from the server both the the data and the data-access pattern. By default, ORAM only hides information from the server; to hide information from both parties, we adopt the method of Gordon et al. [8] and share the client state between the two parties, who can then use the shares as input to a secure computation that outputs a memory address to read, while also updating both users' shares of the state.

In this work, we use ORAM to store both the MIPS program (so parties are oblivious of the instruction being fetched) as well as the contents of main memory (so parties are oblivious about the location of memory being accessed). Note that in the former case, the data is public and read-only, whereas in the latter case the data needs to be kept hidden from both parties (in general), and may be both read and written. We refer to the ORAM storing instructions as the "instruction bank," and the ORAM storing data as the "memory bank."

Security of our emulator. Although we do not provide any proofs of security in this work, an argument as in [8] can be used to prove that our construction is secure (in the semi-honest model) with respect to standard definitions of security [6], with one important caveat: our system leaks the total number of instructions executed in a given run of the program. This is a consequence of the fact that we allow loop conditions based on private data, something that is simply disallowed in prior work. Leaking the running time may leak information about the parties' private inputs; note, however, that this can easily be prevented by using padding to ensure that the running time is always the same. In Sect. 4.3, we will discuss how to reduce this leakage while improving the efficiency at the same time.

3   Basic System Design

In this section we describe the basic design of our system. We describe the overall workflow in Sect. 3.1. In Sect. 3.2, we review relevant aspects of the MIPS architecture, and in Sect. 3.3, we give a high-level overview of how our system works. We provide some low-level details in Sects. 3.4 and 3.5. We defer until Sect. 4 a discussion of several important optimizations that we apply.

3.1   Overall Workflow

Our system enables two parties to securely execute a program described in a MIPS code. Our system works in the following steps:

– It first performs an offline static analysis of the MIPS code to produce a set of CPU circuits and instruction banks, one for each step of the computation. In our basic system described in this section, the offline analysis is rather simple; a more complex analysis, described in Sect. 4, can be used to improve performance.
– During the online phase, the two parties securely execute each instruction, using ORAM to access the appropriate inputs at each step.

As our back-end for secure computation (namely, generation/execution of the garbled circuits, and fetching of inputs using ORAM) we use ObliVM [17]. However, other frameworks [3,21,26] could also potentially be used (in conjunction with other ORAM implementations).

3.2 MIPS Architecture

A MIPS program is an array of instructions, each 32 bits long. In the basic MIPS instruction set (i.e., in MIPS I), there are about 60 instruction types, including arithmetic instructions, memory-related instructions, and branching instructions. Instruction types refer to the operations performed during a CPU cycle. On the other hand, an instruction consists of instruction type and operands. For example, ADD is an instruction type, but ADD $1, $2, $2 is an instruction.

For our purposes, we can view the state of the MIPS architecture during program execution as consisting of (1) the program itself (i.e. the array of instructions), (2) the values stored in a set of 32-bit registers, which include 32 general-purpose registers plus various special registers including one called the *program counter*, and (3) values stored in main memory. To execute a given program, the input(s) are loaded into appropriate positions in memory, and then the following steps are repeated until a special exit instruction is executed:

- Instruction fetch (IF): fetch the instruction according to the program counter.
- Instruction decode (ID): fetch 2 registers according to the instruction.
- Execute (EX): execute the instruction and update the program counter.
- Memory access (MEM): perform load/store operations on memory, if required (depending on the instruction).
- Write back (WB): write a value to one register.

3.3 Overview of Our System

At a high level, two parties use our system to securely execute a MIPS program by maintaining *secret shares* of the current state, and then *updating* their shares by securely emulating each of the steps listed above until the program terminates. We describe each of these next.

We currently support about 37 instruction types (see Table 1), which are sufficient for all the programs used in our experiments. It is easy to add instruction types to our system as needed, using 2–3 lines of code (in the ObliVM framework) per instruction. In our basic system described here, every supported instruction is included in the garbled circuit for every step, thus increasing the run-time of each emulated MIPS cycle. In our optimized system described in Sect. 4, only

Table 1. Set of instruction types currently supported in our system. More instructions can be added easily.

Types	Instruction Type									
R Type	ADDU	MOVZ	MOVN	SLLV	SRLV	MFLO	SLL	SRL	SRA	AND
	MTLO	MFHI	MTHI	MULT	SUBU	SLTU	OR	XOR	NOR	DIV
I Type	BGEZAL	SLTIU	XORI	ANDI	BLEZ	JR	ORI	BNE		
	ADDIU	BLTZAL	BGEZ	BLTZ	BGTZ	BEQ	LUI			
J Type	J	JAL								

instructions that can possibly be executed at some step are included in the garbled circuit for that step, so there is no harm in including support for as many instructions types as desired.

Secret sharing the MIPS state. As mentioned previously, the MIPS state contains the array of program instructions, registers, and memory; all three components are secret shared between the two parties and, in addition, the program instructions and memory are stored in (separate) ORAMs. (Even though the program instructions are known to both parties, it is important that neither party learns which instruction is fetched in any instruction cycle, as this leaks information about the inputs.) The registers could, in principle, also be stored in ORAM, but since there are only 32 registers a trivial ORAM (i.e., a linear scan over all registers) is always better.

By default, all components are secret shared using the mechanism described in Sect. 2. Although this results in shares that are 80–160× larger than the original value (because ObliVM creates garbled circuits with 80-bit keys), this sharing is more efficient for evaluating garbled circuits on those shared values. However, when the allocated memory is larger than 12MB, we switch to a more standard XOR-based secret-sharing scheme, adding an oblivious-transfer step and an XOR operation inside the garbled circuit to reconstruct the secret.

Secure emulation. The parties repeatedly update their state by performing a sequence of secure computations in each MIPS instruction cycle. For efficiency, we reordered the steps described in the previous section slightly. In the secure emulation of a single cycle, the parties:

1. Obliviously fetch the instruction specified by the shared program counter (the IF step).
2. Check whether the program has terminated and, if so, terminate the protocol and reconstruct the output.
3. Securely execute the fetched instruction, and update the registers appropriately (this corresponds to the ID, EX, and WB steps).
4. Obliviously access/update the memory and securely update a register if the instruction is a load or store operation (this corresponds to the MEM and WB steps).

We stress that the parties should not learn whether they are evaluating an arithmetic instruction or a memory instruction, and must therefore execute steps 3 and 4 in every cycle, even if the step has no effect on the shared MIPS state. Our improved design in Sect. 4 provides a way of securely bypassing step 4 on many cycles.

3.4 Setup

Before executing the main loop, we load the MIPS code into the (shared) instruction memory and the users' inputs into the (shared) main memory.

Loading the MIPS code. In our baseline system design, we load the full program (i.e., array of instructions) into an ORAM. Therefore, when emulating each step we incur the cost of accessing an ORAM containing instructions from the entire program. In Sect. 4, we describe improvements to this approach.

In our current implementation, we do not load any code executed before main() is called, e.g., library start-up code, code for managing dynamic libraries, or class-constructor code. The latter is not needed for executing MIPS programs compiled from C code, but would be needed for executing MIPS code generated from object-oriented languages. Note, however, that such operations are data-independent, and can be simulated by the parties locally. Adding support for loading such code would thus be easy to incorporate in our system.

Loading user inputs. We assume a public upper bound on the input size of each party. Each party starts with their input in a local file. When emulation begins, the parties initialize an empty ORAM supporting the maximum input sizes, and the parties' inputs are secret shared and written to some agreed-upon (non-overlapping) segments of memory. The parties also initialize their shares of the register space with pertinent information such as the address and length of the input data. Since no annotation is used, we need to find a way to specify which party each input belongs to. In our system, each party organizes their input as an array, which is passed to the function to compute in an fixed order: generator's array comes first; evaluator's array comes second, followed by the length of two arrays.

Secure computation of MIPS code

Input: $\mathsf{reg}[]$, pc, $\mathsf{ORAM_{inst}}[]$, $\mathsf{ORAM_{MEM}}[]$

Computation:

1. $\mathsf{inst} := \mathsf{FetchInstruction}(\mathsf{pc}, \mathsf{ORAM_{inst}})$
2. $\mathsf{terminateBit} := \mathsf{testTerminate}(\mathsf{inst}, \mathsf{reg})$
3. $\boxed{\text{if (terminateBit) GOTO line 7}}$
4. $\mathsf{ALU}(\mathsf{inst}, \mathsf{pc}, \mathsf{reg})$
5. $\mathsf{MEM}(\mathsf{inst}, \mathsf{reg}, \mathsf{ORAM_{MEM}})$
6. $\boxed{\text{GOTO line 1}}$
7. Reconstruct the output (in reg or $\mathsf{ORAM_{MEM}}$).

Fig. 1. Overview of secure computation of a MIPS program. $\boxed{\text{Boxed lines}}$ are executed outside of secure computation.

3.5   Main Execution Loop

We use $\mathsf{ORAM_{inst}}[]$, $\mathsf{ORAM_{MEM}}[]$, $\mathsf{reg}[]$, pc, and inst to denote, respectively, the (shared) instruction bank, (shared) memory bank, (shared) registers, (shared) value of the program counter, and (shared) current instruction. As shown in Fig. 1, secure execution of a MIPS program involves repeated calls of three procedures: instruction fetch, ALU computation, and memory access.

Secure computation of the MIPS ALU

Input: inst, pc, reg[]

ALU:

1. rs := inst[21:25], funct := inst[0:5],rd := inst[11:15]
   rt := inst[16:20], op := inst[26:31],imm := inst[0:15], ...
2. reg_rs := reg[rs], reg_rt := reg[rt]
3. if op == R_Type and funct == ADD
      reg_rd := reg_rs + reg_rt
    else if op == I_Type and funct == ADDI
      reg_rt := reg_rs + immediate
    else if ... // more arithmetic operations
4. if op == R_Type then pc := pc + 4
    else if op == I_Type and funct == BNE
     if reg_rs! = reg_rt
      pc := pc + 4 + 4 × imm
    else if ... // more cases that update pc
5. if op == R_Type then reg[rd] := reg_rd
    else reg[rt] := reg_rt

Fig. 2. This functionality takes the current instruction, program counter, and registers as input. Depending on the type of the instruction, it performs computation and updates the registers, as well as updating the program counter.

Secure memory access	**Testing termination**
Input: inst, reg[], ORAM$_{MEM}$[] MEM:	Input: inst, reg[31] testTerminate:

1. rs:=inst[21:25], op:=inst[26:31], rt:=inst[16:20], imm:=inst[0:15]
 2. addr := imm+reg[rs]
 3. If op is a load operation code:
  reg[rt] := ORAM$_{MEM}$[addr]
 4. If op is a store operation code:
  ORAM$_{MEM}$[addr] := reg[rt]
	1. terminate := false
	 2. If inst is BEQ \$0,\$0,-1
	  terminate := true
	 3. If inst is jr \$31 and reg[31] == 0
	  terminate := true
	 4. Reveal the bit terminate.

Fig. 3. (a) This functionality takes the instruction, the registers, and the memory as input and accesses the memory and registers according to the instruction. (b) This functionality takes the current instruction and the registers as input. It returns true if these indicate program termination.

Instruction fetch. In the basic system, we put the entire MIPS program into an ORAM. Therefore, fetching the next instruction is simply an ORAM lookup.

ALU computation. The MIPS ALU is securely computed using a universal garbled circuit. As shown in Fig. 2, this involves five stages:

1. Parse the instruction and get fields including operation code, function code, register addresses, and the immediate value. (We use inst[s:e] to denote the s-th bit to the e-th bits of inst.)
2. Retrieve values reg_rs = reg[rs] and reg_rt = reg[rt] from the registers.
3. Perform arithmetic computations.
4. Update the program counter.
5. Write the updated value back to the registers.

The first step is free due to the secret sharing we use and the fact that here we are using a circuit model of computation. The fourth step is very cheap. The second and fifth steps require 3 accesses to the register space in total, which we have implemented using a circuit with 3552 AND gates.

Memory access. Memory-related instructions can either load a value from memory to a register, or store a value from a register to memory. As shown in Fig. 3a, in order to hide the instruction type, every memory access requires one read and one write to the memory ORAM, as well as a read and a write to the registers. The cost of this component depends on how large the memory is, and is often the most expensive part of the entire computation.

Checking for termination. In our basic implementation, we execute a secure computation on each cycle in order to determine whether the program has terminated. (See Fig. 3b.) This is done by checking the current instruction and the contents of the final register (used for storing the return value). Revealing this bit to both parties requires one round trip in each instruction cycle.

4   Improving the Basic Design

The construction described in Sect. 3 requires us to perform a secure emulation of the full MIPS architecture for every instruction cycle. Even if we restrict our system to only include a small number of instruction types, we still have to execute many unnecessary instructions in every step: if a single expensive instruction appears *anywhere* in the program, our basic system would execute this expensive instruction at every step, even though the result is usually ignored. Even worse is the fact that the presence of load/store instructions necessitates expensive accesses to the memory ORAM in every instruction cycle.

4.1   Mapping Instructions to Steps

We improve the efficiency of our system by identifying unnecessary computation. First, we perform static analysis of the MIPS binary code and compute, for every step of the program execution, the set of instructions that might possibly be executed in that step. Then, using this information, we automatically generate a small instruction bank and ALU circuit tailored for each time step. This allows us to improve performance, without affecting security in various ways.

Computing instruction sets for each time step. To compute a set of instructions that might be executed at each time step, we walk through the binary code, spawning a new thread each time we encounter a branching instruction. Each thread steps forward, tagging the instructions it encounters with an increasing time step, and spawning again when it encounters a branch. We terminate our analysis if all threads halt, or if the set of all instructions tagged with current time step L is the same as the set of instructions tagged with some previous time step $k < L$. It is easy to verify that one of these two conditions will eventually be met. Now, the set of instructions that should be executed at time step $i < L$ contains all instructions tagged with time step i.

During the execution, our emulator chooses a circuit according to the following deterministic sequence of time steps: $1, 2, ..., L, k + 1, ..., L, k + 1, ..., L, ...$, until the termination condition is satisfied. In Sect. 5.1, we will discuses in detail how long such static analysis takes on programs of different sizes.

To illustrate this procedure, we provide a very simple example in Fig. 4a. Although there are eight instructions in the code snippet, at most two instructions can possibly be executed in any time step. When the code contains loops, as shown in Fig. 4b, a single instruction might appear in multiple time steps. In this case, our analysis will only terminate when we repeat some prior state, resulting in an instruction set that is identical to one that we previously constructed. In particular, the set of instructions for time step $2k + 4$ is the same as the one for time step $k + 3$.

This analysis does not result in an optimal assignment of instructions to time steps, because it ignores data values. We leave it to future work to explore better methods of performing the mapping of instructions to time steps. On the other hand, because of this it is easy to see that no private information is leaked since the set of instructions corresponding to some time step t includes all possible instructions that could ever be executed at step t for any possible set of inputs.

Instruction mapping makes sure that for each step only the instruction types that can possibly be executed in that step will be included. Therefore, in the optimized system, adding support for more instructions *will not impact the performance*. In particular, although we have not implemented the full MIPS instruction set, doing so would have no impact on the performance results described in Sect. 5 because the unnecessary instructions are automatically excluded by our emulator.

Constructing smaller instruction banks. After performing the above analysis, we can initialize a set of instruction banks in the setup stage, one for each time step, to replace the single, large instruction bank used in Sect. 3. When fetching an instruction during execution, we can simply perform an oblivious fetch on the (smaller) instruction bank associated with the current time step.

When we employ this optimization, using naïve ORAM to store the set of possible instructions for each time step becomes inefficient. Originally, instructions were in contiguous portions of memory, so N instructions could be placed into an ORAM of size N. Now, each instruction set contains only a small number of instructions, say $n < N$, while their address values still span the original range. If we use ORAM to store them, its size would have to be N instead of n. Therefore, we use an oblivious key-value store for the set of instructions at each

```
┌──────────────────────────────────────┐  ┌──────────────────────────────────────┐
│              Example 1               │  │              Example 2               │
│  main:                               │  │  main:                               │
│   MULT $1, $2, $3    //step 1        │  │   ADD $1,$2,$3 //step 1              │
│   BNE $1, $2, else   //step 2        │  │  lo:                                 │
│   Instruction 1      //step 3        │  │   Ins. 1       //step 2, k+3, 2k+4  │
│   Instruction 2      //step 4        │  │   ...                                │
│   J endif            //step 5        │  │   Ins. k       //step k+1, 2k+2     │
│  else:                               │  │   BNE $1,$2,lo //step k+2, 2k+3     │
│   Instruction 3      //step 3        │  │  post-lo:                            │
│   Instruction 4      //step 4        │  │   Ins. k+1     //step k+3, 2k+4     │
│   Instruction 5      //step 5        │  │   ...                                │
│  endif:                              │  │   Ins. 2k+1    //step 2k+3          │
└──────────────────────────────────────┘  └──────────────────────────────────────┘
```

Fig. 4. (a) Assigning instructions to time steps. MULT instruction is not included in any ALU circuit but step 1. (b) An example demonstrating how we map instructions to time steps in a program with loops.

time step. Since the size of each instruction bank is very small for the programs we tested, we implemented an oblivious key-value structure using a simple linear scan; for larger programs with more instructions it would be possible to design a more-complex oblivious data structure with sub-linear access time.

Constructing smaller ALU circuits. Once we have determined the set of possible instructions for a given time step, we can reduce the set of *instruction types* required by that time step. In the offline phase, before user inputs are specified, we generate a distinct garbled ALU circuit for each time step (using ObliVM) supporting exactly the set of possible instructions in that time step. During online execution, our emulator uses the appropriate garbled ALU circuit at each time step.

Skipping unnecessary memory operations. The same idea also allows us to reduce the number of memory operations. There are two types of memory operations: (1) store operations that read a value from a register and write it to memory, and (2) load operations that read a value from memory and write it to a register. When performing the static analysis, we compute two flags for each time step, indicating if any load or store operation could possibly occur in that step. During the run-time execution, our emulator skips the load/store computation depending on the values of these flags.

Improving accesses to the register space. We can additionally improve the efficiency of register accesses. Since register values are hard-coded into the instructions, they can be determined offline, before the user inputs are specified. (This is in contrast to memory accesses, where the addresses are loaded into the registers and therefore cannot be determined at compile time.) For example, the instruction ADD $1, $2, $4 needs to access registers at location 1, 2, and 4. During the offline phase, we compute for each time step the set of all possible register accesses at that time step. Then, in the online phase, only those registers need be included in the secure emulation for that time step.

4.2 Padding Branches

The offline analysis we just described provides substantial improvements on real programs. For example, as we show in Sect. 5.2 for the case of set intersection, this analysis reduces the cost of instruction fetch by $6\times$ and reduces the ALU circuit size by $1.5\times$. This is because the full program has about 150 instructions, while the largest instruction bank after performing our binary analysis contains just 31 instructions; for more than half of the time steps, there are fewer than 20 possible instructions per time step. On the other hand, there is only a small reduction in the time spent performing load and store operations, because these operations are possible in nearly every time step. Load and store operations are by far the most costly instructions to emulate. For example, reading a 32-bit integer from an array of 1024 32-bit integer requires 43K AND gates. So it is important to reduce the number of times we unnecessarily perform these operations.

Before presenting further improvements, it is helpful to analyze the effect of what has already been described. Consider again the simple example in Fig. 4b. Here, with only a single loop, it is easy to calculate how many instructions will be assigned to any particular time step. If the loop has k instructions, and there are n instructions following the loop, then in some time step we might have to execute any of $n/k + 1$ instructions. This should be compared with the worst-case, where we perform no analysis and simply assume that we could be anywhere among the $n + k$ instructions in the program. When k is large and n is small—i.e., if most of the computation occurs inside this loop—our binary analysis provides substantial savings.

Unfortunately, this example is overly simplistic, and in more realistic examples our binary analysis might not be as effective. Let's consider what happens when there is a branch inside the loop, resulting in two parallel blocks of lengths k_1 and k_2. If the first instruction in the loop is reached for the first time at time step x, then it might also be executed at time steps $x + k_1, x + k_2, x + k_1 + k_2, \ldots$, and, more generally, at every time step $x + (i \cdot k_1) + (j \cdot k_2)$ for $i, j \in \mathbb{Z}$. If k_1 and k_2 are relatively prime, then every $i \cdot k_1$ time steps, and every $j \cdot k_2$ time steps, we add another instruction to the instruction set. It follows that in fewer than $k_1 \cdot k_2$ time steps overall, we can be anywhere in the loop! Furthermore, at that point we might exit the loop on any step, so that after executing fewer than $k_1 \cdot k_2 + n$ time steps, we might be anywhere from the start of the loop until the end of the program, and we no longer benefit from our analysis at all.

This motivates the idea of padding parallel blocks with NOPs so the length of one is a multiple of the other. Using the same example of a single if/else statement inside a loop, if the two branches have equal length (i.e., $k_1 = k_2$), then at any time step we will never have more than two instructions from inside the loop—one from each branch—assigned to the same time step. We provide further discussion about the performance improvement in Sect. 5, using set intersection as an example.

4.3 Checking Termination Less Frequently

In our basic system, we test for termination of the program in every instruction cycle, which incurs a round of communication each time. This overhead becomes significant, especially after we performed the optimizations mentioned in the previous sections. For example, for a program with T cycles, our basic system needs $(r_o + 1)T$ roundtrips, where r_o is the number of roundtrips needed by an ORAM access.

In order to avoid such overhead, we modified the system to check for termination only every C instruction cycles, for C a user-specified constant. In every cycle, the parties still compute shares of the bit indicating if the program has terminated, but they do not reconstruct that bit in clear. Instead, memory and register accesses take this bit as input, and do not update the memory or registers if the program has terminated. This ensures that the MIPS state, including registers and memory, will not change after termination, even if additional cycles are executed.

Note that the parties execute up to $C - 1$ extra instruction cycles, but the amortized cost of checking for termination is decreased by a factor of C. One can thus set C depending on the relative speeds of computation and communication to minimize the overall running time. Now for a program with T cycles, and n_o memory accesses, the total number of roundtrips is $n_o \times r_o + \lceil T/C \rceil$, where $n_o < T$. In addition to reducing number of roundtrips, such optimization also reduces the leakage. Instead of leaking total number of cycles T, only $\lceil T/C \rceil$ is leaked.

5 Performance Analysis

Experimental Setup. Our emulator takes MIPS binaries as input and allows two parties to execute that code securely. All binaries we used were generated from C code using a GCC 4.7.3 compiler with `-O2 -std=c99 --save-temps` flags. When specified, we added NOPs to the binary by hand to explore the potential speedup introduced by padding; for all other examples, including binary search, decision trees, and Dijkstra's shortest-path algorithm, we directly used the binaries generated by the GCC compiler without adding any padding. More detailed performance analysis and results for the last two examples can be found in the extended version [22].

All times reported are based on two machines of type `c4.4xlarge` with 3.3 GHz cores and 30 GB memory running in the same region of an Amazon EC2 cluster. Two machines are connected by ethernet with about 1.1 Gbps bandwidth. We did not use parallel cores, except possibly by the JVM for garbage collection. In all our results, we report the time used by the circuit generator, which is the bottleneck in the garbled-circuit protocol. Note that our system is based on ObliVM, with a garbling rate of about 600K AND gates per second. A better garbled circuits implementation can therefore improve the absolute running time. Therefore we report different metrics for a better comparison.

Table 2. Total running time for computing the size of a set intersection.

Input size per party		Memory Access	Instruction Fetch	ALU Computation	Setup	Total Cost
64 Elements	Baseline	18.7 s	25.3 s	14.2 s	0.1 s	58.4 s
	+Inst. Mapping	5.4 s	3.6 s	3.8 s	0.1 s	12.9 s
	+Padding	0.5 s	0.4 s	1.8 s	0.1 s	2.8 s
256 Elements	Baseline	175.9 s	93.6 s	54.5 s	0.2 s	324.1 s
	+Inst. Mapping	51.9 s	14.4 s	14.5 s	0.2 s	81.0 s
	+Padding	4.9 s	1.3 s	6.6 s	0.2 s	13.0 s
1024 Elements	Baseline	2477.4 s	375.2 s	215.2 s	0.4 s	3068.2 s
	+Inst. Mapping	782.5 s	59.4 s	58.7 s	0.4 s	901.0 s
	+Padding	76.3 s	5.5 s	26.3 s	0.4 s	108.5 s

Metrics. Since our emulator uses ALU circuits and instruction banks with different sizes at each time step, and since it may skip memory operations altogether in some time steps, the cost varies between different time steps. Therefore, we report the total cost of execution, amortized over all time steps. We ran each experiment 10 times. Since the standard derivation is never greater than 5 % of the mean, we report the mean of 10 runs if not specified.

5.1   Time for Static Analysis and Compilation

Our system takes MIPS binary code, generated by an off-the-shelf compiler, as input. In all the experiments we ran, our system used less than 0.6 s for the static analysis mapping instructions to time steps, including generation of the code for the CPU circuits for all time steps. Following this step, we run the ObliVM compiler on the code for these CPU circuits; this never took more than 1.5 s for all circuits in any of our examples. Note that compilation time does not include any cryptographic operations; all cryptographic operations, e.g., garbled circuits, oblivious transfer, etc., are all done at runtime, reported separately in the following subsections.

If the program is written in a way such that input size is not fixed at compile time, then we can perform our static analysis and optimization on the binary without prior knowledge of input size. This means that: (1) We only need to perform our static analysis once for all input sizes. (2) The running time of our static analysis is independent of the input size.

The compilation time in our system is within the same range or smaller than systems that report compilation time. For example, two compilers by Kreuter et al. [13,14] both take more than 2000 s to compile a circuit computing matrix multiplication of dimension 16. The time is even higher for larger matrices. In our case, the compilation time is within 2.0 s, independent of the size of the matrices.

5.2   The Effect of Our Optimizations

In this section, we explore the impact of different optimizations on the performance of our emulator. We consider the cost for each component of our emulation, i.e., Instruction Fetch, ALU Computation, and Memory Access. We compare three different approaches:

- **Baseline.** This is the basic system (cf. Sect. 3) with no static analysis.
- **+Instruction Mapping.** For each time step we compute the set of possible instructions at that time step, and use a smaller instruction bank and ALU circuit for each cycle, reduce register accesses, and bypass loads/stores whenever possible, as described in Sect. 4.1.
- **+Padding.** The program is padded (manually) with NOPs as described in Sect. 4.2.

For evaluation we use a program that computes the size of the intersection of two sets. Each party has a sorted array of 32-bit integers as input and wants to compute how many elements are shared by both parties. We report the total running time of the system in Table 2. For all running times shown, including the baseline, we incorporated the optimization that checks termination less frequently, as described in Sect. 4.3.

As shown in Table 2, using static analysis decreases the time used for memory access by $3\times$, the cost of instruction fetching by $6\times$, and the time for ALU computation by $3.5\times$. Using padding gives a further $10\times$ improvement on both instruction-fetch and memory-access time, along with an additional $2\times$ speedup in ALU computation. In total, our optimizations achieve a roughly $28\times$ speedup compared to our baseline system. The cost of instruction fetching is reduced by $67\times$, the cost of memory access is reduced by $33\times$, and the cost of ALU computation is cut by $8\times$.

5.3   Performance of Binary Search

Binary search, where one party holds an array of integers while the other party holds a query, serves as an interesting test case for exploring the (amortized) speedup provided by working in the RAM model of computation. Secure RAM-based computation of binary search was considered by Gordon et al. [8] and Wang et al. [24], both of whom used hand-crafted circuits.

For testing our system, we wrote C code for binary search using a standard iterative implementation (see Fig. 5b), with no annotations or special syntax, and then compiled this to a MIPS binary using GCC. In Fig. 5a, we show the performance of our system when emulating the resulting MIPS binary, when using ObliVM with Circuit ORAM [23] or trivial ORAM as the back-end. In addition, we implemented secure binary search using ObliVM directly as well as via a "trivial" circuit that simply performs a linear scan. Since we only care about the amortized cost, setup time is excluded in all cases. As we can see in Fig. 5a, our emulator with Circuit ORAM outperforms the one with trivial ORAM once the array contains $>2^{16}$ 32-bit integers, and outperforms a linear

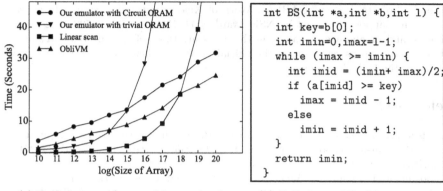

```
int BS(int *a,int *b,int l) {
    int key=b[0];
    int imin=0,imax=l-1;
    while (imax >= imin) {
        int imid = (imin+ imax)/2;
        if (a[imid] >= key)
            imax = imid - 1;
        else
            imin = imid + 1;
    }
    return imin;
}
```

(a) Performance of secure binary search.   (b) C Code used for binary search.

Fig. 5. Binary search example. One party holds an array of 32-bit integers, while the other holds a value to search for.

scan when the array contains $>2^{19}$ 32-bit integers. We can also see that our emulator is only 25 % slower than ObliVM, which requires the programmer to use the domain-specific language supported by ObliVM.

6 Conclusion

In this work, we designed and implemented an emulator that allows two parties to securely execute native MIPS code. Our work fills an important gap in the trade-off between efficiency and generality: by supporting MIPS code, we allow programmers with no knowledge or understanding of secure computation to write and securely execute code of their choice. Contrary to what one might expect, we show that this approach can yield reasonable performance once several automated optimizations are applied. For some programs, our optimized system is competitive with implementations based on state-of-the-art domain-specific languages for secure computation.

There are still many interesting, unexplored optimizations that would further improve the efficiency of our approach: (1) In this work, we demonstrate the potential advantages of padding with NOP instruction, but it remains an interesting challenge to automate and optimize this step. (2) It is also interesting to explore how taint analysis, and other more complex analysis of binary files, can improve the performance by allowing us to further avoid oblivious memory accesses and unnecessary secure computation in the ALU. Our work demonstrates the feasibility of the most general approach to secure computation, opening an avenue for further research and helping to fill a gap in the growing array of options for performing secure computation.

Acknowledgements. The authors thank Elaine Shi for helpful discussions in the early stages. This research was developed with funding from the Defense Advanced

Research Projects Agency (DARPA). Work of Xiao Wang and Jonathan Katz was additionally supported in part by NSF awards #1111599 and #1563722. The views, opinions, and/or findings contained in this work are those of the authors and should not be interpreted as representing the official views or policies of the Department of Defense or the U.S. Government.

References

1. Afshar, A., Mohassel, P., Pinkas, B., Riva, B.: Non-interactive secure computation based on cut-and-choose. In: Nguyen, P.Q., Oswald, E. (eds.) EUROCRYPT 2014. LNCS, vol. 8441, pp. 387–404. Springer, Heidelberg (2014)
2. Bogdanov, D., Laur, S., Willemson, J.: Sharemind: a framework for fast privacy-preserving computations. In: Jajodia, S., Lopez, J. (eds.) ESORICS 2008. LNCS, vol. 5283, pp. 192–206. Springer, Heidelberg (2008)
3. Demmler, D., Schneider, T., Zohner, M.: ABY–a framework for efficient mixed-protocol secure two-party computation. In: NDSS (2015)
4. Ejgenberg, Y., Farbstein, M., Levy, M., Lindell, Y.: SCAPI: the secure computation application programming interface. Cryptology ePrint Archive, Report 2012/629 (2012)
5. Fletcher, C.W., van Dijk, M., Devadas, S.: Towards an interpreter for efficient encrypted computation. In: Proceedings of the 2012 ACM Workshop on Cloud Computing Security Workshop (2012)
6. Goldreich, O.: Foundations of Cryptography: Basic Applications, vol. 2. Cambridge University Press, Cambridge (2004)
7. Goldreich, O., Ostrovsky, R.: Software protection and simulation on oblivious rams. J. ACM 43(3), 431–473 (1996)
8. Gordon, S.D., Katz, J., Kolesnikov, V., Krell, F., Malkin, T., Raykova, M., Vahlis, Y.: Secure two-party computation in sublinear (amortized) time. In: Yu, T., Danezis, G., Gligor, V.D. (eds.) ACM CCS, pp. 513–524. ACM Press, October 2012
9. Henecka, W., Kögl, S., Sadeghi, A.R., Schneider, T., Wehrenberg, I.: TASTY: tool for automating secure two-party computations. In: Al-Shaer, E., Keromytis, A.D., Shmatikov, V. (eds.) ACM CCS, pp. 451–462. ACM Press, October 2010
10. Holzer, A., Franz, M., Katzenbeisser, S., Veith, H.: Secure two-party computations in ANSI C. In: Yu, T., Danezis, G., Gligor, V.D. (eds.) ACM CCS, pp. 772–783. ACM Press, October 2012
11. Huang, Y., Evans, D., Katz, J., Malka, L.: Faster secure two-party computation using garbled circuits. In: Usenix Security Symposium (2011)
12. Keller, M.: The oblivious machine - or: how to put the c into mpc. Cryptology ePrint Archive, Report 2015/467 (2015). http://eprint.iacr.org/
13. Kreuter, B., Mood, B., Shelat, A., Butler, K.: PCF: a portable circuit format for scalable two-party secure computation. In: Usenix Security Symposium (2013)
14. Kreuter, B., Shelat, A., Shen, C.H.: Billion-gate secure computation with malicious adversaries. In: USENIX Security Symposium (2012)
15. Lindell, Y., Riva, B.: Blazing fast 2PC in the offline/online setting with security for malicious adversaries. In: ACM CCS 2015, pp. 579–590. ACM Press (2015)
16. Liu, C., Huang, Y., Shi, E., Katz, J., Hicks, M.: Automating efficient RAM-model secure computation. In: IEEE Security & Privacy (2014)
17. Liu, C., Wang, X.S., Nayak, K., Huang, Y., Shi, E.: Oblivm: a programming framework for secure computation. In: IEEE Security & Privacy (2015)

18. Malkhi, D., Nisan, N., Pinkas, B., Sella, Y.: Fairplay: a secure two-party computation system. In: USENIX Security Symposium (2004)
19. Pinkas, B., Schneider, T., Smart, N.P., Williams, S.C.: Secure two-party computation is practical. In: Matsui, M. (ed.) ASIACRYPT 2009. LNCS, vol. 5912, pp. 250–267. Springer, Heidelberg (2009)
20. Rastogi, A., Hammer, M.A., Hicks, M.: Wysteria: a programming language for generic, mixed-mode multiparty computations. In: 2014 IEEE Symposium on Security and Privacy, pp. 655–670. IEEE Computer Society Press, May 2014
21. Songhori, E.M., Hussain, S.U., Sadeghi, A.R., Schneider, T., Koushanfar, F.: TinyGarble: highly compressed and scalable sequential garbled circuits. In: IEEE Security & Privacy (2015)
22. Wang, X., Gordon, S.D., McIntosh, A., Katz, J.: Secure computation of mips machine code. Cryptology ePrint Archive, Report 2015/547 (2015). http://eprint.iacr.org/2015/547
23. Wang, X.S., Chan, T.H., Shi, E.: Circuit oram: on tightness of the goldreich-ostrovsky lower bound. In: Proceedings of the 2014 ACM SIGSAC Conference on Computer and Communications Security. ACM (2015)
24. Wang, X.S., Huang, Y., Chan, T.H.H., Shelat, A., Shi, E.: SCORAM: oblivious RAM for secure computation. In: Ahn, G.J., Yung, M., Li, N. (eds.) ACM CCS, pp. 191–202. ACM Press, November 2014
25. Yao, A.C.C.: How to generate and exchange secrets (extended abstract). In: 27th FOCS, pp. 162–167. IEEE Computer Society Press, October 1986
26. Zahur, S., Evans, D.: Obliv-c: a language for extensible data-oblivious computation. Cryptology ePrint Archive, Report 2015/1153 (2015)

Secure Logging

Insynd: Improved Privacy-Preserving Transparency Logging

Roel Peeters[1] and Tobias Pulls[2(✉)]

[1] ESAT/COSIC and iMinds, KU Leuven, Leuven, Belgium
roel.peeters@esat.kuleuven.be
[2] Department of Mathematics and Computer Science,
Karlstad University, Karlstad, Sweden
tobias.pulls@kau.se

Abstract. Service providers collect and process more user data then ever, while users of these services remain oblivious to the actual processing and utility of the processed data to the service providers. This leads users to put less trust in service providers and be more reluctant to share data. Transparency logging is about service providers continuously logging descriptions of the data processing on their users' data, where each description is intended for a particular user.

We propose Insynd, a new cryptographic scheme for privacy-preserving transparency logging. Insynd improves on prior work by (1) increasing the utility of all data sent through the scheme thanks to our publicly verifiable proofs: one can disclose selected events without having to disclose any long term secrets; and (2) enabling a stronger adversarial model: Inysnd can deal with an untrusted server (such as commodity cloud services) through the use of an authenticated data structure named Balloon. Finally, our publicly available prototype implementation shows greatly improved performance with respect to related work and competitive performance for more data-intensive settings like secure logging.

1 Introduction

In general, transparency logging allows service providers to show that they are compliant with a certain policy that can be imposed by legislation, sector regulations or internal procedures; but just as well through service level agreements for businesses to keep tabs on subcontractors [10,18]. For personal data, privacy regulations such as the EU General Data Protection Regulation empower users by granting them the right to obtain transparency about their data being processed and by improving their ability to hold the service providers accountable for their actions. Conceptually, through transparency logging, users that wish to know what is happening with their personal data after disclosure to a service provider can see whether or not the processing is inline with the prior agreed upon policy. This could, e.g., be a hospital with a privacy policy for processing patient data. Each access and modification to the patient's health record is logged for the patient. If patients discover someone prying, they can file a complaint with the hospital's ombudsperson.

© Springer International Publishing Switzerland 2016
I. Askoxylakis et al. (Eds.): ESORICS 2016, Part II, LNCS 9879, pp. 121–139, 2016.
DOI: 10.1007/978-3-319-45741-3_7

In the setting of transparency logging [18] as depicted in Fig. 1, the *author* generates *events* intended for *recipients* that describe data processing by the author as it takes place. Events are stored at a *server*: an intermediate party that primarily serves to offload storage of events for authors. The recipient can then at a later point in time get insights into the author's data processing by consulting the events intended for him or her. With these insights, the recipient can hold the author accountable for its actions and if deemed necessary take remediation measures, e.g., file a complaint or switch service providers. Note that this paper focuses on a transparency logging scheme, which is only about the generation, storage and retrieval of events, not on what should be logged to describe data processing, or how policies should be structured to enable the comparison with stated data processing.

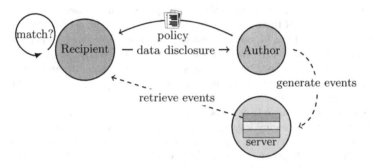

Fig. 1. Recipient comparing actual data processing of its data with the data processing that was agreed upon in the policy prior to data disclosure.

A transparency logging tool must provide security and privacy. The integrity of the stored events has to be guaranteed, as this is where the recipient bases its insights on to hold the author accountable. This means that it should be impossible to alter or delete any events after being stored at the server without being detectable. Data privacy and confidentiality of the stored events are important because the mere existence of events already reveals information, e.g., a patient visiting the hospital. This means that when a transparency logging tool does not consider privacy, one should deploy another transparency enhancing tool for monitoring data processing on the stored events from the first to make sure that data derived from these events are not used instead of the original data.

When users want to take action based upon the messages logged for them, they will inavoidably break some of the privacy properties. What we aim for with Insynd, our proposed cryptographic transparency logging tool, is to limit the privacy breaches to the events disclosed, i.e., enable selective disclosure, and as such greatly increase the utility of the transparency logging tool. Instead of having recipients reveal long term secrets, recipients can generate publicly verifiable proofs which allow them to disclose the content of stored events such that the content and other properties cannot be refuted. Furthermore, Insynd also improves on the scheme that was proposed by Pulls *et al.* [18] by allowing for a stronger adversarial model. While some trust in authors is inevitable (forward security), since authors generate descriptions of their own processing, servers (e.g., commodity cloud services) should not have to be trusted. We primarily achieve the stronger adversary model through the use of Balloon [16], an authenticated data structure that was designed specifically for this setting. Lastly, our performance benchmarks show speeds comparable to state-of-the-art secure logging schemes. In summary, our contributions are:

- Increased utility of a transparency logging scheme through our publicly verifiable proofs: recipients and authors can produce publicly verifiable proofs of all data sent through Insynd, convincing a third-party of who sent what particular message to whom at approximately what time.
- A new transparency logging scheme in our stronger adversarial model where the server does not need to be trusted through the use of Balloon [16]. The resulting scheme also provides publicly verifiable consistency: anyone can verify that all events stored in a Balloon are consistent.
- A publicly available performant proof-of-concept implementation of Insynd using modern cryptographic primitives and benchmark code.

This paper is structured as follows. Section 2 states our assumptions and goals. Section 3 gives a high-level overview of our ideas. Section 4 presents Insynd in detail. Section 5 evaluates Insynd's properties. Section 6 presents related work. Section 7 shows the performance of our implementation.

2   Assumptions and Goals

We assume a setting with three parties: author, server and recipients. The author and recipients only have limited storage capabilities, while the server has high storage capabilities. The author is considered *forward secure*: the author is initially trusted until the time of compromise and the adversary, by compromising the author, gains no advantage towards breaking any of the security and privacy properties related to the events stored before compromise. The server is considered compromised from the start. Recipients are considered honest.

For communication, we assume a secure channel between the author and the server (such as TLS), and a secure and anonymous channel for recipients (such as TLS over Tor [9]) to communicate with the author and server. We explicitly consider availability out of scope, that is, the author and server will always reply (however, their replies may be malicious). For time-stamps, we assume the existence a trustworthy time-stamping authority [7].

For the core security and privacy properties: secrecy, forward integrity with deletion-detection and forward unlinkability of events, we make use of the model of Pulls et al. [18], with some modifications to account for possible information leakage through our introduced publicly verifiable proofs[1] and our stronger

---

[1] Since state is kept by the author instead of the server (which is assumed to be untrusted), the CorruptServer oracle is replaced by a CorruptAuthor oracle. To account for information leakage, additional oracles such as GetState, DecryptEvent and RecipientEvent are introduced.

adversarial setting. The full updated model is available in the extended version of this paper [17]. Secrecy is vital for recipients since events may contain sensitive personal data. Forward integrity with deletion-detection ensures that events are tamper evident: any modifications (including deletion) can be detected. Finally, forward unlinkability of events ensures that prior generated events do not leak information such as the number of events that belong to a particular recipient.

In addition to the core security and privacy properties, we provide publicly verifiable consistency and a number of publicly verifiable proofs to increase the utility of the data sent through the transparency logging scheme. Publicly verifiable consistency can be seen as a form of publicly verifiable deletion-detection and forward integrity for all events produced by the author at a server. Insynd allows for publicly verifiable proofs of (1) the author of an event, (2) the recipient of an event, (3) the message sent in an event, and (4) the time an event existed at a server. While a recipient is always able to produce these proofs, the author has to decide during event generation if it wishes to save material to be able to create these proofs. Each proof is an isolated disclosure and a potential violation of a property of Insynd, like secrecy and forward unlinkability of events.

3   Ideas

To protect the privacy of the recipients, the author turns all descriptions for recipients into events consisting of an identifier and a payload, where the identifiers are unlinkable to each other and the payloads contain the encrypted descriptions for the recipient. It should be noted that the entire events must be unlinkable to each other, hence the encryption scheme must also provide key privacy [2]. Later on the recipient must be able to retrieve its relevant events and decrypt the logged descriptions. For each event, the author updates the symmetric event linking key for the recipient in question using a forward-secure sequential key generator (SKG) in the form of an evolving hash chain [3,13,19]. The recipient can do the same to link the relevant event identifiers together.

To provide the publicly verifiable proofs of message and recipient, we need to go into the details of the used encryption scheme and how the event linking key and nonce for encryption are derived from the forward secure sequential key. We make use of an IND-CCA2[2] *public-key authenticated encryption* scheme [1] in a non-traditional manner. A public key authenticated encryption scheme allows a sender to encrypt a message for a receiver using the receiver's public key and its own private key, such that the receiver can decrypt the message using its own private key and the sender's public key. In this way, both sender and receiver can decrypt the message and be assured that only someone who knows either private key can have created the ciphertext. To avoid a deterministic encryption scheme, a nonce is usually included for each message to be encrypted. Instead of taking the author's private key as input, we generate a fresh ephemeral public private key pair for each message, send along the public key and append the private key

---

[2] Every publicly verifiable proof is an isolated disclosure, hence the encryption scheme must provide secrecy even when the adversary has access to a decryption oracle.

to the message to be encrypted. As such the recipient can prove, by revealing the ephemeral private key and the nonce, that the ciphertext contains the said plaintext. The author can do the same if it stores the ephemeral private key at the time of creating the event. We define the following algorithms, based on the algorithms of the public key authenticated encryption scheme $\Pi = \{(\mathsf{sk}, \mathsf{pk}) \leftarrow \mathbf{KeyGen}(1^\lambda),\ c \leftarrow \mathbf{Enc}^n_{\mathsf{pk}}(m),\ m \leftarrow \mathbf{Dec}^n_{\mathsf{sk}}(c, \mathsf{pk})\}$:

- $(c, \mathsf{pk}') \leftarrow \mathbf{Enc}^n_{\mathsf{pk}}(m)$: Encrypts a message m using an ephemeral key-pair $(\mathsf{sk}', \mathsf{pk}') \leftarrow \mathbf{KeyGen}(1^\lambda)$, the public key pk, and the nonce n. The resulting ciphertext c is $\mathbf{Enc}^n_{\mathsf{pk}'}(m \| \mathsf{sk}')$. Returns (c, pk').
- $(m, \mathsf{sk}') \leftarrow \mathbf{Dec}^n_{\mathsf{sk}}(c, \mathsf{pk}')$: Decrypts a ciphertext c using the private key sk, public key pk', and nonce n where $p \leftarrow \mathbf{Dec}^n_{\mathsf{sk}}(c, \mathsf{pk}')$. If decryption fails $p = \bot$, otherwise $p = m \| \mathsf{sk}'$. Returns p.
- $m \leftarrow \mathbf{Dec}^n_{\mathsf{sk}', \mathsf{pk}}(c, \mathsf{pk}')$: Decrypts a ciphertext c using the private key sk', public key pk, and the nonce n where $p \leftarrow \mathbf{Dec}^n_{\mathsf{sk}'}(c, \mathsf{pk})$. If decryption fails $p = \bot$, otherwise $p = m \| \mathsf{sk}^*$. If $\mathsf{sk}' = \mathsf{sk}^*$ and corresponds to pk', returns m, otherwise $\bot$.

The event linking key k' and nonce n for encryption are derived from the current authentication key k (Fig. 2). The event linking key is used to prove the recipient of the event. By deriving the event linking key from the nonce, we prove that the recipient corresponds to the decrypted message.

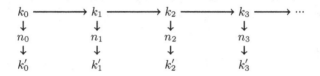

Fig. 2. Deriving the event key k' and nonce n. Each arrow represents a one-way relation, e.g., from k it is easy to compute n, but the other way around is hard.

Through using Balloon [16], an authenticated data structure that was designed for the setting of transparency logging with an untrusted server, we can support our stronger adversarial model and provide publicly verifiable proofs of consistency. Balloon allows for efficient publicly verifiable proofs of both membership and non-membership of keys. This is needed, since otherwise a recipient cannot distinguish between a server denying service and the lack of an event with a specific identifier. The main advantage of Balloon compared to other authenticated data structures that have this property[3], is that the author only needs to keep constant storage (instead of storing a copy of the data structure) and that proof generation is more efficient for the server. The main algorithms from Balloon that are used by Insynd are:

---

[3] For a more in-depth discussion, we refer the reader to Pulls and Peeters [16].

- B.query (**Membership**) and B.verify (**Membership**) to generate as well as verify (non-)membership proofs.
- B.query (**Prune**), B.verify (**Prune**), B.update*, and B.refresh to insert a new set of events into a Balloon and generate a new *snapshot*, which commits the author to all the events that are stored until now.

The full algorithm descriptions can be found in [17]. To support a forward-secure author (preventing it from creating snapshots that delete or modify events inserted prior to compromise), Balloon requires trusted *monitors* and a *perfect gossiping mechanism* for the snapshots. Monitors continuously reconstruct the Balloon and compare calculated snapshots with those gossiped (spread simultaneously to all recipients) by the author. We relax these requirements by linking snapshots together and periodically timestamping these; and by introducing forward integrity with deletion-detection for each recipient.

To provide forward integrity with deletion detection, we rely on the author keeping an evolving forward-secure state for each recipient. By enabling the recipient to query for this state and verifying the response, it is impossible for the author to alter events for this recipient (sent to the server prior to the time of compromise) as it will not be able to generate a valid state to send to the recipient. During recipient registration, cryptographic key material will be set up for the recipient: an asymmetric key-pair, for encryption and decryption, and a symmetric key to be able to link relevant events together. For each recipient, the current values of the forward-secure SKG and the forward-secure sequential aggregate authenticator (FssAgg) [12] over the relevant event values are kept in the author's state.

4   Insynd

Now we will go into the details of the different protocols that make up Insynd. Figure 3 shows five protocols between an author A, a server S, and a recipient R. The protocols are setup (pink box), register (blue box), insert (yellow box), getEvent (red box), and getState (green box). The following subsections describe each protocol in detail.

4.1   Setup and Registration

The author and server each have signature key pairs, (A_{sk}, A_{vk}) and (S_{sk}, S_{vk}), respectively. We assume that A_{vk} and S_{vk} are publicly attributable to the respective entities, e.g., by the use of some trustworthy public-key infrastructure. For the author, the key pair is generated using the B.genkey algorithm of Balloon, as this key pair is also used to sign the snapshots, which are part of Balloon.

Author-Server Setup. The purpose of the setup protocol (pink box in Fig. 3) is for the author and the server to create a new Balloon, stored at the server, with two associated uniform resource identifiers (URIs): one for the author A_{URI},

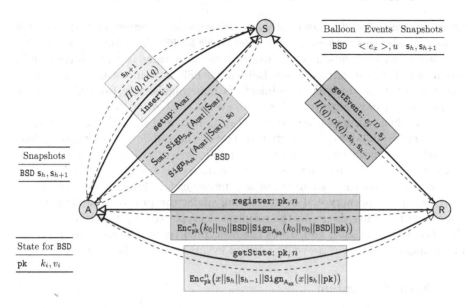

Fig. 3. Insynd consists of five protocols (coloured boxes), between an author A, server S, and recipient R. A solid line indicates the start of protocol and a dashed line a response. (Color figure online)

and one for the server S_{URI}. At the former the recipient can later on query for its current state, while at the latter it can retrieve stored events. The result of this protocol, the *Balloon setup data* (BSD), commits both the author and the server to the newly created Balloon.

The protocol is started by the author sending its A_{URI} to the server. The server replies with S_{URI} and $Sign_{S_{sk}}(A_{URI}||S_{URI})$. The signature commits the server to the specified Balloon. Upon receiving the reply from the server, the author verifies the server's signature. If this verifies, the author creates an empty Balloon $(auth(D_0), s_0) \leftarrow B.setup(D_0, A_{sk}, A_{vk})$ for an empty data structure D_0. The author sends $Sign_{A_{sk}}(A_{URI}||S_{URI})$ together with the initial snapshot s_0 to the server to acknowledge that the new Balloon is now set up. Once the server receives this message, it verifies the author's signature and can complete the setup of the empty Balloon now that it has s_0. The two signatures, the two URIs, and the initial snapshot s_0 together form the BSD.

Recipient Registration. The purpose of the **register** protocol (blue box in Fig. 3) is to enable the author to send messages to the recipient later on, and at the same time have the author commit to the recipient on how these messages will be delivered. Before running the protocol, the recipient is assumed to have generated its encryption key pair (pk, sk).

The protocol is initiated by the recipient sending its public key together with a nonce to the author. The author generates the initial authentication key $k_0 \leftarrow \mathsf{Rand}(|\mathsf{Hash}(\cdot)|)$ and authenticator value $v_0 \leftarrow \mathsf{Rand}(|\mathsf{Hash}(\cdot)|)$ for this recipient and stores these values in its *state table* for BSD. The state table contains the *current* authentication key k_i and authenticator value v_i for each recipient's public key that is registered in the Balloon for BSD. By generating a random v_0, the state of newly registered recipients is indistinguishable from the state of recipients that have already one or more events created for them.

The author returns to the recipient k_0, v_0, BSD, and the following signature: $\mathsf{Sign}_{A_{sk}}(k_0||v_0||\mathsf{BSD}||\mathsf{pk})$. The signature covers the public key of the recipient to bind the registration to a particular public key (and hence recipient). The signature (that commits the author) is necessary to prevent the author from fully refuting that there should exist any messages for this recipient. The reply to the recipient is encrypted by the author under the provided public key and nonce. On receiving the reply, the recipient decrypts the reply, verifies all three signatures (two in BSD), and stores the decrypted reply. The recipient now has everything it needs to retrieve its relevant events and state later on.

4.2 Event Generation

An event $e = (e^{ID}, e^P)$ consists of an identifier and a payload. The event identifier e^{ID} identifies the event in a Balloon and is used by the recipient to retrieve an event. The event payload e^P contains the encrypted message from the author. The nonce n, used for encrypting the event payload, and the event key k', used for generating the event identifier, are derived from the recipient's current authentication key k (which the author retrieves from its state table):

$$n \leftarrow \mathsf{Hash}(1||k) \qquad \text{and} \qquad k' \leftarrow \mathsf{Hash}(n) \tag{1}$$

For deriving the nonce, a prefix 1 is added to k to distinguish between deriving the nonce and updating the authentication key, which is done as follows:

$$k_i \leftarrow \mathsf{Hash}(k_{i-1}) \tag{2}$$

The event identifier is generated by computing a MAC on the recipient's public key using the event key:

$$e^{ID} \leftarrow \mathsf{MAC}_{k'}(\mathsf{pk}) \tag{3}$$

This links the event to a particular recipient, which can be used for publicly verifiable proofs of recipient. The event payload is generated by encrypting the message under the recipient's public key and the generated nonce: $e^P \leftarrow \mathsf{Enc}_{\mathsf{pk}}^n(m)$. Since k' is derived from n, this links the event identifier and event payload together and can be used for publicly verifiable proofs of message.

After generating the event, the author updates its state table, effectively overwriting previous values. First the current authenticator value v for the recipient, which aggregates the entire event, is updated using an FssAgg [12]:

$$v_i \leftarrow \mathsf{Hash}\big(v_{i-1}||\mathsf{MAC}_{k_{i-1}}(e)\big) \tag{4}$$

Then the recipient's current authentication key is updated using Eq. 2.

Insert. The purpose of the `insert` protocol (yellow box in Fig. 3) is for an author to insert a set of generated events u into a Balloon kept by the server. The author sends u to the server and gets back a proof that the events can be correctly inserted. If this proof verifies, the author creates a new snapshot, committing to the current version of the Balloon.

Upon receiving u, the server runs:

$$(\Pi(u), \alpha(u)) \leftarrow \text{B.query}(u, D_h, \text{auth}(D_h), \text{A}_{\text{vk}})(\textbf{Prune})$$

to generate a proof $\Pi(u)$ and answer $\alpha(u)$ and sends these back to the author. To verify the correctness of the server's reply, the author runs:

$$\{\text{accept}, \text{reject}\} \leftarrow \text{B.verify}(u, \alpha, \Pi, s_h, \text{A}_{\text{vk}})(\textbf{Prune})$$

where s_h is the latest snapshot generated by the author. If the verification fails, the author restarts the protocol. Next, the author runs:

$$(s_{h+1}, \text{upd}) \leftarrow \text{B.update*}(u, \Pi, s_h, \text{A}_{\text{sk}}, \text{A}_{\text{vk}})$$

to create the next snapshot s_{h+1} (which is also stored in upd). The author stores the snapshot in its *snapshot table* for BSD, and sends upd to the server. The server verifies the snapshot and then runs:

$$(D_{h+1}, \text{auth}(D_{h+1}), s_{h+1}) \leftarrow \text{B.refresh}(u, D_h, \text{auth}(D_h), s_h, \text{upd}, \text{A}_{\text{vk}})$$

to update the Balloon. Finally, the server stores the snapshot s_{h+1} and events u in its *Balloon table* for BSD.

Snapshots and Gossiping. Balloon assumes perfect gossiping of snapshots. In order to relax this requirement, we modify the snapshot construction. This modification was inspired by CONIKS [15], which works in a setting closely related to ours and links snapshots together into a snapshot chain. We redefine a snapshot as:

$$s_h \leftarrow \left(i, c_i, r, t, \text{Sign}_{\text{A}_{\text{sk}}}(i||c_i||r||s_{h-1}||t)\right)$$

Note that h is an index for the number of updates to Balloon, while i is an index for the number of events in the Balloon. The snapshot s_h contains the latest commitment c_i on the history tree and root r on the hash treap for $\text{auth}(D_h)$, fixing the entire Balloon[4]. The previous snapshot s_{h-1} is included to form the snapshot chain. Finally, an *optional* timestamp t from a trusted time-stamping authority is included both as part of the snapshot and in the signature. The timestamp must be on $(i||c_i||r||s_{h-1})$. How frequently a timestamp is included in snapshots directly influences how useful proofs of time are. Timestamping of snapshots is irrelevant for our other properties.

Gossiping of snapshots is done by having the author and server making all snapshots available, e.g., on their websites. Furthermore, the latest snapshots are gossiped to the recipients as part of the `getState` and `getEvent` protocols (described next). Since snapshots are both linked and occasionally timestamped, this greatly restricts adversaries in the forward-security model.

---

[4] Balloon is the composition of a history tree and hash treap [16].

4.3   Event Reconstruction

A recipient uses two protocols to reconstruct its relevant messages sent by the author: `getEvent` and `getState`. After explaining how to get the relevant events and the current state, we show how recipient can verify the consistency of its retrieved messages.

Getting Events. The purpose of the `getEvent` protocol (red box in Fig. 3) is for a recipient to retrieve an event with a given identifier and an optional snapshot. The server replies with the event (if it exists) and a proof of membership. Before running this protocol, the recipient generates the event identifier it is interested in, by using Eqs. 1–3 together with the data it received from the author during registration.

Upon receiving the event identifier e^{ID} and optional snapshot s_j from the recipient, the server runs for $q = (e^{ID}, s_j)$:

$$\left(\Pi(q), \alpha(q)\right) \leftarrow \text{B.query}(q, D_h, \text{auth}(D_h), A_{vk}) \textbf{(Membership)}$$

If no snapshot is provided, the server uses the latest snapshot s_h. Allowing the recipient to query for any snapshot s_j, where $j \leq h$, is important for our publicly verifiable proofs of time. The server replies to the recipient with $(\Pi(q), \alpha(q), s_h, s_{h-1})$. Including the two latest snapshots s_h and s_{h-1} is part of our gossiping mechanism and allows for fast verification at the recipient without having to download all snapshots separately. The recipient verifies the reply by verifying the last snapshot and running:

$$\{\texttt{accept}, \texttt{reject}\} \leftarrow \text{B.verify}(q, \alpha, \Pi, s_h, A_{vk}) \textbf{(Membership)}$$

Getting State. The `getState` protocol (green box in Fig. 3) plays a central role in determining the consistency of the events retrieved from the server.

The recipient initiates the protocol by sending its public key pk and a nonce $n \leftarrow \text{Rand}(|\text{Hash}(\cdot)|)$ to the author. Upon receiving the public key and nonce, the author validates the public key and sets $x \leftarrow (k_i, v_i)$, with k_i and v_i being the current state for pk, retrieved from its state table. The author replies with $\text{Enc}_{pk}^n\left(x||s_h||s_{h-1}||\text{Sign}_{A_{sk}}(x||s_h||pk)\right)$. This reply also covers the two latest snapshots s_h and s_{h-1}, as part of the gossiping mechanism and a signature of the author over $(x||s_h||pk)$. With this signature the author commits itself to its reply for the recipient with respect to the latest snapshot. The recipient decrypts the reply, verifies the signature and latest snapshot.

The reply to the claimed recipient is encrypted using the provided public key and nonce to ensure that only the recipient with corresponding the private key can decrypt it. Since the encryption is randomised with the nonce and ephemeral key-pair generation (note that the length of the plaintext is fixed), no third party in possession of the recipient's public key can determine if new events are generated for the recipient. The nonce also ensures the *freshness* of the reply.

Verifying Consistency. A recipient can verify the consistency of the messages contained in its events as follows. First, it requests all its events until the server provides a non-membership proof. Next, the recipient retrieves its current state from the author. Note that in order to be able to verify the consistency of the received messages it is essential that the latest snapshot received during getEvent for the last downloaded message (for which a non-membership proof is received) and the latest snapshot received during getState are identical.

With the list of events downloaded and the reply x from getState, the recipient can now use Algorithm 1 to decrypt all events and verify the consistency of the messages sent by the author. First all events (in the order of insertion) are decrypted using the nonce and authentication key generation determined by Eqs. 1 and 2 and the calculated state (Eq. 4) is updated. Finally the calculated state is compared to the x.

Algorithm 1. Verify message consistency for a recipient.

Require: pk, sk, k_0, v_0, the reply x from getState, an ordered list l of events.
Ensure: **true** if all events are authentic and the state x is consistent with the events in l, otherwise **false**.
1: $n \leftarrow \text{Hash}(1\|k), k \leftarrow k_0, v \leftarrow v_0$ ▷ n is the event nonce, k and v the computed state
2: **for all** $e \in l$ **do** ▷ in the order events were inserted
3:     $p \leftarrow \text{Dec}_{sk}^n(e^P)$
4:     **if** $p \overset{?}{=} \bot$ **then**
5:         **return false** ▷ failed to decrypt event
6:     $n \leftarrow \text{Hash}(1\|k), k \leftarrow \text{Hash}(k), v \leftarrow \text{Hash}\big(v\|\text{MAC}_k(e)\big)$ ▷ computed right to left
7: **return** $x \overset{?}{=} (k, v)$ ▷ state should match calculated state

---

4.4 Publicly Verifiable Proofs

Similar to Balloon, Insynd allows for publicly verifiable consistency. On top of this, Insynd allows for four types of publicly verifiable proofs: author, time, recipient, and message. These proofs can be combined to, at most, prove that the author had sent a message to a recipient at a particular point in time. While the publicly verifiable proofs of author and time can be generated by anyone, the publicly verifiable proofs of recipient and message can only be generated by the recipient (always) and the author (if it has stored additional information at the time of generating the event).

Author. To prove who the *author* of a particular event is, i.e., that an author created an event, we rely on Balloon. The proof is the output from B.query (**Membership**) for the event. Verifying the proof uses B.verify (**Membership**).

Time. To prove *when* an event *existed*. The granularity of this proof depends on the frequency of timestamped snapshots. The proof is the output from B.query (**Membership**) for the event from a timestamped snapshot s_j that shows that the event was part of the data structure fixed by s_j. Verifying the proof involves using B.verify (**Membership**) and whatever mechanism is involved in verifying the timestamp from the time-stamping authority. Note that a proof of time proves that an event existed at the time as indicated by the time-stamp, not that the event was inserted or generated at that point in time.

Recipient. To prove who the *recipient* of a particular event is. This proof consists of:

1. the output from B.query (**Membership**) for the event, and
2. the event key k' and public key pk used to generate the event identifier e^{ID}.

Verifying the proof involves using B.verify (**Membership**), calculating $\tilde{e}^{ID} \leftarrow$ MAC$_{k'}$(pk), and comparing it to the event identifier e^{ID}.

The recipient can always generate this proof, while the author needs to store the event key k' and public key pk at the time of event generation. If the author stores this material, then the event is linkable to the recipient's public key. If linking an event to a recipient's public key is not adequately attributing an event to a recipient (e.g., due to the recipient normally being identified by an account name), then the register protocol should also include an extra signature linking the public key to additional information, such as an account name.

Message. The publicly verifiable proof of message includes a publicly verifiable proof of recipient, which establishes that the ciphertext as part of an event was generated for a specific public key (recipient). The proof is:

1. the output from B.query (**Membership**) for the event,
2. the nonce n needed for decryption and used to derive the event key k',
3. the public key pk used to generate e^{ID}, and
4. the ephemeral secret key sk$'$ that is needed for decryption.

Verifying the proof involves first verifying the publicly verifiable proof of recipient by deriving $k' = $ Hash(n). Next, the verifier can use Dec$^n_{sk',pk}(c, pk')$ to learn the message m.

The recipient can always generate this proof, while the author needs to store the nonce n, public key pk, and the ephemeral private key sk' at event generation. Note that even thought we allow the author to save the ephemeral key material to produce publicly verifiable proofs of message, the author is never allowed to do so for the encrypted replies to the getState or register protocols.

5   Evaluation

The proof sketches use the model in the extended version of this paper [17].

5.1 Security and Privacy Properties

Theorem 1. *For an IND-CCA2 secure public-key encryption scheme, Insynd provides computational secrecy of the messages contained in events.*

This follows trivially from the definition of IND-CCA2 security.

Theorem 2. *Given an unforgeable signature algorithm, an unforgeable one-time MAC, and an IND-CCA2 secure public-key encryption algorithm, Insynd provides computational deletion-detection forward integrity in the random oracle model.*

Proof (sketch). This follows from the use of the FssAgg authenticator by Ma and Tsudik [12], which is provably secure in the random oracle model for an unforgeable MAC function.

The register protocol establishes the initial key and value for the forward secure SKG and FssAgg authenticator. These values, together with the BSD and the public key of the recipient, are signed by the author and returned to the recipient. Assuming an unforgeable signature algorithm, this commits the author to the existence of *state*. The recipient gets the current state using the getState protocol for its public key and a fresh nonce. The reply from the author is encrypted under the recipient's provided public key and the nonce provided by the recipient. The nonce ensures the *freshness* of the reply, preventing the adversary from caching replies from the getState protocol made prior to compromise of the author (using the GetState oracle). The current authenticator value and authentication key are updated (and overwritten) by using the FssAgg construction and a forward secure SKG. Note that for each FssAgg invocation, the key for the MAC is unique and derived from the output of a hash function for which the adversary has no information on the input. This means that an unforgeable one-time MAC function is sufficient.

The adversary does not learn any authenticator values and keys through the GetState, DecryptEvent or RecipientEvent oracles. This is due to the use of an IND-CCA2 encryption scheme, and the values k' and n in the proofs Π are derived from the current authentication key at that time using a random oracle. □

Theorem 3. *For a key-private IND-CCA2 secure public-key encryption algorithm, Insynd provides computational forward unlinkability of events within one round of the insert protocol in the random oracle model.*

Proof (sketch). For events created with the CreateEvent' oracle the adversary has access to the following information: $e^{ID} = \text{MAC}_{k'}(\text{pk})$ and $e^P = \text{Enc}_{\text{pk}}^n(m)$ for which $k' = \text{Hash}(n)$ and $n = \text{Hash}(1\|k)$ where k is the current authentication key for the recipient at the time of generating the event.

By assuming the random oracle model, the key to the one-time unforgeable MAC function and the nonce as input of the encryption are truly random. Hence the adversary that does not know the inputs of these hashes, n and k respectively, has no advantage towards winning the indistinguishability game. We will now show that the adversary will not learn these values n and k, even when given the author's entire state (pk, k, v) for all recipients and access to the GetState, DecryptEvent or RecipientEvent oracles. From the previous proof we already know that the adversary does not learn any authenticator values and keys from the latter three oracles. Hence, it will also not learn any n values for events generated with the CreateEvent' oracle, since there is no direct link between the values n_i of multiple events for the same recipient. Instead n is derived from the recipient's current authentication key k at that time, using a random oracle.

The state variable k is generated using a forward-secure sequential key generator in the form of an evolving hash chain. Since the encryption scheme of events is key private, the adversary does not learn anything from all the recipients' public keys pk. Finally, we need to show that the adversary will not be able to link events together from the state variable v. If $v = v_0$, then v is random. Otherwise, $v_i = \text{Hash}(v_{i-1} || \text{MAC}_{k_{i-1}}(e_{i-1}))$. The MAC is keyed with the previous authentication key k_{i-1}, which is either the output of a random oracle (if $i > 1$) or random (k_0). This means the adversary does not know the output of $\text{MAC}_{k_{i-1}}(e_{i-1}^j)$ that is part of the input for the random oracle to generate v. $\square$

5.2   Publicly Verifiable Proofs

Consistency. Assuming a collision resistant hash function, an unforgeable signature algorithm, monitors, and a perfect gossiping mechanism for snapshots, this follows directly from the properties of Balloon (Theorem 3 of [16]). However, our gossiping mechanisms are imperfect. We rely on the fact that (1) recipients can detect any modifications on their own events and (2) snapshots are chained together and occasionally timestamped, to deter the author from creating inconsistent snapshots. The latter one ensures that at least fork consistency as defined by Mazières and Shasha [14] is achieved. This means that in order to remain undetected the adversary needs to maintain a fork for every recipient it disclosed modified snapshots to.

Author. Assuming a collision resistant hash function and an unforgeable signature algorithm, the proof of author cannot be forged. A proof of author for an event is the output from B.query (**Membership**) for the event. Theorem 2 in [16] proves the security of a membership query in a Balloon. For an unforgeable signature algorithm, the existence of a signature is therefore non-repudiable evidence of the snapshot having been created with the signing key.

Time. Assuming a collision resistant hash function, an unforgeable signature algorithm and a secure time-stamping mechanism, the proof of author cannot be forged. A proof of time depends on the time-stamping mechanism, which is used in the snapshot against which the proof of author was created.

Recipient. Assuming a collision resistant hash function, an unforgeable signature algorithm and an unforgeable one-time MAC function, the proof of recipient cannot be forged. A proof of recipient consists of a proof of author, a public key pk, and an event key k'. The proof of author fixes the event, which consists of an event identifier e^{ID} and an event payload e^P. Now that the output of MAC function is fixed by the event identifier $e^{ID} = \text{MAC}_{k'}(\text{pk})$, for the adversary to come up with a different pk and k', it has to break the unforgeability of the one-time MAC function.

Message. Assuming a collision and pre-image resistant hash function, an unforgeable signature algorithm and an unforgeable one-time MAC function, the proof of message cannot be forged. From the proof of message, the proof of recipient can be derived by computing the event key $k' \leftarrow \text{Hash}(n)$. The proof of recipient fixes the payload e^P, the recipient's public key pk and the nonce n, since the prover provided a pre-image to k'. The payload consists of the ciphertext c and the ephemeral public key pk$'$, which also fixes the corresponding sk$'$. The prover provides sk$'$, which can easily be verified to be correct. This fixes all the input to our deterministic decryption function.

6 Related Work

In the setting of transparency logging, we build further upon the model and scheme by Pulls et al. [18] and Balloon [16] as introduced before. The scheme by Pulls et al. is based on hash- and MAC-chains, influenced by the secure log design of Schneier and Kelsey [19].

Ma and Tsudik [12] proposed a publicly verifiable FssAgg scheme by using an efficient aggregate signature scheme. The main drawbacks are a linear number of verification keys with the number of runs of the key update, and relative expensive bilinear map operations. Similarly, Logcrypt by Holt [11] also needs a linear number of verification keys with key updates. The efficient public verifiability, of both the entire Balloon and individual events, of Insynd comes from taking the same approach as (and building upon) the History Tree system by Crosby and Wallach [8] based on authenticated data structures. The main drawback of the work of Crosby and Wallach, and to a lesser degree of Insynd, is the reliance on a gossiping mechanism. Insynd takes the best of both worlds: the public verifiability from authenticated data structures based on Merkle trees, and the private all-or-nothing verifiability of the privately verifiable FssAgg scheme from the secure logging area. Users do not have to rely on perfect gossiping of snapshots, while the existence of private verifiability for recipients deters an adversary from abusing the lack of a perfect gossiping mechanism to begin with. This is similar to the approach of CONIKS [15], where users can verify their entries in a data structure as part of a privacy-friendly key management system. In CONIKS, users provide all data (their public key and related data) in the data structure concerning them. This is fundamentally different to Insynd, where the entire point of the scheme is for the author to inform recipients of the processing performed on their personal data. Therefore, the private verifiability mechanism for Insynd needs to be forward-secure with regard to the author.

PillarBox is a fast forward-secure logging system by Bowers *et al.* [6]. Beyond integrity protection, PillarBox also provides a property referred to as "stealth" that prevents a forward-secure adversary from distinguishing if any messages are inside an encapsulated buffer or not. This indistinguishability property is similar to our forward unlinkability of events property. PillarBox has also been designed to be fast with regard to securing logged messages. The goal is to minimise the probability that an adversary that compromises a system will be able to shut down PillarBox before the events that (presumably) were generated as a consequence of the adversary compromising the system are secured.

Pond and WhisperSystem's Signal[5] are prime examples of related secure asynchronous messaging systems. While these systems are for two-way communication, there are several similarities, such as dedicated servers for storing encrypted messages. Both Pond and Signal use the Signal protocol (previously known as Axolotl) [20]. The Signal protocol is inspired by the Off-the-Record (OTR) Messaging protocol [5] and provides among other things forward secrecy. Note that the goal of Insynd is for messages to be non-repudiable, unlike Pond, Signal and OTR that specifically want *deniability*. Insynd achieves non-repudiation through the use of Balloon and how we encrypt messages.

7   Performance

We implemented Insynd in the Go programming language, making use of the NaCl [4] library for the cryptographic building blocks. The performance benchmark focuses on the `insert` protocol since the other protocols are less frequently used. The source code and steps to reproduce our benchmark are publicly available at http://www.cs.kau.se/pulls/insynd/.

Figure 4 presents our benchmark, based on averages after 10 runs using Go's built-in benchmarking tool. We used a Debian 7.8 (x64) installation on a laptop with an Intel i5-3320M quad core 2.6 GHz CPU and 7.7 GB DDR3 RAM to run both the author and server. Note that the proofs of correct insertion into Balloon between author and server are still generated and verified.

Clearly, the smaller the message are, the more events can be sent (and the more potential recipients that can be served) per second. With at least 100 events to insert per run, we get ≈7000 events per second with 1 KiB messages. Using the same data as in Fig. 4a, Fig. 4b shows the goodput (the throughput excluding the event overhead of 112 bytes per event) for the different message sizes. At ≈800 100-KiB-messages per second (around at least 200 events to insert), the goodput is ≈80 MiB/s. 10 KiB messages offer a trade-off between goodput and number of events, providing 4000 events per second with ≈40 MiB/s goodput.

Insynd improves greatly on related work on transparency logging, and shows comparable performance to state-of-the-art secure logging systems. Ma and Tsudik [12], for their FssAgg schemes, achieve event generation (signing) in the order of milliseconds per event (using significantly older hardware than us).

---

[5] https://whispersystems.org, accessed 2016-07-06.

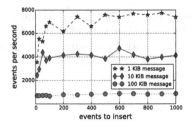
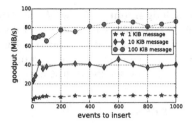

(a) Events per second in a 2^{20} Balloon.   (b) Goodput in a 2^{20} Balloon.

Fig. 4. A performance benchmark related to inserting events. The x-axis specifies the number of events to insert per run of the `insert` protocol.

Marson and Poettering [13], with their seekable sequential key generators, generate *key material* in a few microseconds. Note that for both these schemes, messages are not encrypted and hence the performance results only take into account the time for providing integrity protection. The performance results of Insynd, together with the two following schemes, include the time to encrypt messages in addition to providing integrity protection. Pulls *et al.* [18], for their transparency logging scheme, generate events in the order of tens of milliseconds per event. For PillarBox, Bowers *et al.* [6] generate events in the order of hundreds of microseconds per event, specifying an average time for event generation at 163 μs when storing syslog messages. Syslog messages are at most 1 KiB, so the average for Insynd of 142 μs at 7000 events per second is comparable.

8   Conclusions

Insynd is a cryptographic scheme for privacy-preserving transparency logging where messages are sent through an authenticated data structure (Balloon). The main contribution of Insynd is to provide publicly verifiable proofs of recipient and message of events within the setting of transparency logging, which dictates that events should be encrypted and unlinkable towards non-recipients. This significantly increases the utility of a transparency logging scheme as it enables users to take action without having to disclose everything that was logged for them. On top of this, Insynd improves further on existing transparency logging schemes by combining concepts from authenticated data structures, forward-secure key generation from the secure logging area, and on-going work on secure messaging protocols. Insynd provably achieves the security and privacy properties for a transparency logging scheme, as defined within the general framework of Pulls *et al.* [18], which was adjusted to take into account our publicly verifiable proofs and stronger adversarial model that assumes a forward-secure author and an untrusted server. Furthermore, our freely available proof of concept implementation shows that Insynd offers comparable performance for event generation to state-of-the-art secure logging systems like PillarBox [6].

Acknowledgements. We would like to thank Rasmus Dahlberg, Simone Fischer-Hübner, Stefan Lindskog, and Leonardo Martucci for their valuable feedback. Tobias Pulls has received funding from the Seventh Framework Programme for Research of the European Community under grant agreement no. 317550 and the HITS research profile funded by the Swedish Knowledge Foundation.

References

1. An, J.H.: Authenticated encryption in the public-key setting: Security notions and analyses. IACR Cryptology ePrint Archive 2001, 79 (2001)
2. Bellare, M., Boldyreva, A., Desai, A., Pointcheval, D.: Key-privacy in public-key encryption. In: Boyd, C. (ed.) ASIACRYPT 2001. LNCS, vol. 2248, pp. 566–582. Springer, Heidelberg (2001)
3. Bellare, M., Yee, B.S.: Forward-security in private-key cryptography. In: Joye, M. (ed.) CT-RSA 2003. LNCS, vol. 2612, pp. 1–18. Springer, Heidelberg (2003)
4. Bernstein, D.J., Lange, T., Schwabe, P.: The security impact of a new cryptographic library. In: Hevia, A., Neven, G. (eds.) LatinCrypt 2012. LNCS, vol. 7533, pp. 159–176. Springer, Heidelberg (2012)
5. Borisov, N., Goldberg, I., Brewer, E.A.: Off-the-record communication, or, why not to use PGP. In: WPES, pp. 77–84. ACM (2004)
6. Bowers, K.D., Hart, C., Juels, A., Triandopoulos, N.: PillarBox: combating next-generation malware with fast forward-secure logging. In: Stavrou, A., Bos, H., Portokalidis, G. (eds.) RAID 2014. LNCS, vol. 8688, pp. 46–67. Springer, Heidelberg (2014)
7. Buldas, A., Laud, P., Lipmaa, H., Villemson, J.: Time-stamping with binary linking schemes. In: Krawczyk, H. (ed.) CRYPTO 1998. LNCS, vol. 1462, pp. 486–501. Springer, Heidelberg (1998)
8. Crosby, S.A., Wallach, D.S.: Efficient data structures for tamper-evident logging. In: USENIX Security Symposium, pp. 317–334. USENIX (2009)
9. Dingledine, R., Mathewson, N., Syverson, P.F.: Tor: the second-generation onion router. In: USENIX Security Symposium, pp. 303–320. USENIX (2004)
10. FIDIS WP7: D 7.12: Behavioural Biometric Profiling and Transparency Enhancing Tools. Future of Identity in the Information Society, March 2009
11. Holt, J.E.: Logcrypt: forward security and public verification for secure audit logs. In: Australasian Workshops on Grid Computing and e-Research. ACS (2006)
12. Ma, D., Tsudik, G.: A new approach to secure logging. TOS $5(1)$, 1–21 (2009)
13. Marson, G.A., Poettering, B.: Even more practical secure logging: tree-based seekable sequential key generators. In: Kutyłowski, M., Vaidya, J. (eds.) ICAIS 2014, Part II. LNCS, vol. 8713, pp. 37–54. Springer, Heidelberg (2014)
14. Mazières, D., Shasha, D.: Building secure file systems out of byzantine storage. In: Symposium on Principles of Distributed Computing, pp. 108–117. ACM (2002)
15. Melara, M.S., Blankstein, A., Bonneau, J., Felten, E.W., Freedman, M.J.: CONIKS: a privacy-preserving consistent key service for secure end-to-end communication. In: USENIX Security Symposium, pp. 383–398. USENIX (2015)
16. Pulls, T., Peeters, R.: Balloon: a forward-secure append-only persistent authenticated data structure. In: Pernul, G., Ryan, P.Y.A., Weippl, E. (eds.) ESORICS. LNCS, vol. 9327, pp. 622–641. Springer, Heidelberg (2015). doi:10.1007/978-3-319-24177-7_31
17. Pulls, T., Peeters, R.: Insynd: Improved privacy-preserving transparency logging. Cryptology ePrint Archive, Report 2015/150 (2015)

18. Pulls, T., Peeters, R., Wouters, K.: Distributed privacy-preserving transparency logging. In: WPES, pp. 83–94. ACM (2013)
19. Schneier, B., Kelsey, J.: Cryptographic support for secure logs on untrusted machines. In: USENIX Security Symposium, pp. 53–62. USENIX (1998)
20. Unger, N., Dechand, S., Bonneau, J., Fahl, S., Perl, H., Goldberg, I., Smith, M.: Sok: secure messaging. In: 2015 IEEE Symposium on Security and Privacy, SP 2015, San Jose, CA, USA, 17–21 May 2015. IEEE Computer Society (2015)

Secure Logging Schemes
and Certificate Transparency

Benjamin Dowling[1], Felix Günther[2]([✉]), Udyani Herath[1], and Douglas Stebila[3]

[1] Queensland University of Technology, Brisbane, Australia
[2] Technische Universität Darmstadt, Darmstadt, Germany
guenther@cs.tu-darmstadt.de
[3] McMaster University, Hamilton, ON, Canada

Abstract. Since hundreds of certificate authorities (CAs) can issue browser-trusted certificates, it can be difficult for domain owners to detect certificates that have been fraudulently issued for their domain. *Certificate Transparency (CT)* is a recent standard by the Internet Engineering Task Force (IETF) that aims to construct public logs of all certificates issued by CAs, making it easier for domain owners to monitor for fraudulently issued certificates. To avoid relying on trusted log servers, CT includes mechanisms by which monitors and auditors can check whether logs are behaving honestly or not; these mechanisms are primarily based on Merkle tree hashing and authentication proofs. Given that CT is now being deployed, it is important to verify that it achieves its security goals. In this work, we define four security properties of logging schemes such as CT that can be assured via *cryptographic means*, and show that CT does achieve these security properties. We consider two classes of security goals: those involving security against a malicious logger attempting to present different views of the log to different parties or at different points in time, and those involving security against malicious monitors who attempt to frame an honest log for failing to include a certificate in the log. We show that Certificate Transparency satisfies these security properties under various assumptions on Merkle trees all of which reduce to collision resistance of the underlying hash function (and in one case with the additional assumption of unforgeable signatures).

1 Introduction

The security of web communication via the Transport Layer Security (TLS) protocol relies on safe distribution of public keys in the form of X.509 certificates. *Certificate authorities (CAs)* are trusted third parties that endorse the public keys of *subjects* by performing checks and issuing certificates. Web browsers can accept certificates from hundreds of CAs, and relying parties are unable to determine whether certificates were issued at the request of the subject or fraudulently issued by the CAs, whether by mistake or due to compromise.

In recent years there have been high-profile cases of misissued certificates being used to spoof legitimate websites. For example, in 2011 an intruder managed to

© Springer International Publishing Switzerland 2016
I. Askoxylakis et al. (Eds.): ESORICS 2016, Part II, LNCS 9879, pp. 140–158, 2016.
DOI: 10.1007/978-3-319-45741-3_8

issue itself a valid certificate for the domain `google.com` and its subdomains from the prominent Dutch Certificate Authority DigiNotar [11]. This certificate was issued in July 2011 and may have been used maliciously for weeks before the detection on August 28, 2011, of large-scale man-in-the-middle (MITM) attacks on multiple users in Iran. In another instance, the Comodo Group suffered from an attack which resulted in the issuance of nine fraudulent certificates for domains owned by Google, Yahoo!, Skype, and others [5].

Certificate Transparency (CT) [17,18] is an experimental protocol originally proposed by Google and standardized by the Internet Engineering Task Force (IETF) Public Notary Transparency working group to mitigate the threat of fraudulently issued certificates by publicly logging certificates. CT provides an open auditing and monitoring system which allows domain owners to verify that no fraudulent certificates have been issued for their domains. The end goal of Certificate Transparency is that web clients should only accept certificates that are publicly logged and that it should be impossible for a CA to issue a certificate for a domain without it being publicly visible. Recent incidents demonstrated the effectiveness of CT logs: Google employees detected unrequested certificates for two of their subdomains issued by a Symantec sub-CA Thawte [30]. The certificates were issued on September 14, 2015 and detected by September 17, 2015; the certificates were revoked immediately, limiting the exposure of the certificates to just three days. In another case, the Facebook security team discovered an issuance of two certificates on multiple subdomains violating Facebook's internal security policies [14]. The incident was investigated and both certificates revoked within hours, even before they were deployed to production systems.

1.1 The Web PKI and Certificate Transparency

The basic web public key infrastructure (PKI) includes several types of entities which perform different tasks: web servers, certificate authorities, browser vendors and web browsers. The Certificate Transparency framework adds several new entities which help maintain and monitor public logs:

- *Loggers* or *log servers* maintain publicly accessible append-only logs of certificates. These certificates are received from submitters. As a new entry might not be published immediately for operational reasoning, the logger provides each submitter with a promise to log the certificate within a certain amount of time; the promise is called a *signed certificate timestamp (SCT)*.
- *Submitters*, submit certificates (or partially completed *pre-certificates*) to a log server and receive a signed certificate timestamp from the log.
- *Monitors* are public or private services that watch for misbehaving logs or suspicious certificates by periodically contacting and downloading information from log servers. They inspect every new entry in a log, keep copies of the entire log, and verify the consistency between published revisions of the log.
- *Auditors* verify the correct behaviour of a log, checking that certificates that a logger has promised to include are present in the log. Auditors may be standalone entities or integrated into monitors or web clients.

In CT, the original entities from the web PKI also have some additional tasks:

- CAs should act as submitters above.
- Web servers should include their SCT along with the certificate when communicating with clients. Web servers may choose to submit their certificate to a log server if their CA does not do so for them.
- Web clients, upon receiving an SCT from a web server, may choose to verify that the log named in the SCT actually has publicly logged the certificate (thereby taking on the role of an auditor as above).
- Browser vendors may push updates that remove CAs or revoke certificates based on claims from monitors and web servers about misbehaving CAs.

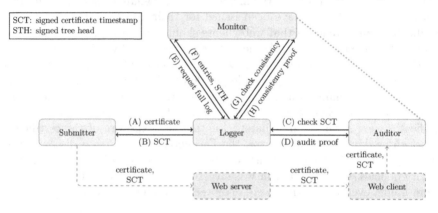

Fig. 1. Overview over the interaction between entities in Certificate Transparency; see Sect. 1.1 for details. Solid-line interactions and solid-line, orange entities are captured by the model in our work while dashed-line interactions and dashed-line, gray entities are not captured. Dotted line–connected entities (monitors and auditors or auditors and web clients) might be the same physical entity. (Color figure online)

Figure 1 provides an overview of the involved parties and their interactions in CT[1]. At the submission of a new certificate entry (step A), the logger returns a signed certificate timestamp (SCT) (step B), which is a promise to include the entry in the log. Every log has a published parameter called a *maximum merge delay (MMD)* which indicates the maximum period between issuing a timestamp and the inclusion of the certificate into the log.

In CT, the logger stores the entries of the log in an append-only Merkle hash tree [24,25], a form of a tamper-evident history tree [6,7]. Recall for Merkle trees, data is placed at the leaves of a binary tree and each intermediate node is the hash of its two child nodes; the root of the trees acts as a fingerprint of all included data. In CT, the root of the tree is signed and published by the logger, and is called the *signed tree head (STH)*. The observed fingerprints are exchanged by all parties in the system through a so-called "gossiping" protocol [27].

---

[1] Note that the labeling of interactions is simply for reference and does not indicate a particular order of the displayed requests.

Gossiping allows monitors, auditors, and web clients to share information they receive from log servers, with the goal of collectively detecting misbehavior of log servers while limiting the damage to user privacy. The parties who hold the same fingerprints of a log are (cryptographically) assured that they have the same view of the log at the point in time represented by the fingerprint. Gossiping can be implemented through SCT feedback (where web clients send SCTs through HTTPS servers), STH pollination (where web clients and CT auditors/monitors use HTTPS servers as STH pools) and trusted auditor streams (where web clients directly communicate with trusted CT auditors/monitors).

To convince other parties that promised certificates are included in a log, and that subsequent published fingerprints are consistent, the logger employs two types of cryptographic proofs: audit proofs and consistency proofs.

An *audit proof* allows an auditor to verify that a particular certificate/SCT that a logger has promised to include is actually included in the log represented by a fingerprint, shown in steps C and D. In CT, an audit proof is essentially an authentication path in the Merkle tree from the leaf containing the certificate in question to the root hash/fingerprint contained in the signed tree hash.

A *consistency proof* allows an auditor or monitor to verify that the log is append-only, in particular that the log represented by a fingerprint at one point in time t_0 is a prefix of the log represented by a fingerprint at a later point in time $t_1 > t_0$, shown in steps G and H. In CT, a consistency proof is a subset of intermediate nodes in the Merkle tree needed to connect the two root hashes.

Monitors can also request that a logger provides them with the full set of entries represented by a fingerprint (steps E and F). In CT, this can be verified by recomputing the Merkle tree hash of the entries.

As a starting point for a threat model, the informational IETF draft "Attack Model for Certificate Transparency" [15] describes potential attack scenarios when Certificate Transparency is used in the context of web public-key infrastructure.

1.2 Our Contribution

Given the practical significance of Certificate Transparency, it is important to have a formal understanding of the security goals of CT and analyse whether CT achieves those goals. The objective of our work is to define security goals of logging schemes using the formalism of provable security, and attempt to prove that CT satisfies these security goals under suitable cryptographic assumptions. Our model of logging schemes does not assume a PKI context, so we do not assume that log entries must have a particular syntax, and thus we leave the threats involving validity or syntax of log entries to existing analyses on certificate validity. Similarly, we omit consideration of threats where an entity *fails* to act.

As noted above, we will focus on two particular threats in the CT threat model: whether a misbehaving log server can present different views of the log and whether a misbehaving monitor can frame an honest log server for bad behaviour. Thus, our model will focus on two entities: the logger and the monitor/auditor.

Definition of Logging Schemes. In Sect. 3 we formally define logging schemes, naming operations that each entity can perform. This model does not attach any semantic meaning to the entries being logged; in particular, we do not assume that log entries are certificates. Subsequently, we describe the operations of Certificate Transparency as a specific instantiation of the logging scheme framework.

Security Definitions. Next, we introduce cryptographic security properties for logging schemes in Sect. 4 that are inspired by the CT threat model but reflect the corresponding ideas in general terms. More specifically, we treat two types of properties. First, we define security notions which concern a malicious logger:

- entry-coll: can a malicious logger present two different sets of entries corresponding to the same fingerprint?
- proof-coll: can a malicious logger present an audit proof that claims a single fingerprint represents both a particular entry as well as a set of entries such that the particular entry is not actually in the list of entries?
- entry-cons: can a malicious logger present two fingerprints connected by a valid consistency proof and two sets of entries such that the entries corresponding to the first fingerprint are not a prefix of the entries corresponding to the second fingerprint?

Second, we define a security notion concerning a malicious monitor:

- promise-incl: can a malicious monitor frame an honest logger for not including a promised entry when it actually has?

Security of Certificate Transparency. Finally, we analyze the security of Certificate Transparency in Sect. 5 and show that CT both prevents logger misbehaviour (i.e., CT satisfies the entry-coll, proof-coll, and entry-cons security properties) as well as protection from framing of honest loggers by misbehaving monitors (i.e., CT satisfies the promise-incl property.) All of these proofs are based on properties of Merkle tree hashing and audit/consistency proofs, all of which ultimately derive from the collision resistance of the hash function. The last property, promise-incl, also depends on the unforgeability of the signature scheme used by loggers.

Generality of Definitions. Our definition of a logging scheme and its security properties are not specific to CT, and have the potential to be applied to other constructions. In Sect. 3.3, we discuss the applicability of our definitions to CONIKS [23], a logging scheme aimed at transparency of user keys: our logging scheme definitions capture some aspects of CONIKS, but also highlights important differences between the functionality and goals of CT versus CONIKS.

1.3   Related Work

New PKI Technologies. Recent certificate mis-issuances and security breaches in CAs have motivated research in alternatives to having a trusted third party vouching for the binding between domain name and its private key. *Public key pinning* [10] and *DANE* [13] are such proposals that allow domain owners to proactively and directly state their trusted public keys for the domain. Certificate Transparency takes a reactive rather than a proactive approach: instead of preventing mis-issuance in the first place, it aims to *detect* mis-issuance by making certificates visible through a public authenticated log.

History Trees. The data structures in CT are similar to the *history trees* of Crosby and Wallach [6,7]. Two of their results [6] connect with our security notions: their Corollary 1 shows that "reconstructed hashes" that are equal imply the entry sets from which they were constructed are equal, where "reconstructed hashes" can mean reconstructed from the leaves directly (like in a full hash tree computation) or from membership proofs. Their Theorem 1 shows that, given a consistency proof between two roots and a membership proof for the same index to each root (two membership proofs total), the leaves at that index must be the same in both trees; this is similar to our entry-cons property, though we focus on entry sets rather than membership proofs. A limitation of Crosby's results is that they assume that each root was computed from an underlying entry set, but one cannot be sure when the adversary generates roots (as in CT); our definitions make no such assumption. We furthermore capture several extensions that CT makes, including delays for entry inclusion and protection of honest loggers from framing (our promise-incl property). Finally, our presentation is notably different: Crosby's descriptions of the history tree operations and the proofs [6, Sect. 3] are generally descriptive rather than algorithmic, whereas we state the operations fully algorithmically and provide complete algorithmic reductions for all proofs.

In recent years a few more approaches have emerged around the concept of *transparency logs*, including revocation [19,29] (which we omit in this work as they are not under consideration by the IETF Public Notary Transparency working group) or limitations on certificate issuance, validation, and update [1,16]. The Electronic Frontier Foundation's *Sovereign Keys Project* [9] combines transparency logs with cross-signing of keys. Melara et al. [23] present *CONIKS*, a system focusing on key transparency in end-to-end encryption/secure messaging scenarios. CONIKS eliminates the need for global third party monitors and aims at additional privacy properties for identity–key bindings, however without providing a formal security model or cryptographic proofs.

Merkle Trees. Introduced by Merkle [24], Merkle trees have been used in many areas of cryptography and computer science, including in the construction of public key signatures from hash functions [25]. Most uses of Merkle trees concern a static dataset, but in CT we are concerned with a dynamic dataset, and in particular the append-only nature of the dataset.

There has been some work on authentication trees and more generally signatures on dynamic data sets. Bellare et al. [2,3] introduced the notion of *incremental cryptography*. Naor and Nissim [26] use dynamic Merkle trees in the context of certificate revocation and updates, Li et al. [20] apply them to authenticate index structures in outsourced databases. Villemson [31] and Ogawa et al. [28] investigated the characteristics of (generalizations of) incremental Merkle trees.

Cryptographic PKI Analyses. Maurer [22] introduced a formal model for public key infrastructures (PKIs) which subsequently was further extended [4,21]. This line of work approaches the dynamic nature of PKI issuance through an event-based system that captures the view of potential users at a certain point in time, using a combination of events that have happened and logical rules that infer certain conclusions from events. Our work differs from this approach by following a game-based approach focusing on the interaction between the parties involved. Our approach also conceptually distinguishes between values generated by honest parties, claims by dishonest parties, and conclusions drawn from events.

2 Cryptographic Building Blocks

Notation. We denote by $\vec{E}$ an ordered list of entries, where () denotes the empty list. Indexing is 0-based: $\vec{E} = (e_0, \ldots, e_{n-1})$, and we write $\vec{E}[i]$ to denote e_i and $\vec{E}[i:j]$ to denote the sublist $(e_i, \ldots, e_{j-1})$. We adopt the convention that $\vec{E}[-1] = ()$. We write $e \in \vec{E}$ to indicate that an entry e is contained in the list $\vec{E}$. We let $\vec{E} \| \vec{E}'$ denote the concatenation of two entry lists and write $\vec{E} \prec \vec{E}'$ if $\vec{E}$ is a prefix of $\vec{E}'$. If we define $P \leftarrow (t, e, \sigma)$, then we can later access fields of P using "object-oriented" notation: $P.t$, $P.e$, $P.\sigma$. Moreover, if $\vec{P}$ is a list $(P_0, \ldots, P_{n-1})$, then the notation $\vec{P}.e$ means the list $(P_0.e, \ldots, P_{n-1}.e)$. The expression $k \leftarrow 2^{\lceil \log_2(n/2) \rceil}$ corresponds to setting k to be the largest power of two less than n, i.e., $\frac{n}{2} \leq k = 2^i < n$.

We rely on the standard notion of signature schemes and existential unforgeability under chosen-message attacks [12], and the corresponding advantage $\mathrm{Adv}_{\mathrm{SIG}}^{\mathrm{euf\text{-}cma}}(\mathcal{A})$ of an adversary $\mathcal{A}$ breaking this notion for a scheme SIG.

Definition 1 (Hash Collision Finding). *Let $\mathcal{M}$ be a set, let $\mathrm{H} : \mathcal{M} \to \{0,1\}^\lambda$ be an unkeyed hash function, and let $\mathcal{A}$ be an algorithm. We say that $\mathcal{A}$ finds a collision in H if $\mathcal{A}$ outputs a pair (m, m') such that $m \neq m'$ and $\mathrm{H}(m) = \mathrm{H}(m')$.*

2.1 Merkle Trees

The use of hash trees for authenticating large amounts of data was first proposed by Merkle [24,25]. Let $\mathrm{H} : \{0,1\}^* \to \{0,1\}^\lambda$ be a hash function. In a Merkle hash tree for $\vec{E}$, the values of $\vec{E}$ are placed at the leaves of a binary tree and each intermediate node is the hash of its two child nodes; the root of the trees acts as a fingerprint of all the data contained in the tree; this is the output of the algorithm $\mathrm{MTH_H}(\vec{E})$ in Fig. 3. Note the use of prefixes 0 and 1 in hash function calculations provides "domain separation" between hash calculations for leaves $(\mathrm{H}(0\| \ldots))$ and intermediate nodes $(\mathrm{H}(1\| \ldots))$; preventing an attacker from gluing part of a tree into a leaf or vice versa.

A common technique is the use of an *authentication path* to demonstrate that a piece of data is in a leaf of a tree corresponding to a particular root. The

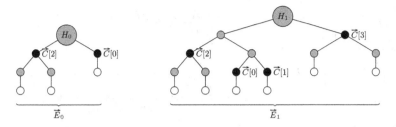

Fig. 2. Merkle tree consistency proof $\vec{C} = (\vec{C}[0], \ldots, \vec{C}[3])$ between roots H_0 (for a tree of size 3) and H_1 (for a tree of size 6). ○ denotes leaf nodes, ◐ denotes inner nodes, ● denotes nodes corresponding to consistency proof values.

authentication path generation algorithm $\text{Path}_\text{H}(m, \vec{E})$ and verification algorithm $\text{CheckPath}_\text{H}(e, H, n, \vec{A}, m)$ are shown in Fig. 3.

A lesser-known technique is the use of a *consistency proof* to demonstrate that the data corresponding to one root is a subset (prefix) of the data corresponding to another root, used, for example, in the context of tamper-evident history trees [6,7]. In Fig. 2, the consistency proof $\vec{C}$ shows that the data corresponding to root H_0 is a prefix of the data corresponding to root H_1. Consistency proofs reconstruct each of the two roots from relevant parts of the proof and compare them against the actual roots; the size of the two trees is essential in verifying a consistency proof. Consistency proofs may be viewed as an authentication path from the inner node immediately above the last leaf node in the first tree (i.e., an authentication path from $\text{H}(e_2) = \vec{C}[0]$ to root H_1 in the right side of Fig. 2). The consistency proof generation algorithm $\text{ConsProof}_\text{H}(m, n, \vec{E})$ and verification algorithm $\text{CheckConsProof}_\text{H}(n_0, H_0, n_1, H_1, \vec{C})$ are shown in Fig. 3. We have reformulated these from how they appear in the RFC [17]: ours use a top-down recursive approach, whereas the RFC versions are bottom-up looping algorithms; the two are equivalent, but our versions are more helpful in proving our theorems.

2.2   Merkle Tree Security Properties

We now note some well-known facts about the collision resistance of Merkle tree hashing and the security of authentication paths in Merkle trees [24,25]. For completeness, full proofs are given in the full version [8].

Lemma 1 (Collision Resistance of Merkle Trees). *If* H *is collision-resistant, then Merkle-tree hashing using* H *is also collision-resistant. More precisely, if $\mathcal{A}$ finds a collision in* MTH_H*, then there exists algorithm $\mathcal{B}_1^\mathcal{A}$ that finds a collision in* H*. Moreover, the runtime of $\mathcal{B}_1^\mathcal{A}$ consists of the runtime of $\mathcal{A}$, plus at most a quadratic (in the size of the larger list) number of hash evaluations.*

Lemma 2 (Authentication Paths Consistency). *If* H *is collision-resistant, then no* $\text{CheckPath}_\text{H}$ *authentication path $\vec{A}$ can be generated*

$\underline{\text{MTH}_H(\vec{E}) \to H:}$
1: $n \leftarrow |\vec{E}|$
2: **if** $n = 1$, **return** $H(0\|\vec{E}[0])$
3: **else** $(n > 1)$
4:   $k \leftarrow 2^{\lceil \log_2(n/2) \rceil}$
5:   **return** $H(1\|\text{MTH}_H(\vec{E}[0:k])$
6:           $\|\text{MTH}_H(\vec{E}[k:n])$

$\underline{\text{Path}_H(m, \vec{E}) \to \vec{A}:}$
1: $n \leftarrow |\vec{E}|$
2: **if** $n = 1$, **return** ()
3: **else** $(n > 1)$
4:   $k \leftarrow 2^{\lceil \log_2(n/2) \rceil}$
5:   **if** $m < k$
6:     **return** $\text{Path}_H(m, \vec{E}[0:k])$
7:           $\|\text{MTH}_H(\vec{E}[k:n])$
8:   **else** $(m \geq k)$
9:     **return** $\text{Path}_H(m - k, \vec{E}[k:n])$
10:          $\|\text{MTH}_H(\vec{E}[0:k])$

$\underline{\text{CheckPath}_H(e, H, n, \vec{A}, m) \to \{0, 1\}:}$
1: $H' \leftarrow \text{RootFromPath}_H(e, n, \vec{A}, m)$
2: **return** $(H = H')$

$\underline{\text{RootFromPath}_H(e, n, \vec{A}, m) \to H:}$
1: **if** $n = 1$, **return** $H(0\|e)$
2: $k \leftarrow 2^{\lceil \log_2(n/2) \rceil}$
3: **if** $m < k$
4:   $\ell \leftarrow \text{RootFromPath}_H(e, k, \vec{A}[0:|\vec{A}|-1], m)$
5:   $r \leftarrow \vec{A}[|\vec{A}|-1]$
6: **else** $(m \geq k)$
7:   $\ell \leftarrow \vec{A}[|\vec{A}|-1]$
8:   $r \leftarrow \text{RootFromPath}_H(e, n - k,$
9:               $\vec{A}[0:|\vec{A}|-1], m - k)$
10: **return** $H(1\|\ell\|r)$

$\underline{\text{ConsProof}_H(m, n, \vec{E}) \to \vec{C}:}$
1: // require: $0 \leq m \leq n \leq |\vec{E}|$
2: **if** $m = n$
3:   **return** ()
4: **else** $(m < n)$
5:   **return** $\text{ConsProofSub}_H(m, \vec{E}[0:n], \text{true})$

$\underline{\text{ConsProofSub}_H(m, \vec{E}, b) \to \vec{C}:}$
1: $n \leftarrow |\vec{E}|$
2: **if** $(m = n) \land (b = \text{false})$
3:   **return** $\text{MTH}_H(\vec{E}[0:m])$
4: **else**
5:   $k \leftarrow 2^{\lceil \log_2(n)/2 \rceil}$
6:   **if** $m \leq k$
7:     **return** $\text{ConsProofSub}_H(m, \vec{E}[0:k], b)$
8:           $\|\text{MTH}_H(\vec{E}[k:n])$
9:   **else** $(m > k)$
10:    **return** $\text{ConsProofSub}_H(m - k, \vec{E}[k:n], \text{false})$
11:          $\|\text{MTH}_H(\vec{E}[0:k])$

$\underline{\text{CheckConsProof}_H(n_0, H_0, n_1, H_1, \vec{C}) \to b:}$
1: **if** n_0 is a power of two, $\vec{C} \leftarrow H_0\|\vec{C}$
2: $H_0' \leftarrow \text{Root0FromConsProof}_H(\vec{C}, n_0, n_1)$
3: $H_1' \leftarrow \text{Root1FromConsProof}_H(\vec{C}, n_0, n_1)$
4: **return** $((H_0 = H_0') \land (H_1 = H_1'))$

$\underline{\text{Root0FromConsProof}_H(\vec{C}, n_0, n_1) \to H:}$
1: $k \leftarrow 2^{\lceil \log_2(n_1)/2 \rceil}$
2: **if** $n_0 < k$
3:   **return** $\text{Root0FromConsProof}_H(\vec{C}[0:|\vec{C}|-1], n_0, k)$
4: **elsif** $n_0 = k$, **return** $\vec{C}[|\vec{C}|-2]$
5: **else**
6:   $\ell \leftarrow \vec{C}[|\vec{C}|-1]$
7:   $r \leftarrow \text{Root0FromConsProof}_H(\vec{C}[0:|\vec{C}|-1],$
8:               $n_0 - k, n_1 - k)$
9:   **return** $H(1\|\ell\|r)$

$\underline{\text{Root1FromConsProof}_H(\vec{C}, n_0, n_1) \to H:}$
1: **if** $|\vec{C}| = 2$, **return** $H(1\|\vec{C}[0]\|\vec{C}[1])$
2: $k \leftarrow 2^{\lceil \log_2(n_1)/2 \rceil}$
3: **if** $n_0 < k$
4:   $\ell \leftarrow \text{Root1FromConsProof}_H(\vec{C}[0:|\vec{C}|-1], n_0, k)$
5:   $r \leftarrow \vec{C}[|\vec{C}|-1]$
6: **else**
7:   $\ell \leftarrow \vec{C}[|\vec{C}|-1]$
8:   $r \leftarrow \text{Root1FromConsProof}_H(\vec{C}[0:|\vec{C}|-1],$
9:               $n_0 - k, n_1 - k)$
10: **return** $H(1\|\ell\|r)$

Fig. 3. Merkle tree algorithms

with respect to Merkle-tree hashing MTH_H for an entry e not contained in the Merkle tree. More precisely, if $\mathcal{A}$ outputs $(e, \vec{E}, \vec{A}, m)$ such that $\text{CheckPath}_H(e, \text{MTH}_H(\vec{E}), |\vec{E}|, \vec{A}, m) = 1$ and $e \notin \vec{E}$, then there exists algorithm $\mathcal{B}_2^{\mathcal{A}}$ that finds a collision in H. Moreover, the runtime of $\mathcal{B}_2^{\mathcal{A}}$ consists of the runtime of $\mathcal{A}$, plus at most a quadratic (in $|\vec{E}|$) number of hash evaluations.

3   Logging Schemes

In this section we specify the algorithms that comprise a logging scheme and formulate CT as a logging scheme.

3.1   Definition of Logging Schemes

Our definition of a logging scheme is based around the certificate transparency functionality, but is designed to be potentially more general. We use non-CT specific language (such as "fingerprint" instead of the CT-specific "signed tree head"), and our logging scheme is not actually about certificates—any type of object can be logged.

Definition 2 (Logging Scheme). *A logging scheme LS consists of the following algorithms, some of which are run by a logger and some of which are run by a monitor/auditor.*

The following algorithm is used by a logger to initialize its log:

- KeyGen() $\xrightarrow{\$}$ (st, pk, sk): *A probabilistic algorithm that returns a state stand a public key/secret key pair (pk, sk).*

The following algorithms are used by a logger to add entries to its log, using a two-step process of promising to add an entry to the log and then a batch update actually adding the entries:

- PromiseEntry(e, t, sk) $\xrightarrow{\$}$ P: *A probabilistic algorithm that takes as input a log entry e, a time t, and the secret key sk and outputs a promise P; the promise contains the entry and time as subfields P.e and P.t.*
- UpdateLog$(st, \vec{P}, t, sk)$ $\xrightarrow{\$}$ (st', F): *A probabilistic algorithm that takes as input a state st, a potentially empty ordered list of promises $\vec{P}$ to add to the log, a time t and the secret key sk and returns an updated state st' and a fingerprint F (where the latter includes the indicated time, denoted as F.t)*

The following algorithms are used by a logger to demonstrate various properties to monitors/auditors:

- PresentEntries(st, F) $\rightarrow$ $\vec{E}$ or $\perp$: *A deterministic algorithm that takes as input a state stand a fingerprint F and outputs an ordered list of log entries $\vec{E}$, or an error symbol $\perp$.*
- ProveMembership(st, e, F) $\xrightarrow{\$}$ $\vec{M}$ or $\perp$: *A probabilistic algorithm[2] that takes as input a state st, a log entry e, and a fingerprint F and outputs a membership proof $\vec{M}$, or an error symbol $\perp$.*
- ProveConsistency(st, F_0, F_1) $\xrightarrow{\$}$ $\vec{C}$ or $\perp$: *A probabilistic algorithm[2] that takes as input a state st and two fingerprints F_0 and F_1 and outputs a consistency proof $\vec{C}$, or an error symbol $\perp$.*

The following algorithms are used by monitors/auditors to check a log:

- CheckPromise(P, pk) $\rightarrow$ $\{0, 1\}$: *A deterministic algorithm that takes as input a promise P (which includes an entry P.e) and a public key pk and outputs a bit $b \in \{0, 1\}$.*

---

[2] In CT, ProveMembership and ProveConsistency are deterministic, though in principle these could be probabilistic in a logging scheme.

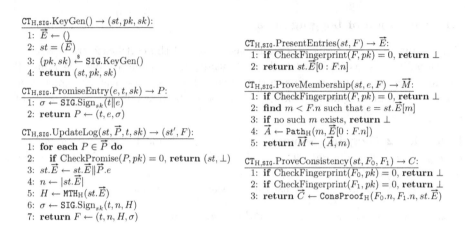

Fig. 4. Certificate Transparency: algorithms run by loggers.

- CheckFingerprint$(F, pk) \rightarrow \{0, 1\}$: *A deterministic algorithm that takes as input a fingerprint F and a public key pk and outputs a bit $b \in \{0, 1\}$.*
- CheckEntries$(\vec{E}, F, pk) \rightarrow \{0, 1\}$: *A deterministic algorithm that takes as input an ordered list of log entries $\vec{E}$, a fingerprint F, and a public key pk and outputs a bit $b \in \{0, 1\}$.*
- CheckMembership$(F, e, \vec{M}, pk) \rightarrow \{0, 1\}$: *A deterministic algorithm that takes as input a fingerprint F, an entry e, a membership proof $\vec{M}$, and a public key pk and outputs a bit $b \in \{0, 1\}$.*
- CheckConsistency$(F_0, F_1, \vec{C}, pk) \rightarrow \{0, 1\}$: *A deterministic algorithm that takes as input two fingerprints F_0 and F_1, a consistency proof $\vec{C}$, and a public key pk and outputs a bit $b \in \{0, 1\}$.*

Correctness of a logging scheme is defined in the natural way and is omitted due to space constraints; see the full version [8].

3.2 Instantiation of Certificate Transparency as a Logging Scheme

Figures 4 and 5 formulate Certificate Transparency using H and SIG as a logging scheme $\mathsf{CT}_{\mathsf{H},\mathsf{SIG}}$ (i.e., following Definition 2). A log entry in CT is a chain of X.509 certificates: the certificate (or partially completed pre-certificate) itself, and each intermediate CA's certificate leading to the root CA's cert. We treat entries in our formalization of logging schemes as opaque bit strings: our fomulation hence omits any syntactical checks for the entries it manages; adding these checks is independent of the logging properties. The promise P is called a *signed certificate timestamp* (SCT). The fingerprint F is called the *signed tree head* (STH).

$\mathrm{CT}_{\mathsf{H,SIG}}.\mathrm{CheckPromise}(P, pk) \to b$:
1: **return** $\mathrm{SIG.Vfy}_{pk}(P.t \| P.e, P.\sigma)$

$\mathrm{CT}_{\mathsf{H,SIG}}.\mathrm{CheckFingerprint}(F, pk) \to b$:
1: **return** $\mathrm{SIG.Vfy}_{pk}(F.t \| F.n \| F.H, F.\sigma)$

$\mathrm{CT}_{\mathsf{H,SIG}}.\mathrm{CheckEntries}(\vec{E}, F, pk) \to b$:
1: **if** $\mathrm{CheckFingerprint}(F, pk) = 0$, **return** 0
2: $H' \leftarrow \mathrm{MTH}_\mathsf{H}(\vec{E})$
3: **return** $(|\vec{E}| = F.n) \wedge (H' = F.H)$

$\mathrm{CT}_{\mathsf{H,SIG}}.\mathrm{CheckMembership}(F, e, \vec{M}, pk) \to b$:
1: **if** $\mathrm{CheckFingerprint}(F, pk) = 0$, **return** 0
2: **return** $\mathrm{CheckPath}_\mathsf{H}(e, F.H, F.n, \vec{M}.\vec{A}, \vec{M}.m)$

$\mathrm{CT}_{\mathsf{H,SIG}}.\mathrm{CheckConsistency}(F_0, F_1, \vec{C}, pk) \to b$:
1: **if** $\mathrm{CheckFingerprint}(F_0, pk) = 0$, **return** 0
2: **if** $\mathrm{CheckFingerprint}(F_1, pk) = 0$, **return** 0
3: **return** $\mathrm{CheckConsProof}(F_0.n, F_0.H, F_1.n, F_1.H, \vec{C})$

Fig. 5. Certificate Transparency: algorithms run by monitors/auditors.

3.3 CONIKS as a Logging Scheme

CONIKS [23] is a recent transparency log scheme that aims to enable privacy-preserving transparency logging for end-user keys, for applications such as secure messaging. Our definition of logging scheme can capture several aspects of CONIKS' functionality and security, but also serves to highlight some significant differences between CT and CONIKS.

CONIKS also uses a Merkle tree structure, but in contrast to CT uses a Merkle *prefix* tree in which some attribute of an entry (e.g., the user's identity) determines its position. The tree root is computed both from present entries and placeholder values for empty subtrees, allowing efficient calculation over very large but mostly empty trees. It is signed and published by the logger as the *signed tree root (STR)*. Membership proofs can be performed in the standard way using Merkle authentication paths. Signed tree roots are linked over time using a hash chain, including the previous signed tree root. However, this does not enable consistency proofs as in CT: verification that a key that was present in STR_i is also present in STR_j requires fresh membership proof of that key's presence in STR_j. Two core security properties of CONIKS are *non-equivocation* (a provider cannot present diverging views) and *privacy-preserving consistency proofs* (privacy here meaning with respect to other entries' information).

CONIKS can be mapped onto the following notions in our definition of a logging scheme. The KeyGen algorithm is run by the logger. CONIKS has no separate notion of promise and log entry, combining PromiseEntry and UpdateLog. CheckFingerprint will verify a signed tree root similarly. Aiming at privacy, CONIKS does not include PresentEntries and CheckEntries. ProveMembership and CheckMembership are supported. ProveConsistency and CheckConsistency are not directly supported; as noted above, an auditor would need to use ProveMembership and CheckMembership for each entry.

In terms of security properties, none of ours directly map onto CONIKS' notions, primarily because of including CheckEntries. However, some notions are similar. Non-equivocation is similar to proof-coll, except that it involves two CheckMembership computations, rather than one CheckMembership and one CheckEntries computation (our entry-coll and proof-coll together imply this new notion). Our promise-incl property matches with a similar change from CheckEntries to CheckMembership, and ignoring maximum merge delays. Consistency of STRs in CONIKS is quite a bit different from our entry-cons property, as CONIKS' involves probabilistic spot-checks using membership proofs.

4 Security Goals

For the security properties of logging schemes that can be proved cryptographically, our security definitions follow a provable security game-based approach. We consider three properties involving security against a malicious logger, in which the experiment acts as an honest monitor/auditor which the logger is trying to fool. We also consider one security property involving security against a malicious monitor/auditor, in which the experiment acts as an honest logger which the monitor/auditor is trying to frame for bad behaviour.

Security Against a Malicious Logger. Since the fingerprint (signed tree hash in CT) is used to concisely represent the contents of the log, the first two cryptographic security properties against a malicious logger, shown in Fig. 6, concern the ability of the logger to make the fingerprint represent different, conflicting information. *Collision resistance of entries*, defined in the experiment entry-coll, requires that it is hard for a malicious logger to come up with a single fingerprint representing two different sets of entries. *Collision resistance of proofs*, formalized in the experiment proof-coll, is about the difficulty for a malicious logger to create a proof that an entry is represented by a fingerprint while simultaneously claiming that the set of entries represented by that fingerprint does not include that particular entry. A scheme that satisfies both of these ensures that a malicious logger cannot make parties who use the same fingerprint believe different things about the log entries represented by that fingerprint.

$\text{Exp}_{\text{LS}}^{\text{entry-coll}}(\mathcal{A})$:
 1: $(\vec{E}_0, \vec{E}_1, F, pk) \xleftarrow{\$} \mathcal{A}()$
 2: **return** 1 iff $(\text{CheckEntries}(\vec{E}_0, F, pk) = 1) \wedge (\text{CheckEntries}(\vec{E}_1, F, pk) = 1) \wedge (\vec{E}_0 \neq \vec{E}_1)$

$\text{Exp}_{\text{LS}}^{\text{proof-coll}}(\mathcal{A})$:
 1: $(e, \vec{E}, F, \vec{M}, pk) \xleftarrow{\$} \mathcal{A}()$
 2: **return** 1 iff $(\text{CheckEntries}(\vec{E}, F, pk) = 1) \wedge (\text{CheckMembership}(e, F, \vec{M}, pk) = 1) \wedge (e \notin \vec{E})$

$\text{Exp}_{\text{LS}}^{\text{entry-cons}}(\mathcal{A})$:
 1: $(\vec{E}_0, \vec{E}_1, F_0, F_1, \vec{C}, pk) \xleftarrow{\$} \mathcal{A}()$
 2: **return** 1 iff $(\text{CheckConsistency}(F_0, F_1, \vec{C}, pk) = 1) \wedge (\text{CheckEntries}(\vec{E}_0, F_0, pk) = 1)$
       $\wedge (\text{CheckEntries}(\vec{E}_1, F_1, pk) = 1) \wedge (\vec{E}_0 \not\prec \vec{E}_1)$

Fig. 6. Security properties of a logging scheme LS against a malicious logger.

Logs are updated over time, but are meant to be append-only. However, since logs are only represented by fingerprints, consistency proofs are used to connect two fingerprints and are meant to prove that the set of entries represented by one fingerprint is a subset of the set of entries represented by a second fingerprint— in other words, that the fingerprints are representative of an append-only log. The final security property in Fig. 6 captures the *consistency of entries*, i.e., the difficulty for a malicious logger to remove an entry from a log: experiment entry-cons is concerned with two fingerprints connected by a single consistency proof. A "multi-hop" version, concerned with a chain of fingerprints connected by consistency proofs, can easily be formulated and shown to follow directly from the "single-hop" version.

Security Against a Malicious Monitor/Auditor. The security properties described above are *cryptographic*, meaning that (under some computational assumptions) it is not possible for a malicious logger to perform certain actions. However, there are some security goals of CT that are not cryptographic. For example, a log could choose to omit an entry that it has promised to log, and no amount of cryptography can prevent it from doing so. Should a log issue a fingerprint after the time by which it has promised to log an entry but the log does not contain an entry, that constitutes evidence of the log's misbehaviour.

However, to protect honest loggers, it should not be possible to frame an honest logger for misbehaviour that did not actually happen, which is the security guarantee formalized as *inclusion of promises* in experiment promise-incl in Fig. 7. Here the experiment plays the role of an honest logger against a malicious monitor/auditor, so we allow the adversary (the malicious monitor/logger) to interact with experiment oracles that carry out the actions of an honest log, such as adding entries or proving membership. The experiment includes a global

$\mathrm{Exp}_{\mathsf{LS},\mathsf{MMD}}^{\mathsf{promise\text{-}incl}}(\mathcal{A})$:

1: $T \leftarrow 0$
2: $\vec{E}_{promised} \leftarrow ()$
3: $(st, pk, sk) \xleftarrow{\$} \mathrm{KeyGen}()$
4: $(F, P, \vec{E}) \xleftarrow{\$} \mathcal{A}^{\mathsf{OTick},\mathsf{OPromiseEntry},\mathsf{OUpdateLog},\mathsf{OProveConsistency},\mathsf{OProveMembership}}(pk)$
5: **return** 1 iff $(\mathrm{CheckFingerprint}(F, pk) = 1) \ \wedge \ (\mathrm{CheckPromise}(P.e, P, pk) = 1)$
   $\wedge \ (\mathrm{CheckEntries}(\vec{E}, F, pk) = 1) \ \wedge \ (P.e \notin \vec{E}) \ \wedge \ (P.t + \mathsf{MMD} \leq F.t)$

OTick():
1: $T \leftarrow T + 1$
2: $\vec{P} \leftarrow \{P \in \vec{E}_{promised} : P.t + \mathsf{MMD} \leq T\}$
3: **if** $\vec{P} \neq ()$,
4:   $F \xleftarrow{\$} \mathrm{OUpdateLog}(\vec{P})$
5:   $\vec{E}_{promised} \leftarrow \vec{E}_{promised} \setminus \vec{P}$
6:   **return** (T, F)
7: **else return** T

OPromiseEntry(e):
1: $(st, P) \xleftarrow{\$} \mathrm{PromiseEntry}(st, e, T, sk)$
2: $\vec{E}_{promised} \leftarrow \vec{E}_{promised} \ || \ \{P\}$
3: **return** P

OUpdateLog($\vec{P}$):
1: $(st, F) \xleftarrow{\$} \mathrm{UpdateLog}(st, \vec{P}, T, sk)$
2: **return** F

OProveConsistency(F_0, F_1):
1: $(st, \vec{C}) \xleftarrow{\$} \mathrm{ProveConsistency}(st, F_0, F_1)$
2: **return** $\vec{C}$

OProveMembership(e, F):
1: $(st, \vec{M}) \xleftarrow{\$} \mathrm{ProveMembership}(st, e, F)$
2: **return** $\vec{M}$

Fig. 7. Security properties of a logging scheme LS against a malicious monitor/auditor framing a log for failing to include a promised entry.

time which advances at the adversary's command, and is parameterized by a *maximum merge delay* MMD > 0, within which an honest log is expected to include a promised entry. The list $\vec{E}_{promised}$ tracks entries that the log has promised to include; in calls to OTick the experiment (acting as the honest log) automatically adds the list of promised entries by the end of the maximum merge delay window.

5   Security of Certificate Transparency

We are now ready to prove the security results on Certificate Transparency, namely that its instantiation $CT_{H,SIG}$ within our logging scheme frameworks guarantees collision resistance of entities and proofs, consistency of entries, and inclusion of promises.

Theorems 1 and 2 below connect rather immediately with the security properties of the underlying Merkle tree hash, so we omit the arguments due to space constraints; they appear in the full version [8]. Lemmas 1 and 2 then connect the Merkle tree hash properties to finding a collision in H, which is infeasible if H is collision-resistant. For Theorem 3 we also provide the proof in the full version due to space restrictions; the proof for Theorem 4 is given in Appendix A.

Theorem 1 (Collision Resistance of Entries). *If hash function* H *is collision-resistant, then, in Certificate Transparency (with hash function* H*), no malicious logger can present different log entries for the same fingerprint. More precisely, if* $\mathcal{A}$ *wins* $\mathrm{Exp}_{CT_{H,SIG}}^{entry\text{-}coll}$*, then algorithm* $\mathcal{B}^{\mathcal{A}}$*, which runs* $\mathcal{A}$ *and then returns the first two components of* $\mathcal{A}$*'s output, finds a collision in* MTH_H*. Moreover, the runtime of* $\mathcal{B}^{\mathcal{A}}$ *is the same as that of* $\mathcal{A}$*.*

Theorem 2 (Collision Resistance of Proofs). *If hash function* H *is collision-resistant then, in Certificate Transparency (with hash function* H*) no malicious logger can present a list of log entries under some fingerprint and a membership proof under the same fingerprint for an entry not contained in this list. More precisely, if* $\mathcal{A}$ *wins* $\mathrm{Exp}_{CT_{H,SIG}}^{proof\text{-}coll}$ *by outputting* $(e, \vec{E}, F, \vec{M}, pk)$*, then algorithm* $\mathcal{B}^{\mathcal{A}}$*, which runs* $\mathcal{A}$ *and then returns* $(e, \vec{E}, \vec{M}.\vec{A}, \vec{M}.m)$*, breaks authentication path consistency in the sense of Lemma 2. Moreover, the runtime of* $\mathcal{B}^{\mathcal{A}}$ *is the same as that of* $\mathcal{A}$*.*

Theorem 3 (Consistency of Entries). *If hash function* H *is collision-resistant, then, in Certificate Transparency (with hash function* H*), no malicious logger can present two lists of entries, two fingerprints, and a consistency proof such that each list corresponds to the fingerprint, and the fingerprints are connected via the consistency proof, but the first list of entries is not a prefix of the second list of entries. More precisely, if* $\mathcal{A}$ *wins* $\mathrm{Exp}_{CT_{H,SIG}}^{entry\text{-}cons}$*, then algorithm* $\mathcal{B}_3^{\mathcal{A}}$ *given in the full version [8] finds a collision in* H*. Moreover, the runtime of* $\mathcal{B}_3^{\mathcal{A}}$ *consists of the runtime of* $\mathcal{A}$*, plus at most a quadratic (in the size of the second list) number of hash evaluations.*

Theorem 4 (Inclusion of Promises). *If hash function* H *is collision-resistant and signature scheme* SIG *is existentially unforgeable under chosen-message attacks, then, in Certificate Transparency (with hash function* H *and signature scheme* SIG*), no malicious monitor/auditor can frame an honest logger of not including a promised entry within the maximum merge delay. More precisely, if algorithm* $\mathcal{A}$ *wins* $\text{Exp}^{\text{promise-incl}}_{\text{CT}_{\text{H,SIG}}}$*, then there exist algorithms* $\mathcal{B}^{\mathcal{A}}$ *and* $\mathcal{C}^{\mathcal{A}}$*, described in the proof, that find a collision in* MTH_{H} *or a forgery in* SIG*, respectively. Moreover, the runtimes of* $\mathcal{B}^{\mathcal{A}}$ *and* $\mathcal{C}^{\mathcal{A}}$ *are approximately the same as that of* $\mathcal{A}$*.*

6   Conclusion and Future Work

Certificate Transparency is a promising approach for providing assurances in the web PKI by using untrusted auditable public logs to detect fraudulently issued certificates. We introduced a generic model for logging schemes and captured Certificate Transparency as one specific instance of our model. Based on the security notions we formalized, we were able to analyze the cryptographic aspects of CT and show how its cryptographic mechanisms prevent both undetected misbehaviour of log servers as well as false accusations of honest loggers.

Although cryptography plays an essential role to establish the trust necessary in a public and auditable logging scheme like Certificate Transparency, there are other components involved that are difficult or even impossible to capture in a cryptographic model. For example, under various conditions on adversary control of the network and with various patterns of honest entity behaviour, how long does it take for the CT gossiping protocol to propagate SCTs and STHs to ensure detection of dishonest log behaviour? Once misbehaviour is detected, what organizational measures should be taken to ensure an appropriate response? Analyzing these components in general as well as their specific relevance in the CT framework is an important task for future work.

Acknowledgements. Benjamin Dowling and Douglas Stebila are supported by Australian Research Council (ARC) Discovery Project grant DP130104304. Felix Günther is supported by the DFG as part of project S4 within the CRC 1119 CROSSING.

A   Proof of Theorem 4 (Inclusion of promises)

Proof. By definition of OTick (cf. Fig. 7), the simulated honest logger will keep track of any promise P issued through OPromiseEntry and will include the P through OUpdateLog by time $T = P.t + \text{MMD}$. As in particular $\text{MMD} > 0$, this ensures that any fingerprint issued by the honest logger at time $T' \geq T$ will include the promised entry $P.e$.

Assume $\mathcal{A}$ wins by outputting $(F, P, \vec{E})$, i.e., F is a valid fingerprint representing entries $\vec{E}$ and P is a promise for an entry $e \notin \vec{E}$ although $P.t + \text{MMD} \leq F.t$. This means either one of the promise P or the fingerprint F (or both) were not issued by the simulated honest logger through an invocation of OPromiseEntry or

OUpdateLog, or that $\mathcal{A}$ repeated an honest F that matches an entry list $\vec{E}$ different from the entry list $\vec{E}'$ hold by the honest logger when creating the fingerprint.

The second case constitutes a Merkle-tree hash collision (as $\text{MTH}_H(\vec{E}) = \text{MTH}_H(\vec{E}')$, but $\vec{E} \neq \vec{E}'$). Hence $\mathcal{A}$'s advantage in winning through this case can be bound by the advantage of an algorithm $\mathcal{B}$ (that simulates the oracles and simply outputs the colliding $\vec{E}$ and $\vec{E}'$) against the collision resistance of MTH_H. (Applying Lemma 1 leads to a collision in H.)

For the first case, we show how this allows constructing a signature forgery attacker $\mathcal{C}$ against the euf-cma security of SIG, which works as follows. First of all, $\mathcal{C}$ creates an initial state with empty list of entries. It then simulates experiment $\text{Exp}_{\text{CT}_{H,\text{SIG}},\text{MMD}}^{\text{promise-incl}}$ for $\mathcal{A}$, providing the public key pk from its euf-cma game as input for $\mathcal{A}$. It furthermore uses its euf-cma signing oracle OSign when required to generate a signature in the simulations of the OPromiseEntry and OUpdateLog oracles and keeps a list of all the values queried to the signing oracle.

If $\mathcal{A}$ halts (outputting $(F, P, \vec{E})$) and wins, as argued above, at least one of P or F was not output through $\mathcal{C}$'s simulation of OPromiseEntry and OUpdateLog (as we excluded the case of a Merkle-tree hash collision). Hence, in particular, the according value was not queried to the euf-cma signing oracle, so $\mathcal{C}$ checks which of the two values is not contained in its list of queries and outputs this as its valid signature forgery. $\square$

References

1. Basin, D.A., Cremers, C.J.F., Kim, T.H.J., Perrig, A., Sasse, R., Szalachowski, P.: ARPKI: attack resilient public-key infrastructure. In: Ahn, G.J., Yung, M., Li, N. (eds.) ACM CCS 2014, pp. 382–393. ACM Press, November 2014

2. Bellare, M., Goldreich, O., Goldwasser, S.: Incremental cryptography: the case of hashing and signing. In: Desmedt, Y.G. (ed.) CRYPTO 1994. LNCS, vol. 839, pp. 216–233. Springer, Heidelberg (1994)

3. Bellare, M., Micciancio, D.: A new paradigm for collision-free hashing: incrementality at reduced cost. In: Fumy, W. (ed.) EUROCRYPT 1997. LNCS, vol. 1233, pp. 163–192. Springer, Heidelberg (1997)

4. Braun, J., Kiefer, F., Hülsing, A.: Revocation and non-repudiation: when the first destroys the latter. In: Katsikas, S., Agudo, I. (eds.) EuroPKI 2013. LNCS, vol. 8341, pp. 31–46. Springer, Heidelberg (2014)

5. Comodo Group: Comodo fraud incident, 31 Mar 2011. https://www.comodo.com/Comodo-Fraud-Incident-2011-03-23.html

6. Crosby, S.A.: Efficient Tamper-Evident Data Structures for Untrusted Servers. Ph.D. thesis, Rice University, Houston, Texas, USA (2009)

7. Crosby, S.A., Wallach, D.S.: Efficient data structures for tamper-evident logging. In: 18th USENIX Security Symposium 2009, pp. 317–334. USENIX Association (2009). http://www.usenix.org/events/sec09/tech/full_papers/crosby.pdf

8. Dowling, B., Günther, F., Herath, U., Stebila, D.: Secure logging schemes and Certificate Transparency (full version). Cryptology ePrint Archive, Report 2016/452 (2016). http://eprint.iacr.org/2016/452

9. Electronic Frontier Foundation: Sovereign Keys. https://www.eff.org/sovereign-keys

10. Evans, C., Palmer, C., Sleevi, R.: Public Key Pinning Extension for HTTP. RFC 7469 (Proposed Standard), April 2015. http://www.ietf.org/rfc/rfc7469.txt
11. Fox, I.T.: Black Tulip: Report of the investigation into the DigiNotar certificate authority breach, August 2012. http://www.rijksoverheid.nl/bestanden/documenten-en-publicaties/rapporten/2012/08/13/black-tulip-update/black-tulip-update.pdf
12. Goldwasser, S., Micali, S., Rivest, R.L.: A digital signature scheme secure against adaptive chosen-message attacks. SIAM J. Comput. **17**(2), 281–308 (1988)
13. Hoffman, P., Schlyter, J.: The DNS-Based Authentication of Named Entities (DANE) Transport Layer Security (TLS) Protocol: TLSA. RFC 6698 (Proposed Standard), August 2012. http://www.ietf.org/rfc/rfc6698.txt
14. Huang, D.: Early impacts of Certificate Transparency, April 2016. https://www.facebook.com/notes/protect-the-graph/early-impacts-of-certificate-transparency/1709731569266987/
15. Kent, S.: Attack model and threat for Certificate Transparency, October 2015. https://tools.ietf.org/html/draft-ietf-trans-threat-analysis-03
16. Kim, T.H., Huang, L., Perrig, A., Jackson, C., Gligor, V.D.: Accountable key infrastructure (AKI): a proposal for a public-key validation infrastructure. In: 22nd International World Wide Web Conference (WWW) 2013, pp. 679–690. ACM (2013)
17. Laurie, B., Langley, A., Kasper, E.: Certificate Transparency. RFC 6962 (Experimental), June 2013. http://www.ietf.org/rfc/rfc6962.txt
18. Laurie, B.: Certificate transparency. ACM Queue Secur. **12**(8), 10 (2014)
19. Laurie, B., Kasper, E.: Revocation Transparency (2012). http://www.links.org/files/RevocationTransparency.pdf
20. Li, F., Hadjieleftheriou, M., Kollios, G., Reyzin, L.: Dynamic authenticated index structures for outsourced databases. In: ACM SIGMOD International Conference on Management of Data 2006, pp. 121–132. ACM (2006)
21. Marchesini, J.C., Smith, S.: Modeling public key infrastructures in the real world. In: Chadwick, D., Zhao, G. (eds.) EuroPKI 2005. LNCS, vol. 3545, pp. 118–134. Springer, Heidelberg (2005)
22. Maurer, U.M.: Modelling a public-key infrastructure. In: Bertino, E., Kurth, H., Martella, G., Montolivo, E. (eds.) Computer Security – ESORICS '96. LNCS, vol. 1146, pp. 325–350. Springer, Heidelberg (1996)
23. Melara, M.S., Blankstein, A., Bonneau, J., Felten, E.W., Freedman, M.J.: CONIKS: bringing key transparency to end users. In: USENIX Security 2015, pp. 383–398. USENIX Association (2015)
24. Merkle, R.C.: Secrecy, authentication, and public key systems. Technical report 1979-1, Information Systems Laboratory, Stanford University, June 1979
25. Merkle, R.C.: A certified digital signature. In: Brassard, G. (ed.) CRYPTO 1989. LNCS, vol. 435, pp. 218–238. Springer, Heidelberg (1990)
26. Nissim, K., Naor, M.: Certificate revocation and certificate update. In: USENIX Security 1998. USENIX Association (1998)
27. Nordberg, L., Gillmor, D., Ritter, T.: Gossiping in CT, August 2015. https://tools.ietf.org/html/draft-ietf-trans-gossip-00
28. Ogawa, M., Horita, E., Ono, S.: Proving properties of incremental merkle trees. In: Nieuwenhuis, R. (ed.) CADE 2005. LNCS (LNAI), vol. 3632, pp. 424–440. Springer, Heidelberg (2005)
29. Ryan, M.D.: Enhanced certificate transparency and end-to-end encrypted mail. In: NDSS 2014, The Internet Society, February 2014

30. Somogyi, S., Eijdenberg, A.: Improved digital certificate security, September 2015. http://googleonlinesecurity.blogspot.de/2015/09/improved-digital-certificate-security.html
31. Villemson, J.: Size-efficient interval time stamps. Ph.D. thesis, Tartu (2002)

Economics of Security

Banishing Misaligned Incentives for Validating Reports in Bug-Bounty Platforms

Aron Laszka[1]([✉]), Mingyi Zhao[2], and Jens Grossklags[2]

[1] University of California, Berkeley, USA
laszka@berkeley.edu
[2] Pennsylvania State University, University Park, USA

Abstract. Bug-bounty programs have the potential to harvest the efforts and diverse knowledge of thousands of white hat hackers. As a consequence, they are becoming increasingly popular as a key part of the security culture of organizations. However, bug-bounty programs can be riddled with myriads of invalid vulnerability-report submissions, which are partially the result of misaligned incentives between white hats and organizations. To further improve the effectiveness of bug-bounty programs, we introduce a theoretical model for evaluating approaches for reducing the number of invalid reports. We develop an economic framework and investigate the strengths and weaknesses of existing canonical approaches for effectively incentivizing higher validation efforts by white hats. Finally, we introduce a novel approach, which may improve efficiency by enabling different white hats to exert validation effort at their individually optimal levels.

Keywords: Bug-bounty programs · Vulnerability discovery · Economics of security · White hat hackers · Misaligned incentives · Crowdsourcing

1 Introduction

In recent years, many organizations have launched independent bug-bounty programs (e.g., Google and Facebook) or have joined bug-bounty platforms, such as HackerOne, Cobalt or Bugcrowd, that facilitate programs for them. These programs allow independent security researchers, so-called white hats, to evaluate the security of a website or software within a set of predefined rules. White hat hackers are encouraged to submit reports for potential vulnerabilities, which after validation by the organization will be rewarded, for example, with monetary bounties. The benefits of these programs are at least twofold. First, the organizations' products are examined by the large and diverse population of white hat hackers, which would be prohibitively expensive to employ directly. White hats' efforts effectively complement the usage of automated web vulnerability scanners, which have been shown to have only limited coverage [8,26]. Second, the public nature of the majority of these programs can signal to third parties the commitment of organizations towards continual security improvements.

© Springer International Publishing Switzerland 2016
I. Askoxylakis et al. (Eds.): ESORICS 2016, Part II, LNCS 9879, pp. 161–178, 2016.
DOI: 10.1007/978-3-319-45741-3_9

The scale of bug-bounty programs is sizable and growing. For example, on HackerOne, more than 20000 security vulnerabilities have been reported and fixed for hundreds of organizations as of May 2016. These contributions are based on reports from over 2500 different white hat hackers, who received bounties totaling over $7.3 M.

However, the public nature of the majority of the programs also poses a challenge since virtually anyone can participate, and organizations may be overwhelmed by low-value reports [28]. In fact, bug-bounty platforms acknowledge that the key challenge "companies face in running a public program at scale is managing noise, or the proportion of low-value reports they receive" [13]. These low-value reports include spam (i.e., completely irrelevant reports), false positives (i.e., issues that do not actually exist or have no security impact), and out-of-scope reports. For the purpose of our work, we will refer to all of these issues as invalid reports.

Invalid reports may be the result of imprecise research approaches or lack of thorough validation by white hats. For example, some hackers utilize automated vulnerability scanners in the discovery process, which typically have a high false-positive rate [8]. Since filtering out false positives is costly, some hackers may prefer to send the outputs of an automated scanner to the bug-bounty program. Further, some discoveries may initially appear to be valid, while they are actually not. For example, a hacker needs to read the participation rules for a program and validate whether an identified issue is out-of-scope. Another important facet is that the hacker needs to demonstrate that a discovered flaw can really lead to a security problem. Finally, writing a good report for a valid discovery requires effort, and can also be seen as a part of the validation process.

In practice, the number of invalid reports is significant. For example, for Bugcrowd's public programs, 34.5 % of all submissions were marked invalid (from January 2013 to June 2015) [7]. HackerOne reported that 54 % of all submissions were marked as invalid before the platform started to proactively improve the signal-to-noise ratio (in 2015) [13].

As a direct response, bug-bounty platforms have started to offer multiple policies that participating organizations can use for reducing the number of invalid reports. For example, HackerOne has introduced "Signal Requirements" and "Rate Limiter" mechanisms, which organizations can use to increase the quality of reports [13]. The former allows only those hackers to submit reports who maintain a given ratio of valid to invalid submissions, while the latter limits the number of reports that a hacker can make in some time interval. These policies aim to incentivize hackers to engage in consistent efforts to validate their reports. According to HackerOne [13], these measures together have decreased the percentage of invalid reports to around 25 %.

Unfortunately, policies may also prevent some hackers, who could contribute valid reports, from participating and may force others to waste effort by being overly meticulous. Consequently, strict policies will result not only in a reduced number of invalid reports, but also in a lower number of valid reports. In summary, finding the right policies and their optimal configuration is a challenging problem since white hat hackers need to be incentivized to produce and submit valid reports, but at the same time, discouraged from submitting invalid reports.

With our work, we provide the first theoretical framework for modeling these policies, finding their optimal configuration, and comparing them with each other. In addition to modeling existing policies, we also propose a new policy, which directly rewards hackers for their accuracy. For each policy, we provide theoretical results on how hackers react to the implementation of the policy, and then complement our analytic results with numerical analyses comparing the policies.

The remainder of this paper is organized as follows. In Sect. 2, we discuss related work on bug-bounty programs, and vulnerability discovery. In Sect. 3, we introduce our economic model of bug-bounty programs. In Sect. 4, we study a set of canonical policies for decreasing the number of invalid reports. In Sect. 5, we present numerical results on these policies. Finally, in Sect. 6, we offer concluding remarks and outline future work.

2   Related Work

2.1   Bug Bounty and Vulnerability Markets

There has been a long-standing interest for using market approaches to address software security problems. Böhme established a terminology for organizational principles of vulnerability markets by comparing bug bounties, vulnerability brokers, exploit derivatives and cyber-insurance [5]. Among these market approaches, bug bounties have received strong attention from both industry and academia. Schechter proposed a testing competition in which multiple testers report security defects to a software company for reward [24]. Ozment further extended Schechter's testing competition into a vulnerability auction to improve its efficiency and better defend against attacks [19]. In both mechanisms, the amount of reward grows linearly with time, and resets to the initial value every time a report is accepted. This reward policy enables the firm to minimize the cost while still offering a fair price for the vulnerabilities discovered by the testers. The reward level at a given time can also serve as a measurement of software security. However, these two mechanisms did not fully consider the problem of invalid reports, which cause high cost for today's bug-bounty programs and the participating organizations. Schechter proposed to require testers to pay the transaction costs of processing reports [24]. However, this idea would prevent many hackers from submitting reports and thus is not implemented in reality. Our research focuses on real bug-bounty programs and their policies, thus complements these early proposed mechanisms.

In recent years, researchers have conducted multiple empirical analyses on bug-bounty programs. Finifter et al. empirically studied the Google Chrome vulnerability reward program (VRP) and the Mozilla Firefox VRP [11], and suggested that VRPs are more cost-effective compared to hiring full-time security researchers in terms of finding security flaws. Zhao et al. conducted a comprehensive study of two bug bounty ecosystems, Wooyun and HackerOne, to understand their characteristics, trajectories and impact [28]. They quantitatively discussed the low signal-to-noise ratio problem which is the focus of this paper. Maillart et al. empirically studied reward distribution and hacker enrollments of public bounty programs on HackerOne and found that growing rewards cannot match the increasing difficulty of vulnerability discovery, and thus hackers tend to switch to newly launched programs to find bugs more easily [18]. Similar to [28], they suggested that a bounty program manager should try to enroll as many hackers as possible to deplete the number of vulnerabilities more effectively. However, this leads to a significant increase of invalid submissions, which we aim to address in this paper.

For other types of market-based vulnerability discovery mechanisms, Kannan and Telang theoretically demonstrated that unregulated vulnerability markets almost always perform worse than regulated ones, or even non-market approaches [15]. They further found that offering rewards for benign vulnerability discoverers is socially beneficial. Frei et al. studied a security ecosystem including discovers, vulnerability markets, criminals, vendors, security information providers and the public, based on 27,000 publicly disclosed vulnerabilities to examine the risk and impact of such an ecosystem [12]. They found that between 10 % and 15 % of the vulnerabilities of major software vendors are handled by commercial vulnerability markets, and exploits become available faster than patches on average. Ransbotham et al. empirically examined the effectiveness of vulnerability markets and concluded that market-based disclosure restricts the diffusion of vulnerability exploits, reduces the risk of exploitation, and decreases the volume of exploitation attempts [22]. Algarni and Malaiya analyzed data of several existing vulnerability markets and showed that the black market offers much higher prices for zero-day vulnerabilities, and government agencies make up a significant portion of the buyers [1]. Bacon et al. have proposed a more general market design that contains bug hunters, developers, and users [4]. Bug bounty, and vulnerability markets in general have also caused debates regarding their ethics. A recent panel discussion of such issues and their implications can be found in [10]. Finally, Libicki et al. conducted a comprehensive study of vulnerability markets and their relevance to cyber security and public policy [17].

2.2 Empirical Analysis of Software Vulnerability Discovery

Previous work has studied various software vulnerability datasets to understand vulnerability discovery. Rescorla studied the ICAT dataset of 1,675 vulnerabilities and found very weak or no evidence of vulnerability depletion. He thus suggested that the vulnerability discovery efforts might not provide much social benefit [23]. This conclusion is being challenged by Ozment and Schechter, who showed that the pool of vulnerabilities in the foundational code of OpenBSD is being depleted with strong statistical evidence [20,21]. Ozment also found that vulnerability rediscovery is common in the OpenBSD vulnerability discovery history [20]. Therefore, they gave the opposite conclusion, i.e., vulnerability hunting by white hats is socially beneficial. More recently, Shahzad et al. [25] conducted a large-scale study of the evolution of the vulnerability life cycle using a combined dataset of NVD, OSVDB and FVDB. Their study provided three positive signs for increasing software security: (1) monthly vulnerability disclosures are decreasing since 2008, (2) exploitation difficulty of the identified vulnerabilities is increasing, and (3) software companies have become more agile in responding to discovered vulnerabilities.

More recently, researchers started to pay attention to the behaviors of vulnerability discoverers. One finding is that vulnerability discoverers are rather heterogeneous. Edmundson et al. conducted a code review experiment for a small web application with 30 subjects [9]. One of their findings is that none of the participants was able to find all 7 Web vulnerabilities embedded in the test code, but a random sample of half of the participants could cover all vulnerabilities with probability of about 95 %, indicating that a sufficiently large group of white hats is required for finding vulnerabilities effectively. Zhao et al. conducted an initial exploratory study of white hats on Wooyun [27] and uncovered the diversity of white hat behaviors regarding productivity, vulnerability type specialization, and discovery transitions. Huang et al. uncovered that hackers at various levels of experience exist in the vulnerability disclosure ecosystem [14]. They found that hackers with different levels of accuracy have diverse strategies in selecting to which programs to contribute [14]. In this paper, we account for these studies by evaluating the effectiveness of bug bounty policies for both homogeneous and heterogeneous white hat hackers.

3   Model

In this section, we introduce our economic model of bug-bounty programs. Note that we will focus on features that are relevant to invalid reports and policies for limiting them. A list of symbols used in this paper can be found in Table 1.

Notation. We use uppercase letters to denote constants (e.g., V) and functions (e.g., $D_i(t_i)$), lowercase letters to denote variables (e.g., b), and bold font to denote vectors (e.g., t). We use Lagrange's notation (i.e., the prime notation) for derivatives of single variable functions (i.e., $D_i'(t_i)$ denotes the first derivative of $D_i(t_i)$). For multivariable functions, we use Leibniz's notation (e.g., $\frac{d}{db}U_O(b, t, v)$ denotes the first derivative of $U_O(b, t, v)$ with respect to b). Finally, we use $^{-1}$ to denote the inverse of a function (e.g., $D_i^{-1}(t_i)$ is the inverse of function $D_i(t_i)$).

In our model, we consider an *organization* that runs a bug-bounty program and *hackers* that may participate in the program. We group hackers who have the same productivity and preferences together into *hacker types*. Since hackers of the same type will respond in the same way to the policies set by the organization, we study their choices as a group instead of as individuals.

The number of *potential vulnerabilities discovered* by hackers of type i is

$$D_i(t_i), \tag{1}$$

where t_i is the amount of time hackers of type i spend on discovery. We assume that $D_i(0) \equiv 0$ and that D_i is a non-negative, increasing, and strictly concave function of t_i. That is, we assume that the marginal productivity of discovery is decreasing, which is supported by experimental results and existing models (e.g., [2,6,29]).

On average, $\Phi_i \cdot D_i(t_i)$ of these discoveries are actual vulnerabilities and $(1 - \Phi_i)D_i(t_i)$ of them are *invalid* $(0 < \Phi_i < 1)$. The number of potential vulnerabilities that are *validated* (i.e., confirmed to be valid or to be invalid) by hackers of type i is

$$I_i(v_i), \tag{2}$$

where v_i is the amount of time hackers of type i spend on validating their discoveries. We assume that $I_i(0) \equiv 0$ and that I_i is a non-negative, increasing, unbounded, and strictly concave function of v_i. The rationale behind the concavity assumption is that some discoveries are easier to validate, and a rational, utility-maximizing hacker starts validation with the easier ones. Finally, we obviously have that

$$v_i \leq I_i^{-1}\left(D_i(t_i)\right). \tag{3}$$

That is, a hacker will not waste time on validation once he has finished with all of his discoveries.

After validating his $I_i(v_i)$ discoveries, the hacker will report all $\Phi_i \cdot I_i(v_i)$ discoveries that he has confirmed to be valid vulnerabilities. Further, he will also report all $D_i(t_i) - I_i(v_i)$ unvalidated discoveries, of which $\Phi_i \cdot (D_i(t_i) - I_i(v_i))$ are valid and $(1 - \Phi_i)(D_i(t_i) - I_i(v_i))$ are invalid. Hence, the number of valid reports made by hackers of type i is

$$\Phi_i \cdot D_i(t_i), \tag{4}$$

Table 1. List of symbols

Symbol	Description
Constants and Functions	
V	average value of a valid report for the organization
C	average cost of processing a report for the organization
W_i	value of time for hackers of type i
Φ_i	fraction of discoveries by hackers of type i that are valid vulnerabilities
$D_i(t_i)$	number of potential vulnerabilities discovered by hackers of type i
$I_i(v_i)$	number of discoveries validated by hackers of type i
Variables	
b	average bounty paid for a valid report
t_i	time spent on vulnerability discovery by hackers of type i
v_i	time spent on validating discoveries by hackers of type i
α	accuracy threshold imposed on participating hackers
ρ	report-rate threshold imposed on participating hackers
δ	validation reward for participating hackers

while the number of invalid reports is

$$(1 - \Phi_i)\left(D_i(t_i) - I_i(v_i)\right). \tag{5}$$

The utility of hackers of type i is

$$\mathcal{U}_{H_i}(b, t_i, v_i) = b \cdot \Phi_i \cdot D_i(t_i) - W_i \cdot (t_i + v_i), \tag{6}$$

where b is the average bounty that the organization pays for a valid report, and $W_i > 0$ is the hacker's utility for spending time on other activities. In other words, W_i is the opportunity cost of the hacker's time.

The organization's utility is

$$\mathcal{U}_O(b, t, v) = \sum_i \underbrace{(V - b)\Phi_i D_i(t_i)}_{\text{net value of valid reports}} - C \cdot \Big(\underbrace{\Phi_i D_i(t_i)}_{\text{valid reports}} + \underbrace{(1 - \Phi_i)\left(D_i(t_i) - I_i(v_i)\right)}_{\text{invalid reports}} \Big),$$
$$\underbrace{}_{\text{cost of processing reports}}$$
$$\tag{7}$$

where $V > 0$ is the average value of a valid report for the organization, and $C > 0$ is the average cost of processing a report. Note that V can incorporate a variety of factors, such as a difference between the processing costs of valid and invalid reports, cost of patching a vulnerability, etc. By letting $\hat{V} = V - C$, we can express the organization's utility as

$$\mathcal{U}_O(b, t, v) = \sum_i (\hat{V} - b)\Phi_i D_i(t_i) - C \cdot (1 - \Phi_i)\left(D_i(t_i) - I_i(v_i)\right). \tag{8}$$

4   Analysis

In this section, we provide theoretical results on our bug-bounty model, and study how hackers respond to various policies. First, as a baseline case, we study the model without any policy against invalid reports. Then, we study two policies, *accuracy threshold* and *report-rate threshold*, which model existing practical approaches for limiting invalid reports. Finally, we propose a novel policy, *validation reward*, which incentivizes hackers to validate their discoveries instead of imposing strict limits on their actions.

4.1   Without an Invalid-Report Policy

First, we consider a baseline case, in which the organization does not have a policy for limiting invalid reports. In this case, the organization's choice is restricted to adjusting the bounty paid for valid reports. The following proposition characterizes the hackers' response to the bounty value chosen by the organization.

Proposition 1. *Without an invalid-report policy, hackers of type i will spend*

$$t_i^*(b) = \begin{cases} (D_i')^{-1}\left(\frac{W_i}{b \cdot \Phi_i}\right) & \text{if } D_i'(0) > \frac{W_i}{b \cdot \Phi_i} \\ 0 & \text{otherwise} \end{cases} \tag{9}$$

time on vulnerability discovery and $v_i^* = 0$ time on validating their discoveries.

Proof. First, it is easy to see that the maximum of

$$\mathcal{U}_{H_i}(b, t_i, v_i) = b \cdot \Phi_i \cdot D_i(t_i) - W_i \cdot (t_i + v_i) \tag{10}$$

is always attained at $v_i = 0$. In other words, hackers have no incentive to validate their discoveries, and their optimal decision is $v_i^* = 0$ for every type i.

Second, to find the optimal t_i for the hackers, we take the first derivative of their utility U_{H_i} with respect to t_i:

$$\frac{d}{dt_i} U_{H_i}(b, t_i, 0) = b \cdot \Phi_i \cdot D_i'(t_i) - W_i. \tag{11}$$

The maximum of U_{H_i} is attained either at the lower bound $t_i = 0$ or when the first derivative is equal to 0:

$$\frac{d}{dt_i} U_{H_i}(b, t_i, 0) = 0 \tag{12}$$

$$b \cdot \Phi_i \cdot D_i'(t_i) - W_i = 0 \tag{13}$$

$$D_i'(t_i) = \frac{W_i}{b \cdot \Phi_i}. \tag{14}$$

Since $D_i(t_i)$ is strictly concave, we have that $D_i'(t_i)$ is strictly decreasing. Consequently, if $D_i'(0) \leq \frac{W_i}{b \cdot \Phi_i}$, then Eq. (14) cannot have a positive solution $t_i > 0$, and the maximum utility is attained at the lower bound $t_i^* = 0$.

On the other hand, if $D_i'(0) > \frac{W_i}{b \cdot \Phi_i}$, then there exists a unique solution

$$\tilde{t}_i = (D_i')^{-1} \left(\frac{W_i}{b \cdot \Phi_i} \right) \tag{15}$$

to Eq. (14). Furthermore, it is easy to see that $t_i = 0$ cannot be an optimum in this case, since an infinitesimal increase to $t_i = 0$ would lead to a higher payoff due to $\frac{d}{dt_i} U_{H_i}(b, 0, 0) = b \cdot \Phi_i \cdot D_i'(0) - W_i > 0$. Thus, $t_i^* = \tilde{t}_i$ is the unique optimal choice in this case. $\square$

4.2   Accuracy Threshold

Second, we consider programs that accept reports only from those hackers who maintain a sufficiently high ratio of valid reports (e.g., invitation-only programs or the "Signal Requirements" mechanisms of HackerOne [13]). We model these programs using a policy that imposes a restriction on the participating hackers' accuracy. We define accuracy formally as the following ratio:

$$\frac{\text{number of valid reports}}{\text{number of valid reports} + \text{number of invalid reports}} \tag{16}$$

$$= \frac{\Phi_i \cdot D_i(t_i)}{\Phi_i \cdot D_i(t_i) + (1 - \Phi_i)(D_i(t_i) - I_i(v_i))} \tag{17}$$

$$= \frac{\Phi_i \cdot D_i(t_i)}{D_i(t_i) - (1 - \Phi_i) I_i(v_i)}. \tag{18}$$

Please recall that $I_i(v_i) \leq D_i(t_i)$ by definition, which ensures that accuracy cannot exceed 1.

Based on the above definition of accuracy, we formalize the accuracy-threshold policy as follows.

Definition 1 (Accuracy-Threshold Policy). *Under an accuracy-threshold policy with threshold* $\alpha \in [0,1]$, *the hackers' choices must satisfy*

$$\frac{\Phi_i \cdot D_i(t_i)}{D_i(t_i) - (1 - \Phi_i)I_i(v_i)} \geq \alpha. \tag{19}$$

The following proposition characterizes the hackers' responses to the accuracy-threshold policy when $\alpha > \Phi_i$ (when $\alpha \leq \Phi_i$ their responses are obviously the same as without a policy).

Proposition 2. *Under an accuracy-threshold policy, if* $\alpha > \Phi_i$, *hackers of type i will spend*

$$t_i^*(b, \alpha) = \begin{cases} 0 & \text{if } D_i'(0) \leq \frac{W_i}{b \cdot \Phi_i - W_i \frac{1}{I_i'(0)} \frac{\alpha - \Phi_i}{\alpha \cdot (1 - \Phi_i)}} \\ \tilde{t}_i & \text{otherwise} \end{cases} \tag{20}$$

time on vulnerability discovery, where $\tilde{t}_i$ *is the unique solution to*

$$D_i'(\tilde{t}_i) \left(b \cdot \Phi_i - W_i \frac{1}{I_i'\left(I_i^{-1}\left(D_i(\tilde{t}_i)\frac{\alpha - \Phi_i}{\alpha \cdot (1 - \Phi_i)}\right)\right)} \frac{\alpha - \Phi_i}{\alpha \cdot (1 - \Phi_i)} \right) = W_i. \tag{21}$$

In addition, they will spend

$$v_i^*(b, \alpha) = I_i^{-1}\left(D_i(t_i^*)\frac{\alpha - \Phi_i}{\alpha \cdot (1 - \Phi_i)}\right) \tag{22}$$

time on validating their discoveries.

Note that even though we cannot express the solution of Eq. (21) in closed form, it can be found easily numerically since the left-hand side is strictly decreasing or negative (see the proof for details). Furthermore, this also holds for the remaining propositions (Propositions 3 and 4).

Proof. Similar to the case without any policy, hackers are interested in minimizing their time spent on validating their discoveries. Consequently, for any given t_i, hackers will choose the minimum validation effort v_i^* that satisfies the accuracy-threshold constraint. Hence, we have

$$\frac{\Phi_i \cdot D_i(t_i)}{D_i(t_i) - (1 - \Phi_i)I_i(v_i^*)} = \alpha \tag{23}$$

$$\Phi_i \cdot D_i(t_i) = \alpha \cdot D_i(t_i) - \alpha \cdot (1 - \Phi_i)I_i(v_i^*) \tag{24}$$

$$I_i(v_i^*) = D_i(t_i)\frac{\alpha - \Phi_i}{\alpha \cdot (1 - \Phi_i)} \tag{25}$$

$$v_i^* = I_i^{-1}\left(D_i(t_i)\frac{\alpha - \Phi_i}{\alpha \cdot (1 - \Phi_i)}\right). \tag{26}$$

Note that I_i^{-1} exists since I_i is strictly increasing.

Next, we study the optimal t_i^* for the hackers. Using the above characterization of v_i^*, we can express the hackers' utility as a function of b and t_i:

$$\mathcal{U}_{H_i}(b, t_i) = b \cdot \Phi_i \cdot D_i(t_i) - W_i \cdot \left(t_i + I_i^{-1} \left(D_i(t_i) \frac{\alpha - \Phi_i}{\alpha \cdot (1 - \Phi_i)} \right) \right). \qquad (27)$$

In order to find the utility-maximizing t_i, we take the first derivative of the hackers' utility with respect to t_i:

$$\frac{d}{dt_i} U_{H_i} = b \cdot \Phi_i \cdot D_i'(t_i) - W_i$$

$$- W_i \cdot (I_i^{-1})' \left(D_i(t_i) \frac{\alpha - \Phi_i}{\alpha \cdot (1 - \Phi_i)} \right) \cdot D_i'(t_i) \frac{\alpha - \Phi_i}{\alpha \cdot (1 - \Phi_i)} \qquad (28)$$

$$= D_i'(t_i) \left(b \cdot \Phi_i - W_i \frac{1}{I_i' \left(I_i^{-1} \left(D_i(t_i) \frac{\alpha - \Phi_i}{\alpha \cdot (1 - \Phi_i)} \right) \right)} \frac{\alpha - \Phi_i}{\alpha \cdot (1 - \Phi_i)} \right) - W_i. \qquad (29)$$

Recall that $D_i(t_i)$ is a strictly increasing function of t_i by definition. Since $\frac{\alpha - \Phi_i}{\alpha \cdot (1 - \Phi_i)} \geq 0$, the argument of I_i^{-1} is increasing in the formula above, which implies that the argument of I_i' is also increasing because I_i^{-1} is an increasing function. Since I_i' is a strictly decreasing function, the value of I_i' is decreasing, which implies that the fraction $\frac{1}{I_i'(\ldots)}$ in the formula above is an increasing function of t_i. Consequently, we have

$$\frac{d}{dt_i} U_{H_i} = \underbrace{D_i'(t_i)}_{\text{strictly decreasing}} \underbrace{\left(b \cdot \Phi_i - W_i \underbrace{\frac{1}{I_i'(\ldots)}}_{\text{increasing}} \underbrace{\frac{\alpha - \Phi_i}{\alpha \cdot (1 - \Phi_i)}}_{\text{non-negative}} \right)}_{\text{decreasing}} - \underbrace{W_i}_{\text{constant}} . \qquad (30)$$

Since $D_i'(t_i)$ is always positive, the first term is either decreasing or negative. Therefore, the following equation has at most one solution for t_i:

$$\frac{d}{dt_i} U_{H_i} = 0. \qquad (31)$$

Using an argument similar to the one used in the proof of Proposition 1, we can show that if the above equation has a solution $\tilde{t}_i$, then the unique optimal choice is $t_i^* = \tilde{t}_i$; otherwise, the unique optimal choice is $t_i^* = 0$. Since the first term on the right-hand side of Eq. (30) is either decreasing or negative, $\frac{d}{dt_i} U_{H_i} = 0$ does not have a solution if and only if $\frac{d}{dt_i} U_{H_i}$ is negative at $t_i = 0$. Therefore, $t_i^* = 0$ is the unique optimal choice if and only if

$$0 \geq D_i'(0) \left(b \cdot \Phi_i - W_i \frac{1}{I_i'(I_i^{-1}(\underbrace{D_i(0)}_{=0} \frac{\alpha - \Phi_i}{\alpha \cdot (1 - \Phi_i)}))} \frac{\alpha - \Phi_i}{\alpha \cdot (1 - \Phi_i)} \right) - W_i \qquad (32)$$

$$W_i \geq D_i'(0) \left(b \cdot \Phi_i - W_i \frac{1}{I_i'(\underbrace{I_i^{-1}(0)}_{=0})} \frac{\alpha - \Phi_i}{\alpha \cdot (1 - \Phi_i)} \right) \qquad (33)$$

$$W_i \geq D_i'(0) \left(b \cdot \Phi_i - W_i \frac{1}{I_i'(0)} \frac{\alpha - \Phi_i}{\alpha \cdot (1 - \Phi_i)} \right) \tag{34}$$

$$D_i'(0) \leq \frac{W_i}{b \cdot \Phi_i - W_i \frac{1}{I_i'(0)} \frac{\alpha - \Phi_i}{\alpha \cdot (1 - \Phi_i)}}. \tag{35}$$

□

4.3   Report-Rate Threshold

Next, we consider programs that limit the number of reports that each hacker can submit in some fixed time interval (e.g., the "Rate Limiter" mechanism of HackerOne [13]). We model these programs using a policy that imposes a restriction on the participating hackers' submission rate $D_i(t_i) - (1 - \Phi_i)I_i(v_i)$. In practice, programs impose these limitations on each hacker individually. To model this, we will assume in this subsection that each hacker type contains only a single hacker. Note that scaling up the analysis to a multitude of hackers is trivial, since hackers having the same parameters will make the same choices, so we can simply add their report numbers together.

We define the rate-threshold policy as follows.

Definition 2 (Rate-Threshold Policy). *Under a rate-threshold policy with threshold $\rho > 0$, the hackers' choices must satisfy*

$$D_i(t_i) - (1 - \Phi_i)I_i(v_i) \leq \rho. \tag{36}$$

The following proposition characterizes the hackers' responses to the rate-threshold policy.

Proposition 3. *Under a rate-threshold policy, hackers of type i will spend*

$$t_i^*(b, \rho) = \begin{cases} 0 & \text{if } D_i'(0) \leq \frac{W_i}{b \cdot \rho} \\ D_i^{-1}(\rho/\Phi_i) & \text{if } D_i'\left(D_i^{-1}(\rho/\Phi_i)\right) \geq \frac{W_i}{b \cdot \Phi_i - W_i \cdot \left(I_i^{-1}\right)'(\rho/\Phi_i)\frac{1}{1-\Phi_i}} \\ \tilde{t}_i & \text{otherwise} \end{cases} \tag{37}$$

time on vulnerability discovery, where $\tilde{t}_i$ is the unique solution to $\frac{d}{dt_i}U_{H_i} = 0$. In addition, they will spend

$$v_i^*(b, \rho) = \begin{cases} 0 & \text{if } D_i(t_i^*) \leq \rho \\ I_i^{-1}\left(\frac{D_i(t_i^*) - \rho}{1 - \Phi_i}\right) & \text{otherwise} \end{cases} \tag{38}$$

time on validating their discoveries.

The proof of Proposition 3 can be found online in the extended version of the paper [16].

4.4   Validation Reward

One of the primary reasons for the large number of invalid reports is the misalignment of incentives: hackers are only interested in increasing the number of valid reports, while organizations are also interested in decreasing the number of invalid reports. Existing approaches try to solve this problem by imposing constraints on the hackers' choices (e.g., imposing a threshold on their accuracy or on their report rate). Here, we propose a novel, alternative approach, which incentivizes hackers to reduce the number of invalid reports by rewarding their validation efforts. The advantage of this approach is that it does not impose strict constraints on the hackers' choices, but instead aligns their incentives with those of the organization, and allows the hackers to optimize their productivity.

A validation-reward policy can be formulated in multiple ways. For example, the organization could slightly lower bounties for valid reports, but give a bonus based on the submitter's accuracy. Alternatively, it could raise bounties, but deduct from the payment based on the submitter's rate of invalid reports. Here, we will study the latter approach since it allows us to align the hackers' incentives with those of the organization in a very straightforward way.

In practice, this policy can be easily implemented in the same way as an accuracy or rate threshold, by keeping track of each hacker's valid and invalid reports. Similar to the rate-threshold policy, we will assume for ease of presentation that each hacker type contains only a single hacker.

We define the validation-reward policy as follows.

Definition 3 (Validation-Reward Policy). *Under a validation-reward policy with incentive $\delta > 0$, a hacker's utility is*

$$\mathcal{U}_{H_i}(b, \delta, t_i, v_i) = b \cdot \Phi_i \cdot D_i(t_i) - W_i \cdot (t_i + v_i) - \delta \cdot (1 - \Phi_i)(D_i(t_i) - I_i(v_i)), \quad (39)$$

and the organization's utility is

$$\mathcal{U}_O(b, \delta, t, v) = \sum_i (\hat{V} - b)\Phi_i \cdot D_i(t_i) - (C - \delta)(1 - \Phi_i)(D_i(t_i) - I_i(v_i)). \quad (40)$$

The following proposition characterizes the hackers' responses to the validation-reward policy.

Proposition 4. *Let*

$$\hat{v}_i = \begin{cases} 0 & if \ I_i'(0) \leq \frac{W_i}{\delta \cdot (1 - \Phi_i)} \\ (I_i')^{-1}\left(\frac{W_i}{\delta \cdot (1 - \Phi_i)}\right) & otherwise. \end{cases} \quad (41)$$

Under a validation-reward policy, hackers of type i will spend

$$t_i^*(b, \delta) = \begin{cases} 0 & if \ \tilde{v}_i = 0 \ and \ D_i'(0) \leq \frac{W_i}{b \cdot \Phi_i - \delta \cdot (1 - \Phi_i)} \\ 0 & if \ \tilde{v}_i > 0 \ and \ D_i'(0) \leq \frac{W_i}{b \cdot \Phi_i - \frac{W_i}{I_i'(0)}} \\ \tilde{t}_i & otherwise \end{cases} \quad (42)$$

time on vulnerability discovery, where $\tilde{t}_i$ is the unique solution to $\frac{d}{dt_i} U_{H_i} = 0$. In addition, they will spend

$$v_i^*(b, \delta) = \min \left\{ \hat{v}_i, I_i^{-1}(D_i(t_i^*)) \right\} \tag{43}$$

time on validating their discoveries.

The proof of Proposition 4 can be found online in the extended version of the paper [16].

5   Numerical Results

In this section, we present numerical results on our bug-bounty model in order to evaluate and compare the policies introduced in Sect. 4. First, in Sect. 5.1, we consider homogeneous hackers by instantiating our model with a single hacker type, and we study the hackers' responses. Second, in Sect. 5.2, we consider heterogeneous hackers and evaluate policies based on the organization's utility.

5.1   Homogeneous Hackers

For the vulnerability-discovery function $D(t)$, we use an instance of *Anderson's thermodynamic model* [3]: $D(t) = \ln(10 \cdot t + 1)$. Note that we added 1 to the argument so that $D(0) = 0$. We instantiate the remainder of our model with the following parameters: $V = 10$, $C = 1$, and a single hacker type with $W_1 = 1$, $\Phi_i = 0.2$, and $I_1(v_1) = \ln(20 \cdot v_1 + 1)$. Notice that these hackers are assumed to be relatively good at validating their discoveries since I_1 grows faster than D. Finally, note that we have experimented with other reasonable parameter combinations as well, and found that the results remain qualitatively the same.

Figure 1 shows the hackers' responses to various policies and the resulting utilities for the organization and the hackers. First, Fig. 1(a) shows that without any policy, the organization attains maximum utility at $b = 2.07$: with lower bounties, hackers dedicate significantly less time to vulnerability discovery (zero time when $b < 0.31$), while with higher bounties, the cost of running the program becomes prohibitively high. In Figs. 1(b), (c), and (d), we set the bounty value to $b = 2.07$ and study the effects of varying the policy parameters.

Figure 1(b) shows that the accuracy-threshold policy is very effective and robust: the organization's utility increases steeply with the threshold α, reaches a 70 % improvement at $\alpha = 0.74$, and declines negligibly after that. In contrast, the rate-threshold policy is considerably less reliable (Fig. 1(c)): the organization's utility is improved by 55 % at $\rho = 0.2$, but it decreases rapidly as the threshold decreases or increases, and it may reach significantly lower values than without a policy. Thus, the organization must implement this policy with great care in order to avoid suppressing productivity. Finally, Fig. 1(d) shows that the validation-reward policy is robust: even though the organization's utility does not increase until the threshold reaches $\delta < 0.66$, it increases steeply after that, reaching and maintaining a 69 % improvement.

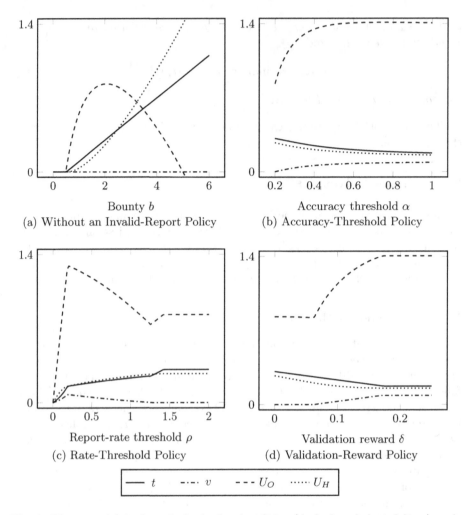

Fig. 1. The organization's and the hackers' utilities (dashed and dotted lines) and the times spent on vulnerability discovery and validation (solid and dash-dotted lines) under various policies as functions of the bounty value.

5.2 Heterogeneous Hackers

Now, we add a second type of hackers, who are worse at validating their discoveries, which we model by letting $I_2(v_2) = \ln(2.5 \cdot v_2 + 1)$ (all other parameters are the same as for the first type). Since we now have multiple hacker types, who may have different responses and utilities, we will plot only the organization's utility for clarity of presentation.

Figure 2 shows the organization's utility under various policies with two types of hackers. Similar to Fig. 1(c), Fig. 2(b) shows that the rate-threshold policy must be implemented carefully since overzealous limiting may signifi-

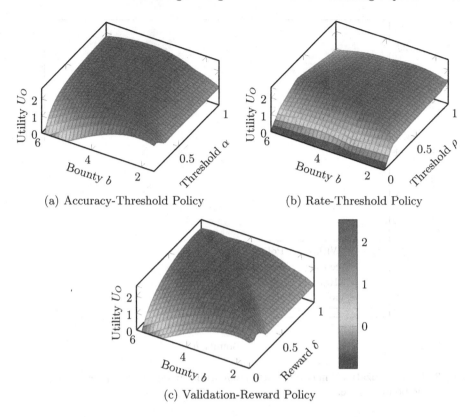

(a) Accuracy-Threshold Policy   (b) Rate-Threshold Policy

(c) Validation-Reward Policy

Fig. 2. The organization's utility under various policies as a function of the bounty value and policy parameter.

cantly decrease the organization's utility, while lenient limiting is ineffective. On the other hand, the accuracy-threshold and validation-reward policies (Figs. 2(a) and (c)) have large "plateaus" around the optimal values, which make them more robust to changes in configuration or parameter values. Nonetheless, if the bounty value is very low, even these policies – especially the validation-reward policy – may be too strict and deter hackers from participating.

Figure 3 shows the organization's maximum attainable utility under various policies with two types of hackers. For each policy and bounty value, we searched over possible values of the policy parameter space (i.e., $\alpha = 0.2, 0.21, \ldots, 1$; $\rho = 0, 0.05, \ldots, 5$; or $\delta = 0, 0.012, \ldots, 1.2$) and plotted the maximum utility. Since the two hacker types differ only in their validation performance, the utility values without a policy shown by Fig. 3 are proportional to the values shown by Fig. 1(a), and the maximum is again attained at $b = 2.07$. Compared to this baseline, the accuracy-threshold, rate-threshold, and validation-reward policies can attain 31 %, 13 %, and 52 % improvement, respectively. However, if the bounty value is not high enough, none of the policies can improve the organization's utility. Finally, offering validation rewards outperforms the other policies

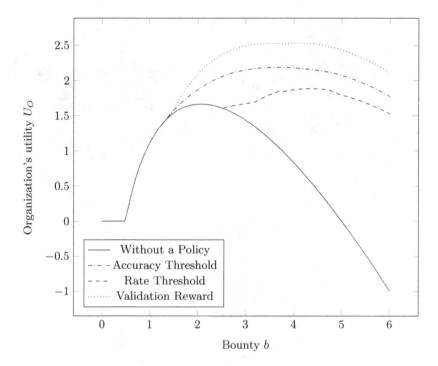

Fig. 3. The organization's maximum attainable utility under various policies as a function of the bounty value.

significantly, since it is able to incentivize heterogeneous hackers to operate at their individual maxima instead of forcing them towards a uniform strategy.

6   Conclusion

In this paper, we provided the first theoretical framework for modeling policies for reducing the number of invalid reports in bug-bounty programs. Using our framework, we investigated a set of canonical policies, and studied the hackers' responses to these policies, showing that each type has a unique response to each policy. In addition to studying existing policies, we also proposed a new policy that incentivizes hackers without restricting their actions.

Based on numerical analyses, we found that all of the considered policies may substantially improve an organization's utility, which explains their widespread use [13]. However, their effectiveness and reliability vary significantly. We found that the rate-threshold policy is not only less effective than the other two, but it must also be configured more carefully. In contrast, the accuracy-threshold and validation-reward policies are less sensitive to changes in parameter and configuration values, and they can also be more effective. However, without adequate bounties, even these policies might "backfire" and actually deter hackers from dedicating time to vulnerability discovery. Finally, we found that the validation-reward policy may significantly outperform the other two when hackers are not homogeneous, since it allows hackers to operate at their individual optima.

In future work, we plan to extend our model and analyses by considering combinations of policies. In other words, we will consider organizations that implement multiple policies at the same time. Building on our current analysis, we will study how hackers respond to various policy-combinations, and we will explore which combinations are the most effective and robust.

Acknowledgements. This work was supported in part by FORCES (Foundations Of Resilient CybEr-Physical Systems), which receives support from the National Science Foundation (NSF award numbers CNS-1238959, CNS-1238962, CNS-1239054, CNS-1239166).

References

1. Algarni, A., Malaiya, Y.: Software vulnerability markets: discoverers and buyers. Int. J. Comput. Inf. Sci. Eng. **8**(3), 71–81 (2014)
2. Alhazmi, O., Malaiya, Y.: Modeling the vulnerability discovery process. In: 16th IEEE International Symposium on Software Reliability Engineering (ISSRE) (2005)
3. Anderson, R.: Security in open versus closed systems - The dance of Boltzmann, Coase and Moore. In: Open Source Software Economics (2002)
4. Bacon, D., Chen, Y., Parkes, D., Rao, M.: A market-based approach to software evolution. In: 24th ACM SIGPLAN Conference Companion on Object Oriented Programming, Systems, Languages, and Applications (2009)
5. Böhme, R.: A comparison of market approaches to software vulnerability disclosure. In: Müller, G. (ed.) ETRICS 2006. LNCS, vol. 3995, pp. 298–311. Springer, Heidelberg (2006)
6. Brady, R., Anderson, R., Ball, R.: Murphy's law, the fitness of evolving species, and the limits of software reliability. Technical Report 471, University of Cambridge, Computer Laboratory (1999)
7. Bugcrowd: The state of bug bounty, July 2015
8. Doupé, A., Cova, M., Vigna, G.: Why Johnny can't pentest: an analysis of black-box web vulnerability scanners. In: Kreibich, C., Jahnke, M. (eds.) DIMVA 2010. LNCS, vol. 6201, pp. 111–131. Springer, Heidelberg (2010)
9. Edmundson, A., Holtkamp, B., Rivera, E., Finifter, M., Mettler, A., Wagner, D.: An empirical study on the effectiveness of security code review. In: Jürjens, J., Livshits, B., Scandariato, R. (eds.) ESSoS 2013. LNCS, vol. 7781, pp. 197–212. Springer, Heidelberg (2013)
10. Egelman, S., Herley, C., van Oorschot, P.: Markets for Zero-Day Exploits: Ethics and Implications. In: New Security Paradigms Workshop (2013)
11. Finifter, M., Akhawe, D., Wagner, D.: An empirical study of vulnerability rewards programs. In: USENIX Security Symposium (2013)
12. Frei, S., Schatzmann, D., Plattner, B., Trammell, B.: Modeling the security ecosystem - The dynamics of (in)security. In: Economics of Information Security and Privacy (2009)
13. HackerOne: Improving public bug bounty programs with signal requirements. HackerOne Blog, March 2016. https://hackerone.com/blog/signal-requirements

14. Huang, C., Liu, J., Fang, Y., Zuo, Z.: A study on web security incidents in China by analyzing vulnerability disclosure platforms. Comput. Secur. **58**, 47–62 (2016)
15. Kannan, K., Telang, R.: Market for software vulnerabilities? Think again. Manage. Sci. **51**(5), 726–740 (2005)
16. Laszka, A., Zhao, M., Grossklags, J.: Optimal policies for bug bounty programs (extended version) (2016). http://aronlaszka.com/papers/laszka2016banishing.pdf
17. Libicki, M., Ablon, L., Webb, T.: The Defenders Dilemma: Charting a Course Toward Cybersecurity. Rand Corporation (2015)
18. Maillart, T., Zhao, M., Grossklags, J., Chuang, J.: Given enough eyeballs, all bugs are shallow? Revisiting Eric Raymond with bug bounty markets. In: Workshop on the Economics of Information Security (WEIS) (2016)
19. Ozment, A.: Bug auctions: Vulnerability markets reconsidered. In: Workshop on the Economics of Information Security (WEIS) (2004)
20. Ozment, A.: The likelihood of vulnerability rediscovery and the social utility of vulnerability hunting. In: Workshop on the Economics of Information Security (WEIS) (2005)
21. Ozment, A., Schechter, S.: Milk or wine: Does software security improve with age? In: USENIX Security Symposium (2006)
22. Ransbotham, S., Mitra, S., Ramsey, J.: Are markets for vulnerabilities effective? MIS Q. **36**(1), 43–64 (2012)
23. Rescorla, E.: Is finding security holes a good idea? IEEE Secur. Priv. **3**(1), 14–19 (2005)
24. Schechter, S.E.: How to buy better testing. In: Davida, G.I., Frankel, Y., Rees, O. (eds.) InfraSec 2002. LNCS, vol. 2437, pp. 73–87. Springer, Heidelberg (2002)
25. Shahzad, M., Shafiq, M., Liu, A.: A large scale exploratory analysis of software vulnerability life cycles. In: International Conference on Software Engineering (2012)
26. Van Goethem, T., Piessens, F., Joosen, W., Nikiforakis, N.: Clubbing seals: Exploring the ecosystem of third-party security seals. In: 21st ACM SIGSAC Conference on Computer and Communications Security (CCS) (2014)
27. Zhao, M., Grossklags, J., Chen, K.: An exploratory study of white hat behaviors in a web vulnerability disclosure program. In: 2014 ACM CCS Workshop on Security Information Workers (2014)
28. Zhao, M., Grossklags, J., Liu, P.: An empirical study of web vulnerability discovery ecosystems. In: 22nd ACM SIGSAC Conference on Computer and Communications Security (CCS) (2015)
29. Zhao, M., Liu, P.: Empirical analysis and modeling of black-box mutational fuzzing. In: Caballero, J., Bodden, E., Athanasopoulos, E. (eds.) ESSoS 2016. LNCS, vol. 9639, pp. 173–189. Springer, Heidelberg (2016)

Efficient Numerical Frameworks
for Multi-objective Cyber Security Planning

MHR. Khouzani[1]([✉]), P. Malacaria[1], C. Hankin[2], A. Fielder[2], and F. Smeraldi[1]

[1] Queen Mary University of London, London, UK
arman.khouzani@qmul.ac.uk
[2] Imperial College London, London, UK

Abstract. We consider the problem of optimal investment in cyber-security by an enterprise. Optimality is measured with respect to the overall (1) monetary cost of implementation, (2) negative side-effects of cyber-security controls (indirect costs), and (3) mitigation of the cyber-security risk. We consider "passive" and "reactive" threats, the former representing the case where attack attempts are independent of the defender's plan, the latter, where attackers can adapt and react to an implemented cyber-security defense. Moreover, we model in three different ways the combined effect of multiple cyber-security controls, depending on their degree of complementarity and correlation. We also consider multi-stage attacks and the potential correlations in the success of different stages. First, we formalize the problem as a non-linear multi-objective integer programming. We then convert them into Mixed Integer Linear Programs (MILP) that very efficiently solve for the exact Pareto-optimal solutions even when the number of available controls is large. In our case study, we consider 27 of the most typical security controls, each with multiple intensity levels of implementation, and 37 common vulnerabilities facing a typical SME. We compare our findings against expert-recommended critical controls. We then investigate the effect of the security models on the resulting optimal plan and contrast the merits of different security metrics. In particular, we show the superior robustness of the security measures based on the "reactive" threat model, and the significance of the hitherto overlooked role of correlations.

1 Introduction

A cyber-security plan is a set of defensive measures (a.k.a., controls) that are applied across an enterprise to improve its overall state of security. There are many cyber-security measures to choose from, and each measure can be implemented at multiple levels of intensity. Examples of these security controls (taken from the list of top-20 critical measures by the UK's Centre for the Protection of National Infrastructure [22]) include: "Inventory of Authorized and Unauthorized Devices", "Inventory of Authorized and Unauthorized Software", "Secure Configurations for Hardware and Software on Mobile Devices, Laptops, Workstations, and Servers", "Malware Defenses", "Wireless Access Control", and so on. Each cyber-security measure addresses a specific set of vulnerabilities. For

© Springer International Publishing Switzerland 2016
I. Askoxylakis et al. (Eds.): ESORICS 2016, Part II, LNCS 9879, pp. 179–197, 2016.
DOI: 10.1007/978-3-319-45741-3_10

instance, while "Access Control" can mitigate "OS Command Injection", it has no effect on "DDoS attacks". Hence a cyber-security plan should be composed of a combination of the measures to provide a well-rounded defense against the range of vulnerabilities that the enterprise faces.

Implementation of each cyber-security measure is not cost-free: it requires monetary investment (direct costs) and can also negatively affect the performance of an enterprise (indirect costs). Therefore, an exhaustive implementation of controls at maximum intensity is likely neither economically feasible nor managerially desirable. In reality, organizations have to deal with cyber-security risk within a limited budget and must be wary of the potential side-effects of the security measures on their existing business processes. Therefore, the mitigation in the security risks has to be judiciously balanced with the direct and indirect costs. A selection analysis should consider the set of controls as well as vulnerabilities jointly. This is because an approach that takes investment decisions for each vulnerability or control separately, ignores the relative importance of the vulnerabilities, and does not optimally use the complementary effects of the controls, and hence, may fail to reach a best overall trade-off. Choosing a desirability metric for a plan is itself a challenging task:

1. The three sources of costs (security, direct and indirect) are not easily combinable. For instance, the investment costs are incurred deterministically and at the present, while the security losses are probabilistic in nature and, if at all, will occur at an unknown future time. Also the monetary conversion is not as clear for indirect costs as for the other two, for instance, it is hard to put a monetary value on the annoyance felt by the staff as a result of a more restrictive access control or a stricter password policy.
2. The trade-off preferences cannot be exactly arbitrated "a priori". For instance, even a "security-concerned" enterprise may choose a different plan if "almost" the same security risk mitigation can be achieved at a much lower direct or indirect cost. Likewise, an enterprise that is very sensitive to indirect costs or extra investment may reconsider if a slight increase in these costs can abate the security risk by a relatively significant amount.

To address these issues we adopt a multi-objective optimization framework. Specifically, we simultaneously minimize the security risk, indirect, and direct costs of the enterprise (the latter within the budget). The "solution" of this three-objective optimization is the set of Pareto-optimal (or non-inferior, or simply, Pareto) plans, that are the solutions with the guarantee that no other plan can simultaneously improve all of these three costs (at least one of them strictly).

Of these three costs, the security risk is the most challenging to model. The effect of an individual security measure (at each implementation intensity) can be represented by its "effectiveness" against different vulnerabilities. That is, the reduction in the success probability of exploitation attempts of each vulnerability when only that control is implemented (stand-alone). Complicating the matter is the fact that, often, the same vulnerability can be (partially) mitigated by more than one security measure. Then a modeling question is how to capture the combined efficacy of controls on their overlapping vulnerabilities.

The simplest approach is an "additive" model, where it is assumed that, per each vulnerability, the (blocking) efficacies of controls are added up, heeding that, logically, none of the overall blocking probabilities should exceed 100 %. This capping of the combined efficacies introduces a degree of non-linearity in the model, but one that can be easily dealt with, as we will show later.

Although computationally the simplest, this model bears the underlying assumption that defensive mechanisms have positive externalities on each others' efficacies. In particular, it potentially allows 100 % efficacy when multiple controls are combined, which is rather unrealistic. A more relaxed modeling assumption is that each control affects the common vulnerabilities independently. Hence, when a vulnerability is attempted, the success chance is the product of successfully bypassing each of its pertaining controls. We will thus refer to this model as "multiplicative". This model is ostensibly nonlinear in the decision variables, and hence, solving the resulting nonlinear integer program accurately can be very inefficient. However, as we will see later, it can be converted into a Mixed Integer Linear Program (MILP) which is much more efficient to solve accurately.

A problem with the previous two models is that they ignore the possible correlations in the defensive mechanisms of security measures. Due to such correlations, it can be argued that if an attempted exploitation bypasses one of the controls, it will be a strong indication for bypassing the other affecting measures as well. The "independent" blocking probabilities in the heart of multiplicative model, although better than the additive model, can still be a significant over-estimation of the overall effectiveness of a security plan. In this paper, we introduce a novel non-linear model, which we call "best-of", that captures such correlations. In particular, the combined effectiveness of implemented controls on a common vulnerability is taken to be (only) the highest effectiveness among them. We then develop a technique to convert the resulting nonlinear integer program into a MILP that is surprisingly quite efficient to solve.

Another challenge in modeling the security losses is anticipating the distribution of exploitation attempts across vulnerabilities. One approach is to use the histogram of the past attempts (retrieved from the logs of the enterprise itself or of any similars), or the publicly available statistics of attacks (*e.g.* [14]). We will refer to this model as the "passive" threat. In reality, the distribution of the attempts may adapt to the implementation of security controls: if a vulnerability is now well-mitigated, then the attempts may shift to other less protected ones. We will refer to this case as "reactive" threat, and establish a connection with a sequential game between the enterprise and attackers. For both passive and reactive cases, we provide methods to solve for the exact Pareto-optimal plans efficiently by converting the nonlinear optimizations into appropriate MILPs.

Finally, we will present a case study and numerical evaluations using our frameworks and a database of major security controls and vulnerabilities. We first compare the derived optimal plans of each model against the expert recommended list of critical controls, which reveals a general consistency, with the best match observed for the "best-of"–"reactive" model. Subsequently, we compare the optimal plans as well as the achieved utilities across our different security risk models. In particular, we observe that the "reactive" threat provides a more robust (and hence more favorable) notion of security risk in the sense that, optimization with respect to reactive threat does not lead to a terribly sub-optimal performance with respect to passive threat, however, the opposite is not true: an optimal plan with respect to passive threat can lead to terrible performance with respect to reactive threat, even for relatively high values of investment budget.

Contributions and Related Works. The main contributions of this work are:

- By reducing the model to MILP we make it possible to compute optimal solutions for cyber-security: the state space we consider in our case study is enormous, of the order of 10^{14} possible plans, and our MILP finds the optimal solution in seconds. The closest work in the cyber-security literature [24] takes instead days to converge and crucially lacks a guarantee of optimality.
- Our case study represents the largest cyber-security modeling to date. The data used in the experiments has been extracted from official government organizations' publications like [4,5,17] as well as the publicly available databases of CVE, CWE and CWSS.

Quantitative risk assessment and mitigation in cyber-security has been a thematic topic of research in security, that has in part lead to established methodologies such as Magerit and NIST800-30 among others [21]. Works that explicitly investigate the problem of investment portfolios in cyber-security include [1–3,7,8,11–13,15,16,18–20,24]. Compared with these references, our work presents a wider modeling framework both in terms of the way controls can be combined (additive, multiplicative, best-of) and in terms of the attacker capabilities and threat types (passive, reactive). Also of the above works only [13,16,24] are based on real world data and only [13,24] model indirect costs. Compared with these last two works their solutions are based on Tabu Search (TS) and genetic algorithms (GA) respectively, and are inherently more inefficient than the solutions here presented and they do not provide any guarantee of optimality within their framework. Also issues like robustness are largely neglected.

2   Modeling and Notations

Let $\mathcal{C}$ represent the set of (cyber-security) *controls*, each with potentially multiple intensity levels of implementation. We will use $\mathcal{L}_c = \{1, \ldots, L_c\}$ to denote the set of available implementation levels of control c. A *cyber-security plan* or a cyber-security investment portfolio $\boldsymbol{x} = (x_c)$ is a vector in $\mathcal{X} := \times_{c \in \mathcal{C}}(\{0\} \cup \mathcal{L}_c)$, where $x_c = l \in \{0\} \cup \mathcal{L}_c$ represents the decision to implement control c at level l, with zero representing the lack of implementation of that control.

Let $B \in \mathbb{R}^+$ be the (hard) constraint on the total cyber-security *budget* of the enterprise. Let $D, I, R : \mathcal{X} \to \mathbb{R}^+$ respectively denote the (total) *direct cost*, (total) *indirect cost*, and the (aggregate) *"security risk"* of the enterprise given a security plan. As we proceed, we explicitly describe each of these functions. But first, we give a high-level description of the problem of cyber-security investment as a (constrained) multi-objective integer programming:

$$\min_{x \in \mathcal{X}} \left(D(x), I(x), R(x) \right) \qquad \text{s.t.:} \ D(x) \le B \qquad (1)$$

Let $d_c(l) \in \mathbb{R}^+$ be the direct cost of implementing control $c \in \mathcal{C}$ at level $l \in \{0\} \cup \mathcal{L}_c$, with the obvious convention that $d_c(0) = 0$. The direct cost is a combination of the (one-time) investment (for obtaining the required hardware, software or staff), and the recurrent monetary expenses associated with the implementation. For controls that are already in place, i.e., existing controls, only the recurrent expenses must be considered. Similarly, let $i_c(l) \in \mathbb{R}^+$ be the indirect cost of implementing control $c \in \mathcal{C}$ at level $l \in \{0\} \cup \mathcal{L}_c$, where $i_c(0) = 0$. The indirect costs are those related to reduced performance (due to introduced overhead on resources), lowered morale (e.g. due to restricting access, false positives, stricter password policies), etc., that are not easily convertible to monetary losses. Using these notations, we simply have:

$$D(x) = \sum_{c \in \mathcal{C}} d_c(x_c), \qquad I(x) = \sum_{c \in \mathcal{C}} i_c(x_c) \qquad (2)$$

We will denote the set of vulnerabilities of the enterprise by $\mathcal{V}$. Let $e_{cv}(l)$ be the stand-alone *effectiveness* of control c at implementation level $l \in \{0\} \cup \mathcal{L}_c$ on vulnerability v, that is, $e_{cv}(l)$ is the probability that an exploitation attempt on vulnerability v is blocked when "only" control c at implementation level l is present. Then $s_{cv}(l) := 1 - e_{cv}(l)$ will represent the success probability of an attempt at exploitation of vulnerability v when no other control than c at level l is implemented. Trivially, $e_{cv}(0) = 0 \ \forall c \in \mathcal{C}$ and $\forall v \in \mathcal{V}$.

Let $\mathcal{C}_v$ be the set of controls that can affect vulnerability v, i.e., $\mathcal{C}_v := \{c \in \mathcal{C} : e_{cv}(l) > 0 \text{ for some } l \in \mathcal{L}_c\}$. If for a vulnerability v, we have $\|\mathcal{C}_v\| > 1$, then the combined effectiveness of the controls on v needs to be modeled. In particular, let $S_v : \mathcal{X} \to [0,1]$ represent the success probability of an exploitation attempt on vulnerability $v \in \mathcal{V}$ given a cyber-security plan. We provide three different candidates for $S_v(x)$, in decreasing order of "complementary" effects among the defensive mechanisms of the controls (using the convention: $a^+ := \max\{a, 0\}$):

Additive: $\qquad\qquad S_v(x) = \left(1 - \sum_{c \in \mathcal{C}_v} e_{cv}(x_c) \right)^+ \qquad (3)$

Multiplicative: $\qquad\qquad S_v(x) = \prod_{c \in \mathcal{C}_v} s_{cv}(x_c) \qquad (4)$

Best-of: $\qquad\qquad S_v(x) = \min_{c \in \mathcal{C}_v} s_{cv}(x_c) \qquad (5)$

Let Λ_v be the random variable representing the losses to the enterprise when vulnerability $v \in \mathcal{V}$ is "successfully" exploited, and let λ_v be its expected value. These losses are due to the interruption in availability, integrity and/or confidentiality of data assets or services of the enterprise (e.g. tampering or theft of intellectual property, financial or client data, disruption of operations, *etc.*) as well as the secondary causes of losses such as reputation damage, loss of clients, legal fees, and so on.[1] We assume a "risk-neutral" decision-maker, and hence take the expected value of losses due to successful exploitations to be the measure of the security risk. In order to represent the expected losses, we need to anticipate the rate with which different vulnerabilities will be target of exploitation. This rate may depend on the profile of the enterprise and may also change in the face of the implemented security plan. Let $\pi : \mathcal{X} \to \Delta(\mathcal{V})$ represent this relation, where $\Delta(\mathcal{V})$ represents the set of all probability distributions over the set of vulnerabilities $\mathcal{V}$. In particular, let $\pi(v; \boldsymbol{x})$ be the rate at which vulnerability $v \in \mathcal{V}$ is attempted, given that the implemented plan is $\boldsymbol{x}$. Then the security risk of the (risk-neutral) enterprise in (1) can be written as:

$$R(\boldsymbol{x}) = \sum_{v \in \mathcal{V}} \pi(v; \boldsymbol{x}) S_v(\boldsymbol{x}) \lambda_v \tag{6}$$

Modeling π requires anticipating the behavior of the attackers. In what follows, we consider two models for this behavior: "passive" and "reactive" threats.

Passive Threat. In this model, the probability distribution of the attacks is assumed given and that it "stays unchanged" irrespective of the implemented plan. In particular, let $\mathbf{P} \in \Delta \mathcal{V}$ be the distribution of attempts across vulnerabilities, and we have $\pi(v; \boldsymbol{x}) = \mathbf{P}(v), \forall \boldsymbol{x} \in \mathcal{X}$. Then the expected loss (as the risk-neutral measure of security risk) is:

$$R(\boldsymbol{x}) = \sum_{v \in \mathcal{V}} \mathbf{P}(v) S_v(\boldsymbol{x}) \lambda_v \tag{7}$$

where $S_v(\boldsymbol{x})$ comes from (3), (4) or (5), depending on the combination model.

Reactive Threat. As we mentioned, the distribution of exploitation attempts on vulnerabilities may evolve in the face of the new implemented security plan. In particular, the attempts on well-protected vulnerabilities may shift to less protected vulnerabilities. The most pessimistic scenario is the assumption that the attempts will shift to a vulnerability that has the most "effective impact", i.e., in (6): $\sum_{v \in \arg\max(S_v(\boldsymbol{x})\lambda_v)} \pi(v; \boldsymbol{x}) = 1$. Then, the corresponding expected loss (as the risk-neutral measure of security risk) is:

$$R(\boldsymbol{x}) = \max_{v \in \mathcal{V}} \left(S_v(\boldsymbol{x}) \lambda_v \right) \tag{8}$$

Next, we show that this notion of security is closely related to a sequential game.

---

[1] The loss Λ_v is enterprise dependent through their evaluation of different sources of disruption: An energy company may be primarily concerned with the availability of their service while a banking firm would assign a large weight to integrity of its data.

Connection to Game Theory. Consider the following non-zero-sum sequential two-player game of "perfect information":

Players: The enterprise 'e' (the leader), and the attacker 'a' (the follower).

Action spaces: The action of the enterprise is its cyber-security investment plan, $\boldsymbol{x}$. The attacker decides on which one of the vulnerabilities to try to exploit (if any). This can be represented by an indicator $\boldsymbol{y}$. Hence, the action spaces are respectively $\mathcal{X}$ and $\mathcal{Y} := \{\boldsymbol{y} \in \{0,1\}^{\mathcal{V}} : \sum_{v \in \mathcal{V}} \boldsymbol{y}(v) \leq 1\}$. The enterprise also has a constraint, defining its set of feasible actions: the total direct cost of its action has to be within its budget, which the attacker may not know the value of.

Information structure & strategies: The enterprise (the leader) makes the first "move", and its action and strategy spaces coincide. The attacker (the follower) observes the "move" of the enterprise $\boldsymbol{x}$ (hence the label: "perfect information") and, after re-assessing the effectiveness of attempts on each of the vulnerabilities, makes its decision of which one to attempt. Hence, a strategy of the attacker, denoted by σ, is a function $\sigma : \mathcal{X} \to \mathcal{Y}$. We will use the notation: $\sigma_v(\boldsymbol{x})$ to represent $\sigma(v; \boldsymbol{x})$, that is, $\sigma_v(\boldsymbol{x}) \in \{0,1\} \; \forall v \in \mathcal{V}$, and $\sum_{v \in \mathcal{V}} \sigma_v(\boldsymbol{x}) \leq 1$.

Payoffs. The negative payoff of the enterprise (which it wants to minimize) is a weighted sum of the three costs. Specifically, let w_d, w_i, and w_r be the weights of the (total) direct and indirect costs and the security damage to the enterprise, respectively, where $w_d, w_i \geq 0$, and $w_r > 0$. Referring to (2) and (6), the expected cost of the enterprise $u_e : \mathcal{X} \times \mathcal{Y} \to \mathbb{R}^+$ is therefore: $u_e(\boldsymbol{x}, \sigma(\boldsymbol{x})) = w_d \sum_{c \in \mathcal{C}} d_c(x_c) + w_i \sum_{c \in \mathcal{C}} i_c(x_c) + w_r \sum_{v \in \mathcal{V}} \sigma_v(\boldsymbol{x}) S_v(\boldsymbol{x}) \lambda_v$. The payoff of the attacker (which it wants to maximize) is (linearly) proportional to the expected security losses of the enterprise due to successful exploitations. In particular, letting $u_a : \mathcal{X} \times \mathcal{Y} \to \mathbb{R}^+$ represent the expected payoff of the attacker, we can write: $u_a(\boldsymbol{x}, \sigma(\boldsymbol{x})) = w'_r \sum_{v \in \mathcal{V}} \sigma_v(\boldsymbol{x}) S_v(\boldsymbol{x}) \lambda_v$, for some $w'_r > 0$, whose exact value may not be known to the enterprise. Note that we assumed exploitation attempts are costless for the attacker. We have the following result:

Proposition 1. *Any strategy of the enterprise in a Subgame Perfect Nash Equilibrium (SPNE) of the above non-zero-sum sequential two player game with "perfect information" is a Pareto-optimal solution to the multi-objective problem of (1) where the security cost is according to the "reactive threat" model in (8).*

Proof. Denoting the attacker's best response correspondence by σ^*, we have:

$$\sigma^*(\boldsymbol{x}) \in \arg\max_{\sigma} w'_r \sum_{v \in \mathcal{V}} \sigma_v(\boldsymbol{x}) S_v(\boldsymbol{x}) \lambda_v,$$

which implies $\sum_{v \in \mathcal{V}} \sigma_v^*(\boldsymbol{x}) S_v(\boldsymbol{x}) \lambda_v = \max_{v \in \mathcal{V}} (S_v(\boldsymbol{x}) \lambda_v)$. Now, using backward induction (for subgame perfection), the problem of the enterprise becomes:

$$\min_{\boldsymbol{x} \in \mathcal{X}} \left[w_d \sum_{c \in \mathcal{C}} d_c(x_c) + w_i \sum_{c \in \mathcal{C}} i_c(x_c) + w_r \max_{v \in \mathcal{V}} (S_v(\boldsymbol{x}) \lambda_v) \right], \quad \text{s.t.} \sum_{c \in \mathcal{C}} d_c(x_c) \leq B.$$

Finally, any solution of the above single optimization is also a Pareto-optimal solution of the multi-objective problem in (8). $\square$

It is worthwhile to note that the set of SPNE stays the same even if the game is converted to a zero-sum game in which the payoff of the attacker (to be maximized) is exactly the same as the total cost of the defender, i.e., if $u_a(\boldsymbol{x}, \sigma(\boldsymbol{x})) = u_e(\boldsymbol{x}, \sigma(\boldsymbol{x})) = w_d \sum_{c \in \mathcal{C}} d_c(x_c) + w_i \sum_{c \in \mathcal{C}} i_c(x_c) + w_r \sum_{v \in \mathcal{V}} \sigma_v(\boldsymbol{x}) S_v(\boldsymbol{x}) \lambda_v$. That is, if the attacker wanted to also maximize the investment and indirect costs of the defender, the optimization problem of the enterprise would not change at all. To see this, note that once the enterprise makes its implementation decision, the attacker cannot affect either the direct or indirect costs of the enterprise. Interestingly, this still holds even if the attacker has its own weights on different components of its overall payoff, i.e., if $u_a(\boldsymbol{x}, \sigma(\boldsymbol{x})) = w'_d \sum_{c \in \mathcal{C}} d_c(x_c) + w'_i \sum_{c \in \mathcal{C}} i_c(x_c) + w'_r \sum_{v \in \mathcal{V}} \sigma_v(\boldsymbol{x}) S_v(\boldsymbol{x}) \lambda_v$, for instance, if the attacker emphatically cares about the investment and indirect costs of the enterprise.[2]

Justifiability of Perfect Information Assumption. The full observability of the action of the enterprise may be unjustifiable in its literal interpretation. However, the critical point here is the much slower variability of security plans and much faster adaptability of attacks. Specifically, once the security plan is implemented, it will not be modified over a relatively long horizon. Hence, the enterprise can be thought of as having committed to its investment decision. In contrast, the exploitation attempts on different vulnerabilities can explore and "learn" the most effective vulnerability. If the transitory learning phase of the attacker is negligible, then the formalism of perfect information is applicable.

3   Solving the Multi-Objective Optimization

An approach to find the Pareto solutions of multi-objective-optimizations (MOO), including multi-objective integer programs (MOIP) and multi-objective combinatorial optimizations (MOCO) as its sub-branches, is through *scalarization*. Here, we provide a brief overview. The reader may consult the survey papers and textbooks on MOO for more detailed treatment, *e.g.* [6,10,23].

In scalarization methods, the MOO is transformed into (parametric) instances of single-objective optimization problems, the optimal solution of each is also a Pareto-optimal solution of the original MOO problem. The most widely known method is the "linear scalarization", where a weighted sum of the individual objectives constitutes the new objective function to be optimized. Specifically, consider a general n-objective optimization problem of $\min_{\boldsymbol{x} \in \mathcal{X}} (F_i(\boldsymbol{x}))$, $i = 1, \ldots, n$. Then a series of single-objective optimizations parametrized by the weight coefficients is constructed as follows: $\min_{\boldsymbol{x} \in \mathcal{X}} \sum_{i=1}^{n} w_i \tilde{F}_i(\boldsymbol{x})$, where $w_i > 0$ and $\sum_{i=1}^{n} w_i = 1$, where $\tilde{F}_i$ is a carefully chosen affine transformation

---

[2] The assumptions that attacks are costless and the reward is linearly proportional to the security damage to the enterprise is important for this observation, and the fact that the attacks do not affect the indirect costs, for instance, through the assumption that if an exploitation attempt fails there is no damage associated with it.

(i.e., normalization) of F_i.[3] Clearly, any solution of the weighted optimization is on the Pareto-front of the original multi-objective problem (because otherwise, there is an alternative solution that simultaneously improves all of the objective functions and at least one of them strictly, which contradicts the optimality in the scalarized problem).[4] The Pareto-optimal solutions are found by "sweeping" the weights over the entire simplex with some granularity, solving each of the single objective optimizations, and storing any "new" solution found.

In our problem, if the weights of the direct, indirect and security costs are respectively $w_d, w_i, w_r \geq 0$, such that $w_d + w_d + w_i = 1$, then, ignoring normalization for brevity, the resulting single objective optimizations (SOO) is:

$$\min_{x \in \mathcal{X}} [w_d D(x) + w_i I(x) + w_r R(x)] \qquad \text{s.t.: } D(x) \leq B. \qquad (9)$$

The form of $R(x)$ in part comes from (7) or (8) depending on the threat model, in which the success rates of each attempted vulnerability comes from (3), (4) or (5) depending on the model for combining efficacies of the controls. Each of these optimizations is an instance of a non-linear integer program, which is NP-hard to solve in general. Exploring the entire set of possible plans can be computationally infeasible since the number of plans is $\prod_{c \in \mathcal{C}} (L_c + 1)$, which grows exponentially in the number of controls (this is, for instance, over 10^{14} for our case study in Sect. 4). In what follows, we describe a series of tricks that help convert each of these nonlinear integer programs into mixed integer linear programs (MILPs) by introducing carefully designed auxiliary variables.[5]

3.1   Conversions to (binary) MILP

Common to all of our models is the introduction of binary decision variables as follows: $x_{cl} \in \{0, 1\}$ for each $c \in \mathcal{C}$ and $l \in \mathcal{L}_c$, which represents whether control c is implemented at level $l \in \mathcal{L}_c$. Using this notation, we first enforce that logically at most only one of the implementation levels per each control is selected:

$$\left(x_{cl} \in \{0, 1\} \ \forall l \in \mathcal{L}_c, \forall c \in \mathcal{C} \right), \quad \left(\sum_{l \in \mathcal{L}_c} x_{cl} \leq 1, \ \forall c \in \mathcal{C} \right). \qquad (10)$$

Recall that $\mathcal{L}_c := \{1, \ldots, L_c\}$, and in particular, it did not include level 0. Then the direct and indirect costs can be represented in linear form as follows:

$$D(x) = \sum_{c \in \mathcal{C}} \sum_{l \in \mathcal{L}_c} d_c(l) x_{cl}, \qquad I(x) = \sum_{c \in \mathcal{C}} \sum_{l \in \mathcal{L}_c} i_c(l) x_{cl}. \qquad (11)$$

Note that $d_c(l)$ and $i_c(l)$ are now just coefficients of the x_{cl} variables.

---

[3] The normalization is for numerical efficiency, such that the range of the objective functions becomes comparable, hence increasing the chances that a uniform sweeping of the weights even with a small number of steps finds all the Pareto solutions.

[4] Note, however, that finding all Pareto solutions is not guaranteed in this method.

[5] An alternative scalarization approach is the "epsilon-constraint" method. All of our MILP conversions can be modified for that method in a straightforward manner.

3.2   Additive Model in (3)

For the passive threat, the expected security damage in the additive model is:

$$R(\boldsymbol{x}) = \sum_{v \in \mathcal{V}} P_v \left(1 - \sum_{c \in \mathcal{C}_v} e_{cv}(x_c)\right)^+ \lambda_v. \tag{12}$$

In order to get rid of the non-linearity introduced by the "positive part" relation, we introduce auxiliary real-valued[6] variables y_v's for each $v \in \mathcal{V}$ such that: $y_v \geq 0$ and $y_v \geq 1 - \sum_{c \in \mathcal{C}} \sum_{l \in \mathcal{L}_c} e_{cv}(l) x_{cl}$. Note that these two inequalities and the goal of the minimization guarantee that at the solution, we have: $y_v = (1 - \sum_{c \in \mathcal{C}} \sum_{l \in \mathcal{L}_c} e_{cv}(l) x_{cl})^+$, as desired. Therefore, we can replace the security cost with $\sum_{v \in \mathcal{V}} P_v y_v \lambda_v$. Hence, we have the following simple proposition:

Proposition 2. *Each of the scalarized single-objective optimizations in* (9) *for the additive–passive risk model is equivalent to the following MILP:*

$$\min_{(x_{cl}, y_v)} \left[w_d \sum_{c \in \mathcal{C}} \sum_{l \in \mathcal{L}_c} d_c(l) x_{cl} + w_i \sum_{c \in \mathcal{C}} \sum_{l \in \mathcal{L}_c} i_c(l) x_{cl} + w_r \sum_{v \in \mathcal{V}} (P_v \lambda_v y_v) \right]$$

$$s.t. : (10), \sum_{c \in \mathcal{C}} \sum_{l \in \mathcal{L}_c} d_c(l) x_{cl} \leq B, \left(y_v \geq 0, \ y_v \geq 1 - \sum_{c \in \mathcal{C}} \sum_{l \in \mathcal{L}_c} e_{cv}(l) x_{cl} : \forall v \in \mathcal{V} \right).$$

For the reactive threat, the expected security damage as the security risk is: $R(\boldsymbol{x}) = \max_{v \in \mathcal{V}} \left\{ \left(1 - \sum_{c \in \mathcal{C}_v} e_{cv}(x_c)\right)^+ \lambda_v \right\}$. This can be made linear by simply introducing (only) one auxiliary variable z and imposing $z \geq 0$ and $z \geq (1 - \sum_{c \in \mathcal{C}} \sum_{l \in \mathcal{L}_c} e_{cv}(l) x_{cl}) \lambda_v$ for "all" $v \in \mathcal{V}$. This yields:

Proposition 3. *Each of the scalarized single objective optimizations in* (9) *for the additive–reactive risk model is equivalent to the following MILP:*

$$\min_{(x_{cl}, z)} \left[w_d \sum_{c \in \mathcal{C}} \sum_{l \in \mathcal{L}_c} d_c(l) x_{cl} + w_i \sum_{c \in \mathcal{C}} \sum_{l \in \mathcal{L}_c} i_c(l) x_{cl} + w_r z \right]$$

$$s.t. : (10), \sum_{c \in \mathcal{C}} \sum_{l \in \mathcal{L}_c} d_c(l) x_{cl} \leq B, \ z \geq 0, \left(z \geq \left(1 - \sum_{c \in \mathcal{C}} \sum_{l \in \mathcal{L}_c} e_{cv}(l) x_{cl}\right) \lambda_v \ \forall v \in \mathcal{V} \right).$$

3.3   Multiplicative Model in (4)

For the multiplicative model, we provide a modification of the method proposed in [19] and modify it for reactive threats too. First, we extend the optimization variables x_{cl} to explicitly include level zero for each control as well. Hence the "logical" choice constraint, as opposed to (10), becomes:

$$\left(x_{cl} \in \{0, 1\} \ \forall l \in \mathcal{L}_c \cup \{0\}, \forall c \in \mathcal{C}\right), \left(\sum_{l \in \mathcal{L}_c \cup \{0\}} x_{cl} = 1, \ \forall c \in \mathcal{C}\right). \tag{13}$$

---

[6] Hence, "mixed" integer linear program, as opposed to pure integer linear program.

Now, for each vulnerability $v \in \mathcal{V}$, we introduce $\sum_{c \in \mathcal{C}_v}(1 + L_c)$ positive real-valued auxiliary ("flow") variables $y_{vcl} \geq 0$, one for each $l \in \mathcal{L}_c \cup \{0\}$ per each control $c \in \mathcal{C}_v$, with the following interpretation: y_{vcl} is the fraction ("flow") of the exploitation attempts on vulnerability v that is "handled" by control c at level l. Let $\mathcal{C}_v$, the set of controls that can affect vulnerability v, be enumerated as follows: $\mathcal{C}_v = \{c_1^v, \ldots, c_{|\mathcal{C}_v|}^v\}$ (the order is immaterial). The total fraction of the exploitation attempts on vulnerability v that is to be handled by the first control in $\mathcal{C}_v$ is 1. That is, for each $v \in \mathcal{V}$, we impose: $\sum_{l \in \mathcal{L}_c \cup \{0\}} y_{vcl} = 1$ where $c = c_1^v$. A portion of these exploitation attempts gets blocked by controls c_1^v, depending on which level it is implemented at, and the "surviving" fraction has to be handled by the next control in $\mathcal{C}_v$. Hence, for each $v \in \mathcal{V}$, we have the following flow-like constraint: $\sum_{l \in \mathcal{L}_c \cup \{0\}} y_{vcl} s_{cv}(l) = \sum_{l \in \mathcal{L}_{c'} \cup \{0\}} y_{vc'l}$, where $c' = c_i^v$ and $c = c_{i-1}^v$ for all $i = 2, \ldots, |\mathcal{C}_v|$. Note that $s_{cv}(l)$ is just a coefficient in this linear equality constraint, and recall the convention that $s_{cv}(0) = 1$ for all $v \in \mathcal{V}$, $c \in \mathcal{C}_v$. The overall probability of success of exploitation attempts of vulnerability v is the fraction that survives the last control in $\mathcal{C}_v$, that is, $\sum_{l \in \mathcal{L}_c \cup \{0\}} y_{vcl} s_{cv}(l)$ where $c = c_{|\mathcal{C}_v|}^v$. Enforcing that only the implemented controls have their blocking effect on the vulnerabilities translates to the following constraint: $y_{vcl} \leq x_{cl}$ $\forall v \in \mathcal{V}$, $\forall c \in \mathcal{C}_v$, $\forall l \in \mathcal{L}_c \cup \{0\}$. This constraint along with (13) ensures that only one level per control is implemented (including level zero) and only the flow-variable corresponding to the implemented level can be nonzero. Now, recursively putting the equalities together will recover the multiplicative form of the overall success probability of exploitation of v. Putting all ingredients together, we have:

Proposition 4. *Each of the scalarized single objective optimizations in (9) for the multiplicative–passive risk model is equivalent to the following MILP:*

$$\min_{(x_{cl}, y_{cvl})} \left[w_d \sum_{c \in \mathcal{C}} \sum_{l \in \mathcal{L}_c} d_c(l) x_{cl} + w_i \sum_{c \in \mathcal{C}} \sum_{l \in \mathcal{L}_c} i_c(l) x_{cl} + w_r \sum_{v \in \mathcal{V}} P_v \lambda_v \sum_{\substack{l \in \mathcal{L}_c \cup \{0\} \\ c = c_{|\mathcal{C}_v|}^v}} y_{vcl} s_{cv}(l) \right]$$

$$\text{s.t.} : (13), \sum_{c \in \mathcal{C}} \sum_{l \in \mathcal{L}_c} d_c(l) x_{cl} \leq B, \left(0 \leq y_{vcl} \leq x_{cl} : \forall v \in \mathcal{V}, \forall c \in \mathcal{C}_v, \forall l \in \mathcal{L}_c \cup \{0\} \right),$$

$$\left(\sum_{l \in \mathcal{L}_c \cup \{0\}} y_{vcl} = 1 : c = c_1^v, \forall v \in \mathcal{V} \right), \tag{14}$$

$$\sum_{l \in \mathcal{L}_{c'} \cup \{0\}} y_{vc'l} = \sum_{l \in \mathcal{L}_c \cup \{0\}} y_{vcl} s_{cv}(l) : c' = c_i^v, c = c_{i-1}^v, \forall i = 2, \ldots, |\mathcal{C}_v|, \forall v \in \mathcal{V}.$$

For the reactive threat model, we can introduce an extra variable z and enforce: $z \geq \lambda_v \sum_{l \in \mathcal{L}_c \cup \{0\}} y_{vcl} s_{cv}(l)$ where $c = c_{|\mathcal{C}_v|}^v$ for all $v \in \mathcal{V}$, along with the rest of the constraints in (14), and change the objective function to the following:

$$\min_{(x_{cl}, y_{cvl}, z)} \left[w_d \sum_{c \in \mathcal{C}} \sum_{l \in \mathcal{L}_c} d_c(l) x_{cl} + w_i \sum_{c \in \mathcal{C}} \sum_{l \in \mathcal{L}_c} i_c(l) x_{cl} + w_r z \right] \tag{15}$$

3.4   "Best-of" Model in (5)

For each vulnerability $v \in \mathcal{V}$ define the set of (flow-based) positive auxiliary variables $y_{v,c,l} \geq 0$ for each $c \in \{0\} \cup \mathcal{C}_v$ and $l \in \mathcal{L}_c$, that is, a flow is considered for each control that affects vulnerability v, along with a "no-control" flow $y_{v,0,0}$. For each $v \in \mathcal{V}$, we impose the total "in-flow" corresponding to vulnerability v to be one, i.e., $\sum_{c \in \{0\} \cup \mathcal{C}_v, l \in \mathcal{L}_c} y_{v,c,l} = 1$. We will also impose the logical "selection" constraints: $y_{v,c,l} \leq x_{cl}$ such that, if a control is not implemented, the corresponding flows will be zero. Then, in (5), we can simply replace $S_v(\boldsymbol{x}) = \min_{c \in \mathcal{C}_v} s_{cv}(x_c)$ with $\sum_{c \in \{0\} \cup \mathcal{C}_v, l \in \mathcal{L}_c} y_{v,c,l} s_{cv}(l)$, where we also define $s_{0v}(0) = 1$ as coefficients of $y_{v,0,0}$. To see that this conversion indeed works, note that when the total sum of the positive flow variables is constant, the minimization problem, trying to minimize the "out-flow" per each vulnerability, chooses the "pathway" with the highest available reduction, i.e. lowest flow coefficient, exactly as the "best-of" model intends. Putting together:

Proposition 5. *Each of the scalarized single objective optimizations in (9) for the best-of–passive risk model is equivalent to the following MILP:*

$$\min_{(x_{cl}, y_{cvl})} \left[w_d \sum_{c \in \mathcal{C}} \sum_{l \in \mathcal{L}_c} d_c(l) x_{cl} + w_i \sum_{c \in \mathcal{C}} \sum_{l \in \mathcal{L}_c} i_c(l) x_{cl} + w_r \sum_{v \in \mathcal{V}} P_v \lambda_v \sum_{\substack{c \in \mathcal{C}_v \cup \{0\} \\ l \in \mathcal{L}_c}} y_{vcl} s_{cv}(l) \right]$$

$$s.t. : \quad \sum_{c \in \mathcal{C}} \sum_{l \in \mathcal{L}_c} d_c(l) x_{cl} \leq B, \quad \left(0 \leq y_{vcl} \leq x_{cl}, \; \forall v \in \mathcal{V}, \forall c \in \mathcal{C}_v, \forall l \in \mathcal{L}_c \right),$$

$$\left(\sum_{\substack{c \in \mathcal{C}_v \cup \{0\} \\ l \in \mathcal{L}_c}} y_{vcl} = 1, \; \forall v \in \mathcal{V} \right), \quad \left(\sum_{l \in \mathcal{L}_c} x_{cl} \leq 1, \; \forall c \in \mathcal{C} \right), \quad \left(x_{cl} \in \{0,1\}, \; \forall l \in \mathcal{L}_c, \forall c \in \mathcal{C} \right).$$

For the "reactive" threat model, the only difference is that the security risk (the third summation in the objective function) is replaced with the extra auxiliary (real-valued) variable z that needs to satisfy the following (linear) constraints:
$z \geq \lambda_v \sum_{c \in \mathcal{C}_v \cup \{0\}, l \in \mathcal{L}_c} y_{vcl} s_{cv}(l), \; \forall v \in \mathcal{V}.$

3.5   From Vulnerabilities to Attacks

The expected losses (λ's) are more accurately related to attacks as opposed to vulnerabilities. For instance, consider an attack A whose success requires successful exploitation of two vulnerabilities v_1 and v_2, as part of the stages of the attack, and if successful inflicts an expected damage of λ_A. Since λ_A is only inflicted when both vulnerabilities are successfully exploited, it is not possible to separate the expected loss among v_1 and v_2 separately. We provide two different models for considering attacks that involve exploiting multiple vulnerabilities and describe how our developed MILPs can be extended to them.

3.6   Independence Across Vulnerabilities

Let $\mathcal{A}$ represent the set of attacks, where the expected inflicted loss if attack $A \in \mathcal{A}$ is successful is λ_A. Consider the multiplicative model in which the effect of controls on a vulnerability was assumed to be independent. Now assume further that the successful exploitation of different vulnerabilities comprising an attack are also independent events. Then, the expected security damages will be:

$$R(x) = \sum_{A\in\mathcal{A}} P_A \lambda_A \prod_{v\in A} \prod_{c\in C_v} s_{cv}(x_c) = \sum_{A\in\mathcal{A}} P_A \lambda_A \prod_{c\in C_v} \prod_{v\in A} s_{cv}(x_c)$$

This shows that, by introducing flow variables y_{Acl} for each attack, and performing a pre-processing by computing $s_{cA}(x_c) := \prod_{v\in A} s_{cv}(x_c)$, the same formulation as in Proposition 4 can be applied with $s_{cv}(l)$ replaced by $s_{cA}(l)$.

3.7 Correlations Across Vulnerabilities

The success of exploitation attempts across different vulnerabilities comprising an attack may have positive correlations. These correlations arise due to skills or resources of the attackers: a successful exploitation of a stage of an attack can be a signal about the higher abilities/resources of the attacker. A model that reflects these correlations is the following: the success chance of carrying out an attack is determined by the lowest probability of success across the vulnerabilities that comprise that attack. Now, combining this model with the "best-of" model that takes the correlations across defensive mechanism of controls, we get:

$$R(x) = \sum_{A\in\mathcal{A}} P_A \lambda_A \min_{v\in A} \min_{c\in C_v} s_{cv}(x_c) = \sum_{A\in\mathcal{A}} P_A \lambda_A \min_{c\in C_v} \min_{v\in A} s_{cv}(x_c)$$

Therefore, by introducing auxiliary variables y_{Acl} per attacks $A \in \mathcal{A}$ as opposed to per vulnerabilities, and performing a pre-processing $s_{cA}(l) := \min_{v\in A} s_{cv}(l)$, we can apply the same formulation as in Proposition 5 with $s_{cv}(l)$ replaced by $s_{cA}(l)$.

3.8 Parameter Uncertainties

The most likely source of uncertainty in the parameters of our models is arguably the effectiveness of the controls against each of the vulnerabilities at different implementation levels, i.e., $e_{cv}(l)$'s. Suppose that each of these parameters are given as an uncertainty interval $[\underline{e}_{cv}(l), \overline{e}_{cv}(l)]$ a subset of $[0,1]$, with the interpretation that the true (realized) value of the parameter can be anywhere in that interval with an unknown distribution. Collating all the efficacy parameters as $[e_{cv}]$, we can show the uncertainty intervals by their lower and upper end in a concise way as: $[\underline{e}_{cv}] \preceq [e_{cv}] \preceq [\overline{e}_{cv}]$, where $\preceq$ denotes element-wise inequalities.

One way to deal with the uncertainty is to optimize for the "worst" combined realization of the uncertain parameters. Consider the optimizations in (9), with the uncertain parameters $[e_{cv}]$ also as variables. Then finding optimal plans with respect to worst case of the uncertainties in efficacies can be expressed as follows:

$$\min_{x\in\mathcal{X}} \left[\max_{[\underline{e}_{cv}]\preceq[e_{cv}]\preceq[\overline{e}_{cv}]} \left\{ w_d \tilde{D}(x) + w_i \tilde{I}(x) + w_r \tilde{R}(x, [e_{cv}]) \right\} \right]$$

$$\text{s.t.:} \quad \max_{[\underline{e}_{cv}]\preceq[e_{cv}]\preceq[\overline{e}_{cv}]} \{D(x) - B\} \le 0 \tag{16}$$

We have the following observation, which we skip the proof of for brevity: For all of the security risk models in this paper, (16) is equivalent to:

$$\min_{x \in \mathcal{X}} \left[w_d \tilde{D}(x) + w_i \tilde{I}(x) + w_r \tilde{R}(x, [\underline{e}_{cv}]) \right] \qquad \text{s.t.: } D(x) \leq B$$

4 Numerical Evaluations

In this section, we first use our frameworks to investigate a list of the most important security controls for a typical SME (Small and Medium Enterprise) given a realistic set of parameters. As a soft method of validation, we compare the controls that most consistently appear in the Pareto-optimal plans against the top critical cyber-security controls as recommended by experts and policy organizations, specifically, SANS [17] and GCHQ [4,5]. Subsequently, we provide some comparisons among the different security models.[7]

Parameters for our Case Study: The vulnerabilities that a typical SME faces can be generally categorized into three groups: I- "Software Vulnerabilities", II- "Social Engineering" (*e.g.* phishing, pretexting, baiting), and III- "Network Vulnerabilities". We incorporated a wide range of vulnerabilities from each of these categories. In total, we consider 37 most common vulnerabilities (Table 1 in the Appendix of our tech. report [9]) which we collected from a combination of the publicly available databases such as the Critical Weakness Enumeration (CWE) and the Common Attack Pattern Enumeration and Classification (CAPEC).

Recall that the "Impact" score for each vulnerability in our models, i.e., I_v, designated the expected damage inflicted on the SME in case of a successful exploitation of that vulnerability. To obtain relative values for I_v, from the vulnerability descriptions in the "Common Weakness Scoring System (CWSS)", we derived a score for the impact of each vulnerability on three sources of damage: (1) "Data Losses", damages as a result of a compromise in the confidentiality or integrity of data; (2) "Business Disruption", losses due to compromise in the availability of services, and (3) "Reputation Damage". For each vulnerability, we considered a weighted average of these three damages as its overall impact. We also estimated the passive probability of exploitation by combining some relevant features from the Common Weakness Scoring System (CWSS) database. Specifically, features regarding their "System Requirement Score" (*e.g.* "required privilege"), "Technical Requirement Score" (*e.g.* "likelihood of discovery" and "ease of execution"), and "Environmental Factor Score" (*e.g.* "exploitability" and "accessibility of information"), were combined to give a measure of the "relative ease" to exploit each vulnerability and hence get a measure of the overall rate of attempts on each vulnerability. The general trend was similar to the measurement reports of [14].

For cyber-security controls, we need each control to be an actionable process as a single independent measure that can be used to help mitigate vulnerabilities

---

[7] Due to space limit, some of our evaluations were relegated to our technical report [9].

in the system. We derived our controls from the "SANS Top 20 Critical Security controls", but we separated some of the controls that were in fact represented by a composition of multiple investment decisions. Therefore, overall, we take into account 27 distinct controls, each with multiple levels of implementation, leading to 75 distinct controls. We estimated and normalized costs parameters (both direct and indirect costs) reported in Table 2 in our tech. report [9]. We also gathered estimates of the efficacy parameters based on the defensive mechanism of each measure in the face of the exploitation requirements of each vulnerability (Table 3 in our tech. report [9]).

Validation. Our overall objective is to provide a cyber-security investment framework which is accurate, credible and relevant to the real world. A rigorous validation should take the form of a field validation in the style of clinical trials. However, at this stage, for both economical and security reasons, this approach is not feasible. In reflecting about what can constitute a reasonable validation of our framework we have decided to concentrate on expert advice, in particular the available recommendations from government agencies. These agencies have studied thousands of cyber-security incidents over many years and as such we consider their advice credible and relevant. In particular, we consult with the SANS institute "The Critical Security Controls for Effective Cyber Defense" [17], and the "10 Steps to Cyber Security" [5] and "Common Cyber Attacks: Reducing The Impact" by GCHQ [4].

A subset of the critical controls is common among all of these documents. For instance from the SANS institute the core of recommended controls are the "5 quick wins" [17]: I- Application whitelisting (found in CSC-2); II- Use of standard, secure system configurations (found in CSC-3); III- Patching application software within 48 hours (found in CSC-4); IV- Patching system software within 48 hours (found in CSC 4); and V- Reducing the number of users with administrative privileges (found in CSC 3 and CSC 12)". A similar set of critical controls is recommended by the latest GCHQ advice [4]: I- Boundary firewalls and Internet gateways; II- Malware protection; III- Patch management; IV- Whitelisting and execution control; V- Secure configuration; VI- Password policy; VII- User access control; It is hence interesting to compare our results with these sets of recommendations and in particular their intersection: I- Patch management; II-Application whitelisting; III- Secure configuration; IV- User access control.

To make a meaningful comparison we have organized the controls appearing in our solutions in a "prevalence ordering". The "most prevalent" controls are the ones that appear across the most number of Pareto-optimal plans for a large range of parameters: we take this as a measure of the relative importance of each cyber-security control. In particular, For each of our models, we computed the number of times each cyber-security control (at any of its implementation levels) appears in the plan across all Pareto-optimal solutions. We then "ranked" the controls based on this measure of prevalence in decreasing order. The resulting ranks are provided in Table 1 in the Appendix. We observed that overall, "patching", "firewalls" and "whitelisting" appear among the top controls for all cases and there is a general consistency with the official recommendations. The best match with the official recommendations pertains to the "Best-of – Reactive" model. This reinforces the intuition that the "Best-of" combination of controls concentrates on the contributions of the most effective controls, and the "Reactive" threat concentrates on the most critical vulnerabilities. This observation also underlines the importance of taking into account the hitherto ignored correlations in the defensive mechanisms of the security controls.

The consistency of our results and the official advice is an encouraging first step. In the longer term we expect our mathematical framework to guide and eventually possibly replace expert advice. Another advantage is that we can customize our data to specific organizations and particular threats and so provide better "individualized" investment portfolios than a generic one-size-fit-all recommendation. We can also extend and edit the data with new controls and attacks as the threat scenarios evolve. Our solutions can be efficiently computed for large sets of controls and attacks, way beyond human manual capabilities. Our framework and the resulting tools hence open the door for customizable and accurate quantitative cyber-security advice.

A note on the computational efficiency of our frameworks. It is worth noting that, with their distinct implementation levels, we are considering 75 distinct security controls, which lead to an order of 10^{14} distinct cyber-security plans. With this size of the problem, an exhaustive search for finding Pareto-optimal plans is outright impractical. Generic heuristic methods such as "Genetic Algorithms" and "Tabu Search" as used in works like [13, 24] will also take "days" to converge, and even after convergence, there is no guarantee of optimality. In contrast, our MILP-based frameworks, using a generic MILP solver (Matlab's `intlinprog` in our case on a typical laptop) solve for an "exact" optimal solution over the following time scales: "additive" (both passive and reactive): fraction of a second; "Multiplicative" (both "passive" and "reactive"): less than a minute; and surprisingly, for the "Best-of" model, about a second for the "passive" case, and less than 10 seconds for the reactive case.

Conclusions and future works. Decision support for cyber-security is a complex multi-objective problem. We modeled a large set of possible vulnerabilities and mitigations, and demonstrated how to efficiently compute Pareto-optimal solutions using Mixed Integer Linear Programming conversions. Many challenges remain, e.g. taking into account the costs of attacks, custom combined efficacies of controls, better approaches to deal with parameter uncertainties, combining learning and optimization, and stronger model validation. Some of these problems are within the realm of optimization engineering, others require more real-world data, which will be direction of our future work.

Acknowledgment. This work was supported by EPSRC project EP/K005820/1.

Appendix

Table 1. Order of prevalence of controls among Pareto-optimal plans, for different security models. In the column-headers, the initials "A.", "M." and "B." stand for "Additive", "Multiplicative" and "Best-of", also, "P." and "R." designate "Reactive" and "Passive", respectively. The table is ordered with respect to the Best-of prevalence rank, as it shows the best match with expert recommendation.

Cyber-security control	B.R	M.R	A.R	B.P	M.P	A.P
Deployment of Network Firewalls	1	1	1	2	2	2
Deploy Web Application Firewalls	2	2	4	4	3	3
Anti-Malware Software	3	7	6	3	4	5
Automated Patching Tools	4	3	2	1	1	1
Use of Secure Config. for OS	5	5	7	5	10	9
Application Whitelisting	6	4	3	10	8	8
Network Data Encryption	7	6	5	7	6	4
Strong Secure Password Policy	8	15	20	13	12	17
User Access Controls	9	12	17	6	7	13
Secure Configuration Controls for All Devices	10	24	26	9	15	22
Penetration Testing	11	13	13	27	27	12
Automated Vulnerability Scanning Tools	12	11	11	17	13	18
Automated Inventory Scanning & Management	13	8	8	16	14	11
Segmentation of Network Based on Trust Levels	14	17	22	23	23	19
Host Based IPS	15	9	16	12	5	7
Deploy DLP Based Systems	16	22	24	8	16	25
Execution Control on Removable Media	17	21	15	18	17	21
Employ Wireless Devices Authentication Config.	18	23	25	19	18	26
Employ Port Scanning & Control Tools	19	25	21	20	19	23
Deploy Network Based IDS	20	20	19	14	20	20
Deploy Network Based Proxies	21	16	14	21	21	14
Deployment of VLANs for Sensitive Operations	22	26	27	22	22	27
Website Whitelisting	23	27	18	11	11	16
Network Log Reporting	24	14	12	24	24	10
Account Management Controls	25	19	23	25	25	24
User Training & Education	26	18	10	26	26	15
Incident Handling & Response Policies	27	10	9	15	9	6

References

1. Anderson, R., Moore, T.: The economics of information security. Science **314**(5799), 610–613 (2006)
2. Butler, S.A.: Security attribute evaluation method: a cost-benefit approach. In: Proceedings of the 24th International Conference on Software Engineering. ACM (2002)
3. Cavusoglu, H., Raghunathan, S., Yue, W.T.: Decision-theoretic and game-theoretic approaches to it security investment. J. Manag. Inf. Syst. **25**(2), 281–304 (2008)
4. CESG: Common cyber attacks: Reducing the impact. https://www.gov.uk/government/uploads/system/uploads/attachment_data/file/400106/Common_Cyber-Attacks-Reducing_The_Impact.pdf. Accessed on 13 April 2016
5. CESG (UK's Nat. Tech. Authority for Inf. Assurance): 10 Steps to Cyber Security. https://www.cesg.gov.uk/10-steps-cyber-security. Accessed on 13 April 2016
6. Chinchuluun, A., Pardalos, P.M.: A survey of recent developments in multiobjective optimization. Ann. Oper. Res. **154**(1), 29–50 (2007)
7. Dewri, R., Poolsappasit, N., Ray, I., Whitley, D.: Optimal security hardening using multi-objective optimization on attack tree models of networks. In: Proceedings of the 14th ACM Conference on Computer and Communications Security. ACM (2007)
8. Gupta, M., Rees, J., Chaturvedi, A., Chi, J.: Matching information security vulnerabilities to organizational security profiles: a genetic algorithm approach. Decis. Support Syst. **41**(3), 592–603 (2006)
9. Khouzani, M., Malacaria, P., Hankin, C., Fielder, A., Smeraldi, F.: Efficient numerical frameworks for multi-objective cyber security planning: Technical report. http://www.eecs.qmul.ac.uk/~khouzani/Papers/ESORICS16Techrep.pdf
10. Marler, R.T., Arora, J.S.: Survey of multi-objective optimization methods for engineering. Struct. Multi. Optim. **26**(6), 369–395 (2004)
11. Nagurney, A., Nagurney, L.S., Shukla, S.: A supply chain game theory framework for cybersecurity investments under network vulnerability. In: Daras, N.J., Rassias, M.T. (eds.) Computation, Cryptography, and Network Security, pp. 381–398. Springer, Switzerland (2015)
12. Ojamaa, A., Tyugu, E., Kivimaa, J.: Pareto-optimal situaton analysis for selection of security measures. In: Military Communications Conference. IEEE (2008)
13. Panaousis, E., Fielder, A., Malacaria, P., Hankin, C., Smeraldi, F.: Cybersecurity games and investments: a decision support approach. In: Poovendran, R., Saad, W. (eds.) GameSec 2014. LNCS, vol. 8840, pp. 266–286. Springer, Heidelberg (2014)
14. Passeri, P.: HACKMAGEDDON, information security timelines and statistics. http://www.hackmageddon.com. Accessed on 19 April 2016
15. Poolsappasit, N., Dewri, R., Ray, I.: Dynamic security risk management using bayesian attack graphs. IEEE Trans. Dependable Secure Comput. **9**(1), 61–74 (2012)
16. Rees, L.P., Deane, J.K., Rakes, T.R., Baker, W.H.: Decision support for cybersecurity risk planning. Decis. Support Syst. **51**(3), 493–505 (2011)
17. SANS: The critical security controls for effective cyber defense. https://www.sans.org/media/critical-security-controls/CSC-5.pdf. Accessed on 13 April 2016
18. Sarala, R., Zayaraz, G., Vijayalakshmi, V.: Optimal selection of security countermeasures for effective information security. In: Padma Suresh, L., Panigrahi, B.K. (eds.) ICSCS 2015. AISC, vol. 398, pp. 345–353. Springer, Heidelberg (2015)

19. Sawik, T.: Selection of optimal countermeasure portfolio in IT security planning. Decis. Support Syst. **55**(1), 156–164 (2013)
20. Schechter, S.E.: Computer security strength & risk: a quantitative approach. Ph.d. thesis, Harvard University Cambridge, Massachusetts (2004)
21. Syalim, A., Hori, Y., Sakurai, K.: Comparison of risk analysis methods: Mehari, magerit, nist800-30 and microsoft's security management guide. In: International Conference on Availability, Reliability and Security. IEEE (2009)
22. UK's Department for Business, Innovation & Skills: Cyber Essentials Scheme. https://www.gov.uk/government/publications/cyber-essentials-scheme-overview. Accessed on 7 January 2016
23. Ulungu, E.L., Teghem, J.: Multi-objective combinatorial optimization problems: a survey. J. Multi Criteria Decis. Anal. **3**(2), 83–104 (1994)
24. Viduto, V., Maple, C., Huang, W., López-Peréz, D.: A novel risk assessment and optimisation model for a multi-objective network security countermeasure selection problem. Decis. Support Syst. **53**(3), 599–610 (2012)

E-voting and E-commerce

On Bitcoin Security in the Presence of Broken Cryptographic Primitives

Ilias Giechaskiel[✉], Cas Cremers, and Kasper B. Rasmussen

University of Oxford, Oxford, UK
{ilias.giechaskiel,cas.cremers,kasper.rasmussen}@cs.ox.ac.uk

Abstract. Digital currencies like Bitcoin rely on cryptographic primitives to operate. However, past experience shows that cryptographic primitives do not last forever: increased computational power and advanced cryptanalysis cause primitives to break frequently, and motivate the development of new ones. It is therefore crucial for maintaining trust in a cryptocurrency to anticipate such breakage.

We present the first systematic analysis of the effect of broken primitives on Bitcoin. We identify the core cryptographic building blocks and analyze the ways in which they can break, and the subsequent effect on the main Bitcoin security guarantees. Our analysis reveals a wide range of possible effects depending on the primitive and type of breakage, ranging from minor privacy violations to a complete breakdown of the currency. Our results lead to several observations on, and suggestions for, the Bitcoin migration plans in case of broken or weakened cryptographic primitives.

1 Introduction

Cryptocurrencies such as Bitcoin rely on cryptographic primitives for their guarantees and correct operation. Such primitives typically get weakened over time, due to progress in cryptanalysis and advances in the computational power of the attackers. It is therefore prudent to expect that, in time, the cryptographic primitives used by Bitcoin will be partially, if not completely, broken.

In anticipation of such breakage, the Bitcoin community has created a wiki page that contains draft contingency plans [46]. However, such plans are hand-wavy and incomplete at best: no adequate transition mechanism has been built into Bitcoin, and no plans for partial breakage (or weakening of a primitive) have been considered. Primitives rarely break abruptly, but instead they break gradually. With hash functions, for example, it is common that first a single collision is found. This is then later generalized to multiple collisions, and only later do arbitrary collisions become feasible to compute. In parallel, the complexity of attacks decreases to less-than-brute-force, and computational power increases. Finally, quantum computing will make some attacks easier, e.g., by Grover's pre-image attack [20], or Shor's algorithm for discrete log computation [40].

Hence, even if such attacks are years away from being practical, it is crucial to anticipate the impact of broken primitives, so that appropriate contingency plans can be put in place. Our work contributes towards filling this gap.

© Springer International Publishing Switzerland 2016
I. Askoxylakis et al. (Eds.): ESORICS 2016, Part II, LNCS 9879, pp. 201–222, 2016.
DOI: 10.1007/978-3-319-45741-3_11

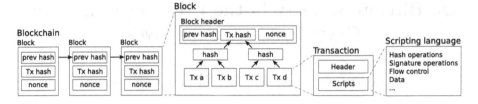

Fig. 1. The blockchain data structure. This forms the basis of the public, append-only ledger where all transactions are recorded.

Contributions. We provide the first systematic analysis of the impact of broken primitives on Bitcoin. By analyzing the failure of primitive properties, both in isolation and in combination, we describe precisely the range of consequences different breaks have, and pinpoint their exact cause. For example, the flexibility of the coinbase transaction is the reason why mining becomes trivial if an adversary can easily compute pre-images of SHA256 hashes. In our analysis, we introduce an oracle model for hash functions that unifies and extends several existing types of breakage, allowing us to analyze more realistic attacks. Our investigations raise concerns about the currently specified migration plans for Bitcoin, being overly conservative in some respects, while inadequate in others. To that end, we make concrete suggestions regarding future iterations of the cryptocurrency in response to entirely broken and partially weakened primitives.

Overview. We provide background in Sect. 2 and propose our adversary model in Sect. 3. We next analyze the effects of broken primitives: hashing in Sect. 4, signature schemes in Sect. 5, and combinations of primitive breaks in Sect. 6. We revisit the current Bitcoin implementation and its contingency plans in Sect. 7. We discuss related work in Sect. 8 and conclude in Sect. 9.

2 Background

In this section, we give a description of Bitcoin, the popular peer-to-peer (P2P) cryptocurrency introduced in 2008 by Satoshi Nakamoto [34]. Figure 1 shows a high-level view of the main component of Bitcoin—the blockchain—which will guide this section. The blockchain is a public log of all Bitcoin transactions that have occurred, combined together in components called blocks. Transactions use a scripting language that determines the owners of coins (Sect. 2.1), and it is up to miners to ensure that only valid transactions occur. To ensure that nobody can change or remove past transactions, miners have to solve a hard computational puzzle, known as a Proof-of-Work (Sect. 2.2). The final component of Bitcoin is its underlying P2P network which enables distributed communication (Sect. 2.3). We do not consider components outside the main protocol, such as wallets.

2.1   Transactions and Scripts

Bitcoin is an electronic cash system [34], so *transactions* to transfer coins between users are central to its structure. A transaction is a list of inputs—unspent transactions in the blockchain—and a list of outputs—addresses to which to transfer the coins, whose unit is a "satoshi", equal to 10^{-8} Bitcoins or BTCs. To ensure that only the owner can spend his coins, each input and output is accompanied by a *script*. For outputs, this "locking" script contains the conditions under which the output can be redeemed (*scriptPubKey*), while for inputs, an "unlocking" script contains a cryptographic signature (*scriptSig*) as proof that these conditions have been met. These *scripts* are sequences of instructions that get executed by special nodes called miners. To prevent Denial-of-Service (DoS) attacks exploiting computationally intensive instructions, most nodes only accept the five *standard scripts*:

1. *Public-Key.* The unlocking script must sign the transaction under this key.
2. *Pay-to-Public-Key-Hash (P2PKH).* The unlocking script must provide a public key which hashes to the given value, and must then sign the transaction.
3. *Multi-Signature.* An M-of-N ($N \leq 15$) multi-signature scheme provides N public keys, and requires M signatures in the unlocking script.
4. *Pay-to-Script Hash (P2SH).* This script is the hash of a non-P2SH standard transaction. The unlocking script provides the full script hashing to this value and any necessary signatures. This script is typically used to shorten the length of multi-signature transactions.
5. *Data Output (OP_RETURN).* The output cannot be redeemed, but can be used to store up to 40 arbitrary bytes, such as human-readable messages.

For a transaction to be valid, it must contain all the required fields, all signatures must be correct, and the scripts must be standard. This is a task that miners undertake for a small fee. Though some non-standard scripts can be accepted by some miners for a higher fee, we do not cover these in our analysis.

2.2   Mining and Consensus

To ensure that no coin is used more than once, every transaction is made public through a global, append-only ledger called the *blockchain*, consisting of *blocks* combining transactions in a Merkle Tree [33]. New blocks become a part of the blockchain through a process called *mining*: miners need to find a value (nonce) such that the hash of a block's header is less than a given target $h(hdr\|nonce) < T$. The idea behind this *proof-of-work* (PoW) scheme is that the probability of creating the next block is proportional to the miner's computational power, and because miners receive transaction fees, they are incentivized to do the work, which includes validating transactions and blocks. A summary is shown in Fig. 2, with the full procedure at [45].

Due to the probabilistic nature of mining, the presence of adversaries, and networking delays, miners may disagree on the current state of the blockchain. This is known as a *fork*. To deal with this issue, there are hard-coded blocks

```
input   : Bitcoin block
output : valid or invalid
/* Verify block header                                                 */
Verify Hash(block header) < target
Verify Merkle hash
Verify Hash(prev block) = prev_hash
/* Verify each transaction input in block                              */
foreach transaction input in the block do
    Check that referenced output transaction exists and hasn't already been spent
    Verify signatures
end
```

Fig. 2. Procedure to verify a block's cryptographic primitives.

included in the clients, known as *checkpoints*, starting from the first block, called the *genesis block*. In addition, honest (non-adversarial) miners work on the longest blockchain they become aware of, when other nodes announce new blocks and transactions. This way, nodes eventually reach consensus [10,17].

These temporary forks enable *double spending*: an adversary can have different transactions in different branches of the fork using the same inputs but different outputs. However, because the probability of "deep" forks where branches differ in the top N blocks drops exponentially in N, receivers usually wait for multiple confirmation blocks. If a miner or a group of collaborating miners (called a *pool*) is in control of a high enough proportion of the total computational power (51 % [29], or even less [16]), then they can possibly destabilize the system.

2.3   Network

The last key component is the Peer-to-Peer (P2P) network for distributed operation. Transactions and blocks are broadcast by nodes to their peers, and then relayed further to flood the network if they meet the relay policies (to prevent DoS attacks). Not every node is a miner or necessarily has access to the full chain: "lightweight" clients that use Simple Payment Verification (SPV) only download headers and the relevant transactions (with the corresponding Merkle Trees).

Over time, the need for extensions or bugfixing motivates protocol changes. Since not all nodes upgrade at the same time, this may introduce forks. If the validation rules in the upgrade become stricter, then the protocol remains backwards-compatible, resulting in a *softfork*. A *hardfork*, on the other hand, is not backwards-compatible, and thus requires the entire network to upgrade, as old software would reject new transactions and blocks as invalid.

3   System and Adversary Model

In this section we describe our Bitcoin model and discuss the adversary's goals and powers in the presence of broken cryptographic primitives. We distinguish between 4 entities: senders, receivers, miners, and networking nodes. Senders and receivers, collectively referred to as users, wish to exchange Bitcoins via transactions. They care about the amount of money under their control, but not about the details of the underlying system.

Transactions are transmitted via the underlying P2P network. Miners have their own (possibly different) copy of the blockchain, and have different hashing capacities. For our model, we consider pools as single miners with a large hashing capability. We distinguish between two adversary roles: user and miner. As a user, the adversary aims to make money, either by successfully double spending or by spending from another user's wallet. As a miner, the adversary controls a proportion $\alpha < 0.5$ of the mining power. We assume the adversary controls a proportion β of the nodes in the P2P network, so that he can attempt to split the network temporarily in the presence of a suitable vulnerability, but cannot be confident that such attempt will succeed.

We consider the economic aspects of Bitcoin out of scope, and we also do not consider developers as a threat. Finally, we do not investigate adversarial attacks of an individual miner against his own pool, thus allowing us to consider pools as single entities of more mining power.

4   Broken Hashing Primitives

In this section we look at the cryptographic hash functions in Bitcoin, and analyze the effect of a break in one of the properties of first and second pre-image and collision resistance. We generalize these into a single property called chosen-format bounded pre-image resistance.

4.1   Hashing in Bitcoin

In the original Bitcoin paper [34], the concrete primitives used are not specified: there were no "addresses" but just public keys, and the hash used for mining and the Merkle tree was just referred to as a hash function. The current Bitcoin implementation, going back to at least version 0.1.0 [35] uses two hash functions.

Main Hash. This hash function has an output of 256 bits and requires applying SHA256 twice: $H_M(x) = \mathrm{SHA256}(\mathrm{SHA256}(x))$. It is the hash used for *mining* (Proof-of-Work): miners need to find a nonce such that the double SHA256 hash of a block header is less than a "target" hash. It is also used to hash transactions within a block into a *Merkle Tree*, a structure which summarizes the transactions present within a block. Finally, it is the hash used for transactions signed with a user's private key (see [39] for details).

Address Hash. The second hash function is used as part of the Pay-to-Public-Key-Hash (P2PKH) and the Pay-to-Script-Hash (P2SH) scripts. Its output is 160 bits, and it is concretely instantiated as $H_A(x) = \mathrm{RIPEMD160}(\mathrm{SHA256}(x))$.

4.2   Modeling Hash Breakage

In this section we analyze how hashes break in terms of their building blocks, and introduce our oracle model for their breakage.

Identifying Hashing Building Blocks. A good cryptographic hash function $h(x)$ should offer three properties:

1. *Pre-image resistance* Given y it is hard to find x with $h(x) = y$.
2. *Second pre-image resistance* Given x_1, it is hard to find $x_2 \neq x_1$ with $h(x_1) = h(x_2)$.
3. *Collision resistance* It is hard to find distinct $x_1 \neq x_2$ such that $h(x_1) = h(x_2)$.

where "hard" refers to computational infeasibility. This is because hash functions have a fixed-length output, so collisions always exist.

We consider attacks against H_A and H_M abstractly, so that our arguments can be extended for any future version that uses the same structure. Currently, H_A and H_M are built using RIPEMD160 and SHA256. To relate the attacks we discover back to the concrete primitives in Sect. 7, we show in Appendix A that for collisions and second pre-images, only one of the two nested hashes needs to be broken, while for pre-images both need to be broken.

Modeling Hash Breakage Variants. The three properties discussed above do not accurately capture all types of breakages, which typically exploit the internal structure of the hash function. Thus, an adversary might have more control over the structure of the pre-image or the target value. For example, mining expects the hash to be smaller than a given target, a property which cannot be expressed using traditional pre-image oracles, as we show in Sect. 4.3.

For this reason, we introduce a more general oracle model to enable our analysis. We call the oracle a *chosen-format bounded pre-image oracle* P, which on input $(a, b, y_l, y_h, i[, s])$ returns an x_i such that $y_l \leq h(a||x_i||b) \leq y_h$ or $\perp$ if none exists. Thus, the oracle returns a value $X_i = a||x_i||b$ such that its beginning and end are caller-supplied, and its hash is within a given target range. Moreover, the oracle is deterministic such that the same x_i is returned each time and $x_i \neq x_j$ for $i \neq j$. If given the optional parameter s, the returned x_i has size s bits. That is to say, the oracle can be called multiple times to get different pre-images, and the user is also able to specify the length of the pre-image in bits.

In Appendix B, we motivate these parameters and show that our oracle captures breakages in the three properties. We summarize our results in Table 1.

4.3   Main Hash

In this section we analyze the main hash H_M, which is used for mining, in Merkle Trees, and with signatures. We discuss all three use-cases separately.

Table 1. Summary of the effects on Bitcoin for different types of hash breakage.

Breakage	Address hash (H_A)	Main hash (H_M)
Collision	Repudiate payment	Steal and destroy coins
Second pre-image	Repudiate payment	Double spend and steal coins
Pre-image	Uncover address	Complete failure of the blockchain ($2n$ calls)
Bounded pre-image	All of the above	Complete failure of the blockchain (n calls)

4.3.1 Mining

We first investigate pre-image attacks against the block headers under three different attack scenarios, before turning to collision and second pre-image attacks.

Attack 1: Pre-Image against Fixed Merkle Root. We show that the probability that an adversary with access to a pre-image oracle can break mining is negligible. Miners search for block headers whose n-bit hash is below a target, which we assume starts with d zeros. This assumption only introduces up to 1 bit of extra work, as there is always a unique d with $T \leq 2^d < 2T$, for any target T.

If the adversary controls $b \leq n$ bits of the input, there are 2^b possible inputs to the hash function. These need to map to one of the 2^{n-d} values in the range $[0, 0^d 1^{n-d})$, and will be uniformly distributed across 2^n values. This gives the expected number of b-bit pre-images as $E[\# \text{ pre-images}] = 2^b \cdot (2^{n-d})/(2^n) = 2^{b-d}$. The adversary can only query the pre-image oracle for specific target hashes. Because there are 2^{b-d} b-bit pre-images, distributed across the 2^{n-d} values, the probability that a given hash in $[0, 0^d 1^{n-d})$ has a b-bit pre-image is: $P[\text{correct pre-image}] = (2^{b-d})/(2^{n-d}) = 2^{b-n}$. This probability does not depend on d, as one might expect. This is because by increasing d to reduce the number of valid hashes, the adversary also reduces the expected number of b-bit pre-images. Assuming the adversary is allowed 2^a queries to the oracle, the probability of breaking mining becomes $P[\text{success}] = 2^a \cdot 2^{b-n} = 2^{a+b-n}$.

To calculate b, we explore all fields in the block header. The version number (`nVersion`), as well as the hashes of the previous block header (`hashPrevBlock`), and of the current Merkle root hash (`hashMerkleRoot`) are fixed. However, the adversary has partial control over the remaining fields in the header. For the timestamp field (`nTime`), the value can be within 7200 seconds of the current median/average, giving the adversary approximately 13 bits of freedom. Moreover, the adversary has complete control over the 32 bits of the nonce (`nNonce`). The `nBits` field $0xAABBCCDD$ describes the target difficulty as $0xBBCCDD \cdot 256^{0xAA-3}$, with the protocol only checking that the produced number is at most the target value given by the consensus. At the time of writing, the target value is $0x180928f0$, granting the adversary 28 bits of freedom.

Together the fields give $b = 73$. With $n = 256$, and allowing 2^{80} calls to the oracle, the probability of success is only $2^{80+73-256} = 2^{-103}$, which is negligible.

Attack 2: Pre-Image against Variable Merkle Root. By varying the Merkle root, an adversary can break mining, though by the discussion of Attack 1, this cannot be achieved by simply reordering or excluding transactions. Instead the adversary must work backwards, by querying the oracle for a target Merkle hash and repeatedly querying the oracle to reconstruct the entire Merkle tree. This would normally fail, as the transactions generated would not be valid due to incorrect signatures, but Bitcoin does not enforce a minimum number of transactions in a block. Hence, miners can mine blocks with just the coinbase transaction which generates new coins, and which has a variable-length input of up to 100 bytes that is controlled by miners [39]. A malicious miner with access to the pre-image oracle can then:

1. Pick an arbitrary target T and get a pre-image for $H_M(a||x||b) = T$ where the desired x is the `hashMerkleRoot` field, and a, b are the remaining fields in a block header. Because the root is 256 bits, there is a pre-image with high-probability, but if not, repeat with some other random target T'.
2. Pick a length l for the script, and fix all other fields for the coinbase transaction. Solve $H_M(a'||y||b') = x$ where a', b' are the remaining fields for the coinbase transaction. Because the number of free bytes is up to 100, there is an l-bit pre-image y with high probability. The miner then generates a coinbase transaction using a', y, b' and combines it into a block using a, b. This block will have a hash of T as desired.

Attack 3: Bounded Pre-Image. An adversary with access to our chosen-format, bounded pre-image oracle P can break mining with half as many calls to the oracle compared to the above attack using the simple pre-image oracle (Attack 2). Indeed, this is accomplished by calling P on $(hdr, \perp, 0, y_t, 0, s)$, where y_t is the target hash, hdr is the beginning of the block header, and $s = 32$ is the size of the required nonce such that $0 \leq H_M(hdr||nonce) \leq y_t$.

Collisions, Second Pre-Images. Collisions and second pre-images are only useful for mining if the pre-images start with d zeros. Assuming the pre-images contain valid transactions and signatures, a miner can fork the chain, but this only occurs with negligible probability.

4.3.2 Merkle Trees

Altering existing blocks. A similar argument as for mining (Attack 1) shows that an adversary cannot find a valid second pre-image of an entire block except with negligible probability. Pre-images do not give the adversary new information, as they already accompany the hash value. Collisions are also not useful, as both values are attacker-controlled and cannot alter existing blocks.

Attacking new blocks. For new blocks and transactions, an adversary with sufficient network control can use a collision or second pre-image to split the network, reject both blocks or reverse transactions, thus enabling double-spending. This can occur even with invalid pre-images: a similar situation occurred when some miners generated invalid blocks which were not detected by clients [1]. Pre-images are again not useful, as they always accompany the hashed value.

4.3.3   Main Hash Usage in Signatures

In Bitcoin, signatures are over messages hashed with H_M. Therefore, a second pre-image attack or a collision on H_M can be used to destroy and possibly steal coins: an adversary can ask for a signature on an innocuous transaction (e.g., pay 1 satoshi to address X), but transmit a malicious one instead (e.g., pay 100 BTC to address Y) since there are enough bytes that the adversary controls to guarantee success with high probability.

Though external to the protocol, signatures of H_M are also used by Bitcoin developers to transmit alerts. A pre-image attack again does not give useful information to the adversary, as the pre-image always accompanies the signature. Collisions are also not useful, as the adversary cannot sign them. However, a second pre-image allows the adversary to reuse an old signature on a new alert.

4.4   Address Hash

The address hash is used in two contexts. First, in Bitcoin addresses, using Pay-to-Public-Key-Hash (P2PKH) scripts: an address is essentially $y = H_A(p) = $ RIPEMD160 (SHA256 (p)) where p is the public key (together with a checksum [4]). Payments to addresses only use the hashed value y, but transactions to addresses require the full public key p and the signature on the transaction. The second use is in Pay-to-Script-Hash (P2SH) scripts. A P2SH is $y = H_A(s)$ where s is a standard script, typically a multi-signature transaction. Payments to a P2SH script do not reveal the pre-image, but transactions spending the coins require it and the signatures of the corresponding parties. We discuss them jointly, since the only difference between a P2PKH and a P2SH in this context is the number of required signatures.

Pre-image. For previously spent outputs, or for reused addresses, H_A is already accompanied by its pre-image. A pre-image thus can only reveal the public key(s) for unspent outputs. This has minimal privacy consequences since public keys are not tied to real identities, but it could enable an offline attack on the key. Assuming that the key was not chosen with bad randomness and there is no weakness in the signature scheme, the probability of success is still negligible.

Second pre-image. A second pre-image gives the adversary access to a different public key or script with the same hash. However, because the adversary does not control the corresponding private key, he cannot use this to change existing transactions or create new ones. This is because pre-images (whether a key or a script) are only revealed and verified when spent in transactions.

Collision. Collisions are similar, though in this case both public keys are under the adversary's control, and again the adversary does not have access to the private keys. In both scenarios, there is a question of non-repudiation external to the protocol itself: by presenting a second pre-image of a key used to sign a transaction, a user/adversary can claim that his coins were stolen.

Table 2. Effects of a broken signature scheme.

Breakage	Effect
Selective forgery	Steal coins from public key
Integrity break	Claim payment not received
Repudiation	-

5   Broken Signature Primitives

In this section we describe the use of digital signatures in Bitcoin, and analyze how a break in their unforgeability, integrity, or non-repudiation impacts Bitcoin. We summarize our results in Table 2.

5.1   Digital Signatures in Bitcoin

Bitcoin's digital signature scheme is the Elliptic Curve Digital Signature Algorithm (ECDSA) with the `secp256k1` [43] parameters, and is used to sign the main hash H_M of transactions. These signatures can be over different parts of the message based on the *hashtype* [39], leading to transaction malleability attacks [13], as the same transaction can be encoded multiple ways without invalidating the signature. The signature scheme is also used for alerts by developers to announce critical information. The signature is over the main hash H_M of the entire alert structure. The effects on alerts are not summarized in the table as they are external to the protocol.

5.2   Modeling Signature Breakage Variants

The security of digital signature schemes is usually discussed in terms of three properties, which we define as follows:

1. *Unforgeability* No-one can sign a message m that validates against a public key p without access to the secret key s.
2. *Integrity* A valid signature $\{m\}_s$ does not validate against any $m' \neq m$.
3. *Non-repudiation* A valid signature $\{m\}_s$ does not validate against any public key $p' \neq p$.

where there is an implicit "except with negligible probability", due to hashing.

These properties are linked and a breakage in one usually implies a breakage in the others. In addition, they are often discussed in a much more abstract way: non-repudiation refers to the property that the signature proves to all parties the origin of the signature, but in this case we introduce it in a way that is more akin to Duplicate Signature Key Selection (DSKS) attacks [9].

5.3   Broken Signature Scheme Effects

We now analyze a break in each of these properties separately, starting with the last two, as neither of them can lead to an attack on their own.

Integrity. In order for a break in the integrity of the signature scheme to be useful in Bitcoin, a signature of $H_M(m)$ must also be valid for $H_M(m')$. This involves H_M in a non-trivial way, so we discuss this further in Sect. 6, but note that transaction malleability can cause the issuer of a transaction to think that his payment was not confirmed [13].

Non-repudiation. For non-repudiation, we note that for transactions, even if a signature verifies under a different key, the address hashes of the two public keys must match. A break thus involves H_A, so we discuss this case further in Sect. 6. For the alert mechanism, however, if given a message m and a public key p, one can find p' (with its secret key s') such that $\{m\}_{s'}$ validates against p, then an adversary can send fake alert messages. This can have an external impact on Bitcoin, for instance by asking users to manually shut down clients.

Unforgeability. When it comes to unforgeability, we can distinguish between various types of breaks [19]: *Total break* to recover the private key, *universal forgery* to forge signatures for all messages, *selective forgery* to forge signature on a message of the adversary's choice, and *existential forgery* to produce a valid signature that is not already known to the adversary.

Because the message to be signed must be the hash of a valid transaction, an existential forgery is not sufficient since the probability that it corresponds to a valid message is negligible. Selective forgery on the other hand can be used to drain a victim's wallets. From this perspective, selective forgery and a total break have the same effect. However, as we discuss later, the type of breakage influences how to upgrade to a new system. It is worth noting that an adversary

Table 3. The effects of a multi-breakage: combining broken hashes and signatures.

	Signature property		
Hash property	Selective forgery	Integrity break	Repudiation
Address hash (H_A)			
Collision	Repudiate transaction	-	Change existing payment[a]
Second pre-image	Steal all coins	-	Change existing payment
Pre-image	Steal all coins	-	-
Bounded pre-image	All of the above	-	Change existing payment
Main hash (H_M)			
Collision	Steal coins	Steal coins[a]	-
Second pre-image	Steal coins	Double spend[a]	-
Pre-image	-	-	-
Bounded pre-image	Steal coins	All of the above	-

[a] Achieving this requires a slight modification of the definitions. See text for details.

does not necessarily have access to a user's public key, since addresses that have not been reused are protected by the address hash H_A.

6   Multi-Breakage

In this section we analyze how combinations of breakages in different primitives can impact Bitcoin. Because H_A and H_M are not used together, we only consider a break in the signature algorithm in combination with a break in one of the two hashes. Since the extra power of our oracle is not needed, we discuss breakage in terms of the three traditional properties. The results are summarized in Table 3.

6.1   Address Hash and Signature Scheme

Signature Forgery. Combining a selective forgery with a *first or second pre-image* break of the address hash can be used to steal all coins that are unspent. Generating two public keys p, p' with $H_A(p) = H_A(p')$ (*collision*) whose signatures the adversary can forge does not have a direct impact, since the adversary controls both addresses. However, it appears as if two different users are attempting to use the same coin, thus raising a question of repudiation, which we discuss in Sect. 7.

Signature Integrity. As the messages signed for alerts or transactions do not involve H_A, this combination does not increase the adversary's power.

Signature Repudiation. A *pre-image* attack on H_A is not useful as the public key is already known. For a *second pre-image*, assume that given a message m (the hash of a transaction) and a public key p, an oracle returns p' such that $H_A(p) = H_A(p')$ and the signature of m under p also validates against p'. Since the same signature validates for both keys, an adversary can replace p by p' in the unlocking script. Though this does not give the adversary immediate monetary gain, a transaction in the blockchain has been partially replaced.

For *collisions*, assume that given a message m, an oracle returns two public keys p, p' such that $H_A(p) = H_A(p')$ and the signature of m under p validates under p'. If the adversary does not have access to the private keys, he cannot sign the transaction. Otherwise, the effect is identical to the second pre-image case, where the adversary can replace part of a transaction in the blockchain.

6.2   Main Hash and Signature Scheme

Signature Forgery. As explained in Sect. 4.3, none of the potential attacks using the hash H_M required a break in the signature scheme. The partial exceptions were mining under a pre-image break, alerts with collisions, and transactions with second pre-image or collision breaks. We discuss each possibility below.

For *mining*, a pre-image attack is useful when working backwards from a fixed target to get a pre-image for the Merkle root, and turn it into a tree of transactions. The problem identified in Sect. 4.3 was that there is only negligible probability that the transactions refer to valid, unspent outputs, so a forgery does not solve this issue. For *alerts*, collisions require forgery. Though the effect of signing and transmitting two different alert messages with the same hash is unclear, it could potentially be used to cause external effects to Bitcoin by making the different messages ask the users to take different actions. Finally, for *transactions*, collisions and second pre-images on their own can be used to destroy coins, or steal coins. If the adversary can also forge signatures, he is guaranteed to be able to steal coins no matter what address they went to, as long as it is not protected by the address hash.

Signature Integrity. A collision or a second pre-image attack trivially breaks the integrity of the scheme as messages are always hashed, and reduces to the case discussed in Sect. 4.3, so we modify the definitions slightly to consider a joint break in the two algorithms.

A *collision integrity* oracle given a public key p produces m, m' such that the signature of $H_M(m)$ is also valid for $H_M(m')$. The adversary can ask for a signature on an innocent transaction, but transmit the malicious one with the still valid signature. Unlike in the regular collision case, the two hashes $H_M(m)$ and $H_M(m')$ are different. Hence, the adversary cannot just replace the transaction in the block, but he can opt never to transmit the innocent one instead.

A *second pre-image integrity* oracle given a public key p and a message m produces m' such that the signature of $H_M(m)$ is also valid for $H_M(m')$. This case also resembles the break on just H_M, but, again, because the hashes are not equal, the adversary cannot simply replace an existing transaction, unless it has not yet been confirmed in a block. This can split the network and destroy coins.

Signature Repudiation. The non-repudiation property of the signature scheme necessarily involves a break of H_A, as was explained in Sect. 5.3. This combination therefore does not increase the adversary's power.

7 Current Bitcoin Implementation

In this section, we revisit the current Bitcoin implementation, its choice of primitives and contingency plans, using observations from the previous sections.

7.1 Current Cryptographic Primitives

In the current version of Bitcoin, $H_A(x) = \text{RIPEMD160}\,(\text{SHA256}\,(x)))$, and $H_M(x) = \text{SHA256}\,(\text{SHA256}\,(x))$. Because there are no critical breaks for H_A, a break in RIPEMD160 is not cause for concern. Moreover, because H_M only uses SHA256, an attack against SHA256 is equivalent to an attack against H_M. We can thus summarize the effect of concrete primitive breakage in Table 4.

Table 4. Effects of concrete primitive breakage on the current version of Bitcoin.

Breakage	Effect
SHA256	
Collisions	Steal and destroy coins
Second pre-image	Double spend and steal coins
Pre-image	Complete failure
Bounded pre-image	All of the above
RIPEMD160	
Any of the above	Repudiate payments
ECDSA	
Selective forgery	Steal coins
Integrity break	Claim payment not received
Repudiation	-

7.2   Existing Contingency Plans

A break of the primitives has interested the community from the early days of Bitcoin. Informal recommendations by Satoshi in forums [36,37] evolved into a "wiki" page which describes contingency plans for "catastrophic failure[s]" [46]. Such a failure for primitives is defined in terms of an adversary that can defeat the algorithm with "a few days of work" [46], and the focus is on notifying users (since alerts may be compromised), and protecting the OP_CHECKSIG operation to prevent people from stealing coins.

Concretely, for a "severe, 0-day failure of SHA-256" [46], the plans propose switching to a new hashing algorithm H', and hard-coding known public keys with unspent outputs as well as the Merkle root of the blockchain under H'. For a broken signature scheme, if the attacker cannot recover the private key, and there is a drop-in replacement using the same key-pair, the plan is to simply switch over to the new algorithm. Otherwise, the new version of Bitcoin "should automatically send old transactions somewhere else using the new algorithm" [46].

7.3   Potential Migration Pitfalls

The contingency plans suggest that "code for all of this should be prepared" [46], but no such mechanism currently exists. Moreover, no plans are in place for a break in RIPEMD160. Since sudden breaks are unlikely, neither is cause for immediate concern, but should be included in future plans.

Broken SHA256. By our analysis, it is clear that new transactions should not use a broken hash. However, existing historical transactions and blocks cannot be altered, except in a majority mining attack. Thus, hard-coding public keys, and rehashing the entire blockchain are more prudent than necessary. It should be noted that a sudden migration necessitates a hardfork for Bitcoin.

Broken ECDSA. For a broken ECDSA, a transition is indeed easy if there is a drop-in replacement and the private key is safe. Otherwise, a gradual transition scheme is necessary as users will need to manually switch over to a new key pair.

7.4 Recommendations

In this section we make recommendations to more properly anticipate primitive breakage. Recognizing that there are financial considerations in addition to the technical ones, we do not propose a full upgrade mechanism, but merely make suggestions to the Bitcoin developers and community.

First of all, our analysis reinforces the idea that users should not reuse addresses, not just for privacy reasons, but also because they protect against some types of primitive breakage. For instance, if the signature scheme is broken, addresses are still protected by the hash.

The plans for a sudden breakage should address when to freeze the blockchain, and whether to roll back transactions in the case of a sudden break. Moreover, the centralized approach of hard-coding well-known keys is perhaps not entirely in line with Bitcoin's decentralized philosophy and can lead to lost coins. If keys are to be hard-coded, there is a trade-off between complexity and risking making coins unspendable: developers must decide whether the migration would occur at once, or whether periodic alert-like messages would be used to distribute new key pairs periodically. An alternative and perhaps better approach would be to use Zero-Knowledge Proofs to tie the old address still protected by their hash to the new public key.

Given that sudden breaks are unlikely, there is a need for a separate plan for weakened primitives. Based on our analysis, we recommend the following:

- Introduce a minimum number of transactions per block to increase the difficulty of performing the pre-image attack against the mining header target (Proof-of-Work or PoW) using the coinbase transaction.
- To migrate from old addresses, whether due to a weakened hash or signature scheme, introduce new address types using stronger hashing and signature schemes. This can be achieved with a softfork by making transactions appear to old clients as "pay-to-anybody", akin to how P2SH was introduced.
- Instead of using nested hashes for H_A, H_M, combine primitives in a way that increases defense-in-depth (see related work in Sect. 8).
- Given that H_M has multiple use-cases, consider whether each of its functions should have a different instantiation, whether through distinct primitives, by pre-pending different values, or by using an HMAC with different keys.
- Since alerts are external to the Bitcoin mechanism itself, send alerts using a new signature and hash scheme to new clients, and duplicate the message using old primitives for old clients.
- Consider a hardfork in response to a weakened H_M, with re-designed headers and transactions, and without any use of the old primitives.

A softfork is insufficient for properly upgrading a weakened hash function $H_M = H_1$ to the stronger H_2, because H_M forms the core of the PoW scheme.

Specifically, since any changes must be backwards compatible, the old validation rules must still apply, so for every new block, $H_1(hdr) < T$, where the target T is still calculated by the same algorithm. New blocks would also need to satisfy some additional constraint $H_2(hdr') < T'$, where the target T' is calculated independently and hdr' is the block header, possibly excluding some fields. As a result, new clients would have to solve two PoW computational puzzles. Though every instance of H_1 (transaction, Merkle root, etc.) could be accompanied by an instance of H_2, fundamentally blocks and transactions are identified by their H_1 hash, which an attacker could exploit. There are also questions of incentives, and whether new iterations of Bitcoin would still use a PoW scheme, but this is left as future work.

8   Related Work

Since no other systematic analysis exists regarding primitive breakage for Bitcoin, we consider papers which have focused on Bitcoin security in general, and also explore related work focusing on the security of the primitives themselves.

Bitcoin. Multiple papers have identified or formalized properties such as stability and anonymity in Bitcoin and other cryptocurrencies [10,17,44]. Anonymity and privacy issues have also been explored extensively [3,8,41,42].

Research on adversarial miners has shown that there are infinitely many Nash equilibria for mining strategies [29], and some strategies allow miners controlling $\alpha < 50\%$ of the power to gain disproportionate rewards [12,15,16]. Other research has demonstrated that double spending attacks are practical against Bitcoin fast payment scenarios [24,25], with some further focus on causing a network split [18] or isolating victims from other peers in the P2P nework [21].

[5] focuses on the economics of Bitcoin, including the effect of a history revision, which is discussed in the contingency plans [46]. [13] investigated transaction malleability attacks which were prevalent in 2014.

Cryptographic Primitives. For combining hashes, [23] shows simultaneous collisions for multiple hash functions are not much harder to find than individual ones. [22] shows that even when the underlying compression functions behave randomly but collisions are easy to generate, finding collisions in the concatenated hash $h_1(x)||h_2(x)$ and the XOR hash $h_1(x) \oplus h_2(x)$ requires $2^{n/2}$ queries. However, when the hash functions use the Merkle-Damgård (MD) construction, there is a generic pre-image attack against the XOR hash with complexity $\tilde{O}\left(2^{5n/6}\right)$ [30].

Neither MD hashes [11] nor $h(h(x))$ [14] behave as random oracles. MD hash functions also behave poorly against pre-image attacks, allowing one to find second pre-images of length 2^{60} for RIPEMD160 in $2^{106} \ll 2^{160}$ time [27]. If an adversary can further find many collisions on an MD construction, he can also find pre-images that start with a given prefix (Chosen Target Forced Prefix) [26]. This notion can be extended to Chosen Target Forced Midfix attacks and it was proven that at least $2^{2n/3}/L^{1/3}$ queries to the compression function are needed where L is the maximum length of the pre-image [2].

Attacks against RIPEMD160 pre-images [38] and collisions [32] as well as SHA256 collisions [31] and pre-images [28] only work for a reduced number of rounds, and typically only incrementally improve upon brute-force solutions. Certain ECDSA parameters can lead to Duplicate Signature Key Selection, where an adversary can create a different key P' that validates against a correct signature under a key P [9]. Implementations of ECDSA can also be vulnerable to side-channel attacks [47], an attack which has also been practically demonstrated against Bitcoin [6]. Finally, [7] showed how hash collisions break the security of protocols like TLS, IPSec, and SSH.

9 Conclusions

We presented the first systematic analysis of the effect of broken primitives on Bitcoin. Our analysis reveals that some breakages cause serious problems, whereas others are inconsequential. The main vectors of attack involve collisions on the double SHA256 hash or attacking the signature scheme, which directly enable coin stealing. In contrast, a break of the hash used in addresses has minimal impact, since they do not meaningfully protect the privacy of a user. Our analysis has also uncovered more subtle attacks. For example, the existence of another public key with the same hash as an address in the blockchain enables parties to claim that they did not make a payment. Such attacks show that an attack on a cryptographic primitive can have social rather than technical implications. We leave the economic impact of such attacks and the extension of our results to other altcoins or blockchain-based schemes as future work. Because our analysis abstracts away from the concrete primitives, our general results extend to future versions that use a similar structure.

We uncovered a worrying lack of defense-in-depth in Bitcoin. In most cases, the failure of a single property in one cryptographic primitive is as bad as multiple failures in several primitives at once. For future versions of Bitcoin, we recommend including various redundancies such as properly combined hash functions, and requiring a minimum number of transactions per block. Bitcoin's migration plans are currently under-specified, and offer at best an incomplete solution if primitives get broken. We offer some initial guidelines for making the cryptocurrency more robust, both for a sudden break, but also in response to weakened primitives. However, future discussions should directly involve the Bitcoin developers and community to propose plans that would be in line with their expectations.

Appendix

A   Breaking Nested Functions

In this section, we investigate the three main hashing properties, for a function $h = h_1 \circ h_2$ which is a composition of two hash functions. We show that for collisions and second pre-images, only one of the two nested hashes needs to be broken, while for pre-images both need to be broken.

Pre-image resistance. h is broken only when both h_1 and h_2 are broken. In one direction, assume that we have a pre-image algorithm for h, that returns x on input y. Then, to find a pre-image for y under h_2, run the algorithm on $h_1(y)$ for output x. If $h_2(x) = y$, then x is a pre-image for y under h_2. Else $h_2(x) \neq y$ and $(h_2(x), y)$ forms a collision (or second pre-image) for h_1. Conversely, if there is an algorithm for both h_1 and h_2 pre-images, then to get a pre-image of y under h, one finds a pre-image x_1 of y under h_1, and then a pre-image x_2 of x_1 under h_2. x_2 is then a pre-image of y under h.

Second pre-image resistance. h is only as strong as the inner function h_2. In one direction, assume that given x_1 one can find $x_2 \neq x_1$ such that $h_2(x_1) = h_2(x_2)$. Then clearly $h(x_1) = h(x_2)$.[1] In the other direction, assuming that given x_1, one can find $x_2 \neq x_1$ such that $h(x_1) = h(x_2)$, then either $h_2(x_1) = h_2(x_2)$ for a second pre-image attack on h_2 or $h_2(x_1) \neq h_2(x_2)$ for a collision (and second pre-image of $h_2(x_1)$) on h_1.

Collision resistance. h is again only as strong as h_2. A collision (x_1, x_2) for h_2 is clearly a collision for h, and a collision (x_1, x_2) for h is either a collision for h_2 or $(h_2(x_1), h_2(x_2))$ is a collision for h_1.

B   Generalizing Hash Oracles

In this section, we first motivate the parameters in our oracle model and then show that our oracle generalizes traditional primitive breakage. We remind the reader that our oracle P on input $(a, b, y_l, y_h, i[, s])$ returns an x_i [of size s] such that $y_l \leq h(a||x_i||b) \leq y_h$ or $\perp$ if none exists, with $x_i \neq x_j$ when $i \neq j$.

First of all, specifying a, b, and the length of the input forces pre-images and collisions to follow the format of transactions and block headers. Using bounds on the target range is necessary to describe some attacks against the proof-of-work (PoW) scheme. In addition, the oracle needs an index parameter to ensure that the adversary is polynomially bounded: when there is no length restriction on the pre-image, there are potentially infinitely many pre-images, and exponentially many for a fixed-length input. Finally, $x_i \neq x_j$ for $i \neq j$ so that the adversary can access as many distinct pre-images as desired. These returned values are distinct, without gaps, i.e., if the oracle returns $\perp$ on i it should also return $\perp$ on $i + 1$, so that the adversary can stop querying the oracle after receiving a $\perp$. We now show how an adversary with access to P can break the three hash properties.

Pre-image. Getting a pre-image of y amounts to calling P on $(\perp, \perp, y, y, 0)$, so the adversary can break pre-image resistance with a single call to the oracle.

Second pre-image. Getting a second pre-image given x is almost identical, but potentially requires two oracle calls: call P on $(\perp, \perp, h(x), h(x), 0)$, and if that returns x, call P on $(\perp, \perp, h(x), h(x), 1)$.

---

[1] The same can be said if h_1 is vulnerable to second pre-image attacks and h_2 is vulnerable to first pre-image attacks.

Collision. Getting a collision is not as straightforward. Let $h : \{0,1\}^* \rightarrow \{0,1\}^n$ be the hash function in question. First of all, it is not always the case that every $y \in \{0,1\}^n$ has a pre-image (let alone two), even though probabilistically this holds true for a well-designed hash function. For instance, consider h', where $h'(x) = 1$ when $h(x) = 0$, and $h'(x) = h(x)$ otherwise. Then, h' is strong if h is strong, but does not hit 0. However, by exploiting the pigeonhole principle and binary search, one can make $\lg(n)$ calls to the oracle to generate a collision.

The idea is to call P on $(\perp, \perp, y_l, y_h, y_h - y_l + 2)$. If the oracle returns anything but $\perp$, there are more pre-images than possible hashes within the range $[y_l, y_h]$. Then, one can perform a binary search with initial $y_l = 0^n$, $y_h = 1^n$ to determine a value y that has at least 2 pre-images.

Chosen-prefix collision. To get a chosen-prefix collision, i.e. given p find two values $x \neq x'$ such that $h(p||x) = h(p||x')$, one performs the same procedure as for getting a normal collision, but with $a = p$.

References

1. Alert, B.: Some miners generating invalid blocks, 4 July 2015. https://bitcoin.org/en/alert/2015-07-04-spv-mining. Accessed: 11 Feb 2016
2. Andreeva, E., Mennink, B.: Provable chosen-target-forced-midfix preimage resistance. In: Miri, A., Vaudenay, S. (eds.) SAC 2011. LNCS, vol. 7118, pp. 37–54. Springer, Heidelberg (2012)
3. Androulaki, E., Karame, G.O., Roeschlin, M., Scherer, T., Capkun, S.: Evaluating user privacy in Bitcoin. In: Sadeghi, A.-R. (ed.) FC 2013. LNCS, vol. 7859, pp. 34–51. Springer, Heidelberg (2013)
4. Antonopoulos, A.M.: Mastering Bitcoin: Unlocking Digital Crypto-Currencies, 1st edn. O'Reilly Media Inc. (2014)
5. Barber, S., Boyen, X., Shi, E., Uzun, E.: Bitter to better — how to make Bitcoin a better currency. In: Keromytis, A.D. (ed.) FC 2012. LNCS, vol. 7397, pp. 399–414. Springer, Heidelberg (2012)
6. Benger, N., van de Pol, J., Smart, N.P., Yarom, Y.: "Ooh Aah.. Just a Little Bit": a small amount of side channel can go a long way. In: Batina, L., Robshaw, M. (eds.) CHES 2014. LNCS, vol. 8731, pp. 75–92. Springer, Heidelberg (2014)
7. Bhargavan, K., Leurent, G.: Transcript collision attacks: breaking authentication in TLS, IKE, and SSH. In: Annual Network and Distributed System Security Symposium (NDSS) (2016)
8. Biryukov, A., Khovratovich, D., Pustogarov, I.: Deanonymisation of clients in Bitcoin P2P network. In: ACM Conference on Computer and Communications Security (CCS) (2014)
9. Blake-Wilson, S., Menezes, A.: Unknown key-share attacks on the station-to-station (STS) protocol. In: Imai, H., Zheng, Y. (eds.) PKC 1999. LNCS, vol. 1560, pp. 154–170. Springer, Heidelberg (1999)
10. Bonneau, J., Miller, A., Clark, J., Narayanan, A., Kroll, J., Felten, E.: SoK: research perspectives and challenges for Bitcoin and cryptocurrencies. In: IEEE Symposium on Security and Privacy (SP) (2015)
11. Nguyên, P.Q., Stern, J., Coron, J.-S., Dodis, Y., Malinaud, C., Puniya, P.: Merkle-Damgård revisited: how to construct a hash function. In: Shoup, V. (ed.) CRYPTO 2005. LNCS, vol. 3621, pp. 430–448. Springer, Heidelberg (2005)

12. Courtois, N.T., Bahack, L.: On subversive miner strategies and block withholding attack in Bitcoin digital currency. ArXiv e-prints 1402.1718 (2014). http://arxiv.org/abs/1402.1718

13. Decker, C., Wattenhofer, R.: Bitcoin transaction Malleability and MtGox. In: Kutyłowski, M., Vaidya, J. (eds.) ICAIS 2014, Part II. LNCS, vol. 8713, pp. 313–326. Springer, Heidelberg (2014)

14. Dodis, Y., Ristenpart, T., Steinberger, J., Tessaro, S.: To hash or not to hash again? (in)differentiability results for H^2 and HMAC. In: Safavi-Naini, R., Canetti, R. (eds.) CRYPTO 2012. LNCS, vol. 7417, pp. 348–366. Springer, Heidelberg (2012)

15. Eyal, I.: The miner's dilemma. In: IEEE Symposium on Security and Privacy (SP) (2015)

16. Eyal, I., Sirer, E.G.: Majority is not enough: Bitcoin mining is vulnerable. In: Christin, N., Safavi-Naini, R. (eds.) FC 2014. LNCS, vol. 8437, pp. 431–449. Springer, Heidelberg (2014)

17. Garay, J., Kiayias, A., Leonardos, N.: The Bitcoin backbone protocol: analysis and applications. In: Oswald, E., Fischlin, M. (eds.) EUROCRYPT 2015. LNCS, vol. 9057, pp. 281–310. Springer, Heidelberg (2015)

18. Gervais, A., Ritzdorf, H., Karame, G.O., Capkun, S.: Tampering with the delivery of blocks and transactions in Bitcoin. In: ACM Conference on Computer and Communications Security (CCS) (2015)

19. Goldwasser, S., Micali, S., Rivest, R.L.: A digital signature scheme secure against adaptive chosen-message attacks. SIAM J. Comput. (SICOMP) **17**(2), 281–308 (1988)

20. Grover, L.K.: A fast quantum mechanical algorithm for database search. In: Annual ACM Symposium on Theory of Computing (STOC) (1996)

21. Heilman, E., Kendler, A., Zohar, A., Goldberg, S.: Eclipse attacks on Bitcoin's peer-to-peer network. In: USENIX Security Symposium (USENIX Security) (2015)

22. Hoch, J.J., Shamir, A.: On the strength of the concatenated hash combiner when all the hash functions are weak. In: Aceto, L., Damgård, I., Goldberg, L.A., Halldórsson, M.M., Ingólfsdóttir, A., Walukiewicz, I. (eds.) ICALP 2008, Part II. LNCS, vol. 5126, pp. 616–630. Springer, Heidelberg (2008)

23. Joux, A.: Multicollisions in iterated hash functions. application to cascaded constructions. In: Franklin, M. (ed.) CRYPTO 2004. LNCS, vol. 3152, pp. 306–316. Springer, Heidelberg (2004)

24. Karame, G.O., Androulaki, E., Roeschlin, M., Gervais, A., Čapkun, S.: Misbehavior in Bitcoin: a study of double-spending and accountability. ACM Trans. Inf. Syst. Secur. (TISSEC) **18**(1), 2 (2015)

25. Karame, G.O., Androulaki, E., Čapkun, S.: Double-spending fast payments in Bitcoin. In: ACM Conference on Computer and Communications Security (CCS) (2012)

26. Kelsey, J., Kohno, T.: Herding hash functions and the nostradamus attack. In: Vaudenay, S. (ed.) EUROCRYPT 2006. LNCS, vol. 4004, pp. 183–200. Springer, Heidelberg (2006)

27. Kelsey, J., Schneier, B.: Second preimages on n-bit hash functions for much less than 2^n work. In: Cramer, R. (ed.) EUROCRYPT 2005. LNCS, vol. 3494, pp. 474–490. Springer, Heidelberg (2005)

28. Khovratovich, D., Rechberger, C., Savelieva, A.: Bicliques for preimages: attacks on Skein-512 and the SHA-2 family. In: Canteaut, A. (ed.) FSE 2012. LNCS, vol. 7549, pp. 244–263. Springer, Heidelberg (2012)

29. Kroll, J.A., Davey, I.C., Felten, E.W.: The economics of Bitcoin mining, or Bitcoin in the presence of adversaries. In: Workshop on the Economics of Information Security (WEIS) (2013)
30. Leurent, G., Wang, L.: The sum can be weaker than each part. In: Oswald, E., Fischlin, M. (eds.) EUROCRYPT 2015. LNCS, vol. 9056, pp. 345–367. Springer, Heidelberg (2015)
31. Mendel, F., Nad, T., Schläffer, M.: Improving local collisions: new attacks on reduced SHA-256. In: Johansson, T., Nguyen, P.Q. (eds.) EUROCRYPT 2013. LNCS, vol. 7881, pp. 262–278. Springer, Heidelberg (2013)
32. Mendel, F., Peyrin, T., Schläffer, M., Wang, L., Wu, S.: Improved cryptanalysis of reduced RIPEMD-160. In: Sako, K., Sarkar, P. (eds.) ASIACRYPT 2013, Part II. LNCS, vol. 8270, pp. 484–503. Springer, Heidelberg (2013)
33. Merkle, R.C.: A digital signature based on a conventional encryption function. In: Pomerance, C. (ed.) CRYPTO 1987. LNCS, vol. 293, pp. 369–378. Springer, Heidelberg (1988)
34. Nakamoto, S.: Bitcoin: a peer-to-peer electronic cash system (2008). http://bitcoin. org/bitcoin.pdf
35. Nakamoto, S.: Bitcoin source code v0.1.0: Util.h. (2009). https://github.com/ trottier/original-bitcoin/blob/4184ab26345d19e87045ce7d9291e60e7d36e096/src/ util.h. Accessed: 11 Feb 2016
36. Nakamoto, S.: Dealing with SHA-256 collisions (msg #6), 14 June 2010. https:// bitcointalk.org/index.php?topic=191.msg1585#msg1585. Accessed: 11 Feb 2016
37. Nakamoto, S.: Hash() function not secure (msg #28), 16 July 2010. https:// bitcointalk.org/index.php?topic=360.msg3520#msg3520. Accessed: 11 Feb 2016
38. Ohtahara, C., Sasaki, Y., Shimoyama, T.: Preimage attacks on step-reduced RIPEMD-128 and RIPEMD-160. In: Lai, X., Yung, M., Lin, D. (eds.) Inscrypt 2010. LNCS, vol. 6584, pp. 169–186. Springer, Heidelberg (2011)
39. Okupski, K.: Bitcoin developer reference working paper (2015). http://enetium. com/resources/Bitcoin.pdf. Accessed: 11 Feb 2016
40. Proos, J., Zalka, C.: Shor's discrete logarithm quantum algorithm for elliptic curves. Quantum Inf. Comput. 3(4), 317–344 (2003)
41. Reid, F., Harrigan, M.: An analysis of anonymity in the Bitcoin system. In: Altshuler, Y., Elovici, Y., Cremers, A.B., Aharony, N., Pentland, A. (eds.) Security and Privacy in Social Networks, pp. 197–223. Springer, New York (2013)
42. Ron, D., Shamir, A.: Quantitative analysis of the full Bitcoin transaction graph. In: Sadeghi, A.-R. (ed.) FC 2013. LNCS, vol. 7859, pp. 6–24. Springer, Heidelberg (2013)
43. Standards for Efficient Cryptography: Sec 2: Recommended elliptic curve domain parameters version 2.0 (2010). http://www.secg.org/sec2-v2.pdf
44. Tschorsch, F., Scheuermann, B.: Bitcoin and beyond: a technical survey on decentralized digital currencies. Cryptology ePrint Archive, Report 2015/464 (2015). https://eprint.iacr.org/2015/464

45. Wiki, B.: Protocol rules, 11 March 2014. https://en.bitcoin.it/wiki/Protocol_rules. Accessed: 11 Feb 2016
46. Wiki, B.: Contingency plans, 15 May 2015. https://en.bitcoin.it/wiki/Contin gency_plans. Accessed: 11 Feb 2016
47. Yarom, Y., Benger, N.: Recovering OpenSSL ECDSA nonces using the FLUSH+RELOAD cache side-channel attack. Cryptology ePrint Archive, Report 2014/140 (2014). https://eprint.iacr.org/2014/140

DRE-ip: A Verifiable E-Voting Scheme Without Tallying Authorities

Siamak F. Shahandashti[(⊠)] and Feng Hao[(⊠)]

School of Computing Science, Newcastle University, Newcastle upon Tyne, UK
{siamak.shahandashti,feng.hao}@ncl.ac.uk

Abstract. Nearly all verifiable e-voting schemes require trustworthy authorities to perform the tallying operations. An exception is the DRE-i system which removes this requirement by pre-computing all encrypted ballots before the election using random factors that will later cancel out and allow the public to verify the tally after the election. While the removal of tallying authorities significantly simplifies election management, the pre-computation of ballots necessitates secure ballot storage, as leakage of precomputed ballots endangers voter privacy. In this paper, we address this problem and propose DRE-ip (DRE-i with enhanced privacy). Adopting a different design strategy, DRE-ip is able to encrypt ballots in real time in such a way that the election tally can be publicly verified without decrypting the cast ballots. As a result, DRE-ip achieves end-to-end verifiability without tallying authorities, similar to DRE-i, but with a significantly stronger guarantee on voter privacy. In the event that the voting machine is fully compromised, the assurance on tallying integrity remains intact and the information leakage is limited to the minimum: only the partial tally at the time of compromise is leaked.

1 Introduction

Direct-recording electronic (DRE) machines have been extensively used for voting at polling stations around the world. In a typical process, a registered voter obtains a token after being authenticated at the polling station. She then enters a private booth and presents the token to a DRE machine. The token is for one-time use and allows the voter to cast only one vote. Usually, the DRE machine has a touch screen to record the vote directly from the voter (hence the name DRE). The machine may tally the votes in real time, or store the votes and tally later. In either case, the machine works like a black box: if an attacker maliciously changes the votes (or the tally thereof), this is likely to go unnoticed.

Lack of assurance on tallying integrity is commonly regarded as a critical weakness of such DRE machines. To address this problem, several cryptographic protocols are proposed in the literature. The seminal work by Chaum in 2004 [16] involves using visual cryptography to allow voters to verify the integrity of an election. The assurance on the integrity includes guarantees that the votes are cast as intended, recorded as cast, and tallied as recorded. The fulfilment of all three constitutes the widely-accepted notion of end-to-end (E2E) verifiability.

© Springer International Publishing Switzerland 2016
I. Askoxylakis et al. (Eds.): ESORICS 2016, Part II, LNCS 9879, pp. 223–240, 2016.
DOI: 10.1007/978-3-319-45741-3_12

Chaum's solution inspired a class of voting systems providing E2E verifiability. Prominent examples include MarkPledge [28], Prêt à Voter [29], Scantegrity [14] (and its predecessor PunchScan [21]), Helios [1], and STAR-Vote [4]. These systems are based on different voting media including physical ballots, optical scanners, DREs and web browsers. They use different tallying techniques, based on mix-nets or homomorphic encryption. But all these schemes allow individual voters to verify if their votes have been cast as intended and recorded as cast, and any observer to verify if all votes have been tallied as recorded.

In this paper we limit our attention to DRE-based elections. We focus on DRE as it has already been widely deployed for national elections worldwide. Today, nearly all of the deployed DRE systems work like a black box and offer no guarantee on integrity; consequently, their use has been abandoned in several countries such as the Netherlands, Germany and Ireland. However, in many other countries, these (unverifiable) DRE machines continue to be extensively used. We believe there is an urgent need to address this real-world problem.

Apart from Chaum's system called Votegrity, other existing E2E verifiable schemes for DRE-based elections include MarkPledge [28], VoteBox [31], STAR-Vote [4], and vVote [18]. These systems may differ significantly in details, but they share some common features. They all offer integrity assurance by introducing a set of trustworthy tallying authorities (TAs). Instead of the DRE directly recording the vote, the machine encrypts the vote on the fly under the joint public key of the TAs. Each TA is responsible for safeguarding a share of the decryption key. When voting is closed, a quorum of TAs jointly perform the tallying process which involves decryption of the ballots (or tally thereof) in a publicly-verifiable manner.

The addition of external TAs however introduces difficulties in the implementation. In theory, the TAs should be selected from parties with conflicting interests. They should have the expertise to independently manage their own key shares and perform cryptographic operations, and if they delegate their key management tasks, the delegates need to be trusted as well. A comparatively high level of cryptographic and computing skills is expected from the TAs. Furthermore, the quorum should be set sufficiently large such that collusion among the TAs is infeasible, but at the same time, sufficiently small such that the process is error-tolerant, since non-availability of TA keys will render the election result non-computable. Reconciling the two is not an easy task. As reported by real-world experience of building E2E verifiable voting based on Helios, the implementation of the TAs proved to be "one particularly difficult issue" [2].

Hao et al. investigated if it was possible to achieve E2E verifiability for a DRE-based election without involving any TAs [24]. They proposed a TA-free E2E verifiable voting system, called DRE-i (DRE with integrity). In DRE-i, the machine directly records the voter's choice as in the existing practice of current DRE-based elections. However, the machine is required to publish additional audit data on a public bulletin board, to enable every voter to verify the integrity of the voting process. In DRE-i, the encryption of votes is based on a variant of the ElGamal encryption scheme: instead of using a fixed public key for encryption as in standard ElGamal, DRE-i uses a dynamically constructed public key for encrypting ballots. The system removes the need for TAs by pre-computing encrypted ballots in a structured manner such that after the election, multiplication of all the published ciphertexts cancels out the random factors that were introduced during the encryption process, and permits anyone to verify the tally.

DRE-i demonstrates that the role of the TAs is not indispensable in achieving E2E verifiability in a DRE-based election. However, its pre-computation strategy inevitably introduces the requirement of ensuring that the pre-computed data is securely stored and accessed during the voting phase. Furthermore, it means that it is possible for an adversary that breaks into the secure storage module to potentially compromise the privacy of all ballots. The authors of DRE-i [24] suggest to use tamper-resistant hardware to protect the pre-computed data in sensitive elections. However, the use of tamper-resistant hardware may significantly drive up the cost of each DRE machine. Furthermore, designing secure API for tamper-resistant hardware is a challenging problem on its own.

It remains an open problem as whether it is possible to achieve the best of both worlds, i.e. strong assurance on the integrity of a DRE-based election without involving any TAs, and simultaneously, a strong guarantee on the privacy of votes without depending on tamper-resistant hardware.

In this paper, we provide a positive answer to this question and present a new E2E verifiable voting system, which we call *DRE-ip* (DRE-i with enhanced privacy). Instead of pre-computing ciphertexts, DRE-ip adopts a more conventional approach, as in other existing DRE-based verifiable systems (see e.g. [4,31]), to encrypt the vote on the fly during voting. DRE-ip achieves E2E verifiability without TAs, but at the same time provides a significantly stronger privacy guarantee than DRE-i.

Our Contributions. We present DRE-ip, an end-to-end verifiable DRE-based voting system that encrypts ballots in real-time, but requires no TAs to decrypt ballots in the tallying phase. We consider intrusive attacks in which the adversary is able to control an arbitrary number of voters and gets read access to the DRE machine for an arbitrary period during the voting phase. We prove that under such attacks, DRE-ip guarantees that elections with the same non-adversarial tally (i.e. tally of the votes neither controlled nor observed by the adversary) remain indistinguishable based on the decision Diffie-Hellman assumption. This shows that in the event of an intrusive attack, only the privacy of the ballots cast during the attack period is lost – a loss which is inevitable – and the ballots cast outside the attack period are guaranteed to remain private. DRE-ip constitutes the first verifiable DRE-based system that removes the need for tallying authorities without introducing new assumptions.

Related Work. In his seminal work on anonymous communications, Chaum put forward e-voting as an application of his technique [15]. This prompted considerable research on e-voting, among which is the work of Benaloh [10] that proposed a formal definition of *ballot secrecy*. Later, Benaloh and Tuinstra argued for *receipt-freeness* [9], and Juels, Catalano, and Jakobsson put forward *coercion-resistance* [25] as progressively stronger notions of privacy. On the other hand, verifiability has evolved as a property guaranteeing the integrity of e-voting systems. Earlier works considered *individual verifiability*. The notion of *universal verifiability* emerged in later works and Sako and Kilian explicitly formalized it [30]. Finally, through the works of Chaum [16] and Neff [28], notions of verifiability were refined into that of *end-to-end verifiability*, which includes guarantees that the votes are cast as intended, recorded as cast, and tallied as recorded. End-to-end verifiability has now become a widely-accepted security requirement for e-voting schemes. Accordingly, in this paper, we limit our attention to end-to-end verifiable voting schemes.

There has been a renewed interest in academic research on e-voting in the past fifteen years and a number of end-to-end verifiable schemes have been designed and used in practice. Among the more influential schemes are Votegrity, proposed by Chaum [16], and MarkPledge, proposed by Neff [28], which are the first end-to-end verifiable schemes. Many other schemes follow similar approaches, including Prêt à Voter [29], a tailored variant of which, vVote, has been used in state elections in Victoria, Australia [18], Scantegrity [14], which was trialled in local elections in Takoma Park, Maryland, USA [13], and STAR-Vote [4], which is scheduled for deployment in elections in Travis County, Texas, USA [26]. Other schemes that have been used in internal university or party elections include PunchScan [21], Bingo Voting [11], Helios [1], Wombat [7], and DRE-i [24].

2   Preliminaries

In this section, we review the preliminaries required for description of DRE-ip, including the notation and cryptographic setting we use.

Notation. Following the notation introduced by Camenisch and Stadler [12], we use $P_K\{\lambda : \Gamma = \gamma^\lambda\}$ to denote a non-interactive *proof of knowledge* of (a secret) λ such that (for publicly-known Γ and γ): $\Gamma = \gamma^\lambda$. Where the context is clear, we shorten the notation to $P_K\{\lambda\}$. We use $P_{WF}\{A : X, Y, Z\}$ to denote a *proof of well-formedness* of A with respect to X, Y, and Z. Where the context is clear, we shorten the notation to $P_{WF}\{A\}$.

2.1   Cryptographic Setting

We assume a DSA-like multiplicative cyclic group setting, where p and q are large primes that satisfy $q \mid p - 1$. We work in the subgroup $\mathbb{G}_q$ of order q of the group $\mathbb{Z}_p^\star$ and assume that g is a generator of $\mathbb{G}_q$. Alternatively, our proposed system can be implemented over an elliptic curve in an ECDSA-like group setting.

The decision Diffie-Hellman (DDH) assumption [19] is defined as follows:

Assumption 1 (DDH). For randomly chosen $a, b \in \mathbb{Z}_q^\star$ and $R \in \mathbb{G}_q$, given (g, g^a, g^b, Ω) where $\Omega \in \{g^{ab}, R\}$, it is hard to decide whether $\Omega = g^{ab}$ or $\Omega = R$.

Zero knowledge proofs, first proposed by Goldwasser, Micali, and Rackoff [22], prove the truth of a statement without conveying any other information, i.e. they guarantee that whatever the verifier can feasibly compute after seeing a proof, they could have computed on their own. Subsequent work by Bellare and Goldreich [5] refined the definition of zero knowledge proofs to distinguish them from proofs of knowledge. Intuitively speaking, proofs of knowledge are guaranteed to be generated by a prover with explicit knowledge of a quantity. In our protocol, the Fiat-Shamir heuristic is employed to construct non-interactive proofs [20]. Consequently, our security proofs are in the Random Oracle Model [6].

3   Our Proposed Solution: DRE-ip

DRE-ip requires a secure and publicly-accessible bulletin board (BB) and incorporates voter-initiated auditing to achieve end-to-end verifiability. We assume the DRE has append-only write access to the BB over an authenticated channel. We assume voting is conducted in supervised polling stations and there are procedures in place to ensure the "one person, one vote" principle, including secure voter registration and authentication. At the time of voting, a voter is authenticated first and issued a token, unlinked to her identity. She then enters a private voting booth and authenticates herself to the DRE using the token. Up to here, the assumptions and mechanisms are similar to those of DRE-i.

We describe DRE-ip for the case where there are only two candidates, i.e. for v_i representing the vote of the i-th ballot, we have $v_i \in \{0,1\}$. In DRE-ip the setup establishes two generators g_1 and g_2, whose logarithmic relationship is unknown. The DRE keeps track of the running tally $t = \sum v_i$ for the cast votes v_i, and the sum $s = \sum r_i$ for random r_i generated on the fly.

To achieve individual verifiability, DRE-ip incorporates Benaloh-style voter-initiated auditing [8], i.e. the voter gets the option to audit the ballot composed by the DRE to gain confidence in that the DRE is preparing the ballots according to her choice. If a ballot is audited, it cannot be used to cast a vote. Therefore, the set of all ballots $\mathbb{B}$ at the closing of the voting phase will be comprised of the audited ballots $\mathbb{A}$ and the cast ballots $\mathbb{C}$, i.e. $\mathbb{B} = \mathbb{A} \cup \mathbb{C}$.

Voting Phase. This phase involves the voter, the DRE, and the BB:

1. The voter enters the booth, initiates voting, and keys in her vote $v_i \in \{0,1\}$.
2. The DRE generates random $r_i \in \mathbb{Z}_q^\star$, calculates

$$R_i = g_2^{r_i}, \quad Z_i = g_1^{r_i} g_1^{v_i}, \quad \mathrm{P_{WF}}\{Z_i : g_1, g_2, R_i\},$$

   and provides a signed receipt including the unique ballot index i and the ballot content R_i, Z_i, and $\mathrm{P_{WF}}\{Z_i\}$ to the voter.
3. The voter observes that the first part of the receipt is provided, and chooses to either audit the ballot or confirm her vote.

In case of audit:

4. The DRE adds i to $\mathbb{A}$, provides a signed receipt of audit, clearly marked **audited**, including r_i and v_i to the voter.
5. The voter takes and keeps the receipt, and verifies that v_i reflects her choice. If the verification succeeds, voting continues to Step 1; otherwise, the voter should raise a dispute immediately.

In case of confirmation:

4. The DRE adds i to $\mathbb{C}$, updates the tally and the sum:

$$t = \sum_{j \in \mathbb{C}} v_j \quad \text{and} \quad s = \sum_{j \in \mathbb{C}} r_j,$$

and provides a signed receipt of confirmation, clearly marked **confirmed**, to the voter, and securely deletes r_i and v_i.
5. The voter leaves the booth with her receipts.

6. The DRE posts on the BB all the receipts provided to the voter.
7. The voter verifies that her receipts match those on the BB.

Tallying Phase. This phase involves the DRE, the BB, and the public:

1. The DRE posts on the BB the final tally t and the final sum s.
2. The public:
   - verify all the well-formedness proofs on the BB (*well-formedness verification*);
   - verify that for all the audited ballots on the BB: R_i and Z_i included in the first part of the receipt are consistent with r_i and v_i included in the second part (and with the system parameters g_1 and g_2) (*audit consistency verification*); and
   - verify that the following equations hold (*tally verification*):

$$\prod_{j \in \mathbb{C}} R_j \stackrel{?}{=} g_2^s \quad \text{and} \quad \prod_{j \in \mathbb{C}} Z_j \stackrel{?}{=} g_1^s g_1^t. \tag{1}$$

If at any point during the voting or tallying phases, any of the verifications carried out by the voter or the public does not succeed, the election staff should be notified and we assume that there are procedures in place dealing with such verification failures. These include voter verifications in Steps 5 (in case of audit) and 7 of the voting phase and public verifications in Step 2 of the tallying phase.

Figure 1 shows the DRE-ip bulletin board. An audited receipt (with index i) and a confirmed receipt (with index j) are shown. Each receipt has two parts: the first part is provided to the voter before she decides to either audit or confirm her ballot and includes similar information for all receipts; the second part is provided after the voter makes her decision and includes different information based on her choice. Both parts of the receipt are signed by the DRE.

The proof of well-formedness $P_{\text{WF}}\{Z_i : g_1, g_2, R_i\}$ can be implemented as a non-interactive proof of knowledge

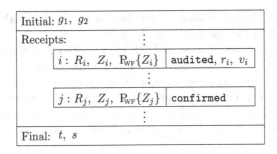

Fig. 1. DRE-ip bulletin board

$$P_{WF}\{Z_i\} = P_K\{r_i : \quad (R_i = g_2^{r_i} \wedge Z_i = g_1^{r_i}) \quad \vee \quad (R_i = g_2^{r_i} \wedge Z_i/g_1 = g_1^{r_i})\}.$$

This proof guarantees that $Z_i \in \{g_1^{r_i}, g_1^{r_i}g_1\}$, or equivalently $v_i \in \{0, 1\}$.

Such a proof can be realized based on Schnorr proofs of knowledge of discrete logarithm [32]. Starting with a Schnorr proof, one can apply techniques proposed by Cramer, Damgård, and Schoenmakers [17] to construct proofs of disjunctive knowledge, conjunctive knowledge, and combinations of both. The Fiat-Shamir heuristic [20] is then applied to make the constructed proofs non-interactive. The index i of the ballot is embedded in the proof (as an input to the hash function) to bind the proof to the ballot.

In practice, truncated hash functions may be used to calculate a short digest, e.g. 4 alphanumeric characters long, of each part of the receipt, so that the voter can easily compare the digests on their receipts with those on the bulletin board. In this case, voters are expected to verify the receipts before leaving the polling station and we assume facilities are provided for them to do so in the station.

4   Security of DRE-ip

In this section we provide proofs to show that DRE-ip is end-to-end verifiable and ensures ballot secrecy under both non-intrusive and intrusive attacks.

4.1   End-to-End Verifiability

We discuss the integrity (i.e. correctness) of the election tally in DRE-ip and show how DRE-ip achieves end-to-end verifiability: we prove that, assuming all proofs of well-formedness are proofs of knowledge, votes are tallied as recorded if public verification succeeds; furthermore, we demonstrate how voter-initiated auditing guarantees that votes are recorded as cast, and cast as intended.

We assume the bulletin board is secure, in particular it is append-only and publicly accessible. Besides, there should be a mechanism to establish an authenticated channel between authorized DRE(s) and the bulletin board, to ensure that only an authorized DRE can append new values to the BB, and also that such values are not modified in transit. This can be achieved using standard techniques such as digital signatures. Furthermore, we assume that the number of voters is less than the size of the group q.

Recall that public verification in DRE-ip, i.e. Step 2 of the tallying phase, includes three types of verification: well-formedness verification, audit consistency verification, and tally verification. The following theorem shows that if well-formedness and tally verifications succeed, DRE-ip achieves the tallied-as-recorded property, that is, DRE-ip guarantees that the tally on the bulletin board is the correct tally of all the confirmed ballots on the bulletin board.

Theorem 1. *In DRE-ip, assuming that all proofs of well-formedness are proofs of knowledge, if the public well-formedness and tally verifications succeed, then the reported tally t is the correct tally of all the confirmed votes on the BB.*

The proof is rather straightforward and hence omitted here. In short, one can demonstrate how the proofs of well-formedness and the first tally verification check (i.e. the first of the two in Eq. 1) collectively guarantee that the second tally verification equation (i.e. the second of the two in Eq. 1) holds if and only if $t = \sum_{i \in \mathbb{C}} v_i$, where $\mathbb{C}$ denotes the set of confirmed votes. Hence, if well-formedness and tally verifications are carried out successfully, the reported tally t is guaranteed to be the correct tally of all the confirmed votes on the BB.

Voter initiated auditing includes the following checks: first, by observing the first part of the receipt is provided before deciding to either audit or confirm a ballot, the voter makes sure that the DRE commits to the first part of the ballot; second, by checking that the receipts match what is published on the BB, the voter makes sure that her interaction with the machine is captured faithfully on the bulletin board. The public verification of the consistency of the audited ballots, i.e. the audit consistency verification, guarantees that DRE has been successful in responding to the challenges made by voter initiated auditing. Hence, the individual verification and the public audit consistency verification collectively ensure that the votes are cast as intended and recorded as cast. Theorem 1 ensures that votes are tallied as recorded.

4.2   Ballot Secrecy

Ballot secrecy corresponds to the natural expectation from a voting system to protect the secrecy of cast ballots. We consider a definition of ballot secrecy which requires that an adversary controlling the voting behaviour of a group of dishonest voters should not be able to distinguish between any two elections, regardless of how honest voters vote, as long as the two elections have the same partial tally of honest votes. This definition originates from Benaloh [10, p. 74].

We assume a secure setup phase; that is, we assume that the discrete logarithm of g_2 in base g_1 is either not known to any party or securely deleted after the two generators are computed. We also assume secure deletion of values x_i, y_i, and v_i after each vote is cast[1].

---

[1] See, for instance, [23] and the references within for an overview of available solutions to secure data deletion.

We consider an intrusive adversary that apart from the ability to determine an arbitrary number of votes, gets read access to the DRE storage for a period during the voting phase. The adversary is able to read the publicly available information on the bulletin board, which includes the total tally. Besides, we assume that the adversary can control an arbitrary number of voters, hence in effect cast an arbitrary number of votes. The adversary is able to observe the votes cast during the access period and also read the running (partial) tally t and (partial) sum s.

Let us call the votes cast or observed by the adversary the *adversarial* votes. Knowledge of the adversarial votes along with the total and partial tallies enables the adversary to find out the tally of the non-adversarial votes cast before and after the adversarial access period. We prove that under the DDH assumption, this is the only information the adversary gains about the non-adversarial votes. In particular, we show that any two elections in which the non-adversarial votes cast before and after the adversarial access period have the same partial tallies are indistinguishable to the adversary. Note that in DRE-i, in case of an adversarial access to the voting machine storage, the privacy of the ballots cast outside the adversarial access period is also lost. Therefore, while DRE-i falls victim to such intrusive attacks, DRE-ip guarantees vote privacy under under such attacks.

We first consider two elections in which all votes are the same except for two votes that are swapped. We show that the bulletin boards of these two elections remain indistinguishable to the adversary as long as these two votes are non-adversarial votes both cast either before or after the adversarial access period. More formally, we have:

Lemma 1. *In DRE-ip, assuming that all proofs of well-formedness are zero knowledge, if the DDH assumption holds, then an adversary that determines an arbitrary number of votes and gets temporary read access to the DRE storage cannot distinguish between two bulletin boards in which two votes both cast either before or after the adversarial access period are swapped.*

The proof of the lemma comes in Appendix A. The proof considers an adversary that not only can determine an arbitrary number of votes except two votes v_i and v_j, but gets access to DRE storage for an arbitrary period. Assuming that such an adversary is able to distinguish the bulletin boards in which v_i and v_j are swapped, we show how it can be used to break the DDH assumption. Basically, the proof shows that the sum s does not leak any extra information other than what the tally t does.

Given Lemma 1, we expand it to prove that any two elections with the same non-adversarial partial tallies of the votes cast before and after the adversarial access period remain indistinguishable to an adversary who controls an arbitrary number of votes. This shows that the only knowledge the adversary can gain about the non-adversarial votes cast before and after the adversarial access period is that disclosed by the partial and total tallies.

Theorem 2. *In DRE-ip, assuming that all proofs of well-formedness are zero knowledge, if the DDH assumption holds, then an adversary that determines an arbitrary number of votes and gets temporary read access to the DRE storage cannot gain any knowledge about the non-adversarial votes cast before and after the adversarial access period other than their partial tallies.*

Proof. To prove this theorem, we show that under the DDH assumption, given any two sets of non-adversarial votes cast before and after the adversarial access period with the same partial tallies, one can simulate two corresponding bulletin boards that are indistinguishable to an adversary that chooses an arbitrary number of adversarial votes.

First, note that any two given sets of non-adversarial votes with the same partial tally differ on an even number of votes, say $2d$. This means that with d "swaps" one set of these votes can be converted to the other, where in each swap, for some i and j, the i-th vote is replaced with the j-th one, and vice versa. In Lemma 1 we proved that the bulletin boards before and after each swap remain indistinguishable to the adversary under DDH. Consequently, the bulletin boards corresponding to the two given sets of non-adversarial votes remain indistinguishable to the adversary and the proof is complete.   □

We discussed the case for a single adversarial access period, but the above theorem guaranteeing ballot secrecy can be easily extended to cover attacks involving multiple adversarial access periods.

5   Comparison

In this section we look at how DRE-ip compares with other DRE-based verifiable e-voting systems. In particular, we consider Chaum's Votegrity [16], Neff's MarkPledge [28], VoteBox [31], STAR-Vote [4], DRE-i [24], and vVote [18].

Votegrity is based on visual cryptography and uses onion encryption. MarkPledge employs a purpose-designed encryption scheme that allows challenge-response-style individual verifiability. VoteBox and STAR-Vote are both based on exponential ElGamal encryption which allows homomorphic tallying. In vVote, ballots are encrypted using elliptic curve ElGamal and later decrypted individually after mixing. DRE-i on the other hand uses encryption that does not admit to a fixed decryption key. DRE-ip basically uses the exponential ElGamal encryption in which no party knows the decryption key. All these systems consider voter registration and voter authentication outside their scope and assume they are carried out correctly and securely.

In general, systems that require tallying authorities, i.e. Votegrity, Mark-Pledge, VoteBox, STAR-Vote, and vVote, assume a minimum number of them are available at the tallying phase to compute the election tally. DRE-i and DRE-ip do not require such an assumption to guarantee availability.

To guarantee integrity, all systems we consider rely on a secure bulletin board and on a sufficient number of voters carrying out individual verification. Systems that require tallying authorities, i.e. Votegrity, MarkPledge, VoteBox, STAR-Vote, and vVote, also require that the tallying authorities perform the decryption of the tally correctly. In a verifiable system, this is enforced by requiring the tallying authorities to produce universally verifiable proofs of correct decryption. Hence, we consider assumptions underlying all the systems to guarantee integrity to be comparable, whether the system requires tallying authorities or not.

To guarantee privacy, all systems we consider assume a secure setup phase to generate and distribute system parameters and keys, as well as secure random number generators to produce the randomness required for probabilistic encryption. Furthermore, all systems assume that the captured votes and any ephemeral secrets generated for the cryptographic operations during the voting phase are securely erased. Votegrity is based on decryption mix-nets and requires that the tallying authorities do not collude to compromise voter privacy. Mark-Pledge and vVote employ re-encryption mix-nets to shuffle encrypted ballots before decryption, and assume that the tallying authorities do not decrypt ballots before mixing although they are available on the bulletin board. VoteBox and STAR-Vote require that the tallying authorities do not collude to decrypt individual ballots. DRE-i does not require this assumption, but instead relies on a secure ballot storage mechanism to keep the pre-computed ballots safe after the setup phase. DRE-ip does not require trust assumptions on tallying authorities or ballot storage.

Table 1 summarizes the main similarities and differences in terms of their underlying security assumptions between the voting systems we consider.

Let us now compare the computation complexity of DRE-ip with that of the other DRE-based verifiable e-voting systems. We do not consider Votegrity, MarkPledge, and vVote since they use mix-nets and their computation complexity depend on how these verifiable mix-nets are implemented. All calculations are based on a two-candidate election, encryption implemented based on exponential ElGamal, and one TA if present. Note that having multiple TAs increases the complexity of tally calculation and verification for all the schemes requiring tallying authorities. We assume in all systems that the TA, if present, provides proofs of correct decryption as required by end-to-end verifiability. We

Table 1. Selected security assumptions for DRE-based verifiable e-voting systems. TA: tallying authority, VIA: voter-initiated auditing, BB: bulletin board, RNG: random number generation, ■: assumption is required, □: assumption is not required.

System	Availability	Integrity		Privacy				
	Reliable TA(s)	Sufficient VIA	Secure BB	Secure setup	Secure RNG	Secure deletion	Secure ballot storage	Trustworthy TA(s)
Votegrity	■	■	■	■	■	■	□	■
MarkPledge	■	■	■	■	■	■	□	■
VoteBox	■	■	■	■	■	■	□	■
STAR-Vote	■	■	■	■	■	■	□	■
DRE-i	□	■	■	■	■	■	■	□
vVote	■	■	■	■	■	■	□	■
DRE-ip	□	■	■	■	■	■	□	□

also assume that the simultaneous multiple exponentiation (SME) technique [27] is used to optimize computations. Using SME, a term of the form $g^x h^y$ costs equivalent to around 1.2 exponentiations to calculate.

The systems considered here use two types of well-formedness proof in general. The first type consists of proofs of (knowledge and) equality of two discrete logarithms and are of the general form

$$P_K\{\lambda : \Gamma_1 = \gamma_1^\lambda \wedge \Gamma_2 = \gamma_2^\lambda\}. \tag{2}$$

Consider an exponential ElGamal encryption scheme with key pair $(k, K = g^k)$ in which a message m is encrypted to the ciphertext $(R = g^r, C = K^r g^m)$. The proof

$$P_{WF}\{m : g, K, (R, C)\} = P_K\{k : K = g^k \wedge C/g^m = R^k\}$$

which is of the form of Eq. 2 can be used as a proof of correct decryption, e.g. in systems like VoteBox and STAR-Vote. Such a proof, when realized as a Fiat-Shamir non-interactive Schnorr proof and optimized using the SME technique, requires 2 exponentiations to generate, and (equivalent to) around 2.4 exponentiations to verify. Algorithms for generation and verification of such proofs are transcribed in the full version of this paper [33].

The second type consists of disjunctive proofs of equality (and knowledge) of either one pair of discrete logarithms or the other, and are of the general form

$$P_K\{\lambda : (\Gamma_1 = \gamma_1^\lambda \wedge \Gamma_2 = \gamma_2^\lambda) \vee (\Gamma_3 = \gamma_3^\lambda \wedge \Gamma_4 = \gamma_4^\lambda)\} \tag{3}$$

Such proof can be constructed as a disjunction of two conjunctive proofs of the form of Eq. 2. These proofs can be used to prove well-formedness of the ballots in all the systems we consider. In DRE-ip, the ballot well-formedness proof $P_{WF}\{Z_i : g_1, g_2, R_i\}$ is of this form. This proof, when realized as a Fiat-Shamir non-interactive Schnorr proof and optimized using the SME technique, requires (equivalent to) around 4.4 exponentiations to generate, and (equivalent to) around 4.8 exponentiations to verify. Algorithms for generation and verification of such proofs are transcribed in the full version of this paper [33].

Table 2. Computation complexity of selected DRE-based verifiable e-voting systems. $\mathbb{B}$, $\mathbb{A}$, $\mathbb{C}$: all, audited, confirmed ballots, $\mathfrak{e}$: exponentiation, $\mathfrak{m}$: multiplication.

System	Ballot calculation	Well-formedness and consistency verification	Tally calculation	Tally verification
VoteBox	$6.4\|\mathbb{B}\|\ \mathfrak{e}$	$(6.8\|\mathbb{A}\| + 4.8\|\mathbb{C}\|)\ \mathfrak{e}$	$\|\mathbb{C}\|\ \mathfrak{m} + 3\ \mathfrak{e}$	$\|\mathbb{C}\|\ \mathfrak{m} + 2.4\ \mathfrak{e}$
STAR-Vote	$6.4\|\mathbb{B}\|\ \mathfrak{e}$	$(6.8\|\mathbb{A}\| + 4.8\|\mathbb{C}\|)\ \mathfrak{e}$	$\|\mathbb{C}\|\ \mathfrak{m} + 3\ \mathfrak{e}$	$\|\mathbb{C}\|\ \mathfrak{m} + 2.4\ \mathfrak{e}$
DRE-i	$10.8\|\mathbb{B}\|\ \mathfrak{e}$	$(9.6\|\mathbb{A}\| + 4.8\|\mathbb{C}\|)\ \mathfrak{e}$		$\|\mathbb{B}\|\ \mathfrak{m} + 1\ \mathfrak{e}$
DRE-ip	$6.4\|\mathbb{B}\|\ \mathfrak{e}$	$(6.8\|\mathbb{A}\| + 4.8\|\mathbb{C}\|)\ \mathfrak{e}$		$2\|\mathbb{C}\|\ \mathfrak{m} + 2\ \mathfrak{e}$

VoteBox and STAR-Vote both encrypt the vote under exponential ElGa-mal, which involves similar computation as that of DRE-ip. In DRE-ip, cal-culating R_i and Z_i take 1 exponentiation each, and calculating $P_{WF}\{Z_i\}$ takes around 4.4 exponentiations. Hence, ballot calculation takes around 6.4 exponen-tiations per ballot in VoteBox, STAR-Vote, and DRE-ip. In DRE-i, two proofs of well-formedness are (pre-)calculated for each ballot and hence ballot calculation requires 10.8 exponentiations per ballot.

In all four systems, checking well-formedness of a confirmed ballot consists of verifying a proof of the second type discussed above, so it takes around 4.8 exponentiations per confirmed ballot. Consistency verification of an audited bal-lot consists of checking well-formedness of the ballot plus verifying whether the revealed audit information is consistent with the ballot. In VoteBox, STAR-Vote, and DRE-ip, the computation involved is similar. In DRE-ip for example, R_i and Z_i are recalculated based on the revealed values of r_i and v_i and the result is compared against reported values of R_i and Z_i on the BB. This takes 2 expo-nentiations, and hence consistency verification takes around 6.8 exponentiations per audited ballot. In DRE-i, there is an extra proof of the second type discussed above to verify for each audited ballot and hence consistency verification takes around 9.6 exponentiations per audited ballot.

In VoteBox and STAR-Vote, tally calculation requires all confirmed vote encryptions to be multiplied, the result decrypted, and finally a proof of correct decryption generated. Decryption and generating the proof of correct decryption require 1 and 2 exponentiations, respectively. These calculations are obviously carried out by the TAs. In DRE-i and DRE-ip, tallies are kept track of and reported by the DRE, so no extra calculation is needed.

Tally verification in VoteBox and STAR-Vote consists of multiplying con-firmed vote encryptions and verifying the proof of correct decryption. The latter costs around 2.4 exponentiations as discussed above. In DRE-i, a tally verifi-cation equation is checked which requires multiplication of all vote encryptions and 1 exponentiation. In DRE-ip, two tally verification equation are checked which require multiplication of all R_i and also all Z_i for confirmed ballots and an exponentiation per equation.

Table 2 summarizes the computation complexity of different operations in the systems we discussed above. Note that our calculations above and figures listed in the table do not include the cost of validating the inputs to the verifi-cation algorithms to ensure that they belong to the right cryptographic groups. In elliptic curve based implementations of the systems discussed above, such validations incur negligible cost.

6   Extension to Multiple Candidates

Although we have described DRE-ip for two candidates only, there are two rather standard ways to extend it to support multiple candidates (see e.g. [3,24]). Here we discuss voting for 1 out of n candidates for $n \geq 3$.

A straightforward method is to essentially run a separate parallel DRE-ip system for each candidate. Let v_{ij} represent the vote in ballot i and candidate

Table 3. Computation complexity of DRE-ip supporting voting for 1 out of $n \geq 3$ candidates. $\mathbb{B}$, $\mathbb{A}$, $\mathbb{C}$: all, audited, confirmed ballots, $\mathfrak{e}$: exponentiation, $\mathfrak{m}$: multiplication.

DRE-ip extension	Ballot calculation	Well-formedness and consistency verification	Tally verification
Parallel	$(6.4n + 2)\|\mathbb{B}\|$ $\mathfrak{e}$	$((6.8n + 2.4)\|\mathbb{A}\| + (4.8n + 2.4)\|\mathbb{C}\|)$ $\mathfrak{e}$	$2n\|\mathbb{C}\|$ $\mathfrak{m}$ + $2n$ $\mathfrak{e}$
Encoded	$(2.4n + 1.6)\|\mathbb{B}\|$ $\mathfrak{e}$	$((2.4n + 2)\|\mathbb{A}\| + 2.4n\|\mathbb{C}\|)$ $\mathfrak{e}$	$2\|\mathbb{C}\|$ $\mathfrak{m}$ + 2 $\mathfrak{e}$

j. 1 out of n votes include a $v_{ij} = 1$ vote for one candidate and $v_{ij} = 0$ votes for all other candidates. Hence, an extra proof of well-formedness is required to guarantee that only one of the votes v_{ij} over all values of j is 1. The i-th ballot in this case will be in the form of a $(3n + 1)$-tuple: $((R_{ij}, Z_{ij}, \mathrm{P_{WF}}\{Z_{ij}\})_{j=1}^{n}, \pi)$, where π represents the extra proof. Since for each j the well-formedness proof $\mathrm{P_{WF}}\{Z_{ij}\}$ already guarantees that $v_{ij} \in \{0,1\}$, it would be sufficient for the extra proof to only show that $\sum_{j=1}^{n} v_{ij} = 1$. Interestingly, given the values $R_{ij} = g_2^{r_{ij}}$, this proof can be easily constructed as the proof of knowledge

$$\mathrm{P_K}\{\sigma_i : (\prod_{j=1}^{n} Z_{ij})/g_1 = g_1^{\sigma_i} \wedge \prod_{j=1}^{n} R_{ij} = g_2^{\sigma_i}\}, \quad \text{where} \quad \sigma_i = \sum_{j=1}^{n} r_{ij}.$$

This is a proof of the first type discussed above (i.e. of the form of Eq. 2). Ballot generation for such a parallel DRE-ip systems costs n times that of a two-candidate DRE-ip plus 2 extra exponentiations to generate the extra proof, i.e. $6.4n + 2$ exponentiations per ballot in total. Verifying the extra proof takes 2.4 exponentiations, thus well-formedness and consistency verification cost $4.8n+2.4$ exponentiations per confirmed ballot and $6.8n+2.4$ exponentiations per audited ballot. Tally verification costs n times that of a two-candidate DRE-ip.

Another method is to extend DRE-ip and encode a vote for candidate j as $v_i = M^{j-1}$, where M is an upper bound on the number of voters. The i-th ballot in this case will be in the form of a triple $(R_i, Z_i, \mathrm{P_{WF}}\{Z_i\})$, where $R_i = g_2^{r_i}$ and $Z_i = g_1^{r_i} g_1^{M^{j-1}}$. The ballot well-formedness proof $\mathrm{P_{WF}}\{Z_i\}$ will be a 1-out-of-n disjunctive proof, rather than 1-out-of-2, and it can be realized as follows:

$$\mathrm{P_K}\{r_i : \bigvee_{j=1}^{n} (R_i = g_2^{r_i} \wedge Z_i/g_1^{M^{j-1}} = g_1^{r_i})\}.$$

This is an extended version of a proof of the second type discussed above (i.e. of the form of Eq. 3). Generation of such a proof costs $2 + 2.4(n - 1) = 2.4n - 0.4$ exponentiations and verifying it $2.4n$ exponentiations. Ballot calculation in such an "encoded" DRE-ip system costs $2.4n + 1.6$ exponentiations per ballot. Well-formedness and consistency verification for the system cost $2.4n$ exponentiations per confirmed ballot and $2.4n + 2$ exponentiations per audited ballot. Tally verification cost is similar to that of a two-candidate DRE-ip.

Table 3 summarizes the computation complexity for the two extensions. Overall, while parallel DRE-ip is more modular and hence more straightforward to implement, encoded DRE-ip is more efficient. A similar observation seems to hold for extended versions of VoteBox, STAR-Vote, and DRE-i.

7   Concluding Remarks

In this paper we revisited the design of the DRE-i voting system and proposed a new system: DRE-ip. On the theoretical level, we have shown that it is possible to have verifiable DRE-based voting systems in which the privacy of the ballots does not rely on trustworthy tallying authorities or trusted hardware. On the practical level, we have shown that DRE-ip provides an efficient and practical verifiable DRE-based voting solution able to preserve the privacy of the ballots even if the adversary gets temporary read access to the voting machine during the voting phase. Designing a system without tallying authorities that can efficiently support more complex electoral systems such as single transferable vote (STV) or write-in candidates remains an open problem.

Acknowledgement. The authors wish to thank Changyu Dong and the anonymous reviewers of ESORICS 2016 for their valuable comments. The authors are supported by the ERC Starting Grant No. 306994.

A   Proof of Lemma 1

We first consider the following assumption and prove that it is implied by DDH:

Assumption 2. For randomly chosen $a, b \in \mathbb{Z}_q^*$, given (g, g^b, g^{ab}, Ω) where $\Omega \in \{g^a, g^{a+1}\}$, it is hard to decide whether $\Omega = g^a$ or $\Omega = g^{a+1}$.

Lemma 2. *The DDH assumption implies Assumption 2.*

Proof. Taking $h = g^b$ as the new generator, and assuming $x = a$ and $y = b^{-1}$, we have $g = h^y$, $g^b = h$, $g^{ab} = h^x$, and $g^a = h^{xy}$. Therefore, the assumption can be rewritten as follows for generator h: for randomly chosen $x, y \in \mathbb{Z}_q^*$, given (h, h^x, h^y, Ω), where $\Omega \in \{h^{xy}, h^{xy+1}\}$, it is hard to decide whether $\Omega = h^{xy}$ or $\Omega = h^{xy+1}$. This assumption is proven to be implied by DDH by Hao et al. [24] and hence the proof is complete.   □

Now we show that Lemma 1 holds under Assumption 2.

Proof (of Lemma 1). Let A be an adversary that, after determining a number of votes and obtaining temporary access to the voting machine, distinguishes the two bulletin boards. We construct an algorithm D that given g, g^b, g^{ab}, and a challenge $\Omega \in \{g^a, g^{a+1}\}$ distinguishes which Ω is given.

Consider an abridged bulletin board resulting from removing the well-formedness proofs. Let us call this the *bare* bulletin board. Let the adversary determine any subset of votes other than the swapped votes v_i and v_j. A has access to the bulletin board. Furthermore, A has temporary access to the voting machine which means it can observe some votes v_k and their respective secret values r_k, and also the value of $s = \sum_{\ell=1}^{k} r_\ell$ for the duration of its access. Therefore, apart from simulating the values on the bulletin board, D ought to provide the adversary with the values of r_k and $s = \sum_{\ell=1}^{k} r_\ell$ for a subset of the votes cast or audited during the adversarial access period.

D simulates the bare bulletin board as follows. We describe how confirmed ballots are constructed. Audited ballots can be easily calculated since r_k and v_k are known to D for all $k \notin \{i, j\}$. Recall that ballots i and j are confirmed ballot, both cast either before or after the adversarial access period.

D posts $g_1 = g$ and $g_2 = g^b$ as the initial parameters on the bulletin board. For all $k \notin \{i, j\}$, D simply chooses r_k randomly and generates the ballot according to the protocol. D generates random α_i and α_j and calculates the i-th and j-th ballots as follows. First, D sets

$$R_i = (g^b)^{\alpha_i} g^{ab}, \qquad Z_i = g^{\alpha_i} \Omega, \qquad R_j = (g^b)^{\alpha_j}/g^{ab}, \qquad Z_j = g^{\alpha_j+1}/\Omega.$$

Assuming implicitly that $r_i = \alpha_i + a$ and $r_j = \alpha_j - a$, we can see that R_i and R_j are well-formed since:

$$R_i = (g^b)^{\alpha_i} g^{ab} = (g^b)^{\alpha_i+a} = g_2^{r_i}, \qquad R_j = (g^b)^{\alpha_j}/g^{ab} = (g^b)^{\alpha_j-a} = g_2^{r_j}.$$

Now if $\Omega = g^a$, then we have

$$Z_i = g^{\alpha_i} \Omega = g^{\alpha_i+a} = g_1^{r_i}, \qquad Z_j = g^{\alpha_j+1}/\Omega = g^{\alpha_j-a} g = g_1^{r_j} g_1.$$

On the other hand, if $\Omega = g^{a+1}$, then we have

$$Z_i = g^{\alpha_i} \Omega = g^{\alpha_i+a} g = g_1^{r_i} g_1, \qquad Z_j = g^{\alpha_j+1}/\Omega = g^{\alpha_j-a} = g_1^{r_j}.$$

In other words, $\Omega = g^a$ corresponds to a bulletin board with $v_i = 0$ and $v_j = 1$, and $\Omega = g^{a+1}$ corresponds to a bulletin board with $v_i = 1$ and $v_j = 0$, with all other votes being identical in the two bulletin boards.

Since all the votes other than v_i and v_j are known to D, it can calculate the partial tallies of the votes other than v_i and v_j cast *before*, *during*, and *after* the adversarial access period. In addition, we have either $v_i = 0$ and $v_j = 1$, or $v_i = 1$ and $v_j = 0$, hence $v_i + v_j = 1$. So whether both v_i and v_j are cast before or after the adversarial access period, the partial tallies of all votes (including v_i and v_j) cast before, during, and after the the adversarial access period can be easily calculated by D.

A similar argument holds for the random values: all random values except for r_i and r_j are known to D, and for r_i and r_j we implicitly have:

$$r_i + r_j = (\alpha_i + a) + (\alpha_j - a) = \alpha_i + \alpha_j$$

which means that $r_i + r_j$ is known to D. Hence following a similar reasoning, whether both v_i and v_j are cast before or after the adversarial access period, the partial sums of all random values (including r_i and r_j) for votes cast before, during, and after the the adversarial access period can be easily simulated by D.

Thus, D is able to simulate all the elements of a bare bulletin board and the internal DRE information revealed to the A during the adversarial access period. Since the well-formedness proofs are assumed to be zero knowledge, they can be simulated in the Random Oracle Model for ballots i and j, and the simulated proofs remain indistinguishable from real proofs. Consequently, D is able to simulate a full bulletin board corresponding to one of the two cases, with $\Omega = g^a$ corresponding to the case where $v_i = 0$ and $v_j = 1$, and $\Omega = g^{a+1}$ corresponding to $v_i = 1$ and $v_j = 0$, with all other votes being identical in the two bulletin boards. Now if A is able to distinguish the two cases, D will be able to distinguish whether $\Omega = g^a$ or $\Omega = g^{a+1}$, and hence the proof is complete. $\square$

References

1. Adida, B.: Helios: web-based open-audit voting. In: USENIX Security Symposium, vol. 17, pp. 335–348 (2008)
2. Adida, B., de Marneffe, O., Pereira, O., Quisquater, J.-J.: Electing a university president using open-audit voting: analysis of real-world use of Helios. In: EVT/WOTE 2009, p. 10. USENIX (2009)
3. Baudron, O., Fouque, P.-A., Pointcheval, D., Stern, J., Poupard, G.: Practical multi-candidate election system. In: ACM Symposium on Principles of Distributed Computing, PODC 2001, pp. 274–283. ACM (2001)
4. Bell, S., Benaloh, J., Byrne, M.D., DeBeauvoir, D., Eakin, B., Fisher, G., Kortum, P., McBurnett, N., Montoya, J., Parker, M., Pereira, O., Stark, P.B., Wallach, D.S., Winn, M.: STAR-Vote: a secure, transparent, auditable, and reliable voting system. USENIX J. Election Technol. Syst. **1**(1), 18–37 (2013)
5. Bellare, M., Goldreich, O.: On defining proofs of knowledge. In: Brickell, E.F. (ed.) CRYPTO 1992. LNCS, vol. 740, pp. 390–420. Springer, Heidelberg (1993)
6. Bellare, M., Rogaway, P.: Random oracles are practical: a paradigm for designing efficient protocols. In: ACM CCS 1993, pp. 62–73. ACM (1993)
7. Ben-Nun, J., Llewellyn, M., Riva, B., Rosen, A., Ta-Shma, A., Wikström, D.: A new implementation of a dual (paper and cryptographic) voting system. In: EVOTE 2012: 5th International Conference on Electronic Voting, pp. 315–329 (2012)
8. Benaloh, J.: Ballot casting assurance via voter-initiated poll station auditing. In: USENIX Workshop on Accurate E-Voting Technology (EVT), p. 14 (2007)
9. Benaloh, J., Tuinstra, D.: Receipt-free secret-ballot elections. In: ACM Symposium on Theory of Computing, STOC 1994, pp. 544–553. ACM (1994)
10. Benaloh, J.D.C.: Verifiable Secret-Ballot Elections. Ph.d. thesis, Department of Computer Science, Yale University (1987)
11. Bohli, J.-M., Müller-Quade, J., Röhrich, S.: Bingo voting: secure and coercion-free voting using a trusted random number generator. In: Alkassar, A., Volkamer, M. (eds.) VOTE-ID 2007. LNCS, vol. 4896, pp. 111–124. Springer, Heidelberg (2007)
12. Camenisch, J.L., Stadler, M.A.: Efficient group signature schemes for large groups. In: Kaliski Jr., B.S. (ed.) CRYPTO 1997. LNCS, vol. 1294, pp. 410–424. Springer, Heidelberg (1997)
13. Carback, R., Chaum, D., Clark, J., Conway, J., Essex, A., Herrnson, P., Mayberry, T., Popoveniuc, S., Rivest, R., Shen, E., Sherman, A., Vora, P.: Scantegrity II municipal election at Takoma Park: the first E2E binding governmental election with ballot privacy. In: USENIX Security Symposium, pp. 291–306 (2010)

14. Chaum, D., Carback, R., Clark, J., Essex, A., Popoveniuc, S., Rivest, R., Ryan, P., Shen, E., Sherman, A., Vora, P.: Scantegrity II: end-to-end verifiability by voters of optical scan elections through confirmation codes. IEEE Trans. Inf. Foren. Secur. 4(4), 611–627 (2009)
15. Chaum, D.L.: Untraceable electronic mail, return addresses, and digital pseudonyms. Commun. ACM 24(2), 84–90 (1981)
16. Chaum, D.L.: Secret-ballot receipts: true voter-vrifiable elections. IEEE Secur. Priv. 2(1), 38–47 (2004)
17. Cramer, R., Damgård, I.B., Schoenmakers, B.: Proof of partial knowledge and simplified design of witness hiding protocols. In: Desmedt, Y.G. (ed.) CRYPTO 1994. LNCS, vol. 839, pp. 174–187. Springer, Heidelberg (1994)
18. Culnane, C., Ryan, P.Y.A., Schneider, S., Teague, V.: vVote: a verifiable voting system. ACM Trans. Inf. Syst. Secur. 18(1), 3:1–3:30 (2015)
19. Diffie, W., Hellman, M.E.: New directions in cryptography. IEEE Trans. Inf. Theor. 22(6), 644–654 (1976)
20. Fiat, A., Shamir, A.: How to prove yourself: practical solutions to identification and signature problems. In: Odlyzko, A.M. (ed.) CRYPTO 1986. LNCS, vol. 263, pp. 186–194. Springer, Heidelberg (1987)
21. Fisher, K., Carback, R., Sherman, A.T.: Punchscan: introduction and system definition of a high-integrity election system. In: Workshop on Trustworthy Elections (WOTE) (2006)
22. Goldwasser, S., Micali, S., Rackoff, C.: The knowledge complexity of interactive proof systems. SIAM J. Comput. 18(1), 186–208 (1989)
23. Hao, F., Clarke, D., Zorzo, A.: Deleting secret data with public verifiability. IEEE Trans. Dependable Secure Comput. PP(99), 1 (2015)
24. Hao, F., Kreeger, M.N., Randell, B., Clarke, D., Shahandashti, S.F., Lee, P.H.-J.: Every vote counts: ensuring integrity in large-scale electronic voting. USENIX J. Election Technol. Syst. 2(3), 1–25 (2014)
25. Juels, A., Catalano, D., Jakobsson, M.: Coercion-resistant electronic elections. In: Privacy in Electronic Society, WPES 2005, pp. 61–70. ACM (2005)
26. Lim, A.: Travis County, TX developing electronic voting system with a paper trail. Government Technology, July 2014. www.govtech.com. Accessed October 2015
27. Menezes, A.J., van Oorschot, P.C., Vanstone, S.A.: Handbook of Applied Cryptography. CRC Press, Boca Raton (1996)
28. Neff, C.A.: Practical high certainty intent verification for encrypted votes (2004). http://citeseer.ist.psu.edu
29. Ryan, P., Bismark, D., Heather, J., Schneider, S., Xia, Z.: Prêt à voter: a voter-verifiable voting system. IEEE Trans. Inf. Foren. Secur. 4(4), 662–673 (2009)
30. Sako, K., Kilian, J.: Receipt-free mix-type voting scheme. In: Guillou, L.C., Quisquater, J.-J. (eds.) EUROCRYPT 1995. LNCS, vol. 921, pp. 393–403. Springer, Heidelberg (1995)
31. Sandler, D., Derr, K., Wallach, D.S.: VoteBox: a tamper-evident, verifiable electronic voting system. In: USENIX Security Symposium, vol. 4, p. 87 (2008)
32. Schnorr, C.-P.: Efficient signature generation by smart cards. J. Cryptology 4(3), 161–174 (1991)
33. Shahandashti, S.F., Hao, F.: DRE-ip: a verifiable e-voting scheme without tallying authorities. Cryptology ePrint Archive, Report 2016/670 (2016). http://eprint.iacr.org/2016/670

When Are Three Voters Enough for Privacy Properties?

Myrto Arapinis[1](✉), Véronique Cortier[2], and Steve Kremer[2]

[1] University of Edinburgh, Edinburgh, UK
marapini@inf.ed.ac.uk

[2] LORIA, CNRS & Inria Nancy & Université de Lorraine, Nancy, France

Abstract. Protocols for secure electronic voting are of increasing societal importance. Proving rigorously their security is more challenging than many other protocols, which aim at authentication or key exchange. One of the reasons is that they need to be secure for an arbitrary number of malicious voters. In this paper we identify a class of voting protocols for which only a small number of agents needs to be considered: if there is an attack on vote privacy then there is also an attack that involves at most 3 voters (2 honest voters and 1 dishonest voter).

In the case where the protocol allows a voter to cast several votes and counts, e.g., only the last one, we also reduce the number of ballots required for an attack to 10, and under some additional hypotheses, 7 ballots. Our results are formalised and proven in a symbolic model based on the applied pi calculus. We illustrate the applicability of our results on several case studies, including different versions of Helios and Prêt-à-Voter, as well as the JCJ protocol. For some of these protocols we can use the ProVerif tool to provide the first formal proofs of privacy for an unbounded number of voters.

1 Introduction

Electronic voting has been adopted in several countries, such as the United States, Estonia, Australia, Norway, Switzerland, and France, to conduct legally binding elections (or at least trials for some of them). Electronic voting systems should ensure the same properties than the traditional paper ballots systems, despite the fact that malicious users may easily intercept ballots and try to forge fake ones. One crucial property is vote privacy: no one should know how a particular voter voted. Symbolic models have been very successful in the analysis of more traditional protocols that aim at confidentiality or authentication. Many decision techniques and several tools have been developed (see [1–3] to cite only a few) which have been successfully applied to a large number of case studies including widely deployed protocols such as TLS [4]. Vote privacy in symbolic models can be expressed through a rather simple and natural property [5]: an attacker should not be able to distinguish the situation where Alice votes 0 and Bob votes 1 from the situation where the votes are swapped:

$$V_{\mathsf{Alice}}(0) \mid V_{\mathsf{Bob}}(1) \approx V_{\mathsf{Alice}}(1) \mid V_{\mathsf{Bob}}(0)$$

© Springer International Publishing Switzerland 2016
I. Askoxylakis et al. (Eds.): ESORICS 2016, Part II, LNCS 9879, pp. 241–260, 2016.
DOI: 10.1007/978-3-319-45741-3_13

Despite its apparent simplicity, this property is difficult to check for several reasons. Firstly, most existing decision techniques apply to reachability properties (such as authentication and confidentiality) but not to indistinguishability properties. Another major difficulty comes from the fact that e-voting systems involve less standard cryptographic primitives and sometimes even specially designed, ad-hoc primitives (like for the protocol used in Norway [6]). Typical primitives in e-voting are homomorphic encryption, zero-knowledge proofs, reencryption mixnets, etc. Some techniques and tools [7–10] for indistinguishability properties have recently been developed to automatically check indistinguishability properties and some of them can handle part of the primitives needed in e-voting. For example, ProVerif and Akiss have both been successfully applied to analyse some voting protocols [5,10–14]. However, a third source of difficulty is the fact that voting systems are typically parametrized by the number of voters: both the bulletin board and the tally processes have to process as many ballots as they receive. This is typically modeled by considering processes parametrized by the number of voters. Even though parameterized protocols can be encoded in a formalism such as the applied pi calculus, such encodings are complicated and generally beyond the capabilities of what automated tools support. ProVerif, which to the best of our knowledge is the only tool that supports verification of indistinguishability properties for an unbounded number of sessions (i.e. allowing replication) generally fails to prove vote privacy. One exception is a case study of the Civitas voting system by Backes et al. [11] using ProVerif. The other tools for indistinguishability (e.g. SPEC [8], Akiss [10], and APTE [9]) can only handle a finite number of sessions. So case studies have to consider a finite number of voters [10,12–14] unless proofs are conducted by hand [13,15].

Contributions. Our main contribution is a reduction result for a reasonably large class of voting protocols. If there is an attack on privacy for n voters, we show that there also exists one that only requires 3 voters: 2 honest voters are necessary to state the privacy property and then 1 dishonest is sufficient to find all existing attacks. This result significantly simplifies security proofs: there is no longer need to consider arbitrarily many voters, even in manual proofs. Moreover, this result allows the use of automated tools for checking equivalence properties and justifies previous proofs conducted for a fixed number of voters (provided at least one dishonest voter was considered).

Several protocols assume voters may revote several times. This is for example the case of Helios or Civitas. Revoting is actually crucial for coercion-resistance in Civitas. When revoting is allowed, this should be reflected in the model by letting the ballot box accept an unbounded number of ballots, and retaining only the valid ones according to the revote policy. This aspect is typically abstracted in any existing formal analysis. We show that we can simplify the analysis by reducing the total number of ballots to 10 for typical revoting policies (e.g. the last vote counts) and typical tally functions. Altogether, our result amounts in a finite model property: if there is an attack on privacy on n voters that may vote arbitrarily, then there is an attack that only requires 3 voters and at most 10 ballots. We can further reduce the number of ballots to 7 for a class of protocols that has *identifiable ballots*, that is ballots that reveal the corresponding public credentials. Of course, only 3 ballots are sufficient when revoting is disallowed.

Our result holds in a rather general setting provided that the e-voting system can be modeled as a process in the applied-pi calculus [16]. Of course, this reduction result cannot hold for *arbitrary* systems. For example, if the tally phase checks that at least 4 ballots are present then at least 4 voters are necessary to conduct an attack. So we model what we think to represent a "reasonable" class of e-voting systems. The process modeling the voter may be an arbitrary process as long as it does not depend on credentials of other voters and provided voters do not need to interact once the tally phase has started. This corresponds to the "vote and go" property, that is often desirable for practical reasons, but also excludes some protocols such as [17]. Once the vote is casted the authorities proceed as follows.

- The bulletin board (if there is one) performs only public actions such as publishing a received ballot, possibly removing some parts and possibly after some public tests, *i.e.* tests that anyone could do as well. Typical public tests are checks of signature validity, well-formedness of the ballots, or validity of zero-knowledge proofs. Alternatively, we may consider an arbitrary bulletin board in case it is corrupted since it is then part of the adversarial environment.
- Next, a revote policy is applied. We consider two particular revote policies: the policy which selects the last ballot, which is the most common one, and the policy that selects the first one, which encodes the situation where revoting is prohibited.
- Finally, the tally is computed according to some counting function. We consider in particular two very common functions: the multiset and the additive counting functions. The multiset counting function returns the votes in an arbitrary order and corresponds for example to the output of a decryption mixnet. The additive counting function returns the number of votes received by each candidate.

We believe that these conditions are general enough to capture many existing e-voting schemes.

Applications. To illustrate the applicability of our result, we re-investigate several existing analyses of e-voting protocols. First, we consider several versions of the Helios protocol [18], both in its mixnet and homomorphic versions. These versions also include the Belenios [19] protocol. We are able to use the ProVerif tool to show privacy for the mixnet versions of these protocols for a bounded number of voters and ballots. Our reduction result allows immediately to conclude that vote privacy also holds for an arbitrary number of voters. The homomorphic version of Helios is out of reach of existing tools due to the presence of associative and commutative symbols. However, our reduction result does apply, which means that the manual proof of Helios conducted in [13] did not need to consider arbitrarily many voters and could be simplified. In case one wishes to adapt this proof to Belenios [19], our reduction result would alleviate the proof. The Prêt-à-Voter [20] protocol (PaV) has been analysed using ProVerif for 2 honest voters [12]. Adding a third, dishonest, voter, we can apply our result and obtain the first proof of vote privacy for an arbitrary number of voters. Unfortunately, ProVerif did not scale up to verify automatically the protocol in presence of a dishonest voter. We were also able to apply our result (and a proof using ProVerif) to a protocol by Moran and Naor and to the JCJ protocol implemented in Civitas (without a ProVerif proof).

Related work. To our knowledge, the only other reduction result applying to voting protocols was proposed by Dreier et al. [21]. Their result states that it is sufficient to prove vote privacy for two honest voters when the protocol is observationally equivalent to a protocol consisting of the parallel composition (not sharing any secret) of a partition of the set of voters. Applicability has however only been shown to examples where this trivially holds, e.g. [17,22] as these protocols use completely public tallying mechanisms. In general, proving the required equivalence does not seem easier than proving directly vote secrecy. Moreover, it does not apply to some well known protocols such as Helios since a dishonest voter is needed to mount the vote replay attack [13].

The results of [23,24] show how to reduce the number of agents, in the case of trace properties [23] and equivalence properties [24]. The major difference with our work is that [23,24] simply reduce the number of *agent identities* while the number of sessions (or processes) remains the same. In contrast, we do not only reduce the number of voter identities but also the number of ballots the ballot box needs to process, yielding a simpler process.

2   Modelling Security Protocols

As usual in symbolic protocol analysis we model protocol messages as terms. Protocols are modelled in a process calculus, similar to the applied pi calculus [16].

2.1   Messages

We assume an infinite set of *names* $\mathcal{N} = \{a, b, k, n, \ldots\}$ (which are used to represent keys, nonces, ...) and an infinite set of *channels* $\mathcal{C}h = \{c, c_1, ch, ch_1, \ldots\}$ (which are used to represent communication channels). We also consider a set of *variables* $\mathcal{X} = \{x, y, \ldots\}$, and a signature Σ consisting of a finite set of *function symbols*.

Terms are defined as names, variables, and function symbols applied to other terms. In particular, a channel is not a term. Let $\mathsf{N} \subseteq \mathcal{N}$ and $\mathsf{X} \subseteq \mathcal{X}$, the set of terms built from N and X by applying function symbols in Σ is denoted by $\mathcal{T}(\Sigma, \mathsf{N} \cup \mathsf{X})$. We write $fv(t)$ (resp. $fn(t)$) for the set of variables (resp. names) occurring in a term t. A term is *ground* if it does not contain any variable.

Example 1. We model asymmetric encryption, signatures, and pairs by the signature

$$\Sigma_{\mathsf{aenc}} \overset{\text{def}}{=} \{\mathsf{aenc}/3, \mathsf{adec}/2, \mathsf{pk}/1, \mathsf{sig}/2, \mathsf{checksig}/2, \mathsf{getmsg}/1, \mathsf{vk}/1, \langle \cdot, \cdot \rangle/2, \pi_1/1, \pi_2/1\}$$

where f/i denotes that f has arity i. Consider term $t \overset{\text{def}}{=} \langle \mathsf{pk}(sk), \mathsf{aenc}(\mathsf{pk}(sk), r, m)\rangle$ where $sk, r, m \in \mathcal{N}$. The term t represents a pair consisting of the public key $\mathsf{pk}(sk)$ associated to the private key sk and the encryption of message m with public key $\mathsf{pk}(sk)$ using randomness r. To improve readability, we may sometimes write $\langle t_1, \ldots, t_n\rangle$ instead of $\langle t_1, \langle \ldots \langle t_{n-1}, t_n\rangle \ldots\rangle\rangle$.

We denote by $\ell = [t_1, \ldots, t_n]$ the list of terms $t_1, \ldots, t_n$ and by $t_0 :: \ell$ the list obtained by adding the term t_0 to the head of the list, i.e., $t_0 :: \ell = [t_0, t_1, \ldots, t_n]$. Sometimes we interpret lists as multisets and we write $\ell_1 =^{\#} \ell_2$ for the equality of the multisets corresponding to these lists.

A *substitution* is a partial function from variables to terms. The substitution σ that maps x_i to t_i ($1 \leq i \leq n$) is denoted $\{x_1 \mapsto t_1, \ldots, x_n \mapsto t_n\}$ and we write $\mathrm{dom}(\sigma) = \{x_1, \ldots, x_n\}$ for the domain of σ. We denote by $\emptyset$ the substitution whose domain is empty. We always suppose that substitutions are acyclic. As usual we extend substitutions to terms and write $t\sigma$ for the application of σ to term t.

To model algebraic properties of cryptographic primitives, we define an *equational theory* by a finite set E of equations $u = v$ with $u, v \in \mathcal{T}(\Sigma, \mathcal{X})$. We define $=_{\mathsf{E}}$ to be the smallest equivalence relation on terms, that contains E and that is closed under application of function symbols and substitutions of terms for variables.

Example 2. Continuing Example 1 we define the equational theory $\mathsf{E}_{\mathsf{aenc}}$ by the following equations.

$$\mathsf{adec}(x_k, \mathsf{aenc}(\mathsf{pk}(x_k), x_r, x_m)) = x_m \qquad \mathsf{checksig}(\mathsf{sig}(x, y), \mathsf{vk}(y)) = \mathsf{ok}$$
$$\pi_i(\langle x_1, x_2\rangle) = x_i \quad (i \in \{1, 2\}) \qquad \mathsf{getmsg}(\mathsf{sig}(x, y)) = x$$

Then we have that $\mathsf{adec}(sk, \pi_2(t)) =_{\mathsf{E}_{\mathsf{aenc}}} m$.

To illustrate our calculus we consider the Helios e-voting protocol as running example. The Helios protocol relies on zero knowledge proofs. We next specify the equational theory for the particular zero knowledge proofs built by the Helios participants.

Example 3. The Helios zero knowledge proofs can be modelled by the signature

$$\Sigma_{\mathsf{zkp}} \overset{\text{def}}{=} \quad \{\mathsf{zkp}_{\mathsf{E}}/3, \mathsf{checkzkp}_{\mathsf{E}}/2, \mathsf{okzkp}_{\mathsf{E}}/0\} \cup \{\mathsf{zkp}_{\mathsf{DM}}^m/3, \mathsf{checkzkp}_{\mathsf{DM}}^m/3, \mathsf{okzkp}_{\mathsf{DM}}^m/0\}_{m \in \mathbb{N}}$$

In case of homomorphic tally, the voters should also prove that their vote is valid, which can be modeled in a similar way. When submitting an encrypted vote, voters are required to prove that the encryption is well-formed, that is to say, that they know the corresponding plaintext and randomness. This is reflected by the following equation.

$$\mathsf{checkzkp}_{\mathsf{E}}(\mathsf{zkp}_{\mathsf{E}}(xr, xv, \mathsf{aenc}(xpk, xr, xv)), \mathsf{aenc}(xpk, xr, xv)) = \mathsf{okzkp}_{\mathsf{E}}$$

In the decryption mixnets-based variant of the Helios protocol, the talliers output a zero knowledge proof of correct mix and decryption. Such a proof establishes that the output of the decryption mixnet is indeed a permutation of the content of the encrypted ballots received as input. This is captured by the following infinite set of equations. For all $m \in \mathbb{N}$, and all $\{i_1, \ldots, i_m\} = \{1, \ldots, m\}$,

$$\mathsf{checkzkp}_{\mathsf{DM}}^m(\mathsf{zkp}_{\mathsf{DM}}^m(xk, xciph, xplain), xciph, xplain) = \mathsf{okzkp}_{\mathsf{DM}}^m$$

with $xciph = (\mathsf{aenc}(\mathsf{pub}(xk), xr_1, xv_1), \ldots, \mathsf{aenc}(\mathsf{pub}(xk), xr_m, xv_m))$ and $xplain = (xv_{i_1}, \ldots, xv_{i_m})$.

In all the examples of this section, we will consider the signature $\Sigma = \Sigma_{\mathsf{aenc}} \cup \Sigma_{\mathsf{zkp}}$ and the equational theory $\mathsf{E} = \mathsf{E}_{\mathsf{aenc}} \cup \mathsf{E}_{\mathsf{zkp}}$.

We say that a symbol $+$ is associative and commutative (AC in short) w.r.t. an equational theory E if E contains the two equations:

$$x + y = y + x \qquad x + (y + z) = (x + y) + z$$

2.2   Processes

We model protocols using a process calculus. Our *plain processes* are similar to plain processes in applied pi calculus [16] and are defined through the grammar given in Fig. 1 where c is a channel, t, t_1, t_2 are terms, x is a variable, n is either a name or a channel, and $i \in \mathbb{N}$ is an integer. The terms t, t_1, t_2 may contain variables.

$$
\begin{aligned}
P, Q := \; & 0 \\
& P \mid Q \\
& \nu n.P \\
& !P \\
& \text{if } t_1 = t_2 \text{ then } P \text{ else } Q \\
& c(x).P \\
& \bar{c}\langle t \rangle.Q \\
& i : P
\end{aligned}
$$

Fig. 1. Syntax of plain processes

The process 0 does nothing. $P \mid Q$ behaves as the parallel execution of processes P and Q. $\nu n.P$ restricts the scope of n. When n is a name, it typically represents a freshly generated, secret value, *e.g.*, a key or a nonce, in P. When n is a channel, it declares a private channel, that cannot be accessed by the adversary. Replication $!P$ behaves as an unbounded number of copies of P. The conditional if $t_1 = t_2$ then P else Q behaves as P if t_1 and t_2 are equal in the equational theory and as Q otherwise. The process $c(x).P$ inputs a message t on channel c, binds it to x and then behaves as P where x has been replaced by t. $\bar{c}\langle t \rangle.Q$ outputs message t on channel c before behaving as Q. Our calculus also introduces a *phase* instruction, in the spirit of [24,25], denoted $i : P$. We denote by $Phase(P)$ the set of phases that appears in P, that is the set of j such that $j : Q$ occurs in P. By a slight abuse of notations, we write $Phase(P) < Phase(Q)$ if any phase in $Phase(P)$ is smaller than any phase in $Phase(Q)$.

As usual, names and variables have scopes, which are delimited by restrictions and inputs. We write $fv(P)$, $bv(P)$, $fn(P)$ and $bn(P)$ for the sets of free and bound variables, and free and bound names of a plain process P respectively.

Example 4. A voter in Helios proceeds as follows. She computes her ballot by encrypting her vote with the public key $\mathsf{pk}(skE)$ of the election. The corresponding secret key is shared among several election authorities, which is not modeled here. Then she casts her ballot together with her identity and a zero knowledge proof through an authenticated channel. All this information will be published on a public bulletin board. The process $V(\mathsf{pk}(skE), cred, id, v)$ models the actions of a voter with identity id and credential $cred$ casting a ballot for candidate v:

$$V(\mathsf{pk}(skE), cred, id, v) \stackrel{\text{def}}{=} \nu r.\, \overline{bb}\langle\langle id, \mathsf{sig}(bal, cred), prf\rangle\rangle$$

where $bal = \mathsf{aenc}(\mathsf{pk}(skE), r, v)$ and $prf = \mathsf{zkp}_\mathsf{E}(r, v, bal)$. The authenticated channel is modelled by a signature although Helios relies on a login/password mechanism.

Extended processes keep track of additional information during an execution: the names that have been bound, the currently active processes that are running in parallel, the history of messages that were output by the process and the current phase.

Definition 1 (Extended process). *An extended process is a tuple* $(\mathcal{E}; \mathcal{P}; \Phi; i)$ *where:*

- $\mathcal{E}$ *is a set of names and channels that are restricted in* $\mathcal{P}$ *and* Φ;
- $\mathcal{P}$ *is a multiset of* plain processes *with* $fv(\mathcal{P}) = \emptyset$;
- $\Phi = \{x_1 \mapsto u_1, \ldots, x_n \mapsto u_n\}$ *is a ground substitution where* $u_1, \ldots, u_n$ *represent the messages previously output to the environment.*
- i *is an integer denoting the current phase.*

Example 5. The following extended process models two honest Helios voters id_A and id_B ready to cast their ballots v_A and v_B respectively in a first phase, and the Helios tallying authorities Tal ready to tally the cast ballots in a second phase

$$\mathsf{Helios}(v_A, v_B) \stackrel{\text{def}}{=} (\mathcal{E}_0, 1 : V_A \mid 1 : V_B \mid 2 : Tal, \emptyset, 1)$$

where $\mathcal{E}_0$ is a set of names with $cred_A; cred_B \in \mathcal{E}_0$,

$$V_A \stackrel{\text{def}}{=} V(\mathsf{pk}(skE), cred_A, id_A, v_A) \text{ and } V_B \stackrel{\text{def}}{=} V(\mathsf{pk}(skE), cred_B, id_B, v_B)$$

model the two honest voters where V is defined in Example 4, and

$$Tal \stackrel{\text{def}}{=} bb(xb_A).bb(xb_B).T$$

for some process T modelling the tallying authorities.

Given $A = (\mathcal{E}; \mathcal{P}; \Phi; i)$, we define the set of free and bound names of A as $fn(A) = (fn(\mathcal{P}) \cup fn(\Phi)) \setminus \mathcal{E}$, and $bn(A) = bn(\mathcal{P}) \cup \mathcal{E}$. Similarly free and bound variables are defined as $fv(A) = (fv(\mathcal{P}) \cup \mathrm{dom}(\varPhi))$, and $bv(A) = bv(\mathcal{P})$. An extended process A is closed if $fv(A) = \mathrm{dom}(\varPhi)$.

The operational semantics of our calculus is defined by a labelled transition system which allows to reason about processes that interact with their environment. The transition relation $A \xrightarrow{\ell} B$ relates two ground extended processes A and B and is decorated by a label ℓ, which is either an input $(c(M))$, an output $(\nu x.\overline{c}\langle x \rangle)$, or a silent action (τ). Silent actions are standard, while visible input and output actions are interactions with the adversary on public channels. An output label $\nu x.\overline{c}\langle x \rangle$ reflects that messages are output "by reference": the label contains the variable added to $\mathrm{dom}(\varPhi)$ which maps to the ground message that was output. The input label $c(M)$ contains the term M used by the adversary to compute the message: M may be constructed from previous outputs (addressed through variables in $\mathrm{dom}(\varPhi)$), but is not allowed to use private names. The transition relation is formally defined in the companion technical report [26].

Notations. Given a set $\mathcal{S}$ we denote by $\mathcal{S}^*$ the set of all finite *sequences* of elements in $\mathcal{S}$. We may also write $\tilde{u}$ for the finite sequence $u_1, \ldots, u_n$. Let $\mathcal{A}$ be the alphabet of actions (in our case this alphabet is infinite and contains the special symbol τ). For every $w \in \mathcal{A}^*$, the relation $\xrightarrow{w}$ on processes is defined in the usual way, i.e., we write $A \xrightarrow{w} A'$ when $w = \ell_1 \ell_2 \cdots \ell_n$ and $A \xrightarrow{\ell_1} A_1 \xrightarrow{\ell_2} \ldots \xrightarrow{\ell_n} A'$. For $s \in (\mathcal{A} \setminus \{\tau\})^*$, the relation $\xRightarrow{s}$ on processes is defined by: $A \xRightarrow{s} B$ if, and only if there exists $w \in \mathcal{A}^*$ such that $A \xrightarrow{w} B$ and s is obtained by erasing all occurrences of τ from w.

Example 6. Continuing our running example we illustrate the operational semantics by the following transitions

$$Helios(v_A, v_B) \xRightarrow{\nu y_A.\overline{bb}\langle y_A \rangle} \xRightarrow{\nu y_B.\overline{bb}\langle y_B \rangle} \xRightarrow{\text{phase 2}} (\mathcal{E}; T; \varPhi; 2) \quad \text{where}$$

- $\mathcal{E} = \mathcal{E}_0 \cup \{r_A, r_B\}$,
- $\varPhi = \{y_A \mapsto \langle id_A, \mathsf{sig}(bal_A, cred_A), prf_A \rangle, y_B \mapsto \langle id_B, \mathsf{sig}(bal_B, cred_B), prf_B \rangle\}$
  where $bal_C = \mathsf{aenc}(\mathsf{pk}(skE), r_C, v_C)$ and $prf_C = \mathsf{zkp}_\mathsf{E}(r_C, v_C, bal_C)$ for $C \in \{A, B\}$.

A *frame* $\varphi = \nu \mathcal{E}.\varPhi$ consists of a set of names $\mathcal{E}$ and a substitution $\varPhi = \{x_1 \mapsto u_1, \ldots, x_n \mapsto u_n\}$. The names $\mathcal{E}$ are bound in φ and can be α-converted. Moreover names can be added (or removed) to (from) $\mathcal{E}$ as long as they do not appear in $\varPhi$. We write $\varphi =_\alpha \varphi'$ when frames φ and φ' are equal up to α-conversion and addition/removal of unused names. In this way two frames can always be rewritten to have the same set of bound names. When $A = (\mathcal{E}; \mathcal{P}; \varPhi; i)$ is an extended process, we define $\phi(A) \overset{\mathrm{def}}{=} \nu \mathcal{E}.\varPhi$.

Given a frame $\varphi = \nu \mathcal{E}.\varPhi$ an attacker can construct new terms building on the terms exposed by φ. For this the attacker applies a *recipe* on the frame. A recipe R for a frame φ is any term such that $fn(R) \cap \mathcal{E} = \emptyset$ and $fv(R) \subseteq \mathrm{dom}(\varPhi)$. An attacker is unable to distinguish two sequences of messages if he cannot construct a test that distinguishes them. This notion is formally captured by *static equivalence* [16] of frames.

Definition 2 (Static equivalence). *Two frames* $\varphi_1 =_\alpha \nu\mathcal{E}.\Phi_1$ *and* $\varphi_2 =_\alpha \nu\mathcal{E}.\Phi_2$ *are statically equivalent, noted* $\varphi_1 \sim \varphi_2$ *when* $\text{dom}(\Phi_1) = \text{dom}(\Phi_2)$, *and for all recipes* M *and* N *of* φ_1 *we have that* $M\Phi_1 =_E N\Phi_1$ *iff* $M\Phi_2 =_E N\Phi_2$.

Note that in the above definition the frames φ_1 and φ_2 have the same set of recipes as they bind the same names $\mathcal{E}$ and their substitutions have the same domain.

Example 7. Let Φ be the substitution of Example 6 and

$$\Phi' = \{y_A \mapsto \langle id_A, \text{sig}(bal'_A, cred_A), prf'_A\rangle, y_B \mapsto \langle id_B, \text{sig}(bal'_B, cred_B), prf'_B\rangle\}$$

where $bal'_C = \text{aenc}(\text{pk}(skE), r_C, v_D)$ and $prf'_C = \text{zkp}_E(r_C, v_D, bal'_C)$ for $C, D \in \{A, B\}$ with $C \neq D$. Since $\text{adec}(skE, \pi_1(\pi_1(\text{getmsg}(y_A))))\Phi =_E v_A$, but $\text{adec}(skE, \pi_1(\pi_1(\text{getmsg}(y_A))))\Phi' \neq_E v_A$, we have that

$$\nu skE.\nu r_A.\nu r_B.\Phi \sim_E \nu skE.\nu r_A.\nu r_B.\Phi' \text{ while } \nu r_A.\nu r_B.\Phi \not\sim_E \nu r_A.\nu r_B.\Phi'$$

Indeed, an attacker may distinguish between these two frames as soon as he has the secret key skE, by simply decrypting the ballots.

Given two extended processes A_1 and A_2, we often write $A_1 \sim A_2$ for $\phi(A_1) \sim \phi(A_2)$. Given an extended process A we define its set of traces as

$$\text{traces}(A) \stackrel{\text{def}}{=} \{(tr, B) \mid A \stackrel{tr}{\Rightarrow} B\}$$

We can now define what it means for an attacker to be unable to *distinguish* two processes even if he is allowed to actively interact with them. This notion of indistinguishability is naturally modelled by *trace equivalence*.

Definition 3 (Trace equivalence). *Let* A *and* B *be two closed extended processes.* A *is trace included in* B, *written* $A \sqsubseteq B$, *if for every trace* $(tr, A') \in \text{traces}(A)$ *there exists* B' *such that* $(tr, B') \in \text{traces}(B)$ *and* $A' \sim B'$. A *and* B *are trace equivalent, denoted* $A \approx B$, *if* $A \sqsubseteq B$ *and* $B \sqsubseteq A$.

Intuitively, as the sequence of visible actions in the labels encode the adversary's actions the definition requires that for the same interaction with the adversary the protocols produce indistinguishable outputs.

3 Modelling E-Voting Protocols

In this section we explain how we formally model e-voting protocols and state the assumptions needed for our results.

Since many e-voting protocols use zero-knowledge proofs, we consider a signature Σ with $\text{zkp}, \text{checkzkp}, \text{okzkp} \in \Sigma$ and we assume an equational theory that can be described by an AC-convergent (possibly infinite) rewrite theory such that the only rules in which zkp, checkzkp, and okzkp occur, are of the form:

$$\text{checkzkp}(\text{zkp}(U_1, \ldots, U_m), V_1, \ldots, V_n) \to \text{okzkp}$$

where zkp, checkzkp, okzkp do not occur in the U_i, V_j. Since the terms U_i, V_j are left unspecified, this captures most existing zero-knowledge proofs. In particular, it covers the zero-knowledge proofs considered in Example 3.

A voting protocol is a family of processes $\{\Pi^{n_h,n_d,m}(Cr^h_{n_h}, Cr^d_{n_d}, \mathcal{K}_{pv}, \mathcal{K}_{pb})\}_{n_h,n_d,m\in\mathbb{N}}$ where

- n_h and n_d are the number of honest and dishonest voters respectively;
- $Cr^h_{n_h}$ (resp. $Cr^d_{n_d}$) is the set of n_h (resp. n_d) voting credentials which determines the set of honest eligible voters (resp. dishonest eligible voters), such that $Cr^h_{n_h} \cap Cr^d_{n_d} = \emptyset$. Each credential $\tilde{c}r \in Cr^h_{n_h} \cup Cr^d_{n_d}$ is a sequence of terms;
- m is the number of ballots accepted during the tally;
- $\mathcal{K}_{pv}$ (resp. $\mathcal{K}_{pb}$) is the set of all private (resp. public) material.

As usual it is sufficient to consider voting processes that model only the honest voters and the tally (the dishonest voters are left unspecified as part of the environment, and their credentials are public). We may assume w.l.o.g. that the tally process starts with a fresh phase and first reads the ballots on the board. Formally, we assume that voting processes are of the form:

$$\Pi^{n_h,n_d,m}(Cr^h_{n_h}, Cr^d_{n_d}, \mathcal{K}_{pv}, \mathcal{K}_{pb}) \overset{\text{def}}{=} V(\tilde{c}r_1) \mid V(\tilde{c}r_2) \mid \cdots \mid V(\tilde{c}r_{n_h}) \mid$$
$$\text{tall}: bb(x_1). \ \dots \ .bb(x_m).T^{n,m}(Cr_n, \mathcal{K}_{pv}, \mathcal{K}_{pb})$$

where $Cr_n = Cr^h_{n_h} \cup Cr^d_{n_d}$, and for all $i \in \{1,\dots,n_h\}$, $\tilde{c}r_i \in Cr^h_{n_h}$. Furthermore, we require that $Phase(V) < \text{tall}$, $Phase(T^{n,m}) = \emptyset$ and $T^{n,m}(Cr_n, \mathcal{K}_{pv}, \mathcal{K}_{pb})$ contains at most one output which is performed on the channel tal. We note that from the above structure of a voting process it follows that all traces are prefixes of traces of the form

$$tr' \cdot \text{phase tall} \cdot bb(RB_1) \dots bb(RB_m) \cdot \nu y . \overline{tal}\langle y \rangle.$$

$V(\tilde{c}r)$ models an honest voter, whose credentials are $\tilde{c}r$. $T^{n,m}(Cr_n, \mathcal{K}_{pv}, \mathcal{K}_{pb})$ is the remainder of the tallier process. It is parameterised by the number m of ballots it accepts and the number n of eligible voters. We require that $V(\tilde{c}r)$ be independent of n and m and does not use any other credentials, i.e. $fn(V(\tilde{c}r)) \cap Cr_n \subseteq \{\tilde{c}r\}$. These are the only restrictions on the voter process and we believe them to be reasonable and natural.

An e-voting protocol proceeds in two phases: vote casting and tallying. During the vote phase all voters simply cast their ballots. The tally phase proceeds as follows. First m ballots are input. Then a *public test* is applied to these ballots to carry out a first validity check, e.g. verify some zero knowledge proofs ensuring that the ballots are well formed. Next, the *revote policy* is applied to remove votes cast by a same voter, e.g., keep only the last one. Finally, the process performs the tally and outputs the result.

3.1   Public Tests

As explained above, the ballot box may apply public tests to the casted ballots. Public tests are Boolean combinations over atomic formulas of the form $M = N$

where $M, N \in \mathcal{T}(\Sigma, \mathsf{X})$, *i.e.* they do not contain any names. An atomic formula is satisfied when $M =_\mathsf{E} N$ and we lift satisfaction to tests as expected.

We assume a family of tests $\{\mathsf{Test}^m\}_{m \in \mathbb{N}}$ where m is the number of casted ballots that are tested and Test^m contains m distinguished variables $x_1, \ldots, x_m$ to be substituted by the ballots. We write $\mathsf{Test}^m([B_1, \ldots, B_m]) = \top$ when the test $\mathsf{Test}^m\{x_1 \mapsto B_1, \ldots, x_m \mapsto B_m\}$ is satisfied. Finally we say that a *test is voting-friendly* whenever satisfaction is preserved on sublists of ballots, that is $\mathsf{Test}^m([B_1, \ldots, B_m]) = \top$ implies $\mathsf{Test}^h([B_{i_1}, \ldots, B_{i_h}]) = \top$ for any $1 \leq i_1 < \cdots < i_h \leq m$.

We believe this condition to be natural. It discards contrived tests that would accept a ballot only if another ballot is present. Conversely, we may consider tests that discard lists with duplicate ballots.

Example 8. The public test applied by the tallying authorities in the Helios protocol consists of two parts. First, a local test that checks the zero knowledge proofs of each submitted ballot, and second, a global test that checks that encrypted votes are pairwise distinct. This is to avoid the replay attack mentioned in [13]. Such checks are formally reflected by the family of tests $\{\mathsf{Test}^m\}_{m \in \mathbb{N}}$ with

$$Test^m([B_1, \ldots, B_m]) \stackrel{\text{def}}{=} \bigwedge_{i=1}^{i=m} \mathsf{lTest}(B_i) \bigwedge_{i,j \in \{1, \ldots, m\}}^{i \neq j} \mathsf{gTest}(B_i, B_j)$$

$$\mathsf{lTest}(B) \stackrel{\text{def}}{=} \begin{cases} \top \text{ if } B = \langle id, bal, prf \rangle \text{ and } \mathsf{checkzkp_E}(\mathsf{getmsg}(bal), prf) =_\mathsf{E} \mathsf{okzkp_E} \\ \bot \text{ otherwise} \end{cases}$$

$$\mathsf{gTest}(B, B') \stackrel{\text{def}}{=} \begin{cases} \top \text{ if } B = \langle id, bal, prf \rangle \text{ and } B' = \langle id', bal', prf' \rangle \\ \quad \text{ and } \mathsf{getmsg}(bal) \neq \mathsf{getmsg}(bal') \\ \bot \text{ otherwise} \end{cases}$$

3.2 Revote Policies

Many e-voting protocols offer voters the possibility to cast several votes, keeping eventually only one vote per voter, e.g. the last submitted ballot. Which vote is kept depends on the particular policy. Re-voting intends to guarantee some protection against coercion. We formalize the notion of policy as a function $\mathsf{Policy}^{n,m}$ which takes a list of m terms (intuitively, the vote and credential) and a set of n credentials (honest and dishonest) and returns the sublist of selected terms to be tallied. A protocol will depend on a family of such policy functions $\{\mathsf{Policy}^{n,m}\}_{n,m \in \mathbb{N}}$. We consider two particular, but standard revote policies. The most usual one selects the last cast vote:

$$\mathsf{Policy}_{\mathsf{last}}^{n,m}([V_1, \ldots, V_m], \mathcal{C}r_n) \stackrel{\text{def}}{=} [V_{i_1}, \ldots, V_{i_k}]$$

where each $V_{i_j} = (v, \tilde{cr})$ is the last occurence of the credential $\tilde{cr} \in \mathcal{C}r_n$ in the list $[V_1, \ldots, V_m]$. We also consider the policy which only keeps the first vote of each voter:

$$\mathsf{Policy}_{\mathsf{first}}^{n,m}([V_1, \ldots, V_m], \mathcal{C}r_n) \stackrel{\text{def}}{=} [V_{i_1}, \ldots, V_{i_k}]$$

where each $V_{i_j} = (v, \tilde{cr})$ is the first occurence of the credential $\tilde{cr} \in Cr_n$ in the list $[V_1, \ldots, V_m]$. Such a policy typically models the norevote policy (a voter cannot revote).

3.3   Extracting Ballots and Counting Votes

A voting protocol should tally the ballots "as expected". Formally, what is expected can be formalized through an *extract* and a *counting* function.

Given a ballot B, and two sets of terms $\mathcal{K}_{pb}$ and $\mathcal{K}_{pv}$ representing the public and private material, the extraction function Extract returns the corresponding vote and credential, or $\bot$ when a ballot is not well formed., i.e., $\text{Extract}(B, \mathcal{K}_{pv}, \mathcal{K}_{pb}) \in (\mathcal{V} \times Cr_n) \cup \{\bot\}$. Moreover, we lift the extract function to lists of m ballots by applying the function pointwise, i.e., $\text{Extract}^m([B_1, \ldots, B_m], \mathcal{K}_{pv}, \mathcal{K}_{pb}) \overset{\text{def}}{=}$

$$[\text{Extract}(B_1, \mathcal{K}_{pv}, \mathcal{K}_{pb}), \ldots, \text{Extract}(B_m, \mathcal{K}_{pv}, \mathcal{K}_{pb})]$$

Similar extract functions have been introduced in [27] to define ballot privacy.

Example 9. The Extract function for the Helios protocol decrypts the encrypted vote and associates it with the signature associated to the ballot:

$$\text{Extract}(B, \{skE\}, \{\text{pk}(skE)\}) \overset{\text{def}}{=}$$

$$\begin{cases} (v, (id, cred)) & \text{if } B = \langle id, bal, prf \rangle \text{ and } bal =_E \text{sig}(\text{aenc}(\text{pk}(skE), r, v), cred) \\ \bot & \text{otherwise} \end{cases}$$

Similarly the counting function defines how the protocol is supposed to tally the votes. The function Count^ℓ takes as input a list of ℓ pairs $(v, cr) \in \mathcal{V} \times Cr$ and returns a list of terms as the election result.

Definition 4. *Let* $\{\text{Count}^\ell\}_{\ell \in \mathbb{N}}$ *be a family of counting functions.* $\{\text{Count}^\ell\}_{\ell \in \mathbb{N}}$ *is voting-friendly if for all* m, n *and lists of terms* W_1 *of size* m, W_2 *of size* n *we have that*

1. *if* $W_1 =^\# W_2$ *then* $\text{Count}^m(W_1) =^\# \text{Count}^n(W_2)$;
2. *if* $\text{Count}^m(W_1) =^\# \text{Count}^n(W_2)$
   then $\text{Count}^{m+1}((v_1, cr_1) :: W_1) =^\# \text{Count}^{n+1}((v_2, cr_2) :: W_2)$ *iff* $v_1 = v_2$

The first assumption requires that the result does not depend on the order in which votes are provided (intuitively, only valid votes are kept at this stage). We believe this property to be natural and it excludes contrived counting functions that would, e.g., only keep votes at even positions. The second assumption states that we may count "step by step". This is more restrictive since it excludes the majority function, i.e., the function that only outputs the name of the candidate that received most votes. But, it captures the most common result functions, namely the multiset and the additive counting functions.

Example 10. The multiset counting function typically arises in mixnet based tallies, which simply output the list of votes (intuitively once votes have been shuffled).

$$\mathsf{Count}^1_{\mathsf{Mix}}([V_1]) \stackrel{\mathrm{def}}{=} [v] \text{ and } \mathsf{Count}^m_{\mathsf{Mix}}([V_1, \ldots, V_m]) \stackrel{\mathrm{def}}{=} v :: Count^{m-1}_{\mathsf{Mix}}([V_2, \ldots, V_m])$$

where $V_1 = (v, \tilde{c}r)$ and $m > 1$. The additive counting function can be defined similarly. For simplicity consider a binary vote, where we just want to count the number of 1's:

$$\mathsf{Count}^1_{\mathsf{HE}}([V_1]) \stackrel{\mathrm{def}}{=} v \text{ and } \mathsf{Count}^m_{\mathsf{HE}}([V_1, \ldots, V_m]) \stackrel{\mathrm{def}}{=} v + Count^{m-1}_{\mathsf{HE}}([V_2, \ldots, V_m])$$

where $V_1 = (v, \tilde{c}r)$, $m > 1$ and $+$ is an AC symbol. Both functions are voting-friendly.

3.4 Properties

When verifying security properties of e-voting protocols it is common to only consider processes whose runs satisfy a particular property. For instance, vote secrecy is typically expressed as the indistinguishability of two processes modelling the situations where two honest voters swap their votes. We need however to ensure that these two honest voters have indeed cast their votes successfully to avoid trivial attacks. Indeed, in a run where the attacker blocks one of these voters, but not the other, the election result will be different and the two processes would be distinguished. Therefore when checking vote secrecy one typically adds a check that guarantees that the two honest votes are counted. We simply require that a *check* check($[b_1, \ldots, b_m]$) applied to a list ballots $[b_1, \ldots, b_m]$ satisfies the two following requirements:

- If check($[b_1, \ldots, b_m]$) holds then we can identify two (intuitively honest) ballots b_{i_1}, b_{i_2} such that check holds for any sublist containing b_{i_1} and b_{i_2}.
- If check($[b_1, \ldots, b_m]$) does not hold then it does not hold either for any sublist of these ballots or if some ballots are replaced by invalid ones (that is replaced by $\perp$).

How such a check is implemented is left unspecified, it could be by listening to private channels, successively checking signatures, etc.

3.5 E-Voting Processes

As often when considering trace equivalence (e.g. [10,24]), we assume processes to be deterministic. More precisely, we require the vote phase to be determinate: if the same sequence of labels leads to two different processes then the two resulting frames have to be statically equivalent. This typically holds for standard voting processes since the voter's behaviour is deterministic. For the tallying phase we slightly relax this notion and require what we call *almost determinate*. This relaxed notion only requires that there exists an output of a tally (among all possible outputs, as the particular tally may be chosen non-deterministically) that ensures static equivalence. This allows us to capture some non-deterministic behaviors such as mixnet tally.

Definition 5. *An e-voting protocol* $\{\Pi^{n_h,n_d,m}(Cr^h_{n_h}, Cr^d_{n_d}, \mathcal{K}_{\mathsf{pv}}, \mathcal{K}_{\mathsf{pb}})\}_{n_h,n_d,m\in\mathbb{N}}$ *is* almost determinate *if for any set of names* $\mathcal{E}_0$, *any initial attacker knowledge* Φ_0, *any* $m, n_h, n_d \in \mathbb{N}$, *and any traces* $(tr, A_1), (tr, A_2) \in$ traces$(\mathcal{E}_0, \Pi^{n_h,n_d,m}(Cr^h_{n_h}, Cr^d_{n_d}, \mathcal{K}_{\mathsf{pv}}, \mathcal{K}_{\mathsf{pb}}), \Phi_0, 0)$ *we have that*

$$\forall A'_1.\ A_1 \xrightarrow{\nu x.\overline{tal}\langle x\rangle} A'_1 \Rightarrow \exists A'_2.\ A_2 \xrightarrow{\nu x.\overline{tal}\langle x\rangle} A'_2 \text{ and } A'_1 \sim A'_2$$

We can now put all the pieces together and link e-voting protocols to the notions of public tests, revote policies, extraction and counting functions and properties.

Definition 6. *An e-voting protocol* $\{\Pi^{n_h,n_d,m}(Cr^h_{n_h}, Cr^d_{n_d}, \mathcal{K}_{\mathsf{pv}}, \mathcal{K}_{\mathsf{pb}})\}_{n_h,n_d,m\in\mathbb{N}}$ *is* voting friendly *w.r.t.* check, $\{\mathsf{Test}^m\}_{m\in\mathbb{N}}$, $\{\mathsf{Policy}^{n,m}\}_{n,m\in\mathbb{N}}$, Extract, $\{\mathsf{Count}^\ell\}_{\ell\in\mathbb{N}}$ *if it is almost determinate, if* $\{\mathsf{Test}^m\}_{m\in\mathbb{N}}$, $\{\mathsf{Policy}^{n,m}\}_{n,m\in\mathbb{N}}$, Extract, *are voting-friendly, and if for any set of names* $\mathcal{E}_0$, *any initial attacker knowledge* Φ_0, *any* m, n_h, n_d, *and any trace* $(tr'\cdot\nu x.$phase tall$.bb(RB_1)\ldots bb(RB_m), A_1)$ *of* $(\mathcal{E}_0, \Pi^{n_h,n_d,m}(Cr^h_{n_h}, Cr^d_{n_d}, \mathcal{K}_{\mathsf{pv}}, \mathcal{K}_{\mathsf{pb}}), \Phi_0, 0)$, *the resulting list of ballots* $BB = [B_1, \ldots, B_m]$ *(where* $B_i = RB_i\phi(A_1)$*) satisfies the following properties.*

1) *The tally is successful (that is* $(\nu y.\overline{tal}\langle y\rangle, A_2) \in$ traces(A_1)*) if and only if* BB *passes the test and the check (*$\mathsf{Test}^m(BB) = \top$ *and* check$(BB) = \top$*)*

2) *Whenever the tally produces an output (that is* $(\nu y.\overline{tal}\langle y\rangle, A_2) \in$ traces(A_1)*) then it outputs a triple* $y\phi(A_2) = \langle res, nvotes, zkp\rangle$ *where*

- *res is the result computed by counting the votes once the extraction function and the revote policy have been applied on the bulletin board;*
- *nvotes is the number of votes that has been counted;*
- *zkp is a (valid) zero-knowledge proof that would not be valid for any other list of ballots different from* BB;
- *either res is the only result the tally can produce from* BB *(typically in the homomorphic case) or the tally can produce any permutation of it (typically in the mixnet case).*

A fully formal definition can be found in the companion technical report [26]. We believe most existing protocols satisfy these requirements.

For many protocols ballots can be associated to the public credentials that were used to cast them. This is the case for Helios and some of its variants where ballots either contain the voter identity (in the original Helios) or are signed using private credentials (in the Belenios system). As we will see in the next section we can get tighter bounds for this class of protocols. Formally we define protocols with identifiable ballots as follows.

Definition 7. *An e-voting protocol* $\{\Pi^{n_h,n_d,m}(\mathcal{C}r^h_{n_h}, \mathcal{C}r^d_{n_d}, \mathcal{K}_{pv}, \mathcal{K}_{pb})\}_{n_h,n_d,m \in \mathbb{N}}$ *has* identifiable ballots *if for all* $n_h, n_d, m \in \mathbb{N}$, *for any trace*

$$(tr' \cdot \nu x.\text{phase tall}.bb(RB_1)...bb(RB_m) \cdot \nu y.\overline{tal}\langle y \rangle, A)$$

of $\Pi^{n_h,n_d,m}(\mathcal{C}r^h_{n_h}, \mathcal{C}r^d_{n_d}, \mathcal{K}_{pv}, \mathcal{K}_{pb}))$ *there exists a recipe* R *and a variable* x *such that*

$$\forall 1 \leq i \leq m. \ \text{if Extract}([RB_i\phi(A)], \mathcal{K}_{pv}, \mathcal{K}_{pb}) = (V, \tilde{cr}) \text{ then } R_i\phi(A) = \text{pub}(\tilde{cr})$$

where $R_i = R\{x \mapsto RB_i\}$.

4 Main Results

Throughout the section we consider two voting protocols

$$\{\Pi_i^{n_h,n_d,m}(\mathcal{C}r^h_{n_h}, \mathcal{C}r^d_{n_d}, \mathcal{K}_{pv}, \mathcal{K}_{pb})\}_{n_h,n_d,m \in \mathbb{N}}$$

for $1 \leq i \leq 2$ which are voting-friendly for check_i, $\{\text{Test}^m\}_{m \in \mathbb{N}}$, $\{\text{Policy}^{n,m}\}_{n,m \in \mathbb{N}}$, Extract_i^m, $\{\text{Count}_i^\ell\}_{\ell \in \mathbb{N}}$. Note that we assume the same public test for both protocols. Moreover we assume that $n_h \geq 2$ and $m \geq n_h + n_d$.

Let $\mathcal{E}_0$ be a set of names, and Φ_0 a ground substitution representing the initial attacker knowledge. $\{A_0^{n_h,n_d,m}\}_{n_h,n_d,m \in \mathbb{N}}$ and $\{B_0^{n_h,n_d,m}\}_{n_h,n_d,m \in \mathbb{N}}$ are two families of extended processes defined as follows

$$A_0^{n_h,n_d,m} \stackrel{\text{def}}{=} (\mathcal{E}_0 \cup \mathcal{C}r^h_{n_h}, \Pi_1^{n_h,n_d,m}(\mathcal{C}r^h_{n_h}, \mathcal{C}r^d_{n_d}, \mathcal{K}_{pv}, \mathcal{K}_{pb}), \Phi_0, 0) \ \forall n_h, n_d, m \in \mathbb{N}$$
$$B_0^{n_h,n_d,m} \stackrel{\text{def}}{=} (\mathcal{E}_0 \cup \mathcal{C}r^h_{n_h}, \Pi_2^{n_h,n_d,m}(\mathcal{C}r^h_{n_h}, \mathcal{C}r^d_{n_d}, \mathcal{K}_{pv}, \mathcal{K}_{pb}), \Phi_0, 0) \ \forall n_h, n_d, m \in \mathbb{N}$$

Our reduction results apply to equivalences of the form $A_0^{n_h,n_d,m} \approx B_0^{n_h,n_d,m}$ for all m, n_h, n_d. Vote privacy is typically modelled in this way [5]. The proofs of the results presented in this section could not be included due to lack of space, but are available in the technical report [26].

Our first result states that attacks on such equivalences require at most 3 voters.

Proposition 1. *If* $A_0^{k_h,k_d,\ell} \not\approx B_0^{k_h,k_d,\ell}$ *then* $A_0^{2,k'_d,\ell} \not\approx B_0^{2,k'_d,\ell}$ *for* $k'_d = 0$ *or* $k'_d = 1$.

Note that this case does not yet bound the number of ballots to be considered. In particular, when re-voting is allowed the attacker may a priori need to submit several ballots in order to distinguish the two processes. In other words, the ballot box is still parameterized by the number of ballots to be received. However, whenever we assume that Π_1 and Π_2 do not allow voters to revote, we can deduce immediately that 3 ballots suffice to capture any attack. More formally, we encode this situation by letting $k = \ell$ and considering the re-vote policy that only keeps the first vote of each voter.

Theorem 1. *If* $\{\text{Policy}^{n,m}\}_{n,m\in\mathbb{N}} = \{\text{Policy}_{\text{first}}^{n,m}\}_{n,m\in\mathbb{N}}$ *and* $A_0^{k_h,k_d,k} \not\approx B_0^{k_h,k_d,k}$ *where* $k = k_h + k_d$, *then* $A_0^{2,k_d',k'} \not\approx B_0^{2,k_d',k'}$ *for* $k_d' = 0$ *or* $k_d' = 1$ *and* $k' = 2 + k_d'$.

Intuitively, the case where $k_d' = 0$ corresponds to the case where an attacker can distinguish the processes playing only with two honest voters. This case for instance arises when analyzing a naive protocol where each voter simply signs his vote, hence offering no anonymity at all. The case where $k_d' = 1$ corresponds to the case where the attacker computes a vote which depends on the honest votes. The above results state that an attacker does not need more then one ballot in that case. An example of such an attack is the vote copy attack on Helios described in [13]. We could actually encode any attack with 2 voters into an attack with 3 voters by letting the adversary play like a useless, honest, voter. This would require however to formalize the fact that the attacker may always simulate an honest voter, that is, the voting process.

We now consider the case where re-voting is allowed. In this case we can bound the number of ballots that need to be considered to $4 + 2k$ (for k number of voters in total).

Proposition 2. *If* $A_0^{k_h,k_d,\ell} \not\approx B_0^{k_h,k_d,\ell}$, *then there exists* $\ell_{min} \leq 4 + 2k$ *such that* $A_0^{k_h,k_d,\ell_{min}} \not\approx B_0^{k_h,k_d,\ell_{min}}$ *where* $k = k_h + k_d$.

Combining the reductions on the number of voters and the number of ballots we obtain the following theorem.

Theorem 2. *If* $A_0^{k_h,k_d,\ell} \not\approx B_0^{k_h,k_d,\ell}$, *then there exists* $k_d' \in \{0,1\}$, $\ell_{min} \leq 4 + 2k$ *such that* $A_0^{2,k_d',\ell_{min}} \not\approx B_0^{2,k_d',\ell_{min}}$ *where* $k = 2 + k_d'$.

This is an immediate consequence of Propositions 1 and 2 and yields a bound of $4 + 2 \times 3 = 10$. When protocols have identifying ballots (Definition 7) we can tighten our reduction of the number of ballots: we only need to consider $4 + k$ ballots.

Corollary 1. *If* Π_1 *and* Π_2 *have identifying ballots and* $A_0^{k_h,k_d,\ell} \not\approx B_0^{k_h,k_d,\ell}$, *then* $\exists \ell_{min} \leq 4 + k$. $A_0^{k_h,k_d,\ell_{min}} \not\approx B_0^{k_h,k_d,\ell_{min}}$ *where* $k = k_h + k_d$.

This is a corollary of the proof of Proposition 2. With identifiable ballots, we know that the ballots selected by the revoting policy on the left and on the right hand-side are the same. Again, we combine this result with the reduction on the number of voters.

Theorem 3. *If* Π_1 *and* Π_2 *have identifying ballots and* $A_0^{k_h,k_d,\ell} \not\approx B_0^{k_h,k_d,\ell}$ *then* $\exists k_d' \in \{0,1\}$, $\ell_{min} \leq 4 + k$ *such that* $A_0^{2,k_d',\ell_{min}} \not\approx B_0^{2,k_d',\ell_{min}}$ *where* $k = 2 + k_d'$.

This follows from Corollary 1 and Proposition 1 and yields a bound of $4 + 3 = 7$ ballots.

5 Case Studies

We apply our results on several case studies: several versions of Helios [18,19,28] and Prêt-à-Voter [20], as well as the JCJ protocol [29] implemented in the Civitas system [30]. For some of these protocols we show that the ProVerif verification tool [1] can be used to perform a security proof that, thanks to our results, is valid for an arbitrary number of voters and ballots.

For the other protocols, ProVerif is not able to verify the protocols, either due to the fact that equational theories with AC symbols are not supported by ProVerif or simply because of a state explosion problem. In these cases we show that our results nevertheless apply. Given recent progress in automated verification for equivalence properties [9,10,31] we hope that verification of some of these protocols will be possible soon. Our results would also be useful to simplify proofs by hand.

The results in this section are summarized in Fig. 2. Our hypotheses were always satisfied wherever applicable. For several protocols, we could not conduct the analysis with ProVerif, either because the equational theory is out of reach of the tool or because we had to stop ProVerif execution after a couple of hours. The case studies are further detailed in the companion report [26]. The results in this section rely on ProVerif scripts available at http://3voters.gforge.inria.fr.

	3 ballots (Theorem 1)	
	Hyp	ProVerif
PaV (DM)	✓	✓
PaV (RM)	✓	✗
Helios mix (weeding)	✓	✓
Helios mix (id in zkp)	✓	✓
Helios hom (weeding)	✓	✗
Helios hom (id in zkp)	✓	✗
Belenios mix	✓	✓
Belenios hom	✓	✗

(a) Protocols without revoting.

	7 ballots (Theorem 3)		10 ballots (Theorem 2)	
	Hyp	ProVerif	Hyp	ProVerif
Helios mix (weeding)	✓	✓	✓	✗
Helios mix (id in zkp)	✓	✓	✓	✗
Helios hom (weeding)	✓	✗	✓	✗
Helios hom (id in zkp)	✓	✗	✓	✗
Belenios mix	✓	✓	✓	✗
Belenios hom	✓	✗	✓	✗
JCJ	✓	✗	✓	✗

(b) Protocols with revoting.

Fig. 2. Summary of application of our results on case studies. A ✗ in the "ProVerif" column indicates that we could not successfully run the analysis with ProVerif.

6 Conclusion

In this paper we propose reduction results for e-voting protocols that apply to vote privacy. We believe they also apply to stronger properties such as receipt-freeness. Our first reduction result states that whenever there is an attack, there is also an attack with only two honest voters and at most one dishonest voter. This considerably simplifies the proofs and encodings otherwise needed to verify such protocols using automated verification tools. We moreover consider the case where the protocol allows a voter to cast multiple votes and selects one vote according to a given re-vote policy, e.g. select the last vote casted. In that case verifying privacy is still complicated even when restricted to three voters. We therefore show a second reduction result that allows to consider at most 10 ballots. In case the protocol has *identifiable ballots* we reduce the number of necessary ballots to 7. We have shown that the hypotheses of our theorems are satisfied by many protocols: several variants of Helios, Prêt-à-Voter, as well as Civitas. For several of these protocols we were able to apply automated tool verification and provide the first automated proofs for an unbounded number of voters and ballots. For the decryption mixnets-based PaV protocol, we even provide the first proof of vote privacy.

An interesting direction for future work is to further tighten the bound on the number of ballots, possibly characterizing properties enjoyed by voting protocols. We also foresee to show similar reduction results for other properties of e-voting, such as verifiability. Given that the result is stated in a symbolic model, we also plan to investigate if the result can be transposed to a computational model.

Acknowledgments. This work has received funding from the European Research Council (ERC) under the EU's Horizon 2020 research and innovation program (grant agreement No 645865-SPOOC) and the ANR project SEQUOIA ANR-14-CE28-0030-01.

References

1. Blanchet, B.: An efficient cryptographic protocol verifier based on Prolog rules. In: 14th Computer Security Foundations Workshop (CSFW 2001), pp. 82–96. IEEE Computer Society (2001)
2. Rusinowitch, M., Turuani, M.: Protocol insecurity with finite number of sessions is NP-complete. In: Proceedings of the 14th Computer Security Foundations Workshop (CSFW 2001), pp. 174–190. IEEE Computer Society (2001)
3. Comon-Lundh, H., Shmatikov, V.: Intruder deductions, constraint solving and insecurity decision in presence of exclusive or. In: Proceedings of the 18th Annual Symposium on Logic in Computer Science (LICS 2003), pp. 271–280. IEEE Computer Society (2003)
4. Bhargavan, K., Corin, R., Fournet, C., Zalinescu, E.: Cryptographically verified implementations for TLS. In: Proceedings of the 15th ACM Conference on Computer and Communications Security (CCS 2008), pp. 459–468, October 2008
5. Kremer, S., Ryan, M.D.: Analysis of an electronic voting protocol in the applied pi calculus. In: Sagiv, M. (ed.) ESOP 2005. LNCS, vol. 3444, pp. 186–200. Springer, Heidelberg (2005)
6. Gjøsteen, K.: Analysis of an internet voting protocol, Cryptology ePrint Archive, Report 2010/380 (2010)
7. Blanchet, B., Abadi, M., Fournet, C.: Automated verification of selected equivalences for security protocols. In: 20th Symposium on Logic in Computer Science (LICS 2005), pp. 331–340, June 2005
8. Tiu, A., Dawson, J.E.: Automating open bisimulation checking for the spi calculus. In: Proceedings of the 23rd Computer Security Foundations Symposium (CSF 2010), pp. 307–321. IEEE Computer Society (2010)

9. Cheval, V., Comon-Lundh, H., Delaune, S.: Trace equivalence decision: negative tests and non-determinism. In: Proceedings of the 18th ACM Conference on Computer and Communications Security (CCS 2011), ACM, October 2011

10. Chadha, R., Ciobâcă, Ş., Kremer, S.: Automated verification of equivalence properties of cryptographic protocols. In: Seidl, H. (ed.) Programming Languages and Systems. LNCS, vol. 7211, pp. 108–127. Springer, Heidelberg (2012)

11. Backes, M., Hritcu, C., Maffei, M.: Automated verification of remote electronic voting protocols in the applied pi-calculus. In: 21st IEEE Computer Security Foundations Symposium (CSF 2008), pp. 195–209. IEEE Computer Society (2008)

12. Arapinis, M., Bursuc, S., Ryan, M.D.: Reduction of equational theories for verification of trace equivalence: re-encryption, associativity and commutativity. In: Degano, P., Guttman, J.D. (eds.) Principles of Security and Trust. LNCS, vol. 7215, pp. 169–188. Springer, Heidelberg (2012)

13. Cortier, V., Smyth, B.: Attacking and fixing helios: an analysis of ballot secrecy. J. Comput. Secur. 21(1), 89–148 (2013)

14. Arapinis, M., Cortier, V., Kremer, S., Ryan, M.: Practical everlasting privacy. In: Basin, D., Mitchell, J.C. (eds.) POST 2013 (ETAPS 2013). LNCS, vol. 7796, pp. 21–40. Springer, Heidelberg (2013)

15. Cortier, V., Wiedling, C.: A formal analysis of the Norwegian E-voting protocol. In: Degano, P., Guttman, J.D. (eds.) Principles of Security and Trust. LNCS, vol. 7215, pp. 109–128. Springer, Heidelberg (2012)

16. Abadi, M., Fournet, C.: Mobile values, new names, and secure communication. In: Proceedings of the 28th ACM Symposium on Principles of Programming Languages (POPL 2001), pp. 104–115. ACM (2001)

17. Okamoto, T.: Receipt-free electronic voting schemes for large scale elections. In: Christianson, B., Crispo, B., Lomas, M., Roe, M. (eds.) Security Protocols 1997. LNCS, vol. 1361, pp. 25–35. Springer, Heidelberg (1998)

18. Adida, B.: Helios: web-based open-audit voting. In: 17th Conference on Security Symposium (SS 2008), pp. 335–348. USENIX Association (2008). http://dl.acm. org/citation.cfm?id=1496711.1496734

19. Cortier, V., Galindo, D., Glondu, S., Izabachène, M.: Election verifiability for helios under weaker trust assumptions. In: Kutyłowski, M., Vaidya, J. (eds.) ICAIS 2014, Part II. LNCS, vol. 8713, pp. 327–344. Springer, Heidelberg (2014)

20. Ryan, P.Y.A., Schneider, S.A.: Prêt-à-voter with re-encryption mixes. In: Gollmann, D., Meier, J., Sabelfeld, A. (eds.) ESORICS 2006. LNCS, vol. 4189, pp. 313–326. Springer, Heidelberg (2006)

21. Dreier, J., Lafourcade, P., Lakhnech, Y.: Defining privacy for weighted votes, single and multi-voter coercion. In: Foresti, S., Yung, M., Martinelli, F. (eds.) ESORICS 2012. LNCS, vol. 7459, pp. 451–468. Springer, Heidelberg (2012)

22. Fujioka, A., Okamoto, T., Ohta, K.: A practical secret voting scheme for large scale elections. In: Zheng, Y., Seberry, J. (eds.) AUSCRYPT 1992. LNCS, vol. 718, pp. 244–251. Springer, Heidelberg (1993)

23. Comon-Lundh, H., Cortier, V.: Security properties: two agents are sufficient. Sci. Comput. Program. 50(1–3), 51–71 (2004)

24. Cortier, V., Dallon, A., Delaune, S.: Bounding the number of agents, for equivalence too. In: Piessens, F., Viganò, L. (eds.) POST 2016. LNCS, vol. 9635, pp. 211–232. Springer, Heidelberg (2016). doi:10.1007/978-3-662-49635-0_11

25. Blanchet, B., Abadi, M., Fournet, C.: Automated verification of selected equivalences for security protocols. J. Logic Algebraic Program. 75(1), 3–51 (2008)

26. Arapinis, M., Cortier, V., Kremer, S.: When are three voters enough for privacy properties? Cryptology ePrint Archive, Report 2016/690, (2016). http://eprint.iacr.org/2016/690

27. Bernhard, D., Cortier, V., Galindo, D., Pereira, O., Warinschi, B.: A comprehensive analysis of game-based ballot privacy definitions. In: Proceedings of the 36th IEEE Symposium on Security and Privacy (S&P 2015), pp. 499–516. IEEE Computer Society, May 2015

28. Bulens, P., Giry, D., Pereira, O.: Running mixnet-based elections with helios. In: 2011 Electronic Voting Technology Workshop/Workshop on Trustworthy Elections, EVT/WOTE 2011, USENIX Association (2011)

29. Juels, A., Catalano, D., Jakobsson, M.: Coercion-resistant electronic elections. In: ACM Workshop on Privacy in the Eectronic Society (WPES 2005), pp. 61–70. ACM (2005)

30. Clarkson, M., Chong, S., Myers, A.: Civitas: toward a secure voting system. In: 29th IEEE Symposium on Security and Privacy (S&P 2008), pp. 354–368. IEEE Computer Society (2008)

31. Cheval, V., Blanchet, B.: Proving more observational equivalences with ProVerif. In: Basin, D., Mitchell, J.C. (eds.) POST 2013 (ETAPS 2013). LNCS, vol. 7796, pp. 226–246. Springer, Heidelberg (2013)

Efficient Zero-Knowledge Contingent Payments in Cryptocurrencies Without Scripts

Wacław Banasik, Stefan Dziembowski, and Daniel Malinowski$^{(\boxtimes)}$

University of Warsaw, Warsaw, Poland
Daniel.Malinowski@crypto.edu.pl

Abstract. One of the most promising innovations offered by the crypto-graphic currencies (like Bitcoin) are the so-called *smart contracts*, which can be viewed as financial agreements between mutually distrusting participants. Their execution is enforced by the mechanics of the currency, and typically has monetary consequences for the parties. The rules of these contracts are written in the form of so-called "scripts", which are pieces of code in some "scripting language". Although smart contracts are believed to have a huge potential, for the moment they are not widely used in practice. In particular, most of Bitcoin miners allow only to post standard transactions (i.e.: those without the non-trivial scripts) on the blockchain. As a result, it is currently very hard to create non-trivial smart contracts in Bitcoin.

Motivated by this, we address the following question: "is it possible to create non-trivial efficient smart contracts using the standard transactions only?" We answer this question affirmatively, by constructing efficient Zero-Knowledge Contingent Payment protocol for a large class of NP-relations. This includes the relations for which efficient sigma protocols exist. In particular, our protocol can be used to sell a factorization (p, q) of an RSA modulus $n = pq$, which is an example that we implemented and tested its efficiency in practice.

As another example of the "smart contract without scripts" we show how our techniques can be used to implement the contract called "trading across chains".

1 Introduction

Cryptographic currencies (also dubbed the *cryptocurrencies*) are a very interesting concept that emerged in the last few years. The most prominent of them, and by far the largest one (in terms of capitalization), is Bitcoin, introduced in 2009 [32]. The main property of these currencies is that their security does not rely on any single trusted third party. The list of transactions in the system is written on a public *ledger* that is maintained jointly by the users. Another

---

This work was supported by the WELCOME/2010-4/2 grant founded within the framework of the EU Innovative Economy Operational Programme and by the Polish National Science Centre grant 2014/13/B/ST6/03540.

© Springer International Publishing Switzerland 2016
I. Askoxylakis et al. (Eds.): ESORICS 2016, Part II, LNCS 9879, pp. 261–280, 2016.
DOI: 10.1007/978-3-319-45741-3_14

reason why these currencies are so interesting is that they allow the users to perform much more than simple money transfers between each other. Namely, several cryptocurrencies, including the Bitcoin, implement an idea of the so-called *smart-contracts*. Such contracts can be viewed as distributed protocols executed between a number of parties. Typically, they have financial consequences, i.e., the users contribute money to them, and these funds are later distributed among the participants according to contract rules. Moreover, these contracts are "self-enforcing", which means that their execution is guaranteed by the rules of the underlying cryptocurrency. In particular, once a party enters into such a contract she cannot "change her mind" and withdraw her invested funds unless the contract specifically allows her to do so.

To be more specific, consider a contract called the *Zero Knowledge Contingent Payment* [16], which is an example on how Bitcoin contracts can provide a solution for the so-called *fair exchange problem* (see, e.g., [34]). It is executed between two parties: the Seller and the Buyer. The Buyer is looking for a value $x \in \{0,1\}^*$, that he does not know, but he is able to specify the conditions of x that make it valuable for him. Namely, he can describe a function $f : \{0,1\}^* \to \{\text{true}, \text{false}\}$ (in a form of a polynomial-time computer program, say), such that every x satisfying $f(x) = \text{true}$, has a value ฿100 for him (here "฿" denotes Bitcoin currency unit). Obviously (assuming that $P \neq NP$), *finding* x such that $f(x) = \text{true}$ is much harder than verifying that $f(x) = \text{true}$ holds. Hence, in many cases it makes a lot of sense for the Buyer to pay for x. As an example: think of a Buyer that wants to buy a factorization p, q of an RSA modulus N. He would then define $f : \mathbb{N} \times \mathbb{N} \to \{\text{true}, \text{false}\}$ as $f(p, q) := \text{true}$ iff $((p \cdot q = N) \wedge p \neq 1 \wedge q \neq 1)$.

Imagine now that the Buyer is approached by a Seller, who is claiming that he knows x such that $f(x) = \text{true}$ and he is willing to sell it. If this happens over the Internet, and the parties do not trust each other then they face the following problem: shall the Seller first send x to the Buyer who later pays to him (after verifying that indeed $f(x)$), or the other way around: shall the Buyer first pay and get x from the Seller? Clearly in the first case a malicious Buyer can refuse to pay ฿100 to the Seller (after receiving x), and in the latter a malicious Seller may not send x to the Buyer (after receiving the payment). Is there a way to sell x in such a way that none of the parties can cheat the other one? Unfortunately, it turns out (see, e.g., [33]), that this fundamental problem, called the *fair exchange* cannot be in general solved without a trusted third party. This is exactly where the contracts come to play. Intuitively, thanks to this feature of the cryptocurrencies, the users can use the ledger as a trusted entity that allows them to perform the exchange x for ฿100 simultaneously. Technically (but still very informally), this is done by placing a contract C on the ledger that has the following semantics: *"The Buyer has to put aside ฿100. This money can be claimed by the Seller only by posting x such that $f(x) = \text{true}$ on the ledger. If he does not do it within time t, then ฿100 goes back to the Buyer."* Now, everybody who observes the ledger can easily verify if the contract obligations were respected by the parties, and decide whether ฿100 should be now "transferred" from the Buyer to the Seller or not.

Another interesting example of a contract is so-called *trading across chains* [12] where users can exchange in a secure and fair way money between different cryptographic currencies. More advanced examples include, the *rapidly-adjusted micro-payments*, the *assurance contracts* [12], the multiparty lotteries [4,6], or general secure multiparty computation protocols [2,11,27]. Some experts predict that the smart contracts will revolutionize the digital economy. It is even envisioned that in the future these contracts may be used to maintain large *distributed autonomous corporations* that would operate without any trusted party control [22].

1.1 Contracts: From Theory to Practice

The above description ignores many technical details, and in particular it does not mention how the contracts are written. The transactions that are used in the contracts contain the so-called *scripts*. In Bitcoin the scripts are written in the so-called *Bitcoin script language* [13], which is not Turing-complete, and hence not every condition can be expressed in it. A serious obstacle when implementing the Bitcoin contracts in real life is that in practice it is currently very hard to post on the ledger a transaction corresponding to a non-trivial contract. Technically, to write a transaction on the ledger one broadcasts it over Bitcoin network and hopes that one of the miners (which are the entities that are maintaining the ledger) will include it into a new block that he mines. This gives the miners power to decide which transactions are included into the blockchain and which are not. Unfortunately, currently most of the miners do not include more complicated transactions into the blockchain. The reasons for this are: (1) such transactions tend to be longer than the "standard" ones, and space in the block is scarce, and (2) writing the transactions is tricky and error-prone, and most of the mining pool operators agreed to disallow them in order to prevent the users from loosing money. Technically deciding whether to accept a transaction or not is done by computing a boolean function `isStandard()` that evaluates to true only if the transaction is "standard", and otherwise it evaluates to false. The vast majority of the miners will include a transaction T in a new block only if `isStandard(`T`) =` true (more on this can be found, e.g., in [5], Chap. 5). Up to our knowledge, the only mining pool that currently accepts the non-standard transactions is *Eligius* that mines less than 1 % of blocks.

Another problem with running the smart contracts in Bitcoin is that the Bitcoin scripting language contains a feature, called the *transaction malleability*, that makes it tricky to implement several natural contracts (for more on this see the extended version of this paper [7], or, e.g., [3]). Although some techniques of dealing with this problem are known [3], they are often hard to use, since they make the contracts unnecessarily complicated (and make the transactions longer), and sometimes force the parties to invest more money than would normally be needed (by requiring them to put aside so-called *deposits*). One interesting new tool for dealing with this problem is the OP_CHECKLOCKTIMEVERIFY instruction [38] that was recently deployed.

After Bitcoin was deployed several other cryptocurrencies were proposed. The most interesting one from the point of view of the smart contracts, is *Ethereum*, which permits to use the Turing-complete scripts. The aforementioned problem of the high time consumption associated with the evaluation of the complicated scripts is solved in Ethereum in the following way. Each step of the computation of a script costs some small amount of money (the currency used for this is called *ether*), and the script evaluates as long as there are enough funds for this. Ethereum has recently been deployed in real life. It is, however, still a very young project and it is unclear how successful it will be in the real life. Moreover, as recently observed by Luu et al. [29] Ethereum may be susceptible to attacks where the adversary wastes miners' computational resources, which, in turn means that the miners might have incentives not to verify the correctness of the scripts. This, at least in theory, puts the whole Ethereum security model at risk.

Some of the other new cryptocurrencies go in the opposite direction by removing the possibility of having scripts at all. Sometimes this is a price for having additional interesting features in a currency. One example is the *Zerocash* [10], where the key new feature is the real anonymity (obtained by using the zero-knowledge techniques). Another, slightly different example is the *Lightning* system, which is a new proposal for micropayments constructed on top of the Bitcoin financial system, that also allows only standard transactions between the parties.

1.2   Our Contribution: Contracts Without Scripts

These observations lead to the following natural question: can we *efficiently* construct non-trivial contracts using only the standard transactions? In this paper we answer this affirmatively. We show (in Sect. 3.2) a general technique for efficiently solving the Zero-Knowledge Contingent Payment problem *using only standard transactions* for any f such that the corresponding language $\{x : f(x) = \mathsf{true}\}$ has an efficient zero-knowledge proof of knowledge of a special (but very broad) form, that, in particular, includes the sigma-protocols (see, e.g., [20]). We define this class of protocols in Sect. 3.3, but for a moment let us only say that it includes many natural languages. As an example we show an efficient protocol for selling a factorization of an RSA modulus, which is a problem that we already discussed at the beginning of this section. We implemented our protocol and confirmed its efficiency (see Sect. 3.4). In our construction we do not rely on any costly cryptographic mechanisms such as the generic secure multiparty computation protocols, or the generic zero-knowledge schemes. Instead, we use the standard and simple cut-and-choose technique. Our techniques can also be used to solve, in a similar way, the "trading across chains" problem. Because of the lack of space this is shown in the extended version of this paper [7].

Our protocols are proven secure in the random oracle model, and are based on standard cryptographic assumptions, an assumption that time-lock encryption of [37] is secure, plus one additional assumption about the strong unforgeability of the Elliptic Curve DSA (ECDSA) signatures used in Bitcoin. We describe this assumption in more detail in Sect. 2. Our protocols have an exponentially small probability of error (i.e.: the probability that the adversary cheats), assuming that we are allowed to use so-called *multisig* transactions, i.e., transactions that can be spent by providing signatures with respect to k public keys (out of $n \geq k$ possible public keys). Currently such transactions are considered standard for $n \leq 15$. We note that if one does not want to use such transactions, then our solution also works, but the error probability is inversely proportional to the running time of the parties.

Related work. As already mentioned, the *Zero-Knowledge Contingent Payment* protocol has been described before in [16] and recently implemented [31] for selling a proof of a sudoku solution. When viewed abstractly, our construction is a bit similar to the one of [16]. There are some important differences, though. Firstly, the protocol of [16] uses some non-standard scripts. Secondly, it is vulnerable to the "malleability attacks": the *refund transaction* depends on an identifier of the *txn* transaction, and becomes meaningless if *txn* is mauled. Finally, the protocol of [16] uses generic zero knowledge protocols, or can be used only for very simple problems (like selling the sudoku solution), while we rely on much simpler and more efficient methods (in particular: the *cut-and-choose* technique).

2   Preliminaries

Definitions. We will sometimes model the hash functions as *random oracles*, see [9]. A *signature scheme* consists of a *key generation algorithm* SignGen, a *signing algorithm* Sign, and a *verification algorithm* Vrfy. For a formal definition of a signature scheme see [26], or the extended version of this paper [7]. The standard security notion for signatures is the *existential unforgeability under a chosen message attack*. In this paper we need a stronger security definition, namely the *strong* existential unforgeability under a chosen message attack. This is formally defined in [1,18]. Essentially, the definition is as follows. Consider the standard chosen-message attack during which the adversary interacts with a signing oracle that knows some secret key sk. We say that $\mathcal{A}$ *mauls a signature* if he is able to produce an output $(\hat{z}, \hat{\sigma})$ such that $\hat{\sigma}$ is a valid signature on $\hat{z}$ with respect to the public key pk (that corresponds to sk), and $\hat{\sigma}$ has not been sent to $\mathcal{A}$ before. A signature scheme is *existentially strongly unforgeable under a chosen message attack* (or: *non-malleable*) if for any polynomial-time adversary the probability that he mauls a signature is negligible.

We will use (*public key* and *private key*) *encryption schemes*, defined in a standard way (see [26] or [7].) We say that a public-key encryption scheme is *additively homomorphic* if for every valid public key pk and private key sk the set of valid messages for pk is an additive group $(\mathbb{H}_{pk}, +)$. Moreover, we require that there exists an operation $\otimes : \{0,1\}^* \times \{0,1\}^* \to \{0,1\}^* \cup \{\bot\}$, such that for every valid (pk, sk) and every pair $z_0, z_1 \in \mathbb{H}_{pk}$ we have that $\mathsf{Dec}_{sk}(\mathsf{Enc}_{pk}(z_0) \otimes \mathsf{Enc}_{pk}(z_1)) = z_0 + z_1$ (where Enc and Dec are the encryption and decryption algorithms, respectively).

Our protocols also rely on the *time-lock commitment schemes* [17,37] (for the definition of the standard commitment schemes see, e.g., [26], or [7]). Informally, $(\mathsf{Commit}, \mathsf{Open})$ is a *time-locked commitment* if it is a standard commitment scheme, except that the receiver can open the commitment by himself (even if the sender is not cooperating). Such *forced opening* requires a significant computational effort. Moreover it is required that this process cannot be parallelized. Every time-lock commitment comes with two parameters: τ_0 and τ_1 (with $\tau_0 \leq \tau_1$), where τ_0 denotes the time (in seconds, say) that everybody, including very powerful adversaries, needs to force open the commitment, and τ_1 denotes time needed by the honest users to force open the commitment. We will call such a commitment scheme (τ_0, τ_1)-secure. Of course, this is not a formal mathematical definition (as it refers to "real time"), but for the purpose of this paper we can stay on this informal level. Later, in Sect. 3.4 we assume that $\tau_1 = 10 \cdot \tau_0$, but this choice is slightly arbitrary, and for real practical applications one would need to perform a more careful analysis of what is the reasonable ratio between τ_0 and τ_1 that one can assume.

For a description of the area of *zero-knowledge* the reader may consult, e.g., [24] (a brief introduction also appears in [7]). In our paper we actually need a stronger notion, namely the *zero-knowledge proofs of knowledge* [8]. Such proofs are defined only if L is in NP, and hence for every $x \in L$ there exists an *NP-witness* w that serves as a proof that $x \in L$. We assume that P knows x and require that the prover not only proves that $x \in L$, but also convinces the verifier that he knows the corresponding witness w. Defining formally the property of a prover "knowing" some value is a bit tricky, and we do not do it here (see, e.g., [24] for such a definition). Very informally, it is usually defined as follows: for every (possibly malicious) prover P^* there exists a polynomial-time machine, called the *knowledge extractor*, that can interact with P^* (possibly even rewinding it), and at the end it outputs x. The definition that we use here is more restrictive. First, suppose without loss of generality, that the last two messages in the protocol are: a challenge c sent by the verifier to the prover, and provers response r. We require (cf. Sect. 3.3) that the extractor extracts the witness after being given transcripts of two accepting executions that are identical except that that the challenge messages are different (and the response messages may also be different). This class of protocols includes our protocol for selling the factorization of the RSA modulus. It is also similar to the sigma-protocols (see, e.g., [20]), except that it may have more rounds than 3, but on the other hand we require that the zero-knowledge property holds also against the malicious verifier. Note that some sigma-protocols, including the Schnorr protocol, are conjectured to be secure also in this case. Observe also that we can easily get rid of the "honest verifier" assumption by requiring the verifier to make his message equal to a hash of some message (chosen by him) [21]. Hence, our method can be used also to efficiently "sell" a witness of any relation for which an efficient sigma-protocol exists.

Instantiations. As explained in the introduction, Bitcoin uses an *Elliptic Curve Digital Signature Algorithm (ECDSA)* [19,25], which is a variant of the *Digital Signature Algorithm (DSA)*. More concretely, it uses the *Secp256k1* curve [14], but to be able to state our theorems in an asymptotic way we will be more general and define our protocol over arbitrary elliptic curve. The description of this algorithm appears in [7].

As it turns out, these signatures are *not* strongly unforgeable: if (r, s) is a valid signature on some message z, then also $(r, -s \bmod p)$ (where p is the order over which the elliptic curve $\mathbb{G}$ is defined) is a valid signature with respect the same public key (see, e.g., [7] for more on this). In order to make our signature scheme strongly-unforgeable we follow the guidelines from [39]. Namely, we assume that the only "legal" signatures have a form (r, s) such that $s \leq (p - 1)/2$. To this end, we simply assume that, whenever our protocol gets as input an ECDSA signature (r, s) with $s > (p - 1)/2$, it converts it to one with $s \leq (p - 1)/2$ by computing $s := -s \bmod p$. An ECDSA scheme with only "legal" signatures being the ones with $s \leq (p - 1)/2$ will be called a *positive ECDSA*.

We can now informally state our strong unforgeability assumption as follows: "*The positive ECDSA defined over Secp256k1 is strongly unforgeable under chosen-message attack*" (or equivalently: the only way to maul the signatures defined over Secp256k1 is to negate the s). Note that this statement is informal, and in order to formalize it we would need to express it in an asymptotic way. See [7] for more on this, and on the general issue of the malleability of Bitcoin transactions.

We will use the additively-homomorphic public key encryption scheme introduced by Pascal Paillier [35]. Below, we describe only the properties of this scheme that are needed in this work. For more details the reader can consult, e.g., [35]. The public key pk of this encryption scheme contains a modulus $n = p \cdot q$, where p and q are large distinct random primes of the same length. The Paillier encryption scheme is homomorphic over $(\mathbb{Z}_n, +)$. It is semantically secure under the *Decisional composite residuosity assumption* [35]. In the sequel we will assume that (AddHomGen, AddHomEnc, AddHomDec) is a Paillier encryption scheme. The elements on which we will perform the addition operations will be the exponents in the elliptic curve group of the ECDSA scheme. Hence, we need $\mathbb{Z}_n$ to be larger than $\mathbb{G}$, and, for the reasons that will become clear later, it will be convenient to have $n \gg |\mathbb{G}|$. We therefore assume that on input 1^λ the algorithm AddHomGen produces as output (pk, sk) such that the corresponding group $\mathbb{Z}_n$ satisfies $n > 2 \cdot |\mathbb{G}|^4$.

We use very standard commitment schemes that are based on the hash functions, and are secure in the random oracle model. Let H be a hash function. In order to commit to $x \in \{0,1\}^*$ the committer chooses random $r \in \{0,1\}^\lambda$ (where 1^λ is the security parameter) and produces as output $\mathsf{Commit}(x) = H(x||r)$. In order to open the commitment it is enough to reveal (x, r). The fact that the scheme is binding follows from the collision-resistance of H. The hiding property follows from the fact that we model H as the random oracle (and hence $H(x||r)$ does not reveal any information about x).

We use the classic timed commitments of [37]. In order to commit to a message $x \in \{0,1\}^{\ell}$ (for some ℓ) the committer chooses an RSA modulus n, i.e., he selects two random primes p and q of length λ (where 1^{λ} is the security parameter) and sets $n = pq$. He then computes $\varphi(n) = (p-1)(q-1)$. Let t be some parameter. The committer takes random $y \in Z_n^*$ and computes $z := y^{2^t} \bmod n$. Since he knows $\varphi(n)$ he can compute it efficiently by first computing $e = 2^t \bmod \varphi(n)$ (doing this using the standard square-and-multiply algorithm takes $\log_2 t$ squaring modulo n), and then letting $z := y^e \bmod n$. Finally, he computes $H(z)$ and outputs y and $H(z) \oplus x$, where $H : \mathbb{Z}_n^* \rightarrow \{0,1\}^{\ell}$ is a hash function. On the other hand, it is conjectured [37] that an adversary, who does not know $\varphi(n)$ needs to perform t squarings to compute z (and hence to compute x). Also, no practical methods of parallelizing the problem of computing z is known. It is also easy to see that this algorithm is a commitment in a standard sense, i.e., if the committer is cooperating with the receiver then he can open the commitment efficiently (by sending (p,q) to the receiver). To set the parameter t let c be the number of squarings that the honest receiver can do in one second. We then let $t = \tau_1 \cdot c$ (where τ_1 is the parameter of the timed commitment scheme).

A short description of the Bitcoin transaction syntax. We now briefly describe the syntax of the Bitcoin transactions. A more complete description can be found, e.g., in [5,7,15]. Since we do not use the non-standard transactions we will provide a simplified description that ignores this feature of Bitcoin. The users in Bitcoin are identified by their public keys in the ECDSA signature scheme (SignGen, Sign, Vrfy). Each such a key pk is called an *address*. In the simplest case transaction T simply sends some amount $\mathbf{B}x$ (where x can be smaller than one) from an address pk_0 (called an *input* of T) to an address pk_1 (called the *output* of T). The amount $\mathbf{B}x$ will also be called the *value of* T. Transaction T must contain a pointer to another transaction T' that appeared earlier on the ledger and has value at least $\mathbf{B}x$, and whose destination is pk_0. We say that T redeems T'. Transaction T is valid only if T' has not been redeemed by some other transaction before. Hence, in the simplest case a transaction contains a following tuple $[T] := (\mathtt{TXid}(T'), \mathtt{value} : \mathbf{B}x, \mathtt{from} : pk_0, \mathtt{to} : pk_1)$, where $\mathtt{TXid}(T')$ denotes the *identifier of* T' (we will define it in a moment), and $[T]$ is called a *simplified transaction* T. Of course, in order for $[T]$ to have any meaning it needs to be signed with the private key sk_0 corresponding to pk_0. Hence, the complete transaction T has a form $([T], \mathsf{Sign}_{sk_0}([T]))$, and is valid if all the conditions described above hold, and the signature on $[T]$ is valid with respect to pk_0. The $\mathtt{TXid}(T)$ is defined simply as a SHA256 hash of $([T], \mathsf{Sign}_{sk_0}([T])))$.

Another standard type of the transactions are the so-called *multisig* transactions. In this case $[T]$ has a form $(\mathtt{TXid}(T'), \mathtt{value} : \mathbf{B}x, \mathtt{from} : pk_0, \mathtt{to} \text{ "}k\text{-out-of-}n\text{"} : pk_1, \ldots, pk_n)$ where $n \leq 15$. It is signed by pk_0. It can be spent by a transaction T'' that is signed by k signatures with respect to k different public keys from the set $pk_1, \ldots, pk_n$. More precisely the transaction

T'' has to have a form $([T''], \sigma_{i_1}, \ldots, \sigma_{i_k})$, where $1 \leq i_1 < \cdots < i_k \leq n$ and for every $1 \leq j \leq k$ holds $\mathsf{Vrfy}_{pk_{i_j}}([T''], \sigma_{i_j}) = \mathsf{ok}$.

3   The Protocols

Our model. We will consider two-party protocols, executed between a Buyer B and a Seller S. If a party is malicious then she may not follow the protocol (in other words: we consider the *active* security settings). The parties are connected by a secure (i.e. secret and authenticated) channel. Such a channel can be easily obtained using the standard techniques, provided that the parties know each others public keys. Observe that in order to do any financial transfers in Bitcoin they anyway need to know each other keys (let (sk_B, pk_B) be the ECDSA key pair of the Buyer, and let (sk_S, pk_S) the key pair of the Seller), and the participating parties can use the same key pairs for establishing the secure channel between each other. How exactly these public keys pk_B and pk_S are exchanged is beyond the scope of this paper.

The security definition. We now outline a construction of our protocol in which the Seller sells to the Buyer x such that $f(x) = \mathsf{true}$ (for some public $f : \{0,1\}^* \to \{\mathsf{true}, \mathsf{false}\}$). We assume that the "price" of x is $\text{\textbaht}d$, and that, before an execution of the protocol starts, there is some unspent transaction T_0 on the blockchain whose value is $\text{\textbaht}d$, and whose output is pk_B (i.e.: it can be spent by the Buyer). The parties initially share the following common input: a security parameter 1^λ, a price $\text{\textbaht}d$ for the secret x, parameters $a, b \in \mathbb{N}$ such that $a > b$, an elliptic curve group $(\mathbb{G}, \mathcal{O}, g, +)$ for an ECDSA signature scheme, such that $\lceil \log_2 |\mathbb{G}| \rceil = \lambda$, and parameters (τ_0, τ_1). We say that the $\mathsf{SellWitness}_f$ protocol is ϵ-*secure* if the following properties hold: (1) except with probability $\epsilon + \mu(\lambda)$ (where μ is negligible), if an honest Buyer loses his funds then he learns x' s.t. $f(x') = \mathsf{true}$, (2) except with negligible probability, if an honest Seller does not get Buyer's funds then the Buyer learns no information about x. We construct a protocol $\mathsf{SellWitness}_f$ (for a large class of functions f) in Sect. 3.3. First, however, we give an outline of our construction. The necessary ingredients are defined and constructed in Sects. 3.1 and 3.2.

Outline of the construction. Our protocol consists of several stages. The main idea can be described as follows (we start with describing an "idealized" protocol and then we show how to modify it to make it efficient and practical). Imagine that the parties first create, in a distributed way, an ECDSA key pair (sk, pk) such that the private key sk is secret-shared between the parties, and the public key pk is known to both of them. Then, the Buyer prepares a transaction T_1 that sends the output of T_0 to the public key pk. Obviously for a moment the Buyer has to keep T_1 private, as posting T_1 on the ledger would put his money at risk (as spending money from T_1 requires cooperation of the Seller). He now creates a simplified transaction[1] $[T_2]$ that redeems T_1 and sends the output to the public key pk_S of the Seller. Then, the parties jointly sign $[T_2]$ with the shared private key sk in such a way that the signature $\sigma = \mathsf{Sign}_{sk}([T_2])$ is known only to the Seller. Note that this is possible without revealing T_1 to the Seller, as the only thing that is needed from T_1 is its transaction identifier, which happens to be equal to the hash $H(T_1)$ of T_1 (in the random oracle model $H(T_1)$ clearly reveals no information about T_1).

Let us now briefly analyze the situation after these steps are executed: the Buyer knows T_1, and the Seller knows T_2 that spends T_1 (but she does not know T_1, so for a moment she cannot make any use of T_2). The key idea now is: the Seller will make a commitment to the signature σ in such a way that opening this commitment will automatically reveal x (and she will convince the Buyer that the commitment was formed in this way). Now the Buyer can post T_1 on the ledger, and wait until the Seller redeems it. The only way in which she can do it, is to publish σ (here we use the assumption that the signatures are strongly unforgeable), so the Buyer can be sure that he learns x.

This construction is similar to the one described in [16]. Unfortunately, in practice there are several problems with it. Firstly, there is no way for the Buyer to "force" the Seller to publish σ, and hence the Buyer's money can be locked forever in T_1. We solve this problem using the time-locked commitments. The Seller has to commit with such a commitment to her private share of sk, so that it can be unlocked by the Buyer after some time. In this way he can get his money back by signing a transaction T_2' that redeems T_1 and sends the money to his key pk_B. As described in Sect. 1, an alternative solution is to use the OP_CHECKLOCKTIMEVERIFY instruction. We describe this solution in the extended version of this paper [7].

Secondly, the currently-known protocols for distributed signing with the ECDSA signatures are rather complicated and involve costly generic zero-knowledge techniques [30] (see also [23]). Also, the generic zero-knowledge would need to be used to prove that the timed commitment above is indeed a commitment to Seller's share in sk.

Our solution to this problem is to use the standard technique, called *cut-and-choose* (see, e.g., [28]). Informally, the idea here is to perform a number a of independent executions of a protocol. Then the Buyer tells the Seller to "uncover" $a - b$ (for some parameter $b < a$) of them, by opening all her commitments related to these executions. It is easy to see that, if all the opened commitments were correct, then most probably a significant fraction of the remaining b ("non-uncovered") executions will also be correct. Since some executions may still be incorrect, we will thus create T_1 as a multisig transaction (so it can be spent with less than b signatures). This is done in Sects. 3.1 and 3.2. Thirdly, we need to describe how to create the commitment to σ in the last step that requires proving that "opening this commitment will automatically reveal x". We do it as follows: we require that the Seller commits to $F(\sigma)$ (where F is some hash function),

---

[1] Recall (cf. Sect. 2) that a "simplified transaction" means a transaction without a signature.

---

1. The parties run a times the SharedKGen protocol to generate secret-shared signing keys.
2. The Buyer selects b of these keys and uses GenMsg_T to produce transactions T_1 and T_2.
3. The parties run the USG protocol to sign T_2 using all a shared keys and the Seller generates commitments. Then the Buyer checks the Seller on the unselected $a - b$ executions.
   - The single signing iteration is performed using the KSignGen procedure.
4. Using the Zero Knowledge protocol (and again the cut-and-choose technique) the Seller proves that by revealing any signature the Buyers will extract the witness x from it.
5. The Buyer broadcasts T_1. Then the Seller uses the signatures to broadcast T_2 and the Buyer can extract the witness x (or solve the timed commitment to get his funds back).

Fig. 1. The outline of the SellWitness$_f$ protocol and the subprotocols.

and then we use again the cut-and-choose technique (on the elements of $F(\sigma)$) to prove that if the whole $F(\sigma)$ is opened then x is revealed. Technically, this is done by showing that revealing $F(\sigma)$ opens commitments to messages from a zero-knowledge proof of knowledge of x. For the details see Sect. 3.3. The outline of the SellWitness$_f$ protocol and the subprotocols is presented on Fig. 1.

3.1 The Two-Party ECDSA Key Generation Protocol

The first ingredient of our scheme is a protocol in which two parties, the Seller and the Buyer, generate a (public key, private key) key pair for the ECDSA signatures, in such a way that the secret key is secret-shared between the Seller and the Buyer. To be more precise, fix an elliptic curve $(\mathbb{G}, \mathcal{O}, g, +)$ constructed over a field $\mathbb{Z}_p$ and recall that the secret key in the ECDSA signatures is a private integer $d \in \mathbb{Z}_{|\mathbb{G}|}$. We construct a two-party protocol, that we call SharedKGen, in which both parties take as input a security parameter 1^λ and at the end they both know an ECDSA public key $pk = d \cdot g$ (where d is secret), and additionally the Seller knows $d_S \in \mathbb{Z}_{|\mathbb{G}|}$ and the Buyer knows $d_B \in \mathbb{Z}_{|\mathbb{G}|}$ such that $d_S \cdot d_B = d$ (mod $|\mathbb{G}|$) is a secret-sharing. The protocol is very similar to the classic actively-secure key generation protocols for the discrete log signatures [36]. Because of the lack of space it is presented in the extended version of this paper [7].

3.2 The Unique Signature Generation Protocol

After the parties generate a key pairs $(sk^1, pk^1), \ldots, (sk^a, pk^a)$ using the SharedKGen protocol, they perform an additional procedure, called *unique signature generation (USG) protocol*, whose goal is to sign a message $z \in \{0, 1\}^*$ with respect to these keys. The message z is chosen by the Buyer and may depend on the public keys that were generated in the SharedKGen phase, and on the Buyer's private randomness. During the execution of the USG protocol $a - b$ private keys are "uncovered" (here $b < a$ is some parameter), i.e., they are reconstructed by the parties. At the end of the execution they are discarded and the output of the protocol depends only on the key pairs whose private keys were not uncovered. Let $(\hat{sk}_1, \hat{pk}_1), \ldots, (\hat{sk}_b, \hat{pk}_b)$ denote these key pairs. Each $\hat{pk}_i$ is known to both parties, and each $\hat{sk}_i$ remains secret and is shared between the parties (as a pair $(\hat{d}_S^i, \hat{d}_B^i)$ of shares). Moreover the Seller knows the ECDSA signatures $\hat{\sigma}_1, \ldots, \hat{\sigma}_b$ on z with respect to $\hat{pk}_1, \ldots, \hat{pk}_b$ (respectively). The Buyer does not know these signatures, but we require that the Seller is committed (again: using COM) to each $F(\hat{\sigma}_i)$, where F is a hash function (modeled as a random oracle). Let $\Gamma_1, \ldots, \Gamma_b$ denote the commitments created this way. Finally, we want the Buyer to be able to "force open" the values $\hat{d}_S^1, \ldots, \hat{d}_S^b$ after some time τ_1, so that he can reconstruct the private keys $\hat{sk}_1, \ldots, \hat{sk}_b$ and sign any message that he wants using these keys. This is achieved using a (τ_0, τ_1)-secure time-locked commitment scheme TLCOM = (TLCommit, TLForceOpen). Let $\Phi_1, \ldots, \Phi_b$ denote the timed-commitments that were created this way.

To explain informally our security requirements, first let us say what are the goals of a malicious Seller. One obvious goal is to produce a signature on some message $z^* \neq z$ (with respect to some $\hat{pk}_i$). A more subtle (and more specific to our applications) goal for the Seller is to learn some signature σ_i^* on z (with respect to one of $\hat{pk}_1, \ldots, \hat{pk}_b$) other than $\hat{\sigma}_1, \ldots, \hat{\sigma}_b$. Finally, she could try to time-commit to some value other than $\hat{d}_S^i$ (so that, after time τ_1 passes, the Buyer cannot reconstruct $\hat{sk}_i$). Formally, we say that the malicious Seller S^* *breaks the key i (for $i = 1, \ldots, b$)* if the Buyer did not abort the protocol and one of the following holds:

– after the execution of the protocol S^* produces as output $(\hat{\sigma}_i^*, \hat{z}_i)$ such that $\hat{\sigma}_i^*$ is a valid signature on $\hat{z}_i \neq z$ with respect to $\hat{pk}_i$,
– after the execution of the protocol S^* produces as output $\hat{\sigma}_i^*$ such that $\hat{\sigma}_i^*$ is a valid signature on z with respect to $\hat{pk}_i$, and S^* opens the commitment Γ_i to a value different than $F(\hat{\sigma}_i^*)$,
– the value d_B^{i*} that results from forced opening of Φ_i is such that $\hat{d}_S^i \cdot d_B^{i*} \neq \hat{d}^i$.

Now, consider a malicious Buyer. Informally, his goal is to learn any valid signature on z with respect to any key $\hat{pk}_1, \ldots, \hat{pk}_b$. If he does not succeed in this, then another goal that he could try to achieve is to learn at least one of the $F(\hat{\sigma}_i)$'s. Recall also that the secrets of the Seller are time-locked. Hence after time τ_0 the Buyer can easily "break" the protocol, and our definition has to take care of it. Formally, we say that a malicious Buyer B^* *wins* if the Seller did not abort the protocol and before time τ_0 one of the following holds:

– the B^* produces as output a signature on z^* (either $z^* = z$ or $z^* \neq z$) that is valid with respect to one of the $\hat{pk}_i$'s,
– the B^* learns some information about one of the $F(\hat{\sigma}_i)$'s.

We say that a USG *protocol is* $(\epsilon, \hat{b})$-*secure* if (a) for every polynomial-time malicious Seller the probability that she breaks at least $\hat{b}$ keys is at most $\epsilon + \mu(\lambda)$, where μ is negligible, and (b) for every polynomial-time malicious Buyer the probability that he wins is negligible.

The implementation of the USG protocol. Our USG protocol is depicted on Fig. 2. We assume that before it is executed the parties run the SharedKGen procedure a times (on input 1^λ). We denote these executions as $\mathsf{SharedKGen}^i(1^\lambda)$ for $i = 1, \ldots, a$. As a result of each execution $\mathsf{SharedKGen}^i$, both parties learn the public keys pk^i and they secret-share the corresponding secret keys sk^i (let (d_S^i, d_B^i) be the respective shares).

The USG protocol uses as a subroutine the protocol $\mathsf{KSignGen}$ from Fig. 3. This protocol allows the parties to sign a message z using the secret key that is secret shared $d = d_S \cdot d_B$. First they jointly create signing randomness K. Then the Seller creates a new key in the Paillier encryption scheme and sends the encryption of his share d_S of the signing key d to the Buyer. The Buyer calculates the encryption of the unfinished signature (using the homomorphic properties of the Paillier cryptosystem) and sends it to the Seller. Then the Seller decrypts it and completes the signature σ. At the end the Seller commits to $F(\sigma)$ and creates a timed commitment to d_S. We now have the following lemma, its proof appears in [7].

Lemma 1. *Suppose Paillier encryption is semantically secure, COM and TLCOM are secure commitment schemes, and the ECDSA scheme used in the construction of the USG is Strongly Unforgeable signature scheme. Then the USG protocol constructed on Fig. 2 is $(\epsilon, \hat{b})$-secure for $\epsilon = (b/a)^{\hat{b}}$.*

---

1. The Buyer chooses a random subset $\mathcal{J} \subset \{1, \ldots, a\}$, such that $|\mathcal{J}| = a - b$. Let $\{j_1, \ldots, j_b\}$ denote the set $\{1, \ldots, a\} \setminus \mathcal{J}$.
2. The Buyer chooses a message z to be signed and sends it to the Seller.
3. For $i = 1$ to a the parties execute the $\mathsf{KSignGen}(1^\lambda)$ procedure depicted on Fig. 3. As a result of each such execution, the Seller is committed to $S^i = F(\sigma^i)$ and timed-committed to d_S^i.
4. The Buyer sends $\mathcal{J}$ to the Seller.
5. For every $j \in \mathcal{J}$ the Seller opens the commitments to S^j and d_S^j, and sends σ^j, k_S^j and sk_{AH}^j to the Buyer.
6. The Buyer aborts if any of the commitments did not open correctly. Otherwise he verifies if the following holds (for every $j \in \mathcal{J}$): (a) $\mathsf{Vrfy}_{pk^j}(z, \sigma^j) = \mathsf{ok}$, (b) $F(\sigma^j) = S^j$, (c) $d_S^j \cdot d_B^j \cdot g = pk^j$, and (d) $\mathsf{Dec}_{sk_{\mathrm{AH}}^j}(c_S^j) = d_S^j$,
7. If the verification fails then the Buyer aborts. If he did not abort then the parties use as output the values that were not open in Step 5. More precisely, the parties set $(\hat{sk}_i, \hat{pk}_i, \hat{\sigma}_i) := (sk^{j_i}, pk^{j_i}, \sigma^{j_i})$.

Fig. 2. The USG protocol.

3.3 The Construction of the $\mathsf{SellWitness}_f$ Protocol

In this section we show how to use the USG protocol to construct the $\mathsf{SellWitness}_f$ protocol (defined in Sect. 3). Our assumption is that f has a zero-knowledge proof of knowledge protocol, that we denote $\mathcal{F}$, in which the Seller can prove that she knows an x such that $f(x) = \mathsf{true}$. Additionally $\mathcal{F}$ consist of two phases: $\mathsf{Setup}_{\mathcal{F}}$ and $\mathsf{Challenge}_{\mathcal{F}}$. Let the values $A_{\mathcal{F}}$ and $B_{\mathcal{F}}$ denote the views of the Seller and the Buyer (respectively) after executing

Seller | | **Buyer**

sample: $k_S \leftarrow \mathbb{Z}^*_{|\mathbb{G}|}$
compute: $K_S := k_S \cdot g$

$\xrightarrow{\mathsf{Commit}(K_S)}$

$\xleftarrow{K_B}$ sample: $k_B \leftarrow \mathbb{Z}^*_{|\mathbb{G}|}$,
compute: $K_B := k_B \cdot g$

$\xrightarrow{\mathsf{Open}(K_S)}$

$K := k_S \cdot K_B$
if $K = \mathcal{O}$ then abort

$K := k_B \cdot K_S$
if $K = \mathcal{O}$ then abort

The parties now know $pk, K \in \mathbb{G}$. The corresponding discrete logs of these values are multiplicatively shared between the parties as pairs (d_S, d_B) and (k_S, k_B).

parse K as (x, y)
$r := x \bmod |\mathbb{G}|$
if $r = 0$ then abort

parse K as (x, y)
$r := x \bmod |\mathbb{G}|$
if $r = 0$ then abort

$(pk_{\mathrm{AH}}, sk_{\mathrm{AH}}) :=$
$\mathsf{AddHomGen}(1^\lambda)$
$c_S := \mathsf{AddHomEnc}_{pk_{\mathrm{AH}}}(d_S)$

$\xrightarrow{pk_{\mathrm{AH}}, c_S}$

$c_0 := (k_B)^{-1} \cdot H(z) \bmod |\mathbb{G}|$
$c_1 := \mathsf{AddHomEnc}_{pk_{\mathrm{AH}}}(c_0)$
$t := (k_B^{-1}) \cdot r \cdot d_B \bmod |\mathbb{G}|$
$c_2 := c_1 \otimes (c_S)^t$
samples $u \leftarrow \{1, \ldots, |\mathbb{G}|^2\}$

$s_0 := \mathsf{AddHomDec}_{sk_{\mathrm{AH}}}(c_B)$ $\xleftarrow{c_B}$ $c_B := c_2 \otimes \mathsf{AddHomEnc}_{pk_{\mathrm{AH}}}(u \cdot |\mathbb{G}|)$
$s := (k_S)^{-1} \cdot s_0 \bmod |\mathbb{G}|$
if $s = 0$ then abort
$\sigma := (r, s)$
if $\mathsf{Vrfy}_{pk}(z, \sigma) = \bot$ then abort
$S = F(\sigma)$
$\Gamma_i := \mathsf{Commit}(S)$ $\xrightarrow{\Gamma_i, \Phi}$
$\Phi := \mathsf{TLCommit}(d_S)$

Fig. 3. The $\mathsf{KSignGen}(1^\lambda)$ procedure. Recall that $\mathbb{G}$ is an elliptic curve group for ECDSA, and $(\mathsf{AddHomGen}, \mathsf{AddHomEnc}, \mathsf{AddHomDec})$ is a Paillier encryption scheme which is additively homomorphic over $\mathbb{Z}_n$, where $n > 2 \cdot |\mathbb{G}|^4$.

the $\mathsf{Setup}_{\mathcal{F}}$ phase. In the $\mathsf{Challenge}_{\mathcal{F}}$ phase the Buyer generates a challenge message $c_{\mathcal{F}} = \mathsf{GenChallenge}_{\mathcal{F}}(B_{\mathcal{F}})$ and sends it to the Seller. Then the Seller calculates the response $r_{\mathcal{F}} = \mathsf{GenResponse}_{\mathcal{F}}(x, A_{\mathcal{F}}, c_{\mathcal{F}})$ and sends it to the Buyer. At the end the Buyer accepts according to the output of the function $\mathsf{VerifyResponse}_{\mathcal{F}}(B_{\mathcal{F}}, c_{\mathcal{F}}, r_{\mathcal{F}}) \in \{\mathsf{true}, \mathsf{false}\}$. The fact that $\mathcal{F}$ is a proof of knowledge is formalized as follows: we require that there is also a function $\mathsf{Extract}_{\mathcal{F}}$ s.t. $\mathsf{Extract}_{\mathcal{F}}(B_{\mathcal{F}}, c^1_{\mathcal{F}}, r^1_{\mathcal{F}}, c^2_{\mathcal{F}}, r^2_{\mathcal{F}}) = x'$ and $f(x') = \mathsf{true}$ if only $\mathsf{VerifyResponse}_{\mathcal{F}}$ $(B_{\mathcal{F}}, c^i_{\mathcal{F}}, r^i_{\mathcal{F}}) = \mathsf{true}$ for $i = 1, 2$ and $c^1_{\mathcal{F}} \neq c^2_{\mathcal{F}}$. That means that the witness x' can be computed from the correct answers to two different challenges. We also assume that from the point of view of the Seller the challenge $c_{\mathcal{F}}$ is chosen uniformly from the set $X_{A_{\mathcal{F}}}$. Without loss of generality we also assume that $X_{A_{\mathcal{F}}} = \{0, 1\}$.

The parties use the USG protocol, so we have to describe how the Buyer produces the message z to be signed. Given the public keys $\hat{pk}_1, \ldots, \hat{pk}_b$ the Buyer first creates a transaction T_1 that takes ₿d from his funds and sends them to a multisig escrow "b-out-of-$(2b-1)$" using public keys $\hat{pk}_1, \ldots, \hat{pk}_b$ and $b-1$ times his own public key pk_B. The Buyer does not broadcast T_1 yet. Then he creates a transaction T_2 that spends the transaction T_1 and sends all the funds (₿d minus fee) to the public key pk_S owned by the Seller. The simplified transaction $z := [T_2]$ is the message that the parties later sign. We call this procedure GenMsg_T. We assume that each S^i from the USG protocol is divided into 2λ parts $S^{i,1}, \ldots, S^{i,2\lambda}$ each of size λ. Additionally we assume that each part $S^{i,j}$ is committed separately. To explain the idea behind our protocol assume for simplicity that $b = 1$. Recall that at the end of the USG protocol the Buyer knows the transaction T_1 that sends his funds to the key secret-shared between the Seller and the Buyer. Both parties know the transaction T_2 that is redeeming the transaction T_1 and sends the money to the Seller. The Seller knows the signature σ on T_2, but she cannot use T_2 yet, because the Buyer did not broadcast T_1. When the Buyer learns σ then he will be able to learn the secret random values $S^1, \ldots, S^{2\lambda}$ to which the Seller is committed. Additionally after some (long) time the Buyer will learn the secret key needed to redeem T_1 when only he force-opens the time-locked puzzle hiding d_S.

Now the Seller and the Buyer will use cut-and-choose technique again. They run 2λ times the first part $\mathsf{Setup}_{\mathcal{F}}$ of the zero knowledge proof of knowledge $\mathcal{F}$ of the x satisfying f. Each time the Seller calculates the responses r_0^i and r_1^i to the challenges $c = 0$ and $c = 1$. The Seller encrypts r_0^i and r_1^i using the same key S^i to get γ_0^i and γ_1^i and she commits to each ciphertext. Then the Buyer selects λ indices $j_1, \ldots, j_\lambda$ and challenges the Seller on them using $c_1, \ldots, c_\lambda \in \{0,1\}$. The Seller opens commitments to $S^{j_1}, \ldots, S^{j_\lambda}$ and to $\gamma_{c_1}^{j_1}, \ldots, \gamma_{c_\lambda}^{j_\lambda}$ (the Seller opens only one of $\gamma_0^{j_k}, \gamma_1^{j_k}$) and the Buyer uses secrets S^{j_k} to decrypt $\gamma_{c_k}^{j_k}$ and verify the response. If the Buyer verifies everything without an error, then the Seller opens the commitments to γ_0^k and γ_1^k (but not S^k) for $k \neq j_1, \ldots, j_\lambda$.

Now the Buyer broadcasts the transaction T_1. The Seller can spend it by revealing σ — in that case the Buyer can compute S^k, decrypt γ_0^k and γ_1^k to learn responses r_0^k and r_1^k and from them extract the value x. And if the Seller does nothing then after some time the Buyer will solve his time-locked puzzle, learn the secret key and take his funds back. The $\mathsf{SellWitness}_f$ protocol is depicted on Fig. 4. We have the following lemma, its proof appears in [7].

Lemma 2. *Suppose Paillier encryption and symmetric encryption are semantically secure,* COM *and* TLCOM *are secure commitment schemes, and the ECDSA scheme used in the construction of the* USG *is Strongly Unforgeable signature scheme. Assume additionally that there is a zero knowledge proof $\mathcal{F}$ of knowledge of x s.t. $f(x) = \mathsf{true}$ of the required form. Then the* $\mathsf{SellWitness}_f$ *constructed on Fig. 4 is ϵ-secure for $\epsilon = \left(\frac{b}{a}\right)^b$.*

1. The parties execute the USG protocol using the provided parameters. The Buyer will generate transaction T_2 to be signed as defined earlier in the procedure GenMsg_T.
2. For $i = 1$ to b:
   a) For $j = 1$ to 2λ: the parties execute the $\mathsf{Setup}_{\mathcal{F}}^{i,j}$ phase and the Seller and the Buyer learns $A_{\mathcal{F}}^{i,j}$ and $B_{\mathcal{F}}^{i,j}$ respectively.
   b) For $j = 1$ to 2λ: the Seller calculates the two challenges (in random order) that can be chosen by the Buyer $c_1^{i,j}$ and $c_2^{i,j}$. Then she calculates the responses $r_k^{i,j} = \mathsf{GenResponse}_{\mathcal{F}}(x, A_{\mathcal{F}}^{i,j}, c_k^{i,j})$ for $k = 1, 2$.
   c) For $j = 1$ to 2λ: The Seller uses the secret $S^{i,j}$ as a key in the symmetric cypher and encrypts $\gamma_k^{i,j} = \mathsf{Enc}_{S^{i,j}}(c_k^{i,j}, r_k^{i,j})$ for $k = 1, 2$. Then she commits to $\gamma_k^{i,j}$ for $k = 1, 2$.
   d) The Buyer chooses random subset $\mathcal{J}^i \subset \{1, \ldots, 2\lambda\}$ of size λ. Then he sends to the Seller $(j, c_B^{i,j} := \mathsf{GenChallenge}_{\mathcal{F}}(B_{\mathcal{F}}^{i,j}))$ for $j \in \mathcal{J}^i$.
   e) For $j \in \mathcal{J}^i$: the Seller opens her commitment to $S^{i,j}$ and checks that $c_B^{i,j} = c_k^{i,j}$ for $k = 1$ or $k = 2$. She opens the commitments to $\gamma_k^{i,j}$ for only this k.
   f) For $j \notin \mathcal{J}^i$: the Seller opens her commitments to $\gamma_k^{i,j}$ for $k = 1, 2$.
   g) The Buyer verifies all the commitments.
   h) For $j \in \mathcal{J}^i$: the Buyer decrypts $(c^{i,j}, r^{i,j}) = \mathsf{Dec}_{S^{i,j}}(\gamma_k^{i,j})$. Then he checks that $c^{i,j} = c_B^{i,j}$ and $\mathsf{VerifyResponse}_{\mathcal{F}}(B_{\mathcal{F}}^{i,j}, c_B^{i,j}, r^{i,j}) = \mathsf{true}$.
3. The Buyer broadcasts T_1 and the parties wait until it becomes final.
4. The Seller broadcasts T_2 using the signatures $\hat{\sigma}_1, \ldots, \hat{\sigma}_b$ to get her payment.
5. The Buyer uses signatures $\hat{\sigma}_i$ to calculate secrets $S^{i,j}$. Then he decrypts all the values $\gamma^{i,j}$ to get all the challenges and responses $c_k^{i,j}, r_k^{i,j}$. At the end using any pair of responses he calculates $x' = \mathsf{Extract}_{\mathcal{F}}(B_{\mathcal{F}}^{i,j}, c_1^{i,j}, r_1^{i,j}, c_2^{i,j}, r_2^{i,j})$.
6. If the Seller do not redeem the Buyer's transaction then the Buyer force-opens time-locked puzzles Φ_i and uses any of the opened values d_S^i to get his funds back.

Fig. 4. The $\mathsf{SellWitness}_f$ protocol.

Fig. 5. The $\mathsf{ZKFactorization}(n)$ protocol

3.4 Protocol for Selling a Factorization of an RSA Modulus

In this section we use the SellWitness protocol to construct the protocol for selling a factorization of an RSA modulus. To do it, we introduce the ZKFactorization protocol depicted on Fig. 5 — a zero knowledge proof of knowledge of the factorization of the RSA modulus. We now have the following lemma, whose proof appears in [7].

Lemma 3. *Assume that the commitment scheme is hash based and we model the hash function as a programmable oracle. Then the protocol* ZKFactorization *depicted on Fig. 5 is a zero knowledge proof of knowledge of the factorization of the RSA modulus.*

Implementation of the protocol for selling a factorization of an RSA modulus. We have created a prototype implementation of the protocol for selling a factorization of an RSA modulus. The main part of the protocol is written in C++, it is using the Crypto++ library for cryptographic functions. The Bitcoin related functionality is written in Java using the *bitocinj* library. The communication between C++ and Java is operated by *Apache Thrift*. The implementation is only a proof of concept but we were able to verify the feasibility and efficiency of the protocol. The current version of the protocol can be found on github.com/SellWitness/ZKFactorization. When using the ZKFactorization protocol in the SellWitness protocol we were able to simplify the main protocol a little. In the ZKFactorization protocol the Seller sends the commitments to the square roots of y but now it is not necessary because we do similar step in the SellWitness protocol. This is why the only messages exchanged between the parties before the Buyer sends the challenge are: first the Buyer sends $y^{i,j}$, then the Seller calculates the square roots $r_0^{i,j}, r_1^{i,j}$ of y, encrypts them $\gamma_k^{i,j} = Enc_{S^{i,j}}(r_k^{i,j})$ and commits to both $r_k^{i,j}$. In the implementation we use the following parameters: $a = 512$, $b = 8$ and $\lambda = 1024$. We use $b = 8$ because it means "b-out-of-$(2b-1)$" multisig transactions, and this kind of multisig transaction are standard in Bitcoin (for greater b they would be non-standard). We set $\lambda = 1024$, so the

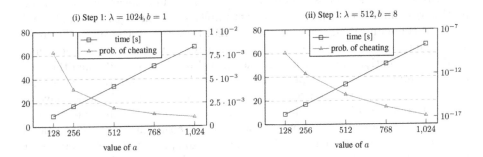

Fig. 6. The running time of the Step 1 and the probability that the Seller successfully cheats the Buyer in the Step 1 of the SellWitness protocol for the following fixed parameters: (i) $\lambda = 1024$ and $b = 1$ (i.e. using only standard single-signature transactions), and (ii) $\lambda = 512$ and $b = 8$ (i.e. using multi-signature transactions with the greatest parameters that are standard in Bitcoin) and different values of a. The running time of Step 1 is proportional to a and does not depend on other parameters. Using greater b gives much better security.

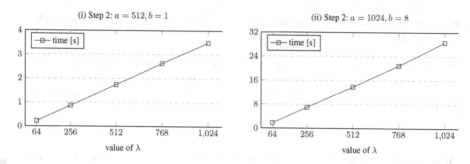

Fig. 7. The running time of the Step 2 of the SellWitness protocol for the following fixed parameter: (i) $a = 512$ and $b = 1$ (i.e. using only standard single-signature transactions), and (ii) $a = 1024$, and $b = 8$ (i.e. using multi-signature transactions with the greatest parameters that are standard in Bitcoin) and different values of λ. The running time of Step 2 is proportional to $b \cdot \lambda$ and does not depend on a. The probability of successfully cheating (by either the Buyer or the Seller) in step 2 is negligible in λ.

ZKFactorization protocol is executed $b \cdot 2\lambda = 8 \cdot 2048$ times. Fortunately this phase does not require any costly public key cryptography operations and therefore it is still very efficient. We set $a = 512$ and $b = 8$, and hence the probability of cheating is at most $(b/a)^b = 2^{-48}$. The running time of our protocol (i.e. the time until the Buyer broadcasts T_1) for this configuration (and primes of size about 512 bits each) is about 1 min — the running time of the USG protocol is about 33 s and Step 2 in the SellWitness$_f$ protocol takes about 28 s. The numbers are an average over 10 runs of the algorithm using a single thread on a standard personal computer. We note that the running time could be improved by using multiple threads. Additional measurements are presented on Figs. 6 and 7.

We run our protocol on a single machine, and local testing blockchain (testnet-box) and hence posting on blockchain, and communication between the parties was almost immediate (our current implementation takes 12 rounds, and the total communication size is about 60 MB). However, since we use the time-lock commitment schemes we need a conservative estimate on how much time would the execution of our protocol take on real blockchain, and when the parties are running in different physical locations. As in our protocol the parties have to wait for two transactions to be included into the blockchain, we have to assume that the whole protocol may take up to two hours[2]. Taking into account time needed to post messages on the blockchain the running our protocol takes on average 2 h, we have to have at least $\tau_0 = 5$ h, so τ_1 should be set to 50 h. Our tests has shown that an honest user (on an standard personal computer) can compute about 2^{19} squares (modulo n of size $\lambda = 1024$ bits) per second. That is why in our protocol we set the hardness of the timed commitment to $t = 2^{37}$.

---

[2] It takes on average 10 min for a transaction to be included into the blockchain but the users are advised to wait for 6 blocks (≈ 1 h) on top of the transaction.

References

1. An, J.H., Dodis, Y., Rabin, T.: On the security of joint signature and encryption. In: Knudsen, L.R. (ed.) EUROCRYPT 2002. LNCS, vol. 2332, pp. 83–107. Springer, Heidelberg (2002)
2. Andrychowicz, M., Dziembowski, S., Malinowski, D., Mazurek, Ł.: Fair two-party computations via bitcoin deposits. In: Böhme, R., Brenner, M., Moore, T., Smith, M. (eds.) FC 2014 Workshops. LNCS, vol. 8438, pp. 105–121. Springer, Heidelberg (2014). doi:10.1007/978-3-662-44774-1_8. http://dx.doi.org/10.1007/978-3-662-44774-1_8. ISBN: 978-3-662-44773-4
3. Andrychowicz, M., Dziembowski, S., Malinowski, D., Mazurek, Ł.: On the malleability of bitcoin transactions. In: Brenner, M., Christin, N., Johnson, B., Rohloff, K. (eds.) FC 2015 Workshops. LNCS, vol. 8976, pp. 1–18. Springer, Heidelberg (2015). doi:10.1007/978-3-662-48051-9. http://dx.doi.org/10.1007/978-3-662-48051-9. ISBN: 978-3-662-48050-2
4. Andrychowicz, M., Dziembowski, S., Malinowski, D., Mazurek, L.: Secure multi-party computations on bitcoin. In: 2014 IEEE Symposium on Security and Privacy, pp. 443–458. IEEE Computer Society Press, Berkeley (2014). doi:10.1109/SP.2014.35
5. Antonopoulos, A.M.: Mastering Bitcoin: Unlocking Digital Crypto-Currencies, 1st edn. O'Reilly Media, Inc., Sebastopol (2014). ISBN: 1449374042, 9781449374044
6. Back, A., Bentov, I.: Note on fair coin toss via Bitcoin. CoRR abs/1402.3698 (2014). http://arxiv.org/abs/1402.3698
7. Banasik, W., Dziembowski, S., Malinowski, D.: Efficient Zero-Knowledge Contingent Payments in Cryptocurrencies Without Scripts. Cryptology ePrint Archive (2016). http://eprint.iacr.org/2016/451.pdf
8. Bellare, M., Goldreich, O.: On defining proofs of knowledge. In: Brickell, E.F. (ed.) CRYPTO 1992. LNCS, vol. 740, pp. 390–420. Springer, Heidelberg (1993)
9. Bellare, M., Rogaway, P.: Random oracles are practical: a paradigm for designing efficient protocols. In: Ashby, V. (ed.) ACM CCS 1993, pp. 62–73. ACM Press, Fairfax (1993)
10. Ben-Sasson, E., Chiesa, A., Garman, C., Green, M., Miers, I., Tromer, E., Virza, M.: Zerocash: decentralized anonymous payments from bitcoin. In: 2014 IEEE Symposium on Security and Privacy, pp. 459–474. IEEE Computer Society Press, Berkeley (2014). doi:10.1109/SP.2014.36
11. Bentov, I., Kumaresan, R.: How to use bitcoin to design fair protocols. In: Garay, J.A., Gennaro, R. (eds.) CRYPTO 2014, Part II. LNCS, vol. 8617, pp. 421–439. Springer, Heidelberg (2014). doi:10.1007/978-3-662-44381-1_24
12. Bitcoin Wiki: Construct
13. Bitcoin Wiki: Script
14. Bitcoin Wiki: Secp256k1
15. Bitcoin Wiki: Transaction
16. Bitcoin Wiki: Zero Knowledge Contingent Payment
17. Boneh, D., Naor, M.: Timed commitments. In: Bellare, M. (ed.) CRYPTO 2000. LNCS, vol. 1880, pp. 236–254. Springer, Heidelberg (2000)
18. Boneh, D., Shen, E., Waters, B.: Strongly unforgeable signatures based on computational diffie-hellman. In: Yung, M., Dodis, Y., Kiayias, A., Malkin, T. (eds.) PKC 2006. LNCS, vol. 3958, pp. 229–240. Springer, Heidelberg (2006)
19. Brown, D.R.L.: Standards for Efficient Cryptography SEC 2: Recommended Elliptic Curve Domain Parameters, Version 2.0 (2010)

20. Damgard, I.: On Sigma-Protocols (2015). http://www.cs.au.dk/~ivan/Sigma.pdf
21. Fiat, A., Shamir, A.: How to prove yourself: practical solutions to identification and signature problems. In: Odlyzko, A.M. (ed.) CRYPTO 1986. LNCS, vol. 263, pp. 186–194. Springer, Heidelberg (1987)
22. Filippi, P.D.: Tomorrow's apps will come from brilliant (and risky) Bitcoin code. Wired magazine
23. Goldfeder, S., Gennario, R., Kalodner, H., Bonneau, J., Felten, E.W., Kroll, J.A., Narayanan, A.: Securing bitcoin wallets via a new DSA/ECDSA threshold signature scheme (manuscript, 2015)
24. Goldreich, O.: Foundations of Cryptography, vol. 1. Cambridge University Press, New York (2006). ISBN: 0521035368
25. Johnson, D., Menezes, A., Vanstone, S.: The elliptic curve digital signature algorithm (ECDSA). Int. J. Inf. Secur. 1(1), 36–63 (2001)
26. Katz, J., Lindell, Y.: Introduction to Modern Cryptography (Chapman & Hall/Crc Cryptography and Network Security Series). Chapman & Hall/CRC, Boca Raton (2007). ISBN: 1584885513
27. Kumaresan, R., Moran, T., Bentov, I.: How to use bitcoin to play decentralized poker. In: Ray, I., Li, N., Kruegel, C. (eds.) Proceedings of the 22nd ACM SIGSAC Conference on Computer and Communications Security, Denver, CO, USA, pp. 195–206. ACM, 12–16 October 2015. doi:10.1145/2810103.2813712. http://doi.acm.org/10.1145/2810103.2813712. ISBN: 978-1-4503-3832-5
28. Lindell, Y., Pinkas, B.: Secure two-party computation via cut-and-choose oblivious transfer. In: Ishai, Y. (ed.) TCC 2011. LNCS, vol. 6597, pp. 329–346. Springer, Heidelberg (2011)
29. Luu, L., Teutsch, J., Kulkarni, R., Saxena, P.: Demystifying incentives in the consensus computer. In: ACM CCS 2015, pp. 706–719. ACM Press (2015)
30. MacKenzie, P., Reiter, M.K.: Two-party generation of DSA signatures. English. Int. J. Inf. Secur. 2(3–4), 218–239 (2004). doi:10.1007/s10207-004-0041-0. http://dx.doi.org/10.1007/s10207-004-0041-0. ISSN: 1615-5262
31. Maxwell, G.: The first successful Zero-Knowledge Contingent Payment (2016)
32. Nakamoto, S.: Bitcoin: A Peer-to-Peer Electronic Cash System (2009). http://bitcoin.org/bitcoin.pdf
33. Pagnia, H., Gartner, F.C.: On the impossibility of fair exchange without a trusted third party. Technical report Darmstadt University of Technology (1999)
34. Pagnia, H., Vogt, H., Gärtner, F.C.: Fair Exchange. Comput. J. 46(1), 55–75 (2003). doi:10.1093/comjnl/46.1.55. http://dx.doi.org/10.1093/comjnl/46.1.55
35. Paillier, P.: Public-key cryptosystems based on composite degree residuosity classes. In: Stern, J. (ed.) EUROCRYPT 1999. LNCS, vol. 1592, pp. 223–238. Springer, Heidelberg (1999)
36. Pedersen, T.P.: A Threshold cryptosystem without a trusted party (Extended Abstract) (Rump Session). In: Davies, D.W. (ed.) EUROCRYPT 1991. LNCS, vol. 547, pp. 522–526. Springer, Heidelberg (1991)
37. Rivest, R.L., Shamir, A., Wagner, D.A.: Time-lock puzzles and timed-release Crypto. Technical report Cambridge, MA, USA (1996)
38. Todd, P.: OP_CHECKLOCKTIMEVERIFY. Bitcoin Improvement Proposal 0062. https://github.com/bitcoin/bips/blob/master/bip-0062.mediawiki
39. Wuille, P.: Bitcoin Improvement Proposal 062: Dealing with malleability

Security of the Internet of Things

LeiA: A Lightweight Authentication Protocol for CAN

Andreea-Ina Radu[✉] and Flavio D. Garcia[✉]

School of Computer Science,
University of Birmingham, Birmingham, UK
{a.i.radu,f.garcia}@cs.bham.ac.uk

Abstract. Recent research into automotive security has shown that once a single vehicle component is compromised, it is often possible to take full control of the vehicle. This paper proposes LEIA, a lightweight authentication protocol for the Controller Area Network (CAN). This protocol allows critical vehicle Electronic Control Units (ECUs) to authenticate each other providing compartmentalisation and preventing a number of attacks e.g., where a compromised CD player is able to accelerate the vehicle. LEIA is designed to run under the stringent time and bandwidth constraints of automotive applications and is backwards compatible with existing vehicle infrastructure. The protocol is suitable to be implemented using lightweight cryptographic primitives yet providing appropriate security levels by limiting the usage of every key in the system. The security of LEIA is proven under the unforgeability assumption of the MAC scheme under chosen message attacks (UF-CMA).

1 Introduction

The automotive industry has recently faced a massive transformation which has enabled serious security threats [4,8,15]. The increasing number of (wireless) interfaces available in today's cars exposes it to new attack vectors. Modern Cars have dozens and sometimes even over a hundred of *Electronic Control Units* (ECUs). While more technology is being introduced in modern vehicles, transforming them into smart, connected cars, the underlying security infrastructure has struggled to keep up with the pace of these changes.

The Controller Area Network (CAN), standardised in [13], is the most commonly used serial bus nowadays. Its purpose is to connect the ECUs of a car, and allow them to communicate without a source or destination address. As the in-vehicle network has been traditionally considered a safe, trusted environment, and there were no wireless interfaces, resilience against cyber-attacks has not been of prime concern. Also, the security of ECUs, which provide a significant part of the functionality of a modern vehicle, has been overlooked. The CAN bus is a broadcast network, whereby any message sent can be read by all connected ECUs. By design, it does not provide security features, such as confidentiality (messages are not encrypted, therefore they can be eavesdropped), or authenticity (the source or destination of a message is unknown) [18]. Most attacks

© Springer International Publishing Switzerland 2016
I. Askoxylakis et al. (Eds.): ESORICS 2016, Part II, LNCS 9879, pp. 283–300, 2016.
DOI: 10.1007/978-3-319-45741-3_15

presented in the literature could be prevented if authentication was present on the network, or at least their impact would be localised and mitigated.

While transitioning from mostly mechanical systems to complex systems with digital components, manufacturers overlooked the possibility of a cyber-attacker in their designs. The KeeLoq block cipher, used by various car manufacturers in anti-theft mechanisms, was first attacked by Bogdanov in [2]. Later, this attack was improved in [5,12,14]. Verdult et al. proposed an attack against the Megamos Crypto [21,24] and Hitag2 [22] vehicle immobilisers. These attacks allow an adversary to start the vehicle without the car key. Automotive remote keyless entry systems have also been shown to use weak key management and cryptographic primitives, enabling an eavesdropping adversary to clone the car key [7].

Koscher et al. [15] provide an extensive description of attack vectors under the assumption that an attacker has direct access to the vehicle, focusing on the security of the in-vehicle networks. Their research shows it is possible to compromise the radio, instrument panel cluster, HVAC, BCM (which controls door locks, interior and exterior lights, horn, windows, wipers, ignition), as well as safety-critical functionality of the engine and brakes. They launched a generic denial of service attack which disabled communication on the CAN bus and froze the instrument panel cluster. Part of the attacks were then tested on the road, proving their viability in a real-world scenario.

The work of Koscher et al. raises a key issue: *how* would an attacker get access to the vehicle. Under the assumption that prior physical access to the vehicle is deemed as an unrealistic scenario, Checkoway et al. [4] explore the external attack surface of automotive vehicles. They successfully used the entertainment system, radio, Bluetooth interface, Tire Pressure Monitoring System (TPMS) and cellular network to compromise a vehicle. They also identified weaknesses and exploited a PassThru device, used for servicing and diagnostics by dealerships. They have shown that a malicious PassThru device can be used to send CAN messages to a vehicle and install malware onto the car's telematics unit.

Miller et al. [17] provide an extensive analysis of the wireless interfaces of a Jeep Cherokee as potential attack surfaces. Most notably, they took advantage of vulnerabilities in the Jeep's UConnect system, which provides a cellular connection to the vehicle, and showed how they could completely control the vehicle over the Internet. They were able to control the car's dashboard functions, steering, brakes, heating system, radio, windshield wipers, the car's digital display and transmission. They demonstrated the attacks live, on the road, for Wired [8].

Ultimately, these attacks all rely on the fact that messages can be sent on the CAN network by a malicious attacker or a compromised ECU, and they are accepted by all other ECUs as if they were legitimate. The lack of source authentication is an enabler for all these types of attacks. While vehicles are designed to tolerate random failures, they cannot currently cope with malicious cyber-attacks. The lock-down of components is not a viable solution, both from a legislative point of view (e.g., right-to-repair legislation) or from the economic point of view of the manufacturer.

The AUTOSAR [1] specifications are a set of standards for ECU software functionality. The purpose of the standard is to reduce the development cost of ECU software and increase its scalability. The 4.2 release of the specification includes provisions for security on CAN. It provides interfaces and guidelines for authentication of messages, but leaves the implementation up to the manufacturer. The documents introduce the *Secure On-board Communication* module and provide guidelines for implementing authentication. They recommend using 128-bit keys, 64-bit MACs, and counters or timestamps to provide freshness. The MAC computation should be based on the data identifier, the data to be sent and the freshness value.

Our contribution. This paper proposes LEIA, the first AUTOSAR compliant, lightweight authentication protocol in the literature. The protocol respects the requirements laid out to become a standard in the automotive industry, as described in the Secure On-board Communication Module Specification, AUTOSAR Release 4.2.

LEIA does not require additional hardware components or substantial implementation costs thus is less expensive than previously proposed solutions, while providing higher security levels. The protocol has been designed by taking into consideration real-world requirements and limitations of the CAN bus such as limited bandwidth, short data frames and publisher-subscriber broadcast architecture where newly arrived messages overwrite older ones in the receiver's buffer.

Furthermore, LEIA is fully backwards compatible with existing CAN configuration, and is designed such that it can be flexibly implemented, providing different security vs bandwidth, computational overhead trade-offs.

Finally, we have proven the protocol to provide secure authentication under the unforgeability assumption of the MAC scheme under chosen plaintext attacks. Since we use the same MAC scheme for key diversification, we have the additional requirement that the produced MAC values are indistinguishable from the output of the key generation function.

Related work. CANAuth [19] and LiBrA-CAN [9] are two protocols for lightweight authentication over CAN. Both solutions make use of the CAN+ protocol, an improvement of the existing CAN. The CAN+ protocol was introduced by Ziermann et al. in [23]. It takes advantage of the fact that additional data can be sent in time intervals where the nodes conforming to the original CAN protocol do not listen. Therefore, CAN+ is backwards compatible and allows CAN-conform nodes to operate undisturbed alongside CAN+ nodes. This solution allows the transmission of 16 CAN+ bits, for one CAN bit transmitted.

Both solutions require replacing the CAN transceivers, and therefore imply a large cost for the manufacturers. Also, the logistics that would be involved in upgrading vehicles already in use are unclear.

Several solutions which do not require modified hardware have been proposed. We discuss them below and highlight their differences in respect with our proposed protocol, LEIA.

MaCAN is an authenticated protocol described in [10]. It is designed specifically for the CAN bus and takes into account the network's constraints, such as message length and available resources. MaCAN authenticates 4-byte messages with 4-byte MACs, in bidirectional communication. Timestamps are used as source of freshness, therefore, a *time server* is added into the system, which broadcasts a timestamp at regular intervals. Also, a *key server* is added, which shares a symmetric long term key with each security-enabled node. The key server mediates the establishment of keys between two nodes that want to securely communicate. In the case multiple nodes need to be able to verify the authenticity of a message, they propose using group keys. Bruni et al. give a formal analysis of the MaCAN protocol in [3]. They formally prove the secrecy of both long term keys and session keys used by the protocol. However, they found an attack through which one node is left unauthenticated and proposed a corrected version of the protocol. MaCAN introduces two new elements in the network, a time server and a key server. In LEIA, we remove the need for these components by using counters, instead of the time server, and by having each node derive the session keys locally, instead of having a key server.

LCAP was proposed by Hazem et al. in [11] and is a lightweight broadcast authentication protocol, which closely follows the CAN specification. The authors propose the use of a "magic number", which is appended to the message, instead of MACs. The number is part of a chain, which is obtained by applying a transformation function on an initial value, multiple times. Given the end of the chain, the sender and receiver can both verify if a value belongs to it. The magic number is 2 bytes in length. Handshakes are used in order to establish the secure channel and keep the nodes synchronised. This requires a significant number of CAN message identifiers be added to the network (five new IDs for each sender-receiver pair). The advantage of LCAP is that it only uses 2 bytes of the payload in order to achieve the authentication property, thus having a small overhead for authenticated message exchange. However, due to the high number of new IDs to be introduced in the network configuration, LCAP requires a large address space. Also, the channel setup and soft/hard synchronisation functions require a significant number of messages to be exchanged, thus adding to the overhead.

CaCAN has been introduced in [16], by Kurachi et al. Their approach is to use a *monitor node*, which authenticates the other nodes in the network. It detects and destroys unauthorised data frames by overwriting them with an error frame in real time. Challenge-response authentication is used in order to establish the secure channel. This approach requires a modified CAN controller, the monitor node, to be fitted in every car. Also, as is the general case with centralised authorities, if the monitor node is compromised or removed, the entire network is compromised as well.

Overview. This paper is organised as follows. Section 2 introduces standard security definitions, most of it is (adapted) from the literature. Section 3 provides the design and specification of our protocol. We give a formal security evaluation in Sect. 4. In Sect. 5 we discuss how we deal with the shortcomings of CAN and we provide guidelines for implementing the protocol in practise. We conclude in Sect. 6.

2 Security Notions and Adversarial Model

An authentication protocol is an interactive cryptographic protocol executed between a prover $\mathcal{P}$ and a verifier $\mathcal{V}$. In an initial phase, both parties run a setup(η) function, which produces a shared secret s and, potentially, public parameters ns. After an execution of the protocol, $\mathcal{V}$ outputs the identity of the prover, id, and the message *data*. We say that the protocol has completeness error α if for all secrets s generated by setup(η), the honestly executed protocol rejects the identity and message with a probability at most α.

We will show that our protocol is secure against active attacks. These allow the adversary $\mathcal{A}$ to interact with the honest prover a polynomial amount of times. Then, $\mathcal{A}$ interacts with the verifier only, and wins if the verifier returns accept. The adversary interacts with $\mathcal{V}$ only once. An authentication protocol is (t, Q, η)-*secure against active adversaries* if every probabilistic polynomial time (PPT) adversary $\mathcal{A}$, running at most t times and making Q queries to the honest prover, has probability at most ε to win the above game.

We first need to introduce some notation. Let $\mathbb{F}_2 = \{0, 1\}$ be the field of two elements (or the set of Booleans). $\mathbb{F}_2^l$ denotes a bitstring of length l and $\mathbb{F}_2^*$ is a bitstring of arbitrary length. $\|$ stands for the concatenation of two bitstrings.

Execution environment. Let n be the number of identifiers in the system, and $\mathcal{I} = \{\text{id}_0, \ldots, \text{id}_{n-1}\}$ be the set of all identifiers. Let $\mathsf{P} = \{P_0, \ldots, P_{n-1}\}$ be the set of all protocol participants, where participant P_i knows the secret parameter s_i and public parameters ns.

Definition 1 (Protocol setup). Let the function setup : $\eta \rightarrow (s, ns)$ be the initialisation procedure of the protocol parties, where η is the security parameter and (s, ns) is a tuple formed by the secret parameter s and the public parameters ns.

Definition 2 (Authentication oracles). Let $\Pi = \{\pi(s_i) \mid s_i \in s\}$ be a set of oracles such that $\pi(s_i)$ emulates party P_i of the authentication protocol.

Definition 3 (Protocol output). Let output: $\mathsf{P} \rightarrow \mathcal{I} \times \mathbb{F}_2^*$ be the protocol output function of a protocol participant P_i and outputs a tuple (id$_j$, *data*) corresponding to the last successful protocol instance of P_i, where id$_j \in \mathcal{I}$ is the identity of sender and *data* is the message that was sent.

We will now introduce the security notions for symmetric key authentication protocols. Most of it is standard, most of the definitions proposed here are adapted from [20].

Definition 4 (Matching conversations [20]). We define *matching conversations* as a successful execution of the authentication protocol, between two parties.

We introduce the authentication game $\mathbf{Auth}_\Pi(\eta, \mathcal{A})$ and give a formal definition below. The public and secret parameters are generated by calling the $\mathsf{setup}(\eta)$ function. Then adversary $\mathcal{A}$ interacts with the oracles $\pi(s_i)$ which emulate the protocol participants which respond according to the protocol description. At some point the adversary $\mathcal{A}$ terminates. $\mathcal{A}$ wins if there is a party P_i which has accepted, and thus outputs, $(\mathsf{id}_j, data)$ while P_i and P_j did not have any matching conversation.

We denote by $\mathsf{Adv}_{\mathsf{MAC}}^{\mathsf{Auth}}(\eta, \mathcal{A})$ the advantage of the adversary $\mathcal{A}$ in breaking the authentication protocol.

Experiment $\mathbf{Auth}_\Pi(\eta, \mathcal{A})$

$ns, s \leftarrow \mathsf{setup}(\eta)$

$\mathcal{B}^{\Pi(ns,s)}(\eta, ns)$

winif $\exists\, i, j, data : \mathsf{output}(P_i) = (\mathsf{id}_j, data)$ is the output of a party P_i and, parties P_i and P_j did not have any *matching conversation*.

Definition 5 (Authentication Protocol Security). An authentication protocol is said to be *secure* if for all PPT adversaries $\mathcal{A}$, the probability that $\mathcal{A}$ wins the game $\mathbf{Auth}_\Pi(\eta, \mathcal{A})$ is a negligible function of η:

$$\mathsf{Adv}_{\mathsf{MAC}}^{\mathsf{Auth}}(\eta, \mathcal{A}) \le \varepsilon(\eta)$$

Message Authentication Codes

A message authentication code is a set of three algorithms {KG, MAC, Verify}, with associated key space $\mathcal{K}$, message space $\mathcal{M}$ and MAC space Φ.

The standard security notion for a MAC is *unforgeability under a chosen message attack (uf-cma)*. The secret key K is generated by calling the key generation algorithm KG of the MAC. Then, adversary $\mathcal{B}$ makes up to Q queries to the $\mathsf{MAC}(K, \cdot)$ and $\mathsf{Verify}(K, \cdot, \cdot)$ algorithms. At some point, $\mathcal{B}$ terminates and outputs a tuple $(\mathbf{m}, \phi)$, where $\mathbf{m} \in \mathcal{M}$ is a message and $\phi \in \Phi$ is a MAC. Adversary $\mathcal{B}$ wins if it did not query $\mathsf{MAC}(K, \mathbf{m})$ and ϕ verifies for message $\mathbf{m}$, under the secret key K.

We denote by $\mathsf{Adv}_{\mathsf{MAC}}^{\mathsf{uf\text{-}cma}}(\eta, \mathcal{B}, Q)$ the advantage of the adversary $\mathcal{B}$ in forging a messaged under a chosen message attack for MAC, on the security parameter η.

Experiment $\mathbf{UF\text{-}CMA}_{\mathsf{MAC}}(\eta, \mathcal{B}, Q)$

$K \leftarrow \mathsf{KG}(1^\eta)$

Invoke $\mathcal{B}^{\mathsf{MAC}(K,\cdot),\mathsf{Verify}(K,\cdot,\cdot)}$ which can make up to Q queries to $\mathsf{MAC}(K, \cdot)$ and $\mathsf{Verify}(K, \cdot, \cdot)$.

$(\mathbf{m}, \phi) \leftarrow \mathcal{B}^{\mathsf{MAC}(K,\cdot),\mathsf{Verify}(K,\cdot,\cdot)}$

winif

1. $\mathsf{Verify}(K, \mathbf{m}, \phi) = \mathtt{accept}$
2. $\mathcal{A}$ did not already request $\mathsf{MAC}(K, \mathbf{m})$

Definition 6 (UF–CMA Security). We say that MAC is (t, Q, η)-secure against uf–cma adversaries if for any adversary $\mathcal{B}$ running in time t the experiment above, we have:

$$\mathsf{Adv}_{\mathsf{MAC}}^{\mathrm{uf-cma}}(\eta, \mathcal{B}, Q) \leq \varepsilon(\eta)$$

Assumption 1 (MAC indistinguishability from random). We assume that the output of the MAC algorithm is computationally *indistinguishable from random* and, the output of the key generation (KG) function of the MAC algorithm and the output of the MAC function have the same distribution.

Adversarial model. We consider a Dolev-Yao adversary [6], who controls the network. In particular, she can passively monitor the network, reading all data passing through the CAN and send messages with any id. She can also send error frames to destroy current data or remote frames. However, in practise, the CAN error handling limits the attacker's capabilities in this respect.

3   LeiA: A Lightweight Authentication Protocol for CAN

This section outlines the design of LEIA, with a detailed description of each function of the authentication protocol.

The CAN bus uses a publish-and-subscribe architecture model, where one ECU can broadcast a message with a certain identifier (id_i). The identifier is not a way to identify the source or destination of a message, therefore, our protocol provides unidirectional authentication, with a method of signalling if any of the subscribed ECUs have gone out of sync/authentication failed.

Each protocol participant which needs to authenticate data, will need to store a tuple $\langle \mathsf{id}_i, K_{\mathsf{id}_i}, e_{\mathsf{id}_i}, K_{\mathsf{id}_i}^e, c_{\mathsf{id}_i} \rangle$ per relevant CAN identifier, where:

- the identifier id_i is a CAN ID;
- the key K_{id_i} is a 128-bit long term symmetric key that is used to derive the session key;
- the epoch e_{id_i} is a 56-bit counter; the value is incremented at every vehicle start-up or when the counter c_{id_i} overflows; participates in the generation of the session key;
- the session key $K_{\mathsf{id}_i}^e$ is a 128-bit key used for generating the MAC; re-generating the session key when the epoch e_{id_i} changes ensures that only a small amount of data is authenticated under the same key; also, if the session key becomes compromised, the attacker can compute valid MACs only until the epoch changes (limited time);
- the counter c_{id_i} is a 16-bit counter included in the Message Authentication Code (MAC) and is sent within the Data Frame containing the MAC, in order to provide freshness.

The long term keys and epochs are assumed to be stored in tamper-resistant memory. Updating the set of keys (e.g. if adding or replacing a node in the network) should require direct physical access to the involved nodes and, therefore, could only be done by an authorised repairs shop. How exactly this is done is beyond the scope of this paper.

We describe below the functions of the protocol for a pair of nodes: sender S, which is the broadcaster of messages with the identifier id_i, and receiver R, which is the node subscribed to messages broadcast on the identifier id_i.

The authentication protocol LEIA has an associated key space $\mathcal{K} \in \mathbb{F}_2^{128}$, message space $\mathcal{M} \in \mathbb{F}_2^*$ and MAC space $\Phi \in \mathbb{F}_2^{64}$.

Protocol setup. The function $\mathsf{setup}\colon \eta \to (s, ns)$ is the initialisation procedure of the ECUs, where η is the security parameters and (s, ns) is a tuple formed by the secret parameter s and the public parameters ns. The secret parameter $s = \langle K_{id_0}, \ldots K_{id_{n-1}} \rangle$ is computed by running the key generation algorithm $\mathsf{KG}(1^\eta)$ of the MAC for each identity id_i, with $K_{id_i} \in \mathcal{K}$. The public parameters are $ns = \langle (c_{id_0}, e_{id_0}), \ldots, (c_{id_{n-1}}, e_{id_{n-1}}) \rangle$, where $c_{id_i} \in \mathbb{F}_2^{16}$ is the counter and $e_{id_i} \in \mathbb{F}_2^{56}$ is the epoch. Both the counter and epoch are initialised to zero, for each identity id_i. The session key generation function is then called for each identity id_i, in order to generate the session key $K_{id_i}^e$.

Session key generation (Fig. 1). Let $\mathsf{session\_key\_gen}\colon \mathcal{K} \times \mathbb{F}_2^{56} \to \mathcal{K}$ be the session key generation function. This function takes as input a long term symmetric key K_{id_i} and an epoch e_{id_i}, both associated with an identity id_i, and outputs the session key $K_{id_i}^e$ computed as follows:

1. increment epoch: $e_{id_i} \leftarrow e_{id_i} + 1$
2. apply the MAC algorithm on the epoch:

$$K_{id_i}^e \leftarrow \mathsf{MAC}(K_{id_i}, e_{id_i})$$

3. reset counter to zero: $c_{id_i} \leftarrow 0$

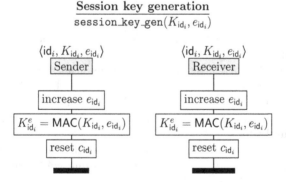

Fig. 1. Session key generation between sender S and receiver R for message with identifier id_i.

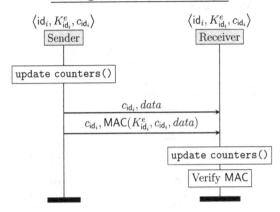

Fig. 2. Message authentication between sender S and receiver R for message with identifier id_i.

Sending authenticated messages (Fig. 2). In order to send an authenticated message, the sender first needs to update the counter c_{id_i}. If c_{id_i} overflows, then the epoch e_{id_i} is incremented and c_{id_i} is reset to 0 (see Algorithm 1). It then calls the MAC algorithm which takes as input the session key $K^e_{\mathrm{id}_i}$, the counter c_{id_i} and the message $data$, and produces as output a MAC $\phi \in \Phi$ computed as:

$$\phi = \mathsf{MAC}(K^e_{\mathrm{id}_i}, c_{\mathrm{id}_i}, data)$$

The sender then transmits the counter, data and MAC. After reading the values, the receiver updates the counters and verifies the MAC.

Algorithm 1. `update_counters()` function

Require: counter c_{id_i}, epoch e_{id_i}, LTSK K_{id_i}
Ensure: c_{id_i} and e_{id_i} are incremented accordingly
1: **if** $c_{\mathrm{id}_i} = $ 0xFFFF **then**
2:     **if** $e_{\mathrm{id}_i} = $ 0xFFFFFFFFFFFFFF **then**
3:         $e_{\mathrm{id}_i} \leftarrow$ 0x00000000000000
4:     **else**
5:         $e_{\mathrm{id}_i} \leftarrow e_{\mathrm{id}_i} + 1$
6:     **end if**
7:     $c_{\mathrm{id}_i} \leftarrow$ 0x0000
8:     call `session_key_gen`$(K_{\mathrm{id}_i}, e_{\mathrm{id}_i})$
9: **else**
10:     $c_{\mathrm{id}_i} \leftarrow c_{\mathrm{id}_i} + 1$
11: **end if**

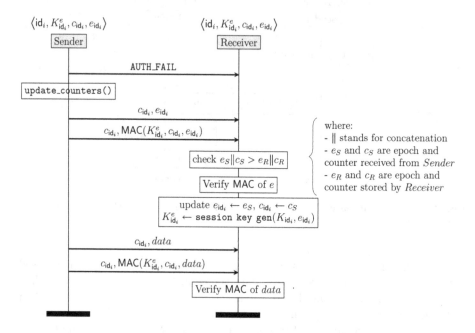

Fig. 3. Message authentication failure and resynchronisation procedure, between sender S and receiver R for message with identifier id_i.

Resynchronisation (Fig. 3). If a MAC cannot be verified, the receiver sends an AUTH_FAIL signal to the sender. When an AUTH_FAIL message is read, the sender S broadcasts a message containing its current epoch value, a MAC of the epoch and counter c_{id_i}, then proceeds with normal data transmission. This will help the receiver nodes resynchronise their epoch and counter.

R will only update e_{id_i} and c_{id_i} if the values are higher (e_{id_i} received can be equal to e_{id_i} stored) than the stored ones. If the new counter is lower than the receiver's counter, it means there is an attacker performing a replay attack, therefore the data is discarded and the counter not incremented.

Most common cause for a MAC to fail verification, in the context of the CAN, is the de-synchronisation of counter c_{id_i} and epoch e_{id_i} values. Not all nodes join the network at the same time, therefore the counters will be outdated and the receiver will need to request the current values from the sender. A complete protocol outline is given in Fig. 4.

4   Security Analysis

This section analyses the security of LEIA under the unforgeability assumption of the MAC scheme under chosen message attacks.

Protocol outline

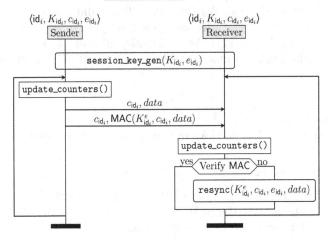

Fig. 4. Communication between sender S and receiver R for message with identifier id_i – LEIA protocol outline: first, the session keys are generated by both participants; then, S can send authenticated message to R; R verifies the MAC of the received message; if the verification fails, the resynchronisation is initialised, otherwise, the message is accepted.

Theorem 2. *The* LEIA *authentication protocol is secure with respect to Definition 5 (see Sect. 2).*

Proof. Assume that there is an adversary $\mathcal{A}$ that breaks the $\mathbf{Auth}_\Pi(\eta, \mathcal{A})$ security of the authentication protocol LEIA. Then, we build an adversary $\mathcal{B}$ that breaks the (t, Q, η)-security of the $\mathbf{UF\text{–}CMA}_{\mathsf{MAC}}$ scheme.

At the beginning, the adversary $\mathcal{B}$ randomly picks one target identifier $id^\star$ and a target epoch $e^\star$. Then, $\mathcal{B}$ runs the protocol setup function for each identity id_i.

The adversary $\mathcal{B}$ executes $\mathcal{A}$. For this, $\mathcal{B}$ needs to emulate oracles $\pi(K_{id_i})$. Emulating party P_i means generating the session key, and keeping track of the counters c_{id_i} and epochs e_{id_i}, as specified in the protocol description. The session key for an identity is regenerated every time the associated epoch is incremented. The adversary $\mathcal{A}$ has access to the oracles in Π.

When transitioning from $e^\star - 1$ to $e^\star$, for identity $id^\star$, $\mathcal{B}$ will not use the MAC algorithm, as described in the protocol, to generate the session key $K_{id^\star}^{e^\star}$. Instead, whenever a MAC needs to be computed under the key $K_{id^\star}^{e^\star}$, the adversary will use the $\mathsf{MAC}(\cdot, \cdot)$ oracle from the $\mathbf{UF\text{–}CMA}_{\mathsf{MAC}}$ game. Note that due to Assumption 1, this will be indistinguishable from the case of using the key generation algorithm $\mathsf{KG}(\cdot)$. For all other cases, it will compute it herself, by running the MAC algorithm.

At some point, $\mathcal{A}$ terminates. With non-negligible probability, there must exist a P_i which outputs an identity id_j and a message $\mathbf{m}$, without having a matching conversation between P_i and P_j. In order for P_i to produce this output, it means $\mathcal{A}$ has sent a message $\mathbf{m} = (c\|data)$ and a MAC $\phi = \mathsf{MAC}(K^e_{\mathsf{id}}, \mathbf{m})$ which P_i has verified, and therefore this must be a valid MAC.

If $\mathsf{id}_j = \mathsf{id}^\star$ and $e = e^\star$, the adversary $\mathcal{B}$ will output $(\mathbf{m}, \phi)$; otherwise, it will output a tuple of random strings. As the identity $\mathsf{id}^\star$ and epoch $e^\star$ are chosen at random before the $\mathsf{setup}(\eta)$ phase, the probability that $\mathcal{A}$ also attacks $\mathsf{id}^\star$ and $e^\star$ is:

$$\mathcal{P}(K^{e^\star}_{\mathsf{id}^\star} = K^e_{\mathsf{id}_j}) = \frac{1}{n} \cdot \frac{1}{2^{56}}$$

and we recall that n is the number of identifiers in the system.

In order to win the **UF–CMA**$_{\mathsf{MAC}}$ game, the adversary needs:

1. $\mathsf{Verify}(K^{e^\star}_{\mathsf{id}^\star}, \mathbf{m}, \phi) = \mathsf{accept}$;
2. the MAC ϕ was never queried to the MAC oracle.

Condition 1. holds because ϕ is a valid MAC, as it was verified by party P_i. Condition 2. holds because the MAC was never queried to the MAC oracle, as P_i and P_j do not have a matching conversation.   □

5   Dealing with the Shortcomings of CAN

As some of the ECUs are involved in safety-critical functions such as acceleration and ABS, latency is of prime concern. Any solution aiming at providing extra security features, such as authentication, cannot introduce significant latency. To this end, lightweight cryptography is best suited. Furthermore, many ECUs have limited memory available, therefore the implementation of the protocol should be compact as well. For this reason, our solution uses a MAC algorithm for two different purposes: authenticating data and deriving session keys.

In order to compensate for the modest security provided by lightweight cryptographic primitives, we do not use the long term secret key directly, but generate session keys, which are used to authenticate the messages exchanged. A session key is used to authenticate at most 2^{16} messages, after which a new session key is derived. This limits the amount of key-dependent data an attacker has access to. In case a session key is compromised, an attacker can use it either until 2^{16} messages have been authenticated, or until the vehicle is restarted, whichever comes first.

LEIA makes use of the extended identifier data frames. It uses the Extended Identifier 18-bit field in order to send the 16-bit counter and a 2-bit command code, as explained below (Fig. 5). The 29-bit identifier data frames co-exist with the 11-bit data frames without interfering with the arbitration process of CAN, as the priority of a message is decided based on the 11-bit Identifier field. We define three transmission channels over CAN:

Data Channel
   All ids which are used to transmit data and signals constitute the data channel. The data is transmitted within the payload field of the frame. The counter c_{id_i} which is used to generate the MAC is placed in the extended identifier field. The two leftmost bits are the *command code* 00, and signal that data is being transmitted in the frame.

Fig. 5. Extended Data Frame CAN 2.0B (29-bit identifier) – placement of command code and counter within Extended Identifier field.

Authentication Channel

All ids which are used to transmit MACs make up the Authentication Channel. The MACs are transmitted on a different identifier than the data. We propose this id be a fixed offset from the base id on which the data is sent. It should be as close as possible to the base id, in order to avoid scheduling issues caused by arbitration. In our example, $id_{MAC} = id_{data} + 1$. This will avoid messages with the same identifier being overwritten in the CAN controller *buffer*. The counter is placed in the extended identifier field. The two leftmost bits, which represent the *command code*, are defined as follows:

01: the data frame contains a MAC of data;

10: the data frame contains an epoch value e_{id_i};

11: the data frame contains a MAC of an epoch e_{id_i}.

Authentication Error Channel (AEC)

Each node connected to CAN has an Authentication Error Channel, AEC. This is used for resynchronisation purposes. The `AUTH_FAIL` signal is sent on the AEC. Nodes which are broadcasters of messages with id_i become subscribers of the AEC of the nodes listening to id_i. The `AUTH_FAIL` signal is defined as a set of two messages. The first data frame contains the id of the message which failed MAC verification (id_{failed}), concatenated with the lower 53 bits of the AEC epoch counter ($lsb_{53}(e_{id_{AEC}})$). Sending the epoch within the data frame ensures the receiving nodes can verify they have the correct values, and a resynchronisation procedure for the AEC is not needed. The second message contains the MAC of the previous one, as shown in Fig. 6. Sending an `AUTH_FAIL` signal is considered a rare event, therefore overwriting messages within the buffer are not of concern, in contrast to data transmission. Thus, we can use the same identifier (id_{AEC}) for both message types.

Table 1 shows a small example of an extended communication matrix. The *identifiers* highlighted are the additional identifiers introduced by LEIA. Identifiers 0x005, 0x011 and 0x016 correspond to the *Authentication Channel*, while identifiers 0x7FD, 0x7FE and 0x7FF correspond to the *Authentication Error Channel*.

The procedures of sending authenticated messages and re-synchronisation, complete with *command code* placement are shown in Figs. 7 and 8.

The CAN bus has a static configuration. Due to this, LEIA can be implemented in two ways, depending on the functionality of the ECU. As described above, the protocol requires each message to be accompanied by a MAC. If

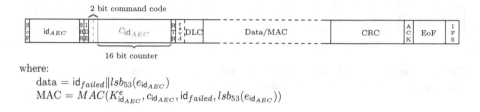

where:

$$\text{data} = \text{id}_{failed} \| lsb_{53}(e_{\text{id}_{AEC}})$$
$$\text{MAC} = MAC(K^e_{\text{id}_{AEC}}, c_{\text{id}_{AEC}}, \text{id}_{failed}, lsb_{53}(e_{\text{id}_{AEC}}))$$

Fig. 6. Data frame structure for AUTH_FAIL signal.

Table 1. Extended communication matrix example. 'S' stands for Sender and 'R' for Receiver.

Identifier	Node A	Node B	Node C	Node D
id = 0x004	S		R	
id = 0x010		R	R	S
id = 0x015		S		R

$\rightarrow$

Identifier	Node A	Node B	Node C	Node D
id = 0x004	S		R	
id = 0x005	S		R	
id = 0x010		R	R	S
id = 0x011		R	R	S
id = 0x015		S		R
id = 0x016		S		R
id = 0x7FD		S		R
id = 0x7FE	R		S	R
id = 0x7FF		R		S

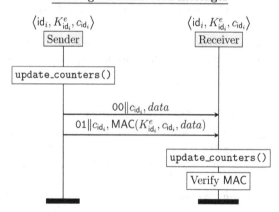

Fig. 7. Message authentication between sender S and receiver R for message with identifier id_i, with command code.

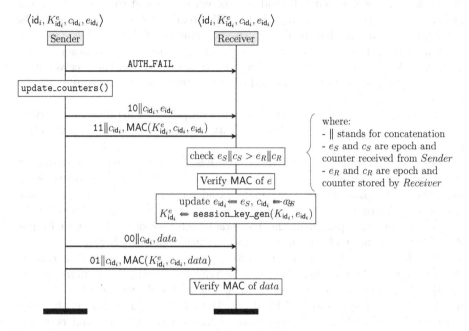

Fig. 8. Message authentication failure and resynchronisation procedure, between sender S and receiver R for message with identifier id_i, with command code placement.

applied to all ECUs, this doubles the communication overhead. However, for nodes not involved in safety-critical functions, the protocol can be implemented such that one MAC is sent after n messages, where n can be decided based on the node's security requirements. This allows manufacturers to choose a most suitable trade-off between security and bandwidth for their vehicles.

The CAN is an architecture which is highly susceptible to denial of service (DoS) attacks. LEIA is not a solution that tackles this issue, as it is out of the scope of our goals. However, DoS attacks do not affect the security of the protocol. In fact, under LEIA, messages that are not correctly authenticated are not parsed, saving ECUs time and computation energy.

In the case an attacker fully compromises and takes control of an ECU, for the ids the node broadcasts or listens on, the attacker will unavoidably be able to generate valid MACs, but not for any other id. This is not a problem of our protocol but an inherit limitation of using symmetric key cryptography.

An attacker can collect some AUTH_FAIL answers from the sender, knowing one of the receiver nodes is offline. When the receiver node joins the network and sends the AUTH_FAIL signal, as it does not have the correct counter and epoch values, the attacker sends a stored answer. The receiver will accept the message, provided the stored counter and epoch are lower than the received ones. However, due to the design of CAN, the initial AUTH_FAIL signal is also received by the sender node, which will send the correct epoch and counter values. The attacker can destroy these frames, but S will broadcast them again, due to the error handling mechanism of CAN. After a number of destroyed frames, the CAN flags the attacker as error passive, meaning it cannot destroy other frames. Therefore, the correct message of S will be transmitted and the receiver node will be able to update its values accordingly. Communication then resumes under the protocol.

We would like to emphasize that all other proposed authentication protocols from the literature are susceptible to DoS attacks and do not deal with attackers taking full control over an ECU.

Next we elaborate on how LEIA satisfies the requirements laid out by AUTOSAR 4.2, Secure On Board Communication Module. Regarding freshness, the specification states both sending and receiving sides need to maintain a Freshness Value (e.g. counter, timestamp). In LEIA, this is achieved by the 16-bit counters c_{id_i}, placed in the Extended Identifier field of a Data Frame. AUTOSAR recommends the use of 128-bit keys, which LEIA respects though K_{id}. It also states that, depending on the authentication algorithm chosen, the Message Authentication Code can be truncated, with a minimum recommended length of 64-bit. As described in our protocol, we use 64-bit MACs, which fit in the 8-byte Payload Field of a Data Frame. Furthermore, the standard requires the MAC to be calculated based on the id, data and complete freshness value. In LEIA, the MAC is computed based on the session key $K_{id_i}^e$, which is uniquely associated with an identifier id_i, the counter c_{id_i} and the data to be transmitted. Regarding MAC verification failure, SecOC requires the receiver to attempt to verify for a number of times (defined by the parameter SecOCFreshnessCounterSyncAttempts), after which the data is dropped. LEIA uses the resync procedure, in order to keep the protocol in synch, and avoid a possible internal denial of service attack due to the de-synchronisation of counters.

6   Conclusion

We have proposed a new lightweight authentication protocol for CAN, LEIA, that allows ECUs to authenticate each other, therefore preventing a number of attacks presented in the literature. We have proven the protocol secure under the unforgeability assumption of the MAC scheme under a chosen message attack. LEIA has been designed to run under the stringent time and bandwidth constraints of automotive applications, and is backwards compatible with existing CAN configuration. LEIA is the first AUTOSAR compliant lightweight authentication protocol available in the literature. Also, our protocol achieves higher security levels than previously proposed solutions, without the need of additional hardware components or substantial implementation costs. Finally, we have taken into consideration the real-world requirements and constraints of the

CAN bus, and discussed how we mitigated and overcame them. The properties of LEIA make it suitable for deployment in automotive applications as it strikes the right balance between practicality, cost, latency and security.

Acknowledgements. This research was partly sponsored by EPSRC, through industrial CASE award 14220107. The authors are thankful to Paul Sanderson and David Battersby for their support.

References

1. AUTOSAR: AUTOSAR Specification 4.2. http://www.autosar.org/specifications/release-42/
2. Bogdanov, A.: Linear slide attacks on the keeloq block cipher. In: Pei, D., Yung, M., Lin, D., Wu, C. (eds.) Inscrypt 2007. LNCS, vol. 4990, pp. 66–80. Springer, Heidelberg (2008)
3. Bruni, A., Sojka, M., Nielson, F., Nielson, H.R.: Formal security analysis of the MaCAN protocol. In: Albert, E., Sekerinski, E. (eds.) IFM 2014. LNCS, vol. 8739, pp. 241–255. Springer, Heidelberg (2014)
4. Checkoway, S., McCoy, D., Kantor, B., Anderson, D., Shacham, H., Savage, S., Koscher, K., Czeskis, A., Roesner, F., Kohno, T., et al.: Comprehensive experimental analyses of automotive attack surfaces. In: 20th USENIX Security Symposium (USENIX Security 2011), San Francisco (2011)
5. Courtois, N.T., Bard, G.V., Wagner, D.: Algebraic and slide attacks on KeeLoq. In: Nyberg, K. (ed.) FSE 2008. LNCS, vol. 5086, pp. 97–115. Springer, Heidelberg (2008)
6. Dolev, D., Yao, A.C.: On the security of public key protocols. IEEE Trans. Inf. Theory **29**(2), 198–208 (1983)
7. Garcia, F.D., Oswald, D., Kasper, T., Pavlidès, P.: Lock it and still lose it - on the (in)security of automotive remote keyless entry systems. In: 25nd USENIX Security Symposium (USENIX Security 2016). USENIX Association (to appear, 2016)
8. Greenberg, A.: Hackers Remotely Kill a Jeep on the Highway - with me in it (2015). http://www.wired.com/2015/07/hackers-remotely-kill-jeep-highway/
9. Groza, B., Murvay, S., van Herrewege, A., Verbauwhede, I.: LiBrA-CAN: a lightweight broadcast authentication protocol for controller area networks. In: Pieprzyk, J., Sadeghi, A.-R., Manulis, M. (eds.) CANS 2012. LNCS, vol. 7712, pp. 185–200. Springer, Heidelberg (2012)
10. Hartkopp, O., Reuber, C., Schilling, R.: MaCAN - message authenticated CAN. In: 10th International Conference on Embedded Security in Cars (ESCAR 2012), Berlin, Germany, vol. 6 (2012)
11. Hazem, A., Fahmy, H.A.: LCAP - a lightweight CAN authentication protocol for securing in-vehicle networks. In: 10th International Conference on Embedded Security in Cars (ESCAR 2012), Berlin, Germany, vol. 6 (2012)
12. Indesteege, S., Keller, N., Dunkelman, O., Biham, E., Preneel, B.: A practical attack on KeeLoq. In: Smart, N.P. (ed.) EUROCRYPT 2008. LNCS, vol. 4965, pp. 1–18. Springer, Heidelberg (2008)
13. ISO: 11898–1: 2003 - Road Vehicles - Controller Area Network. International Organization for Standardization, Geneva, Switzerland (2003)

14. Kasper, M., Kasper, T., Moradi, A., Paar, C.: Breaking KEELOQ in a flash: on extracting keys at lightning speed. In: Preneel, B. (ed.) AFRICACRYPT 2009. LNCS, vol. 5580, pp. 403–420. Springer, Heidelberg (2009)
15. Koscher, K., Czeskis, A., Roesner, F., Patel, S., Kohno, T., Checkoway, S., McCoy, D., Kantor, B., Anderson, D., Shacham, H., et al.: Experimental Security Analysis of a Modern Automobile. In: 31st IEEE Symposium on Security & Privacy (S&P 2010), pp. 447–462. IEEE (2010)
16. Kurachi, R., Matsubara, Y., Takada, H., Adachi, N., Miyashita, Y., Horihata, S.: CaCAN - centralised authentication system in CAN. In: 12th International Conference on Embedded Security in Cars (ESCAR 2014) (2014)
17. Miller, C., Valasek, C.: Remote Exploitation of an Unaltered Passenger Vehicle (2015). http://illmatics.com/Remote%20Car%20Hacking.pdf
18. Studnia, I., Nicomette, V., Alata, E., Deswarte, Y., Kaâniche, M., Laarouchi, Y.: Survey on security threats and protection mechanisms in embedded automotive networks. In: 2013 43rd Annual IEEE/IFIP Conference on Dependable Systems and Networks Workshop (DSN-W 2013), pp. 1–12. IEEE (2013)
19. Van Herrewege, A., Singelee, D., Verbauwhede, I.: CANAuth - a simple, backward compatible broadcast authentication protocol for CAN bus. In: ECRYPT Workshop on Lightweight Cryptography 2011 (2011)
20. Vaudenay, S.: On privacy models for RFID. In: Kurosawa, K. (ed.) ASIACRYPT 2007. LNCS, vol. 4833, pp. 68–87. Springer, Heidelberg (2007)
21. Verdult, R., Garcia, F.D.: Cryptanalysis of the megamos crypto automotive immobilizer. In: USENIX; login, vol. 40(6), pp. 17–22. USENIX Association (2015)
22. Verdult, R., Garcia, F.D., Balasch, J.: Gone in 360 seconds: Hijacking with Hitag2. In: 21st USENIX Security Symposium (USENIX Security 2012), pp. 237–252 (2012)
23. Ziermann, T., Wildermann, S., Teich, J.: CAN+: A new backward-compatible controller area network (CAN) Protocol with up to 16x Higher Data Rates. In: Design, Automation & Test in Europe Conference & Exhibition (DATE 2009), pp. 1088–1093. IEEE (2009)
24. Verdult, R., Garcia, F.D., Ege, B.: Dismantling megamos crypto: wirelessly lockpicking a vehicle immobilizer. In: 22nd USENIX Security Symposium (USENIX Security 2013), pp. 703–718. USENIX Association (2015)

Privacy, Discovery, and Authentication for the Internet of Things

David J. Wu[1(✉)], Ankur Taly[2], Asim Shankar[2], and Dan Boneh[1]

[1] Stanford University, Stanford, USA
dwu4@cs.stanford.edu
[2] Google, Mountain View, USA

Abstract. Automatic service discovery is essential to realizing the full potential of the Internet of Things (IoT). While discovery protocols like Multicast DNS, Apple AirDrop, and Bluetooth Low Energy have gained widespread adoption across both IoT and mobile devices, most of these protocols do not offer any form of privacy control for the service, and often leak sensitive information such as service type, device hostname, device owner's identity, and more in the clear.

To address the need for better privacy in both the IoT and the mobile landscape, we develop two protocols for private service discovery and private mutual authentication. Our protocols provide private and authentic service advertisements, zero round-trip (0-RTT) mutual authentication, and are provably secure in the Canetti-Krawczyk key-exchange model. In contrast to alternatives, our protocols are lightweight and require minimal modification to existing key-exchange protocols. We integrate our protocols into an existing open-source distributed applications framework, and provide benchmarks on multiple hardware platforms: Intel Edisons, Raspberry Pis, smartphones, laptops, and desktops. Finally, we discuss some privacy limitations of the Apple AirDrop protocol (a peer-to-peer file sharing mechanism) and show how to improve the privacy of Apple AirDrop using our private mutual authentication protocol.

1 Introduction

Consider a smart home with dozens of IoT devices: an alarm system, a nanny camera, health monitoring devices, house controls (e.g., lighting, heating), and electronics. Many of these devices need to be controlled by multiple people, including residents, guests, employees, and repairmen. The devices must be easily discoverable by all these people.

To provide a good experience, IoT devices advertise the services they offer using a service discovery mechanism. Examples include Multicast DNS (mDNS) [24,25], Apple Bonjour [3], Bluetooth Low Energy (BLE) [5], and Universal Plug-N-Play (UPnP) [6]. These mechanisms require only a broadcast communication channel between the devices (unlike older discovery protocols [4,27,57] that need a directory service). Moreover, these protocols adhere to

The full version of this paper with complete proofs is available at http://arxiv.org/abs/1604.06959.

© Springer International Publishing Switzerland 2016
I. Askoxylakis et al. (Eds.): ESORICS 2016, Part II, LNCS 9879, pp. 301–319, 2016.
DOI: 10.1007/978-3-319-45741-3_16

the zero configuration networking charter (*Zeroconf*) [2] and can operate with minimal user intervention.

Privacy is an important feature often missing in zero-configuration service discovery protocols (e.g., Zeroconf) [37,38,40,49]. Services broadcast extensive information about themselves in the clear to make it easy for clients to discover them. Advertisements often include sensitive information such as service type, device hostname, and the device owner's identity. This poses a threat when the service is running on a private device (e.g., an alarm system or a smart watch). Identities obtained from personal devices can be used for user profiling, tracking, and launching social engineering attacks. A recent study [40] revealed that 59 % of all devices advertise their owner's name in the clear, which is considered harmful by more than 90 % of the device owners. Indeed, one would not want random visitors, or passerbys, to "discover" the alarm system in their home. Only authorized clients, such as the home owner and her family, a technician, or local police, should be able to discover this device.

In this work, we address this problem by building a new discovery and authentication mechanism that respects the privacy of both sides.

Private service discovery. Our goal is to ensure that services are only discoverable by an authorized set of clients. This problem is challenging as on one hand, services want to advertise themselves only after confirming that the client trying to discover them is authorized to see them. On the other hand, clients want to reveal their identity only after verifying that the service they are talking to is the desired one. In particular, a client device, such as a smartphone, should not simply identify itself to every device in the wild that requests it. This leads to a chicken-and-egg problem reminiscent of the settings addressed by secret handshakes and hidden credentials [11,12,31,35,36,46].

Private mutual authentication. A closely related privacy problem arises during authentication between mutually suspicious entities. Most existing mutual authentication protocols (SIGMA [23,41], JFK [10], and TLS [28]) require one of the parties (typically the server) to reveal its identity to its peer before the other, effectively making that party's identity public to anyone who communicates with it. This is undesirable when the participants are personal end-user devices, where neither device is inclined to reveal its identity before learning that of its peer. Private mutual authentication is the problem of designing a mutual authentication protocol wherein each end learns the identity of its peer only if it satisfies the peer's authorization policy.[1]

An application. Our private discovery protocols apply broadly to many identification and key-exchange settings. Here we describe a common mobile-to-mobile example: peer-to-peer file sharing. Protocols such as AirDrop and Shoutr have become popular among mobile users for sharing photos and other content with their friends. These peer-to-peer protocols typically work by having a participant

---

[1] While protocols like SIGMA-I [23,41] and TLS 1.3 [43,50] can ensure privacy against passive adversaries, they do *not* provide privacy against active attackers.

start a sharing service and making it publicly discoverable. The other device then discovers the service and connects to it to complete the file transfer. While this offers a seamless sharing experience, it compromises privacy for the device that makes itself discoverable—nearby devices on the same network can also listen to the advertisement and obtain identifiers from it. A private service discovery mechanism would make the service advertisement available only to the intended devices and no one else. The AirDrop protocol offers a "contacts-only" mode for additional privacy, but as we show in Sect. 2.1, this mechanism leaks significant private information. The private discovery protocols we develop in this paper provide an efficient solution to these problems.

1.1   Our Contributions

This paper presents private mutual authentication and service discovery protocols for IoT and mobile settings. Given the network connectivity constraints implicit to these settings, our protocols do not require devices to maintain constant connectivity to an external proxy or directory service in the cloud. Furthermore, the protocols do not require the participants to have an out-of-band shared secret, thereby allowing devices with no pre-existing relationships to discover each other (in accordance with their respective privacy policies).

Protocol construction. Our protocols are designed for distributed public-key infrastructures, such as the Simple Distributed Security Infrastructure (SDSI) [51]. Each principal has a public and private key-pair (for a signature scheme), and a hierarchical human-readable name bound to its public key by a certificate chain. The key primitive in our design is an encryption scheme that allows messages to be encrypted under an authorization policy so that it can be decrypted only by principals satisfying the policy. Using this primitive, we design a mutual authentication protocol where one party sends its identity (certificate chain) encrypted under its authorization policy. This protects the privacy of that party. The other party maintains its privacy by revealing its identity only *after* verifying the first party's identity. The same primitive is also used to construct a private service discovery protocol by having a service encrypt its advertisement under its authorization policy before broadcasting.

The service advertisements in our discovery protocol carry a signed semi-static Diffie-Hellman (DH) key. The signature provides authenticity for the advertisements and protects clients from connecting to an impostor service. The semi-static DH key enables clients to establish a secure session with the service using zero round-trips (0-RTT), similar to what is provided in TLS 1.3 [43,50].

The authorization policies considered in this work are based on name prefixes. For instance, a technician Bob from HomeSecurity Corp. may have the name HomeSecurityCorp/Technician/Bob, and a home security system might have a policy that only users whose name starts with HomeSecurityCorp/Technician are allowed to discover it. Encrypting messages under a prefix-based authorization policy is possible using a prefix encryption scheme [44], which can be constructed using off-the-shelf identity-based encryption (IBE) schemes [19,20].

Protocol analysis. We give a full specification of our private mutual authentication and service discovery protocols in Sects. 4 and 5. We also discuss a range of practical issues related to our protocol such as replay protection, ensuring perfect forward secrecy, and amortizing the overhead of the prefix encryption. In the full version [54], we provide a rigorous proof of the security and privacy of both protocols in the Canetti-Krawczyk key-exchange model [22,23,41].

Implementation and evaluation. We implemented and deployed our protocols in the *Vanadium* open-source distributed application framework [1]. We measured the end-to-end latency overhead for our private mutual authentication protocol on an Intel Edison, a Raspberry Pi, a smartphone, a laptop, and a desktop. On the desktop, the protocol completes in 9.5 ms, which corresponds to a 1.8x slowdown over the SIGMA-I protocol that does *not* provide mutual privacy. On the Nexus 5X and the Raspberry Pi, the protocol completes in just over 300 ms (about a 3.8x slowdown over SIGMA-I), which makes it suitable for user-interactive services such as AirDrop and home security system controls that do not have high throughput requirements.

For the discovery protocol, a service's private discovery message consists of approximately 820 bytes of data. Since mDNS broadcasts support up to 1300 bytes of data, it is straightforward to deploy our discovery protocol over mDNS. Based on our benchmarks, our protocols are practical on a range of IoT devices, such as thermostats (e.g., Nest), security systems (e.g., Dropcam), and smart switches (e.g., Belkin Wemo). All of these devices have hardware comparable to a Pi or an Intel Edison. In fact, the Intel Edison is marketed primarily as a platform for building IoT applications. Moreover, as our AirDrop analysis demonstrates, many of the privacy issues we describe are not limited to only the IoT setting. Indeed, in Sect. 6.4, we show how our private mutual authentication and discovery protocols can be efficiently deployed to solve privacy problems in peer-to-peer interactions on smartphones. On more constrained processors such as the ARM Cortex M0, however, we expect the handshakes to take several seconds to complete. This makes our protocols less suitable in Cortex M0 applications that require fast session setup. Nonetheless, our protocols are sufficient for a wide range of existing IoT and mobile scenarios.

2   Desired Protocol Features

In this section, we define the privacy properties and features that we seek in our protocols. We begin with a case study of Apple's AirDrop protocol, and use it to motivate our privacy concerns and desired features.

2.1   Case Study: Apple AirDrop

AirDrop is a protocol for transferring files between two devices running recent versions of OS X or iOS. It is designed to work whenever two AirDrop-enabled devices are close to each other and even when they do not have Internet access.

AirDrop uses both Bluetooth Low Energy (BLE) and Apple's peer-to-peer WiFi technology (awdl) for device discovery and file transfer.

To receive files, devices make themselves discoverable by senders. AirDrop offers two modes for making devices discoverable: *everyone*, which makes the device discoverable by all nearby devices, and *contacts-only* (default), which makes the receiving device discoverable only by senders in its contacts. The contacts-only mode is meant to be a privacy mechanism and can be viewed as a solution to the private service discovery problem for the "contacts-only" policy.

Protocol overview. We analyzed the AirDrop protocol to understand its privacy properties and see how it solves the chicken-and-egg problem of private mutual authentication. We describe the protocol in the full version of this paper.

Privacy weaknesses in Apple AirDrop. Our analysis indicates that AirDrop employs two main privacy checks in contacts-only mode. First, a receiving device responds only if the sender's identifier (received over BLE) matches one of its contacts, and second, a communication channel is established (via TLS 1.2 with client authentication[2]) between a sender and receiver only if their respective certificates match a contact on their peer's device. While necessary, these checks are insufficient to protect the privacy of the sender and receiver. Below, we enumerate some of the privacy problems with the existing protocol.

- **Sender and receiver privacy and tracking.** The use of TLS 1.2 with client authentication causes both the sender and receiver to exchange certificates in the clear. This makes their identities, as specified by their certificates, visible to even a *passive* eavesdropper on the network. Moreover, the public keys in the certificates allow the eavesdropper to track the sender and receiver in the future. Protecting the privacy of *both* parties against active attackers, requires *private* mutual authentication, as constructed in Sect. 4.
- **Sender impersonation.** Another privacy problem is that the sender's identifier advertised over BLE can be forged or replayed by an attacker to trick an honest receiver into matching it against its contacts. Based on the receiver's response, the attacker learns whether the receiver has the sender in their contacts, and moreover, could try to initiate a TLS session with the receiver to obtain its certificate. To protect against this kind of impersonation attack, discovery broadcasts must provide some kind of *authenticity*, as in Sect. 5.

2.2   Protocol Design Goals

The privacy properties of AirDrop are insufficient to solve the private service discovery problem. While our case study in Sect. 2.1 focuses exclusively on the AirDrop protocol, most existing key-exchange and service discovery protocols do not provide robust privacy and authenticity guarantees. We survey some of these alternative protocols in Sect. 8. At a high level, our primary privacy objectives,

---

[2] All AirDrop-enabled devices have an RSA public and private key pair and an iCloud certificate for the owner's identity.

which should hold in the presence of both passive and active network attackers, are as follows:

- **Mutual privacy.** The protocols must ensure that the identities and any identifying attributes of the protocol participants are only revealed to authorized recipients. For service discovery, this applies to both the service being advertised and the clients trying to discover it.
- **Authentic advertisements.** Service advertisements should be unforgeable and authentic. Otherwise, an attacker may forge a service advertisement to determine if a client is interested in the service.

Finally, to ensure that our protocols are applicable in both IoT and peer-to-peer settings, we impose additional constraints on the protocol design:

- **No out-of-band pairing for participants.** The protocol should not require participants to exchange certain information or secrets out-of-band. This is especially important for the discovery protocol as the service may not know all the clients that might try to discover it in the future.
- **No cloud dependency during protocol execution.** The protocol should not rely on an external service in the cloud, such as a proxy or a directory service. Protocols that depend on cloud-based services assume that the participating devices maintain reliable Internet access. This assumption fails for many IoT devices, including devices that only communicate over Bluetooth, or ones present in spaces where Internet access is unreliable.

3   Preliminaries

In this section, we describe our identity and authorization model, as well as introduce the cryptographic primitives we use in our constructions.

Identity and authorization model. We define our protocols for a generic distributed public-key infrastructure, such as SDSI [51]. We assume each principal has a public and private key-pair for a signature scheme and one or more hierarchically-structured human-readable names bound to its public key via a certificate chain. For instance, a television set owned by Alice might have a certificate chain binding the name Alice/Devices/TV to it. Our protocols are agnostic to the specific format of certificates and how they are distributed.

Principals authenticate each other by exchanging certificate chains and providing a signature on a fresh (session-specific) nonce. During the authentication protocol, a principal validates its peer's certificate chain, and extracts the name bound to the certificate chain. Authorization decisions are based on this extracted name, and *not* the public key. For example, Alice may authorize all principals with names matching the prefix pattern Alice/Devices/* to access her television set. In this work, we consider prefix-based authorization policies. These prefix-based policies can be used to support group-based access control policies by viewing "subdomains" (e.g., Alice/Family) as groups.

3.1 Cryptographic and Protocol Building Blocks

We write $\mathbb{Z}_p$ to denote the group of integers modulo p. For a distribution $\mathcal{D}$, we write $x \leftarrow \mathcal{D}$ to denote that x is drawn from $\mathcal{D}$. For a finite set S, we write $x \xleftarrow{\text{R}} S$ to denote that x is drawn uniformly at random from S.

Identity-based encryption and prefix encryption. Identity-based encryption (IBE) [19,20,26,53] is a generalization of public-key encryption where public keys can be arbitrary strings, or *identities*. We give more details in the full version [54]. Prefix encryption [44] is a generalization of IBE where the secret key SK_{ID} for an identity ID can decrypt all ciphertexts encrypted to any identity ID' that is a prefix of ID (in IBE, decryption succeeds only if ID = ID'). Prefix encryption allows for messages to be encrypted under a prefix-based policy such that the resulting ciphertext can only be decrypted by principals satisfying the policy.

It is straightforward to construct prefix encryption from IBE. The following construction is adapted from the Lewko-Waters scheme [44]. The key for an identity ID $= s_1/s_2/\cdots/s_n$ consists of n different IBE keys for the following sequence of identities: $(s_1), (s_1/s_2), \ldots, (s_1/s_2/\cdots/s_n)$. Encryption to an identity ID' is just IBE encryption to the identity ID'. Given a secret key SK_{ID} for ID, if ID' is a prefix of ID, then SK_{ID} contains an IBE identity key for ID'.

The syntax of a prefix encryption scheme is very similar to that of an IBE scheme. Secret keys are still associated with identities, but ciphertexts are now associated with prefix-constrained policies. In the following, we write PE.Enc(MPK, π, m) to denote an encryption algorithm that takes as input the public key MPK, a message m, a prefix-constrained policy π, and outputs a ciphertext CT. When there is no ambiguity, we will treat MPK as an implicit parameter to PE.Enc. We write PE.Dec(SK_{ID}, CT) for the decryption algorithm that takes in a ciphertext CT and a secret key SK_{ID} (for an identity ID) and outputs a message if ID matches the ciphertext policy π, and a special symbol $\perp$ otherwise.

Other cryptographic primitives. We write $\{m\}_k$ to denote an authenticated encryption [13,15,52] of a message m under a key k, and KDF($\cdot$) to denote a key-derivation function [29,42]. We describe these additional primitives as well as the cryptographic assumptions (Hash Diffie-Hellman and Strong Diffie-Hellman [9]) we use in our security analysis in the full version.

Key-exchange model. We analyze the security of our private mutual authentication and privacy service discovery protocols in the Canetti-Krawczyk [22,23,41] key-exchange model, which models the capabilities of an active network adversary. We defer the formal specification of this model and our generalization of it to the service discovery setting to the full version.

4   Private Mutual Authentication Protocol

In this section, we describe our private mutual authentication protocol and discuss some of its features and limitations. We use the identity and authorization model described in Sect. 3.

Protocol execution environment. In our setting, each principal has a signing/verification key-pair and a set of names (e.g., Alice/Devices/TV) bound to its public verification key via certificate chains. For each name, a principal possesses an identity secret key (for the prefix encryption scheme) extracted for that name. The secret key extraction is carried out by IBE root authorities (who possess the IBE master secret key MSK), which may coincide with certificate authorities. Finally, each principal also has one or more prefix-constrained authorization policies.

In our protocol description, we refer to the initiator of the protocol as the *client* and the responder as the *server*. For a party P, we write ID_P to denote a certificate chain binding P's public key to one of its identities. For a message m, we write $\text{SIG}_P(m)$ to denote P's signature on m. We refer to each instantiation of the key-exchange protocol as a "session," and each session is identified by a unique session id, denoted sid.

Protocol specification. Our starting point is the 3-round SIGMA-I protocol [23,41] which provides mutual authentication as well as privacy against passive adversaries. Similar to the SIGMA-I protocol, our protocol operates over a cyclic group $\mathbb{G}$ of prime order where the Hash-DH [9] assumption holds. Let g be a generator of $\mathbb{G}$. We now describe our private mutual authentication protocol. The message flow is illustrated in Fig. 1.

1. To initiate a session with id sid, the client C chooses $x \xleftarrow{\text{R}} \mathbb{Z}_p$, and sends (sid, g^x) to the server.
2. Upon receiving a start message (sid, g^x) from a client, the server S chooses $y \xleftarrow{\text{R}} \mathbb{Z}_p$, and does the following:
   (a) Encrypt its name ID_S using the prefix encryption scheme under its policy π_S to obtain an encrypted identity $\text{CT}_S \leftarrow \text{PE.Enc}(\pi_S, \text{ID}_S)$.
   (b) Derive authenticated encryption keys $(\text{htk}, \text{atk}) = \text{KDF}(g^x, g^y, g^{xy})$ for the handshake and application-layer messages, respectively.
   (c) Compute a signature $\sigma = \text{SIG}_S(\text{sid}, \text{CT}_S, g^x, g^y)$ on its encrypted identity and the ephemeral session state, and encrypt (CT_S, σ) using htk to obtain a ciphertext c.

   The server replies to the client with (sid, g^y, c).
3. When the client receives a response (sid, g^y, c), it derives the keys $(\text{htk}, \text{atk}) = \text{KDF}(g^x, g^y, g^{xy})$. It tries to decrypt c with htk and aborts if decryption fails. It parses the decrypted value as (CT_S, σ_S) and checks whether its identity ID_C satisfies the server's policy π_S (revealed by CT_S). If the client satisfies the server's policy, it decrypts CT_S using its identity key SK_C to obtain the server's identity ID_S. If ID_S satisfies the client's policy π_C and σ_S is a valid signature on $(\text{sid}, \text{CT}_S, g^x, g^y)$ under the public key identified by ID_S,

$$C(\text{ID}_C, \pi_C) \xrightarrow{\quad \text{sid}, \; g^x \quad} S(\text{ID}_S, \pi_S)$$

$$\xleftarrow{\quad \text{sid}, \; g^y, \; \{\text{PE.Enc}(\pi_S, \text{ID}_S), \text{SIG}_S(\text{sid}, \text{CT}_S, g^x, g^y)\}_{\text{htk}} \quad}$$

$$\xrightarrow{\quad \text{sid}, \; \{\text{ID}_C, \text{SIG}_C(\text{sid}, \text{ID}_C, g^x, g^y)\}_{\text{htk}} \quad}$$

Fig. 1. Message flow between the client C (with certificate ID_C and policy π_C) and the server S (with certificate ID_S and policy π_S) for the private mutual authentication protocol. Both the client and the server possess a secret signing key. The associated verification keys are bound to their identities via the certificates ID_C and ID_S, respectively. For a message m, $\text{SIG}_C(m)$ and $\text{SIG}_S(m)$ denote the client's and server's signature on m, respectively. Both the client and server know the master public key for the prefix-based encryption scheme, and the client possesses a secret key SK_C for the prefix-based encryption scheme for the identity associated with its certificate ID_C.

the client replies to the server with the session id sid and an encryption c' of $(\text{ID}_C, \text{SIG}_C(\text{sid}, \text{ID}_C, g^x, g^y))$ under htk. Otherwise, the client aborts.

4. Upon receiving the client's response (sid, c'), the server tries to decrypt c' using htk and aborts if decryption fails. It parses the decrypted value as (ID_C, σ_C) and verifies that ID_C satisfies its policy and that σ_C is a valid signature on $(\text{sid}, \text{ID}_C, g^x, g^y)$ under the public key identified by ID_C. If so, the handshake completes with atk as the shared session key and where the client believes it is talking to ID_S and the server believes it is talking to ID_C. Otherwise, the server aborts.

4.1 Protocol Analysis

In this section, we highlight some properties of our private mutual authentication protocol. In the full version [54], we also discuss policy privacy, unlinkability, and caching the encrypted certificate chains.

Comparison with SIGMA-I. Our authentication protocol is very similar to the SIGMA-I key-exchange protocol [41, Sect. 5.2], but with the following key difference: the server's certificate, ID_S, is sent encrypted under a prefix encryption scheme. Moreover, instead of deriving separate MAC and encryption keys from the shared DH key, we combine the two primitives by using an authenticated encryption scheme. Since we have only added an additional layer of prefix encryption to the certificates, each party's signature verification key is still bound to its identity as before. Thus, the proof that the SIGMA-I protocol is a secure key-exchange protocol [23, Sect. 5.3] (with perfect forward secrecy) translates to our setting.

Identity privacy. The identity of the server is sent encrypted under its prefix policy, so by security of the prefix encryption scheme, it is only revealed to clients that satisfy the policy. Conversely, an honest client only reveals its identity after it has verified that the server's identity satisfies its policy. We formally define our notion of mutual privacy and show that the protocol in Fig. 1 achieves this notion in the full version. In contrast, the SIGMA-I protocol does not provide such a guarantee as the identity of the server is revealed to active adversaries.

Security theorem. We state the security theorem for our private mutual authentication protocol here, but defer the formal proof to the full version [54].

Theorem 4.1 (Private Mutual Authentication). *The protocol in Fig. 1 is a secure and private key-exchange protocol in the Canetti-Krawczyk key-exchange model assuming the Hash Diffie-Hellman assumption in $\mathbb{G}$ and the security of all underlying cryptographic primitives.*

5   Private Service Discovery Protocol

In this section, we describe our private service discovery protocol. The primary goal is to make a service discoverable only by parties that satisfy its authorization policy. Additionally, once a client has discovered a service, it should be able to authenticate to the server using zero round-trips (0-RTT), i.e., include application data on the first flow of the handshake. 0-RTT protocols are invaluable for IoT since devices are often constrained in both computation and bandwidth.

The key idea in our design is to have the service include a fresh DH share and a signature in its advertisement. The DH share allows 0-RTT client authentication, and the signature provides authenticity for the service advertisement. Next, the service encrypts its advertisement under its policy π_S before broadcasting to ensure that only authorized clients are able to discover it. A similar mechanism for (non-private) 0-RTT authentication is present in OPTLS and the TLS 1.3 specification [43,50], although OPTLS only provides server authentication.

Protocol specification. Our protocol works over a cyclic group $\mathbb{G}$ of prime order p with generator g where the Strong-DH and Hash-DH assumptions [9] hold. The private discovery protocol can be separated into a broadcast protocol and a 0-RTT mutual authentication protocol. Each broadcast is associated with a unique broadcast identifier bid and each session with a unique session identifier sid. The protocol execution environment is the same as that described in Sect. 4. The basic message flow for the private discovery protocol is illustrated in Fig. 2.

Service broadcast message. To setup a new broadcast with broadcast id bid, the server S chooses a fresh DH exponent $s \xleftarrow{\text{R}} \mathbb{Z}_p$, and encrypts $(\text{ID}_S, g^s, \text{SIG}_S(\text{bid}, \text{ID}_S, g^s))$ using the prefix encryption scheme under its authorization policy π_S to obtain a broadcast ciphertext CT_S. The server broadcasts $(\text{bid}, \text{CT}_S)$.

0-RTT mutual authentication. Upon receiving a broadcast $(\text{bid}, \text{CT}_S)$, a client performs the following steps to establish a session sid with the server:

1. The client C checks that its identity ID_C satisfies the server's authorization policy π_S (included with CT_S). If so, it decrypts CT_S using its prefix encryption secret key and parses the decrypted value as $(\text{ID}_S, g^s, \sigma_S)$. It verifies that ID_S satisfies its policy π_C and that σ_S is a valid signature on $(\text{bid}, \text{ID}_S, g^s)$ under the public key identified by ID_S. If any step fails, the client aborts.

2. Next, the client chooses an ephemeral DH exponent $x \xleftarrow{\text{R}} \mathbb{Z}_p$. It derives authenticated encryption keys $(\text{htk}, \text{htk}', \text{eadk}) = \text{KDF}(g^s, g^x, g^{sx})$, where htk and htk' are used to encrypt handshake messages, and eadk is used to encrypt any early application data the client wants to include with its connection request. The client encrypts the tuple $(\text{ID}_S, \text{ID}_C, \text{SIG}_C(\text{bid}, \text{sid}, \text{ID}_S, \text{ID}_C, g^s, g^x))$ under htk to obtain a ciphertext c_1 and any early application data under eadk to obtain a ciphertext c_2. It sends $(\text{bid}, \text{sid}, g^x, c_1, c_2)$ to the server.

3. When the server receives a message from a client of the form $(\text{bid}, \text{sid}, g^x, c_1, c_2)$, it first derives the encryption keys $(\text{htk}, \text{htk}', \text{eadk}) = \text{KDF}(g^s, g^x, g^{sx})$, where s is the DH exponent it chose for broadcast bid. Then, it tries to decrypt c_1 with htk and c_2 with eadk. If either decryption fails, the server aborts the protocol. Otherwise, let $(\text{ID}_1, \text{ID}_2, \sigma)$ be the message obtained from decrypting c_1. The server verifies that $\text{ID}_1 = \text{ID}_S$ and that ID_2 satisfies its authorization policy π_S. Next, it checks that σ is a valid signature on $(\text{bid}, \text{sid}, \text{ID}_1, \text{ID}_2, g^s, g^x)$ under the public key identified by ID_2. If all these checks pass, the server chooses a new ephemeral DH exponent $y \xleftarrow{\text{R}} \mathbb{Z}_p$ and derives the session key $\text{atk} = \text{KDF}(g^s, g^x, g^{sx}, g^y, g^{xy})$.[3] The server encrypts the tuple $(\text{bid}, \text{sid}, \text{ID}_1, \text{ID}_2)$ under htk' to obtain a ciphertext c_1', and any application messages under atk to obtain a ciphertext c_2'. It replies to the client with $(\text{bid}, \text{sid}, g^y, c_1', c_2')$.

4. When the client receives a response message $(\text{bid}, \text{sid}, g^y, c_1', c_2')$, it first decrypts c_1' using htk' and verifies that c_1' decrypts to $(\text{bid}, \text{sid}, \text{ID}_S, \text{ID}_C)$. If so, it derives $\text{atk} = \text{KDF}(g^s, g^x, g^{sx}, g^y, g^{xy})$ and uses atk to decrypt c_2'. The handshake then concludes with atk as the shared session key.

5.1   Protocol Analysis

We now describe some of the properties of our private service discovery protocol in Fig. 2. We give a more detailed discussion in the full version of this paper.

0-RTT security. The security analysis of the 0-RTT mutual authentication protocol in Fig. 2 is similar to that of the OPTLS protocol in TLS 1.3 [43] and relies on the Strong-DH and Hash-DH assumptions [9] in the random oracle model [14]. Note that in contrast to the OPTLS protocol which only provides client authentication, our protocol provides *mutual authentication*.

---

[3] In this step, the server samples a fresh ephemeral DH share g^y that is used to derive the application-traffic key atk. This is essential for ensuring perfect forward secrecy for all subsequent application-layer messages (encrypted under atk). We discuss the perfect forward secrecy properties of this protocol in Sect. 5.1.

Server's Broadcast:

$$\mathsf{bid}, \mathsf{PE.Enc}(\pi_S, (\mathrm{ID}_S, g^s, \mathrm{SIG}_S(\mathsf{bid}, \mathrm{ID}_S, g^s)))$$

0-RTT Mutual Authentication:

$$C(\mathrm{ID}_C, \pi_C) \xrightarrow{\begin{array}{c} \mathsf{bid}, \mathsf{sid}, g^x, \{\mathrm{ID}_S, \mathrm{ID}_C, \mathrm{SIG}_C(\mathsf{bid}, \mathsf{sid}, \mathrm{ID}_S, \mathrm{ID}_C, g^s, g^x)\}_{\mathsf{htk}} \end{array}} S(\mathrm{ID}_S, \pi_S)$$
$$\xleftarrow{\mathsf{bid}, \mathsf{sid}, g^y, \{(\mathsf{bid}, \mathsf{sid}, \mathrm{ID}_S, \mathrm{ID}_C)\}_{\mathsf{htk'}}}$$

Fig. 2. Basic message flow between the client C (with certificate ID_C and policy π_C) and the server S (with certificate ID_S and policy π_S) for the private discovery protocol. The client can also include early application data in the first flow of the 0-RTT mutual authentication protocol.

Replay attacks. One limitation of the 0-RTT mode is that the early-application data is vulnerable to replay attacks. A typical replay-prevention technique (used by QUIC [47]) is to have the server maintain a list of client nonces in the 0-RTT messages and reject duplicates for the lifetime of the service advertisement.

Authenticity of broadcasts. Because the service broadcasts are signed, a client is assured of the authenticity of a broadcast before establishing a session with a service. This ensures that the client will not inadvertently send its credentials to an impostor service. However, an adversary that intercepts a service broadcast and recovers the associated semi-static DH exponent can replay the broadcast for an honest client. If the client then initiates a session using the DH share from the replayed advertisement, the adversary compromises the client's privacy. To protect against this kind of replay attack, the server should include an expiration time in its broadcasts, and more importantly, sign this expiration.

Forward secrecy. Since the server's semi-static DH share persists across sessions, perfect forward secrecy (PFS) is lost for early-application data and handshake messages sent during the lifetime of each advertisement. To mitigate this risk in practical deployments, it is important to periodically refresh the DH-share in the server's broadcast (e.g., once every hour). The refresh interval corresponds to the window where forward secrecy may be compromised.

While PFS is not achievable for early-application and handshake messages for the lifetime of a service's broadcast, PFS is ensured for all application-layer messages. In particular, after processing a session initiation request, the server responds with a fresh ephemeral DH share that is used to derive the session key for all subsequent messages. In the full version, we show that the security of the session is preserved even if the server's semi-static secret is compromised but the ephemeral secret is uncompromised. This method of combining a semi-static key with an ephemeral key also features in the OPTLS [43] and QUIC [47] protocols.

Identity privacy. As was the case in our private mutual authentication protocol from Sect. 4, privacy for the server's identity is ensured by the prefix-based encryption scheme. Privacy for the client's identity is ensured since all handshake messages are encrypted under handshake traffic keys htk and htk'. We formally state and prove mutual privacy for the protocol in the full version.

Security theorem. We conclude by stating the security theorem for our private service discovery protocol. We give the formal proof in the full version [54].

Theorem 5.1 (Private Service Discovery). *The protocol in Fig. 2 is a secure and private service discovery protocol in a Canetti-Krawczyk-based model of key-exchange in the random oracle model, assuming the Hash Diffie-Hellman and Strong Diffie-Hellman assumptions in* $\mathbb{G}$, *and the security of the underlying cryptographic primitives.*

6   Protocol Evaluation and Deployment

In this section, we describe the implementation and deployment of our private mutual authentication and service discovery protocols in the Vanadium framework [1]. We benchmark our protocols on a wide range of architectures: an Intel Edison (0.5 GHz Intel Atom), a Raspberry Pi 2 (0.9 GHz ARM Cortex-A7), a Nexus 5X smartphone (1.8 GHz 64-bit ARM-v8A), a Macbook Pro (3.1 GHz Intel Core i7), and a desktop (3.2 GHz Intel Xeon).

Vanadium. We implement our private mutual authentication and service discovery protocols as part of the Vanadium framework for developing secure, distributed applications. The Vanadium identity model is based on a distributed PKI. All principals in Vanadium possess an ECDSA P-256 signing and verification key-pair. Principals have a set of human-readable names bound to them via certificate chains, called *blessings*. Blessings can be extended locally and delegated from one principal to another. Interactions between parties are encrypted and mutually authenticated based on the blessings bound to each end.

We implement our protocols to enhance the privacy of the Vanadium discovery framework. Our entire implementation is in Go (with wrappers for interfacing with third-party C libraries).

6.1   Identity-Based Encryption

The key primitive we require for our protocols is prefix-based encryption, which we can construct from any IBE scheme (Sect. 3.1). For our experiments, we implemented the Boneh-Boyen (BB$_2$) scheme [19, Sect. 5] over the 256-bit Barreto-Naehrig (bn256) [48] pairings curve. We chose the BB$_2$ IBE scheme for its efficiency: it only requires a single pairing evaluation during decryption. We apply the Fujisaki-Okamoto transformation [32] to obtain CCA-security. For the underlying symmetric encryption scheme in the Fujisaki-Okamoto transformation, we use the authenticated encryption scheme from NaCl [16,17]. All of our cryptographic primitives are chosen to provide at least 128 bits of security. In the full version, we give some microbenchmarks of the different IBE operations on several devices and describe how we integrate IBE into the Vanadium infrastructure.

6.2   Private Mutual Authentication

We implemented the private mutual authentication protocol from Sect. 4 within the Vanadium RPC system as a means to offer a "private mode" for Vanadium services. We implemented the protocol from Fig. 1 that allows caching of the encrypted server certificate chain. The implementation uses a prefix encryption primitive implemented on top of our IBE library.

Benchmarking. We measure the end-to-end connection setup time for our protocol on various platforms. To eliminate network latency, we instantiate a server and client in the same process. Since the encrypted server certificate chain can be reused across multiple handshakes, we precompute it before executing the protocol. Both the client and the server use a prefix-based policy of length three. Note that the encryption and decryption times in our prefix encryption scheme are not affected by the length of the policy.

Results. We compare the performance of our protocol to the traditional SIGMA-I protocol in Table 1. The end-to-end latency on the desktop is only 9.5 ms, thanks to an assembly-optimized IBE implementation. The latency on smaller devices is typically around a third of a second, which is quite suitable for user-interactive applications like AirDrop. Even on the Intel Edisons (a processor marketed specifically for IoT), the handshake completes in just over 1.5 s, which is still reasonable for many applications. Moreover, with an optimized implementations of the IBE library (e.g., taking advantage of assembly optimizations like on the desktop), these latencies should be significantly reduced.

The memory and storage requirements of our protocol are very modest and well-suited for the computational constraints of IoT and mobile devices. Specifically, the pairing library is just 40 KB of code on the ARM processors (and 64 KB on x86). The public parameters for the IBE scheme are 512 bytes, and each IBE secret key is just 160 bytes. For comparison, a typical certificate chain (of length 3) is about 500 bytes in Vanadium. Also, our protocols are not memory-bound, and in particular, do not require much additional memory on top of the existing non-private SIGMA-I key-exchange protocol supported by Vanadium.

Table 1. Private mutual authentication benchmarks.

	Intel Edison	Raspberry Pi 2	Nexus 5X	Laptop	Desktop
SIGMA-I	252.1 ms	88.0 ms	91.6 ms	6.3 ms	5.3 ms
Private mutual auth.	1694.3 ms	326.1 ms	360.4 ms	19.6 ms	9.5 ms
Slowdown	6.7x	3.7x	3.9x	3.1x	1.8x

6.3   Private Discovery

We also integrated the private discovery protocol from Sect. 5 into Vanadium.

Benchmarks. We benchmark the cryptographic overhead of processing service advertisements, and measure the size of the service advertisements. Processing service advertisements requires a single IBE decryption and one ECDSA signature verification. For instance, on the Nexus 5X smartphone, which is a typical client for processing service advertisements, the cost is approximately 236 ms (IBE decryption) + 11 ms (ECDSA signature verification) = 247 ms.

The advertisement size can also be estimated analytically from the structure shown in Fig. 2. Our implementation of prefix encryption (PE.Enc) has a ciphertext overhead of 208 bytes on top of the plaintext. The Diffie-Hellman exponent (g^s) is 32 bytes, the broadcast id (bid) is 16 bytes, the ECDSA signature is 64 bytes, and a certificate chain (ID_S) of length three is approximately 500 bytes in size. The overall service advertisement is about 820 bytes.

Deployment. We deploy our service discovery protocol within the Vanadium discovery framework. The protocol allows services to advertise themselves while restricting visibility to an authorized set of clients. The Vanadium discovery API allows services to advertise over both mDNS and BLE. An mDNS TXT record has a maximum size of 1300 bytes [24,25], which suffices for service advertisements.

When the policy has multiple prefixes, our advertisements would no longer fit in a single mDNS TXT record. Furthermore, BLE advertisement payloads are restricted to 31 bytes [5], which is far too small to fit a full service advertisement. In the full version [54], we show how an auxiliary service can be used to host the encrypted advertisements, and thus, enable private service discovery over BLE and other similarly space-constrained advertisement protocols.

6.4 Fixing AirDrop

Recall from Sect. 2.1 that during an AirDrop file exchange in contacts-only mode, a hash of the sender's identity is advertised over BLE and matched by potential receivers against their contacts. If there is a match, the receiver starts a service that the sender can connect to using TLS (version 1.2). In the TLS handshake, the sender and receiver exchange their certificates in the clear, which makes them visible to eavesdroppers on the network. This privacy vulnerability can be fixed using the private mutual authentication protocol from Sect. 4. In particular, once the receiver matches the sender's hash against one of its contacts, it uses the prefix encryption scheme to encrypt its identity under the name of the contact that matched the sender's hash. We provide more details in the full version [54].

7 Extensions

In the full version, we describe several ways to extend our protocols. These include ways to hide the server's authorization policy and allowing non-IBE roots to manage and issue prefix encryption keys for their subdomains.

8   Related Work

Private mutual authentication. The term "private authentication" was first introduced by Abadi and Fournet [7,8]. However, the protocols in [8] require the authorization policy to be specified by a set of public keys and do not scale when the set of public keys is very large. Many other cryptographic primitives have also been developed for problems related to private mutual authentication, including secret handshakes [11,12,36], oblivious signature-based envelopes [46], oblivious attribute certificates [45], hidden credentials [21,31,35], and more.

Secret handshakes and their extensions are protocols based on bilinear pairings that allow members of a group to identify each other privately. A key limitation of secret handshakes is that the parties can only authenticate using credentials issued by the same root authority. Oblivious signature-based envelopes [46], oblivious attribute certificates [45] and hidden credentials [21,31,35] allow a sender to send an encrypted message that can be decrypted only by a recipient that satisfies some policy. Hidden credentials additionally hide the sender's policy. Closely related are the cryptographic primitives of attribute-based encryption [18,33] and predicate encryption [34,39], which allow more fine-grained control over decryption capabilities.

The protocols we have surveyed here are meant for *authentication*, and not authenticated key-exchange, which is usually the desired primitive. Integrating these protocols into existing key-exchange protocols such as SIGMA or TLS 1.3 is not always straightforward and can require non-trivial changes to existing protocols. In contrast, our work shows how IBE-based authentication can be very naturally integrated with existing secure key-exchange protocols (with minimal changes) to obtain private mutual authentication. Moreover, our techniques are equally applicable in the service discovery setting, and can be used to obtain 0-RTT private mutual authentication.

Service discovery. There is a large body of work on designing service discovery protocols for various environments—mobile, IoT, enterprise and more; we refer to [57] for a survey. Broadly, these protocols can be categorized into two groups: "directory-based" protocols and "directory-free" protocols.

In directory-based discovery protocols [4,27,55], there is a central directory that maintains service information and controls access to the services. Clients query directories to discover services while services register with the directory to announce their presence. While directory-based protocols allow for centralized management and tend to be computationally efficient, their main drawback is that they force dependence on an external service. If the directory service is unavailable then the protocol ceases to work. Even worse, if the directory service is compromised, then both server and client privacy is lost. Besides, mutually suspicious clients and servers may not be able to agree on a common directory service that they both trust. In light of these downsides, we designed decentralized, peer-to-peer protocols in this work.

Directory-free protocols, such as [37,38,56,58], typically rely on a shared key established between devices in a separate, out-of-band protocol. The shared key is then used to encrypt the private service advertisements so that only paired devices can decrypt. Other protocols like UPnP [30] rely on public key encryption, where each device maintains a set of public keys for the peers it is willing to talk to. In contrast, key-management in our IBE-based solution is greatly simplified—devices do not have to maintain long lists of symmetric or public keys. Our protocol is similar to the Tryst protocol [49], which proposes using an anonymous IBE scheme for encrypting under the peer's name (based on using a mutually agreed upon convention). A distinguishing feature of our protocol over Tryst is the support for prefix-based authorization policies.

Acknowledgments. We thank Martín Abadi, Mike Burrows, and Adam Langley for many helpful comments and suggestions. This work was supported by NSF, DARPA, a grant from ONR, the Simons Foundation, and an NSF Graduate Research Fellowship. Opinions, findings and conclusions or recommendations expressed in this material are those of the authors and do not necessarily reflect the views of DARPA.

References

1. Vanadium. http://vanadium.github.io/
2. IETF zero configuration networking (zeroconf) (2004). https://datatracker.ietf.org/doc/charter-ietf-zeroconf
3. Bonjour printing specification version 1.2 (2013)
4. Jini(TM) network technology specifications - Apache river version 2.2.0 (2013)
5. Bluetooth specification version 4.2 (2014)
6. UPnP(TM) device architecture 2.0 (2015)
7. Abadi, M.: Private authentication. In: PETS, pp. 27–40 (2003)
8. Abadi, M., Fournet, C.: Private authentication. Theoret. Comput. Sci. **322**, 427–476 (2004)
9. Abdalla, M., Bellare, M., Rogaway, P.: The oracle Diffie-Hellman assumptions and an analysis of DHIES. In: Naccache, D. (ed.) CT-RSA 2001. LNCS, vol. 2020, pp. 143–158. Springer, Heidelberg (2001)
10. Aiello, W., Bellovin, S.M., Blaze, M., Canetti, R., Ioannidis, J., Keromytis, A.D., Reingold, O.: Just fast keying: key agreement in a hostile internet. ACM Trans. Inf. Syst. Secur. **7**(2), 242–273 (2004)
11. Ateniese, G., Kirsch, J., Blanton, M.: Secret handshakes with dynamic and fuzzy matching. In: NDSS (2007)
12. Balfanz, D., Durfee, G., Shankar, N., Smetters, D.K., Staddon, J., Wong, H.-C.: Secret handshakes from pairing-based key agreements. In: 2003 IEEE S&P 2003, pp. 180–196 (2003)
13. Bellare, M., Namprempre, C.: Authenticated encryption: relations among notions and analysis of the generic composition paradigm. In: Okamoto, T. (ed.) ASIACRYPT 2000. LNCS, vol. 1976, pp. 531–545. Springer, Heidelberg (2000)
14. Bellare, M., Rogaway, P.: Random oracles are practical: a paradigm for designing efficient protocols. In: ACM CCS, pp. 62–73 (1993)
15. Bellare, M., Rogaway, P., Wagner, D.: EAX: a conventional authenticated-encryption mode. IACR Cryptology ePrint Archive, 2003:69 (2003)
16. Bernstein, D.J.: Cryptography in NaCl (2009)
17. Bernstein, D.J., Lange, T., Schwabe, P.: The security impact of a new cryptographic library. In: Hevia, A., Neven, G. (eds.) LatinCrypt 2012. LNCS, vol. 7533, pp. 159–176. Springer, Heidelberg (2012)

18. Bethencourt, J., Sahai, A., Waters, B.: Ciphertext-policy attribute-based encryption. In: IEEE S&P, pp. 321–334 (2007)
19. Boneh, D., Boyen, X.: Efficient Selective-ID secure identity-based encryption without random oracles. In: Cachin, C., Camenisch, J.L. (eds.) EUROCRYPT 2004. LNCS, vol. 3027, pp. 223–238. Springer, Heidelberg (2004)
20. Boneh, D., Franklin, M.: Identity-based encryption from the Weil pairing. In: Kilian, J. (ed.) CRYPTO 2001. LNCS, vol. 2139, pp. 213–229. Springer, Heidelberg (2001)
21. Bradshaw, R.W., Holt, J.E., Seamons, K.E.: Concealing complex policies with hidden credentials. In: ACM CCS, pp. 146–157 (2004)
22. Canetti, R., Krawczyk, H.: Analysis of key-exchange protocols and their use for building secure channels. In: Pfitzmann, B. (ed.) EUROCRYPT 2001. LNCS, vol. 2045, pp. 453–474. Springer, Heidelberg (2001)
23. Canetti, R., Krawczyk, H.: Security analysis of IKE's signature-based key-exchange protocol. In: Yung, M. (ed.) CRYPTO 2002. LNCS, vol. 2442, pp. 143–161. Springer, Heidelberg (2002)
24. Cheshire, S., Krochmal, M.: DNS-Based Service Discovery. RFC 6763 (Proposed Standard), February 2013
25. Cheshire, S., Krochmal, M.: Multicast DNS. RFC 6762 (Proposed Standard), February 2013
26. Cocks, C.: An identity based encryption scheme based on quadratic residues. In: Honary, B. (ed.) Cryptography and Coding 2001. LNCS, vol. 2260, pp. 360–363. Springer, Heidelberg (2001)
27. Czerwinski, S.E., Zhao, B.Y., Hodes, T.D., Joseph, A.D., Katz, R.H.: An architecture for a secure service discovery service. In: MobiCom, pp. 24–35 (1999)
28. Dierks, T., Rescorla, E.: The Transport Layer Security (TLS) Protocol Version 1.2. RFC 5246 (Proposed Standard), August 2008
29. Dodis, Y., Gennaro, R., Håstad, J., Krawczyk, H., Rabin, T.: Randomness extraction and key derivation using the CBC, cascade and HMAC modes. In: Franklin, M. (ed.) CRYPTO 2004. LNCS, vol. 3152, pp. 494–510. Springer, Heidelberg (2004)
30. Ellison, C.M.: Home network security. Intel Technol. J. 6(4), 37–48 (2002)
31. Frikken, K.B., Atallah, M.J., Li, J.: Hidden access control policies with hidden credentials. In: ACM WPES, p. 27 (2004)
32. Fujisaki, E., Okamoto, T.: Secure integration of asymmetric and symmetric encryption schemes. In: Wiener, M. (ed.) CRYPTO 1999. LNCS, vol. 1666, pp. 537–554. Springer, Heidelberg (1999)
33. Gorbunov, S., Vaikuntanathan, V., Wee, H.: Attribute-based encryption for circuits. In: STOC, pp. 545–554 (2013)
34. Gorbunov, S., Vaikuntanathan, V., Wee, H.: Predicate encryption for circuits from LWE. In: Gennaro, R., Robshaw, M. (eds.) CRYPTO 2015. LNCS, vol. 9216, pp. 503–523. Springer, Heidelberg (2015)
35. Holt, J.E., Bradshaw, R.W., Seamons, K.E., Orman, H.K.: Hidden credentials. In: ACM WPES, pp. 1–8 (2003)
36. Jarecki, S., Kim, J.H., Tsudik, G.: Authentication for paranoids: multi-party secret handshakes. In: Zhou, J., Yung, M., Bao, F. (eds.) ACNS 2006. LNCS, vol. 3989, pp. 325–339. Springer, Heidelberg (2006)
37. Kaiser, D., Waldvogel, M.: Adding privacy to multicast DNS service discovery. In: IEEE TrustCom, pp. 809–816 (2014)
38. Kaiser, D., Waldvogel, M.: Efficient privacy preserving multicast DNS service discovery. In: IEEE CSS (2014)

39. Katz, J., Sahai, A., Waters, B.: Predicate encryption supporting disjunctions, polynomial equations, and inner products. In: Smart, N.P. (ed.) EUROCRYPT 2008. LNCS, vol. 4965, pp. 146–162. Springer, Heidelberg (2008)

40. Könings, B., Bachmaier, C., Schaub, F., Weber, M.: Device names in the wild: investigating privacy risks of zero configuration networking. In: IEEE MDM, pp. 51–56 (2013)

41. Krawczyk, H.: SIGMA: the 'SIGn-and-MAc' approach to authenticated Diffie-Hellman and its use in the IKE protocols. In: Boneh, D. (ed.) CRYPTO 2003. LNCS, vol. 2729, pp. 400–425. Springer, Heidelberg (2003)

42. Krawczyk, H.: Cryptographic extraction and key derivation: the HKDF scheme. In: Rabin, T. (ed.) CRYPTO 2010. LNCS, vol. 6223, pp. 631–648. Springer, Heidelberg (2010)

43. Krawczyk, H., Wee, H.: The OPTLS protocol and TLS 1.3. IACR Cryptology ePrint Archive, 2015:978 (2015)

44. Lewko, A., Waters, B.: Why proving HIBE systems secure is difficult. In: Nguyen, P.Q., Oswald, E. (eds.) EUROCRYPT 2014. LNCS, vol. 8441, pp. 58–76. Springer, Heidelberg (2014)

45. Li, J., Li, N.: OACerts: oblivious attribute certificates. IEEE Trans. Dependable Sec. Comput. 3(4), 340–352 (2006)

46. Li, N., Wenliang, D., Boneh, D.: Oblivious signature-based envelope. Distrib. Comput. 17(4) (2005). Extended abstract in ACM PODC 2003

47. Lychev, R., Jero, S., Boldyreva, A., Nita-Rotaru, C.: How secure and quick is quic? Provable security and performance analyses. In: IEEE Symposium on Security and Privacy, pp. 214–231 (2015)

48. Naehrig, M., Niederhagen, R., Schwabe, P.: New software speed records for cryptographic pairings. In: Abdalla, M., Barreto, P.S.L.M. (eds.) LATINCRYPT 2010. LNCS, vol. 6212, pp. 109–123. Springer, Heidelberg (2010)

49. Pang, J., Greenstein, B., McCoy, D., Seshan, S., Wetherall, D.: Tryst: the case for confidential service discovery. In: HotNets (2007)

50. Rescorla, E.: The transport layer security (TLS) protocol version 1.3, July 2015

51. Rivest, R.L., Lampson, B.: SDSI - a simple distributed security infrastructure. Technical report (1996)

52. Rogaway, P.: Authenticated-encryption with associated-data. In: ACM CCS, pp. 98–107 (2002)

53. Shamir, A.: Identity-based cryptosystems and signature schemes. In: Blakely, G.R., Chaum, D. (eds.) CRYPTO 1984. LNCS, vol. 196, pp. 47–53. Springer, Heidelberg (1985)

54. Wu, D.J., Taly, A., Shankar, A., Boneh, D.: Privacy, discovery, and authentication for the Internet of Things. CoRR, abs/1604.06959 (2016). http://arxiv.org/abs/1604.06959

55. Zhu, F.W., Mutka, M.W., Bivalkar, A., Demir, A., Yue, L., Chidambarm, C.: Toward secure and private service discovery anywhere anytime. Front. Comput. Sci. China 4(3), 311–323 (2010)

56. Zhu, F.W., Mutka, M.W., Ni, L.M.: PrudentExposure: a private and user-centric service discovery protocol. In: IEEE PerCom, pp. 329–340 (2004)

57. Zhu, F.W., Mutka, M.W., Ni, L.M.: Service discovery in pervasive computing environments. IEEE Pervasive Comput. 4(4), 81–90 (2005)

58. Zhu, F.W., Mutka, M.W., Ni, L.M.: A private, secure, and user-centric information exposure model for service discovery protocols. IEEE Trans. Mob. Comput. 5(4), 418–429 (2006)

Secure Code Updates for Mesh Networked Commodity Low-End Embedded Devices

Florian Kohnhäuser[✉] and Stefan Katzenbeisser

Security Engineering Group, Technische Universität Darmstadt, Darmstadt, Germany
{kohnhaeuser,katzenbeisser}@seceng.informatik.tu-darmstadt.de

Abstract. Mesh networked low-end embedded devices are increasingly used in various scenarios, including industrial control, wireless sensing, robot swarm communication, or building automation. Recently, more and more software vulnerabilities in embedded systems are disclosed, as they become appealing targets for cyber attacks. In order to patch these systems, an efficient and secure code update mechanism is required. However, existing solutions are unable to provide verifiable code updates for networked commodity low-end embedded devices. This work presents a novel code update scheme which verifies and enforces the correct installation of code updates on all devices in the network. After update distribution and installation, devices mutually attest and verify each others' software state. Devices being in an untrustworthy state are excluded from the network. In this way, the scheme enforces software integrity as well as software up-to-dateness on all devices in the network. Issuing a secure code update, the network operator is able to learn the identity of all trustworthy and all untrustworthy devices. We demonstrate that the proposed scheme is applicable to a wide range of existing commodity low-end embedded systems. Furthermore, we show that the scheme is practically usable in networks with tens of thousands of devices.

1 Introduction

The continuous cost reduction and miniaturization of electronic devices commences a new technological revolution of omnipresent embedded devices. Trends like the Internet of Things, Smarter Planet, Industry 4.0, or Smart Cities aim at applying networked embedded systems in virtually every aspect of our life. Wireless technologies like IEEE 802.11s, IEEE 802.15.4, ZigBee, Z-Wave, or Bluetooth facilitate the establishment of large mesh networks consisting of numerous embedded systems. In a mesh network, all devices cooperate in the distribution of data in the network, forming a decentralized and self-organized network topology. Nowadays, wireless mesh networked embedded devices are already widely used in industrial control, wireless sensor networks, home automation, building automation, military communication, or community networks. These systems often perform security or safety-critical tasks, or process privacy-sensitive information. In addition, they commonly lack effective security mechanisms due to their low production costs as well as their small and simple system architecture.

© Springer International Publishing Switzerland 2016
I. Askoxylakis et al. (Eds.): ESORICS 2016, Part II, LNCS 9879, pp. 320–338, 2016.
DOI: 10.1007/978-3-319-45741-3_17

These circumstances made them appealing targets for cyber attacks. Consequently, many software vulnerabilities in embedded systems have been revealed lately [10,17,31]. In order to fix such vulnerabilities, it is vital that low-end embedded devices provide secure code update mechanisms.

A secure code update scheme for the above described application must provide several features. First, it has to ensure that devices verify the novelty, integrity, and authenticity of code updates before installation. This feature is necessary to prevent misuse of the code update mechanism, e.g., by downgrading a software or installing malicious code. Second, the scheme must ensure that, appropriately executed, it restores the integrity of the software state on a device, even if the device was compromised before. Thus, an attacker who exploited a vulnerability in the old software to compromise and gain control over a device is removed from the device. However, compromised devices can simply deny the execution of code updates or execute them inappropriately without restoring software integrity. Therefore, after code update execution, the scheme must verify whether all devices are in a trustworthy, i.e., an unmodified and up-to-date, software state. To reduce potential damage caused by compromised devices, the secure code update scheme should exclude untrustworthy devices from the network. Furthermore, the scheme must be scalable, as it should allow for an efficient update of all devices in large mesh networks. Moreover, it should be applicable to already existing commodity low-end embedded devices. In this way, the scheme can be retrofitted to currently deployed systems. Finally, a network operator issuing a secure code update should eventually be informed about the integrity of the software state of all devices in the network.

However, to the best of our knowledge, there is no solution which satisfies all these requirements. Software- and PoSE-based (Proofs of Secure Erasure) approaches are applicable to commodity devices, but rely on strong security assumptions which are hard to achieve in practice [2,14,19,30,35]. Additionally, they allow a verifier to attest only one device but not a group of devices, as they rely on the assumption that during attestation an adversary is unable to communicate with any other party, except for the verifier. By contrast, hardware-based solutions provide much stronger security guarantees by relying on secure hardware modules. Yet, security architectures which are applicable to low-end embedded systems such as TyTAN, SMART, TrustLite, or SANCUS are still in research stage [8,13,21,28]. These architectures have only been implemented as prototypes and their future availability in commodity devices is uncertain.

Contributions. In this work, we present a novel secure code update scheme for wireless mesh networked commodity low-end embedded devices. As opposed to existing hardware-based approaches, we require only minimal assumptions on secure hardware, which makes our scheme applicable to many existing low-end embedded devices. Nevertheless, by relying on lightweight secure hardware, we achieve much stronger security guarantees than existing software- and PoSE-based approaches. This, in particular, allows us to provide secure code updates for groups of devices. Our scheme allows only fresh and authenticated updates to be installed on devices. During a proper code update execution, each device verifies its local software integrity and ensures that only unmodified and up-to-date software runs on the device. To enforce a proper execution of the code update, neighboring devices mutually verify each others' genuine and up-to-date software state and establish secure channels only if the verification succeeds. Thus, compromised devices can either refuse an appropriate execution of the code update, whereupon they are excluded from the network, or perform a correct code update, whereby any present malware gets eliminated. Issuing a secure code update for the network, the operator is able to learn the identity of all trustworthy and all untrustworthy network devices. We implemented the scheme on exemplary low-end embedded systems that are interconnected via ZigBee. Simulation results demonstrate that our scheme scales well and is practically usable in networks with tens of thousands of devices.

Structure. In Sect. 2, we summarize existing work. Section 3 presents our system model, device requirements, and our adversary model. In Sect. 4, we show how the device requirements can be implemented on commodity devices. Section 5 describes our secure code update scheme. In Sect. 6, we evaluate the performance of the proposed scheme. Finally, Sect. 7 concludes this work.

2 Related Work

Code Updates. The process of updating software or firmware present in embedded devices is referred to as over-the air programming (OTA), firmware over-the-air (FOTA), code update, software update, or firmware update. Common research topics are transmission reliability, transmission scalability, update size minimization, and energy efficiency [12,16,23,32]. Moreover, several papers explicitly focus on security aspects and use digital signatures to ensure code update freshness, authenticity, and integrity [18,25,38]. In addition, these works offer features like denial-of-service resilience, extra small or efficient signatures, or support for multiple code update initiators with different privileges. However, conventional code update techniques only perform unidirectional verification. Embedded systems verify the integrity and authenticity of code updates, but the initiator of the code update is unable to verify whether embedded systems indeed install the code update appropriately.

Remote Attestation. Remote attestation is a mechanism that allows a third party to verify the software state of a remote system. Consequently, by performing remote attestation after the execution of a code update, its correct installation can be verified. Software-based attestation mechanisms do not require secure hardware and thus can be applied in commodity low-end embedded systems or legacy systems [9,22,26,34]. However, they rely on various assumptions like exact time measurements, optimal protocol implementation and execution, or the adversary being passive during attestation. Those assumptions are hard to achieve in practice [2]. By contrast, hardware-based attestation mechanisms provide much stronger security guarantees by relying on secure hardware. As standardized and commercial secure hardware components like ARM TrustZone,

TPM, Intel TXT, or Intel SGX are too complex and too expensive to be used in low-end embedded systems, new security architectures, such as SMART [13], SANCUS [28], TrustLite [21], or TyTan [8], have recently been proposed. Nevertheless, these architectures have only been implemented as prototypes and their future availability in commodity low-end embedded devices is uncertain. In addition, their remote attestation mechanisms only target the attestation of a single device, which is impractical in mesh network scenarios due to a large communication overhead. We are only aware of two approaches that address efficient attestation of multiple embedded devices. SMATT [29] verifies multiple devices at once by comparing their integrity measurements. On the downside, SMATT requires identical devices, relies on special copy-proof memory, and only enables a probabilistic attack detection rate. SEDA [3] is an efficient and scalable attestation scheme for large heterogeneous embedded system networks. Yet, as SEDA relies on secure hardware that is not available in commodity devices, it is not applicable to currently deployed systems. Regarding secure code updates, SEDA provides only a brief protocol extension that leaves several design decisions open (e.g., protection against rollback attacks) and lacks desirable features (e.g., the exclusion of compromised devices from the network).

Secure Code Updates. Work on secure code updates specifically addresses the problem of verifying that a code update has been securely distributed and correctly installed on a remote embedded system. Seshadri et al. [35] applied a software-based approach to ensure an untampered execution of the software update protocol on a single remote device. However, as already mentioned, software-based solutions provide questionable security guarantees due to their strong assumptions [2]. Perito and Tsudik [30] pursued a different approach and introduced the concept of Proofs of Secure Erasure (PoSE) to secure software updates. PoSE allow a device to prove to a remote party that it is free of malicious code by attesting that it has erased all its memory. In a second step, cleaned devices download the software update and send a MAC of the downloaded code to the verifier to prove the storage of the software update. Recently, Karame et al. [19] enhanced this concept by combining PoSE with All or Nothing Transforms to reduce the time and energy overhead. Nevertheless, both software and PoSE-based approaches rely on the strong assumption that a device proving its correct code update installation is only able to communicate with the verifier, and no other party. Thus, both approaches are impractical for updating multiple networked devices, since they can only provide security if the adversary is not physically present and has not gained control of more than one device in the network.

3   System Requirements and Adversary Model

System Model. We consider a mobile wireless mesh network that consists of various interconnected commodity low-end embedded devices. The devices can be of different type and model, having, for instance, varying computational power, storage capacity, or security functionalities. Devices in the network can move, but the network topology is assumed to remain static during a single run of the secure code update protocol. We assume that all correctly functioning devices are reachable in the network. Unreachable devices are ignored and they are temporarily regarded as compromised, since it is uncertain whether they will ever contribute to the network again. We further assume that each device $\mathcal{D}_i$ gets initialized and deployed by a trusted network operator $\mathcal{O}$ once (see Sect. 5.1).

After deployment, the goal of $\mathcal{O}$ is to perform a secure and efficient code update for all devices in the network. Devices conducting a secure code update should ensure that only authentic, untampered, and fresh code updates are installed and that the installation establishes software integrity, thereby undoing potential manipulations made by an attacker. Devices that refuse a correct installation should be identified as manipulated and excluded from the network. This prevents compromised devices from eavesdropping, manipulating transmitted data, or communicating with a remote attacker. Finally, $\mathcal{O}$ should get a report listing all devices that are in a trustworthy, i.e., an up-to-date and unmodified, software state. During code update execution, we assume $\mathcal{O}$ to be connected to at least one device in the network.

Hardware Security Requirements. Our secure code update solution requires the following properties from each device $\mathcal{D}_i$:

(1) *Immutable Code:* A static non-volatile write-protected memory region $\mathcal{R}$ which contains code and data;
(2) *Secure Storage:* A device-dependent unique secret $\mathcal{SK}$ that can only be accessed during the execution of code in $\mathcal{R}$;
(3) *Uninterruptible Execution:* Once code in $\mathcal{R}$ gets executed, execution cannot be interrupted until the control flow intentionally leaves $\mathcal{R}$.

In Sect. 4, we discuss how these properties can be implemented on commodity low-end embedded devices. We will see that many existent devices provide hardware features that allow for the implementation of these requirements.

Adversary Model. We assume that an adversary has full control over the execution state of a compromised device, and can read all readable storage and write to all writable storage. Furthermore, the adversary has complete control over the communication medium, i.e., all messages sent between devices can be eavesdropped and manipulated. In addition, we assume that the adversary can be physically present and introduce additional hardware to the network.

In contrast, we assume that the adversary does not perform physical attacks on the hardware of the embedded devices. In particular, we presume that the adversary cannot bypass any of the hardware protections described above. Moreover, we do not consider Denial of Service (DoS) attacks in the immediate vicinity of the attacker, since there is no defense against a physically present attacker who cuts the wire or jams the wireless communication medium. We would like to point out that the described limitations on the adversary's capabilities are common for hardware-based attestation or code update schemes [3,8,13,21,28].

4 Requirements on COTS Low-End Embedded Systems

In the following, we demonstrate how each of the stated hardware security requirements (see Sect. 3) can be implemented on existing commercial off-the-shelf (COTS) low-end embedded devices.

1st Requirement: Immutable Code. Nowadays, it is common for commodity low-end embedded devices to provide protection of Flash memory. On some devices, the Flash memory can be separated into multiple sections which have dedicated lock bits for read protection, write protection, and also interrupt prevention [4]. Most commonly, the Flash memory is divided into one boot loader section (BLS) and one application section. If the device at hand offers this feature, we propose so store the code region $\mathcal{R}$ in the BLS and the rest of the program in the application section. Afterwards, we advise to set the lock bits in a way that write access to the BLS is denied. This makes $\mathcal{R}$ immutable. Other devices provide a more fine-grained Flash protection, where memory regions of different sizes can be marked as read-only memory (ROM) or potentially also as execute-only memory (XOM) [36]. If the device at hand offers XOM or ROM, we propose to protect $\mathcal{R}$ using the strongest supported memory protection available on the device, i.e., XOM if available and ROM otherwise. Note that once Flash protection is set, it can only be unset by physically accessing the system. This process typically involves the erasure of the entire Flash memory [4,36].

2nd Requirement: Secure Storage. If the particular device offers separable memory (e.g., a BLS) with lock bits, we suggest that $\mathcal{R}$ and the protected secret $\mathcal{SK}$ are stored in an extra section, isolated from the application code. Next, we propose to configure the lock bits in a way that read access to the separated section is denied if it is performed by code stored outside the separated memory region [4]. Thus, $\mathcal{SK}$ can only be read during the execution of $\mathcal{R}$. If the particular device offers XOM, we propose that $\mathcal{SK}$ is stored in XOM using constants that are loaded into the CPU by MOV instructions during execution. Since the content of XOM cannot be read out, $\mathcal{SK}$ only gets revealed during the execution of $\mathcal{R}$. If the particular device only supports ROM, we suggest to store the code region $\mathcal{R}$ in the boot loader and enforce that $\mathcal{R}$ immediately gets executed when the device starts. Consequently, in order to execute $\mathcal{R}$, the device must restart. In addition, we propose to store $\mathcal{SK}$ in a secure key storage whose access can intentionally be denied until the next device restart. In this way, code in $\mathcal{R}$ can read out $\mathcal{SK}$ once during device start and afterwards deny access to $\mathcal{SK}$. As $\mathcal{R}$ is immutable and immediately gets executed when the device starts, an attacker is unable to access $\mathcal{SK}$. A secure key storage which provides this functionality is, for instance, an SRAM PUF. Previous works have shown that the SRAM modules present in several low-end embedded devices can be used as PUF instances, so that cryptographic keys can be derived from the SRAM start-up values [20,33]. Note that the start-up values can be deleted after they have been read out, so keys are only accessible at boot time. A further possible key storage is memory which provides the functionality to hide blocks, e.g., EEPROM block hide [36].

Once an EEPROM block is hidden, it is not accessible until the next reboot of the device.

3rd Requirement: Uninterruptible Execution. If the device at hand provides separable memory with lock bits, we suggest to set the lock bits of a separated memory section containing $\mathcal{R}$ such that interrupts are denied during the execution of code in that section. On other devices, we propose to store both the interrupt vector table (IVT) and a default interrupt handler in write-protected memory (i.e., XOM or ROM). All interrupts in the IVT are configured to refer to the default interrupt handler. When an interrupt occurs and the default interrupt handler gets executed, it checks whether the interrupt was triggered during the execution of code in $\mathcal{R}$. If this is the case, the default interrupt handler denies interrupt processing. If this is not the case, the interrupt handler redirects execution to a user-defined interrupt handler which processes the particular interrupt [15]. A further approach is to let the default interrupt handler clean up sensitive data before control is handed over to the particular user-defined interrupt handler [37]. Both approaches impose no restrictions, since custom interrupts can still be deployed by modifying the user-defined interrupt handlers.

Summary. This section has shown various measures to implement the three required device properties on low-end embedded systems. Because the described measures are frequently available, our scheme is applicable to a wide range of commodity low-end embedded devices. In the full version of the paper, we provide an overview of popular low-end embedded development devices and show which of the described security mechanisms are available on each device [1].

5   Secure Code Update Scheme

Our secure code update scheme comprises two phases: an offline phase (see Sect. 5.1) and an online phase (see Sect. 5.2). The offline phase is executed once, before the initial deployment of all devices. In the offline phase, each low-end embedded device $\mathcal{D}_i$ is initialized by the trusted network operator $\mathcal{O}$. After the devices have been deployed, the online phase is executed repeatedly, once for every code update. In the online phase, $\mathcal{O}$ issues a secure code update for all devices in the network.

5.1   Offline Phase

For the purpose of authenticating devices and for implementing a challenge-based protocol to attest and verify appropriate update installations, we use public-key cryptography. In the offline phase, $\mathcal{O}$ thus generates a unique identifier i and a unique signature key pair, consisting of a public key $\mathcal{PK}_i$ and a private key $\mathcal{SK}_i$, for each device $\mathcal{D}_i$. $\mathcal{SK}_i$ is stored in a protected storage, which can only be accessed during the execution of code in the static protected memory region $\mathcal{R}$ (see device requirements in Sect. 3). Furthermore, each device is equipped with a device certificate $\mathcal{DC}_i$ and a software certificate $\mathcal{SC}_i$, both signed by $\mathcal{O}$ with $\mathcal{SK}_O$

Table 1. Notation

$\mathcal{O}$	Trusted network operator	$\mathcal{SK}_i$	Secret signing key of entity i
$\mathcal{R}$	Static protected code region	$\mathcal{PK}_i$	Public signing key of entity i
$\mathcal{D}_i$	Device with identity i	$\mathcal{DC}_i$	Device certificate of entity i
$\mathcal{SH}_i$	Secret ECDH key of entity i	$\mathcal{SC}_i$	Software certificate of entity i
$\mathcal{PH}_i$	Public ECDH key of entity i	$\mathcal{CU}_c$	Code update for device class c

($\mathcal{DC}_i.sig, \mathcal{SC}_i.sig$). $\mathcal{DC}_i$ stores the device class c of $\mathcal{D}_i$, the public key $\mathcal{PK}_i$ of $\mathcal{D}_i$, and the identifier i. $\mathcal{SC}_i$ lists all memory regions on $\mathcal{D}_i$ where the code update routine and the firmware is stored. In addition, $\mathcal{SC}_i$ provides hash values over the data of these memory regions ($\mathcal{SC}_i.hash$). Thus, $\mathcal{SC}_i$ can be used to verify the integrity of the installed software on $\mathcal{D}_i$. In order to indicate the freshness of the software, $\mathcal{SC}_i$ also stores a software version number ($\mathcal{SC}_i.ver$). Moreover, each device initially stores the public key of the trusted network operator $\mathcal{PK}_\mathcal{O}$ in $\mathcal{R}$. $\mathcal{SC}_i$ and $\mathcal{DC}_i$ are stored in a mutable and unprotected memory region.

Additionally, $\mathcal{O}$ equips each device with the functionality to perform a secure code update. Our scheme relies on the untampered execution of code that attests the integrity of the local software state. For this reason, code that implements the attestation routine is stored in $\mathcal{R}$, while the rest of the code (including the actual code update functionality) is stored in a mutable and unprotected memory region (see Fig. 1). Table 1 summarizes relevant definitions used in the offline and the online phase.

5.2 Online Phase

The online phase consists of four different stages. In the first stage, $\mathcal{O}$ prepares a code update package, which is distributed in the network and installed on the devices. In the second stage, devices invoke the execution of the attestation routine in $\mathcal{R}$. The attestation routine verifies the integrity of the installed software and ensures that a device passes execution to an unmodified and up-to-date software. Additionally, the attestation routine generates an attest which proves a trustworthy software state by certifying an untampered and complete execution of the attestation routine. In the third stage, neighboring devices verify each others' software integrity attest. If the verification is successful, devices establish a secure channel. As untrustworthy devices are unable to attest their valid software integrity, they cannot establish communication channels and thus are excluded from the network. In the fourth stage, $\mathcal{O}$ obtains an installation report, which exhibits the software state of all devices in the network. Figure 1 shows the memory layout of the code update scheme and illustrates the control flow throughout all stages. In the following, we will explain each stage in detail.

Stage 1: Code Update Distribution and Installation. The online phase starts with $\mathcal{O}$ preparing a code update package *cupkg*. *Cupkg* includes an ascending version number *cupkg.no* and a signature by $\mathcal{O}$, in order to prevent replay

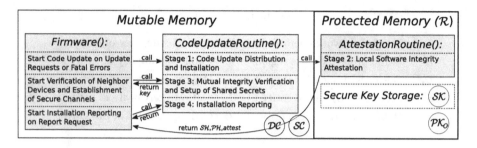

Fig. 1. Illustration of memory layout and control flow of the online phase.

attacks and tampering with the code update package. Since devices in the network may be heterogeneous, *cupkg* must be able to address multiple device classes. For each device class c in the network, *cupkg* contains a software certificate $\mathcal{SC}_c$. $\mathcal{SC}_c$ specifies the correct software configuration for a device of type c, after the installation of the code update. In addition, all contained $\mathcal{SC}$s store the current *cupkg* version number ($\mathcal{SC}.ver = cupkg.no$). Furthermore, for each device class c that should be updated, *cupkg* contains code update data $\mathcal{CU}_c$. $\mathcal{CU}_c$ comprises the binary code of the update and installation instructions (e.g., addresses where to store the binary code during installation).

After preparing *cupkg*, $\mathcal{O}$ sends a code update request followed by *cupkg* to an arbitrary device in the network. This causes the recipient device to execute stage one in the code update routine (see Fig. 1). Next, the code update routine receives *cupkg* and stores it in a free memory region. Devices that received *cupkg* check whether it contains a valid signature by $\mathcal{O}$ and whether its version number is higher than the last received *cupkg* version number. If both checks pass, devices send a code update request to their immediate neighboring devices and subsequently forward *cupkg* to them. In this way, a flooding propagation of *cupkg* is initiated (see Fig. 2). Since efficient and secure code disseminations in wireless mesh networks are well-understood [12,16,18,23,25,32,38], we will not dwell on the distribution of *cupkg*, but instead assume that eventually each device in the network receives *cupkg*. This also includes scenarios in which *cupkg* is too large to fit into the free memory of devices and must be transmitted in multiple smaller chunks.

Devices that received, verified, and forwarded *cupkg* to their neighbors check whether *cupkg* comprises a new code update for their device class. Thereto, each device $\mathcal{D}_i$ examines whether *cupkg* contains a $\mathcal{CU}_k$ for the local target device class specified in $\mathcal{DC}_i$. If this is the case, a device uses the installation instructions in $\mathcal{CU}_k$ to install the update binary code. Note that, since the code update routine is stored in mutable memory, the update routine itself may also be updated during update installation. Furthermore, all devices in the network update their local software certificate to the new software certificate for their device class and issue an attestation of the local software configuration (see next stage).

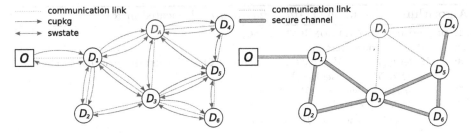

Fig. 2. *Cupkg* distribution in stage 1 and *swstate* message exchange in stage 3.

Fig. 3. Establishment of secure channels in stage 3 in presence of an adversary $\mathcal{D}_A$.

We propose that devices also invoke the execution of the code update routine on fatal errors that render devices non-functional. This allows $\mathcal{O}$ to recover devices whose software accidentally became misconfigured or defective remotely.

Stage 2: Local Software Integrity Attestation. In order to attest an untampered and up-to-date software state, devices invoke the execution of the attestation routine. Since the attestation routine is stored in the protected memory region $\mathcal{R}$ (see Fig. 1), this process requires a reboot on certain commodity devices (see Sect. 4). As illustrated in Algorithm 1, the attestation routine starts with the retrieval of the protected secret signing key $\mathcal{SK}$. Next, the authenticity of the software certificate $\mathcal{SC}$ is ensured by verifying whether $\mathcal{SC}$ was signed by $\mathcal{O}$. If this is the case, $\mathcal{SC}$ is used to check the local software integrity (denoted by the execution of CheckCodeIntegrity()). Consequently, hash values over all memory regions that are listed in $\mathcal{SC}$ are taken and compared to the expected reference values specified in $\mathcal{SC}.hash$. If all measurements match their reference value, the verification of the software integrity is successful. Upon a successful verification, the device generates a new Elliptic curve Diffie-Hellman (ECDH) key pair $(\mathcal{SH}, \mathcal{PH})$ [24] and computes *attest* by signing $\mathcal{PH}$ and $\mathcal{SC}.ver$ with $\mathcal{SK}$. Afterwards, it is ensured that no information about the secret signing key $\mathcal{SK}$ gets leaked (denoted by the execution of HideSecret()). As shown in Sect. 4, this may involve the erasure of certain memory regions or the execution of specific instructions on some commodity devices. Finally, the firmware is executed and $\mathcal{SH}$, $\mathcal{PH}$, and *attest* are passed to the firmware (see Fig. 1). The entry point of the firmware is hardcoded in $\mathcal{R}$. This ensures that the control flow is indeed passed to the firmware, whose integrity was just verified, and not to malicious code that hides somewhere in memory. However, if the verification of the software integrity is unsuccessful, stage one in the code update routine is executed all over again. In this way, devices are able to recover from situations where $\mathcal{O}$ accidentally distributed a buggy *cupkg*.

We would like to point out, that a valid *attest* proves that $\mathcal{D}$ runs a firmware as well as a code update routine whose integrity was successfully verified using a software certificate with the version $\mathcal{SC}.ver$. One reason for this are the three device properties (see Sect. 4). They prevent an adversary from tampering with

---

Algorithm 1. Execution of *AttestationRoutine()* (located in $\mathcal{R}$).

```
 1: procedure ATTESTATIONROUTINE(SC)
 2:     SK ← RetrieveSecret()
 3:     if Verify(PK_O; SC.sig; SC.content) and CheckCodeIntegrity(SC.hash) then
 4:         (SH, PH) ← GenKey()
 5:         attest ← Sign(SK; PH||SC.ver)
 6:         HideSecret(SK)
 7:         StartFirmware(SH, PH, attest)
 8:     else
 9:         HideSecret(SK)
10:         StartCodeUpdateRoutine()
11: end procedure
```

---

the attestation routine, accessing $\mathcal{SK}$ outside of the attestation routine, and interrupting the execution of the attestation routine. Another reason is the design of the attestation routine, which prevents an adversary from generating a valid *attest* while not executing the attestation routine from the beginning. This is due to the first instructions of the attestation routine which retrieve $\mathcal{SK}$ and thus must initially be executed to sign *attest* correctly. However, executing the attestation routine from the beginning leads to its execution in entirety (see third device property). This inevitably executes code which ensures that no information about $\mathcal{SK}$ gets leaked, that the software integrity of $\mathcal{D}$ conforms to $\mathcal{SC}$, and that the firmware, and no unverified code, gets executed next. Tampering with the input of the attestation routine is also not promising for the adversary. The only mutable data that the attestation routine relies on is $\mathcal{SC}$. However, $\mathcal{SC}$'s integrity is verified before it is used to check the local software integrity. Using old $\mathcal{SC}$s as input for the attestation routine, devices can pass the local software integrity verification with an outdated software state. Nevertheless, as we will see in the next stage, this will be detected during the verification of *attest* by neighboring nodes.

Stage 3: Mutual Integrity Verification and Setup of Shared Secrets. In the third stage, each device looks for immediate neighbor devices in the network. If a device $\mathcal{D}_i$ finds a neighbor $\mathcal{D}_n$ whose software state has not yet been verified, it invokes a mutual verification. Thereto, $\mathcal{D}_i$ generates a *swstate_i* message comprising *attest_i*, $\mathcal{PH}_i$, and $\mathcal{DC}_i$, and sends this message to $\mathcal{D}_n$. Upon receiving *swstate_i*, $\mathcal{D}_n$ generates a *swstate_n* message and sends it to $\mathcal{D}_i$ (see Fig. 2). Next, both devices invoke the execution of stage three in their code update routines (see Fig. 1) to verify each others' integrity of the software state and to establish a shared secret. Algorithm 2 illustrates this process in pseudocode.

In order to verify the software state of $\mathcal{D}_n$, $\mathcal{D}_i$ initially checks $\mathcal{DC}_n$ using $\mathcal{PK}_O$. Next, $\mathcal{D}_i$ verifies whether *attest_n* corresponds to the received $\mathcal{PH}_n$ and the latest software version, which $\mathcal{D}_i$ stores in its local software certificate ($\mathcal{SC}_i.ver$). A successful verification ensures that $\mathcal{D}_n$ is in a software state that corresponds to an $\mathcal{SC}$ from $\mathcal{O}$'s latest *cupkg*. Thus, it ensures the integrity as well as the up-to-dateness of $\mathcal{D}_n$'s software state. In addition, verifying *attest_n* confirms the

---

Algorithm 2. Software integrity verification of a neighbor device $\mathcal{D}_n$ on $\mathcal{D}_i$.

1: **procedure** VERIFYNEIGHBORSOFTWAREINTEGRITY($swstate_n$)
2:     $attest_n, \mathcal{DC}_n, \mathcal{PH}_n := swstate_n$
3:     $key \leftarrow \bot$
4:     **if**   Verify($\mathcal{PK}_O$; $\mathcal{DC}_n.sig$; $\mathcal{DC}_n.content$)
5:     **and** Verify($\mathcal{DC}_n.\mathcal{PK}_n$; $attest_n$; $\mathcal{PH}_n \| \mathcal{SC}_i.ver$)
6:     **then** $key \leftarrow$ KeyExchange($\mathcal{SH}_i, \mathcal{PH}_n$)
7:     **return** key
8: **end procedure**

---

integrity and the authenticity of $\mathcal{PH}_n$. If the verification of $\mathcal{DC}_n$ and $attest_n$ is successful, $\mathcal{D}_i$ uses its own secret ECDH key $\mathcal{SH}_i$ and $\mathcal{D}_n$'s public ECDH key $\mathcal{PH}_n$ to perform a key exchange and establish a shared secret key. Note that if $\mathcal{D}_n$'s verification of $\mathcal{D}_i$'s software state is likewise successful, both parties agree on the same key. However, if any of the verifications fail, $\mathcal{D}_i$ regards the software state of $\mathcal{D}_n$ as untrustworthy and does not reconstruct a shared secret. Next, the attestation routine returns and passes key to the firmware (see Fig. 1). If the verification failed, the firmware causes $\mathcal{D}_i$ to send $\mathcal{D}_n$ a message that indicates a failure. Nevertheless, $\mathcal{D}_n$ can re-request a mutual integrity verification with $\mathcal{D}_i$ to recover from connection breaks or other avoidable errors. If the verification was successful on both sides, $\mathcal{D}_i$ and $\mathcal{D}_n$ use key to establish a confidential and authenticated channel. This channel is used for any further communication between both parties. In this way, devices whose software is in an untrustworthy state are effectively excluded from communication. An adversary may try to pass the mutual software state verification by replaying a $swstate$ messages recorded from a trustworthy device. However, in doing so, the adversary is not in the possession of the $\mathcal{SH}$ that correspond to the replayed $swstate$ message. For this reason, the adversary is not able to reconstruct the correct key and the attack will be detected during the establishment of the secure channel. Figure 3 illustrates a scenario in which a compromised device $\mathcal{D}_A$ is unable to attest its software state towards its neighboring devices and thus is unable to establish a communication channel with them.

Stage 4: Installation Reporting. The fourth stage starts with $\mathcal{O}$ requesting an installation report from the network. For this purpose, $\mathcal{O}$ initially uses the approach explained in stage three to establish a secure channel with an arbitrary trustworthy device $\mathcal{D}_i$ in the network. In order to pass the integrity verification by $\mathcal{D}_i$, $\mathcal{O}$ generates a signature key pair, issues a $\mathcal{DC}$ that authenticates the generated key, and uses the key to compute $attest$. Next, $\mathcal{O}$ sends $\mathcal{D}_i$ a request for an installation report over the established channel. Devices that receive a report request invoke the execution of stage four in their code update routines (see Fig. 1). The report request is used to construct a spanning tree whose root is $\mathcal{O}$. Thereto, $\mathcal{D}_i$ broadcasts the request over secure channels to all trustworthy neighboring devices, which in turn broadcast the request. Broadcasting is repeated until the report request reaches leaf nodes in the spanning tree, i.e., nodes whose neighbors all have received the request. Leaf nodes then generate an installation report, which initially contains the identifier of the particular leaf node. Afterwards, the installation report incrementally gets propagated back to the root of the spanning tree. At each hop, a node aggregates the report from its child nodes, includes its own identifier, and then forwards the aggregated report to its parent node. Above a certain number of aggregated identifiers, it is useful to encode the report as an n-bit array, where a flipped bit at position k indicates that $\mathcal{D}_k$ is in a trustworthy state. Eventually, the installation report gets transmitted from $\mathcal{D}_i$ to $\mathcal{O}$. Since $\mathcal{O}$ knows the identifiers of all deployed devices, $\mathcal{O}$ can also assess the precise identifiers of all untrustworthy devices. This may serve as a first step towards physically locating and recovering compromised devices.

Nevertheless, listing the precise identifiers of all devices in the network causes a considerable transmission overhead in large mesh networks with many devices. If $\mathcal{O}$ does not require detailed information about the identity of trustworthy and untrustworthy devices, it is reasonable to implement a more coarse-grained report type. For instance, $\mathcal{O}$ could initially only request for the total number of trustworthy devices or the number of trustworthy devices per device class.

6   Evaluation

Setup. We implemented the proposed secure code update scheme on Stellaris EK-LM4F120XL microcontrollers. The Stellaris is a low-cost embedded system from Texas Instrument which features an 80 MHz ARM Cortex-M4F microprocessor and provides 256 kB of protectable Flash memory. To enable wireless mesh connectivity based on the ZigBee standard, we equipped the Stellaris microcontrollers with CC2530 BoosterPacks from Anaren. In the following, we consider a homogeneous network of Stellaris microcontrollers in a static network topology. We measured network and computational delays of our implementation in small real word mesh networks. In order to evaluate the scalability of the secure code update scheme, we simulated large-scale networks based on our measurements. We found out that the network topology plays an important role for the code update runtime. This is due to the high communication costs for the transmission of the binary code updates.

We implemented the key exchange using Elliptic Curve Diffie-Hellman (EC-DH) with Curve25519 [6]. For the signature scheme, we used an Edwards-curve Digital Signature Algorithm (EdDSA) called Ed25519, which is based on Curve25519 [7]. We implemented the hash function using SHA-512, while the secure and authentic channel uses AES in Galois/Counter Mode (AES-GCM). In the full paper [1], we outline measurements of the network performance and the cryptographic implementations.

Storage Consumption. Compared to a naïve code update approach that only distributes the binary code of the update but provides no security, our scheme requires additional storage for data. In fact, each device must store $\mathcal{SC}$ (ca. 212 byte), $\mathcal{DC}$ (100 byte), $\mathcal{PK}_\mathcal{O}$ (32 byte), $\mathcal{SK}$ (64 byte), ECDH keys (96 byte), and shared secrets (32 byte per neighbor). Hence, with k being the number of neighboring devices, the storage overhead for data adds up to $504 + 32 \cdot k$ bytes.

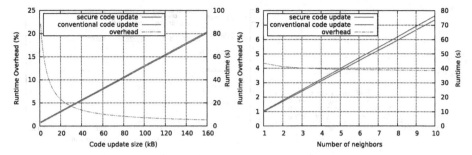

Fig. 4. Single device runtime performance with varying code update sizes.

Fig. 5. Single device runtime performance with a varying number of neighbors.

Another storage consumption arises due to the size of the code. Our reference implementation, which we use throughout this performance evaluation, requires 66 kB of protected storage in $\mathcal{R}$. However, almost all the storage is spent for the implementation of the Ed25519 signature scheme. By using an Ed25519 implementation that is particularly suited for low-memory systems [5], we were able to reduce the size of $\mathcal{R}$ to 7.7 kB, albeit increasing the runtime for cryptographic operations.[1] This smaller implementation makes our scheme applicable to all commodity low-end embedded devices listed in the full paper [1], since all of them offer at least 8 kB of protectable Flash memory. Reusing the signature scheme in $\mathcal{R}$, further 15.1 kB of code in mutable memory are consumed to implement, among others, the network communication, the key exchange, and the encryption and decryption for the secure channel. In total, our reference implementation consumes 81.1 kB and our code size optimized implementation consumes 22.9 kB of storage. This is an acceptable overhead of respectively 31.6 % and 8.9 % of the totally available storage on the Stellaris platform.

Single Device Secure Code Update Runtime. We simulated the runtime of our code update scheme under various conditions and compared it to a conventional code update approach. The conventional code update approach distributes and installs code updates and ensures the authenticity, integrity, and freshness of updates on the devices. However, it does not exclude devices that are in an untrustworthy software state from the network and also provides no report listing all trustworthy devices for the network operator.

Figure 4 compares the runtime on a single device between our secure code update approach and the conventional code update approach with varying code update sizes. It shows the runtime of both approaches in seconds as well as the percentage overhead of our secure approach. The mesh network consists of 1024 nodes which are arranged in a binary tree topology. Since devices in the network require different amounts of time to perform the code update, e.g., some devices transmit a smaller installation report or they need not forward

---

[1] Yet, existing works have shown that a signature scheme which achieves about the same runtime performance than our reference implementation can be implemented in less than 4 kB of code by using platform dependent assembler directives [11,27].

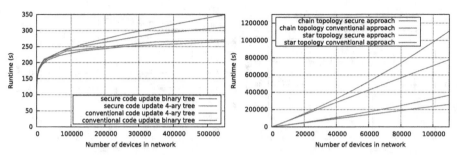

Fig. 6. Network runtime performance with varying network sizes.

Fig. 7. Network runtime performance with varying network sizes.

the new code update to neighboring devices, we averaged the runtime over all devices in the network. The figure illustrates that the size of the code update has a linear impact on the code update runtime. This is almost entirely due to the transmission time of the code update. In fact, the runtime overhead of our secure approach is nearly independent of the code update size, as it increases only slightly from 0.7 s with a 1 kB code update to 1.1 s with a 160 kB code update. For that reason, the runtime overhead decreases from 22.0 % down to 1.4 % with an increasing size of the code update.

Figure 5 shows the runtime for a 30 kB code update on a single device with a varying number of neighbor devices. We distributed the code update to the measured device first, which is why all surrounding neighbor devices are supplied with the code update during protocol execution. This causes a linear increase of the code update runtime. However, the additional runtime of our secure update approach also increases linearly with the number of neighbor devices. This is due to the time neighboring devices require to mutually verify each others' software state during protocol execution. Thus, with a varying number of neighbor devices, the runtime overhead remains rather constant at circa 4 %.

Network Secure Code Update Runtime. We further evaluated the total runtime required to perform a secure code update with all nodes in the mesh network. Figure 6 shows the total runtime for a 30 kB code update with varying numbers of nodes, using the secure or the conventional code update approach. The network topology is arranged as a binary tree or a 4-ary tree. The figure demonstrates that due to the tree network topologies, the code update runtime increases logarithmically with the number of devices in the network. We configured our secure update scheme to report the precise device ids of all trustworthy devices to the network operator. As this causes the installation report to grow proportional with the network size, the gap between the runtime of our secure approach and the conventional approach increases considerably when the network contains more than 100.000 devices. In such large network, our secure code update scheme performs better if the network is arranged in a broader but flatter network topology, as this decreases the average size of the report (e.g., it increases the number of leaf nodes that must only transmit their own id to the parent node). Therefore, in networks with more than 106.000 devices, our code update scheme performs better in a 4-ary tree network topology than in a binary tree topology. Nevertheless, for smaller networks, the runtime overhead is quite low in tree network topologies. To be precise, the runtime overhead remains below 2 % for up to 25.000 devices and is less than 5 % for up to 100.000 devices.

However, mesh networks could also embrace unfavorable topologies. Figure 7 depicts the total runtime performance for a 30 kB secure code update in a network with a chain topology and a star topology. The star topology is constituted of three device chains branching off a central star device. Figure 7 shows that in such an inconvenient network topology, the runtime for a code update attains extremely high values. This is caused by the long transmission time for the code update and the installation report. Nevertheless, even in the worst case, which is the chain topology, the overhead of our secure approach compared to the conventional approach is below 2 % for up to 4.000 devices and less than 11 % for up to 30.000 devices in the network.

We would like to stress that the overhead is largely introduced by transmitting the precise ids of trustworthy devices to the network operator. If we instead configure our scheme to report only the total number of trustworthy devices to the operator, the network runtime overhead becomes almost negligible compared to the conventional approach. In fact, this way, the runtime overhead is less than 1.5 % for 10 devices and less than 0.35 % for networks with 500.000 devices.

7 Conclusion

In this work, we presented a novel secure code update scheme for large mesh networks composed of commodity low-end embedded devices. Our scheme offers desirable security features for the application scenario of patching software vulnerabilities in these systems. Properly executed, our scheme enforces that after code update installation a device runs only unmodified and up-to-date software. Devices that refuse a proper execution of our scheme, and thus run outdated or compromised software, are detected by their neighboring devices and excluded from the network. Issuing a secure code update, the network operator learns which devices are in a trustworthy and which devices are in an untrustworthy software state. We demonstrated that our scheme is applicable to a broad range of popular low-end embedded systems without requiring any hardware modifications. Therefore, our solution can be retrofitted to many currently deployed systems. In addition, we showed that the scheme scales well and is practically usable in networks with tens of thousands of devices. Compared to a conventional code update, which offers none of the described security features, our scheme imposes a runtime overhead of 2.1 % in the best case and 11.9 % in the worst case for a network with 30.000 devices and a firmware update size of 30 kB. Thus, our solution is also well suited for future developments, where we expect low-end embedded device networks to increase in size.

Acknowledgment. This work has been co-funded by the LOEWE initiative (Hesse, Germany) within the NICER project and the DFG as part of project P3 within CROSSING.

References

1. Secure Code Updates for Mesh Networked Commodity Low-End Embedded Devices –Full Version. http://www.seceng.informatik.tu-darmstadt.de/assets/kohnhaeuser/esorics16full.pdf
2. Armknecht, F., Sadeghi, A.R., Schulz, S., Wachsmann, C.: A security framework for the analysis and design of software attestation. In: ACM SIGSAC Conference on Computer & Communications Security (CCS) (2013)
3. Asokan, N., Brasser, F., Ibrahim, A., Sadeghi, A.R., Schunter, M., Tsudik, G., Wachsmann, C.: SEDA: scalable embedded device attestation. In: ACM SIGSAC Conference on Computer & Communications Security (CCS) (2015)
4. Atmel: Atmel ATmega640/V-1280/V-1281/V-2560/V-2561/V Datasheet (2014)
5. Beer, D.: Curve25519 and Ed25519 for low-memory systems (2014). http://www.dlbeer.co.nz/oss/c25519.html
6. Bernstein, D.J.: Curve25519: new Diffie-Hellman speed records. In: Yung, M., Dodis, Y., Kiayias, A., Malkin, T. (eds.) PKC 2006. LNCS, vol. 3958, pp. 207–228. Springer, Heidelberg (2006)
7. Bernstein, D.J., Duif, N., Lange, T., Schwabe, P., Yang, B.Y.: High-speed high-security signatures. J. Crypt. Eng. **2**, 77–89 (2012)
8. Brasser, F., El Mahjoub, B., Sadeghi, A.R., Wachsmann, C., Koeberl, P.: TyTAN: tiny trust anchor for tiny devices. In: Design Automation Conference (DAC) (2015)
9. Butterworth, J., Kallenberg, C., Kovah, X., Herzog, A.: Bios chronomancy: fixing the core root of trust for measurement. In: ACM SIGSAC Conference on Computer & Communications Security (CCS) (2013)
10. Costin, A., Zaddach, J., Francillon, A., Balzarotti, D., Antipolis, S.: A large-scale analysis of the security of embedded firmwares. In: USENIX Security (2014)
11. De Clercq, R., Uhsadel, L., Van Herrewege, A., Verbauwhede, I.: Ultra low-power implementation of ECC on the ARM Cortex-M0+. In: Design Automation Conference (DAC) (2014)
12. Dong, W., Chen, C., Bu, J., Liu, W.: Optimizing relocatable code for efficient software update in networked embedded systems. ACM Trans. Sens. Netw. (TOSN) **11**(2), 22–34 (2014)
13. Eldefrawy, K., Tsudik, G., Francillon, A., Perito, D.: SMART: secure and minimal architecture for (establishing dynamic) root of trust. In: NDSS (2012)
14. Francillon, A., Nguyen, Q., Rasmussen, K.B., Tsudik, G.: Systematic treatment of remote attestation. In: IACR Cryptology ePrint Archive (2012)
15. Freesale Semiconductor: Using the Kinetis Flash ExecuteOnly Access Control Feature - 6.3 Entry into execute-only code on the ARM Cortex-M4 core (2015)
16. Hagedorn, A., Starobinski, D., Trachtenberg, A.: Rateless deluge: over-the-air programming of wireless sensor networks using random linear codes. In: IEEE International Conference on Information Processing in Sensor Networks (2008)
17. Hanna, S., Rolles, R., Molina-Markham, A., Poosankam, P., Fu, K., Song, D.: Take two software updates and see me in the morning: the case for software security evaluations of medical devices. In: Proceedings of the 2nd USENIX Workshop on Health Security and Privacy (HealthSec) (2011)

18. He, D., Chen, C., Chan, S., Bu, J.: SDRP: a secure and distributed reprogramming protocol for wireless sensor networks. IEEE Ind. Electron. **59**, 4155–4163 (2012)
19. Karame, G.O., Li, W.: Secure erasure and code update in legacy sensors. In: Conti, M., Schunter, M., Askoxylakis, I. (eds.) TRUST 2015. LNCS, vol. 9229, pp. 283–299. Springer, Heidelberg (2015)
20. Katzenbeisser, S., Kocabaş, Ü., Rožić, V., Sadeghi, A.-R., Verbauwhede, I., Wachsmann, C.: PUFs: myth, fact or busted? a security evaluation of physically unclonable functions (PUFs) cast in silicon. In: Prouff, E., Schaumont, P. (eds.) CHES 2012. LNCS, vol. 7428, pp. 283–301. Springer, Heidelberg (2012)
21. Koeberl, P., Schulz, S., Sadeghi, A.R., Varadharajan, V.: TrustLite: a security architecture for tiny embedded devices. In: ACM European Conference on Computer Systems (2014)
22. Kovah, X., Kallenberg, C., Weathers, C., Herzog, A., Albin, M., Butterworth, J.: New results for timing-based attestation. In: IEEE Security and Privacy (S&P) (2012)
23. Kulkarni, S., Wang, L.: Energy-efficient multihop reprogramming for sensor networks. ACM Trans. Sens. Netw. (TOSN) **5**, 16 (2009)
24. Law, L., Menezes, A., Qu, M., Solinas, J., Vanstone, S.: An efficient protocol for authenticated key agreement. Des. Codes Crypt. **28**, 119–134 (2003)
25. Law, Y.W., Zhang, Y., Jin, J., Palaniswami, M., Havinga, P.: Secure rateless deluge: pollution-resistant reprogramming and data dissemination for wireless sensor networks. EURASIP J. Wirel. Commun. Network. **2011**, 5–22 (2011)
26. Li, Y., McCune, J.M., Perrig, A.: VIPER: verifying the integrity of PERipherals' firmware. In: ACM SIGSAC Conference on Computer & Communications Security (CCS) (2011)
27. Mackay, K.: Micro-ECC. http://kmackay.ca/micro-ecc/
28. Noorman, J., Agten, P., Daniels, W., Strackx, R., Van Herrewege, A., Huygens, C., Preneel, B., Verbauwhede, I., Piessens, F.: Sancus: low-cost trustworthy extensible networked devices with a zero-software trusted computing base. In: USENIX Security (2013)
29. Park, H., Seo, D., Lee, H., Perrig, A.: SMATT: smart meter ATTestation using multiple target selection and copy-proof memory. Computer Science and its Applications, vol. 203, pp. 875–887. Springer, Heidelberg (2012)
30. Perito, D., Tsudik, G.: Secure code update for embedded devices via proofs of secure erasure. In: Gritzalis, D., Preneel, B., Theoharidou, M. (eds.) ESORICS 2010. LNCS, vol. 6345, pp. 643–662. Springer, Heidelberg (2010)
31. Rios, B.: Owning a Building: Exploiting Access Control and Facility Management Systems. Black Hat ASIA (2014)
32. Rossi, M., Bui, N., Zanca, G., Stabellini, L., Crepaldi, R., Zorzi, M.: SYNAPSE++: code dissemination in wireless sensor networks using fountain codes. IEEE Trans. Mob. Comput. **9**, 1749–1765 (2010)
33. Schrijen, G.J., van der Leest, V.: Comparative analysis of SRAM memories used as PUF primitives. In: Conference on Design, Automation & Test in Europe (DATE) (2012)
34. Seshadri, A., Luk, M., Perrig, A.: SAKE: software attestation for key establishment in sensor networks. Distributed computing in sensor systems. LNCS, vol. 5067, pp. 372–385. Springer, Heidelberg (2008)
35. Seshadri, A., Luk, M., Perrig, A., van Doorn, L., Khosla, P.: SCUBA: secure code update by attestation in sensor networks. In: Proceedings of the 5th ACM workshop on Wireless security, ACM (2006)

36. Texas Instruments: Stellaris LM4F120H5QR Microcontroller Data Sheet (2013)
37. Texas Instruments: Software IP Protection on MSP432P4xx Microcontrollers -10.1 Interrupt Handling in IP Protected Secure Zone (2015)
38. Ugus, O., Westhoff, D., Bohli, J.M.: A ROM-friendly secure code update mechanism for WSNs using a stateful-verifier τ-time signature scheme. In: Proceedings of the Second ACM Conference on Wireless Network Security, ACM (2009)

Authenticated Key Agreement Mediated by a Proxy Re-encryptor for the Internet of Things

Kim Thuat Nguyen[1(✉)], Nouha Oualha[1], and Maryline Laurent[2]

[1] CEA, LIST, Communicating Systems Laboratory,
91191 Gif-sur-yvette Cedex, France
{kimthuat.nguyen,nouha.oualha}@cea.fr
[2] Institut Mines-Telecom, Telecom SudParis, UMR CNRS 5157 SAMOVAR,
9 Rue Charles Fourier, 91011 Evry, France
maryline.laurent@telecom-sudparis.eu

Abstract. The Internet of Things (IoT) is composed of a wide range of heterogeneous network devices that communicate with their users and the surrounding devices. The secure communications between these devices are still essential even with little or no previous knowledge about each other and regardless of their resource capabilities. This particular context requires appropriate security mechanisms which should be well-suited for the heterogeneous nature of IoT devices, without pre-sharing a secret key for each secure connection.

In this work, we first propose a novel symmetric cipher proxy re-encryption scheme. Such a primitive allows a user to delegate her decryption rights to another with the help of a semi-trusted proxy, but without giving this latter any information on the transmitted messages and the user's secret keys. We then propose AKAPR, an Authenticated Key Agreement mediated by a Proxy Re-encryptor for IoT. The mechanism permits any two highly resource-constrained devices to establish a secure communication with no prior trust relationship. AKAPR is built upon our proposed proxy re-encryption scheme. It has been proved by ProVerif to provide mutual authentication for participants while preserving the secrecy of the generated session key. In addition, the scheme benefits from the lightness of our proxy re-encryption algorithm as it requires no expensive cryptographic operations such as pairing or modular exponentiation.

Keywords: Authenticated key agreement · Proxy re-encryption · Security · Internet of Things

1 Introduction

The Internet of Things (IoT) paradigm implies a network of heterogeneous devices (*things*) that evolves constantly in terms of complexity and scale. According to Garner's forecast [1], the number of active wireless devices will exceed 25

© Springer International Publishing Switzerland 2016
I. Askoxylakis et al. (Eds.): ESORICS 2016, Part II, LNCS 9879, pp. 339–358, 2016.
DOI: 10.1007/978-3-319-45741-3_18

billions of units by 2020. More connected devices mean more attack vectors and more difficulties to protect these devices. In addition, IoT security issues concern not only civil applications (e.g. monitoring live home temperature and humidity) but also critical applications, for instance, the Internet-connected cars or the remote patient monitoring in healthcare. These applications can be compromised when secure channels are not properly implemented. Hence, secure communications between IoT devices become no longer an option, but a requirement.

Due to limited resources and highly interconnected objects, there is a strong need to design lightweight and scalable key establishment protocols. The existing solutions that require the pre-distribution of secret keys cannot be envisioned. Indeed, we cannot pre-share every time a common secret key in each device because the number of connected devices composing the network is very important. If the key pre-distribution is not considered, most of the existing schemes require expensive cryptographic operations to establish a session key between entities that do not share common credentials *a priori* such as ECDH-based approaches [26]. Indeed, Sciancalepore et al. [26] propose a key agreement protocol with implicit certificates in the context of IoT. Their approach requires four costly operations in order to negotiate a common key between two parties. In addition, the negotiation algorithm always produces the same key for a given couple of devices, which can be vulnerable to known-key attacks. Many other efforts (e.g. in [23,24]) have been undertaken to reduce the overhead of standard security protocols so that they can fit in low power computing sensor platforms. However, these solutions still require the executions of costly cryptographic operations on such platforms.

The aforementioned heavyweight computations can be handled by a resource-rich server. Server-assisted approaches for key establishment protocols have been proposed in this respect for IoT. As such, Fouladgar et al. [17] introduce an adaption and an extension of TLS (Transport Layer Security) handshake to the Wireless Sensor Network. Their solution describes an ECDH key establishment between a constrained sensor node and an external entity mediated by a partially trusted gateway. Such solution requires only two costly operations on the constrained node side. However, the gateway is able to launch a man-in-the-middle attack and to establish a common Diffie-Hellman key with each party without anyone noticing. Saied et al. [25] propose a lightweight collaborative key agreement based on Diffie-Hellman (DH) key establishment. Their idea is to delegate the heavyweight cryptographic calculation of DH values to the resource-unconstrained trusted proxies in neighborhood. Such mechanism requires a sufficient number of non-colluding neighbors in proximity. Besides, it may seem unpractical, since the two end nodes, which do not share any relation, may not be in possession of a secure established link with those common proxies. Several works attempt to build a common secret key for any two entities using the DTLS (Datagram TLS) protocol in the context of IoT. Their approach is to delegate partially [18,29] or totally the DTLS handshake [20] to a third party. Such mechanism removes the overhead of intensive calculations for the constrained-devices. However, the third party can read all communications between sensor nodes and the Internet hosts. This feature is not desirable in certain scenarios especially when we do not trust the server. We remove such inconvenience by applying a lightweight proxy re-encryption mechanism in our proposed key establishment mechanism.

Lighter proxy re-encryption schemes can help to design scalable key establishment mechanisms. The proxy can translate a ciphertext encrypted under one key to another but is not allowed to learn anything on either keys. There exists many PRE schemes in the literature (e.g. in [2,7,19,22]). Their applications are diverse such as encrypted mail forwarding system, secure data storage on semi-trusted servers. In this paper, we present an application of PRE to build a server-assisted key agreement protocol where the server is unable to recover not only the secret keys of communicating parties but also the negotiated session keys.

Our contribution: In this work, we first propose a lightweight proxy re-encryption that uses a symmetric cipher to encrypt data. Our scheme is able to convert a ciphertext from one key to another without placing trust entirely on the proxy and without computing heavyweight computational operations. Second, based on the proposed re-encryption scheme, we build an efficient authenticated key agreement mediated by a proxy re-encryptor, namely AKAPR, for IoT services. The scheme allows us to establish common secret keys between devices, even highly resource-constrained ones (e.g. class 1 devices [9]). Third, we present a formal security validation of AKAPR using ProVerif [6]. The results show that AKAPR provides mutual authentication for participants and ensures the secrecy of the generated session keys.

Paper outline: The rest of this paper is organized as follows. Section 2 provides several notations and recalls cryptographic definitions of a proxy re-encryption scheme. We present a novel lightweight proxy re-encryption construction in Sect. 3. Section 4 describes in detail our proposed authenticated key agreement AKAPR for IoT. Section 5 provides an informal security analysis of AKAPR against common attacks with a formal security validation done by the cryptographic verifier ProVerif [6]. Finally, the conclusion remarks are given in Sect. 6.

2 Preliminaries

2.1 Notations and Abbreviation

The definitions and terms used throughout the rest of this paper are presented in Table 1.

Definition 1 (Symmetric cipher proxy re-encryption). *A symmetric cipher proxy re-encryption consists of five algorithms (*KeyGen, ReKeyGen, Encrypt, Decrypt, Reencrypt*) with the following functionalities:*

- KeyGen$(k) \rightarrow (id_A, id_B, sk_A, sk_B)$. *Given a security level parameter k, output the identifiers and the secret keys for two entities A and B. These keys are to be used in the encryption and decryption processes.*

Table 1. Abbreviations

Abbreviation	Definition
$s\|\|t$	Concatenation of two strings s and t
PRE	Proxy re-encryption
KDC	Key Distribution Center
I	Initiator
R	Responder
DG	Delegatee
KDF	Key Derivation Function
MAC	Message Authentication Code
WSN	Wireless Sensor Network

- ReKeyGen$(id_A, id_B, sk_A, sk_B) \rightarrow rk_{A \rightarrow B}$. *Given the identifiers and secret keys of A and B, output the re-encryption key $rk_{A \rightarrow B}$.*
- Encrypt$(id_A, sk_A, M, id_B) \rightarrow C_A$. *Given the identifiers (id_A, id_B), the secret key sk_A and a message M, return the ciphertext C_A.*
- Reencrypt$(rk_{A \rightarrow B}, C_A) \rightarrow C_B$. *Given a ciphertext C_A encrypted by the entity A and the re-encryption key $rk_{A \rightarrow B}$, return a ciphertext C_B to be decrypted by B.*
- Decrypt$(id_B, sk_B, C_B, id_A) \rightarrow M$. *Given a secret sk_B and a ciphertext C_B and the identifiers (id_A, id_B), return the plaintext M.*

3   The Basic Idea: Lightweight Bi-directional Proxy Re-encryption Scheme with Symmetric Cipher

In this section, we first specify general definitions and the most useful properties of a PRE scheme. We present subsequently several related PRE propositions in the literature. Then, the concrete description of our proposed symmetric cipher PRE scheme is given which is followed by a comparison with related solutions in terms of supported properties and performance.

3.1   Properties of a Proxy Re-encryption Scheme

In a proxy re-encryption scheme, Alice can delegate the decryption right on an encryption to Bob with the help of a *semi-trusted* proxy (i.e. An entity that acts and returns correct results according to demanded tasks but can be untrusted when processing sensitive data). In general, the proxy uses a prior provided secret, namely, proxy key or re-encryption key, to translate a ciphertext dedicated to Alice to another one dedicated to Bob. However, it cannot gain any information on the secret keys of Alice or Bob and is unable to read the content of the encrypted messages.

Proxy re-encryption schemes are characterized according to different criteria. The works in [19] and [7] provide several properties by which to compare different proxy re-encryption schemes. We briefly redefine these desirable properties as follows.

- Uni-directionality: The proxy re-encryption scheme is said to be *unidirectional* if the re-encryption key of the proxy can be used in only one direction. In contrast, a *bidirectional* proxy re-encryption scheme permits the re-encryption key to be used to translate encrypted messages from Alice to Bob and vice versa.
- Non-Interactivity: In a *non-interactive* scheme, Alice can generate a re-encryption key, while offline, from its secret key and Bob's public values without the participation of the Key Distribution Center (KDC), the proxy, or Bob. On the other hand, *interactive* schemes require the participation of parties (including KDC) to generate the re-encryption keys.
- Multiple-use: Some proxy re-encryption schemes can re-encrypt a ciphertext multiple times. For example, Bob can demand a re-encryption of a ciphertext re-encrypted for him which is previously intended to Alice to obtain a ciphertext dedicated to Charlie without actually decrypting the message. Such scheme is called *mutiple-use*. In opposition, a *single-use* proxy re-encryption scheme permits the proxy to perform only one re-encryption on a ciphertext.
- Non-transitivity: In a *non-transitive* scheme, the proxy cannot combine provided re-encryption keys to re-delegate decryption rights. For example, given three entities A, B and C, the proxy is unable to construct the re-encryption key $rk_{A \to C}$ from A to C from the two supplied re-encryption keys $rk_{A \to B}$ and $rk_{B \to C}$.
- Collusion resistance: In a proxy re-encryption scheme, it is desirable that Bob even colluding with the proxy, can not guess the secret key of Alice.

3.2 Existing Approaches on Proxy Re-encryption

Blaze et al. [7] first proposed the notion of proxy cryptography where Alice (A) can securely delegate her decryption rights or her digital signatures to

Table 2. Two existing approaches of a proxy re-encryption scheme

Type	Typical operations of a proxy re-encryption scheme	Examples
PRA	$A \xrightarrow{E_{pub_A}(M)} PR \xrightarrow{E_{pub_B}(M)} B$	[7], [2], [19, 22]
PRS	$A \xrightarrow{E_{sk_A}(M)} PR \xrightarrow{E_{sk_B}(M)} B$	[13, 27]

Meaning of abbreviations: PRA: Proxy re-encryption schemes that employ asymmetric ciphers; PRS: Proxy re-encryption schemes that employ symmetric ciphers; E: An encryption function; M: Message; pub_X: public key of the entity X; sk_X: secret key of the entity X; PR: the proxy.

another party Bob (B) with the help of a proxy. Many works on proxy re-encryption schemes have been proposed in the literature. We classify these schemes into two categories as depicted in Table 2: (a) Proxy re-encryption schemes that employ asymmetric ciphers (public key cryptography) to encrypt the message and (b) Proxy re-encryption schemes that employ symmetric ciphers to encrypt the message. Most of the proposed schemes use a public key primitive to encrypt the message. In [7], the authors propose the very first proxy re-encryption scheme based on Elgamal cryptosystem [15]. Alice first generates the ciphertext $C_A = (m.g^r, g^{ar})$ on message m using its pair of public/private key $(sk_A = a, pk_A = g^a)$. The proxy uses subsequently the re-encryption key $rk_{A \to B} = b/a$ to obtain $g^{br} = (g^{ar})^{rk_{A \to B}}$. Hence, B receives the new ciphertext $C_B = (m.g^r, g^{br})$ encrypted under his secret key. This scheme is bidirectional, transitive and exposed to collusion attacks. As such, the proxy can compute $(rk_{A \to B})^{-1}$ to obtain the re-encryption key in the opposite direction from B to A. In addition, the proxy can combine the two re-encryption keys $rk_{A \to B}$ and $rk_{B \to C}$ to get the valid re-encryption key from A to C $(rk_{A \to C} = a/c = (a/b).(b/c))$. Such property is sometimes unwanted. Furthermore, if the proxy colludes with one party, it is trivial for them both to learn the secret key of the other party. Ateniese et al. [2] proposed an unidirectional pairing-based proxy re-encryption scheme that fixes the above issues. They use a proxy key in the form of $rk_{A \to B} = g^{a/b}$. Such configuration provides non-transitivity and collusion-resistance properties. Indeed, the possession of $(rk_{A \to B} = g^{a/b}, rk_{B \to C} = g^{b/c})$ does not permit the proxy to find out $rk_{A \to C} = g^{a/c}$ due to the Decisional Diffie-Hellman Problem [8]. In addition, colluding with Bob does not help the proxy to discover the secret key of Alice and vice versa since having $g^{a/b}$ and b does not help him to recover a due to the Discrete Logarithm Problem. From then onwards, many schemes based on pairing operations have been proposed including Identity-based (IBE) proxy re-encryption schemes [19,22]. They are proved to be secure under chosen ciphertext attack (CCA) assumption. Pairing-free proxy re-encryption schemes exist, for example [11,12], but multiple modular exponentiations are still required.

There are several propositions on proxy re-encryption that employ symmetric ciphers to encrypt the message such as [13,27]. The main advantage of symmetric cipher proxy re-encryption approach is the lightness of the employed symmetric cryptographic operations in terms of complexity and memory usage. In [13], Cook et al. propose two conversion functions for symmetric ciphers. In their first attempt, they assume that Alice shares with Bob a secret key k_{ab}. In addition, Alice and the proxy must share k_a. Then, Alice sends $E_{k_a}(E_{k_{ab}}(M))$ to the proxy. The proxy decrypts the obtained ciphertext with k_a and sends the result $E_{k_{ab}}(M)$ to Bob. Hence, Bob does not need to share a key with the proxy and yet he can still get the message M. However, this assumes Alice and Bob must always share a common secret. Such assumption is not trivial when there exists a significant number of devices in the network, such as in the context of IoT. In their second attempt (termed as CK to be used in Table 3), the authors provide the proxy the key $k_p = k_a \oplus k_b$, built from the secret keys (k_a, k_b) of A and B, respectively. A computes $C = M \oplus k_a$ and sends it to the proxy. The proxy performs the conversion by computing $C' = k_p \oplus C = k_b \oplus M$. B can then decrypts C' to get the message using its secret key k_b. This approach is efficient but not secure. Indeed, B can easily retrieve the secret key of A by computing $k_b \oplus C \oplus C' = k_a$. In [27], Syalim et al. propose a pure symmetric cipher proxy re-encryption algorithm. However, this approach requires that A and B share common secret keys *a priori*. Moreover, it is assumed that the proxy cannot collude with any previous users since a compromised user can recover the current encryption key if he/she has the re-encryption key.

3.3 Our Proposed Lightweight Proxy Re-encryption

In this section, we present in detail our proposed symmetric cipher proxy re-encryption. A symmetric cipher proxy re-encryption consists of five algorithms (KeyGen, ReKeyGen, Encrypt, Decrypt, Reencrypt). In addition, we define (Enc, Dec) as the encryption and decryption algorithms of a symmetric encryption scheme. A key distribution center (KDC) is responsible for providing keying material. As such, KDC runs the two algorithms KeyGen and ReKeyGen to generate the needed security parameters. We suppose that Alice (A) desires to delegate the decryption right of a ciphertext C_A encrypted under her secret key to Bob (B) with the help of the proxy (PR). Figure 1 describes the message exchanges of our proposed PRE scheme. The procedure is detailed as follows.

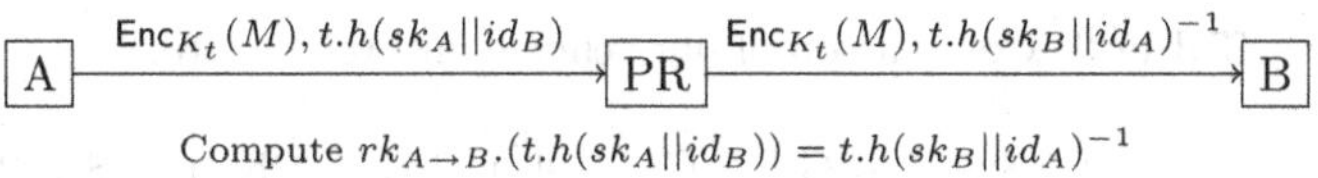

$$\boxed{A} \xrightarrow{\mathsf{Enc}_{K_t}(M),\, t.h(sk_A||id_B)} \boxed{PR} \xrightarrow{\mathsf{Enc}_{K_t}(M),\, t.h(sk_B||id_A)^{-1}} \boxed{B}$$

$$\text{Compute } rk_{A \to B}.(t.h(sk_A||id_B)) = t.h(sk_B||id_A)^{-1}$$

Fig. 1. Our proposed symmetric cipher proxy re-encryption scheme

- KeyGen$(k) \to (id_A, id_B, sk_A, sk_B)$: Given the security parameter k, this algorithm outputs the identifiers (id_A, id_B) and the secret keys (sk_A, sk_B) for A and B, respectively.
- ReKeyGen$(id_A, sk_A, id_B, sk_B) \to rk_{A \to B}$: Given the identifiers and the secret keys of A and B, this algorithm returns the re-encryption key $rk_{A \to B} = (h(sk_A||id_B).h(sk_B||id_A))^{-1}$, where $h : \{0,1\}^* \to \mathbb{Z}_p$ is a hash function that converts a string to a number on $\mathbb{Z}_p$. As we shall see, our construction results in the fact that $rk_{A \to B} = rk_{B \to A}$. This property makes our proxy-encryption scheme *bidirectional* meaning that the proxy only needs to store one re-encryption key to re-encrypt messages from A to B and vice versa.
- Encrypt$(id_A, sk_A, M, id_B) \to C_A$: Given the identifier of B and a message M, A uses its identifier id_A and its secret key sk_A to generate a ciphertext C_A. A first chooses a random number $t \leftarrow \mathbb{Z}_p$. Then, it generates a symmetric key $K_t \leftarrow KDF(t)$, where KDF is a Key Derivation Function. Finally, it outputs the ciphertext $C_A = (\mathsf{Enc}_{K_t}(M), t.h(sk_A||id_B))$.

– Reencrypt($rk_{A \to B}, C_A$) → C_B: Upon receiving the ciphertext $C_A = (C_1, C_2)$, PR keeps C_1 unchanged while multiplying C_2 with the re-encryption key $rk_{A \to B}$ to obtain the new ciphertext $C_B = (\mathsf{Enc}_{K_t}(M), t.h(sk_B \| id_A)^{-1})$.

– Decrypt(id_B, sk_B, C_B, id_A) → M: Upon receiving $C_B = (C_1', C_2') = (\mathsf{Enc}_{K_t}(M), t.h(sk_B \| id_A)^{-1})$, B first calculates the value of $l = h(sk_B \| id_A)$ from its secret key and the identifier of A. Then, it obtains the value of t by multiplying l to C_2'. From t, B generates the symmetric key $K_t \leftarrow KDF(t)$. Then, it gets the message M by decrypting C_1' using the generated key K_t: $M = \mathsf{Dec}_{K_t}(\mathsf{Enc}_{K_t}(M))$.

Correctness. The correctness of our proposed scheme is straightforward.

3.4   Comparison of Our PRE Scheme to Related Work

In Table 3, we compare several proxy re-encryption schemes in related work with our scheme based on the properties provided in Sect. 3.1. In comparing with asymmetric cipher PRE schemes, our scheme is much lighter in terms of computational cost. Indeed, the proposed construction does not necessitate any pairing or exponentiation operation. On the other hand, while providing equivalent performance compared with symmetric cipher proxy re-encryption schemes, our scheme is more robust against attacks from compromised receiver, semi-honest proxy and their corporation. We argue that our scheme provides most of the desirable properties as described in the following.

Table 3. Comparison of our scheme and related work

Property	BBS [7]	AFG [2]	GG [19]	CH [11]	CK [13]	SN [27]	Ours
Type	PRA	PRA	PRA	PRA	PRS	PRS	PRS
Directionality	bi-d	uni-d	uni-d	bi-d	bi-d	bi-d	bi-d
Non-interactivity	No	No	Yes	No	No	No	No
Multiple-use	Yes	No	Yes	Yes	Yes	No	No
Non-transitivity	No	Yes	Yes	No	No	Yes	Yes
Collusion resistance	No	Yes	Yes	No	No	No	Yes
Pairing-free	Yes	No	No	No	Yes	Yes	Yes
Exponentiation-free	No	No	No	No	Yes	Yes	Yes

Meaning of abbreviations: bi-d: Bidirectional; uni-d: Unidirectional; PRA: Proxy re-encryption scheme that uses asymmetric ciphers; PRS: Proxy re-encryption scheme that uses symmetric ciphers.

First, our scheme is *bidirectional* since $rk_{A \to B} = rk_{B \to A}$. This can be an advantage in the considered scenario (e.g. IoT) where the proxy has to store only one proxy key for any pair of devices. Second, in our construction, only KDC can provide the re-encryption key because it is generated from the secret keys of participants. This property makes our scheme *interactive*. However, the scheme can be made partially *non-interactive* such that A and B can negotiate a new proxy re-encryption key even when KDC is offline. In fact, A may generate a new secret key sk'_A and compute $k_1 = h(sk'_A||id_B).h(sk_A||id_B)$. B generates also a new secret key sk'_B and compute $k_2 = h(sk'_B||id_A).h(sk_B||id_A)$. k_1, k_2 are then sent to the proxy. The latter can now obtain the new proxy re-encryption key by computing $1/(k_1.k_2.rk_{A\rightarrow B})$ in $\mathbb{Z}_p$. Finally, as each proxy key is generated specifically for a pair of users, the proxy can only re-encrypt the ciphertext a *single* time. Such construction makes our scheme unconditionally *non-transitive* and *collusion-resistant*. Indeed, providing $rk_{A\rightarrow B} = (h(sk_A||id_B).h(sk_B||id_A))^{-1}$ and $rk_{B\rightarrow C} = (h(sk_B||id_C).h(sk_C||id_B))^{-1}$, the only way that the proxy can get $rk_{A\rightarrow C}$ is to have the secret keys of A and C due to one-way property of hash function. Even if B colludes with the proxy, they only have the value of $h(sk_A||id_B)$ which is only used in the communication between A and B. Such knowledge will not help them to find out A's secret key sk_A. In addition, to obtain $rk_{A\rightarrow C}$, they still need both the secret keys of A and C.

4 Lightweight Authenticated and Mediated Key Agreement for IoT

In this section, we present the application of our PRE scheme presented in Sect. 3.3 to obtain a very lightweight key establishment mechanism. Our protocol is relevant even with highly resource-constrained devices in the context of IoT. The first subsection presents the network architecture and our considered scenarios. The second subsection provides the security assumptions needed for the description of the protocol. Then, we describe concretely the message exchanges of our proposal.

4.1 Network Architecture and Scenario Description

Figure 2 describes the network architecture of our proposal. The considered network of *things* consists of a number of tiny nodes communicating with each other and with an unconstrained resource border router (or gateway). The gateway is the bridge between the sensor network and the outside world. It may take part in the communication between two entities in a passive (transparent to the communicating parties) or active (as a mediator in the communication process) manners.

Our key establishment protocol involves the four following actors:

- Two parties: an Initiator (I) and a Responder (R), which respectively initiates the communication and responds to incoming requests.
- A partial trusted party, named as Delegatee (DG), which is responsible for assisting the key establishment process between I and R. In fact, DG is provided with a re-encryption key that allows it to translate the ciphertext from I to R. In addition, it is considered as a *semi-trusted* party that acts and returns correct results according to the protocol but can be curious on transmitted messages.

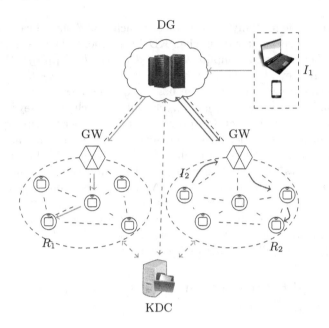

Fig. 2. Network architecture and considered scenarios (→: KDC provides keying material for all actors in the system. Examples of scenario: (1) —: The external user I_1 initiates a key agreement process (mediated by DG) with the resource-constrained sensor node R_1; (2) →: Two unknown resource-constrained nodes (I_2 and R_2) initiate a key agreement process with the help of DG and then GW.)

– A trusted Key Distribution Center (KDC), which is responsible for generating keying material and acts as the root of trust of the whole system. Besides, KDC is also in charge of delegation credential management and distribution.

In our considered scenario, I and R can be both resource-constrained devices. At the beginning, KDC provisions the keying material for all users on the system. Hence it can stay offline until the security parameters need to be refreshed. On the other hand, DG must stay online and participate actively in the key establishment procedure. Our motivation is that DG acts as a partially-trusted third party helping the constrained devices to negotiate session keys without obtaining any knowledge about these keys.

As depicted in Fig. 2, the initiator can be an external entity requesting for information of the Responder - a sensor platform device lying in a Wireless Sensor Networks (WSN). The key negotiation process is assisted by DG. In addition, when I and R are in the same WSN, DG can provide the delegation keys for the border router (or gateway) so that the key agreement process can be done locally. Note that the gateway is also considered *semi-trusted* as a consequence of which it only knows the delegation keys and is not able to recover the secret keys of I and R. We provide more details on the security analysis of our proposal in Sect. 5.

4.2   Security Assumptions and Notations

We suppose that I and R possess their own secret keys (sk_I and sk_R, accordingly). However, they do not have any common secrets *a priori*. On the other hand, DG shares with each communicating entity X a secret symmetric key K_{xd} which is employed to protect the integrity of the traffic between X and DG. As a result, DG shares the secret keys K_{id} and the secret key K_{rd} with I and R, respectively. In addition, we use an incremental counter in both communicating parties to mitigate the replay attacks. For example, we maintain the counter CT_{IR} in I's side for all exchanges with R. If this is the first time that I communicates with R, CT_{IR} is set to 0. It is increased by 1 after every successful key agreement. Furthermore, for each entity X, we denote its identifier as id_X. Such identifier must be unique for each entity. We also define (Enc, Dec) as the encryption and decryption algorithms of a symmetric encryption scheme. While, (AEnc, ADec) is an authenticated encryption algorithm such that $\mathsf{AEnc}_{K_1,K_2}(M) = \mathsf{Enc}_{K_1}(M)||MAC_{K_2}(\mathsf{Enc}_{K_1}(M))$ and $\mathsf{ADec}_{K_1,K_2}(\mathsf{Enc}_{K_1}(M)||MAC_{K_2}(\mathsf{Enc}_{K_1}(M))) = M$, for each message M and two secret keys K_1, K_2. Each key agreement exchange of order i between I and R (Message i, for $i = 1, 2, 3$) has two components ED_i and $MAC_i(K)$. ED_i defines the appended security parameters and the encrypted data, while $MAC_i(K)$ denotes the MAC of ED_i computed with the symmetric key K.

In addition, two hash function $h : \{0,1\}^* \to \mathbb{Z}_p$ and $H : \{0,1\}^* \to \{0,1\}^n$ are also defined, where n is an integer number generated from the input security level. These functions are modeled as random oracles [5]. Such oracle produces a random value for each new query. Of course, if an input is asked twice, identical answers are returned. In this work, we also use a Key Derivation Function (KDF) for generating a symmetric key. KDF is based on a solid pseudorandom number generator (PRNG) (e.g. in [3]). This function is initialized with several secret values, called seeds. An attacker with the knowledge of PRNG output should not be able to guess the seeds other than by exhaustive guessing.

4.3   AKAPR Message Sequence Chart

The proposed key establishment protocol AKAPR consists of four messages as depicted in Fig. 3. The key negotiation process is mediated by DG. The detailed description of the key agreement process is given as follows.

Message 1 from I to DG: To start a new session, I first increases CT_{IR} by one, where CT_{IR} denotes the current counter of I for all communications with R. CT_{IR} is set to zero if this is the first time I communicates with R. Next, it generates a session identifier SID at random (e.g. $SID = H(id_I||id_R||w)$, where w is randomly chosen in $\mathbb{Z}_p$). Then, I chooses at random two fresh numbers N_i and t from $\mathbb{Z}_p$. The ephemeral authentication keys $AK = (AK_e, AK_a)$ are then generated from id_I, id_R and t using a key derivation function (KDF). To construct the Message 1, I concatenates the session identifier SID, its identifier id_I and R's identifier id_R to (N_i, CT_{IR}). The concatenation is then encrypted using the algorithm AEnc. As we shall see, the resulting ciphertext is the encryption and MAC of the concatenation by the pair of keys (AK_e, AK_a). This guarantees that the attacker (including DG) cannot modify the encrypted text of the concatenation. Second, I masks the value of t by multiplying it with the hashed value $h(sk_I||id_R)$, where sk_I is the secret key of I. As we shall see, the result of such multiplication is randomly distributed in $\mathbb{Z}_p$ since the two used operands are also randomly generated in $\mathbb{Z}_p$. Then, the first five components of the message $(SID, id_I, id_R, \mathsf{AEnc}_{AK_e, AK_a}(id_I||id_R||N_i||CT_{IR}), t.h(sk_I||id_I))$ is completed by a MAC computed with K_{id}, to form the Message 1.

Message 2 from DG to R: Upon receiving the Message 1 from I, DG first verifies that SID is fresh. We suppose that DG stores a list of SID values for each pair of I and R. Next, DG validates that the message has not been modified by an attacker by verifying its MAC using K_{id}. If the verification holds, DG is also certain that the Message 1 has not been replayed. Then, it modifies the fifth component of the encryption part (ED_1) in the Message 1 with the delegation key dk_{IR}. Indeed, it multiplies $t.h(sk_I||id_R)$ with $dk_{IR} = (h(sk_I||id_R).h(sk_R||id_I))^{-1}$ to obtain $t.h(sk_R||id_I)^{-1}$. DG now concatenates the obtained result to the first four components of the Message 1 to form ED_2. The encryption part of the Message 2, $ED_2 = (SID, id_I, id_R, \mathsf{AEnc}_{AK_e, AK_a}(id_I||id_R||N_i||CT_{IR}), t.h(sk_R||id_I)^{-1})$, is then appended with a MAC computed with K_{rd}.

Message 3 from R to I: When receiving the Message 2 from DG, R first verifies the authenticity of the message by employing its shared key with DG, K_{rd}. Then, by multiplying the hashed value of its secret key sk_R and the identifier of I (id_I) to the fifth part of ED_2, $(t.h(sk_R||id_I)^{-1})$, it obtains t, which is a number on $\mathbb{Z}_p$. From t, I generates the secret ephemeral authentication keys $AK = KDF(id_I, id_R, t) = (AK_e, AK_a)$. Next, it decrypts the fourth part of the Message 2 using (AK_e, AK_a) to get the value of $(id_I, id_R, N_{i1}, CT')$. It verifies subsequently that CT' is superior or equal to its counter number CT_{RI} to be sure about the freshness of the Message 2 (see Sect. 5.1). The counter value of R, CT_{RI}, is now set to the value of CT'. To construct the Message 3, R first chooses randomly N_r from $\mathbb{Z}_p$. Next, it increases CT_{RI} by one. R now encrypts the concatenation of $(SID, id_R, id_I, N_{i1}, t, N_r)$ with the generated key AK_e. The encrypted data is then appended with the session identifier SID to obtain the encryption part. The latter is finally integrity protected with a MAC based on the generated secret key AK_a.

Message 4 from I to R: After receiving the Message 3 from R, I first approves the authenticity of the message using AK_a. Next, it decrypts the encrypted part by employing the secret key AK_e to get the values of $(SID_1, id_R, id_I, N_{i2}, t_1, N_{r1}, CT_{RI1})$. I verifies that (SID_1, N_{i2}, t_1) is equal to the generated values (SID, N_i, t). It also verifies that $CT_{RI1} = CT_{IR} + 1$. Finally, the session keys are generated from the values (CT_{RI1}, N_i, N_{r1}) and the identifiers of I and R: $K_s = KDF(CT_{RI1}, id_I, id_R, N_i, N_{r1})$. I macs the concatenation of $(SID, id_I, id_R, N_i, N_{r1})$ using the session key K_s and sends directly to R the hashed value appended with the session identifier SID as a key confirmation message.

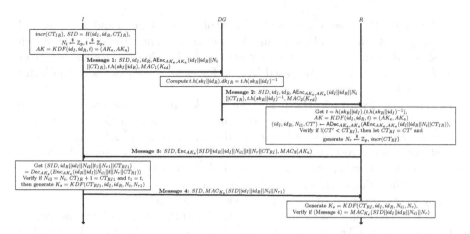

Fig. 3. Lightweight Secure Key Agreement for IoT (Meaning of abbreviations: $dk_{IR} = (h(sk_I||id_R).h(sk_R||id_I))^{-1}$; $incr(CT)$: $CT = CT + 1$; Message $i = (ED_i, MAC_i(K))$ for $i = 1, 2, 3$, e.g. $ED_1 = (id_I, id_R, \mathsf{AEnc}_{AK_e, AK_a}(id_I||id_R||N_i||CT_{IR}), t.h(sk_I||id_R))$, $MAC_1(K_{id}) = MAC_{K_{id}}(ED_1)$. Security keys needed for each participant: I (CT_{IR}, sk_I, K_{id}), DG (K_{id}, K_{rd}, dk_{IR}), R (CT_{RI}, sk_R, K_{rd}).)

Upon receiving the Message 4, R first generates the session key K_s from the identifiers (id_I, id_R), the obtained N_{i1} in the Message 2, the generated value N_r and its counter number CT_{RI}. Then, it calculates a MAC from the concatenation of $(SID, id_I, id_R, N_{i1}, N_r)$ using the generated session key K_s. If the latter is identical to the received Message 4, I and R can now start secure communications, e.g. using standard security protocols such as DTLS-PSK [16] where the pre-shared keys are provided beforehand by our proposal.

5 Security Analysis

In this section, we first provide an informal security analysis of AKAPR by describing its resistance against common security attacks. Then, we validate the security of AKAPR using the cryptographic protocol analyzing tool ProVerif [6].

5.1 Resistance Against Attacks

Our proposal is resistant to the following attacks:

- Replay attack: This attack is mitigated by the used counter numbers (CT_{IR}, CT_{RI}) and the random numbers (N_i, N_r) at run-time. The replays of messages 1 and 2 are detected thanks to the counter numbers (CT_{IR}, CT_{RI}). Indeed, for any new session, I increases the value of CT_{IR} by one. This value is then encrypted inside the Message 1. Upon receiving the Message 2, R can be sure about the freshness of this message by comparing its counter number CT_{RI} with CT'. If the latter is inferior than CT_{RI} then the message is detected as replayed. On the other hand, the freshness of the Messages 3 and 4 are assured by the pair of random values N_r and N_i since they are newly generated for each session. DG can also prevent replay attacks by keeping the session identifier SID. Because CT_{IR} is increased by one for each communication, the latter will vary in each session.

- Denial-of-service attack (DoS): The Dos attacks aiming at each participant are reduced in our proposal because all exchanges between parties are authenticated. Indeed, each message is appended with an authentication code (MAC) that permits the receiving party to verify if the message is altered during the transmission. Further operations are canceled if the verification fails.

- Man in the middle attack (MITM): The attacker cannot impersonate any party in our protocol since each message is protected by the secret keys that are unknown to him. As such, the Message 1 and the Message 2 are encrypted-then-maced by (AK_e, K_{id}) and (AK_e, K_{rd}), respectively. The Message 3 is encrypted then maced by the ephemeral secret keys $AK = (AK_e, AK_a)$, while, the Message 4 is protected by the new generated session key K_s.

- Key escrow attack: DG is a blind participant in the key agreement procedure. It aids the key negotiation without having any knowledge on the agreed session key and the secret keys of I and R. Indeed, although DG participates in the key negotiation process, it possesses only the delegation key $dk_{IR} = (h(sk_I||id_R).h(sk_R||id_I))^{-1})$ for each pair of Initiator and Responder. In addition, without knowing the secret key of I and R, DG cannot distinguish dk_{IR}, $t.h(sk_R||id_I)$ and $t.h(sk_I||id_R)^{-1}$ from a random number on $\mathbb{Z}_p$. The only actor that can intercept message exchanges between I, R and DG is the KDC. However, we have assumed that KDC is a totally trusted party which is responsible for the keying material generations and stays offline.

- Collusion attack: This feature inherits the collusion-resistance property of the proposed PRE scheme in Sect. 3. As such, even if DG colludes with one party, it cannot retrieve the secret key of the other party thanks to the one-way property of the hash function h. Indeed, if R collaborates with DG, they will get the values of t, AK, N_i and N_r. However, only the messages dedicated for R of I are affected. In fact, DG can only have the value of $h(sk_I||id_R)$ which does not help him to find the secret key of I, sk_I. If DG colludes with I, I can then decrypt itself the Message 3, which contains no secret information of R. The colluding parties can achieve the value of $h(sk_R||id_I)$. However, they are unable to guess the secret sk_R of R thanks again to the one-way property of hash functions.

The above security attacks except the MITM attacks, are usually impossible to be detected by an automatic software verifier (e.g. ProVerif [6]). In practice, the latter is used to verify if the essential security properties, such as mutual authentication and secret key protection, are provided in the testing cryptographic protocol. We provide more details on such software verification in the next section.

5.2 Formal Security Validation with ProVerif

In this section, we present a formal verification of AKAPR using ProVerif [6]. Our verification ensures that the proposed protocol provides the secrecy of the generated session keys and the authentication of participants.

ProVerif is an automatic verifier for cryptographic protocols defined in the Dolev-Yao model [14]. In such model, the attacker is an *active* eavesdropper, capable of obtaining any message passing in the network, initiating a conversation with any other users and impersonating as a legitimate receiver. It is only limited by the restrictions of the cryptographic methods used. In other words, the cryptographic primitives is considered idealized in the sense that they are unbreakable without knowing the employed secret keys.

In Listing 1.2, we provide the ProVerif verification code of our protocol AKAPR while respecting the description written in Sect. 4.3. A protocol description in ProVerif is divided into three parts: the *declarations*, the *process macros* and the *main process*. As described in Lines 1–44, the declaration part consists of the *user types*, the *security properties*, the cryptographic primitive *functions* and the list of defined *events* and *queries*. We define the types, the communication channel and the identifiers of the participating parties in Lines 1–6. The tables specified in Lines 8–11 are employed to model the storage of keys in a server. Only I, R and DG can use these tables to get the associations between host names and keys. Note that we use the table $ctr(host, Zp)$ to store the counter value of a specific host. To describe the synchronization of the counter values in both sides (I and R), we model only the ideal situation where there is no failed session between them. In such case, the counter values of I and R are equal. The detailed synchronization process is described in Lines 52–54, 68, 87 and 90 of Listing 1.2. Furthermore, the secrecy assumptions are specified in Lines 13–16. For example, sk_I and K_id define the secret key of I and its shared key with DG. These keys are kept secret to the attackers. Then, Lines 18–30 describe the cryptographic functions needed in our protocol. For example, the function $(kdf\_h(Zp, host) : Zp)$ generates the hashed value $h(aZpNumber\|aHostName)$. On the other hand, the function $(mask(Zp, Zp) : Zp)$ denotes a simple multiplication on $\mathbb{Z}_p$. Other functions are self-explained according to the protocol specification as depicted in Sect. 4. As we shall see, the correctness of the re-encryption process is modeled in Lines 32–35 based on the commutativity of multiplication on $\mathbb{Z}_p$. Finally, we introduce a list of events and queries in Lines 37–44. For example, the event $beginRkey(host, host, key)$ represents the request from I to create a trusted session with R. The defined events play as reference points for the protocol execution order.

In ProVerif, we can ensure the authentication by testing the correspondence assertions between the aforementioned events. Indeed, we verify the mutual authentication between I and R using queries defined in Lines 43–44. For example, the first query in Line 43 says that, if event $endRkey(host, host, key)$ occurs then, event $beginRkey(host, host, key)$ must have occurred before. Furthermore, our second interest of this protocol modeling is to verify the secrecy of the negotiated session key K_s. To do so, I and R choose a random number in each side and output the ciphertext encrypted with K_s. Then, they challenge the attacker to find the encrypted data by the queries specified in Lines 41–42. The attacker can obtain the underlying data if and only if having the secret key K_s since the cryptographic primitives are considered as black-boxes in ProVerif.

The second part of AKAPR ProVerif program describes the process macros for participants I, R and DG. They are specified in Lines 46–74, Lines 76–99 and Lines 101–109, respectively. These macros present the operations of I, R and DG during AKAPR execution. Note that in lines 57, 71, 86 and 98, we insert the events that we specified earlier. The other four process macros processDK, processKD, processK and processCTR fill the four tables of secret keys defined in Lines 8–11.

In the last part of Listing 1.2, we specify the main process (Lines 127–141) of the AKAPR ProVerif program. It instantiates the keying materials needed, inserts these keys to the right tables and runs the defined macros unlimited times.

The output of the program when running with ProVerif is summarized in Listing 1.1.

```
1 RESULT event(endIkey(x_72,y_73,z)) ==> event(beginIkey(x_72,
      y_73,z)) is true.
2 RESULT event(endRkey(x_3724,y_3725,z_3726)) ==> event(
      beginRkey(x_3724,y_3725,z_3726)) is true.
3 RESULT not attacker(secretI[!1 = v_7305]) is true.
4 RESULT not attacker(secretR[]) is true.
```

Listing 1.1. AKAPR verification results

The result in Lines 1–2 informs us that AKAPR provides mutual authentication of the two participants I and R. As such, the proved correspondence property in Line 1 implies that R authenticates I by the fact that I can correctly retrieve the session key K_s. On the other hand, Line 2 shows that I authenticates R since the latter can obtain the correct ephemeral key AK after receiving the Message 2. In addition, Lines 3–4 show the results of the queries not attacker(secretI[]) and not attacker(secretR[]) returned by ProVerif. As we shall see, these results are true, which means that the secrecy of the random values secretI and secretR are preserved by the protocol. In other words, the secrecy of the session key generated by AKAPR is also preserved.

The above ProVerif verification has several limitations. Indeed, in ProVerif, the hypothesis of perfect cryptography is considered, meaning that the only way to decrypt an encrypted message is to use the right secret key. Besides, in Line 18–35, we have to model the modular multiplication and its commutative property required in the re-encryption process by defining several new functions. This is necessary because real modular multiplication cannot be handled by ProVerif. In fact, ProVerif verification might not terminate when dealing with protocols that use algebraic operations such as modular multiplication or Exclusive-or. In addition, several security protocols that are conceptually safe, but are found flawed when considering algebraic properties as described in [21]. As a result, one can complete the above formal verification using other tools such as CryptoVerif [10], CL-Atse [28] or OFMC [4], which support most of algebraic properties and provide more realistic assumptions, e.g. the hypothesis of perfect cryptography is not required.

6   Conclusion

In this paper, we first introduced a novel proxy re-encryption scheme that requires only symmetric cipher to encrypt data. We showed that although our scheme is bidirectional and single-use, it provides the most important features: non-transitivity and collusion-resistance. Furthermore, the scheme is much more efficient when compared with related solutions that use asymmetric approaches. Second, we proposed a novel authenticated delegation-based and lightweight key agreement protocol to be used in the Internet of Things. This protocol is built upon the proposed proxy re-encryption scheme. The security of our solution has been formally validated by ProVerif. In addition, thanks to the used symmetric primitives, the proposed key agreement mechanism is very lightweight since it does not require any expensive cryptographic operations such as pairing operation or modular exponentiation. The proposed protocol can be applied even in class 1 devices with extremely resource-constrained profile.

Appendix

```
 1  type host.
 2  type key.
 3  type mkey.
 4  type Zp.
 5  free c: channel.
 6  free I, R: host.
 7
 8  table msKey(host, Zp).
 9  table transMsKey(host, host, Zp).
10  table keys(host, mkey).
11  table ctr(host, Zp).
12
13  not attacker(new K_id).
14  not attacker(new K_rd).
15  not attacker(new sk_I).
16  not attacker(new sk_R).
17
18  fun addone(Zp): Zp.
19  fun enc(bitstring, key): bitstring.
20  reduc forall x: bitstring, y: key; denc(enc(x,y),y) = x.
21  fun mac(bitstring, mkey): bitstring.
22  fun kdf_AK(host, host, Zp): key.
23  fun mkdf_AK(host, host, Zp): mkey.
24  fun kdf_h(Zp, host): Zp.
25  fun kdf_fn(Zp, host, host, Zp, Zp): key.
26  fun mkdf_fn(Zp, host, host, Zp, Zp): mkey.
27  fun mask(Zp, Zp): Zp.
28  fun kdf_rk(Zp, Zp): Zp.
29  fun inv(Zp): Zp.
30  fun sid_gen(host, host, Zp): bitstring.
31
32  reduc forall r:Zp, k1:Zp, k2:Zp;
33      reenc(mask(r, k1), kdf_rk(k1, k2)) = mask(r, inv(k2)).
34  reduc forall r:Zp, k:Zp;
35      unmask(mask(r, inv(k)), k) = r.
36
37  event beginIkey(host, host, key).
38  event endIkey(host, host, key).
39  event beginRkey(host, host, key).
40  event endRkey(host, host, key).
41  query attacker(new secretI);
42      attacker(new secretR).
```

```
43  query x: host, y: host, z: key; event(endRkey(x, y, z)) ==> event(beginRkey(x, y
        , z)).
44  query x: host, y: host, z: key; event(endIkey(x, y, z)) ==> event(beginIkey(x, y
        , z)).
45
46  let processI =
47    new secretI: bitstring;
48    in(c, hostR: host);
49    get keys(=I, kid) in
50    new Ni: Zp;
51    new t: Zp;
52    get ctr(=I, ct_i0) in
53    let ct_i: Zp = addone(ct_i0) in
54    insert ctr(I, ct_i);
55    let AK_e: key = kdf_AK(I, hostR, t) in
56    let AK_a: mkey = mkdf_AK(I, hostR, t) in
57    event beginRkey(I, hostR, AK_e);
58    new w: Zp; let SID: bitstring = sid_gen(I, hostR, w) in
59    let e1: bitstring = enc((I, hostR, Ni, ct_i), AK_e) in
60    let me1: bitstring = mac(e1, AK_a) in
61    get msKey(=I, ki) in
62    let tb: Zp = mask(t, kdf_h(ki, hostR)) in
63    let mac1: bitstring = mac((SID, I, hostR, e1, me1, tb), kid) in
64    out (c, (SID, I, hostR, e1, me1, tb, mac1));
65    in(c, (=SID, e2: bitstring, mac2: bitstring));
66    if mac((SID, e2), AK_a) = mac2 then
67    let (=SID, =hostR, =I, =Ni, =t, Nrp: Zp, ct_rp: Zp) = denc(e2, AK_e) in
68    if (ct_rp = addone(ct_i)) then
69    let K_s: key = kdf_fn(ct_rp, I, hostR, Ni, Nrp) in
70    let m_Ks: mkey = mkdf_fn(ct_rp, I, hostR, Ni, Nrp) in
71    event beginIkey(I, hostR, K_s);
72    let mac3: bitstring = mac((SID, I, hostR, Ni, Nrp), m_Ks) in
73    out(c, (SID, mac3));
74    out(c, enc(secretI, K_s)).
75
76  let processR =
77    new secretR: bitstring;
78    in(c, (SID: bitstring, hostI: host, =R, e4: bitstring, me4: bitstring, tbp: Zp,
        mac4: bitstring));
79    get keys(=R, krd) in
80    if mac((SID, hostI, R, e4, me4, tbp), krd) = mac4 then
81    get msKey(=R, kr) in
82    let tp: Zp = unmask(tbp, kdf_h(kr, hostI)) in
83    let AK_ep: key = kdf_AK(hostI, R, tp) in
84    let AK_ap: mkey = mkdf_AK(hostI, R, tp) in
85    if mac(e4, AK_ap) = me4 then
86    event endRkey(hostI, R, AK_ep);
87    get ctr(=R, ct_r) in
88    let (=hostI, =R, Nip: Zp, =ct_r) = denc(e4, AK_ep) in
89    new Nr: Zp;
90    insert ctr(R, addone(ct_r));
91    let e5: bitstring = enc((SID, R, hostI, Nip, tp, Nr), AK_ep) in
92    let mac5: bitstring = mac((SID, e5), AK_ap) in
93    out(c, (SID, e5, mac5));
94    in(c, (=SID, mac6: bitstring));
95    let K_s: key = kdf_fn(addone(ct_r), hostI, R, Nip, Nr) in
96    let m_Ks: mkey = mkdf_fn(addone(ct_r), hostI, R, Nip, Nr) in
97    if mac((SID, hostI, R, Nip, Nr), m_Ks) = mac6 then
98    event endIkey(hostI, R, K_s);
99    out(c, enc(secretR, K_s)).
100
101 let processDG =
102   in(c, (SID: bitstring, hostI: host, hostR: host, e7: bitstring, td: Zp, mac7:
        bitstring));
103   get keys(=hostI, kd1) in
104   if mac((SID, hostI, hostR, e7, td), kd1) = mac7 then
105   get transMsKey(=hostI, =hostR, dk_ir) in
106   let tdr: Zp = reenc(td, dk_ir) in
107   get keys(=hostR, kd2) in
108   let m7: bitstring = mac((SID, hostI, hostR, e7, tdr), kd2) in
109   out(c, (SID, hostI, hostR, e7, td, m7)).
110
111 let processDK =
112   in(c, (hi: host, hr: host, k: Zp));
113   if (hi <> I) && (hr <> R) then insert transMsKey(hi, hr, k).
114
115 let processKD =
116   in(c, (h: host, k: mkey));
117   if (h <> I) && (h <> R) then insert keys(h, k).
118
119 let processK =
120   in(c, (h: host, r: Zp));
121   if (h <> I) && (h <> R) then insert msKey(h, r).
122
123 let processCTR =
124   in(c, (h: host, r: Zp));
125   if (h <> I) && (h <> R) then insert ctr(h, r).
126
127 process
128   new sk_I: Zp;
```

```
129    new sk_R: Zp;
130    new K_id: mkey;
131    new K_rd: mkey;
132    new cpt: Zp;
133    insert ctr(I, cpt);
134    insert ctr(R, cpt);
135    insert msKey(I, sk_I);
136    insert msKey(R, sk_R);
137    insert keys(I, K_id);
138    insert keys(R, K_rd);
139    let dgIR: Zp = kdf_rk(kdf_h(sk_I, R), kdf_h(sk_R, I)) in
140    insert transMsKey(I, R, dgIR);
141    ((!processI) | (processR) | (! processDG) | (! processK) | (! processKD) | (!
           processDK) | (! processCTR))
```

Listing 1.2. ProVerif code of AKAPR

References

1. Gartner inc., forecast: The internet of things, worldwide (2013)
2. Ateniese, G., Kevin, F., Green, M., Hohenberger, S.: Improved proxy re-encryption schemes with applications to secure distributed storage. ACM Trans. Inf. Syst. Secur. (TISSEC) **9**(1), 1–30 (2006)
3. Barker, E.B., Kelsey, J.M.: Recommendation for random number generation using deterministic random bit generators (revised) (2007)
4. Basin, D., Mödersheim, S., Viganò, L.: An on-the-fly model-checker for security protocol analysis. In: Snekkenes, E., Gollmann, D. (eds.) ESORICS 2003. LNCS, vol. 2808, pp. 253–270. Springer, Heidelberg (2003)
5. Bellare, M., Rogaway, P.: Random oracles are practical: a paradigm for designing efficient protocols. In: Proceedings of the 1st ACM Conference on Computer and Communications Security, pp. 62–73. ACM (1993)
6. Blanchet, B.: Automatic verification of correspondences for security protocols. J. Comput. Secur. **17**(4), 363–434 (2009)
7. Blaze, M., Bleumer, G., Strauss, M.J.: Divertible protocols and atomic proxy cryptography. In: Nyberg, K. (ed.) EUROCRYPT 1998. LNCS, vol. 1403, pp. 127–144. Springer, Heidelberg (1998)
8. Boneh, D.: The decision Diffie-Hellman problem. In: Buhler, J.P. (ed.) ANTS 1998. LNCS, vol. 1423, pp. 48–63. Springer, Heidelberg (1998)
9. Bormann, C., Ersue, M., Keranen, A.: Terminology for constrained-node networks. Internet Engineering Task Force (IETF), RFC, 7228 (2014)
10. Cadé, D., Blanchet, B.: Proved generation of implementations from computationally secure protocol specifications1. J. Comput. Secur. **23**(3), 331–402 (2015)
11. Canetti, R., Hohenberger, S.: Chosen-ciphertext secure proxy re-encryption. In: Proceedings of the 14th ACM Conference on Computer and Communications Security, pp. 185–194. ACM (2007)
12. Chow, S.S.M., Weng, J., Yang, Y., Deng, R.H.: Efficient unidirectional proxy re-encryption. In: Bernstein, D.J., Lange, T. (eds.) AFRICACRYPT 2010. LNCS, vol. 6055, pp. 316–332. Springer, Heidelberg (2010)
13. Cook, D.L., Keromytis, A.D.: Conversion functions for symmetric key ciphers. J. Inf. Assur. Secur. **2**, 41–50 (2006)
14. Dolev, D., Yao, A.C.: On the security of public key protocols. IEEE Trans. Inf. Theory **29**(2), 198–208 (1983)
15. El Gamal, T.: A public key cryptosystem and a signature scheme based on discrete logarithms. In: Blakely, G.R., Chaum, D. (eds.) CRYPTO 1984. LNCS, vol. 196, pp. 10–18. Springer, Heidelberg (1985)
16. Eronen, P., Tschofenig, H.: Pre-shared key ciphersuites for transport layer security (TLS). Technical report, RFC 4279, December 2005

17. Fouladgar, S., Mainaud, B., Masmoudi, K., Afifi, H.: Tiny 3-TLS: a trust delegation protocol for wireless sensor networks. In: Buttyán, L., Gligor, V.D., Westhoff, D. (eds.) ESAS 2006. LNCS, vol. 4357, pp. 32–42. Springer, Heidelberg (2006)
18. Granjal, J., Monteiro, E., Silva, J.S.: End-to-end transport-layer security for internet-integrated sensing applications with mutual and delegated ECC public-key authentication. In: 2013 IFIP Networking Conference, pp. 1–9. IEEE (2013)
19. Green, M., Ateniese, G.: Identity-based proxy re-encryption. In: Katz, J., Yung, M. (eds.) ACNS 2007. LNCS, vol. 4521, pp. 288–306. Springer, Heidelberg (2007)
20. Hummen, R., Shafagh, H., Raza, S., Voig, T., Wehrle, K.: Delegation-based authentication and authorization for the IP-based internet of things. In: 2014 Eleventh Annual IEEE International Conference on Sensing, Communication, and Networking (SECON), pp. 284–292. IEEE (2014)
21. Lafourcade, P., Terrade, V., Vigier, S.: Comparison of cryptographic verification tools dealing with algebraic properties. In: Degano, P., Guttman, J.D. (eds.) FAST 2009. LNCS, vol. 5983, pp. 173–185. Springer, Heidelberg (2010)
22. Matsuo, T.: Proxy re-encryption systems for identity-based encryption. In: Takagi, T., Okamoto, E., Okamoto, T., Okamoto, T. (eds.) Pairing 2007. LNCS, vol. 4575, pp. 247–267. Springer, Heidelberg (2007)
23. Ray, S., Biswas, G.P.: Establishment of ECC-based initial secrecy usable for ike implementation. In: Proceedings of World Congress on Expert Systems (WCE) (2012)
24. Raza, S., Shafagh, H., Hewage, K., Hummen, R., Voigt, T.: Lithe: lightweight secure CoAP for the internet of things. IEEE Sens. J. $13(10)$, 3711–3720 (2013)
25. Ben Saied, Y., Olivereau, A., Zeghlache, D., Laurent, M.: Lightweight collaborative key establishment scheme for the internet of things. Comput. Netw. 64, 273–295 (2014)
26. Sciancalepore, S., Capossele, A., Piro, G., Boggia, G., Bianchi, G.: Key management protocol with implicit certificates for IoT systems. In: Proceedings of the 2015 Workshop on IoT Challenges in Mobile and Industrial Systems, pp. 37–42. ACM (2015)
27. Syalim, A., Nishide, T., Sakurai, K.: Realizing proxy re-encryption in the symmetric world. In: Abd Manaf, A., Zeki, A., Zamani, M., Chuprat, S., El-Qawasmeh, E. (eds.) ICIEIS 2011, Part I. CCIS, vol. 251, pp. 259–274. Springer, Heidelberg (2011)
28. Turuani, M.: The CL-Atse protocol analyser. In: Pfenning, F. (ed.) RTA 2006. LNCS, vol. 4098, pp. 277–286. Springer, Heidelberg (2006)
29. Van den Abeele, F., Vandewinckele, T., Hoebeke, J., Moerman, I., Demeester, P.: Secure communication in IP-based wireless sensor networks via a trusted gateway. In: 2015 IEEE Tenth International Conference on Intelligent Sensors, Sensor Networks and Information Processing (ISSNIP), pp. 1–6. IEEE (2015)

Data Privacy

Information Control by Policy-Based Relational Weakening Templates

Joachim Biskup$^{(\boxtimes)}$ and Marcel Preuß$^{(\boxtimes)}$

Technische Universität Dortmund, Dortmund, Germany
{joachim.biskup,marcel.preuss}@cs.tu-dortmund.de

Abstract. We conceptually design, formally verify and experimentally evaluate a sophisticated information control mechanism for a relational database instance. The mechanism reacts on access requests for data publishing or query answering with a granularity of either the whole instance or individual tuples. The reaction is based on a general read access permission for the instance combined with user-specific exceptions expressed as prohibitions regarding particular pieces of information declared in a confidentiality policy. These prohibitions are to be enforced in the sense that the user should neither be able to get those pieces directly nor by rational reasoning exploiting the interaction history and background knowledge about both the database and the control mechanism. In an initial off-line phase, the control mechanism basically determines instance-independent weakening templates for individual tuples and generates a policy-compliant weakened view on the stored instance. During the system-user interaction phase, each request to receive data of the database instance is fully accepted but redirected to the weakened view.

Keywords: Distortion · Confidentiality · Background knowledge · History-awareness · Information control · Read access · Relational database · Query access · View generation · Weakened information

1 Introduction

Early versions of access control deal with objects as containers on the layer of an *operating system*. Basically, the control intercepts any request issued by a process to read, write or execute the content of a container and then either accepts or denies the request. The decision is taken according to previously granted access rights, but without inspecting the actual content of the container. Access control primarily aims at enforcing requirements of confidentiality, integrity and availability. In this article, we focus on *confidentiality* regarding processes of a *single user* or a group of potentially colluding users. Accordingly, requests to read or, more generally, to *receive data* are our main concern.

Since early days, many refinements of access control have been proposed and have come into operation. In particular, the concepts of *granularity, history-awareness* and *content-sensitivity* are important for access control on the layer of a *database management system*. Going even further, managing data can be

© Springer International Publishing Switzerland 2016
I. Askoxylakis et al. (Eds.): ESORICS 2016, Part II, LNCS 9879, pp. 361–381, 2016.
DOI: 10.1007/978-3-319-45741-3_19

seen as the fundament of providing knowledge or some kind of belief, by assigning some well-defined meaning to raw data. Typically, such semantics are defined for the syntax of a formal logic. For example, first-order logic is employed for query answering in a relational database management system. Dealing with sophisticated notions of information – whether seen as knowledge or as belief – rather than with raw data might be even more ambitious, leading to a further layer of a *knowledge-and-belief management system*. Accordingly, access control for such a system demands for further concepts, namely of *information* control and *entailment*.

If a process running on behalf of an intelligent agent issues access requests, the results of an accepted access might be further exploited by computational rational reasoning, in order to determine the information actually gained. Roughly described, this gain is the new information inferred by reasoning about recently directly received data together with the already previously held information. Hence, the control has to confine the information content of data delivered such that any information gain by a "too curious" receiver does not comprise information to be kept confidential.

To still achieve best availability of information, the control should then be further enhanced by more sophisticated reactions on a request: rather than simply either accepting or denying a request, the control can react by a larger range of options, including the mediation of *distorted* data. However, distortions might lead to new vulnerabilities by so-called *meta-inferences*. Accordingly, on the layer of a *multi-(intelligent-)agent system*, it is necessary to also deal with adversarial reasoning including meta-inferences based on advanced background knowledge about the protection mechanism.

During this development rather straightforward access control gradually matured to highly sophisticated inference control. Unfortunately, the increase of functionality comes along with a decline of efficiency and scalability. One line of answers to this challenge is known as *confidentiality/privacy-preserving data publishing* [11], which in particular includes the technique of value generalization by k-anonymization as a special case of information weakening. In a first precomputation *offline phase*, the control system generates a sanitized view such that all concerns regarding inferences are already provably captured. In a second *system-user interaction phase*, access to the original data is completely prohibited, but full read access rights on the view are granted.

A particular instantiation of this approach applied to relational databases even goes a step further. In this instantiation [5], access rights for receiving data are expressed by the combination of (i) a *general permission* to see the tuples of a fixed database instance and (ii) exceptions in the form of *user-specific prohibitions* to acquire specific pieces of information. These forbidden pieces are expressed as queries in terms of the database schema and declaratively stated in a *confidentiality policy*. Notably, a security officer should declare such prohibitions independently of the actual instance. Given a confidentiality policy and the database instance, the control system splits the offline phase into two stages, which can be roughly rephrased as follows:

– For each forbidden piece of information listed in the policy, the system generates a suitable *weakening* by individually assigning a disjunctive and thus a less informative template to it, such that all these templates seen together with any non-distorted data are totally non-interferential regarding the information to be kept confidential.
– In any sequence inspecting each *actual* tuple of the instance in turn, the system checks whether the tuple is related to one or more of the disjunctive templates generated from the policy, and if this is the case the system replaces the tuple by the set of all pertinent templates.

Our contributions generalize and substantially extend that particular instantiation of confidentiality/privacy-preserving data publishing:

– We propose a *generic approach* consisting of first generating weakening templates from the policy and afterwards applying these templates on the instance tuple-wise, whether *dynamically* and interactively while reacting on query requests, or *statically* for defining a view.
– We design and verify a powerful method to handle *a priori knowledge*, in particular in the form of relational *data dependencies*.
– We employ a flexible scheme to declare and enforce *prohibitions*.
– We reduce the conceptual requirements to graph problems for which well-established *scalable graph algorithms* are known.

In the remainder of this article, we first introduce an example in Sect. 2. In Sect. 3, we briefly summarize basic notions and present the new generic approach. In Sect. 4, we refine the generic approach for data dependencies as a priori knowledge. Moreover, in Sect. 5, we discuss the practical efficiency on the basis of an experimental evaluation of a prototype implementation. Finally, we further relate our contributions to previous work and conclude in Sect. 6.

2   Running Example

We consider a simple relation instance r over a schema $R(A, B, C)$, so far without any data dependencies. For confining the interactions with some user, the security officer declares a confidentiality policy *ppol* with the *prohibitions* shown in Fig. 1a, formalized as sentences of first-order logic as any other items. This confidentiality requirement implies in particular that the user should neither be able to infer that the hidden instance contains any of the listed ground facts, nor should he be able to reason that the instance contains any ground fact that *entails* some of the listed existential facts. But the requirement still accepts that the user infers the validity of strict disjunctions of the listed items, as long as the user cannot strengthen such a disjunction to just one disjunct, i.e., to one of the prohibited items.

Accordingly, in the *first stage* of the weakening method, the prohibited items are suitably clustered into mutually independent groups in order to define for each of these groups a *weakening template* in the form of the *disjunction* of the

$ppol = \{\ R(a,a,a),\ R(a,b,a),\ R(a,b,c),\ R(a,b,d),\ R(a,b,e),\ R(a,c,a),$
$\qquad\quad (\exists X)\,R(a,e,X),\ (\exists X)\,R(b,e,X),\ (\exists X)\,R(c,e,X),\ (\exists X)\,R(b,X,e)\ \}$

(a) Confidentiality policy $ppol$

$\{\ R(a,b,c),\ R(a,b,d)\qquad\qquad\ \}$, $\{\ R(a,a,a),\ R(a,c,a)\qquad\qquad\ \}$,

$\{\ (\exists X)\,R(b,X,e),\ (\exists X)\,R(b,X,d)^A\ \}$, $\{\ R(a,b,a),\ R(a,b,e)\qquad\qquad\ \}$,

$\{\ (\exists X)\,R(a,e,X),\ (\exists X)\,R(a,f,X)^A\ \}$ $\{\ (\exists X)\,R(b,e,X),\ (\exists X)\,R(c,e,X)\ \}$

(b) Groups for templates that are satisfied by the instance   (c) Groups for templates that are *not* satisfied by the instance

$r = \{\ (a,b,c),\ (a,f,g),\ (b,a,e),\ (b,b,d),\ (b,d,f),\ (g,e,i),\ (g,h,i)\ \}$

(d) Original database instance r

$R(b,d,f)$
$R(g,e,i)$
$R(g,h,i)$

$R(a,b,c) \vee R(a,b,d)$
$(\exists X)\,R(a,e,X) \vee (\exists X)\,R(a,f,X)$
$(\exists X)\,R(b,X,d) \vee (\exists X)\,R(b,X,e)$

$\neg\,[\,R(a,a,a) \vee R(a,c,a)\,]$
$\neg\,[\,R(a,b,a) \vee R(a,b,e)\,]$
$\neg\,[\,(\exists X)\,R(b,e,X) \vee (\exists X)\,R(c,e,X)\,]$

$(\forall X)(\forall Y)(\forall Z)\,[$
$(\ X \equiv a \wedge Y \equiv b \wedge Z \equiv c\ ) \vee$
$(\ X \equiv a \wedge Y \equiv b \wedge Z \equiv d\ ) \vee$
$(\ X \equiv a \wedge Y \equiv e \qquad\qquad\ ) \vee$
$(\ X \equiv a \wedge Y \equiv f \qquad\qquad\ ) \vee$
$(\ X \equiv b \wedge \qquad\qquad Z \equiv d\ ) \vee$
$(\ X \equiv b \wedge \qquad\qquad Z \equiv e\ ) \vee$
$(\ X \equiv b \wedge Y \equiv d \wedge Z \equiv f\ ) \vee$
$(\ X \equiv g \wedge Y \equiv e \wedge Z \equiv i\ ) \vee$
$(\ X \equiv g \wedge Y \equiv h \wedge Z \equiv i\ ) \vee$
$\neg R(X,Y,Z)\,]$

(e) Confidentiality-preserving weakened view

Fig. 1. Groups for weakening templates generated from a confidentiality policy, a database instance, and the resulting confidentiality-preserving weakened view

group members. In case that the clustering leaves some items isolated, suitable further items are added, in our example $(\exists X)\,R(a,f,X)^A$ and $(\exists X)\,R(b,X,d)^A$. Figure 1b and c show the resulting groups, though at this stage the partitioning into the two parts is not relevant.

The weakening method computes that partitioning only in the *second stage*, when the stored instance r as shown in Fig. 1d is treated: one part contains the templates that are entailed by the instance; the other part contains the remaining templates. Finally, the weakening method generates the confidentiality-preserving *weakened view* that consists of three kinds of sentences, as shown in Fig. 1e (though in the presence of a priori knowledge, we might need to deal with a fourth kind of totally *refused knowledge*).

- *positive knowledge* about the instance, $R(b,d,f)$, $R(g,e,i)$ and $R(g,h,i)$;
- *disjunctive knowledge*, the templates of the first part;
- *negative knowledge*, a first sentence capturing all facts not entailing the other knowledge and further sentences capturing all templates of the second part.

3   Generic Approach

Stored Data. We consider data stored by means of a *relational database* management system, for which a single relational *schema* is declared. A schema comprises a relation *symbol* (table name) R, a finite set of *attributes* (column names) $\mathcal{A} = \{A_1, \ldots, A_n\}$, each of which has the same *infinite domain Dom* of constants, and some set SC of semantic *constraints*. In the running example we have three attributes A, B and C and, so far, an empty set of constraints.

The system maintains a database *instance* r, which is a finite set of tuples over $\mathcal{A}$ with values in *Dom*, satisfying the semantic constraints in SC. Intuitively, such an instance is treated as being *complete* in the following sense: each tuple in r represents a fact that is *true* in some fictitious "real world"; whereas, by Closed World Assumption (CWA), each other tuple over $\mathcal{A}$ with values in *Dom* represents a possible fact which is *false* in that world. Figure 1d shows an example of a database instance, leaving the CWA implicit.

We follow a foundation of the relational model of data in terms of first-order logic with equality, as also used in [3]. Syntactically, the logic is specified by a language $\mathscr{L}$ over $\equiv$, R, $\mathcal{A}$, *Dom*, variables, propositional connectives and first-order quantifiers in the usual way. Semantically, for this logic we treat a database tuple $(a_1, \ldots, a_n)$ as a ground fact $R(a_1, \ldots, a_n) \in \mathscr{L}$ and a database instance as a finite Herbrand interpretation of $\mathscr{L}$ with the infinite universe *Dom* assuming *unique names*. Using an instance in this way, we can inductively assign a truth value to each sentence in $\mathscr{L}$. This foundation also provides us with the pertinent notions of *satisfaction* and *entailment*: an instance r, seen as an Herbrand interpretation of the kind described above, *satisfies* a sentence $\Phi \in \mathscr{L}$ (r is a model of Φ, $r \models \Phi$) iff the truth evaluation according to r returns the truth value *true*; a set $S \subseteq \mathscr{L}$ of sentences *entails* a sentence $\Phi \in \mathscr{L}$ ($S \models \Phi$) iff each instance r satisfying S also satisfies Φ.

Given an instance $r = \{(a_{1,1}, \ldots, a_{1,n}), \ldots, (a_{m,1}, \ldots, a_{m,n})\}$ consisting of m tuples $(a_{j,1}, \ldots, a_{j,n})$, we can formalize our completeness assumption, specified above in natural language, by the following sentence in $\mathscr{L}$, denoted by $Comp(r)$:

$$(\forall X_1) \ldots (\forall X_n) [\bigvee_{(a_{j,1}, \ldots, a_{j,n}) \in r} (\bigwedge_{i \in \{1, \ldots, n\}} X_i \equiv a_{j,i}) \vee \neg R(X_1, \ldots, X_n)].$$

The control system should be effective for any fixed instance r. But the user is assumed to have some *a priori knowledge prior* $\subseteq \mathscr{L}$ that includes the semantic constraints SC, i.e., only instances with $r \models prior$ are seen as being possible. Extending the running example in Sect. 4 below, we will consider the a priori knowledge shown in Fig. 2b.

Confidentiality Policy. Confidentiality requirements are expressed in the form of *user-specific prohibitions*. Syntactically, most generally each prohibition would just be a sentence Ψ in $\mathscr{L}$. However, facing the well-known difficulty of the computational unsolvability of the general entailment problem for the full first-order logic language $\mathscr{L}$, in this work we restrict prohibitions to sentences in the sublanguage $\mathscr{L}_{exist}$ of existential facts. A security officer is assumed to declare all prohibitions as a finite subset $ppol \subseteq \mathscr{L}_{exist}$. The prohibitions dealt within the running example are gathered in the confidentiality policy shown in Fig. 1a.

More formally, an *existential fact* is a sentence of the form $(\exists X_{i_1}) \ldots (\exists X_{i_m}) R(t_1, \ldots, t_n)$ with pairwise different variables $X_{i_1}, \ldots, X_{i_m}$ and terms $t_{i_j} = X_{i_j}$ for $i_j \in \{i_1, \ldots, i_m\} \subseteq \{1, \ldots, n\}$ and $t_i \in Dom$ otherwise. Such a sentence corresponds to a subtuple where the components for the attributes in $\{A_{i_1}, \ldots, A_{i_m}\}$ are dropped. We also see ground facts as elements of $\mathscr{L}_{exist}$. The *entailment problem* for existential facts, i.e., whether for some Ψ_1 and Ψ_2 in $\mathscr{L}_{exist}$ we have $\Psi_1 \models \Psi_2$, is known to be easily solvable by a simple *term matching*, namely if and only if the following holds: whenever Ψ_2 has a constant $a \in Dom$ for an attribute A, then Ψ_1 has the same constant for that attribute. Consequently, we have both $\Psi_1 \not\models \Psi_2$ and $\Psi_2 \not\models \Psi_1$ if and only if at least one of the following alternatives holds: Ψ_1 and Ψ_2 have different constants $a_1 \neq a_2$ on some attribute A, or Ψ_1 has a constant a_1 for some attribute A_1 but Ψ_2 has a variable there and, vice versa, Ψ_2 has a constant a_2 for a different attribute $A_2 \neq A_1$ but Ψ_1 has a variable there. Each $\Psi \in \mathscr{L}_{exist}$ determines its *sphere* (of ground facts) defined by $Sp(\Psi) := \{\Phi \mid \Phi \text{ is ground fact in } \mathscr{L} \text{ and } \Phi \models \Psi\}$. Obviously, we have $\Psi_1 \models \Psi_2$ if and only if $Sp(\Psi_1) \subseteq Sp(\Psi_2)$. Moreover, even if both $\Psi_1 \not\models \Psi_2$ and $\Psi_2 \not\models \Psi_1$, the spheres might be overlapping, i.e., $Sp(\Psi_1) \cap Sp(\Psi_2) \neq \emptyset$, namely if only the second alternative discussed above holds.

Semantically, a prohibition sentence $\Psi \in ppol$ intuitively requires the following: from the point of view of the user, it should always appear to be *possible* that the prohibition sentence Ψ is *not true* [12]. More formally, the *view generation* mechanism to be designed gets three inputs, namely (i) the actually stored database instance r, together with (ii) the (assumed) a priori knowledge $prior$ with $r \models prior$, and (iii) a confidentiality policy $ppol$ with $prior \not\models \Psi$ for each $\Psi \in ppol$. Thus in the running example the input consists of the database instance shown in Fig. 1d, the empty a priori knowledge, and the confidentiality policy shown in Fig. 1a.

Given the inputs, the mechanism should return a consistent weakened view $v(r, prior, ppol)$ on r such that for all prohibition sentences $\Psi \in ppol$ there exists an alternative instance r^Ψ that

1. satisfies the a priori knowledge $prior$, i.e., $r^\Psi \models prior$,
2. does not satisfy Ψ, i.e., $r^\Psi \not\models \Psi$, and
3. generates the same weakened view, i.e., $v(r, prior, ppol) = v(r^\Psi, prior, ppol)$.

Since the view $v(r, prior, ppol)$ will be both a joint weakening of all these alternative instances and consistent, it should not entail any prohibition sentence $\Psi \in ppol$. In particular, this implies that for all $\Phi \in Sp(\Psi)$ we should have $v(r, prior, ppol) \not\models \Phi$. Notably, in general the latter property is only *necessary* for achieving our strong notion of *semantic confidentiality*, but it is *not sufficient* to guarantee the third property of *indistinguishability*.

Weakened Views. We aim at designing a control mechanism that applied to any possible instance r generates a sanitized *view* by *weakening* the information content of individual tuples as far as needed to preserve confidentiality. Such a view will again be formally specified in terms of the first-order logic language $\mathcal{L}$, in particular employing the sublanguage $\mathcal{L}_{exist}^{\vee}$ of strict and non-redundant *disjunctions* over $\mathcal{L}_{exist}$, i.e., all sentences of the form $\Psi_1 \vee \Psi_2 \vee \ldots \vee \Psi_k$ such that $k \geq 2$, $\Psi_i \in \mathcal{L}_{exist}$ and $\Psi_i \not\models \Psi_j$ for $i \neq j$.

As far as needed for confidentiality, a tuple/ground fact $R(a_1,\ldots,a_n)$ in the stored instance is disjunctively *weakened* by replacing it in a *context-free* way by a disjunction $\Psi_1 \vee \Psi_2 \vee \ldots \vee \Psi_k$ taken from a predefined finite set of *templates* $\mathcal{T} \subset \mathcal{L}_{exist}^{\vee}$ such that $R(a_1,\ldots,a_n) \models \Psi_1 \vee \ldots \vee \Psi_k$. In fact, in order to conveniently capture many simultaneous threats to confidentiality, the replacement is performed with *all* such disjunctions. To avoid unnecessary distortions, the disjunctions should only be formed by prohibitions of the confidentiality policy. Moreover, all disjunctions for all tuples seen together should be *mutually independent* in the following sense: for each two different disjunctions $\Psi_1 \vee \Psi_2 \vee \ldots \vee \Psi_k$ and $\bar{\Psi}_1 \vee \bar{\Psi}_2 \vee \ldots \vee \bar{\Psi}_{\bar{k}}$ we have $\Psi_i \not\models \bar{\Psi}_j$ and $\bar{\Psi}_j \not\models \Psi_i$.

Lines 1 to 6 of the left side of Fig. 1e indicate that the last three tuples of the example database instance remain undistorted, whereas the first four tuples are replaced by suitable disjunctions. Each of the distorted tuples entails a prohibition sentence and is thus replaced by the disjunction of the pertinent group for templates shown in Fig. 1b.

All replacements have to be reflected in a corresponding *partial* completeness assertion. Now, a tuple/ground fact Φ is treated as *false* if at least one of the following two properties holds: (i) Φ does neither entail an unreplaced tuple/ground fact nor an existential fact occurring in the weakening disjunctions; (ii) Φ does entail an existential fact occurring in $\mathcal{T}$ but not in the weakening disjunctions. If $\mathcal{G}$ is the set of unreplaced ground facts and $\mathcal{R} \subseteq \mathcal{T}$ is the set of weakening disjunctions used for replacements, then the completeness assertion is expressed by the following two sentences in $\mathcal{L}$, denoted by $Comp(\mathcal{G}, \mathcal{R}, \mathcal{T})$:

$$(\forall X_1)\ldots(\forall X_n)[\bigvee_{R(a_1,\ldots,a_n)\in\mathcal{G}} (\bigwedge_{i\in\{1,\ldots,n\}} X_i \equiv a_i)$$
$$\vee \bigvee_{(\exists X_{i_1})\ldots(\exists X_{i_m})R(t_1,\ldots,t_n) \text{ occurs in } \mathcal{R}} (\bigwedge_{i\in\{1,\ldots,n\} \text{ with } t_i \in Dom} X_i \equiv t_i)$$
$$\vee \neg R(X_1,\ldots,X_n)],$$
$$(\forall X_1)\ldots(\forall X_n)[\bigvee_{(\exists X_{i_1})\ldots(\exists X_{i_m})R(t_1,\ldots,t_n) \text{ occurs in } \mathcal{T} \text{ but not in } \mathcal{R}}$$
$$(\bigwedge_{i\in\{1,\ldots,n\} \text{ with } t_i \in Dom} X_i \equiv t_i) \Rightarrow \neg R(X_1,\ldots,X_n)].$$

Lines 7 to 9 of the left side of Fig. 1e show an equivalent reformulation of the second completeness assertion, and the right side of Fig. 1e exemplifies the first completeness assertion.

For some syntactically possible tuples the exact status of being either *true* or *false* deliberately remains unknown. Instead, the status is only determined up to the specified entailment relationships to disjunctions in $\mathcal{T}$, and in this sense the view might become only *partially complete*. Moreover, we will have to ensure that a weakened view is *consistent* even under consideration of the semantic constraints SC and possibly further *a priori knowledge*.

Two-Stage Weakening Method for View Generation. To achieve the goal of employing weakened views to enforce the confidentiality requirements of the prohibition sentences by means of context-free replacements of ground facts by weakening disjunctions, we propose the following two-stage *weakening method*. Given a database instance r, the a priori knowledge *prior*, and a confidentiality policy *ppol* such that $prior \not\models \Psi$ for all $\Psi \in ppol$, a weakened view $v(r, prior, ppol)$ is created as follows:

Stage 1 (independent of r) **Safe Templates**
Determine a finite set $\mathcal{T} \subset \mathscr{L}^\vee_{exist}$ with the following properties:

Property 1. $\mathcal{T}$ *covers ppol*, i.e., for each prohibition sentence $\Psi \in ppol$ there is a template $\tau \in \mathcal{T}$ such that $\Psi \models \tau$.
Property 2. The templates in $\mathcal{T}$ are *independent*, i.e., for each two different elements $\Psi_1 \vee \Psi_2 \vee \ldots \vee \Psi_k$ and $\bar{\Psi}_1 \vee \bar{\Psi}_2 \vee \ldots \vee \bar{\Psi}_{\bar{k}}$ of $\mathcal{T}$ we have $\Psi_i \not\models \bar{\Psi}_j$ and $\bar{\Psi}_j \not\models \Psi_i$.
Property 3. $\mathcal{T}$ is *non-interferential* under *prior*, i.e., for each finite set $\mathcal{G}$ of ground facts Φ such that $\Phi \not\models \tau$ for all $\tau \in \mathcal{T}$, for each finite set $\mathcal{R} \subseteq \mathcal{T}$ such that $\mathcal{R} = \{\tau \mid \tau \in \mathcal{T}$ and there exists $\Phi \in \mathcal{D} : \Phi \models \tau\}$ for some set $\mathcal{D}$ of ground facts, and for each $\Psi \in \mathscr{L}_{exist}$ occurring in $\mathcal{T}$, we have $\mathcal{G} \cup \mathcal{R} \cup \{Comp(\mathcal{G}, \mathcal{R}, \mathcal{T})\} \cup prior \not\models \Psi$.

Stage 2 (dependent on r) **Weakened View**
Define and (to block any information gain from the syntactic appearances) suitably normalize the following outputs:

1. *positive knowledge:*
   $v(r, prior, ppol)^+ := \{\Phi \mid \Phi \in r$ and for all $\tau \in \mathcal{T} : \Phi \not\models \tau\}$;
2. *disjunctive knowledge:*
   $v(r, prior, ppol)^\vee := \{\tau \mid \tau \in \mathcal{T}$ and there exists $\Phi \in r : \Phi \models \tau\}$;
3. *negative knowledge:*
   $v(r, prior, ppol)^- := Comp(v(r, prior, ppol)^+, v(r, prior, ppol)^\vee, \mathcal{T})$.

Quite obviously, the task of achieving the non-interferential Property 3 of $\mathcal{T}$ is the only conceptually difficult one. However, Stage 1 can be executed as a precomputation without even having an actual instance so far. In many applications we expect the costs to be affordable, at least under some reasonable restrictions. This claim will be further treated in the remaining sections.

Regarding the running example, still not considering a priori knowledge, in Stage 1 the safe templates are determined by the groups shown in Fig. 1b and c, which are straightforwardly formed by putting together two prohibitions that differ in exactly one attribute with constants. As explained before, the weakened view of our running example generated in Stage 2 is shown in Fig. 1e as follows: lines 1 to 3 of the left side form the positive knowledge; lines 4 to 6 of the left side comprise the disjunctive knowledge; and lines 7 to 9 of the left side together with the right side yield the negative knowledge.

Total Refusals. In some cases, it is impossible to achieve the wanted weakening of information *only* by means of weakening disjunctions. Intuitively, such an unfortunate event can be caused by a prohibition sentence Ψ that in some sense is conflicting with the a priori knowledge such that *every candidate* for a covering template is *not* safe, i.e., including it into the set $\mathcal{T}$ to be determined would violate the non-interferential property. We escape from this seemingly hopeless situation by complementing the set of templates $\mathcal{T}$ with a set $\mathcal{C} \subset \mathscr{L}_{exist}$ of such *conflicting* prohibition sentences and by adapting the generic approach accordingly, as sketched in the following. In Stage 1, we now require that

1. *ppol* is *covered* by $\mathcal{T} \cup \mathcal{C}$,
2. the *independence* property also applies for $\mathcal{C}$, and
3. the *non-interferential* property is adapted by (i) considering sets $\mathcal{G}$ of ground facts that additionally do not entail any prohibition sentence in $\mathcal{C}$, (ii) modifying the definition of $\mathcal{R}$ accordingly, and (iii) inserting the clauses corresponding to $\mathcal{C}$ into the first completeness sentence (thus *excluding* the ground facts in their spheres from known to be *not true*).

And in Stage 2, we generate an additional output $v(r, prior, ppol)^? := \mathcal{C}$ representing *refused knowledge*, meaning that any nontrivial information about the truth value of a ground fact in the sphere of an element of $\mathcal{C}$ is totally refused. Accordingly, we (i) strengthen the positive knowledge into $v(r, prior, ppol)^{+?}$ by additionally requiring that no prohibition sentence in $\mathcal{C}$ is entailed, (ii) change the disjunctive knowledge into $v(r, prior, ppol)^{\vee?}$ by insisting that only those $\Phi \in r$ are replaced that do not entail a prohibition sentence in $\mathcal{C}$, and (iii) modify the negative knowledge into $v(r, prior, ppol)^{-?}$ as just outlined.

Information Control. The output of the weakening method can be employed in essentially two ways: The weakened view $v(r, prior, ppol)$ is used for *data publishing* and thus the anticipated user is granted the full read access right to it, whereas all rights on the actually stored instance r are revoked. Alternatively, the anticipated user keeps his previously granted rights for *reading* or *querying*, but his requests are redirected to the weakened view. In the latter case we can even easily implement *content-dependent* query access rights with the granularity of single tuples/ground facts. More specifically, a *query request* regarding the (truth evaluation by the instance) of a ground fact Φ is handled as follows:

- If $\Phi \in v(r, prior, ppol)^{+?}$, then return Φ.
- If $v(r, prior, ppol)^{-?} \models \neg\Phi$, then return $\neg\Phi$.
- If $\Phi \models \Psi$ for some $\Psi \in v(r, prior, ppol)^? = \mathcal{C}$, then return MUM (a refusal).
- Otherwise, implying that there exists $\tau \in v(r, prior, ppol)^{\vee?}$ such that $\Phi \models \tau$, then return the pertinent weakening disjunctions in $v(r, prior, ppol)^{\vee?}$.

For each possible tuple/ground fact Φ exactly one of the four cases applies. Moreover, the third case applies for all tuples – whether in r or not – that entail an element in the refused knowledge. Similarly, the fourth case applies not only for the replaced tuples of r but also for all tuples – whether in r or not – that entail an element in the disjunctive knowledge about r without being affected by the second completeness sentence. Furthermore, since the fact of a refusal is explicitly indicated, a total refusal is only slightly related to simple tuple suppressions, which cannot be recognized in general.

Basic Assurance. To complete the presentation of our generic approach to generate weakened views, we formally verify the following assurance.

Theorem 1. *The weakening method of Subsect. 3.4 always returns a view that complies with the semantic confidentiality property defined in Subsect. 3.2.*

Proof. We consider appropriate inputs r, *prior* and *ppol* such that Stage 1 of the method successfully determines a finite set $\mathcal{T}$ of templates together with a set $\mathcal{C}$ of conflicting prohibitions with the required properties and Stage 2 defines the view $v := v(r, prior, ppol)$. Let then $\Psi \in ppol$ be a prohibition sentence. The non-interferential Property 3 guarantees that $v^{+?} \cup v^{\vee?} \cup \{v^{-?}\} \cup prior \not\models \Psi$. Hence, there exists an alternative instance r^{Ψ} such that $r^{\Psi} \models v^{+?} \cup v^{\vee?} \cup \{v^{-?}\} \cup prior$, but $r^{\Psi} \not\models \Psi$. Define $v^{\Psi} := v(r^{\Psi}, prior, ppol)$ to be the view generated for r^{Ψ}. It remains to show that $v = v^{\Psi}$.

In fact, the mutually exclusiveness of the four cases for a query request implies that r and r^{Ψ} can only differ in tuples for which the fourth case applies. Regarding that case, $r^{\Psi} \models v^{\vee?}$ means that for each disjunction $\tau \in v^{\vee?}$ there exists a tuple/ground fact $\Phi \in r^{\Psi}$ such that $\Phi \models \tau$. So, we verify that r^{Ψ} does not satisfy any further disjunctions in $\mathcal{T}$.

Assume indirectly that there is some $\tau = \Psi_1 \vee \ldots \vee \Psi_k \in \mathcal{T} \setminus v^{\vee?}$ such that $r^{\Psi} \models \tau$. On the other hand, since $\tau \notin v^{\vee?}$ and by step 2 of Stage 2, none of the existential facts Ψ_i of τ does occur in any of the disjunctions in $v^{\vee?}$. Hence, since $r^{\Psi} \models v^{-?}$, the second completeness sentence in $v^{-?}$ implies that for all $\Phi \in r^{\Psi}$ we have $\Phi \not\models \Psi_i$ for each Ψ_i of τ, and thus $r^{\Psi} \not\models \tau$, resulting in a contradiction.□

The non-interferential Property 3 of Stage 1 is also *necessary* to uniformly guarantee semantic confidentiality of the view constructed in Stage 2 for all situations. For assume that there are $\mathcal{G}$, $\mathcal{R}$, $\mathcal{D}$ and Ψ violating that property. Then the construction of Stage 2 for the instance $r := \mathcal{G} \cup \mathcal{D}$ would return a view that entails Ψ, and thus semantic confidentiality could not be achieved.

Availability, Admissibility and Interchangeability. In general *formal confidentiality* has to be balanced with and complemented by further possibly conflicting goals. First of all, we comply with *availability* by weakening information only if seen to be (locally) necessary. Moreover, best availability is achieved if the templates in $\mathcal{T}$ are as short as possible, i.e., are disjunctions of length 2, and additional prohibitions to complete a clustering are avoided as far as possible.

However, favoring better confidentiality than formally required, we might want to generate longer templates. Furthermore, as already discussed in [5], a weakening disjunction used as replacing template should be *admissible* in some application-oriented sense. In the next section, we will instantiate admissibility by *interchangeability* (of length 2), requiring that a template should be formed from two existential facts that only differ in *one* attribute with *constants*.

4 Data Dependencies as a Priori Knowledge

As captured by the non-interferential Property 3 of Stage 1, controlling information requires us to consider the *a priori knowledge*. Of course, for arbitrary a priori knowledge expressed in first-order logic we cannot algorithmically decide in general whether or not the crucial non-entailment actually holds. Thus, to come up with algorithmic solutions, we have to suitably restrict the expressiveness of the a priori knowledge that we aim to consider. In this section, we elaborate an example of such a restriction, focussing on single-premise tuple-generating dependencies as an important class of sentences capturing background knowledge about an application. Other examples would have to be treated in a similar way.

A *single-premise tuple-generating dependency* (called *dependency* for short) is a sentence Γ in the underlying first-order logic $\mathscr{L}$ of the syntactic form

$$(\forall X_1) \ldots (\forall X_k) [R(t_1, \ldots, t_n) \Rightarrow (\exists Y_1) \ldots (\exists Y_l) R(\bar{t}_1, \ldots, \bar{t}_n)],$$

where $X_1, \ldots, X_k, Y_1, \ldots, Y_l$ are pairwise different variables, each universally quantified variable X_i occurring exactly once in $R(t_1, \ldots, t_n)$ and at most once in $R(\bar{t}_1, \ldots, \bar{t}_n)$, each existentially quantified variable Y_j occurring exactly once in $R(\bar{t}_1, \ldots, \bar{t}_n)$, and – preferably to avoid an overall refusal – in both $R(t_1, \ldots, t_n)$ and $R(\bar{t}_1, \ldots, \bar{t}_n)$ at least one constant of Dom occurs. We will extract from Γ two existential facts in $\mathscr{L}_{exist}$, basically by taking the *existential closure* of each of the atomic formulas occurring in Γ:

$$prem^{\exists}(\Gamma) := (\exists X_1) \ldots (\exists X_k) R(t_1, \ldots, t_n) \text{ and}$$
$$concl^{\exists}(\Gamma) := (\exists X_{\bar{i}_1}) \ldots (\exists X_{\bar{i}_k}) (\exists Y_1) \ldots (\exists Y_l) R(\bar{t}_1, \ldots, \bar{t}_n).$$

Instead of converting originally universally quantified variables into existentially quantified ones, we might want to replace them by constants, basically by applying a *constant substitution* $\sigma : \{ X_1, \ldots, X_n \} \to Dom$:

$$prem^{\sigma}(\Gamma) := R(t_1, \ldots, t_n)[\sigma] \text{ and}$$
$$concl^{\sigma}(\Gamma) := (\exists Y_1) \ldots (\exists Y_l) R(\bar{t}_1, \ldots, \bar{t}_n)[\sigma].$$

A dependency establishes knowledge about the relationships between the validity of one single fact with another single fact, and can be used for reasoning in two ways. By *forward chaining*, knowing the validity of a fact that can be unified with the premise, we can infer the *validity* of the fact resulting from applying the unifier involved to the conclusion. By *backward chaining*, knowing the *non-validity* of a fact unifiable with the conclusion – as possibly enabled by our treatment of *partial completeness sentences* – we can infer the non-validity of the fact resulting from applying the unifier involved with the premise.

Regarding weakened views, basically, we have to avoid in an *instance-independent* way that for some possible instance such kinds of reasoning enable the adversary to exploit what we call an *interference* of a dependency with a prohibition: namely, to infer from the validity of both a weakening disjunction $\Psi_1 \vee \Psi_2$ of two prohibitions and a dependency Γ – together with the validity of positive or negative knowledge – that either Ψ_1 or Ψ_2 is *not* valid, i.e., that the other one is entailed. Technically, it can be shown that this unwanted effect can happen under three conditions: (i) a prohibition Ψ entails the existential closure $prem^\exists(\Gamma)$ of a dependency Γ; (ii) the sphere $Sp(\Psi)$ of a prohibition and the sphere of the existential closure $concl^\exists(\Gamma)$ of the conclusion of a dependency Γ have a nonempty intersection (which includes the case that $concl^\exists(\Gamma)$ entails Ψ); and (iii) a prohibition Ψ at the same time equals the existential closure of the conclusion of some dependency and for some constant substitution σ, $\Psi[\sigma]$ entails the existential closure $prem^\exists(\Gamma)$ of the premise of a dependency Γ.

These conditions will be blocked (step 1 below) by extending the policy with both the existential closure of the premise and the existential closure of the conclusion of the dependency Γ involved, thus excluding their spheres from published positive or negative knowledge. Unfortunately, in some cases this main measurement has to be complemented by further ones (steps 3 and 4/5 below). In a nutshell, the refinement for data dependencies proceeds as follows:

Refined Stage 1 (independent of r) **Safe Templates**

1. *extend* the policy by *implicit prohibitions* caused by a single dependency;
2. *clean* the policy from semantically *redundant prohibitions*;
3. *reject* conflicting prohibitions and establish total *refusals* instead;
4. *partition* the set of dependencies according to interactions with prohibitions;
5. respecting the partitioning, *cluster* prohibitions into admissible groups;
6. if possible, *add synthetic prohibitions* for completing a partial match;
7. *reject* prohibitions remained isolated and establish additional total *refusals*;
8. *form templates* of $\mathcal{T}$ as disjunctions, one for each group of the clustering.

We will only briefly explain the many subtle details by means of an example, reusing the confidentiality policy and the database instance of Sect. 2.

0. Input: The input is now given in Fig. 2. One can easily see that the given instance r complies with the given a priori knowledge *prior*.

1. Policy extension: As a basic step to achieve the most crucial non-interferential Property 3, the given confidentiality policy *ppol* is exhaustively extended according to each dependency in the given a priori knowledge *prior*. The dependencies Γ_1, Γ_2, Γ_3 and Γ_5 immediately interfere with *ppol*, and thus we have to add $prem^\exists(\Gamma_i)$ and $concl^\exists(\Gamma_i)$ for $i = 1, 2, 3, 5$. Afterwards, the dependency Γ_4 interferes with an added element, due to a suitable constant substitution of $concl(\Gamma_4) = (\exists X)\, R(g, e, X)$ and $(\exists X)(\exists Y)\, R(X, e, Y)$, requiring to add $prem^\exists(\Gamma_4)$ and $concl^\exists(\Gamma_4)$ as well. This leads to the *extended* policy

$$ppol_{prior} = ppol \cup \{\ (\exists X)\, R(a, X, c),\ (\exists X)\, R(X, d, f),\ (\exists X)\, R(X, a, e),$$
$$(\exists X)\, R(a, X, d),\ (\exists X)\, R(X, b, e),\ (\exists X)\, R(a, X, a),$$
$$(\exists X)(\exists Y)\, R(X, e, Y),\ (\exists X)\, R(g, h, X),\ (\exists X)\, R(g, e, X)\}.$$

$$r = \{\,(a,b,c),\ (a,f,g),\ (b,a,e),\ (b,b,d),\ (b,d,f),\ (g,e,i),\ (g,h,i)\,\}$$

(a) Original database instance r (complying with $prior$)

$$
\begin{aligned}
prior = \{\ \ \Gamma_1 &= (\forall X)\,[\,R(a,X,c) \Rightarrow R(X,d,f)\,] \\
\Gamma_2 &= (\forall X)\,[\,R(X,d,f) \Rightarrow R(X,a,e)\,] \\
\Gamma_3 &= (\forall X)\,[\,R(a,X,d) \Rightarrow R(X,b,e)\,] \\
\Gamma_4 &= (\forall X)\,[\,R(g,h,X) \Rightarrow R(g,e,X)\,] \\
\Gamma_5 &= (\forall X)\,[\,R(a,X,a) \Rightarrow (\exists Y)\,R(X,e,Y)\,]\ \ \}
\end{aligned}
$$

(b) Adversary's a priori knowledge $prior$

$$
\begin{aligned}
ppol = \{\ &R(a,a,a),\ R(a,b,a),\ R(a,b,c),\ R(a,b,d),\ R(a,b,e),\ R(a,c,a), \\
&(\exists X)\,R(a,e,X),\ (\exists X)\,R(b,e,X),\ (\exists X)\,R(c,e,X),\ (\exists X)\,R(b,X,e)\,\}
\end{aligned}
$$

(c) Confidentiality policy $ppol$

Fig. 2. Example input with a priori knowledge for refined weakening method

2. Policy cleaning: We then ensure the *independence* Property 2 of Stage 1 but without affecting the *covering* Property 1 of Stage 1. To do so, the extended policy $ppol_{prior}$ is cleaned by removing those elements that entail another element, which is still kept. Thus, the policy is reduced to the "core" subset of its weakest sentences. This leads to the *cleaned* (extended) confidentiality policy

$$
\begin{aligned}
\widehat{ppol}_{prior} = \{\ &(\exists X)\,R(b,X,e),\ (\exists X)\,R(a,X,c),\ (\exists X)\,R(X,d,f), \\
&(\exists X)\,R(X,a,e),\ (\exists X)\,R(a,X,d),\ (\exists X)\,R(X,b,e), \\
&(\exists X)\,R(a,X,a),\ (\exists X)(\exists Y)\,R(X,e,Y),\ (\exists X)\,R(g,h,X)\}.
\end{aligned}
$$

3. Rejecting prohibitions and establishing refusals: If a prohibition of $\widehat{ppol}_{prior}$ is entailed by $concl^\sigma(\Gamma)$ for some constant substitution σ for some dependency Γ, then it always needs to be rejected. This results in the set of *conflicting* prohibitions to be refused:

$$
\begin{aligned}
\mathcal{C} = \{\ &(\exists X)\,R(b,X,e),\ (\exists X)\,R(X,d,f), \\
&(\exists X)\,R(X,a,e),\ (\exists X)\,R(X,b,e),\ (\exists X)(\exists Y)\,R(X,e,Y)\,\}.
\end{aligned}
$$

4. Partitioning dependencies: To decisively ensure the crucial non-interferential Property 3, we have to take provisions against unwanted *joint* effects of two or more dependencies. Accordingly, we partition the given a priori knowledge $prior$ with respect to $\widehat{ppol}_{prior}$, with the intention to block forming templates of prohibitions that are affected by dependencies of the same partition.

The dependencies Γ_1 and Γ_2 need to be in the same partition, as the existential closure of the conclusion of Γ_1 implies the existential closure of the premise of Γ_2. Further, Γ_3 also needs to be in this partition, because there is the prohibition $(\exists X)\,R(b,X,e) \in \widehat{ppol}_{prior}$, for which both implications $concl^{\sigma_2}(\Gamma_2) \models (\exists X)\,R(b,X,e)$ and $concl^{\sigma_3}(\Gamma_3) \models (\exists X)\,R(b,X,e)$ hold under constant substitutions σ_2 and σ_3 with $\sigma_2(X) = \sigma_3(X) = b$. Similarly, the dependencies Γ_4 and Γ_5 need to be in the same partition, as $\widehat{ppol}_{prior}$ contains the prohibition $(\exists X)(\exists Y) R(X, e, Y)$ with both $concl^{\sigma_4}(\Gamma_4) \models (\exists X)(\exists Y) R(X, e, Y)$ and $concl^{\sigma_5}(\Gamma_5) \models (\exists X)(\exists Y) R(X, e, Y)$ under arbitrary constant substitutions σ_4 and σ_5. As a consequence, the algorithm creates the partitioning $\mathcal{P} = \{P_1, P_2\}$ with $P_1 = \{\Gamma_1, \Gamma_2, \Gamma_3\}$ and $P_2 = \{\Gamma_4, \Gamma_5\}$.

$$
\begin{aligned}
&R(a, f, g) \\
&R(b, b, d) \\
\\
&(\exists X)\, R(a, X, a) \vee (\exists X)\, R(a, X, c) \\
&(\exists X)\, R(g, c, X) \vee (\exists X)\, R(g, h, X) \\
\\
&\text{Refused: } \{\ (\exists X)\, R(X, a, e), \\
&\qquad\qquad (\exists X)\, R(X, b, e), \\
&\qquad\qquad (\exists X)\, R(X, d, f), \\
&\qquad\qquad (\exists X)(\exists Y)\, R(X, e, Y), \\
&\qquad\qquad (\exists X)\, R(a, X, d), \\
&\qquad\qquad (\exists X)\, R(b, X, e) \qquad \}
\end{aligned}
$$

$$
(\forall X)(\forall Y)(\forall Z)\,[
$$
$$
\begin{aligned}
&(\qquad\qquad\quad Y \equiv a \wedge Z \equiv e\ )\ \vee \\
&(\qquad\qquad\quad Y \equiv b \wedge Z \equiv e\ )\ \vee \\
&(\qquad\qquad\quad Y \equiv d \wedge Z \equiv f\ )\ \vee \\
&(\qquad\qquad\quad Y \equiv e \qquad\qquad\ )\ \vee \\
&(X \equiv a\ \wedge \qquad\qquad Z \equiv a\ )\ \vee \\
&(X \equiv a\ \wedge \qquad\qquad Z \equiv c\ )\ \vee \\
&(X \equiv a\ \wedge \qquad\qquad Z \equiv d\ )\ \vee \\
&(X \equiv a\ \wedge Y \equiv f \wedge Z \equiv g\ )\ \vee \\
&(X \equiv b\ \wedge \qquad\qquad Z \equiv e\ )\ \vee \\
&(X \equiv b\ \wedge Y \equiv b \wedge Z \equiv d\ )\ \vee \\
&(X \equiv g\ \wedge Y \equiv c \qquad\qquad)\ \vee \\
&(X \equiv g\ \wedge Y \equiv h \qquad\qquad)\ \vee \\
&\neg R(X, Y, Z)\,]
\end{aligned}
$$

Fig. 3. Inference-proof weakened view for inputs of Fig. 2

5. Admissible clustering: To prepare the clustering by means of an efficient graph algorithm, the prohibitions in the set $\widehat{ppol}_{prior} \setminus C$ are used as vertices to generate an *indistinguishability-graph*. Although the prohibitions $(\exists X)\, R(a, X, c)$ and $(\exists X)\, R(a, X, d)$ are obviously interchangeable, the indistinguishability-graph does *not* contain an edge connecting the corresponding vertices of the graph, as both of these prohibitions entail an existential closure of a premise of the *same* partition P_1 due to $prem^{\exists}(\Gamma_1) = (\exists X)\, R(a, X, c)$ and $prem^{\exists}(\Gamma_3) = (\exists X)\, R(a, X, d)$. Then we employ a suitable *graph algorithm* to compute a clustering as a maximum matching on the considered indistinguishability-graph, getting (in this simple example trivially) $M = \{\ \{(\exists X)\, R(a, X, a),\ (\exists X)\, R(a, X, c)\}\ \}$.

6. Adding synthetic prohibitions. To tentatively maintain the covering Property 1, the prohibition $(\exists X)\, R(g, h, X)$, which is uncovered by the matching M, is admissibly paired with the additional synthetic prohibition $(\exists X)\, R(g, c, X)$.

7. Rejecting isolated prohibitions: To decisively maintain the covering Property 1, we still have to treat the prohibition $(\exists X)\, R(a, X, d)$, which remains isolated so far. Each interchangeable additional prohibition must differ either in the constant symbol at first position or in the constant symbol at the third position, and in both of these cases a dependency of *prior* would interfere with it. Accordingly, the prohibition $(\exists X)\, R(a, X, d)$ is additionally rejected and added to the set of conflicting prohibitions $\mathcal{C}$, to be used for total refusals.

8. Forming templates: We form a disjunction for each group of the clustering.

Stage 2 of the weakening method: We get the view given in Fig. 3.

Theorem 2. *The output $\mathcal{T}$ of the refined Stage 1 complies with the required properties of the generic weakening method, namely (i) covering the confidentiality policy ppol, (ii) having mutually independent templates, and (iii) being non-interferential under the a priori knowledge prior.*

Proof. Elaborated arguments following the explanations given for the example.

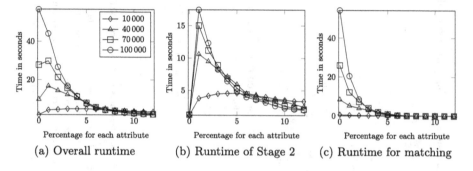

(a) Overall runtime   (b) Runtime of Stage 2   (c) Runtime for matching

Fig. 4. Experiment 1: Varying *existential quantification* in confidentiality policy

5   Experimental Evaluation and Practical Efficiency

To experimentally confirm the practical efficiency of the generic approach under the refinement for data dependencies we provided a prototype implementation and performed several experiments. The prototype is implemented in Java 8, except for the C++ implementation of the matching algorithm. All experiments were run under Ubuntu 14.04 on a machine with 2 CPU sockets, each of which is equipped with an "Intel Xeon E5-2690" with 8 physical cores running at 2.9 GHz. As each CPU core can logically handle two threads due to hyperthreading, the machine has a total number of 32 logical CPU cores. To benefit from the modern hardware, the algorithms used for cleaning the policy, partitioning the a priori knowledge and constructing the weakened view have been parallelized (but we could not find a suitable parallelization for the maximum matching algorithm).

To compute a maximum matching (cf. [13,15]), the prototype benefits from the "Boost"-library [8]. Although a maximum matching on a general graph

Table 1. Parameters of experiments (varying parameter values in boldface)

Parameter	Experiment 1	Experiment 2	Experiment 3	Experiment 4	Experiment 5
Relation instance:					
Number of tuples	10^6	10^6	10^6	10^6	10^6
Number of constants used	20	20	20	20	20
Instance generation	fully random	fully random	random/chased	random/chased	random/chased
Confidentiality policy:					
Number of prohibitions	$1, 4, 7, 10 \times 10^4$	$1, 4, 7, 10 \times 10^4$	$1, 4, 7, 10 \times 10^4$	$1, 4, 7, 10 \times 10^4$	$1, 4, 7, 10 \times 10^4$
Number of constants used	12	**from 10 to 22**	12	12	12
Existential quantification	**from 0 % to 12 %**	5 %	5 %	5 %	5 %
Policy generation	fully random	fully random	fully random	fully random	fully random
A priori knowledge:					
Number of dependencies	-	-	**from 100 (200) to 2500**	1200	1200
Constants used	-	-	as for instance	as for instance	as for instance
Universal quantification	-	-	15 %	**from 5 % to 29 %**	15 %
Universal variables in concl.	-	-	10 %	**5 % less than above**	10 %
Existential variables in concl.	-	-	5 %	5 %	5 %
Knowledge generation	-	-	random/corrected	random/corrected	random/corrected
Parallelization:					
Number of threads	64	64	64	64	**from 1 (2) to 25**

Explanations:
existential quantification: for each attribute, the percentage of existential facts used as a prohibition which have an existentially quantified variable in that attribute
universal quantification: for each attribute, the percentage of premises of a dependency which have a universally quantified variable in that attribute
universal variables in conclusion: for each attribute, the wanted percentage of conclusions of a dependency which have a universally quantified variable in that attribute, subject that the dependency has enough such variables
existential variables in conclusion: for each attribute, the percentage of conclusions of a dependency which have an existentially quantified variable in that attribute
randomness: always coupled with the removal of semantic(ally equivalent) duplicates

$G = (V, E)$ can be computed in $O(\sqrt{|V|} \cdot |E|)$ (cf. [19]), common implementations as provided by "LEDA" [16] or "Boost" [8] prefer an algorithm performing in $O(|V| \cdot |E| \cdot \alpha(|E|, |V|))$ with $\alpha(|E|, |V|) \leq 4$ for any feasible input.

We only outline and briefly comment on five experiments, in each of them *varying one* specific generation parameter. We always employ the schema $R(A, B, C, D, E)$ and fix the generation parameters of the database *instances* (but not the instances themselves!): complying with the schema, having about 1 000 000 tuples, using 20 constants in *Dom* as an active domain, and for each repetition being fully randomly generated and then chased to enforce compliance with the a priori knowledge. Moreover, we always vary the following parameter of the confidentiality policy: having either 10 000, 40 000, 70 000 or 100 000 semantically different prohibitions, in each case being fully randomly generated. Table 1 provides an overview about the parameters considered. In the figures below, each evaluation curve is based on the average results of 100 experiments.

Experiment 1 studies the impact of allowing arbitrary existential facts (corresponding to subtuples) rather than only ground facts (corresponding to full tuples) in the confidentiality policy, thus leading to improved *flexibility to declare prohibitions*. First of all, the results shown in Fig. 4 clearly indicate the practical feasibility of our weakening method, which needs at most 1 min for both stages together. If about so much time is needed at all, then it is spent in the instance-independent first stage, in particular for the matching computation, while for the instance-dependent second stage only a few seconds suffice.

Experiment 2 deals with the number of *constants affected by prohibitions*. Figure 5 indicates an increase of the runtime nearly linear in that number at the beginning, but a somewhat surprising pique for the matching computation.

Experiment 3 starts investigating the runtime consequences of taking care of *data dependencies*, at the beginning varying the number of dependencies considered. Figure 6 confirms that introducing a priori knowledge essentially affects the overall runtime, but fortunately still keeps it practically feasible. For the instance-dependent second stage the runtime even decreases when more dependencies are considered, among others caused by the strong impact of cleaning the policy. Moreover, Fig. 6d shows that the impact of rejecting conflicting

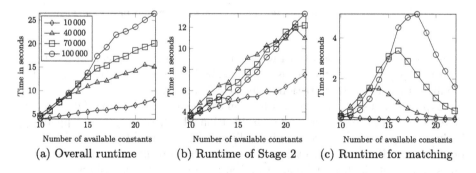

(a) Overall runtime   (b) Runtime of Stage 2   (c) Runtime for matching

Fig. 5. Experiment 2: Varying *number of constants used* in confidentiality policy

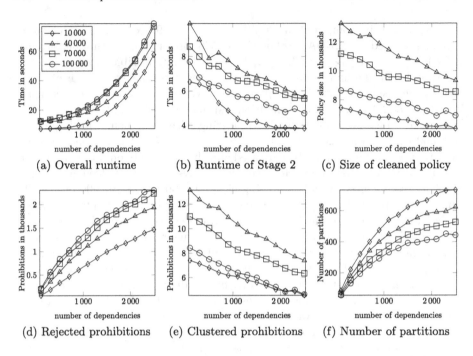

Fig. 6. Experiment 3: Varying *number of dependencies* in a priori knowledge

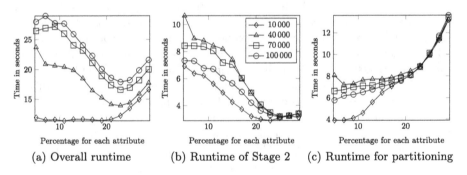

Fig. 7. Experiment 4: Varying *universal quantification* in a priori knowledge

prohibitions is acceptable. And Fig. 6e and f indicate the behavior of partition-ing the dependencies, which causes increasing costs but nevertheless keeps the number of the resulting partitions manageably bounded.

Experiment 4 serves for a closer look on the *syntactic structure of data depen-dencies* in terms of the occurring quantifications. Intuitively, a data dependency is the more powerful the more universally quantified variables are used. As can be seen from Fig. 7 among others, if we vary the percentage of universal vari-ables as indicated, then at about a percentage of 20 % the interferential effects

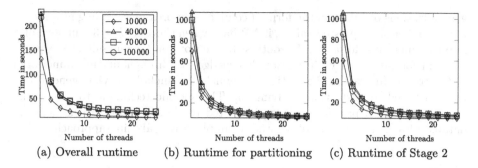

Fig. 8. Experiment 5: Varying number of threads

substantially grow leading in Stage 1 to more runtime needed for (parallelized) partitioning and thus overall as well, whereas the task of Stage 2 becomes easier.

Experiment 5 inspects the merits of *parallelization*. The curves shown in Fig. 8 indicate that we profit nearly optimally from parallelization, reducing the runtime to a half when the number of threads is doubled.

6 Conclusion

Our contribution constitutes a successful compromise between several potentially conflicting requirements: strong semantic confidentiality in terms of indistinguishability according to a declared policy representing pieces of information prohibited to be gained from interactions of data transfer, background knowledge and rational reasoning; expressive language for a "too curious" user's assumed a priori knowledge about the database content; flexible language for declaring prohibitions; uniform applicability for both data publishing and query answering; high availability of only correct information; application-dependent admissibility of weakening distortions; conformity to completeness assumptions regarding the actually stored data; and last but not least practical feasibility and scalability.

Though the concrete weakening method is novel, both its aims and its structure have been inspired by various previous work in the already very wide field of confidentiality preservation. Though often neglected, the ambitious aim of semantic confidentiality has already been considered in early work on confidentiality-preserving statistical databases, see [9], has explicitly and uniformly been used for the framework of Controlled Interaction Execution [2], and is in the spirit of many other approaches as highlighted by [12]. The further aim of providing only correct but if necessary explicitly weakened information has a long research tradition as well, in particular including the seminal work on refusals in information systems [17] and the extensive research on k-anonymity [14, 18].

The structure of our weakening method generalizes a more special case [5] and is related to k-anonymization [14, 18] by replacing sensitive data in a context-free way. Accordingly, our method also shares their complexity restrictions identified in [1, 7]. Basically, the optimization problem for k-anonymization by maximum generalizations of values in the form of complete suppressions, aiming at a minimum number of suppressed values, is NP-hard when choosing $k \geq 3$, but solvable in polynomial time for $k = 2$. In contrast to the work on k-anonymity, we explicitly and formally deal with a priori knowledge, as throughout the framework of Controlled Interaction Execution [2], which also includes a view generation method based on distortion by lying [6]. The specific technique to deal with dependencies as a priori knowledge is related to similar efforts in the field of database fragmentation [4,10], another example of a weakening approach.

References

1. Aggarwal, G., Feder, T., Kenthapadi, K., Motwani, R., Panigrahy, R., Thomas, D., Zhu, A.: Anonymizing tables. In: Eiter, T., Libkin, L. (eds.) ICDT 2005. LNCS, vol. 3363, pp. 246–258. Springer, Heidelberg (2005)
2. Biskup, J.: Inference-usability confinement by maintaining inference-proof views of an information system. Int. J. Comput. Sci. Eng. **7**(1), 17–37 (2012)
3. Biskup, J., Bonatti, P.A.: Controlled query evaluation with open queries for a decidable relational submodel. Ann. Math. Artif. Intell. **50**(1–2), 39–77 (2007)
4. Biskup, J., Preuß, M.: Database fragmentation with encryption: under which semantic constraints and a priori knowledge can two keep a secret? In: Wang, L., Shafiq, B. (eds.) DBSec 2013. LNCS, vol. 7964, pp. 17–32. Springer, Heidelberg (2013)
5. Biskup, J., Preuß, M.: Inference-proof data publishing by minimally weakening a database instance. In: Prakash, A., Shyamasundar, R. (eds.) ICISS 2014. LNCS, vol. 8880, pp. 30–49. Springer, Heidelberg (2014)
6. Biskup, J., Wiese, L.: A sound and complete model-generation procedure for consistent and confidentiality-preserving databases. Theoret. Comput. Sci. **412**(31), 4044–4072 (2011)
7. Blocki, J., Williams, R.: Resolving the complexity of some data privacy problems. In: Abramsky, S., Gavoille, C., Kirchner, C., Meyer auf der Heide, F., Spirakis, P.G. (eds.) ICALP 2010. LNCS, vol. 6199, pp. 393–404. Springer, Heidelberg (2010)
8. Boost Graph Library: Maximum cardinality matching (2014). http://www.boost. org/doc/libs/1_55_0/libs/graph/doc/maximum_matching.html
9. Denning, D.E.: Cryptography and Data Security. Addison-Wesley, Reading (1982)
10. De Capitani di Vimercati, S., Foresti, S., Jajodia, S., Livraga, G., Paraboschi, S., Samarati, P.: Fragmentation in presence of data dependencies. IEEE Trans. Dependable Sec. Comput. **11**(6), 510–523 (2014)
11. Fung, B.C.M., Wang, K., Fu, A.W.-C., Yu, P.S.: Introduction to Privacy-Preserving Data Publishing - Concepts and Techniques. Chapman & Hall/CRC, Boca Raton (2010)
12. Halpern, J.Y., O'Neill, K.R.: Secrecy in multiagent systems. ACM Trans. Inf. Syst. Secur. **12**(1), 5.1–5.47 (2008)
13. Korte, B., Vygen, J.: Combinatorial Optimization: Theory and Algorithms. Algorithms and Combinatorics, 5th edn. Springer, Heidelberg (2012)
14. Machanavajjhala, A., Kifer, D., Gehrke, J., Venkitasubramaniam, M.: ℓ-diversity: privacy beyond k-anonymity. ACM Trans. Knowl. Discov. Data **1**(1) (2007)
15. Magun, J.: Greedy matching algorithms: an experimental study. ACM J. Exp. Algorithmics **3**(6) (1998)

16. Mehlhorn, K., Näher, S.: LEDA: a platform for combinatorial and geometric computing. Cambridge University Press, Cambridge (1999)
17. Sicherman, G.L., de Jonge, W., van de Riet, R.P.: Answering queries without revealing secrets. ACM Trans. Database Syst. **8**(1), 41–59 (1983)
18. Sweeney, L.: k-anonymity: a model for protecting privacy. Int. J. Uncertainty Fuzziness Knowl. Based Syst. **10**(5), 557–570 (2002)
19. Vazirani, V.V.: A theory of alternating paths and blossoms for proving correctness of the $O(\sqrt{|V|} \cdot |E|)$ general graph maximum matching algorithm. Combinatorica **14**(1), 71–109 (1994)

Quantifying Location Privacy Leakage
from Transaction Prices

Arthur Gervais[1(✉)], Hubert Ritzdorf[1], Mario Lucic[1], Vincent Lenders[2],
and Srdjan Capkun[1]

[1] ETH Zurich, Zurich, Switzerland
arthur.gervais@inf.ethz.ch
[2] Armasuisse, Thun, Switzerland

Abstract. Large-scale datasets of consumer behavior might revolutionize the way we gain competitive advantages and increase our knowledge in
the respective domains. At the same time, valuable datasets pose potential privacy risks that are difficult to foresee. In this paper we study the
impact that the prices from consumers' purchase histories have on the
consumers' location privacy. We show that using a small set of low-priced
product prices from the consumers' purchase histories, an adversary can
determine the country, city, and local retail store where the transaction
occurred with high confidence. Our paper demonstrates that even when
the product category, precise time of purchase, and currency are removed
from the consumers' purchase history (e.g., for privacy reasons), information about the consumers' location is leaked. The results are based
on three independent datasets containing thousands of low-priced and
frequently-bought consumer products. The results show the existence of
location privacy risks when releasing consumer purchase histories. As
such, the results highlight the need for systems that hide transaction
details in consumer purchase histories.

1 Introduction

Making data publicly available creates unexpected privacy risks. Recent examples include AOL's release of users' search keywords [30], which has led to the
identification of users and their profiles [1]. Data released by Netflix was de-
anonymized by leveraging IMDB and dates of user ratings [28], showing that
the release of data cannot be analyzed in isolation. The privacy risks of combining different public records have led to several [36] de-anonymization attacks.
Recent studies of anonymized mobility data showed that mobility traces can be
de-anonymized by leveraging a few observations [19]. One source of consumer
information involves their spending patterns. To date however, it was unclear to
what extent consumer prices leak information about the respective purchase.

Consumer purchase histories are typically recorded by store chains with loy-
alty programs and are used to compute consumer spending profiles [6]. Banks,
payment card issuers, and point-of-sale system providers collect this data at different levels of granularity. In a number of scenarios, it might be desirable to

© Springer International Publishing Switzerland 2016
I. Askoxylakis et al. (Eds.): ESORICS 2016, Part II, LNCS 9879, pp. 382–405, 2016.
DOI: 10.1007/978-3-319-45741-3_20

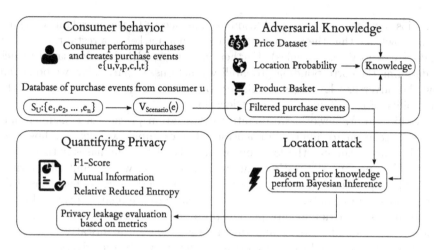

Fig. 1. Framework overview for quantifying location privacy leakage from consumer price datasets.

share this data within different departments of a company, across companies, or with the public [7]. Before disclosure, the data is sanitized so that it does not leak sensitive data, such as personally identifiable information and that it (partially or fully) hides location information. In new digital currency systems such as Bitcoin [33] and Ripple [10], transaction values stored on a public ledger. Irrespective of whether transaction values are made available so that a system can fulfill its functions or are being disclosed for research purposes, it is important to understand the privacy implications of such disclosures.

In this paper we focus on quantifying location disclosure resulting from the release of prices from consumer's purchase histories. Intuitively, the price distribution for a product differs from country to country, which allows us to identify possible purchase locations. We focus on consumer products which are generally inexpensive (≤ 25 USD) and frequently-bought. More precisely, based on global prices (leveraging the Numbeo dataset [9]), we show that given access to a few consumer prices (and even without the product categories, precise times of purchase or currency), an adversary can determine the country in which the purchase occurred. Similarly, given the country, the city can be determined and within a city (leveraging the Chicago dataset [11]), the *local store* can be identified. We further demonstrate that it is possible to distinguish purchases among store chains (leveraging the Kaggle dataset [7]).

We present a generic framework (cf. Fig. 1) that allows the modeling and quantitative evaluation of location leakage from consumer price datasets. In our framework we model the adversarial knowledge, composed of a public dataset of consumer prices and location-specific information. We assume that the adversary has access to the individual product prices of a purchase (similar to the Kaggle dataset) and a coarse-grained value of the purchase time. In order to make the framework more flexible, our model supports different prior knowledge scenarios, e.g., the adversary additionally has access to the merchant category (e.g., knowledge that the product was bought in a market or a restaurant) or the product category (e.g., apples). Furthermore, we model the adversarial attack by detailing the corresponding probability functions. In particular, we point out how the adversary leverages multiple product prices in order to increase the probability of identifying the correct location.

Within our framework, we quantify the location privacy of consumer purchases in relation to different dimensions. For example, we measure how well the adversary estimates the location probability of the purchases with the F_1-score [35], capturing the test's accuracy. Furthermore, we use mutual information [18] to quantify the absolute location privacy loss of consumers, based on the considered price dataset. In addition, we capture the relative privacy loss by measuring the reduction in entropy. The proposed metrics are independent of the choice of adversarial strategy and therefore allow us to quantitatively measure the privacy loss induced from any price dataset known to the adversary.

We apply our framework to three real-world datasets: (i) the *Numbeo dataset* [9] contains, after outlier filtering, crowd-sourced real-world consumer prices from 112 countries and 23 US cities for 23 distinct product categories; (ii) the *Chicago dataset* [11] contains 24 million prices for 28 product categories capturing on average of 6304 products sold in Dominick's stores within the Chicago metropolitan area; finally, (iii) the *Kaggle dataset* [7] contains 350 million purchases from 311,541 consumer across 134 store chains.

Our evaluation shows that in order to infer the country based on a vector of purchases, an adversary often needs to observe less than 30 prices. Similarly, after having identified the country of the purchases and given roughly 30 prices, we show that we can reliably predict among 23 major cities within the United States. Finally, when the adversary narrowed down the coarse location, such as the Chicago metropolitan area, we show that based on a regional price dataset, and given a vector of purchases, an adversary can distinguish with high confidence *among local stores* using 100 purchases. For comparison, a weaker adversary with access only to coarse-grained time, i.e., the day of the purchase and price information, requires 50 purchases to identify the country. Furthermore, to establish practical utility of our methodology, we evaluate it on a dataset of purchase records (Kaggle [7]) and show that an adversary requires approximately 250 purchases to distinguish with high confidence among 134 store chains.

The main contributions of this paper are as follows:

- We propose a generic quantitative framework for evaluating attacks against the location privacy of consumer purchases. We validate our framework on three independent price datasets of real-world consumer prices and show that location information can be extracted reliably.
- We introduce three privacy metrics to capture the performance of the adversary in the attack as well as the extent to which location privacy of consumers is reduced when the adversary has access to a specific dataset of purchases.

To the best of our knowledge, this is the first work to infer the location of a purchase based on the price value in consumer purchases. The remainder of this paper is organized as follows. In Sect. 2, we model purchase history and describe the adversarial model. In Sect. 3, we present the datasets selected for our evaluation in Sect. 4. We survey the related work in Sect. 5 and conclude the paper in Sect. 6.

2 Model

In this section we introduce our system and adversarial model. We present the privacy metrics that quantify the probability of location disclosure based on the assumption that the adversary has access to a part of a consumer's purchase history.

2.1 System Model

A consumer interacts with merchants and performs purchases of one or more products. This interaction leaves a trace of purchase activity as a sequence of *purchase events*. We model each of the consumer's purchase events together with their contextual information as e: {consumer u, value v, product p, product category c, location l, time t}, where v is the price value spent on product p of product category c at location l and time t. In our model, one purchase event is limited to one product, similar to the data contained in the Kaggle dataset. In addition, the price value is given in a global currency, which usually is different from the local currency of the purchase (e.g., the original price is SEK, but recorded in USD). The trace of purchases performed by the target consumer U, given as a series of purchase events, is denoted by S_U:{$e_1, e_2, \ldots, e_n$}. We define the following functions to represent the adversarial knowledge:

LOCATION PROBABILITY: It describes the prior probability of a purchase event taking place in a specific location, e.g., $P(\text{USA})$ is the prior probability with which a random purchase event e has $e.l = \text{USA}$. We define $\mathbb{L}$ as the set of all considered locations.

CATEGORY PROBABILITY: Given location l, $P(c \mid l)$ describes the conditional probability of a purchase event to belong to a certain product category, e.g., $P(\text{Milk} \mid \text{USA})$ is the conditional probability with which a random event e from the USA has $e.c = \text{milk}$. This conditional probability models the product category preferences in a location. We define $\mathbb{C}$ as the set of all considered product categories.

VALUE PROBABILITY: Given location l and product category c, $P(v \mid l, c)$ describes the conditional probability of a purchase event at a given price value. It models the price distributions for different product categories in different locations, e.g., $P(1.5 \mid \text{USA}, \text{Milk})$ is the conditional probability with which milk can be bought in the USA for 1.5 worth of a global currency.

The adversary can now model the spending behavior and identify likely candidate locations. Specifically, the adversary computes the posterior probability that a single price value v for a product category c originated from a location l. The computation involves the prior and the conditional probabilities described above and the application of Bayes' theorem:

$$P(l \mid c, v) = \frac{P(l) \cdot P(c, v \mid l)}{P(c, v)} \tag{1}$$

In order to infer the location without knowing the product category, the adversary computes the probability that a price value v originates from location l:

$$P(l \mid v) = \frac{P(l) \cdot P(v \mid l)}{P(v)} \tag{2}$$

2.2 Adversarial Model

The adversary's goal is to identify the location of the events in S_U. In this section we present two different adversaries: (1) an adversary with complete knowledge and (2) an adversary with only public knowledge.

Adversary with Complete Knowledge. The ideal adversary represents a strong adversary with complete access to global purchase events. In particular, the adversary has access to the following prior knowledge:

GLOBAL PURCHASE HISTORY: The complete series of purchase events in the history of global purchases[1], denoted by $\mathcal{H}_G$. The adversary computes the posterior probability of a location based on $\mathcal{H}_G$.

HISTORY FOR TARGET CONSUMER: The adversary might have access to prior information about the target consumer's purchase history, denoted by $\mathcal{H}_U$. This could help the adversary to optimize the model for the target consumer[2].

Based on this knowledge, the ideal adversary computes the probabilities in Eqs. 1 and 2.[3]

Adversary with Public Knowledge. Our second adversarial model is a more realistic one, where the adversary only makes use of public information.

POPULATION: Given the population at each location, the adversary estimates the location probability $P(l)$.

PRODUCT BASKET: A product basket indicates which products an average consumer purchases during a year, both in terms of quantity and monetary amount. We leverage the product basket in order to estimate the probability of a product category given the location $(P(c \mid l))$.[4]

---

[1] The area of the attacker's interest can be restricted, e.g., when the adversary knows that its victim is somewhere in that restricted area.

[2] For example, by only considering the locations of previous purchases.

[3] The intermediate steps are given in the Appendix A.

[4] We currently use a single product basket for all locations.

PRICE DATASET: For each location and product category combination, a price value distribution D is available, e.g., the Numbeo or the Chicago dataset. The adversary can use the distribution to estimate $P(v \mid l, c)$. We define $D(l, c, v)$ as the number of occurrences of price value v for product category c in location l and $D(l, c)$ as the number of price values for product category c and location l.

Since D might be imperfect, the adversary can have incomplete or incorrect knowledge about the price value probabilities (i.e. unknown or rounded product prices). In this case the adversary should perform additive smoothing, which assigns a small probability α to each event [26]. On the contrary, if the adversary has or assumes complete knowledge of the price value probabilities, additive smoothing is not required.

The adversary with public knowledge computes the following probabilities:

$$P(l) = \frac{\text{Population}(l)}{\sum\limits_{l' \in \mathbb{L}} \text{Population}(l')} \tag{3}$$

$$P(c \mid l) = \frac{\text{Basket}(l, c)}{\sum\limits_{c' \in \mathbb{C}} \text{Basket}(l, c')} \tag{4}$$

$$P(v \mid l, c) = \frac{D(l, c, v) + \alpha}{D(l, c) + \alpha \cdot |S_U|} \tag{5}$$

In order to compute the probabilities defined earlier in Eqs. 1 and 2, the adversary requires access to either $P(l \mid c, v)$ or $P(l \mid v)$. Next, we describe how the adversary computes these probabilities and we define the adversary's knowledge.

2.3   Knowledge Scenarios

As mentioned, the adversary's objective is to identify the location of the events in S_U. The adversary is given a finite set of events S_U on which the attack is executed—the adversary is not allowed to choose or request new purchase events e. We consider an adversary with public knowledge and distinguish among three distinct adversarial knowledge scenarios, each consisting of a subset of the public knowledge. Depending on the knowledge scenario, the adversary might not have access to all information from a purchase event e. Therefore, we define a family of functions $V_{\text{scenario}}(e) = V(e)$ that filter, depending on the given scenario, the public knowledge accessible to the adversary.

PRICE: This scenario corresponds to an adversary that has access to multiple purchase events e, *only* the corresponding *price value* and a notion of the purchase time $e.t$. The adversary is not aware of the product $e.p$ or the product category $e.c$. The precision of the purchase time depends on further specifications of the scenario. More formally, $V_{\text{price}}(e) = \{e.v, e.t\}$. Given the public knowledge modeled by Eqs. 3, 4 and 5, the adversary computes the posterior probability

$P(l \mid v)$ of a price value v from location l. The intermediate steps for computing $P(v \mid l)$ and $P(v)$ are detailed in the Appendix A in Eqs. 10 and 12.

PRICE_MERCHANT: Similar to the former knowledge scenario, the adversary here has access to S_U, a series of multiple purchase events. In this scenario, however, the adversary knows the price value $e.v$ of the event as well as which merchant category m sold the product. Formally, for each purchase event e, $V_{\text{price}}\_\text{merchant}(e) = \{e.v, e.t, m\}$, where $V_{\text{price}}\_\text{merchant}$ requires a function $M(e) = m$. We consider three merchant categories: restaurant, market and local transportation. The $V_{\text{price}}\_\text{merchant}(e)$ function estimates the merchant category m from the product category $e.c$ of the respective event[5]. Analogously, using Eq. 1, the adversary computes the probability of a location, based on the merchant and the price value:

$$P(l \mid m, v) = \frac{P(l) \cdot P(m, v \mid l)}{P(m, v)} \tag{6}$$

where $P(m, v \mid l)$ is computed as follows:

$$P(m, v \mid l) = \sum_{c \in M^{-1}(m)} P(c, v \mid l) \tag{7}$$

PRICE_PRODUCT-CATEGORY: This scenario corresponds to the most knowledgeable adversary with public knowledge. Similarly to the former scenarios, the adversary receives multiple purchase events S_U. In addition, the adversary has access to the product category $e.c$ as well as the price value $e.v$. Note that $e.c$ implicitly assumes knowledge of the merchant, resulting in more formally $V_{\text{price}}\_\text{product-category}(e) = \{e.v, e.t, e.c\}$.

Given the public knowledge described in Sect. 2.2, the adversary computes the probability $P(l \mid c, v)$ of a purchase event with product category c and price value v originating in location l. The intermediate steps for computing $P(c, v \mid l)$ and $P(c, v)$ are detailed in the appendix in Eqs. 11 and 13.

In the following section we provide an intuitive perspective on the probabilities $P(l \mid v)$ and $P(l \mid c, v)$.

2.4   Conditional Probability Intuition

$P(l \mid v)$ is the probability of a location, given a price value in a purchase event. An example plot based on our evaluation can be found in Fig. 2. We have chosen the purchase event e with a price value of $e.v = 1$ Euro and estimated the location of the price. The figure shows that the most likely location for 1 Euro is France, closely followed by Germany, Italy and Spain. The plot also shows $P(l \mid c, v)$ for a purchase event with $e.v = 1$ Euro and the product category is milk. The most likely country is again France, followed by Germany and Italy. Surprisingly, China ranks as 5th. This can be explained by the fact that (i) some prices from

---

[5] In the following we refer to the merchant category as merchant.

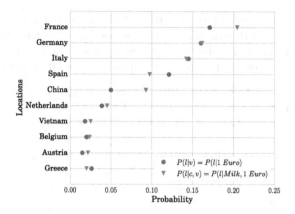

Fig. 2. Probability distribution of $P(l \mid v)$ and $P(l \mid c, v)$, given 1 Euro and milk.

China in the dataset were erroneously reported in Euros and (ii) that the location probability $P(l)$ influences the overall outcome, and, since China's population is considerable, there is an increased probability of purchases occurring there. Overall we observed that the probability distribution changes when the product category is known, i.e., France is more likely to have a 1 Euro price for milk, than a 1 Euro price in general.

2.5 Multiple Purchase Events

Up to this point, the analysis has been based on a single purchase event. To naturally combine multiple purchase events, we assume that the purchase events are conditionally independent, given the location l. Therefore, the probability of a location l, given a set of purchase events S_U, is calculated as follows:

$$P(l \mid S_U) = P(l \mid V(e_1), V(e_2), \dots, V(e_n))$$

$$= \frac{P(l) \cdot \prod_{e \in S_U} P(V(e) \mid l)}{P(V(e_1), \dots, V(e_n))} \qquad (8)$$

The intermediate steps for computing $P(l \mid S_U)$ can be found in the appendix in Eq. 18. We experimentally verified the conditional independence of $V(e)$ given l for the three knowledge scenarios and therefore Eq. 8 applies equally to the different adversarial knowledge scenarios. Note that we effectively weaken the adversary by considering the products of different purchases independent from each other.

2.6 Privacy Metrics

We introduce three privacy metrics in order to capture the privacy of consumers revealing their purchase histories across different dimensions: We (i) measure the performance of the adversary in identifying the true location with the F_1-score. Then, (ii) using the notion of mutual information [18], we quantify the absolute privacy loss of the consumer due to the adversary's knowledge of a price dataset. Finally, (iii) we use the relative reduced entropy as a relative privacy metric[6].

F_1-SCORE: The objective of the adversary is to assign the purchase events to the correct location. In the worst case, the adversary is forced to randomly guess among all possible locations. If the adversary, however, can estimate location probabilities more accurately, location privacy is reduced. Our problem corresponds to a multi-class classification problem and we therefore quantify the adversarial performance by averaging the F_1-score [35] of each individual class. The F_1-score corresponds to the harmonic mean of recall and precision, measuring the test's accuracy.

MUTUAL INFORMATION: A purchase event dataset enables the adversary to infer the distribution of prices among locations. Therefore, we want to measure how much privacy consumers lose when their purchase events are revealed and when the adversary has access to a dataset of purchase events. We quantify this privacy objective by measuring the *absolute* reduced location entropy given the purchase events. To this extent, we use the Mutual Information [18], denoted by $I(l, V(e))$, which measures how much the entropy of the locations is reduced given the purchase events (cf. Eq. 9).

$$I(l, V(e)) = \sum_{l \in \mathbb{L}, e \in S_U} P(l, V(e)) \cdot \log_2 \frac{P(l, V(e))}{P(l)P(V(e))} \tag{9}$$

RELATIVE REDUCED ENTROPY: Recall that the mutual information quantifies what we call the absolute privacy loss. In fact, there is an inherent randomness in the price distribution among locations. It is important to capture to what extent the original uncertainty about the locations can be reduced when a dataset of purchase events is given. The relative reduced entropy therefore captures the *relative* privacy, as the complement of the fraction of the conditional entropy over the location entropy. Given $H(l) = I(l, V(e)) + H(l \mid V(e))$, we compute the relative reduced entropy as $1 - \frac{H(l|V(e))}{H(l)}$ over all purchase events.

The proposed evaluation metrics are independent of a particular adversarial strategy. In return, the output of the privacy leakage quantification only depends upon the employed dataset of purchase events. In the next section we present the datasets utilized for our experimental evaluation.

3   Datasets

There are only a couple of datasets accurately accumulating the worldwide product price information. For individual products (e.g., a Big Mac [5] or Starbucks

---

[6] Defined as the complement of the fraction of conditional entropy over the location entropy.

coffee [8]), the average price values per country are available. Because a product often appears multiple times with different price values in the same country or city, the average is not a good estimator for elaborate studies. In the following, we describe the three independent price datasets considered in our work.

The first dataset, Numbeo [9], is a crowd-sourced dataset containing world-wide price values per product category, city and country. It is the most complete dataset of worldwide harvested prices available to our knowledge. We restricted our analysis to 23 frequently bought product categories, and split the Numbeo dataset into two separate datasets: (i) two years of data as the Numbeo dataset and (ii) five months of data as the Numbeo test dataset (cf. Table 3). Numbeo performs sanity checks on the crowdsourced inputs, and we additionally filtered extreme outlier [3]⁷ from the data to account for possible mistakes from crowd-sourced data. We identified 112 countries, with a total of 328,720 price values. Note that the provided data mostly contains prices from the US (18 %) and India (14 %).

The second dataset, referred to as the Chicago dataset [11], covers 84 stores in the Chicago metropolitan area over a period of five years. The data is sourced on a weekly basis from Dominick's supermarket stores. We sample 85 weeks with the most data, each containing on average 283,181 prices, spanning 28 product categories for an average of 6304 different products.

The third dataset originates from Kaggle [7], a Machine Learning competition platform. The dataset contains 350 million purchase events from 311,539 consumers across 134 store chains. The data is anonymized, but contains the individual product price, product category, date of purchase and purchase amount. Most purchase events cost less than 25 USD. The country of the dataset is not disclosed, but purchase prices are given in USD and purchase amounts are described in the imperial system.

In order to estimate the location probability, an adversary requires the knowledge of the population in each location. On the country granularity, we use the data available from the World Bank [12] for the year 2013, while for the US city granularity we used the data from the US Census Bureau [37].

As described in Sect. 2.2, we increase the knowledge of the adversary with the product basket. A product basket details which and how many products an average person purchases, both in terms of quantity and monetary amount. We leverage a national product basket [4] from 2010 containing over 300 product categories in order to infer the ratio in which different products are bought over the year.

4 Experimental Evaluation

In this section we evaluate the adversarial models designed in Sect. 2.2. We start by presenting the assumptions and choices made for the evaluation.

---

⁷ $price < 25^{th}$ percentile $- 3 \cdot$ interquartile range, and
$price > 75^{th}$ percentile $+ 3 \cdot$ interquartile range.

4.1 Experimental Considerations

With respect to the value probability $P(v \mid l, c)$, we assume that the frequency of price values in the Numbeo dataset reflects the frequency of real-world purchase events with the corresponding price values. This is a natural assumption and is further motivated by the fact that e.g., Numbeo contributors likely entered the most popular price values for the considered product categories. Because our datasets contain a limited amount of products and product categories, our analysis is naturally confined to the available products. Note that, if the adversary knows the product categories of the purchases, e.g. milk, other categories such as apples can be ignored, which allows precise predictions with knowledge about few products. In order to compute the product category probability, $P(c \mid l)$, we only consider one national product basket and apply it to every country. Note that we do not use the product basket as an indicator of how much money is spent on average by a person, but rather as an indicator in which ratio products are bought.

SAMPLING PRICE VALUES: Given a location l, we generate *synthetic* consumer purchase events by sampling price values from the respective dataset. For the three datasets we consider adversaries with complete knowledge of the price values. In addition we instantiate an adversary with incomplete knowledge with the Numbeo test dataset. Given the product basket of the location l we compute the probability of a product category being sampled (cf. Eq. 4). Thus, we sample each product category with the product category probability $P(c \mid l)$. For each location we repeat the sampling of the price values $n = 1000$ times and average the result.

ADDITIVE SMOOTHING PARAMETER: In the case of an adversary with incomplete knowledge, we make use of additive smoothing to avoid zero probabilities when aggregating the probabilities of multiple purchase events for locations (see Sect. 2.2). We choose a smoothing parameter $\alpha = 0.01$ which provides us with the best results on our data (cf. appendix Fig. 6).

In the following, we evaluate up to three knowledge scenarios (cf. Sect. 2.3) for four location granularities: (i) across 112 countries worldwide; (ii) across 23 cities within the United States; (iii) across 84 stores within the Chicago metropolitan area; (iv) we distinguish among 134 store chains in a country.

4.2 Country Granularity

The adversary has to distinguish 112 candidate countries for each purchase event. We quantify the privacy given the three privacy metrics defined in Sect. 2.6. In particular, we performed our study in two settings. First, (i) we assumed that the adversary does not have complete knowledge. This means that the adversary receives purchase events from the Numbeo test dataset and estimate their location based on the Numbeo dataset. In the second case, (ii) the adversary assumes complete knowledge of price values, and therefore, the sampled prices are included in the price dataset which is adversarial knowledge.

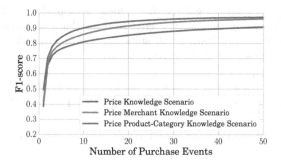

Fig. 3. F_1-score for identifying the country given purchase events *sampled from the Numbeo test dataset*, corresponding to incomplete knowledge. We are not overfitting as we successfully classify new prices based on previously known prices.

Figure 3 shows the F_1-score for the first case based on the number of purchase events accessible to the adversary. Given one purchase event, the price, price_merchant and price_product-category knowledge scenario achieve an average of 0.38, 0.41 and 0.49 respectively. The high F_1-score after one purchase event shows, that even one event allows a decent prediction. We observe that the adversary is more likely to identify the correct location when it knows the product category of the purchase event. On the contrary, if the adversary has access to 10 purchase events, the respective F_1-scores are 0.80, 0.85 and 0.90. In other words, 10 purchase events significantly improve the ability of the adversary to identify the location of the purchase events. The reported values are averaged over $n = 1000$ iterations.

Fig. 4. F_1-score for identifying the country given purchase events *sampled from the Numbeo dataset*, corresponding to complete knowledge. Averaging does not hide poorly performing countries (cf. appendix).

Figure 4 corresponds to the second case, where the adversary assumes complete knowledge of the price values. We observe that the adversary can distinguish more accurately between the possible locations. The F_1-scores are averaged

Table 1. Mutual information and relative reduced entropy for the three knowledge scenarios when estimating the country, city, store or chain of purchase events. The respective abbreviations P., PM., PPC. stand for Price, Price Merchant and Price Product-Category knowledge scenario respectively.

Knowledge scenarios	112 countries			23 US cities			84 stores		134 chains	
	P	PM	PPC	P	PM	PPC	P	PPC	P	PPC
Mutual information	0.539	0.841	1.703	0.368	0.572	1.164	0.280	0.569	0.456	2.256
Relative reduced E.	0.114	0.178	0.360	0.101	0.157	0.319	0.044	0.089	0.068	0.337

over all considered countries. For each considered country in the price knowledge scenario, we verify that averaging does not hide poorly performing countries (cf. Fig. 7 in the appendix).

Table 1 presents the results of the mutual information and the relative reduced entropy for each knowledge scenario. We observe that the price_product-category knowledge scenario reduces the entropy more significantly than the other knowledge scenarios. Naturally, this is because the price_product-category knowledge scenario provides the adversary with more information than the price knowledge scenario, thus effectively reducing uncertainty when identifying the location.

4.3   US City Granularity

In this section we analyze an adversary that aims to distinguish among the purchase events of 23 US cities. As before, we quantify the privacy based on the three privacy metrics defined in Sect. 2.6. We sample and test purchase events on the Numbeo dataset only, since our test dataset does not contain sufficiently many purchase events per considered US city.

Figure 10 illustrates the F_1-score depending on the number of purchase events. We observe, that after 10 purchase events, the F_1-score is greater than 0.7. Therefore, our methodology also provides accurate estimations on a city granularity. Table 1 reports the mutual information and relative reduced entropy when estimating the US city. We observe that the relative reduced entropies of country and city granularity match across the knowledge scenarios. This exemplifies the usefulness of the relative reduced entropy to highlight similarities across different price datasets.

4.4   Chicago Metropolitan Granularity

In this section, we analyze an adversary that aims to distinguish among the purchase events of 84 Dominick's stores within the Chicago metropolitan area.

We sample the price values from the Chicago dataset, and assume an adversary with complete knowledge; we therefore do not apply additive smoothing. We consider the location prior probability $P(l)$ to be uniform, because we do not have reliable store popularity information for the Chicago area.

In Fig. 11 we can observe that the adversary can identify a local store given 100 purchase events with high confidence. We expected a weaker result, since all stores are operated by the same chain, implying relatively similar price structures. We ran our attack on each of the 85 weeks with most data, averaged the results and report the standard deviation as shown in the blue area of Fig. 11.

Table 1 shows that the Chicago price dataset reveals less information about the considered locations than the Numbeo dataset. This observation holds for both knowledge scenarios, and is consistent with the result that more price points are required to localize purchase events within the Chicago area.

4.5 Store Chain Granularity

The large-scale Kaggle dataset does not provide precise location information of purchase events, but allows the adversary to distinguish among 134 store chains. Knowing the store chain of purchase events effectively reduces the possible locations of the purchases. Note, that the prices of Kaggle are distributed over a year and the adversary therefore does not know the precise time of the purchase events.

We uniformly sample purchase events of different consumers and perform our attack on the Kaggle dataset. Figure 5 reveals that given approximately 250 price values we achieve an F_1-score of over 0.95 for the origin of the purchase events. Note, that the price_product-category knowledge scenario is particularly strong due to many product categories. This is reflected by the particularly high Mutual Information (cf. Table 1).

Fig. 5. F_1-score for identifying the store chain. The purchase events are sampled from the Kaggle dataset.

Given these results, we conclude, that our framework and methodology apply to a wide variety of different price datasets and allow us to quantitatively compare their respective privacy leakage. In the following, we extract further insights from our data to strengthen the attack.

4.6 Most Revealing Product Category

In this section we investigate which of the 23 considered product categories from the Numbeo dataset leak more information. This is a useful insight since an adversary would pick purchase events of this product category in order to increase the probability of correctly identifying their location. Therefore, with the mutual information we measure the extent to which the location entropy is reduced, given the purchase events of a particular product category. Contrary to the previous analysis, we evaluate the mutual information *per product category* based on the price_product-category knowledge scenario defined in Sect. 2.3. More specifically, we compute the mutual information using only purchase events of a particular product category.

The results of the evaluation can be found in Fig. 13. According to this metric, the most revealing product categories are milk, a one-way ticket for local transportation, and a loaf of white bread. On the contrary, the product categories that disclose less information about a location are oranges, chicken breasts and rice.

4.7 Required Time Precision

Previously, we assumed that knowledge of the exact currency conversion rates is required to compare non-localized purchase events. Exact currency conversion rates, however, require a precise knowledge of the purchase event times. In this section, we show that our attack does not require the exact currency conversion rates, but also works if the adversary knows only the date or even week of the purchase, i.e. it has an uncertainty of 24 h or 7 days in relation to the conversion rates. We therefore relax the requirements on the time precision.

Due to the conversion rate differences, the adversarial estimation of $P(v \mid l, c)$ is inaccurate. To compensate for the conversion rate differences, the adversary can use a price tolerance. We study two options for the tolerance: a static tolerance and a dynamic tolerance. For the static tolerance, the adversary estimates $P(v \mid l, c)$ in the presence of uncertainty by considering price values in the interval $[v - tol_s, v + tol_s]$ where the static tolerance tol_s is a small amount in global currency (e.g., 0.02 USD). The dynamic tolerance value tol_d is a percentage-wise estimate of uncertainty (e.g., 2 %). To estimate $P(v \mid l, c)$ the adversary considers price values from the interval $[v \cdot (1 - tol_d), v \cdot (1 + tol_d)]$.

We evaluated the attack to infer the country of purchase events with imprecise purchase times and compensated the time error with different tolerance values. To simulate imprecise purchase times, we converted the adversarial knowledge using conversion rates of 30 different days from the year 2014 and then converted the non-localized purchase events S_U using the previous days' conversion rates. As before, we computed the F_1-score to evaluate the quality of the estimated $P(l \mid S_U)$.

For static and dynamic tolerance values, we found that the attack is still accurate, i.e. reaches an F_1-score above 95 % with less than 50 purchase events. A higher tolerance value has two opposing effects: (i) it compensates for differences in currency conversion rates and increases the number of correctly considered price values; (ii) a higher tolerance, however, also increases the number of incorrectly considered price values which fall into larger intervals. Therefore, the tolerance value presents a trade off between the true-positive and true-negative rate. Our experimental results reflect this trade off both for static and dynamic tolerance values (cf. Appendix B). Based on our experimental results we propose a dynamic tolerance of 2 % for a 24 h time imprecision.

We also evaluated the uncertainty of one week on the currency conversion rates. We used real-world currency conversion rates that were seven days apart from each other. Figure 14 shows the result of this experiment for the different knowledge scenarios and a dynamic tolerance value of 2 % on the Numbeo dataset. We conclude that our attack does not require precise purchase event times.

5   Related Work

Location Privacy. Blumberg [16] *et al.* provide a non-technical discussion of location privacy, its issues and implications. Gruteser and Grunwald [23] initiate major research in the area of the anonymization approaches to location privacy. Further, Narayanan *et al.* [29] investigate location privacy from a theoretical standpoint and present a variety of cryptographic protocols motivated by and optimized for practical constraints while focusing on proximity testing. Shokri *et al.* [34] propose a formal framework for quantifying location privacy in the case where users expose their location sporadically. They model various location-privacy-preserving mechanisms, such as location obfuscation and fake location injections. This work is orthogonal to ours, since in our setting the consumers are not willingly revealing their locations. Voulodimos *et al.* [38] address the issue of privacy protection in context-aware services through the use of entropy as a means of measuring the capability of locating a user's whereabouts and identifying personal selections. Narayanan [28] and Shmatikov propose statistical de-anonymization attacks against high-dimensional micro-data. We do not rely on their methods, since we are not aiming to de-anonymize the consumers. De Montjoye *et al.* [39] show that consumers can be uniquely identified within credit card records with only a few spatiotemporal triples containing location, time and price value. Contrary to their work, we focus on the price values and we localize instead of identify consumers.

Payment systems. The privacy implications of public transaction prices have been widely ignored. One prominent example is Bitcoin [17,33], where transactions are exchanged between peers by means of pseudonyms. The actual transaction prices are archived and publicly available. The literature features many different methods for analyzing the privacy implications of Bitcoin, e.g., by means of appropriate heuristics [13], tainting [22], or other techniques [21,32]. Reid and Harrigan [31] analyze the flow of Bitcoin transactions in a small part of the Bitcoin log, and show that external information like publicly-announced addresses, can be used to link identities and organizations to some transactions. In [27] the authors propose Zerocoin, a cryptographic extension to Bitcoin that augments the protocol to allow for fully anonymous currency transactions using a distributed ECash scheme. To the best of our knowledge only two contributions [14,15] have aimed to hide the transaction prices in Bitcoin.

Price rigidity. Herrmann and Moeser [24] perform a quantitative analysis on price variability and conclude that prices are often rigid for several weeks. Pricing strategies for identical brands, however, vary significantly among retailers. Their observations match the studies of the Big Mac index [5] (the Economist), the Starbucks coffee index [8] (the Wall Street Journal) and the Ikea Billy Bookshelf index [2] (Bloomberg). The former studies show that prices of identical products from a single brand vary across locations. Dutta *et al.* [20] find that retail prices respond promptly to direct cost changes as well as upstream manufacturers' costs. Hosken and Reiffen [25] find that each product has a price mode—a price that the product stays at most of the time. Note that Hosken's non-public dataset contains nearly as many price observations as our Numbeo dataset.

6   Conclusion

Having a systematic methodology to reason quantitatively about the privacy leakage from datasets containing price relevant information is a necessary step to avoid privacy leakages. While further tests with more datasets will help to generally claim that price values alone can reveal the location of a purchase, our empirical results provide evidence that with relatively few purchase events it is possible to identify a consumer's location. In this paper, we have raised the following two questions: How much location information is leaked by consumer purchase datasets? How can it be quantified with the considered adversarial model and knowledge? In our proposed framework, we have modeled several adversaries and quantified the privacy leakage according to different dimensions. We make extensive use of Bayesian inference in our framework to model the different attack strategies. Our framework can be easily applied to any price dataset of consumer purchases and allows one to compare the privacy leakage of different datasets. We applied our methodology to three real-world datasets and achieve comparable results. The results presented in this paper strongly motivate the need for careful consideration when sharing price datasets and should be considered when designing public ledger cryptocurrencies.

Appendix A: Probability Calculations

In the following we clarify the individual steps for calculating the probabilities derived in Sect. 2.

$$P(v) = \sum_{l \in \mathbb{L}} P(l, v) = \sum_{l \in \mathbb{L}} \sum_{c \in \mathbb{C}} P(l, c, v)$$
$$= \sum_{l \in \mathbb{L}} \sum_{c \in \mathbb{C}} P(l) \cdot P(c \mid l) \cdot P(v \mid l, c) \tag{10}$$

$$P(c, v) = \sum_{l \in \mathbb{L}} P(l, c, v)$$
$$= \sum_{l \in \mathbb{L}} P(l) \cdot P(c \mid l) \cdot P(v \mid l, c) \tag{11}$$

$$P(v \mid l) = \frac{P(l, v)}{P(l)} = \frac{\sum\limits_{c \in \mathbb{C}} P(l, c, v)}{P(l)}$$
$$= \sum_{c \in \mathbb{C}} P(c \mid l) \cdot P(v \mid l, c) \tag{12}$$

$$P(c, v \mid l) = \frac{P(l, c, v)}{P(l)} = \frac{P(l) \cdot P(c \mid l) \cdot P(v \mid l, c)}{P(l)}$$
$$= P(c \mid l) \cdot P(v \mid l, p) \tag{13}$$

$$P(l \mid v) = \frac{P(l) \cdot P(v \mid l)}{P(v)}$$
$$= \frac{P(l) \cdot \sum\limits_{c \in \mathbb{C}} [P(c \mid l) \cdot P(v \mid l, c)]}{\sum\limits_{l' \in \mathbb{L}} \sum\limits_{c \in \mathbb{C}} [P(l') \cdot P(c \mid l') \cdot P(v \mid l', c)]} \tag{14}$$
$$= \frac{P(l) \cdot \sum\limits_{c \in \mathbb{C}} [P(c \mid l) \cdot P(v \mid l, c)]}{\sum\limits_{l' \in \mathbb{L}} P(l') \cdot \sum\limits_{c \in \mathbb{C}} [P(c \mid l') \cdot P(v \mid l', c)]}$$
$$= \frac{\frac{\text{Population}(l)}{\sum\limits_{l' \in \mathbb{L}} \text{Population}(l')} \cdot \sum\limits_{c \in \mathbb{C}} [\frac{\text{Basket}(l,c)}{\sum\limits_{c' \in \mathbb{C}} \text{Basket}(l,c')} \cdot \frac{D(l,c,v)}{D(l,c)}]}{\sum\limits_{l' \in \mathbb{L}} \frac{\text{Population}(l')}{\sum\limits_{l'' \in \mathbb{L}} \text{Population}(l'')} \cdot \sum\limits_{c \in \mathbb{C}} [\frac{\text{Basket}(l',c)}{\sum\limits_{c' \in \mathbb{C}} \text{Basket}(l',c')} \cdot \frac{D(l',c,v)}{D(l',c)}]} \tag{15}$$

$$P(l \mid c, v) = \frac{P(l) \cdot P(c, v \mid l)}{P(c, v)}$$
$$= \frac{P(l) \cdot [P(c \mid l) \cdot P(v \mid l, p)]}{\sum\limits_{l' \in \mathbb{L}} [P(l') \cdot P(c \mid l') \cdot P(v \mid l', c)]} \tag{16}$$

$$= \frac{\dfrac{\text{Population}(l)}{\sum\limits_{l'\in\mathbb{L}}\text{Population}(l')} \cdot \dfrac{\text{Basket}(l,c)}{\sum\limits_{c'\in\mathbb{C}}\text{Basket}(l,c')} \cdot \dfrac{D(l,c,v)}{D(l,c)}}{\sum\limits_{l'\in\mathbb{L}}[\dfrac{\text{Population}(l')}{\sum\limits_{l''\in\mathbb{L}}\text{Population}(l'')} \cdot \dfrac{\text{Basket}(l',c)}{\sum\limits_{c'\in\mathbb{C}}\text{Basket}(l',c')} \cdot \dfrac{D(l',c,v)}{D(l',c)}]} \tag{17}$$

$$P(l \mid S_U) = P(l \mid V(e_1), V(e_2), \ldots, V(e_n))$$

$$= \frac{\prod\limits_{i=1..n} P(V(e_i))}{P(V(e_1), V(e_2), \ldots, V(e_n))}$$

$$= \frac{\dfrac{\prod\limits_{i=1..n} P(l \mid V(e_i))}{P(l)^{n-1}}}{\tag{18}}$$

$$= \frac{P(l) \cdot \prod\limits_{e\in S_U} P(V(e) \mid l)}{P(V(e_1), \ldots, V(e_n))}$$

Appendix A.1: Probability Calculations

Based on its knowledge, the ideal adversary computes the following probabilities by computing the fractions of events.

$$P(l) = \frac{|\{e|e \in \mathcal{H}_G : e.l = l\}|}{|\mathcal{H}_G|} \tag{19}$$

$$P(v) = \frac{|\{e|e \in \mathcal{H}_G : e.v = v\}|}{|\mathcal{H}_G|} \tag{20}$$

$$P(c,v) = \frac{|\{e|e \in \mathcal{H}_G : e.c = c \wedge e.v = v\}|}{|\mathcal{H}_G|} \tag{21}$$

$$P(v \mid l) = \frac{|\{e|e \in \mathcal{H}_G : e.l = l \wedge e.v = v\}|}{|\{e|e \in \mathcal{H}_G : e.l = l\}|} \tag{22}$$

$$P(c,v \mid l) = \frac{|\{e|e \in \mathcal{H}_G : e.l = l \wedge e.c = c \wedge e.v = v\}|}{|\{e|e \in \mathcal{H}_G : e.l = l\}|} \tag{23}$$

Appendix B: Further Experimental Results

Appendix B.1: Required Time Precision

Figure 8 shows, that a larger tol_s will improve the overall F_1-score, but more purchase events are needed to filter out the false positives. Similarly, for the dynamic tolerance in Fig. 9, a higher value for tol_d provides a better prediction for many purchase events, but a worse prediction for few purchase events. The figures show the experiments for the price_product-category knowledge scenario, however, we note that the results are analogous to the other scenarios. Based on these results we propose a dynamic tolerance of 2 % in the case of a 24 h time imprecision on the conversion rate.

Fig. 6. Comparison of different α-parameters for additive smoothing based on the price_product-category knowledge scenario.

Fig. 7. F_1-score of each individual country for the price knowledge scenario. The purchase events are sampled from Numbeo. We observe that no country performs poorly.

Fig. 8. Using static tolerance values to compensate for imprecise time information (one day uncertainty) in the price_product-category knowledge scenario.

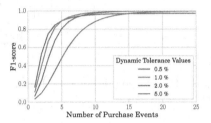

Fig. 9. Using dynamic tolerance values to compensate for imprecise time information (one day uncertainty) in the price_product-category knowledge scenario.

Fig. 10. F_1-score for identifying the US city given purchase events for different knowledge scenarios. The purchase events are sampled from the Numbeo dataset.

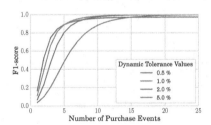

Fig. 11. F_1-score and standard deviation over 85 weeks for identifying the store in the price knowledge scenario. Data sampled from the Chicago dataset among 84 stores.

Appendix B.2: Motivating Example

Since products appear in a multitude of price values, it is at first unclear how accurately price values can identify a location. To illustrate why purchases can be localized, we focus on an example of the product category *domestic beer (0.5 L bottle)*, which can be bought in nearly every country. The price values are taken from the Numbeo dataset [9]. Figure 12 shows the distribution of price values of beer in USD for four countries. We observe that ranges of prices clearly differ for India and the other countries, while prices in Australia are more likely to be higher than in the US and Canada, where distributions of prices are similar. Given a beer price above 3 USD, in this case, it is highly likely that the purchase has not occurred in India.

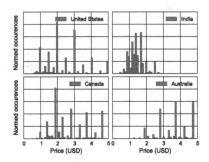

Fig. 12. Distribution of domestic beer prices (0.5 L) in 4 countries from Numbeo in USD.

Appendix C

See Figures 13, 14, Tables 2 and 3.

Fig. 13. The higher the mutual information, the more revealing is the product category.

Fig. 14. Dynamic tolerance of 2 % with one week time uncertainty on the Numbeo dataset while estimating the country. Precise time allows an F_1-score of 0.95 after 10 purchase events whereas a one week time uncertainty achieves an F_1-score of 0.63.

Table 2. Product categories of the Numbeo dataset.

Category and merchant	Unit	Prices
Market product categories		
Apples	1 kg	11876
Chicken Breasts	1 kg	11893
Cigarettes (Marlboro)	1 pack	12712
Domestic Beer	One 0.5 L bottle	10243
Eggs	12 units	14617
Imported Beer	One 0.33 L bottle	9484
Lettuce	1 head	8966
Loaf of White Bread	0.5 kg	14633
Local Cheese	1 kg	10975
Milk (regular)	1 L	17197
Oranges	1 kg	10289
Potato	1 kg	10891
Rice (white)	1 kg	10924
Tomato	1 kg	10539
Water	1.5 L bottle	12762
Wine (Mid-Range)	1 bottle	11893
Restaurant product categories		
Cappuccino (regular)	1 unit	21539
Coke/Pepsi	One 0.33 L bottle	21351
Fast Food Combo Meal	1 unit	21794
Domestic Beer	One 0.5 L bottle	19128
Imported Beer	One 0.33 L bottle	18048
Water	One 0.33 L bottle	21691
Local transportation categories		
One-way Ticket	1 unit	15275

Table 3. Statistics about the three price datasets

Numbeo dataset (2 years)	
Number of countries	112
Number of prices	328,720
Number of cities in the US	23
Number of prices in the US cities	11,686
Number of distinct product categories	23
Numbeo test dataset (5 months)	
Number of countries	47
Number of prices	40,968
Number of distinct product categories	23
Chicago dataset (5 years)	
Number of stores	84
Number of total prices in top 85 weeks	24,070,437
Average number of prices per week	283,181 ± 6790
Number of distinct product categories	28
Average number of products per week	6304 ± 461
Kaggle dataset (1 year)	
Number of store chains	134
Number of purchase events	349,655,789
Number of consumers	311,539
Number of distinct product categories	836

References

1. A Face Is Exposed for AOL Searcher No. 4417749 (2006). http://www.nytimes.com/2006/08/09/technology/09aol.html
2. Ikea Billy Bookshelf Index, Bloomberg (2009). http://www.bloomberg.com/apps/news?pid=newsarchive&sid=a.K4T4ypP9ko
3. NIST/SEMATECH e-Handbook of Statistical Methods (2013). http://www.itl.nist.gov/div898/handbook/
4. Anonymized for review (2015)
5. Big Mac Index, The Economist (2015). http://www.economist.com/content/big-mac-index
6. Consumer panel data and retail scanner data across the United States (2015). http://research.chicagobooth.edu/nielsen/
7. Kaggle, Acquire Valued Shoppers Challenge (2015). https://www.kaggle.com/c/acquire-valued-shoppers-challenge
8. More (or Less) Brew for your Buck, Starbucks coffee price (2015). http://online.wsj.com/news/articles/SB10001424127887324048904578319783080709860
9. Numbeo, database of user contributed data about cities and countries worldwide (2015). http://www.numbeo.com
10. Ripple, cryptocurrency (2015). https://ripple.com/
11. Store-level scanner data collected at Dominick's Finer Foods (2015). http://research.chicagobooth.edu/kilts/marketing-databases/dominicks/dataset
12. World Population, The world bank (2015). http://data.worldbank.org/indicator/SP.POP.TOTL?order=wbapi_data_value_2009+wbapi_data_value+wbapi_data_value-first&sort=asc
13. Androulaki, E., Karame, G.O., Roeschlin, M., Scherer, T., Capkun, S.: Evaluating user privacy in bitcoin. In: Sadeghi, A.-R. (ed.) FC 2013. LNCS, vol. 7859, pp. 34–51. Springer, Heidelberg (2013). http://eprint.iacr.org/2012/596.pdf
14. Androulaki, E., Karame, G.O.: Hiding transaction amounts and balances in bitcoin. In: Holz, T., Ioannidis, S. (eds.) Trust 2014. LNCS, vol. 8564, pp. 161–178. Springer, Heidelberg (2014)
15. Ben-Sasson, E., Chiesa, A., Garman, C., Green, M., Miers, I., Tromer, E., Virza, M.: Zerocash: decentralized anonymous payments from bitcoin. In: 2014 IEEE Symposium on Security and Privacy (SP). IEEE (2014)
16. Blumberg, A.J., Eckersley, P.: On locational privacy, and how to avoid losing it forever. EEF (2009)
17. Bonneau, J., Miller, A., Clark, J., Naryanan, A., Kroll, J.A., Felten, E.W.: SoK: bitcoin and second-generation cryptocurrencies. In: IEEE Security and Privacy, May 2015
18. Cover, T.M., Thomas, J.A.: Elements of Information Theory. John Wiley and Sons, Hoboken (2012)
19. de Montjoye, Y.-A., Hidalgo, C.A., Verleysen, M., Blondel, V.D.: Unique in the crowd: the privacy bounds of human mobility. Sci. Rep. 3 (2013)
20. Dutta, S., Bergen, M., Levy, D.: Price flexibility in channels of distribution: evidence from scanner data. J. Econ. Dyn. control 26(11), 1845–1900 (2002)
21. Meiklejohn, S., et al.: A fistful of bitcoins: characterizing payments among men with no names. In: Proceedings of the 2013 Conference on Internet Measurement Conference, IMC 2013, pp. 127–140. ACM, New York (2013)
22. Gervais, A., Karame, G., Capkun, S., Capkun, V.: Is bitcoin a decentralized currency? IEEE Secur. Priv. Mag. 12, 54–60 (2014)

23. Gruteser, M., Grunwald, D.: Anonymous usage of location-based services through spatial and temporal cloaking. In: Proceedings of the 1st International Conference on Mobile Systems, Applications and Services, pp. 31–42. ACM (2003)
24. Herrmann, R., Möser, A.: Price variability or rigidity in the food-retailing sector? theoretical analysis and evidence from german scanner data. Technical report (2003)
25. Hosken, D., Reiffen, D.: Patterns of retail price variation. RAND J. Econ., 128–146 (2004)
26. Manning, C.D., Raghavan, P., Schütze, H.: Introduction to Information Retrieval, vol. 1. Cambridge University Press, Cambridge (2008)
27. Miers, I., Garman, C., Green, M., Rubin, A.D.: Zerocoin: anonymous distributed e-cash from bitcoin. In: 2013 IEEE Symposium on Security and Privacy (SP), pp. 397–411. IEEE (2013)
28. Narayanan, A., Shmatikov, V.: Robust de-anonymization of large sparse datasets. In: IEEE Symposium on Security and Privacy, SP 2008. IEEE (2008)
29. Narayanan, A., Thiagarajan, N., Lakhani, M., Hamburg, M., Boneh, D.: Location privacy via private proximity testing
30. Pass, G., Chowdhury, A., Torgeson, C.: A picture of search. In: Proceedings of the 1st International Conference on Scalable Information Systems, InfoScale 2006. ACM, New York (2006)
31. Reid, F., Harrigan, M.: An analysis of anonymity in the bitcoin system
32. Ron, D., Shamir, A.: Quantitative analysis of the full bitcoin transaction graph (2013). http://eprint.iacr.org/2012/584.pdf
33. Nakamoto, S.: Bitcoin: a peer-to-peer electronic cash system (2009)
34. Shokri, R., Theodorakopoulos, G., Danezis, G., Hubaux, J.-P., Le Boudec, J.-Y.: Quantifying location privacy: the case of sporadic location exposure. In: Fischer-Hübner, S., Hopper, N. (eds.) PETS 2011. LNCS, vol. 6794, pp. 57–76. Springer, Heidelberg (2011)
35. Sokolova, M., Lapalme, G.: A systematic analysis of performance measures for classification tasks. Inf. Process. Manag. **45**(4), 427–437 (2009)
36. Sweeney, L.: Simple demographics often identify people uniquely. Health (San Francisco) **671**, 1–34 (2000)
37. U.S. Census Bureau, Population Division. Annual Estimates of the Resident Population for Incorporated Places of 50,000 or More, Ranked by July 1, 2013 (2014)
38. Voulodimos, A.S., Patrikakis, C.Z.: Quantifying privacy in terms of entropy for context aware services. Identity Inf. Soc. **2**(2), 155–169 (2009)
39. Singh, V.K., Pentland, A.S., de Montjoye, Y.-A., Radaelli, L.: Unique in the shopping mall: on the reidentifiability of credit card metadata. Science **347**, 536–539 (2015)

A Formal Treatment of Privacy in Video Data

Valerie Fetzer[1], Jörn Müller-Quade[1], and Tobias Nilges[2]([✉])

[1] Karlsruhe Institute of Technology, Karlsruhe, Germany
[2] Aarhus University, Aarhus, Denmark
tobias.nilges@cs.au.dk

Abstract. Video surveillance has become prevalent both in public spaces, e.g. to prevent crimes, and in private areas, e.g. in order to assist the staff in assisted living communities. This leads to privacy concerns regarding the ability of third parties to create profiles and track individuals, possibly across several services.

Usually, techniques such as pixelation and silhouettes are used to anonymize individuals. However, no formal treatment of privacy for video data has been proposed and current anonymization techniques are simply "best practice". To resolve this unsatisfactory state of affairs, we initiate a formal treatment of privacy in video data and propose a game-based notion for privacy in video data that is inspired by cryptographic security games.

We show for an exemplary video privacy scheme that this scheme satisfies our notion with good parameters. In order to evaluate these parameters, we conduct a user study where the users essentially play the role of the adversary in the privacy game. Our approach can be used as a blueprint to evaluate the privacy of other video privacy schemes.

1 Introduction

The advent of video mass surveillance [16,25] in public requires an increased effort to maintain the privacy of individuals, especially since all the collected data can be combined from different sources, allowing tracking of individuals over large time and space intervals [17]. It is obvious that this data can be used to solve crimes after they happened, but it can also be used as a deterrent to *prevent* crimes [31]. Nevertheless, innocent citizens are captured on video, and they should be protected against misuse of the collected video data by anonymization.

Video surveillance is not only used in public, but also as a helpful tool in assisted living homes and retirement homes [1,13]. In this setting, privacy is even more important, because the daily lives of the residents are monitored, including their private rooms. However, providing privacy in such an environment is even more difficult, since an operator of such a surveillance system might learn the habits of the residents and has a lot more side information about the individuals than an operator in public surveillance scenarios.

Over the years it has become apparent that it is notoriously difficult to define privacy. This difficulty spawns from the conflicting goals of releasing anonymous

© Springer International Publishing Switzerland 2016
I. Askoxylakis et al. (Eds.): ESORICS 2016, Part II, LNCS 9879, pp. 406–424, 2016.
DOI: 10.1007/978-3-319-45741-3_21

data: on the one hand the individuals want to remain private, on the other hand the released data should give the receiver of the data some utility. In the context of databases, notions such as k-anonymity [27], l-diversity [19] and t-closeness [23] tried to formally capture anonymity of individuals in a database, but all of these notions have some drawbacks [19,23]. The first formal guarantee for database privacy was presented by Dwork [12] with the notion of differential privacy, albeit only for real-valued data. Even in these scenarios, finding an adequate level of privacy and utility turns out to be non-trivial [20].

For privacy in video data, the state of the art is even worse: we largely rely on techniques such as bounding boxes, blurring, pixelation, edge detection and silhouettes [9,32] that *seem* to be good heuristics to give at least some privacy to individuals. Nevertheless, to the best of our knowledge, formal models for privacy in video data have not been proposed so far. This is at least in part due to the difficulty of formally defining the content of images or video data. Without a way to formally describe the features that are shown in the data, it is also very difficult to formally argue about the features that are hidden by the above mentioned heuristics.

Our contribution. We propose a formal security notion for privacy in video data that is applicable to many scenarios. In particular, this notion is also applicable to scenarios where the operator has a lot of side information about the individuals that are shown in the anonymized videos[1]. The privacy notion is inspired by cryptographic security notions, but evaluated empirically so that we can achieve a good understanding of the privacy of the anonymization algorithm/heuristic.

In more detail, we first define an anonymization scheme with respect to a set of features that it *does not* hide. This formally captures the utility of the anonymization scheme. Given such an anonymization scheme, we define a game-based security definition for privacy in video data, *indistinguishability under individual selection and anonymization* (IND-ISA), that is inspired by semantic security for encryption (IND-CPA) [14]. Overly simplified, we let an adversary choose two individuals from a set of individuals, for which he believes that he can distinguish the anonymized videos. The adversary is given an anonymized video of one of the individuals, and he has to decide which of the individuals is shown in the video. Privacy holds with respect to a parameter ε, i.e. an adversary wins if he decides correctly with probability greater than $\frac{1}{2} + \varepsilon$. The aforementioned notion is impossible to satisfy due to a trivial attack, but we propose a relaxed variant that is actually satisfiable.

We then exemplarily investigate the scenario of an assisted living community, where a possibly malicious operator controls several video cameras, similar to [18]. We focus on the case of individuals that fall to the floor, where the operator has to decide if the individual is actually falling down or just sitting down.

---

[1] We focus on hiding information about individuals in video data. This does *not* directly translate into anonymity. Instead, it limits the number of features that are available to identify individuals, which in turn can lead to (some form of) anonymity, depending on the scenario.

As a dataset, we use the publicly available [6]. Previously, a silhouette view has been proposed to provide privacy in this scenario [13]. We therefore implement an algorithm that creates a silhouette view and prepare a user study where the users essentially play the role of the adversary in the privacy game.

Our results from the evaluation of the user study show that our anonymization algorithm satisfies our privacy notion in the investigated scenario with $\varepsilon = 0.04$, i.e. the users' answers were essentially as good as random guesses[2]. Our analysis (although based on a very limited dataset) shows that the intuitive idea of using a silhouette view can provide privacy in complex scenarios. But we also show that great care has to be taken when applying the same algorithm to other situations. The same algorithm applied to videos of people sitting down allows to identify the individuals in the videos with significantly higher probability. Our analysis shows that this is due to the fact that the individuals in the anonymized video first take several steps and then sit down, whereas in the individuals in the other videos directly fall to the floor. These steps provides enough information to increase ε to 0.25, which means that the adversary can (with high probability) identify an individual with probability close to 75 %.

Related work. Automatic surveillance systems have seen a rise in the last years, an overview of automated visual surveillance systems can be found in [29]. Senior et al. [26] develop the *PrivacyCam*, where a processing unit in the camera itself takes measures to ensure privacy before sending the video data to the central server. Similarly, Cavallera [5] proposes an architecture of a privacy-preserving video surveillance system, which segments the video stream into privacy-preserving behavioral video data and personal video data. Thorpe et al. [28] also develop a model to split a video stream into an anonymized and a non-anonymized stream. Winkler and Rinner [33] invent the *TrustCam*, a camera with hardware security support, to ensure privacy protection in hardware. The same authors [34] also give an overview about security requirements and privacy protection techniques in the context of visual sensor networks.

Chen et al. [8] present a work that is concerned with the effectiveness of anonymization by only replacing the face of a person with a black box. The authors come to the conclusion that this is by no means satisfactory. A similar result is obtained by Neustaedter et al. [24]. They study a scenario where the privacy of a person working at home should be preserved in a video conference with colleagues at work through blurring the image. The authors find that the blur has to be so intense that the video conference is not worthwhile.

A wide range of techniques for video anonymization have been developed, e.g. [2,3,7,10]. However, there have been very few studies about the quality of anonymization techniques. One of the few studies is the work of Birnstill et al. [4]. They conduct a user study to empirically evaluate different anonymization techniques. The techniques silhouette, pixelization, gray blurring, color blurring and

---

[2] Please note that we only had a limited dataset available. In real scenarios, the operators of surveillance systems should be able to obtain a larger dataset and more representative results.

edge detection are evaluated with regard to utility and privacy protection. It is empirically shown that the utility of all techniques is very high and most of the techniques achieve acceptable privacy protection. The quality of the anonymization techniques, however, is only indicated through the opinions of the participants of the user study, no formal definition of video anonymization quality has been introduced.

2   Defining Privacy for Video Anonymization Algorithms

Our main goal is to define a security notion for anonymization algorithms on video data. Towards this goal, we first have to define an abstract notion of such an algorithm. Lacking a better term, in the following we will use "anonymize" to describe the process of applying an algorithm to video data that removes certain features. This "anonymization" does not in itself provide *anonymity* for the individuals in the video data.

In general, the motivation behind anonymization of video data is to give privacy to the individual(s) that are shown in the video, while still allowing a third party to use the anonymized video for a specific purpose. Put differently, an anonymization method finds a trade-off between the conflicting goals of providing complete anonymity to the individual on the one hand and providing optimal utility of the video data to a third party on the other. Utility of video data is very hard to formalize, but it is possible to test whether a video allows to learn a certain set of features (e.g. height, physique, etc.).

Thus, for our formalization, we take into account both the privacy and the utility of the data. We do so by explicitly stating a set of features that the anonymization algorithm will *not* hide[3]. A similar approach was recently taken in the context of database privacy by Kifer and Machanavajjhala [21]. However, they explicitly state the data that is supposed to be *hidden*, while we define the features that are not hidden. In most countries, collecting video data must already be justified by a specific purpose, e.g. observing thefts. This purpose implicitly specifies the features that are necessary to accomplish the task. Contrary to database privacy, where the utility of the data is unclear at the time of anonymization, all other information in the video data can be removed by the anonymization process.

Explicitly stating the features of an algorithm that remain unchanged allows to decide whether a specific algorithm is suitable for the given scenario, both with respect to the privacy of the individuals and the utility for the third party. Please note the fundamental difference between e.g. an encryption scheme and an anonymization scheme: the anonymization scheme provides anonymity only in certain scenarios, where the features that remain in the clear do not jeopardize anonymity. In particular, the same algorithm cannot be used blindly in related scenarios without careful consideration (cf. Sect. 4.4).

---

[3] One might argue that it is very difficult to explicitly state all features that are not hidden, but we show in Sect. 4.4 that a good approximation seems to be sufficient in most cases.

Each anonymization scheme is defined with respect to a set of features that will not be hidden after anonymizing a video.

Definition 1. *A set of features $\mathcal{F}$ is defined as a set of tuples $(f, \mathcal{D})$, where f denotes the name of the feature, and $\mathcal{D}$ the domain of this specific feature. We write $\mathcal{F}(v)$ to denote the specific manifestations of the features in video v.*

Consider for example the features Age and Height. Then $\mathcal{D}_{\text{Age}}$ could be $[0, 100]$ and $\mathcal{D}_{\text{Height}}$ could be $[30, 220]$. For a specific video v, $\mathcal{F}(v)$ could be e.g. $\{(\text{Age}, 32), (\text{Height}, 178)\}$. In the following we define the abstract notion of an anonymization scheme. The anonymization algorithm has to preserve the features in the set $\mathcal{F}_{\text{AS}}$, which implicitly defines the utility of the scheme.

Definition 2. *An anonymization scheme AS consists of two algorithms (PGen, Anonymize) and an associated feature set $\mathcal{F}_{\text{AS}}$.*

- *PGen() outputs a set of public parameters pp.*
- *Anonymize(pp, v) outputs an anonymized video $\tilde{v}$ such that $\mathcal{F}_{\text{AS}}(\tilde{v}) = \mathcal{F}_{\text{AS}}(v)$.*

In some cases the anonymization algorithm might add some noise to the preserved features, e.g. the age of an individual might be harder to decide in the anonymized video. This would mean that the equality of $\mathcal{F}_{\text{AS}}(\tilde{v})$ and $\mathcal{F}_{\text{AS}}(v)$ does not hold, instead the features in $\mathcal{F}_{\text{AS}}(\tilde{v})$ are from a smaller domain than $\mathcal{F}_{\text{AS}}(v)$. This influences both utility and privacy of the anonymization scheme. On the one hand, partially hiding some of the features in $\mathcal{F}_{\text{AS}}$ will increase the privacy. On the other hand, the utility of the anonymized video decreases. We do not consider this in our formal definition, since the exact loss of utility/gain of privacy is very hard to quantify, which in turn might make it a lot harder to work with a definition covering this case. One can interpret our definition as a "better safe than sorry" variant, that gives more privacy at the cost of some utility. But verifying the utility of an anonymization scheme in a real world scenario should be fairly simple.

It is obvious that the above definition of an anonymization scheme does not give any privacy. Instead, we want to define a security notion for anonymization schemes analogous to the notion of indistinguishability under chosen plaintext-attack (IND-CPA) in the context of semantically secure encryption [14]. Informally, IND-CPA states that an adversary cannot even learn a single plaintext bit of an encrypted message. For the purpose of defining a formal security notion for privacy in video data, a similar approach would yield a desirable level of privacy: an adversary cannot identify an individual in an anonymized video. However, in contrast to an encrypted message, an anonymized video still has to provide some non-trivial utility (otherwise we could just encrypt it). We will show that this enforces a weaker notion of security, compared to a direct translation of IND-CPA to the scenario of video anonymization.

First, let us briefly recall the IND-CPA security game for an encryption scheme ES. The experiment executes the key generation of the encryption scheme (depending on the security parameter k) and sends the resulting public key pk to the adversary $\mathcal{A}$. The adversary is now allowed to choose two messages m_0 and m_1, for which he believes that he can distinguish the respective ciphertexts. He sends both messages to the experiment, which in turn randomly selects a bit b and encrypts m_b. This encrypted message $c = \mathsf{Enc}(\mathsf{pk}, m_b)$ is then given to the adversary. The adversary now has to output a bit b' indicating whether the encrypted message is m_0 or m_1. The adversary wins this game if $b = b'$. This game is formalized in Fig. 1.

$$\textbf{Experiment } \mathsf{Exp}_{\mathsf{ES},\mathcal{A}}^{\mathsf{ind-cpa}}(k)$$

$$(\mathsf{pk}, \mathsf{sk}) \leftarrow \mathsf{ES.KeyGen}(1^k)$$
$$(m_0, m_1) \leftarrow \mathcal{A}(\mathsf{pk}, 1^k)$$
$$b \leftarrow \{0, 1\}$$
$$c \leftarrow \mathsf{ES.Enc}(\mathsf{pk}, m_b)$$
$$b' \leftarrow \mathcal{A}(\mathsf{pk}, c)$$
$$\text{return } b = b'$$

Fig. 1. The IND-CPA security game for encryption schemes.

Obviously, an adversary can always guess the random bit. Therefore the security requirement states that an adversary only breaks the security of an encryption scheme if his chance of winning the game is bigger or equal to $\frac{1}{2} + \epsilon(k)$, where $\epsilon(k)$ is a non-negligible function in the security parameter.

2.1 From IND-CPA to IND-ISA

Our goal is to provide a security notion that basically states that an adversary cannot guess which individual is shown in the anonymized video. As indicated above, we cannot directly apply the approach of the IND-CPA notion to privacy in video data, as we will show in the following. Imagine a security game where the experiment first samples some parameters for the anonymization algorithm, then the adversary is allowed to choose two arbitrary videos. He receives an anonymized version of one of the videos, and then has to decide what the underlying video was. This is basically the IND-CPA game with video data. The crucial difference between encryption and anonymization is that we require some utility from the anonymized video. In particular, there has to exist at least one predicate or feature in both videos that has to be recognizable (otherwise we would have no utility). Now an adversary can just select two videos that differ in this predicate, which will result in the adversary winning the game with probability 1.

We thus have to restrict the adversary's power to prevent this trivial attack. This means in particular that the adversary may only indirectly select the video: the video that the experiment anonymizes differs from all the videos that the adversary has at his disposal. While this might seem to be a strong restriction, we argue that this is the case in all scenarios where anonymization is required. The adversary might have some knowledge–not just in the form of video data–about the individual(s) that appear in the anonymized video, but he should obviously not have access to the exact same video without anonymization. The adversary can still choose videos based on individuals for which he believes that he can distinguish the anonymizations, e.g. due to the height, clothing or physique of the individuals.

Additionally, we have to restrict the choice of videos with respect to the feature set $\mathcal{F}_{AS}$ of the anonymization algorithm. To obtain a meaningful notion, we require that the experiment picks only videos that are indistinguishable with respect to these features; the videos can be completely arbitrary with respect to all other features. An anonymization algorithm satisfying our notion thus implies that the adversary cannot distinguish the anonymized videos depending on all the other features, i.e. these features are effectively removed by the anonymization algorithm.

We model the requirement of videos that are indistinguishable with respect to $\mathcal{F}_{AS}$ by defining an extraction algorithm Ext. This algorithm extracts the features included in $\mathcal{F}_{AS}$ from a given video.

Definition 3. *An* extraction algorithm Ext *for a feature set* $\mathcal{F}_{AS}$ *gets as input a video* v *and returns the manifestations* $\mathcal{F}_{AS}(v)$.

We are now ready to propose the notion of *indistinguishability under individual selection and anonymization*, or IND-ISA. The adversary selects two individuals from a set of individuals, the experiment selects two videos containing the individuals and uses the extractor Ext to verify that the videos are indeed indistinguishable with respect to $\mathcal{F}_{AS}$. It then anonymizes one video at random and sends it to the adversary, who has to guess which individual is shown in the video. This notion captures the goal of hiding the identity of an individual, even if the adversary is allowed to select the individuals that the experiment has to choose from. The game is depicted in Fig. 2. Let $\mathcal{A}$ denote the adversary, I denote the set of individuals and $\mathcal{V}$ the set of videos from which the experiment can choose to create an anonymized challenge. We write $\mathcal{V}_{|i}$ to denote the subset of $\mathcal{V}$ showing individual $i \in I$.

Remark 1. In some scenarios, it might be possible to allow the adversary to actually choose two videos directly and only require that the features that are not hidden have to be identical. While this yields a stronger notion of privacy, we believe that such a notion is hard to achieve in general. Our notion on the other hand provides a (weaker) guarantee, but is applicable in most realistic scenarios.

Remark 2. Obviously, IND-ISA only states that given two videos with the same manifestations of features regarding $\mathcal{F}_{AS}$ an adversary cannot distinguish the anonymized videos. This does not necessarily guarantee anonymity: in a scenario where one individual has a specific set of feature manifestations that no other individual shares, the anonymized video might still leak the identity. Thus, in order to achieve anonymity of individuals in a specific scenario, it has to be

Experiment $\mathsf{Exp}_{\mathsf{AS},\mathcal{A}}^{\mathsf{ind-isa}}$

$$(\mathsf{pp}) \leftarrow \mathsf{AS.PGen}()$$

$$(i_0, i_1) \leftarrow \mathcal{A}(\mathsf{pp})$$

return 0 if $i_0 = i_1$ or $i_0, i_1 \notin I$

$$v_0 \leftarrow \mathcal{V}_{|i_0}$$

$$v_1 \leftarrow \mathcal{V}_{|i_1}$$

return 0 if $\mathsf{Ext}(\mathcal{F}_{\mathsf{AS}}, v_0) \neq \mathsf{Ext}(\mathcal{F}_{\mathsf{AS}}, v_1)$

$$b \leftarrow \{0, 1\}$$

$$\tilde{v} \leftarrow \mathsf{AS.Anonymize}(\mathsf{pp}, v_b)$$

$$b' \leftarrow \mathcal{A}(\mathsf{pp}, \tilde{v})$$

return $b = b'$

Fig. 2. The IND-ISA privacy game for video anonymization schemes.

ensured that at least two individuals with the same feature manifestations actually exist.

In comparison to standard cryptographic notions, it is at the very least unclear how to achieve asymptotic security. Instead, we measure the success probability of an adversary with a statistical parameter ε that is supposed to indicate his success probability in comparison to simply guessing the result. We defer a detailed discussion on the parameter ε to Sect. 3, where we propose a method to determine ε. Given the definition of IND-ISA, we are able to define the privacy of an anonymization scheme.

Definition 4. *We say an anonymization scheme* AS *is* $\varepsilon-IND\text{-}ISA\text{-}secure$, *if any adversary wins* $\mathsf{Exp}_{\mathsf{AS},\mathcal{A}}^{\mathsf{ind-isa}}$ *with probability at most* $\frac{1}{2} + \varepsilon$ *averaged over all videos in* $\mathcal{V}$.

At first sight, the above definition of privacy for anonymization schemes might seem very weak, because we only require an *average* distinguishing advantage. In particular, there might exist an adversary that identifies an individual in a certain video with very high probability. This lies in stark contrast to the classical cryptographic security notions, but it still gives us a meaningful measure of the quality of an anonymization scheme.

3   On Obtaining IND-ISA-Secure Anonymization Schemes

Before we describe our anonymization scheme and discuss the results, let us first elaborate on how one can actually obtain IND-ISA security. The main problem that we face is that we have no underlying cryptographic assumptions or statistical data on the image to work with, on which we could base the security for an algorithm.

Our idea is to take an empirical approach to verify the security of a specific algorithm. Instead of assuming hardness of some underlying assumption, we actually implement the IND-ISA game with videos and an anonymization scheme. In contrast to cryptographic games, where we make no assumptions about the adversary apart from possibly polynomial efficiency, we now use a "constructive" approach.

The approach that we use for our example implementation is as follows: We create a user study, in which users essentially take the role of the adversary (a human adversary is the most likely case in real world scenarios). Using a statistical analysis, it is possible to measure the indistinguishability of anonymized videos in a meaningful way. Given enough participants for such a study, we can make a fairly good assumption on the IND-ISA security of the anonymization algorithm. We propose the following method to determine the value ε. The user study is basically a Bernoulli process, i.e. the game that the user plays is independent of the games that other users played. This means that the results should be distributed according to a binomial distribution. We can thus sum up all the answers from the study and compute the Clopper-Pearson interval [11] with confidence e.g. 95 % and $p = \frac{1}{2}$. This results in two values $[a, b]$, and we set $\varepsilon = \max\{b - \frac{1}{2}, 0\}$. Taking the value b of the interval corresponds to a "worst-case" choice for the parameter ε.

Another approach based on the same idea is to use learning algorithms to play the IND-ISA game, e.g. PAC learning [30]. This would yield several advantages over the approach with user studies: first of all it is much cheaper and less time consuming than a user study while additionally shedding light on the question whether an adversary can learn to distinguish the anonymized videos over time. We leave this research direction as an open question for future work.

In the following section, we give two examples of such studies with somewhat surprising results.

4   An IND-ISA-Private Anonymization Scheme

In the following we will present an exemplary instantiation of an anonymization scheme applied to two real world scenarios to illustrate our approach. In order to do so, we first have to define an anonymization scheme according to Definition 2 and a scenario to apply it to.

4.1   Scenario

In recent years, supporting the staff of an assisted living community with privacy preserving video surveillance has been the focus of research, both with respect to feature recognition and privacy [1,13,18,22,35]. In a little more detail, the idea is to enhance the apartments of an assisted living community with video cameras that help the staff detecting accidents and emergencies. One line of research focuses on fully automated systems that incorporate e.g. fall detection algorithms [13]. However, the detection rate is not perfect and in the case of an emergency a falling resident *must* be detected, which inevitably leads to possibly many false positive alarms. Another aspect is the problem that in some countries fully automated systems are not allowed to make decisions without human verification. Thus, in a realistic scenario an operator has to access the video data and can evaluate whether an emergency arises. This operator can observe the individuals in their private rooms, therefore anonymization methods have to be applied to ensure privacy of the residents.

We study two situations that are closely related: an individual falling to the floor and an individual sitting down. These situations are difficult to distinguish by an algorithm and therefore sometimes require human verification. We assume that the operator knows the individuals that are shown by the surveillance system, but he only sees the anonymized video of the presumed fall. The video data recorded before the incident and afterwards cannot be accessed by the operator. Further, the operator is supposed to verify that the individual fell or recognize an error by the algorithm. This implies that the anonymization scheme must provide enough utility to make this distinction.

4.2 Anonymization Scheme

In the literature, the anonymization technique of choice for this scenario is a silhouette view. On the one hand, it still allows to discern the movements of an individual, on the other hand most features like colors and environment are removed. However, there is no formal treatment regarding the validity of this approach. We thus implemented an anonymization algorithm that realizes a blurred silhouette view of a video. The blurring is added to remove the exact outline of the individual, which might give away too much information. The implementation is based on the OpenCV library and written in C++.

The generation of the public parameters for our anonymization scheme AS_{sil} is implicit, they are included in the anonymization algorithm Anonymize. It proceeds in three steps:

1. For each frame: calculate the silhouette view by means of background subtraction
2. For each frame: blur the image with median filter and Gaussian blur
3. Normalize the whole video by zooming to the relevant section and then scaling the video to a fixed width

The public parameters pp_{sil} are the parameters used for each step: in the first step any parameters that are needed to produce the silhouette view, for the second step the parameters for the median filter and Gaussian blur and in the last step the width the video is scaled to. Figure 3 shows the intermediate results of the algorithm when applied to an example video.

In accordance with our definition of anonymization schemes, our algorithm must be defined with respect to a feature set $\mathcal{F}_{AS_{sil}}$. Finding a formal specification for the feature set is highly nontrivial, because some features are a superset of other features. These features are therefore also distinguishable after

(a) The raw image

(b) After silhouette extraction

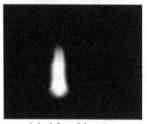

(c) After blurring

(d) After normalizing

Fig. 3. An example for the use of AS_{sil}. In (a) the original image can be seen, picture (b) and (c) are intermediate steps and the finished anonymization is shown in (d). The video data is taken from Gorelick et al. [15].

anonymization. Thus, we define a rather coarse feature set that should cover all distinguishable features, but might include some features that are actually hidden by the scheme AS_{sil}. In the following, let

$$\mathcal{F}_{AS_{sil}} = \{\text{physique}, \text{movements}, \text{accessories}\}.$$

Note that it is e.g. possible to derive knowledge about the age from the sequence of movements and the physique of an individual. By accessories we mean objects like an umbrella, a bag or a walking aid.

4.3   Dataset

We use a dataset due to Charfi et al. [6]. It contains 191 videos of individuals walking, falling down and sitting down. The resolution of the videos is 320×240 px and the frame rate is 25 frames/second. Only 60 of these videos were suitable for our study. The amount was further limited because the number of videos of each individual fluctuates. There are only four videos of one individual falling down, and 3 videos of another individual sitting down. The videos of falling and sitting individuals were used as the set $\mathcal{V}$ in the IND-ISA game. Videos of individuals walking through the room were given the users to get some background information on the individuals. Therefore the four individuals of the dataset add up to the set I in the IND-ISA game.

The camera is placed in a corner of the room, comparable to the installation in a real assisted living community. The room contains a table, a chair and a sofa. In some videos, a carpet or blanket is put on the floor. Based on this dataset we can test several aspects.

- Is it possible to discern whether an individual is falling down or sitting down? This is one situation that might occur if an automated system misclassifies a situation and describes the utility of the data.
- Is it possible to identify an individual if one knows only the video of the person falling down? This reflects our definition of privacy in video data.

Our user study covers both of these aspects. We cut the videos that we wanted to anonymize such that they only show the respective action, i.e. an individual falling down or sitting down[4].

4.4 User Study

We prepared a user study that evaluated two aspects. On the one hand, users had to decide whether an individual was falling down or sitting down in an anonymized video. On the other hand, we let each user play the IND-ISA privacy game for the anonymization scheme AS_{sil} based on the aforementioned video dataset. The study was conducted similar to our proposal from Sect. 3. Each user was shown four videos of different individuals that walk through a room (cf. Fig. 4), i.e. these individuals represent the set I of the IND-ISA game. These individuals were (supposedly) chosen in a way that they were indistinguishable with respect to $\mathcal{F}_{AS_{sil}}$ (because we did not have a feature extraction that could have been used). The user had to select two of the four videos, i.e. individuals, for which he believed he could distinguish an anonymized version.

After the selection the user was shown one anonymized video of one of the selected persons falling down or sitting down, respectively. Then the user had to decide which person was anonymized in the video. Answer options were "Person X", "Person Y" and "I don't know", where X and Y were replaced with the letters corresponding to the chosen persons. We added the "I don't know"-option to get a better understanding of how the users felt when seeing the anonymized video. For the analysis, we assumed that in the case of the "I don't know"-option an IND-ISA-adversary would just guess an option with probability $\frac{1}{2}$. Additionally, the user had the option to describe the feature(s) that helped him identify the individual.

We let each user play several games (four, respectively two) with new anonymized videos to increase the number of samples that we could use, which in turn breaks the independence of the sequential games. Thus, if we use the approach from Sect. 3 to compute the value ε, the result is less accurate, because we introduce learning effects. Due to the structure and low sample size of our user study, however, it is not possible to quantify these learning effects in a

---

[4] Our discussion in Sect. 4.5 elaborates on the problems that arise when cutting the videos.

| Person A | Person B | Person C | Person D |

Fig. 4. Parts of the videos that provide the user of the study with some knowledge about the individuals which he has to distinguish. Each video shows the corresponding individual walking around.

meaningful way, so we stick to the same approach to compute ε in this example implementation. Usually, one would have to calculate the multidimensional confidence interval with respect to several identically distributed games.

All in all, we obtained results from 248 users, but only 103 users answered the complete study. The results show that the anonymization method is suitable to discern between individuals falling down and individuals sitting down. The detection rate of individuals sitting down in the anonymized videos was 100 %, and the detection rate of individuals falling down was between 97 % and 99 %. Our results concerning the privacy of the individuals are summarized in the following two paragraphs.

Evaluation of the Fall Detection Study. Due to the small amount of available videos, we let each user play four games with individuals falling down. Figure 5 shows images from the anonymized videos. The set of videos that was used for the anonymization is disjoint from the set of videos that the users saw in order to select their "challenge" identity in the IND-ISA game.

An analysis of the data shows that, generally, the users had difficulties in identifying the correct individual in the anonymized video. Averaged over all four games, 60 % of the users selected the "I don't know"-option, with values ranging from 52 to 69 %. Of all the users that identified an individual, averaged over all four games, the answers were close to uniformly distributed (19 % selected the

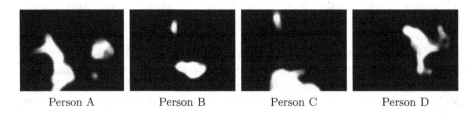

| Person A | Person B | Person C | Person D |

Fig. 5. Images of some of the anonymized videos used in the fall detection study. Each anonymized video shows the corresponding individual falling down.

Individuals	Game 1			Game 2			Game 3			Game 4		
	[1]	[2]	IDK	[1]	[2]	IDK	[1]	[2]	IDK	[1]	[2]	IDK
A,B	3	**3**	4	**4**	12	5	**3**	8	9	2	**3**	12
A,C	9	**10**	41	**6**	20	22	**10**	8	20	3	**4**	31
A,D	0	**7**	2	**2**	1	6	**4**	5	6	4	**3**	6
B,C	3	**6**	28	**5**	6	23	**5**	2	23	3	**2**	25
B,D	0	**1**	1	**1**	1	3	**0**	1	4	2	**1**	5
C,D	4	**6**	2	**1**	1	8	**6**	1	11	7	**3**	5
Total	**19**	33	78	**19**	41	67	**28**	25	73	21	**16**	84

Fig. 6. This table shows the number of answers for each of the four games. Each game is split into 6 separate games due to the choices of individuals by the users. [1] and [2] specify the first individual and the second individual from the first column, respectively. Correct answers are written in bold font.

correct answer, 21 % the wrong answer, 60 % did not recognize the individual). A more detailed breakdown is shown in Fig. 6.

While the first game might be interpreted as an indication that it is possible to identify the individuals, we have to consider that the sample size is very small. When we look at the actual detection rates for each possible pair of choices by the users, we observe that except for one pair of individuals in the first game (Individuals A and D), the answers are nearly uniformly distributed. The users that selected this constellation of individuals described that the gait and speed of movements of the individuals convinced them that the anonymized video showed the correct individual. Upon inspection of the videos, we noticed that the anonymized video shows the individual taking two steps before falling to the floor.

There are several possible interpretations. On the one hand, the sample size is far too small to rule out a statistical fluke (9 users, 7 correct answers). Additionally, the users' answers with regard to the identifiable feature have to be taken with a grain of salt, because many users claimed to have identified individuals according to e.g. gait, even in cases where they chose the wrong individual. On the other hand, in combination with the results from the videos of individuals sitting down (cf. Sect. 4.4), we believe that the two steps shown in the video are indeed enough information to correctly identify an individual.

We now want to fix a value for ε. As mentioned above, we will ignore learning effects and just calculate ε as described in Sect. 3. We split the "I don't know"-answers evenly between correct and incorrect guesses, which results in a success probability of 49.01 % based on our study, i.e. the wrong answer is given with 50.99 %. By computing the Clopper-Pearson confidence interval [11] for the success probability we get the interval [44.56 % , 53.47 %]. Thus, $\varepsilon = 0.5347 - 0.5 = 0.0347$, which rounds up to $\varepsilon = 0.04$.

Evaluation of the Sitting Detection Study. In comparison to the fall detection study, we had less videos available so that we let each user play only

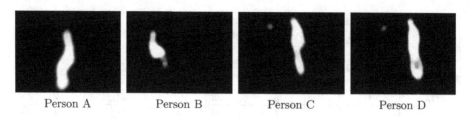

Person A   Person B   Person C   Person D

Fig. 7. Parts of some of the anonymized videos used in the sitting detection study. Each video shows the corresponding individual sitting down in anonymized form.

two games. Apart from this and the fact that the individuals sit down in the anonymized videos, the setup is identical to the fall detection study. Examples for the anonymized videos used in the sitting detection study are shown in Fig. 7.

Our results are shown in Fig. 8. On average, 55 % of the users identified the correct individual, but only 18 % identified the wrong individual, leaving 27 % of undecided users. Looking closer into the data, it seems as if the first game was more or less uniformly distributed averaged over all 6 possible choices of the users, but in the second game 75 % of the users selected the correct individual. Even worse, a closer look at the individual games shows that the users identified some individuals with probability (close to) 1, even for certain choices of individuals in game 1.

Most users claimed to have identified the individuals due to the walking style in the videos. In comparison to the videos that show individuals falling down, nearly all anonymized videos include two steps taken by the individual before sitting down. As in the previous study, this seems to give the users a high probability in identifying the anonymized individual.

Obviously, the value ε is much worse than in the previous case. Again, we distribute the "I don't know"-answers evenly between the right and the wrong answers. The success probability of an IND-ISA-adversary is therefore 69 % and

Individuals	Game 1			Game 2		
	[1]	[2]	IDK	[1]	[2]	IDK
A,B	4	**6**	11	2	**12**	3
A,C	4	**20**	21	2	**32**	8
A,D	2	**1**	3	0	**5**	0
B,C	**17**	7	5	0	**27**	7
B,D	**1**	0	3	4	**2**	1
C,D	**12**	0	2	0	**11**	2
Total	40	34	46	8	89	21

Fig. 8. This table shows the number of answers for both games. Each game is split into 6 separate games due to the choices of individuals by the users. [1] and [2] specify the first individual and the second individual from the first column, respectively. Correct answers are written in bold font.

the error probability 31 %. The calculation of the Clopper-Pearson interval yields [62.02 %, 74.22 %]. Thus, $\varepsilon = 0.7422 - 0.5 = 0.2422$, which rounds up to $\varepsilon = 0.25$.

4.5 Discussion

We believe that the main reason that users could identify an individual in an anonymized video was that the anonymized videos included one or two steps of the individual. We cut the videos in this way to help the users identify the action, but our results concerning the privacy show that this allows the identification of anonymized individuals with high probability.

Intuitively, this already follows from the definition of the privacy game IND-ISA and our anonymization scheme: the anonymization scheme does not hide sequences of movements, therefore the IND-ISA game would require us to select videos that are indistinguishable with respect to these movements. From an adversarial point of view, seeing an individual walk will not give him much information about an individual falling down (in our scenario). However, if the anonymized video includes, apart from the falling or sitting individual, some steps of the individual, the adversary can use his knowledge to identify this individual. When we selected videos that include both walking and falling down, we did not (manually) check whether the individuals were indistinguishable with respect to the walking movements. Our results clearly show that the individuals are not indistinguishable in that regard. We believe that removing the part of the videos that shows the steps of the individuals would greatly reduce the users' ability to identify the individuals and yield a smaller value for ε. In turn, the measured utility of the anonymization might drop a bit.

This highlights a very important aspect of anonymizing video data: even if an anonymization method is very good in one scenario, it is not possible to incorporate it into another scenario without considering all aspects of the anonymization process.

To finish our evaluation, we want to discuss a value ε_t that describes the anonymity of individuals in the above described scenario, i.e. an operator is shown anonymized videos of alleged falls of individuals. The overall identification probability in this scenario is dependent on the accuracy of the fall detection system. If we assume the detection algorithms of Charfi et al. [6], a fall is correctly detected with probability 99.6 %. Thus, despite the poor performance of the anonymization due to videos showing the walking movements, the privacy of the individuals in the scenario is very close to $\varepsilon_t = 0.04$.

5   Conclusion and Future Work

Currently, privacy in video data is only argued on a very informal level, and the applied anonymization algorithms are more or less chosen because they are "best practice". As our second example showed, this can be a dangerous way to approach privacy in complex systems. We started a formal treatment of the problem of privacy in video data and laid a formal foundation for future research in this area. We believe that an interdisciplinary effort is required to find widely applicable anonymization algorithms, together with good formal guarantees. This is due to the fact that for anonymization methods, we need knowledge from security/cryptography, feature recognition and machine learning. Additionally, a large dataset for the evaluation of the anonymization schemes seems essential, because it is not possible to create large amounts of realistic videos in software.

Using the approach that we presented, it is possible to define a set of candidates for IND-ISA secure anonymization algorithms that cover a wide range of applications. Being able to abstract from the anonymization method allows the design of *provably private* video surveillance systems. The system itself can be proven private, while the anonymization algorithm is then chosen according to the scenario in which the surveillance system is used. Thus, the security analysis is simplified and modularized.

References

1. Abowd, G.D., Bobick, A.F., Essa, I.A., Mynatt, E.D., Rogers, W.A.: The aware home: a living laboratory for technologies for successful aging. In: Proceedings of AAAI Workshop and Automation as a Care Giver, pp. 1–7 (2002)
2. Bamba, B., Liu, L.: Privacygrid: supporting anonymous location queries in mobile environments. Technical report, Defense Technical Information Center (2007)
3. Berger, A.M.: Privacy mode for acquisition cameras and camcorders. US Patent 6,067,399 (2000)
4. Birnstill, P., Ren, D., Beyerer, J.: A user study on anonymization techniques for smart video surveillance. In: 2015 12th IEEE International Conference on Advanced Video and Signal Based Surveillance (AVSS), pp. 1–6. IEEE (2015)
5. Cavallaro, A.: Adding privacy constraints to video-based applications. In: European Workshop on the Integration of Knowledge, Semantics and Digital Media Technology (2004)
6. Charfi, I., Miteran, J., Dubois, J., Atri, M., Tourki, R.: Definition and performance evaluation of a robust SVM based fall detection solution. In: Eighth International Conference on Signal Image Technology and Internet Based Systems (SITIS), pp. 218–224. IEEE (2012)
7. Chen, D., Chang, Y., Yan, R., Yang, J.: Tools for protecting the privacy of specific individuals in video. EURASIP J. Adv. Sig. Process. **2007**(1), 075427 (2007)
8. Chen, D., Chang, Y., Yan, R., Yang, J.: Protecting personal identification in video. In: Senior, A. (ed.) Protecting Privacy in Video Surveillance, pp. 115–128. Springer, London (2009)
9. Chinomi, K., Nitta, N., Ito, Y., Babaguchi, N.: Prisurv: privacy protected video surveillance system using adaptive visual abstraction. In: Satoh, S., Nack, F., Etoh, M. (eds.) MMM 2008. LNCS, vol. 4903, pp. 144–154. Springer, Heidelberg (2008)
10. Cichowski, J., Czyzewski, A.: Reversible video stream anonymization for video surveillance systems based on pixels relocation and watermarking. In: IEEE International Conference on Computer Vision Workshops (ICCV Workshops), pp. 1971–1977 (2011)
11. Clopper, C.J., Pearson, E.S.: The use of confidence or fiducial limits illustrated in the case of the binomial. Biometrika **26**(4), 404–413 (1934)

12. Dwork, C.: Differential privacy. In: Bugliesi, M., Preneel, B., Sassone, V., Wegener, I. (eds.) ICALP 2006. LNCS, vol. 4052, pp. 1–12. Springer, Heidelberg (2006)
13. Fleck, S., Straßer, W.: Smart camera based monitoring system and its application to assisted living. Proc. IEEE **96**(10), 1698–1714 (2008)
14. Goldwasser, S., Micali, S.: Probabilistic encryption. J. Comput. Syst. Sci. **28**(2), 270–299 (1984)
15. Gorelick, L., Blank, M., Shechtman, E., Irani, M., Basri, R.: Actions as space-time shapes. Trans. Pattern Anal. Mach. Intell. **29**(12), 2247–2253 (2007)
16. Haering, N., Venetianer, P.L., Lipton, A.: The evolution of video surveillance: an overview. Mach. Vis. Appl. **19**(5–6), 279–290 (2008)
17. Hampapur, A., Brown, L., Connell, J., Ekin, A., Haas, N., Lu, M., Pankanti, S.: Smart video surveillance: exploring the concept of multiscale spatiotemporal tracking. IEEE Sig. Process. Mag. **22**(2), 38–51 (2005)
18. Huber, M., Müller-Quade, J., Nilges, T., Thal, C.: A provably privacy preserving video surveillance architecture for an assisted living community. In: GI-Jahrestagung, pp. 563–574 (2014)
19. Kifer, D., Gehrke, J.: L-diversity: privacy beyond k-anonymity. In: ICDE, p. 24 (2006)
20. Kifer, D., Machanavajjhala, A.: No free lunch in data privacy. In: Proceedings of the 2011 ACM SIGMOD International Conference on Management of Data, SIGMOD 2011, pp. 193–204. ACM, New York (2011)
21. Kifer, D., Machanavajjhala, A.: Pufferfish: a framework for mathematical privacy definitions. ACM Trans. Database Syst. **39**(1), 3:1–3:36 (2014)
22. Kleinberger, T., Becker, M., Ras, E., Holzinger, A., Müller, P.: Ambient intelligence in assisted living: enable elderly people to handle future interfaces. In: Stephanidis, C. (ed.) UAHCI 2007 (Part II). LNCS, vol. 4555, pp. 103–112. Springer, Heidelberg (2007)
23. Li, N., Li, T., Venkatasubramanian, S.: t-Closeness: privacy beyond k-anonymity and l-diversity. In: ICDE, pp. 106–115 (2007)
24. Neustaedter, C., Greenberg, S., Boyle, M.: Blur filtration fails to preserve privacy for home-based video conferencing. ACM Trans. Comput. Hum. Interact. (TOCHI) **13**(1), 1–36 (2006)
25. Norris, C., McCahill, M., Wood, D.: The growth of CCTV: a global perspective on the international diffusion of video surveillance in publicly accessible space. Surveill. Soc. **2**(2/3), 110–135 (2002)
26. Senior, A., Pankanti, S., Hampapur, A., Brown, L., Tian, Y.L., Ekin, A., Connell, J., Shu, C.F., Lu, M.: Enabling video privacy through computer vision. IEEE Secur. Priv. **3**(3), 50–57 (2005)
27. Sweeney, L.: k-anonymity: a model for protecting privacy. Int. J. Uncertainty Fuzziness Knowl. Based Syst. **10**(5), 557–570 (2002)
28. Thorpe, C., Li, F., Li, Z., Yu, Z., Saunders, D., Yu, J.: A coprime blur scheme for data security in video surveillance. IEEE Trans. Pattern Anal. Mach. Intell. **35**(12), 3066–3072 (2013)
29. Valera, M., Velastin, S.A.: Intelligent distributed surveillance systems: a review. In: IEEE Proceedings - Vision, Image and Signal Processing, vol. 152, pp. 192–204. IET (2005)
30. Valiant, L.G.: A theory of the learnable. Commun. ACM **27**(11), 1134–1142 (1984)
31. Welsh, B.C., Farrington, D.P.: Evidence-based crime prevention: the effectiveness of CCTV. Crime Prev. Community Saf. **6**(2), 21–33 (2004)

32. Wickramasuriya, J., Datt, M., Mehrotra, S., Venkatasubramanian, N.: Privacy protecting data collection in media spaces. In: Proceedings of the 12th Annual ACM International Conference on Multimedia, pp. 48–55. ACM (2004)

33. Winkler, T., Rinner, B.: Privacy and security in video surveillance. In: Atrey, P.K., Kankanhalli, M.S., Cavallaro, A. (eds.) Intelligent Multimedia Surveillance, pp. 37–66. Springer, Heidelberg (2013)

34. Winkler, T., Rinner, B.: Security and privacy protection in visual sensor networks: a survey. ACM Comput. Surv. (CSUR) **47**(1), 2 (2014)

35. Wood, A.D., Stankovic, J.A., Virone, G., Selavo, L., He, Z., Cao, Q., Doan, T., Wu, Y., Fang, L., Stoleru, R.: Context-aware wireless sensor networks for assisted living and residential monitoring. IEEE Netw. **22**(4), 26–33 (2008)

Security of Cyber-Physical Systems

On Attacker Models and Profiles
for Cyber-Physical Systems

Marco Rocchetto[1]([✉]) and Nils Ole Tippenhauer[2]

[1] iTrust, Singapore University of Technology and Design, Singapore, Singapore
macro_rocchetto@sutd.edu.sg
[2] ISTD, Singapore University of Technology and Design, Singapore, Singapore

Abstract. Attacker models are a fundamental part of research on security of any system. For different application scenarios, suitable attacker models have to be chosen to allow comprehensive coverage of possible attacks. We consider Cyber-Physical Systems (CPS), that typically consist of networked embedded systems which are used to sense, actuate, and control physical processes. The physical layer aspects of such systems add novel attack vectors and opportunities for defenses, that require extended models of attackers' capabilities. We develop a taxonomy to classify and compare attacker models in related work. We show that, so far, there are no commonly used attacker models for such CPS. In addition, concepts of what information belongs in an attacker model are widely different among the community. To address that problem, we develop a framework to classify attacker models and use it to review related work on CPS Security. Using our framework, we propose a set of attacker profiles and show that those profiles capture most types of attackers described in the related work. Our framework provides a more formal and standardized definition of attacker model for CPS, enabling the use of well-defined and uniform attacker models in the future.

1 Introduction

In recent years, security of Cyber-Physical Systems (CPS) has received increasing attention by researchers from the domain of computer science, electrical engineering, and control theory [15,24,28,31]. We use the term CPS to refer to systems that consist of networked embedded systems, which are used to sense, actuate, and control physical processes. Examples of such CPS include industrial water treatment facilities, electrical power plants, public transportation infrastructure, or even smart cars. All those systems have seen a rapid increase in automation and connectivity, which threatens to increase vulnerability to malicious attacks.

In contrast to the domain of information security , where the Dolev-Yao attacker model [11] (DY) is widely used for protocol analysis, the state-of-the-art for CPS security does not have a common terminology for attacker models. Instead, attacker-models are usually defined ad-hoc for the specific setting considered. Even if the topic has been broadly discussed in the CPS research community (e.g., in [15,28,31]) only a small number of tentative works [18,37] have tried to overcome this problem.

© Springer International Publishing Switzerland 2016
I. Askoxylakis et al. (Eds.): ESORICS 2016, Part II, LNCS 9879, pp. 427–449, 2016.
DOI: 10.1007/978-3-319-45741-3_22

In this work, we provide a comprehensive overview of work on CPS attacks. We find that in most cases, the authors show how to attack the system without defining attacker models [2,3,16] or propose their own attacker model(s) depending on the system they are considering (e.g., [8]) or leave to the users the (non trivial) problem of defining their own attacker models [2]. In general, authors often prefer to use their own attacker model with an *ad hoc* set of constraints on the attacker. In addition, we review attempts to provide more general attacker models or frameworks, e.g., [18,37].

Based on our findings of related work, we show commonalities and differences in existing attempts to generalize attacker models for CPS, and provide recommendations for future attacker models in that direction.

We summarize our main contributions as follows:

- We define and apply a taxonomy of 10 different features to classify and compare attacker models in related work
- We provide a detailed overview of work discussing attacks and attackers on CPS
- We propose an attacker framework and a more formal and standardized definition of attacker model for CPS
- Using that framework, we extract attacker profiles from related work, analyze those profiles, and propose six attacker profile archetypes that distill common intuition behind related work

In addition, we developed a complementary tool to support our review of the related work. The tool allows the application of our taxonomy to classify related work, comparisons between profiles and export filters, and contains the results of our analysis. The tool is called APE (Attacker Profile Examiner) available at [29].

Structure. In Sect. 2, we describe the scope of our review and aspects considered. We review the literature in Sect. 3 (attacks on CPS, categorizations of attackers, (semi-) formal model of attacker). In Sect. 4 we analyze the related works, showing a list of commonalities and metrics that we use to categorize the related work. We propose an attacker model framework in Sect. 5, apply it to the related work to obtain their attacker profiles, and analyze those profiles and propose a set of our own profiles. We conclude the paper in Sect. 6.

2   Scope and Taxonomy for Related Work Review

We start by defining the scope of our related work review, we then provide definitions which help us to classify the related work. Finally, we present the taxonomy we use to summarize related work.

2.1   Scope of Our Review

We review the related work on: (i) attacks on CPS and their ad-hoc attacker models, (ii) works which profile attackers for CPS and (iii) works on generic attacker models for CPS. We start by reviewing works that discuss specific attackers who target or leverage the physical layer in their attacks (mechanical, electrical interactions). These works are found in the domain of public infrastructure (e.g., water [2] and power [20]). To limit the scope, we do not focus on attacks that are only related to physical-layer wireless communication (e.g., key establishment, jamming, anti-jamming, friendly jamming).

In addition, we review works that provide profiles for different attackers on CPS, and works that consider more generic attacker models that include the physical layer.

2.2 Terminology

Interestingly, we did not find general definitions of central terms related to models for CPS attackers. In [7], there is a first attempt in providing general definitions for CPS security but the authors focus on attacks and properties rather than attacker model. For that reason, we now provide a short description of the central terminology we use in the remainder of this work.

A *System under attack* is an interacting or connected group of components (soft- and hardware, humans) forming a unified whole and serving a common purpose.

An *Attacker* is a group of human actors that collaborate to achieve a goal related to the system under attack.

An *Attacker Profile* describes templates or classes of attackers. These profiles are a generic description of the setting and intuition, and not an exhaustive listing of possible actions, motivations, or capabilities of the attacker.

An *Attacker Model* (together with compatible system models) will ideally fully characterize the possible interactions between the attacker and the system under attack. In particular, the model will define constraints for the attacker (e.g. finite computational resources, no access to shared keys)

A *System Model* characterizes relevant components of the system under attack, to a level of detail that allows to determine all possible interaction of the attacker with the system. We will not go into the details of the system model since our work focuses on the attacker. Therefore, we will not distinguish between system models which consider (or not) risk or threat linked to components of the system.

An *Attack Model* characterizes all potential interactions between the attacker and a specific configuration of the system under attack and the specification of the goal that the attacker wants to achieve with respect to the system under attack. One can consider an attack model as an instantiation of the attacker model on a specific scenario (i.e., system configuration).

2.3 Taxonomy

In our review of related work, we systematically analyze and summarize the attacker models (or related models) that are used to describe the attacker. In particular, we focus on the following aspects:

1. If different attacker profiles are discussed, and how many
2. The dimensions used by authors to define the attacker
3. The number of actions types available to the attacker
4. Use of a system model (or constraints on the type of system)
5. Validation of attack(er) models
6. Generality of model (i.e., specific for one CPS or general attacker model)
7. Supporting case studies (and if they are ad-hoc, real)
8. Whether the authors considered time in their models
9. Terminology used by authors for the model, and how it fits to our terminology
10. The main research goal of the reviewed work

3   Review of Attacker Definitions in Related Work

The idea of attacker models for CPS has been explored from different perspectives. In this section, we provide a review of related works that focus on a specific case study or attacks which can be exploited on a CPS or a class of CPS (Sect. 3.1). We then review common informal and semi-formal *attacker profiles* that are often used in research and by the public (Sect. 3.2). Afterwards, we review CPS-related attacker models (Sect. 3.3). We *emphasize* the key points we have used in our taxonomy. For a more detailed description of our review we refer to our tool available at [29].

3.1   Attacks on CPS

In the following, we provide a review of works which focuses on specific attacks or (class of) CPS.

Amin et al. In [2], the authors perform security *threat assessment* of networked control systems and Supervisory Control and Data Acquisition (SCADA) systems with regulatory and supervisory control layers. Authors *do not define a model of the system* and their technique is *specific* for one case study. No dimensions are explicitly considered, some assumptions are made on the *knowledge* of the attacker and his *resources*. Specific actions for the attacker are not discussed, *attacks* are considered as a general action.

Esfahani et al. In [12], the authors propose an approach for the identification of security flaw in of electric power transmission systems. The authors do not discuss *profiles*, *dimensions* or *actions* of the attacker model because the study is focused on the *modeling of the system* and the aim is to perform *risk analysis*.

Krotofil et al. In [17], the authors discuss the importance of *time* in security attacks to CPS. The discussion is *specific* for electric power grid. An *attacker model* (called adversary model in the paper) is defined with DoS and false data injection attacks as only *actions*. The only *dimension* of the attacker model is identified with his goals. Authors apply their results to *one case study*.

Lin et al. In [19], the authors study vulnerabilities of distributed energy routing processes by *attack simulation*. Authors focus on false data injection attacks and analyze their impact on the *system model*. The *attacker model* (called threat model in [19]) can modify data and compromise component injecting malicious codes. Authors consider the attacker's *knowledge of the system* and ability to *attack* the system (node compromise).

Liu et al. In [20], the authors define a new attack class against electric power systems. The basic idea is that an attacker can inject malicious measurements (attack) *without being detected* by any of the existing techniques for bad measurement detection. Authors describe how to formally represent a *system model* of a power grid and test their attacks against *two ad-hoc examples*.

Taormina et al. In [33], the authors define how to *simulate cyber-physical attacks* on water distribution systems. EPANET [35] (a numerical modeling environment) is used to define the *system model* along with the properties of each component. The *attacker model* is informally defined by two *actions*: direct and indirect attacks. These actions represent the *knowledge of physical and virtual attacks*. The effectiveness of the technique is motivated on *one case study*.

Urbina et al. In [36], the authors discuss practical MitM (Man in the Middle) *attacks* on ICS Fieldbus communications. They perform such an attack on a water treatment testbed. The *attacker model* consists in a description of his main characteristics which are divided into two different *dimensions*: objective and resources.

3.2   Attacker Profiles

A number of authors defined, formally or semi-formally, attacker profiles. In the following, we provide a summary of that related work.

Cardenas et al. In [5], the authors informally discuss some challenges for securing CPS. They start by identifying the lack of terminology and attacker models for CPS. Authors informally define *four attacker profiles* (*adversary models* in the paper) with respect to *two dimensions*. The authors highlight the importance of defining which are the specific *attacks* targeting CPS. No formal attack model or case studies are provided.

Cardenas et al. In [7], the authors address the problem of sensor network security focusing on SCADA systems. They propose a taxonomy for security of sensor networks discussing security *properties*, the *attacker model* (*threat model* in [7]). They distinguish between *insider and outsider attacks* and several dimensions and sub-dimensions to rank the attacker (attacker profiles). *Skills*, *costs* and *distance* are discussed in the paper. Authors do not define specific *actions* of the attacker since they focus on the system model but they discuss a number of *attacks*.

The physical distance between the attacker and the target (for wireless networks) is discussed in [8,27,32]. In particular, in [8], the authors define an insider attacker and locality dimension to describe attackers for securing wireless authentication.

Corman et al. In a talk at the RSA conference [9] in 2012, the authors presented an high-level definition of several *attacker profiles* which they call adversaries.

The authors defined several *dimensions*. Authors do not define a set of possible attacks but provide some examples. Finally, we highlight that the work is not published and no or a few details about profiles and the model in general are provided.

Heckman. In [15] a comprehensive informal proposal of several attacker profiles is presented in an industrial white paper. The author shows several *dimensions* to categorize different *attacker profiles*. Even if the categorization describes several different attacker profiles, there is no formal definition of attacker model and there is no clear distinction between terrorists and hacktivists, and between basic users and cybercriminals. Furthermore, the categorization does not consider any physical aspect of the attacker focusing on cyber actions only. The author uses the dimensions to *rate the threat risk* of each attacker profiles over one ad-hoc case study.

A similar categorization for cyber attacker is defined in [28]. The authors performed an extensive description of concrete metrics to categorize an attacker. The work focuses on a subset of profiles without going too much into the details of the dimensions distinguishing these profiles.

3.3   Formal Models for Attackers

We now provide an overview of related work on formal models for CPS attackers.

Adepu et al. In [1], the authors defines how to model a CPS along with an attacker. The study focuses on a *specific* CPS (a water treatment system) and the *dimensions* that are used to define the attacker can be summarized as: components of the CPS (the target), the property an attacker wants to violate and performance (impact of the attack). *Actions* are defined as steps of the attack model.

Basin et al. In [4], the authors present a formal model for modeling and reasoning on security protocols that are using physical-layer properties such as the *distance* between communication partners. The authors define several dimensions (*time*, agent locations, and physical properties of the communication network) to describe physical properties of CPS (such as the physical distance between communication partners). They then define the intruder as set of nodes of the formalized CPS. Authors apply their model to *four case studies*.

Le May et al. In [13,18], the authors formally define a framework for the identification of attacks in CPS. The authors define a set of abstract components to describe an attack execution graphs (AEG) and an *attacker model*. The AEG represents potential attack steps against the system, together with a formal definition of the attacker using a set of six *dimensions*. This formalization has been implemented in a framework called ADVISE where users can define their own attacker models, e.g., defining the *knowledge* of the attacker with respect to the AEG. Some *attacker profiles* are defined with respect to cost, payoff and detection.

McEvoy et al. In [22], the authors present a variant of π-calculus to prove security properties in the context of intrusion detection for SCADA systems.

Authors define how to *model a SCADA network* along with an *attacker model* (called agent-based adversary capability model in the paper). In contrast with the DY model, the intruder is not the source and sink of all communications but he can communicate by request. The dimensions considered are: *distance*, topology of the network related to attacker actions and *skills*, the attacker can subvert any process.

Mo et al. A survey on CPS security, but specific for power grid, is presented in [24]. The authors formally describe how to *model a power grid* and provide a description of possible *attackers' actions* and goals. There is no mention to attacker profiles but several general actions to describe the attacker are provided. Finally, we notice that the terms adversary, attack and attacker model are used as synonyms in the paper.

Orojloo et al. In [25], authors define an approach for *modeling* and evaluating the security of CPS. They propose a model, based on semi-Markov chain, which aims at predicting possible attacker's decisions with respect to the search of both cyber and physical attacks. The authors define five different *dimensions*. Finally, they show how their technique can concretely be used against a simple ad hoc case study.

Teixeira et al. In [34], authors define an approach for the modeling of attacks and scenarios in network controlled system. They describe how to define an *attacker model* using three main *dimensions* (along with several sub-dimensions): knowledge, disclosure resources and disruption resources available to the attacker. The authors take into account the *stealthiness* of an attacker. The attacker model is *general* but constrained to networked controlled systems and is tested on *one test case*.

Vigo. In [37], the author presents a formal definition of an *attacker model* for CPS. The attacker model is presented along with a *system model*. The attacker is define as a set of pairs representing locations in the network topology and capabilities. *Capabilities* are defined as a set of tuples expressing actions, cost (energy/time) and range (with respect to the topology) of the attacker. The attacker is believed to perform two types of attacks: *physical*, against a device and *cyber* against the communications

4 Discussion of Attackers in Related Work

We now summarize our findings, and show the results of applying our taxonomy to the related work in Table 1. Then, we discuss each aspect of the taxonomy in detail.

Profiles, Dimensions, and Actions. Seven works explicitly use different attacker profiles, seventeen define dimensions and the vast majority use actions to characterize the attacker. Just two works define a system model and perform risk analysis without explicitly considering an attacker model. This shows the trend of defining an attacker model to perform security analysis on CPS and, at the same time, that there exist various way to model the attacker.

Table 1. Summary of taxonomy of related work on attacker models and profiles for CPS

Publication	#Profiles	#Dimensions	#Actions	System Modeling	Validation	Generic/Specific	#Test Cases	Time	Terminology used	Our terminology	Research Goal
Amin et al. [2]	1	2	1	○	○	S	1	●	AtkM	AtkM	Threat Assessment
Esfahani et al. [12]	0	0	0	●	●	S	1	●	SM	SM	Risk Analysis
Krotofil et al. [17]	0	1	1	○	○	S	1	●	AdM	AtM	Security Analysis
Lin et al. [19]	0	1	1	●	●	S	1	●	TM	AtM	Attack Simulation
Liu et al. [20]	0	3	1	●	●	S	2	●	SM	SM	Attack Simulation
Taormina et al. [33]	0	2	1	●	●	S	1	●	AtM	AtM	Attack Simulation
Urbina et al. [36]	1	4	1	○	○	S	1	●	AtM	AtkM	Testing
Adepu et al. [1]	0	1	1	●	○	S	1	○	AtM	AtM	Security Analysis
Cardenas et al. [5]	4	2	1	○	○	G	0	●	AdM	AtP	Overview
Cardenas et al. [7]	2	4	1	○	○	G	0	●	TM	AtM	Risk Analysis
Corman et al. [9]	4	4	0	○	○	G	0	○	Ad	AtP	Risk Analysis
Heckman [15]	9	5	0	○	○	G	1	○	TM	AtP	Risk Analysis
Basin et al. [4]	0	2	2	●	○	G	4	●	IM	AtM	Security Analysis
Le May et al. [18]	4	8	0	●	●	G	2	●	AdP	AtM	Risk Analysis
McEvoy et al. [22]	0	2	3	●	●	G	1	○	Ad	AtM	Intrusion Detection
Mo et al. [24]	0	0	8	●	○	G	0	●	AtM	AtM	Survey
Orojloo et al. [25]	0	5	0	●	○	G	1	●	SM	SM	Quantitative Evaluation
Teixeira et al. [34]	0	4	0	●	○	G	1	●	AdM	AtM	Security Analysis
Vigo [37]	0	2	5	●	○	G	0	○	AtM	AtM	Definition

●= argument discussed, ○= not discussed, At=Attacker, I=Intruder, Ad=Adversary, T=Threat, S=System, Atk=Attack, M=Model, P=Profile

One common aspect of the related work is that the attacker actions should consider all the actions of the usual cyber attacks, e.g., read the network communication (sniffing) and modifying all or some of the messages (spoofing) with the ability of injecting new values. The authors commonly assume that the attacker should not be identified with the network itself but, instead, be located somewhere in the network. In other words, following the rules defined by the topology of the network. This gives to the attacker the possibility to divert a node and then to decrypt (encrypt) the network traffic if the node contains the proper key.

System Modeling, Validation, and Test Cases. Roughly half of the reviewed papers define how to create a model of a CPS, but only a few (six) validate their model against an attacker model. Considering validation, simulation, and implementation, we note that in general, only three papers show their results on more than one test case.

Time. Most of the works take into account the notion of time as an important feature to perform attacks since a CPS very often has different (sequential and/or parallel) phases. An attack then has to be carefully timed to go through some of these phases in a particular order or to not be detected by intrusion detection systems.

Terminology. We note that there is no common terminology and attacker, attack and threat model are usually used as synonyms. In Table 1 we propose a mapping from the various terminologies used in the papers to the one we proposed in Sect. 2.2.

Summary. From our review, we notice that the actions for the attacker model for CPS have been defined in a common way, i.e., all the papers share the same actions or the same intuitions on this aspect. However, they apply those actions to different definitions of the concept of attacker models. We can group the reviewed papers into two different categories, (i) the ones which use different attacker profiles with different properties (e.g., to distinguish between insider and a nation-state attackers) and (ii) the ones which define a set of dimensions, e.g., knowledge, to define one specific attacker model. Both groups aim at identifying a set of useful characteristics of the attacker but the former, as showed in Table 1 is more focused on risk analysis and tries to handle several different attacker instantiations while the latter is more system-specific and focuses on one generic description of the attacker model.

One might ask which is the best way to define an attacker model or if there exist a way to define *one* general attacker model in the context of CPS (e.g., as the DY model for security protocols); or if CPS are so heterogeneous that we should define a variety of different profiles for the attacker. In the remainder of this section, we provide insights to answer to these questions by discussing different attacker profiles and dimensions found in the related work. We believe that a common understanding of what are thought to be the key aspects of the attacker model (in the context of CPS) can be useful for the identification of a common definition. In Sect. 5 we propose a first steps in this direction by providing an attacker framework and a more formal definition of attacker model and profile.

4.1 Profiles

The following classification is a collection of all the attacker profiles we have found in the literature. The boundary between the different attacker profiles are not well defined, and sometimes it is hard to classify a specific real-life attacker as one specific profile.

Basic user [9,15], also known as *script kiddie, unstructured hacker, hobbyist* or even *crackers*. Someone who uses already established and potentially automated techniques to attack a system. This attacker has average access to hardware, software, and Internet connectivity, similar to what an individual can obtain through purchase with personal funds or by theft from an employer.

Insider [5,7,15,18], which for example can be *disgruntled employees* or a *social engineering victims*. The employment position or the system privileges he owns (e.g., user, supervisor, administrator) are tightly related to the damage he can cause to the target. This type of attacker is of high importance for systems that are mainly protected through air-gaps between the system network and the outside world (often used in CPS).

Hacktivist [5,9,15]. A portmanteau word which combines hacker and activist, as defined in [10]. This class of attackers uses their hacking abilities to promote a political agenda. Often related to freedom of information (e.g., Anonymous).

Terrorist [5,15,18], also known as *cyber-terrorist*. Is a politically motivated attacker who uses computers and information technology in general to cause severe disruption or widespread fear [10,21].

Cybercriminal [5,7,9,15,18], sometimes generally called *black hat hacker* or *structured hacker*. An attacker with an extensive security knowledge and skills. This category of attackers takes advantage of known vulnerabilities, and potentially has the knowledge and intention of finding new zero-day vulnerabilities. The cyber-criminals' goals can range from blackmailing to espionage (industrial, foreign) or sabotage.

Nation-State [9,15,18], an attacker sponsored by a nation/state. Possibly belonging to (or that used to belong to) a state organization for carrying out offensive cyber operations [26]. His targets usually are public infrastructure systems, mass transit, power or water systems, and general intelligence.

4.2 Dimensions

By assigning quantitative or qualitative scores on the dimensions, a large set of potential attacker configurations could be described. We now define a set of dimensions extracted from the related work. The application of those definitions to the related work is summarized in Table 2. Note that we have standardized the names used for dimensions. Therefor, the names of the dimensions in Table 2 might be different from the one used in the related work. For readability and lack of space we do not go into the details of the mapping which is defined in the APE.

Table 2. Dimensions proposed in the related work

	Aim-Physical	Aim-Virtual	Resources	Offensive	Distance	System	Manpower	Tools	Credentials	Camouflage	Motivation	Target Asset	Aim	Honesty	Determination	Likelihood	Knowledge	Attack Step	Financial Support	Psychology	Reward	Easy Of Access	Physical	Network	Disclosure Resources	Disruption Resources	Aim-Virtual (Availability)	Protocols
Adepu et al. [1]	●	●																										
Amin et al. [2]			●	●	●																							
Basin et al. [4]				●	●																							
Cardenas et al. [5]				●			●																					
Cardenas et al. [7]				●				●	●	●																		
Corman et al. [9]								●				●	●	●														
Esfahani et al. [12]																												
Heckman [15]			●	●											●	●	●											
Krotofil et al. [17]	●	●																										
Le May et al. [18]	●	●	●	●						●	●								●	●	●	●						
Lin et al. [19]							●																					
Liu et al. [20]							●			●																		
McEvoy et al. [22]			●	●																								
Mo et al. [24]																												
Orojloo et al. [25]				●	●																●		●	●				
Taormina et al. [33]																									●	●		
Teixeira et al. [34]				●						●																●	●	
Urbina et al. [36]				●			●																				●	●
Vigo [37]				●	●																							

- *Financial support*, expresses the budget that an attacker has to perform his attacks.
- *Manpower available*, is used to differentiate between lone attackers and (small to large) groups. This dimension expresses quantitatively the human resources available to perform the attack.
- *Tools (Resources) available*, also known as attacklets, or actions in abstract definition of attacker model, defines which types of tools are available to the attacker. This dimension can be used to better understand which are the countermeasures needed to protect a CPS.
- *Camouflage* or preference to stay hidden, expresses the aim and/or the ability of the attacker to not be tracked down after or while performing an attack.
- *Distance* to the CPS. An attacker can be located in another country, within WiFi range or possibly have direct access to the system.
- *Knowledge*, defines the knowledge of the attacker. It may refer to the knowledge of the *System*, the technical knowledge (distinguish between *Physical*, *Network* and *Protocols*) and attack knowledge (*Offensive*) which can be considered as sub-dimensions. In addition, some of the authors consider the *Credentials* dimension as related to the knowledge of the system.

Note here that the knowledge of the attacker is intuitively always considered. However, sometimes the knowledge (of the system or attacks) is hard-coded into the system model and not explicitly considered as part of the attacker model.

- *Attack*, defines which type of attack an attacker can perform, e.g., white, gray or black box attack. This dimension can be used to determine whether obfuscation should be take into consideration as a protection against a particular attacker profile.
- *Target* (e.g., CPS, valves, pumps, access points, information) identifies which physical and logical parts of the system under attack are targeted by an attacker profile.
- *Motivations* and *Aim*, which can be considered as a sub-dimension of target, refer to the objective of the attacker. In some work, the authors details the aim distinguishing between *Physical* or *Virtual* components of the system.

5   Profiles and a Generic Attacker Framework

In this section, we propose the draft of a formalized *attacker framework* that is designed to encompass commonly used informal attacker models in other works. The framework allows to define *attacker profiles* characterized by a number of dimensions.

The idea behind our framework is that an *attacker model* can be described by a set of dimensions. These dimensions can be instantiated to define an *attacker profile* which characterize the key aspects of an attacker. We cannot prove that our framework is complete, however, we have considered, expanded and structured all the aspects extrapolated from our review, i.e., the ones in Table 2.

5.1   Attacker Framework, Profile, Model, and System Model

From our literature review in Sect. 3, we found that attacker models are often defined on different layer of abstractions. Before going into the details of our framework, we propose a terminology to differentiate between those different layers, and show how they are related (see Fig. 1).

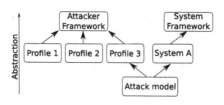

Fig. 1. Proposed hierarchy of attacker framework, profiles, attack models and system models.

An *attacker framework* is defined as a set of different, structured *dimensions* which quantitatively represent a characteristic of an attacker. A *metric* is associated to each dimensions and when the dimensions are instantiated, the framework produces an *attacker profile*. An attacker profiles is then an instantiation of the set of dimensions defined by the attacker framework. For the sake of readability, we provide the details of each dimension and sub-dimension in the Appendix A.

Correspondingly, we define a *system framework* as a paradigm which provides different aspects (dimensions) of a CPS. By instantiating these aspects we produce a *system model*. In practice, system models are often only considering a small subset of the system under consideration due to the involved complexity. Such reduced system models are nevertheless useful to define the scope of the analysis. When we combine attacker profiles and system model (e.g., we run the attacker profiles against a system model) searching for attacks, we obtain an *attack model*.

There is a strong connection between the DY model and the attacker models we have found in our literature review. One intuitive question is how we position the DY model in our definitions. The DY model is defined as a set of actions (e.g., encryption, decryption, concatenation), usually formalized as set of deduction rules. However, a set of constraints over the attacker capabilities is usually defined along with the actions. To give some examples, in the verification of security protocols, the DY is usually identified with the network (i.e., he can read all the messages that are passing through the network) and perfect cryptography is often assumed. In our review, the DY model is always defined along with some constrains. As an example, the attacker's position on the network topology is considered in [4]. These constraints can be defined in one or more profiles of the DY attacker model. Due to lack of space we will not go into the details of the DY profile. A more detailed discussion on an extension of the DY (with physical layer interactions) that takes into account some of the dimensions of our framework can be found in [30]. In the remainder of this section, we standardize the attacker profiles proposed in the related work.

5.2   Mapping Profiles in Related Work to Our Profiles

In order to standardize the attacker profiles we have first mapped the profiles in the related work into our framework as showed in Table 3. Using WEKA [14] (a machine learning tool) we have applied several machine learning algorithm for clustering the profiles (results reported at [29]). However, the results show that there is no general agreement between different authors on the definition of the same or similar profiles (with an incorrectly clustered instances parameter above 47 %). The only exceptions are the insider profiles which are correctly clustered together. We have then defined six archetypal profiles, based on the descriptions in the related work, and showed that they are generalization of the ones proposed in the related work.

We now define a *profile distance metric* to measure the distance between two attacker profiles, and analyzed how well the profiles of related work cluster, and fit to our generic profiles as defined in Sect. 5.3.

Table 3. Categorization of attacker profiles found in the related work

Dimensions	Cardenas [5] Cybercriminal	Cardenas [5] Insider	Cardenas [5] NationState	Cardenas [5] Terrorist	Corman [9] AdaptivePersistent	Corman [9] Hacktivist	Corman [9] OrganizedCrime	Corman [9] Skiddie	Heckman [15] Hacktivist	Heckman [15] Hobbyist	Heckman [15] Insider	Heckman [15] NationState	Heckman [15] OrganizedCrime	Heckman [15] ScriptKiddie	Heckman [15] StructuredHacker	Heckman [15] Terrorist	Heckman [15] UnstructuredHacker	Le May [18] DisgruntledEmployee	Le May [18] LoneHacker	Le May [18] NationState	Le May [18] SystemAdministrator	Le May [18] Terrorist	Urbina [36] Insider
Knowledge	●								◑	◑	◑	●	●	○	●	●	◑	◑	◑	◑	●	○	●
Offensive									◑	◑	○	●	●	○	●	●	◑		◑	●		○	●
Physical																							
Network																							●
Software																							●
System	●																	◑	○	○	●	○	●
Source code																							
Protocols																							●
Credentials	●																	◑	○	○	●	○	◑
Resources	◑		●	●	◑	◑	○		●	○	◑	●	●	○	◑	●	◑	◑	○	◑	◑	○	◑
Distance	●																	●	○	○	●	○	●
Manpower					●														○				
Effort																							
Tools					●	◑	◑	○															○
Financial support	○								●						●				○		●	○	
Psychology	◑	◑	◑	●	◑	●	●	◑	●	○	●	●	●	●	◑	●	◑	◑	●	●	◑	◑	◑
Honesty	●	●	●	●	●	●	●	●	●	○	●	●	●	●	●	●	●	●	●	●	●	●	●
Periodicity																							
Camouflage																		○	◑	●	○	○	
Aim-Physical					●																		◑
Integrity																							●
Confidentiality																							○
Availability					●																		●
Determination									●	○	◑	●	◑	○	◑	●	◑	●	●	●	●	●	
Strategy	◑																	●	○	●	●	●	●
Aim-Virtual	●		○	●	◑	●	●	◑															◑
Integrity																							●
Confidentiality					●	●	●	◑															○
Availability	●				●	○	●	○															○

A metric on each dimensions is expressed on the (strict) partially ordered set [○<◑<●]

5.3   Attacker Profile Archetypes

In Table 4, we give a more rigorous definition of the six common attacker profiles (we described in Sect. 4.1) using our framework.

As it can be seen in Table 4, the honesty dimension is the same on all the archetype. This is because all but one work [15] only consider dishonest attacker profiles. Our terrorist profile is classified with low knowledge of offensive skills. Changing this metric to an higher metric leads to a mismatch between the terrorist profiles in the literature and the archetype.

Table 4. Categorization of proposed attacker profile archetypes

	Knowledge	Offensive	Physical	Network	Software	System	Source code	Protocols	Credentials	Resources	Distance	Manpower	Effort	Tools	Financial support	Psychology	Honesty	Periodicity	Camouflage	Strategy	Determination	Aim-Physical	Integrity	Confidentiality	Availability	Aim-Virtual	Integrity	Confidentiality	Availability
B	○	○	○	○	○	○	○	○	○	○	○	○	○	○	○	○	●	○	○	○	○	○	○	○	○	○	○	○	○
C	◐	◐	○	●	◐	○	○	○	○	○	◐	○	○	●	◐	●	◐	●	◐	●	◐	●	○	○	○	○	●	◐	●	●
H	◐	◐	○	●	●	◐	○	○	○	◐	○	●	◐	●	○	●	◐	●	○	◐	◐	●	○	○	○	○	◐	○	●	●
I	◐	○	○	○	◐	●	●	●	●	●	○	◐	●	○	○	◐	◐	○	◐	●	○	◐	●	◐	◐	◐	◐	◐	◐	◐
N	◐	●	●	●	●	●	○	○	○	○	●	○	●	●	●	●	◐	●	○	●	●	●	●	●	●	●	○	○	◐	○
T	○	○	○	○	○	○	○	○	○	◐	○	○	◐	●	◐	◐	◐	●	○	○	○	●	◐	○	○	●	◐	◐	◐	◐

B=BasicUser,   C=Cybercriminal,   H=Hacktivist,   I=Insider,   N=NationState, T=Terrorist. A metric on each dimensions is expressed on the (strict) partially ordered set [○<◐<●]

1. *Basic User.* Represents the lower bound of our profiles with all the dimensions set to the lowest value. Usually, attacks from this type of profile are believed to be very frequent. However, in the case of CPS might not be the case.
2. *Cybercriminal.* Advanced knowledge of network attacks but low of physical layer attacks. Advanced tools and average financial support.
3. *Hacktivist.* Similar to the cybercriminal but with a lower financial support but higher manpower support.
4. *Insider.* It is the only profile which has an advance knowledge of the system because it has physical access to it. He has a structured strategy to perform his attacks. His aim are physical properties of the system (e.g., damage the system to attack its availability). He acts alone, with low budgets but with dedicated tools.
5. *Nation-State.* On average the most powerful profile between the archetypes. High offensive skills and tools, high resources and determination. The stealthiness of the attacks is very important.
6. *Terrorist.* Low offensive skills and average resources. The attacks mainly targets the physical availability of the system and their stealthiness is not important.

5.4   Validation of Proposed Profiles and Discussion

Motivated by the results obtained by the machine learning clustering phase, we investigated if our archetypes generalize the related work. We used the Euclidean distance on a n-dimensional space to calculate the distance between profiles as $\sqrt{\sum_{i=1}^{n} (q_i - p_i)^2}$, where two profiles p and q are represented as two points in an Euclidean n-dimensional space: $p = (p_1, \ldots, p_n)$ and $q = (q_1, \ldots, q_n)$. Each point is defined by the metric associated to a dimension, mapping the poset $[\bigcirc < \mathbb{O} < \bullet]$ to $[1 < 2 < 3]$ $(1, 2, 3 \in \mathbb{N})$.

In 21 cases out of 23, our profile archetype correctly matches to the expected profile (see Table 5). That implies that (a) attacker models in related work are based on commonly used implicit profiles, and (b) our profiles are closely approximating the underlying intuition behind the commonly used profiles. That result now allows to relate attacker profiles from related work with each other, and could be used to complement those profiles with additional missing information based on our archetypes.

There are two cases in which the expected mapping is not found. In [15] the authors do not distinguish between a terrorist and a Nation-State profiles. In fact, the nearest profile to Heckman [15] Terrorist is Nation-State. Furthermore, the difference between an Hacktivist and Nation-State and Terrorist is not well defined. As [15] is an industrial white paper, it could be that the author's views are somewhat diverging from the academic security community. In addition, we note that there are six cases in which a profile has the same distance to multiple archetypes. In that case, the archetypes cannot be distinguished only by the subset of dimensions considered by the profile analyzed. That could indicate that (a) the profiles in the related work are vaguely defined, or (b) our dimensions do not yet appropriately capture all aspects intended by the original authors.

5.5   APE (Attacker Profile Analyzer)

To support our work we developed APE, an interactive command-line tool, using Python. The tool is available as open source at [29]. APE allows the application of our taxonomy to classify related work, definition of own attacker profiles using our framework, and comparisons between profiles. Profiles can be exported to several different formats (e.g. WEKA .arff), and the profiles we defined in this paper are part of the tool.

We envision that other researchers can use our framework and APE to define constraints during the security analysis, verification, or testing of CPS. Most of the related work (e.g., in [4,18,37]) base their analysis on some constraints (the same applies for security protocols when the DY is assumed to control the network). One relevant example is the physical distance between the attacker and the CPS which has a severe impact on the physical layer interactions of the attacker. This and other dimensions have been used in a number of works (e.g., [1,4,15,18]) to show different security flaws or attacks based on different profiles. Our framework supports the modeler or the security analyst in the generation of such constraints. In addition to theoretical analysis, our tool can

Table 5. Distance of attacker profiles from related work to our proposed six profiles. Columns represent the first, second, ..., sixth best fit and the respective distance metric value.

Profile	#1	#2	#3	#4	#5	#6
Cardenas [5] Cybercriminal	C (1.0)	H (1.0)	I (1.73)	T (1.73)	N (3.0)	B (3.16)
Cardenas [5] Insider	I (1.0)	H (3.60)	C (3.74)	T (4.12)	B (4.24)	N (4.24)
Cardenas [5] NationState	N (0.0)	I (1.0)	H (1.0)	T (1.0)	B (1.0)	C (2.0)
Cardenas [5] Terrorist	T (2.44)	N (3.0)	I (3.16)	H (3.46)	C (3.74)	B (5.29)
Corman [9] AdaptivePersistent	N (1.41)	I (2.0)	T (2.0)	H (2.44)	C (2.44)	B (3.74)
Corman [9] Hacktivist	H (1.41)	C (1.41)	I (2.0)	T (2.0)	N (3.46)	B (4.24)
Corman [9] OrganizedCrime	T (2.0)	I (2.0)	C (2.44)	H (2.44)	N (2.82)	B (3.74)
Corman [9] Skiddie	B (1.73)	T (1.73)	I (1.73)	H (2.64)	N (3.0)	C (3.31)
Heckman [15] Hacktivist	N (1.41)	C (2.0)	T (2.23)	H (2.44)	I (2.82)	B (4.24)
Heckman [15] Hobbyist	B (1.73)	C (2.0)	I (2.23)	H (2.64)	T (3.0)	N (3.31)
Heckman [15] Insider	I (1.0)	C (1.41)	H (1.73)	T (1.73)	B (2.64)	N (2.64)
Heckman [15] NationState	N (1.41)	H (2.0)	C (2.23)	I (2.82)	T (3.16)	B (4.47)
Heckman [15] OrganizedCrime	N (1.73)	C (2.0)	H (2.23)	I (2.64)	T (3.31)	B (4.12)
Heckman [15] ScriptKiddie	B (2.0)	I (2.0)	C (2.23)	T (2.44)	H (2.82)	N (3.74)
Heckman [15] StructuredHacker	C (1.41)	N (1.73)	H (2.0)	I (2.23)	T (3.60)	B (3.87)
Heckman [15] Terrorist	N (1.41)	C (2.44)	H (2.82)	T (3.31)	I (3.46)	B (4.89)
Heckman [15] UnstructuredHacker	H (1.41)	T (1.73)	C (2.0)	I (2.23)	B (2.23)	N (2.64)
Le May [18] Disgruntled Employee	I (2.0)	H (2.82)	C (3.0)	T (3.46)	N (3.87)	B (4.12)
Le May [18] LoneHacker	C (1.73)	H (2.0)	T (3.16)	N (3.31)	B (3.87)	I (4.0)
Le May [18] NationState	N (1.41)	C (2.23)	H (2.82)	T (3.87)	I (4.79)	B (5.09)
Le May [18] System Administrator	I (1.73)	H (3.87)	C (4.0)	T (4.58)	N (4.69)	B (5.09)
Le May [18] Terrorist	T (2.23)	H (2.23)	C (2.23)	B (3.0)	N (3.60)	I (4.0)
Urbina [36] Insider	I (4.58)	N (5.56)	H (6.16)	C (6.24)	T (6.63)	B (7.0)
#Expected	21	0	0	2	0	0

B=BasicUser, C=Cybercriminal, H=Hacktivist, I=Insider, N=NationState, T=Terrorist, (Float)=Euclidean distance, X(x.x)=Expected mapping

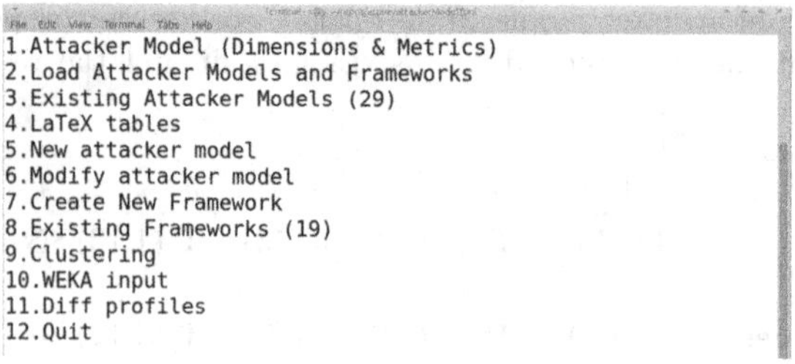

Fig. 2. Features available in Attacker Profile Examiner

be used to output constraints that can be applied when concretely testing a CPS (Fig. 2).

6 Conclusion

In this work, we discussed attacker models for security research, in particular for CPS. We started with a literature review, and defined a taxonomy of 10 different features that we applied to the literature. This lead us to the identification of discrepancies and commonalities between different works. We grouped the reviewed papers into two main classes (discussing profiles and dimensions): publications that aim at profiling attackers, and that propose an attacker model. We argued that these classes and dimensions should be the starting point for a definition of a comprehensive attacker model. We then defined an attacker framework and mapped the 23 attacker profiles from related work into that framework, and defined a distance metric that allows us to compute overlap/discrepancies between attacker models in related work. We used machine learning approaches to cluster the attacker models from related work, but did not obtain good results so far. We then manually constructed 6 attacker profiles, and show that they match the profiles from the literature in 21/23 cases.

We wrote a tool to capture our attacker framework, and profiles proposed by us and the related work. The tool showcases some of the benefits of more structured approaches to attacker models: we use it to compare different profiles, export profiles to tools such as WEKA, and produce structured representations such as the tables in this work.

Acknowledgments. This work was supported by the National Research Foundation of Singapore under grant NRF2014NCR-NCR001-40.

A   Appendix: Subdimensions

We now summarize each top-most dimension: knowledge, resources, and phychology. Each metric is defined between square brackets with the following order: $[1 < 2 < 3]$.

Finally, in Appendix A.4 we clarify the relation between a subset of our dimensions and time.

A.1   Knowledge

The knowledge dimension ([low, medium, high]) represents the understanding of the system under attack and the expertise of the attacker (as in, [11,18,37] to give some examples). The dimension is structured as follows.

– *Offensive* ([basic, intermediate, advanced]), determines the expertise of the attacker with regard to the attacks known, e.g., attack methodologies, attack patterns [23]. It is composed by three sub-dimensions: *Physical* ([basic, intermediate, advanced]), *Network* ([basic, intermediate, advanced]) and *Software* ([basic, intermediate, advanced]) which can be used to define the offensive knowledge with a finer granularity considering different expertise of the attacker.
– *System* ([basic, intermediate, advanced]), expresses the knowledge of the system under attack/analysis, e.g., the set of components of a CPS [37] or entities in a security protocol [11]. It is composed by three sub-dimensions: *Source code* ([blackBox, grayBox,whiteBox]), *Protocols* ([blackBox, grayBox,whiteBox]), and *Credentials* ([user, supervisor, admin]) which can be used to define the knowledge with respect to the these three general aspects of the system (e.g., CPS).

A.2   Resources

The resource dimension ([low, medium, high]) represents the resources available to the attacker [15,28,32]. It can be used to limit the practical capabilities of the attacker. This dimension is widely accepted in our related work. This dimension is structured in the following different sub-dimensions.

– *Distance* ([far, near, physicalAccess]), expresses the physical distance of the attacker with respect to the target and may limit his interactions with the system. This is particularly important with respect to CPS which can be isolated from the Internet or when using WiFi networks, e.g., [32].
– *Manpower* ([low, medium, high]), represents the human resources available to the attacker, e.g., to distinguish between lone attackers and (small to large) groups.
– *Tools* ([basic, intermediate, advanced]), also know as attacklets, defines which types of tools are available to the attacker for performing the attack.
– *Financial support* ([low, medium, high]), expresses which is the budget that an attacker has in order to perform an attack. Discriminating between attacker with low or high budget can be helpful, e.g., for risk assessments.
– *Effort* ([low, medium, high]), defines the effort an attacker will put into his attacks. How deeply the attacker will explore possible/different attacks of the system.

A.3   Psychology

The psychology dimension ([weak, average, strong]) represents a set of aspects which are not directly related to the knowledge or resources of the attacker.

These aspects are related to the motivations or behavioral aspects of the attacker [5, 6, 15, 18]. This dimension is structured in the following different sub-dimensions.

- *Aim* ([knowledge, manipulation, damage]), identifies which parts of the system are more likely to be interesting for the attacker. There are two sub-dimensions which discriminates between virtual and physical components: *Virtual* ([knowledge, manipulation, damage]) and *Physical* ([knowledge, manipulation, damage])
- *Periodicity* ([once, anytime, continuous]), defines which is the frequency with which an attacker will try to attack the system. Some system are more incline to be attacked than other, for example, if a CPS is exposed on the Internet the periodicity of attacks will be higher with respect to a CPS isolated from the Internet.
- *Determination* ([firstAttempt, severalAttempts, untiring]), Defines how long the attacker will perform the attacks on the system. As an example, the effort of the attacker should grow after each assessment performed on a system.
- *Honesty* ([malicious, benign]), discriminates between benign (White Hat attackers or "honest but curious" [15]) and malicious attackers (Black Hat).
- *Camouflage* ([visible, stealthy, invisible]), is the ability or preference of an attacker to stay hidden.
- *Strategy* ([random, brute-force, structured]), refers to the attack strategy adopted by the attacker. Random if an attacker will randomly select some attacks or some attack patterns. Brute-force when the attacker tries all possible attack pattern and structured when an optimal subset of attack patter is chosen.
- *Aim-Physical* and *Aim-Virtual* ([low, medium, high]), represent the objective of the attacker with respect to physical and virtual components. They are both divided into the three sub-dimensions: *Integrity*, *Confidentiality*, *Availability*.

A.4   Time

As depicted in Fig. 3, different aspects related to time have been captured as a combination of the three dimensions: effort, periodicity and determination.

The effort represents how deeply the attacker will try to attack the system during each attack. The determination is the duration of each attack and the periodicity expresses the distribution of attacks over time.

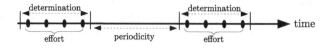

Fig. 3. Time related metrics

References

1. Adepu, S., Mathur, A.: An investigation into the response of a water treatment system into cyber attacks. In: IEEE Symposium on High Assurance Systems Engineering (HASE) (2015)
2. Amin, S., Litrico, X., Sastry, S., Bayen, A.: Cyber security of water SCADA systems; Part I: analysis and experimentation of stealthy deception attacks. IEEE Trans. Control Syst. Technol. **21**(5), 1963–1970 (2013)
3. Amin, S., Litrico, X., Sastry, S., Bayen, A.: Cyber security of water SCADA systems; Part II: attack detection using enhanced hydrodynamic models. IEEE Trans. Control Syst. Technol. **21**(5), 1679–1693 (2013)
4. Basin, D., Capkun, S., Schaller, P., Schmidt, B.: Formal reasoning about physical properties of security protocols. Trans. Inf. Syst. Secur. (TISSEC) **14**(2), 16 (2011)
5. Cárdenas, A.A., Amin, S.M., Sinopoli, B., Giani, A., Perrig, A., Sastry, S.S.: Challenges for securing cyber physical systems. In: Workshop on Future Directions in Cyber-physical Systems Security, DHS, July 2009
6. Cárdenas, A.A., Baras, J.S., Evaluation of classifiers: practical considerations for security applications. In: AAAI Workshop on Evaluation Methods for Machine Learning (2006)
7. Cárdenas, A.A., Roosta, T., Sastry, S.: Rethinking security properties, threat models, and the design space in sensor networks: a case study in SCADA systems. Ad Hoc Netw. **7**(8), 1434–1447 (2009)
8. Chang, S.-Y., Hu, Y.-C., Liubook, Z.: Securing wireless medium access control against insider denial-of-service attackers. In: Proceedings of Conference on Communications and Network Security (CNS) (2015)
9. Corman, J., Etue, D.: Adversary ROI.: Evaluating security from the threat actor's perspective (2012)
10. Denning, D.E.: Activism, hacktivism, and cyberterrorism: the internet as a tool for influencing foreign policy. In: Ronfeldt, D. (ed.) Networks and Netwars: The Future of Terror, Crime, and Militancy. RAND Corporation, Santa Monica (2001)
11. Dolev, D., Yao, A.C.: On the security of public key protocols. IEEE Trans. Inf. Theor. **29**(2), 198–207 (1983)
12. Esfahani, P., Vrakopoulou, M., Margellos, K., Lygeros, J., Andersson, G., Cyber attack in a two-area power system: impact identification using reachability. In: American Control Conference (ACC), pp. 962–967, June 2010
13. Ford, M.D., Keefe, K., LeMay, E., Sanders, W.H., Muehrcke, C.: Implementing the ADVISE security modeling formalism in möbius. In: IEEE/IFIP Conference on Dependable Systems and Networks (DSN) (2013)
14. Hall, M.A., Frank, E., Holmes, G., Pfahringer, B., Reutemann, P., Witten, I.H.: The WEKA data mining software: an update. SIGKDD Explor. **11**(1), 10–18 (2009)
15. Heckman, R.: Attacker classification to aid targeting critical systems for threat modelling and security review (2005). www.rockyh.net/papers/AttackerClassification.pdf. Accessed 23 Oct 2015
16. Knapp, E.D., Samani, R.: Applied Cyber Security and the Smart Grid. Elsevier Syngress, Boston (2013)
17. Krotofil, M., Cárdenas, A.A., Manning, B., Larsen, J., CPS: driving cyber-physical systems to unsafe operating conditions by timing dos attacks on sensor signals. In: Proceedings of the Computer Security Applications Conference (ACSAC), pp. 146–155. ACM (2014)

18. LeMay, E., Ford, M.D., Keefe, K., Sanders, W.H., Muehrcke, C.: Model-based security metrics using adversary view security evaluation (ADVISE). In: Proceedings of Conference on Quantitative Evaluation of Systems, QEST (2011)
19. Lin, J., Yu, W., Yang, X., Xu, G., Zhao, W.: On false data injection attacks against distributed energy routing in smart grid. In: Proceedings of the Conference on Cyber-Physical Systems (ICCPS) (2012)
20. Liu, Y., Ning, P., Reiter, M.K.: False data injection attacks against state estimation in electric power grids. ACM Trans. Inf. Syst. Secur. (TISSEC) 14, 13 (2011)
21. Matusitz, J.: Cyberterrorism: postmodern state of chaos. Inf. Secur. J. Glob. Perspect. 17(4), 179–187 (2008)
22. McEvoy, T.R., Wolthusen, S.D.: A formal adversary capability model for SCADA environments. In: Xenakis, C., Wolthusen, S. (eds.) CRITIS 2010. LNCS, vol. 6712, pp. 93–103. Springer, Heidelberg (2011)
23. MITRE. Common attack pattern enumeration and classification (capec)
24. Mo, Y., Kim, T.-H., Brancik, K., Dickinson, D., Lee, H., Perrig, A., Sinopoli, B.: Cyber-physical security of a smart grid infrastructure. Proc. IEEE 100(1), 195–209 (2012)
25. Orojloo, H., Azgomi, M.A.: A method for modeling and evaluation of the security of cyber-physical systems. In: ISC Conference on Information Security and Cryptology (ISCISC) (2014)
26. Ottis, R.: Theoretical model for creating a nation-state level offensive cyber capability. In: European Conference on Information Warfare and Security (2009)
27. Papadimitratos, P., Poturalski, M., Schaller, P., Lafourcade, P., Basin, D., Capkun, S., Hubaux, J.-P.: Secure neighborhood discovery: a fundamental element for mobile ad hoc networking. IEEE Commun. Mag. 46(2), 132–139 (2008)
28. Parker, T., Shadow, E., Stroz, E., Devost, M.G., Sachs, M.H.: Cyber Adversary Characterization: Auditing the Hacker Mind. Syngress Publishing Inc., Rockland (2004)
29. Rocchetto, M., Tippenhauer, N.O.: APE (Attacker Profile Examiner) (2016). http://research.scy-phy.net/ape/
30. Rocchetto, M., Tippenhauer, N.O., CPDY: extending the Dolev-Yao attacker with physical-layer interactions. In: Proceedings of the International Conference on Formal Engineering Methods (ICFEM) (2016). Preprint available on arXiv
31. SPaCIoS. Deliverable 3.3.2: Methodology and technology for vulnerability-driven security testing (final version) (2014). http://www.spacios.eu
32. Steinmetzer, D., Schulz, M., Hollick, M., Lockpicking physical layer key exchange: weak adversary models invite the thief. In: Proceedings of the ACM Conference Wireless Security (WiSeC) (2015)
33. Taormina, R., Galelli, S., Tippenhauer, N.O., Salomons, E., Ostfeld, A.: Simulation of cyber-physical attacks on water distribution systems with EPANET. In: Proceedings of Singapore Cyber Security R&D Conference (SG-CRC), January 2016
34. Teixeira, A., Pérez, D., Sandberg, H., Johansson, K.H.: Attack models and scenarios for networked control systems. In: Proceedings of the Conference on High Confidence Networked Systems (HiCoNS), pp. 55–64. ACM (2012)
35. United States Environmental Protection Agency. Epanet: Software that models the hydraulic and water quality behavior of water distribution piping systems. www.epa.gov/nrmrl/wswrd/dw/epanet.html

36. Urbina, D., Giraldo, J., Tippenhauer, N.O., Cardenas, A.: Attacking fieldbus communications in ICS: applications to the SWaT testbed. In: Proceedings of Singapore Cyber Security R&D Conference (SG-CRC), January 2016
37. Vigo, R.: The cyber-physical attacker. In: Ortmeier, F., Daniel, P. (eds.) SAFECOMP Workshops 2012. LNCS, vol. 7613, pp. 347–356. Springer, Heidelberg (2012)

Towards the Automated Verification of Cyber-Physical Security Protocols: Bounding the Number of Timed Intruders

Vivek Nigam[1]([⊠]), Carolyn Talcott[2], and Abraão Aires Urquiza[1]

[1] Federal University of Paraíba, João Pessoa, Brazil
vivek@ci.ufpb.br, abraauc@gmail.com
[2] SRI International, Menlo Park, USA
clt@csl.sri.com

Abstract. Timed Intruder Models have been proposed for the verification of Cyber-Physical Security Protocols (CPSP) amending the traditional Dolev-Yao intruder to obey the physical restrictions of the environment. Since to learn a message, a Timed Intruder needs to wait for a message to arrive, mounting an attack may depend on where Timed Intruders are. It may well be the case that in the presence of a great number of intruders there is no attack, but there is an attack in the presence of a small number of well placed intruders. Therefore, a major challenge for the automated verification of CPSP is to determine how many Timed Intruders to use and where should they be placed. This paper answers this question by showing it is enough to use the same number of Timed Intruders as the number of participants. We also report on some preliminary experimental results in discovering attacks in CPSP.

1 Introduction

The Dolev-Yao intruder model is one of the cornerstones for the success of protocol verification being used in most verification tools. The protocol security literature contains a number of properties about the Dolev-Yao intruder, many of them vital for automated verification. For instance, it has been shown that protocol security verification is complete when considering only a single Dolev-Yao intruder in the following sense: if there is an attack in the presence of one or more (colluding) Dolev-Yao intruders, then the same attack with a single Dolev-Yao intruder is possible [4]. Such result greatly simplifies the implementation of tools as it is enough to use only one Dolev-Yao intruder.

However, for the important class of Cyber-Physical Security Protocols (CPSP), the Dolev-Yao intruder model is not suitable. CSPS normally rely on the physical properties of the environment where sessions are carried out to establish some physical properties. For example, Distance Bounding Protocols are used to infer an upper-bound on the distance between two players V, the verifier, and P, the prover. It works as follows:

$$V \longrightarrow P : m$$
$$P \longrightarrow V : m'$$

© Springer International Publishing Switzerland 2016
I. Askoxylakis et al. (Eds.): ESORICS 2016, Part II, LNCS 9879, pp. 450–470, 2016.
DOI: 10.1007/978-3-319-45741-3_23

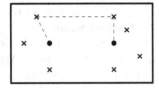 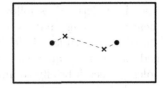

Fig. 1. The dots are protocol participants and the crosses are intruders.

The verifier sends a challenge m remembering the time t_1, when this message is sent. The prover responds to the challenge, m', and by measuring the round-trip time of the challenge response round, the verifier can compute (using assumptions on the transmission channel used) an upper bound on the distance to the prover.

It is easy to check that the Dolev-Yao intruder is not suitable for CPSP verification, as the Dolev-Yao intruder does not obey the physical properties of the system. As the Dolev-Yao intruder controls the network, he can receive the challenge m and instantaneously respond m' to the verifier's challenge. There have been, therefore, proposals to amend the Dolev-Yao intruder model to CSPS [3,16] in the form of Timed Dolev-Yao models. These have been used to prove general decidability of important properties of CSPS [3,15] and prove the security of protocols using theorem provers.

In contrast with the traditional Dolev-Yao intruder, who is the whole network, a timed intruder is placed at some location and in order to learn a message, must wait until the message arrives to that location. A consequence of this is that a greater number of colluding intruders may not do as much damage as a smaller number of intruders that are better placed. For example, consider Fig. 1. With a distribution of intruders shown to the left, there may not be an attack as it might take too long for intercepting and forwarding messages among intruders (illustrated by the dashed lines), while there may be an attack with the distribution of intruders shown to the right.

The main contribution of this paper is to answer the question: *How many intruders are enough for verification and where should they be placed?* We prove that it is enough to consider one intruder per protocol participant, thus bounding the number of timed intruders. This result greatly simplifies automated CSPS verification as the specifier no longer has to guess how many timed intruders to consider and where to place them.

Our second contribution is a general specification language, which extends strand spaces [25] by allowing for the symbolic representation of time. Instead of instantiating time variables and time constraints with explicit values, the semantics of our language accumulates symbolic time constraints. An execution using symbolic time constraints corresponds to a set of possible concrete executions, considerably reducing state-space. We implemented a prototype of our language in Maude [8] with SMT support. Our preliminary experiments show that it is possible to find attacks traversing few states. While we do not claim (yet) to have a complete tool, our first results are promising.

This paper is structured as follows: Sect. 2 specifies the syntax of our protocol specification language and its semantics extending Strand Spaces [25]. We introduce the Timed Intruder Model in Sect. 3. Section 4 contains the definition of the Timed Intruder Completeness problem and a solution to it. We revisit some examples in Sect. 5 briefly commenting on our prototype implementation. Finally we conclude by reviewing related and future work in Sect. 6.

2   A Specification Language for Cyber-Physical Security Protocols

We start first by specifying the syntax of our CPSP specification language with symbolic time variables and symbolic time constraints. We exemplify the specification of protocols using our language. Then, we formalize the operational semantics of our language by extending Strand Spaces [25] to include time variables.

2.1   Syntax

Message Expressions. We assume a message signature Σ of constants, and function symbols. Constants include nonces, symmetric keys and player names. The set of messages is constructed as usual using constants, variables and at least the following function symbols:

$sk(p)$	Denoting the secret key of the player p;
$pk(p)$	Denoting the public key of the player p;
$enc(m, k)$	Encryption function denoting the encryption of m using key k;
$\{m_1, m_2, \ldots, m_n\}$	Tuple function denoting a list of messages $m_1, m_2, \ldots, m_n$;

where $c_1, c_2, \ldots$ range over constants, $n_1, \ldots, n_n$ range over nonces, $k_1, k_2, \ldots$ range over symmetric keys, $p_1, p_2 \ldots$ range over player names, $v_1, v_2, \ldots$ range over variables, and $m_1, m_2, \ldots$ range over messages. For example, the message $enc(\{v_1, enc(c, k)\}, pk(p))$ denotes the encryption using the public key of p of the pair of messages v_1 (not instantiated) and $enc(c, k)$. We define $(pk(p))^{-1} = sk(p)$ and $k^{-1} = k$ if k is a symmetric key. We also write interchangeably the singleton tuple $\{m\}$ and m.

For a given scenario with some protocol session instances, we are going to distinguish the players that are participating in the protocol sessions, *e.g.*, as verifiers and as provers, which we call *protocol participants* (briefly *participants*), from the *Timed Intruders* which are not participating explicitly in the protocol sessions in the given scenario, but are simply manipulating messages and possibly interacting with the participants. The symbols $p_1, p_2 \ldots$ will range over participant names while $ti_1, ti_2, \ldots$ will range over the names of such Timed Intruders.

Time Expressions. We also assume a time signature Ξ which is disjoint to the message alphabet Σ. It contains:

$r_1, r_2, \ldots$	A set of numbers;
$tt_1, tt_2, \ldots,$	A set of time variables including the special variablecur;
$+, -, \times, /, \text{floor}, \text{ceiling}, \ldots$	A set of arithmetic symbols and other function symbols.

Time Expressions are constructed inductively by applying arithmetic symbols to time expressions. For example $\text{ceiling}((2 + tt + cur)/10)$ is a Time Expression. The symbols $tr_1, tr_2, \ldots$ range over Time Expressions. We do not constrain the set of numbers and function symbols in Ξ. However, in practice, we allow only the symbols supported by the SMT solver used. All examples in this paper will contain SMT supported symbols (or equivalent). Finally, the time variable cur will be a keyword in our protocol specification language denoting the current global time.

Definition 1 (Symbolic Time Constraints). *Let Ξ be a time signature. The set of symbolic time constraints is constructed using time expressions. Let tr_1, tr_2 be time expressions, then*

$$tr_1 = tr_2, \qquad tr_1 \geq tr_2 \qquad tr_1 > tr_2, \qquad tr_1 < tr_2, \qquad \text{and} \quad tr_1 \leq tr_2$$

are Symbolic Time Constraints.

For example, $cur + 10 < \text{floor}(tt - 5)$ is a Time Constraint. The symbols $tc_1, tc_2, \ldots$ will range over Time Constraints.

Finally, we let $b_1, b_2, \ldots$, range over boolean expressions, which include timed comparison constraints. We also allow for checking whether two messages m_1 and m_2 can be unified, *e.g.*, $\{v_1, v_2\} :=: \{p_1, k_1\}$ evaluates to true as they can be unified by the substitution $\{v_1 \mapsto p_1, v_2 \mapsto k_1\}$.

Definition 2 (Timed Protocols). *The set of Timed Protocols, $\mathcal{PL}$, is composed of Timed Protocol Roles, pl, which are constructed by using commands as specified by the following grammar, where b is a boolean expression:*

pl	:=	nil	*Empty Protocol*
	|	(new v), pl	*Fresh Constant*
	|	(+m), pl	*Message Output*
	|	(+m # tc), pl	*Timed Message Output*
	|	(−m), pl	*Message Input*
	|	(−m # tc), pl	*Timed Message Input*
	|	(if b then pl_1 else pl_2)	*Conditional*
	|	(if b # tc then pl_1 else pl_2)	*Timed Conditional*

We explain some examples intuitively before we formalize the semantics of our language in the following section. We will elide nil whenever it is clear from the context.

Example 1. The following program specifies the verifier of a (very simple) distance bounding protocol:

$$(\mathsf{new}\ \mathsf{v}), (+\mathsf{v}\ \#\ \mathsf{tt} = \mathsf{cur}), (-\mathsf{v}\ \#\ \mathsf{cur} \le \mathsf{tt} + 4)$$

It creates a fresh constant and sends it to the prover, remembering the current global time by assigning it to the time variable tt. Finally, when it receives the response v it checks whether the current time is less than $\mathsf{tt} + 4$.

Example 2. Timed conditionals can be used to specify the duration of operations, such as checking whether some message is of a given form. In practice, the duration of these operations can be measured empirically to obtain a finer analysis of the protocol [6].

For example, consider the following protocol role:

$$
\begin{aligned}
&(\mathsf{new}\ \mathsf{v}), (+\mathsf{v}), (-\{\mathsf{v}_{enc}, \mathsf{v}_{mac}\}\ \#\ \mathsf{tt}_0 = \mathsf{cur}), \\
&\mathsf{if}\ (\mathsf{v}_{mac} :=: \mathsf{enc}(\mathsf{v}_{enc}, \mathsf{k}_M))\ \#\ \mathsf{tt}_1 = \mathsf{tt}_0 + \mathsf{tt}_{Mac} \\
&\mathsf{then}\ (\mathsf{if}\ (\mathsf{v}_{enc} :=: \mathsf{enc}(\mathsf{v}, \mathsf{k}_E))\ \#\ \mathsf{tt}_2 = \mathsf{tt}_1 + \mathsf{tt}_{Enc}) \\
&\qquad \mathsf{then}\ (+done\ \#\ \mathsf{cur} = \mathsf{tt}_2)\ \mathsf{else}\ (+error\ \#\ \mathsf{cur} = \mathsf{tt}_2)) \\
&\mathsf{else}\ (+error\ \#\ \mathsf{cur} = \mathsf{tt}_1)
\end{aligned}
$$

This role creates a fresh value v and sends it. Then it is expecting a pair of two messages v_{mac} and v_{enc}, remembering at time variable tt_0 when this message is received. It then checks whether the first component v_{mac} is of the form $\mathsf{enc}(\mathsf{v}_{enc}, \mathsf{k}_M))$, *i.e.*, it is the correct MAC. This operation takes tt_{mac} time units. The time variable tt_1 is equal to the time $\mathsf{tt}_0 + \mathsf{tt}_{mac}$, *i.e.*, the time when the message was received plus the MAC check duration. If the MAC is not correct, an *error* message is sent exactly at time tt_1. Otherwise, if the first component, v_{MAC}, is as expected, the role checks whether the second component, v_{enc}, is an encryption of the form $\mathsf{enc}(\mathsf{v}, \mathsf{k}_E))$, which takes (a longer) time tt_{enc}. If so it sends the *done* message, otherwise the *error* message, both at time tt_2 which is $\mathsf{tt}_1 + \mathsf{tt}_{enc}$.

We will need to identify a particular command in a Timed Protocol Role. We use a string of the form $i_1.i_2.i_3.\ldots.i_n$, called position and denoted by $\bar{i}$, where each $i_j \in \{1, 2\}$ to specify a path in the control flow of the Timed Protocol. For example, 1.1.1.1.2 in Example 2 leads to $(+error\ \#\ \mathsf{cur} = \mathsf{tt}_1)$. We denote by $\mathcal{PS}(\mathsf{pl})$ the set of strings representing the paths in the Timed Protocol Role pl.

2.2   Timed Strand Spaces and Bundles

We formalize the semantics of Timed Protocols by extending Strand Spaces and Bundles [25] to include time constraints and a network topology.

Network Topology. Messages take time to travel between agents, both honest players and intruders. The network model is specified by representing the time a message needs to travel from any agent a to any agent b, specified by $\mathsf{td}(a, b)$ using a function that takes two names and returns a number. Typically, $\mathsf{td}(a,a) = 0$, that is the time for a message sent from a player to reach himself is 0, but we do not need to enforce this. We also assume the following axiom for all players $a, a_1, \ldots, a_n, a'$ (with $1 \leq n$):

$$\mathsf{td}(a,a') \leq \mathsf{td}(a,a_1) + \mathsf{td}(a_1,a_2) + \cdots + \mathsf{td}(a_n,a') \tag{1}$$

That is, it is faster for a message to travel directly from a to a', then to first travel through $a_1, \ldots, a_n$. This is similar to the usual triangle inequality in basic geometry.

A given scenario with some protocol session instances includes the protocol participants (or simply participants), $\mathcal{P} = \{\mathsf{p}_1, \ldots, \mathsf{p}_n\}$ and a set of Timed Intruders $\mathcal{I} = \{\mathsf{ti}_1, \ldots, \mathsf{ti}_m\}$, who may be manipulating messages. The Network Topology is composed by two disjoint functions $\mathsf{td} = \mathsf{td}_{\mathcal{P}} \uplus \mathsf{td}_{\mathcal{I}}$ defined as follows:

$$\mathsf{td}(a,b) = \begin{cases} \mathsf{td}_{\mathcal{P}}(a,b) \text{ if } a,b \in \mathcal{P} \\ \mathsf{td}_{\mathcal{I}}(a,b) \text{ otherwise} \end{cases}$$

Thus, $\mathsf{td}_{\mathcal{P}}$ specifies the time messages take to travel among participants, while $\mathsf{td}_{\mathcal{I}}$ specifies the time messages take to travel between Timed Intruders, between a Timed Intruder and a participant and between a participant and a Timed Intruder.

Remark 1. Here we are assuming that two agents share a single transmission channel. We leave to future work how to incorporate different transmission channels. One way to do so is to add another parameter to td, which would imply the addition of more axioms. If multiple transmission channels are allowed, then it may well be the case that Eq. 1 does not hold as some participants might use much faster transmission channels. While we leave a more careful analysis of such cases to future work, we strongly believe that our completeness theorem (Theorem 1) still holds (see Remark 2) as one can assume that intruders communicate among themselves using the fastest available transmission medium.

The following definitions extend Strands and Bundles to include time variables capturing the semantics of Timed Protocols. A Timed Protocol Role is ground if it does not contain variables.

Definition 3. *A Timed Strand Space is a set Π and a trace mapping $tr : \Pi \longrightarrow \mathcal{P} \times \mathcal{GPL}$, where $\mathcal{P}$ is the set of player names $\{\mathsf{p}_1, \ldots, \mathsf{p}_n\}$ and $\mathcal{GPL}$ is the set of Ground Timed Protocol Roles. We denote by $tr(s)_1$ the player name and $tr(s)_2$ the Timed Protocol Role of a strand $s \in \Pi$.*

For the remainder we fix a Timed Strand Space $[\Pi, tr]$.

Definition 4. *The Timed Strand Space Graph, $\mathcal{G} = \langle \mathcal{N}, \Rightarrow \cup \rightarrow \rangle$, has nodes $\mathcal{N}$ and edges $\Rightarrow$ and $\rightarrow$ as defined below.*

1. *A node n is a tuple $\langle \mathsf{p}, s, \bar{\imath} \rangle @\mathsf{tt}$ with $s \in \Pi$, $\mathsf{p} = tr(s)_1$, $\bar{\imath} \in \mathcal{PS}(tr(s)_2)$ is a string identifying a command in the Timed Protocol, and tt is a time variable timestamping the node n. The set of nodes is denoted by $\mathcal{N}$;*

2. If $n = \langle \mathsf{p}, s, \overline{i} \rangle @\mathsf{tt}$, we denote by $term(n)$, the command at position $\overline{i}$ in $tr(s)_2$;
3. If $n_1 = \langle \mathsf{p}, s, \overline{i} \rangle @\mathsf{tt}_1$ and $n_2 = \langle \mathsf{p}, s, \overline{i}.j \rangle @\mathsf{tt}_2$ are in $\mathcal{N}$, then there is an edge $n_1 \Rightarrow n_2$;
4. For two nodes $n_1, n_2 \in \mathcal{N}$, there is an edge $n_1 \rightarrow n_2$ if and only if $term(n_1)$ is of the form $+\mathsf{m}$ or $+\mathsf{m} \# \mathsf{tc}_1$ and $term(n_2)$ is of the form $-\mathsf{m}$ or $-\mathsf{m} \# \mathsf{tc}_2$;
5. If a node $n \in \mathcal{N}$, $term(n) = \mathsf{new}\ \mathsf{c}$, then c originates on n, that is, all nodes n' such that $term(n')$ contains c are such that $n\ (\Rightarrow \cup \rightarrow)^*\ n'$, where $(\cdot)^*$ is the reflexive and transitive closure operator.

Definition 5. Let td be a Network Topology and let $\mathcal{C} = \langle \mathcal{N}_C, \rightarrow_C \cup \Rightarrow_C \rangle$ be a subgraph of $\mathcal{G} = \langle \mathcal{N}, \Rightarrow \cup \rightarrow \rangle$. The Timed Constraint Set of $\mathcal{C}$ over td, denoted by $\mathcal{TC}(\mathcal{C}, \mathsf{td})$, is the smallest set of Time Constraints specified as follows:

1. If $n = \langle \mathsf{p}, s, \overline{i} \rangle @\mathsf{tt} \in \mathcal{N}_C$, such that $term(n)$ is of the form $\pm\mathsf{m} \# \mathsf{tc}$ or if $\mathsf{b} \# \mathsf{tc}$, then $\mathsf{tc}' \in \mathcal{TC}(\mathcal{C}, \mathsf{td})$ where tc' is the Time Constraint obtained by replacing cur by tt;
2. If $\langle \mathsf{p}, s, \overline{i} \rangle @\mathsf{tt}_1 \Rightarrow_C \langle \mathsf{p}, s, \overline{i}.j \rangle @\mathsf{tt}_2$, then $\mathsf{tt}_2 \geq \mathsf{tt}_1 \in \mathcal{TC}(\mathcal{C}, \mathsf{td})$;
3. If $\langle \mathsf{p}_1, s_1, \overline{i}_1 \rangle @\mathsf{tt}_1 \rightarrow_C \langle \mathsf{p}_2, s_2, \overline{i}_2 \rangle @\mathsf{tt}_2$, then $\mathsf{tt}_2 \geq \mathsf{tt}_1 + \mathsf{td}(\mathsf{p}_1, \mathsf{p}_2) \in \mathcal{TC}(\mathcal{C}, \mathsf{td})$.

Intuitively, the $\Rightarrow$ specifies the sequence of actions carried out by a protocol session participant, while the $\rightarrow$ specifies the interactions between protocol session participants. However, not all timed strand space graph will correspond to possible executions. Thus, we introduce Timed Bundle which is a subset of the Timed Strand space graph, playing a similar role of Bundles for Strand Spaces.

Definition 6. Let td be a Network Topology. Let $\rightarrow_C \subseteq \rightarrow$ and $\Rightarrow_C \subseteq \Rightarrow$ and suppose $\mathcal{C} = \langle \mathcal{N}_C, \rightarrow_C \cup \Rightarrow_C \rangle$ is a sub-graph of $\langle \mathcal{N}, \Rightarrow \cup \rightarrow \rangle$. $\mathcal{C}$ is a Timed Bundle over td if:

1. $\mathcal{C}$ is finite and acyclic;
2. $n_2 \in \mathcal{N}_C$ is Message Input or a Timed Message Input, then there is a unique $n_1 \in \mathcal{N}_C$ such that $n_1 \rightarrow_C n_2$;
3. $n_2 \in \mathcal{N}_C$ and $n_1 \Rightarrow n_2$, then $n_1 \in \mathcal{N}_C$, and $n_1 \Rightarrow_C n_2$;
4. $n = \langle \mathsf{p}, s, \overline{i} \rangle$ is a node such that $term(n)$ is of the form if b or if $\mathsf{b} \# \mathsf{tc}$ and b is evaluated to true, then $n \Rightarrow_C \langle \mathsf{p}, s, \overline{i}.1 \rangle$ and $n \not\Rightarrow_C \langle \mathsf{p}, s, \overline{i}.2 \rangle$; otherwise $n \Rightarrow_C \langle \mathsf{p}, s, \overline{i}.2 \rangle$ and $n \not\Rightarrow_C \langle \mathsf{p}, s, \overline{i}.1 \rangle$;
5. the Timed Constraint Set of $\mathcal{C}$ over td is satisfiable, i.e., there is a substitution σ, called model of $\mathcal{TC}(\mathcal{C}, \mathsf{td})$, replacing all time variables in $\mathcal{TC}(\mathcal{C}, \mathsf{td})$ by Real numbers so that all inequalities in $\mathcal{TC}(\mathcal{C}, \mathsf{td})$ are true.

Example 3. The following is a graphical representation for a Timed Bundle using the Distance Bounding Protocol described in Example 1:

$$\langle \mathsf{p}_1, \mathsf{new}\ \mathsf{c} \rangle @\mathsf{tt}_1$$
$$\Downarrow$$
$$\langle \mathsf{p}_1, +\mathsf{c} \# \mathsf{tt} = \mathsf{cur} \rangle @\mathsf{tt}_2 \longrightarrow \langle \mathsf{p}_2, -\mathsf{c} \rangle @\mathsf{tt}_4$$
$$\Downarrow \qquad\qquad\qquad \Downarrow$$
$$\langle \mathsf{p}_1, (-\mathsf{c} \# \mathsf{cur} \leq \mathsf{tt} + 4) \rangle @\mathsf{tt}_3 \longleftarrow \langle \mathsf{p}_2, +\mathsf{c} \rangle @\mathsf{tt}_5.$$

It involves two participants p_1 and p_2 which simply exchange a fresh value c.[1] Its Timed Constraint Set should be satisfiable for the assumed Network Topology specified by the function td:

$$\{\, tt_5 \geq tt_4, tt_3 \geq tt_2, tt_2 \geq tt_1, tt = tt_2, tt_4 \geq tt_2 + td(p_1, p_2), tt_3 \geq tt_5 + td(p_2, p_1), tt_3 \leq tt + 4 \,\}$$

Notice that the use of the time symbols in this representation means that this single object specifies a possibly infinite collection of executions of the Distance Bounding Protocol, where the time symbols are instantiated by concrete timestamps taken from the set of non-negative Real numbers $\mathbb{R}^+$. This compact representation greatly reduces the state space during automated protocol verification. In our prototype implementation, we use an SMT solver to check whether the set of Time Constraints is satisfiable or not.

Finally, consider the following specification (new v), (−v). This specification creates a fresh constant and then expects v as input. Since this is a fresh constant and is never sent, it will never be received. The condition (5) in Definition 4 captures this restriction, as it disallows an → edge to $\langle p, (-v) \rangle$

3   Timed Intruder Model

The Timed Intruder Model is similar to the usual Dolev-Yao Intruder Model in the sense that it can compose, decompose, encrypt and decrypt messages provided it has the right keys. However, unlike the Dolev-Yao intruder, a Timed Intruder is constrained by the physical properties of the systems, namely, an intruder is not able to learn any message instantaneously, instead, must wait until the message arrives.

A Timed Intruder Set is a set of intruder names $\mathcal{I} = \{ti_1, \ldots, ti_n\}$ a set of initially known keys K_P, which contain all public keys, all private keys of all the intruders, all symmetric keys initially shared between intruders and honest players, and may contain "lost keys" that an intruder learned previously by, for instance, succeeding in some cryptoanalysis. Recall that Timed Intruders are situated at locations specified by the Network Topology. For instance, $td(p_1, ti_1) = td_{\mathcal{I}}(p_1, ti_1) = 4$ denotes that the timed needed for a message to travel from participant p_1 to intruder ti_1 is 4.

Definition 7. *An intruder trace is one of the following, where* ti *is a Timed Intruder Name,* tt, tt$_1$, tt$_2$, tt$_3$ *are time variables, and* m, m$_1$, \ldots, m$_n$, m$'_1$, \ldots, m$'_p$ *are messages:*

- *Text Message:* $\langle ti, +t \rangle$@tt, *where* t *is a text constant;*
- *Flushing:* $\langle ti, -m \rangle$@tt;

---

[1] For readability we display graph nodes using the player's id paired with the node term, rather than using the strand identifier and trace position.

- *Forward:* $\langle ti, -m, +m \rangle @(tt_1, tt_2)$ *denoting the strand* $\langle ti, -m \rangle @tt_1 \Rightarrow \langle ti, +m \rangle$ $@tt_2;$
- *Concatenation:* $\langle ti, -\{m_1, \ldots, m_n\}, -\{m'_1, \ldots, m'_p\}, +\{m_1, \ldots, m_n, m'_1, \ldots, m'_p\}\rangle @(tt_1, tt_2, tt_3)$ *denoting the strand*
  $\langle ti, -\{m_1, \ldots, m_n\}\rangle @tt_1 \Rightarrow \langle ti, -\{m'_1, \ldots, m'_p\}\rangle @tt_2 \Rightarrow \langle ti, +\{m_1, \ldots, m_n, m'_1, \ldots, m'_p\}\rangle @tt_3$
- *Decomposing:* $\langle ti, -\{m_1, \ldots, m_n\}, +\{m_1, \ldots, m_i\}, +\{m_{i+1}, \ldots, m_n\}\rangle @(tt_1, tt_2, tt_3)$ *denoting the strand*
  $\langle ti, -\{m_1, \ldots, m_i, m_{i+1}, \ldots, m_n\}\rangle @tt_1 \Rightarrow \langle ti, +\{m_1, \ldots, m_i\}\rangle @tt_2 \Rightarrow \langle ti, +\{m_{i+1}, \ldots, m_n\}\rangle @tt_3$
- *Key:* $\langle ti, +k \rangle @tt$ *if* $k \in K_P$;
- *Encryption:* $\langle ti, -k, -m, +enc(m, k)\rangle @(tt_1, tt_2, tt_3)$ *denoting the strand*
  $\langle ti, -k \rangle @tt_1 \Rightarrow \langle ti, -m \rangle @tt_2 \Rightarrow \langle ti, +enc(m, k)\rangle @tt_3$
- *Decryption:* $\langle ti, -k^{-1}, -enc(m, k), +m \rangle @(tt_1, tt_2, tt_3)$.
  $\langle ti, -k^{-1} \rangle @tt_1 \Rightarrow \langle ti, -enc(m, k)\rangle @tt_2 \Rightarrow \langle ti, +m \rangle @tt_3$

As with the the usual Dolev-Yao intruder model as, e.g., in [25], the Timed Intruder can send text messages and known keys, receive a message, replay a message, concatenate and decompose messages, and finally encrypt and decrypt messages. There are, however, two differences with respect to the usual Dolev-Yao intruder model as defined in [25]. Each node of the trace is associated with an intruder name ti and a time variable tt. These are necessary for extracting the Time Constraints of a Strand Graph (as described in Definition 5), specifying the physical restrictions of the Timed Intruder.

As the time when timed intruders receive and manipulate messages cannot be measured by the protocol participants, they do not have control over the time variables of timed intruder strands. The following assumption captures this intuition:

Time Variable Disjointness Assumption. For any Bundle $\mathcal{B}$, the set of time variables appearing in protocol participant strands in $\mathcal{B}$ is disjoint from the set of time variables appearing in timed intruder strands in $\mathcal{B}$.

Example 4. Let us return to the distance bounding protocol described in Example 1. The following is an attack, where two colluding intruders ti_1, who is close to p_1, and ti_2, who is close to p_2, collude by sharing a fast channel to fool p_1 into thinking that p_2 is closer than he actually is.

The intruders ti_1 and ti_2 simply forward messages between each other and the players p_1 and p_2. However, this is a Bundle only if the following Time Constraint Set is satisfiable:

$$\left\{ \begin{array}{c} tt_2 \geq tt_1, tt = tt_2, tt_6 \geq tt_2 + td(p_1, ti_1), tt_7 \geq tt_6, tt_8 \geq tt_7 + td(ti_1, ti_2), tt_9 \geq tt_8, \\ tt_4 \geq tt_9 + td(ti_1, p_2), tt_5 \geq tt_4, tt_{10} \geq tt_5 + td(p_2, ti_1), tt_{11} \geq tt_{10}, tt_{12} \geq tt_{11} + td(ti_2, ti_1), \\ tt_{13} \geq tt_{12}, tt_3 \geq tt_{13} + td(ti_1, p_1), tt_3 \leq tt_2 + 4 \end{array} \right\}$$

This set of constraints represents a set of concrete executions, where the Timed Intruders ti_1 and ti_2 collude. There is a concrete execution only if the set of Time Constraints is satisfiable, which depends on the Network Topology, that is, on the function td.

4   Timed Intruder Completeness

Standard Security Protocol Verification is already very challenging. However, automated verification has been very successful in discovering new attacks. A good part of this success is due to the Dolev-Yao intruder model, which greatly simplifies the design of verification tools. Tools can rely on the important result that just a single Dolev-Yao intruder is enough, in the sense that if there is an attack in the presence of multiple (colluding) Dolev-Yao intruders, then there is also an attack in the presence of a single Dolev-Yao intruder [4].

Unfortunately, for Cyber-Physical Security Protocols, it is not the case that a single Timed Intruder is enough for verification. Consider the attack illustrated in Example 4. There may be a great number of Timed Intruders, but none of them situated between p_1 and p_2, as illustrated by Fig. 1. In such a scenario there might not be an attack as the round time to receive and return a message between such a display of intruders may never be less than the distance bound (4). On the other hand, two strategically placed Timed Intruders, as in the second picture in Fig. 1, may lead to an attack.

Clearly there is an unbounded number of choices based on deciding:

- How many Timed Intruders are there?
- Where are these Timed Intruders located?

This is similar to the challenge in usual security protocol verification of determining how many protocol sessions running in parallel should the scenario have, which is undecidable [20]. Fortunately, we are able to prove a completeness result which answers the two questions above. In order to formalize the completeness statement, we introduce some notation.

Definition 8. *Let $\mathcal{B}$ be a Timed Bundle over the Network Topology* td *involving the participants $\mathcal{P} = \{p_1, \ldots, p_n\}$ and the Timed Intruders $\mathcal{I} = \{ti_1, \ldots, ti_n\}$. The graph $\mathcal{B}$ restricted to participants $\mathcal{P}$, written $\mathcal{B}_\mathcal{P}$, is the graph $\langle \mathcal{N}_\mathcal{B}^\mathcal{P}, (\Rightarrow_\mathcal{B}^\mathcal{P} \cup \rightarrow_\mathcal{B}^\mathcal{P}) \rangle$ specified as follows:*

- $\mathcal{N}_\mathcal{B}^\mathcal{P}$ *contains only the nodes in $\mathcal{B}$ belonging to a participant in $\mathcal{P}$, i.e., of the form $\langle p, s, \bar{i} \rangle$ where $p \in \mathcal{P}$;*
- *For two nodes n_1, n_2 in $\mathcal{N}_\mathcal{B}^\mathcal{P}$, if $n_1 \Rightarrow n_2$ in $\mathcal{B}$, then $n_1 \Rightarrow_\mathcal{B}^\mathcal{P} n_2$;*

- *If n is a node in $\mathcal{N}_\mathcal{B}^P$ whose term is a message receive, $-m$ or $-m \ \# \ tc$, and n' is a maximal element of the set of predecessors of n in $\mathcal{N}_\mathcal{B}^P$ under the relation $(\Rightarrow \cup \rightarrow)^*; \rightarrow$ then $n' \rightarrow_\mathcal{B}^P n$. We let $\mathcal{P}(n, \mathcal{B})$ denote this set of predecessors.*

Intuitively, a Bundle restricted to the set of participants specifies the events observable by the participants without including the moves corresponding to the timed intruders. It includes all the edges of the original bundle connecting two nodes of $\mathcal{N}_\mathcal{B}^P$. The "maximal predecessor" in $\mathcal{N}_\mathcal{B}^P$ is the first element of $\mathcal{N}_\mathcal{B}^P$ encountered when following edges in the predecessor direction. It is maximal in the partial order on nodes induced by the edges of the bundle. Thus the terms of nodes in $\mathcal{P}(n, \mathcal{B})$ contain all the terms used by the intruders to derive the term at node n.

The Bundle shown in Example 4 restricted to the participants $\{p_1, p_2\}$ is

$$\langle p_1, \text{new } c\rangle @tt_1$$
$$\Downarrow$$
$$\langle p_1, +c \ \# \ tt = cur\rangle @tt_2 \longrightarrow \langle p_2, -c\rangle @tt_4$$
$$\Downarrow \qquad\qquad\qquad\qquad \Downarrow$$
$$\langle p_1, (-c \ \# \ cur \leq tt + 4)\rangle @tt_3 \longleftarrow \langle p_2, +c\rangle @tt_5.$$

The edge $\langle p_1, +c \ \# \ tt = cur\rangle @tt_2 \rightarrow \langle p_2, -c\rangle @tt_4$ in this figure simply specifies that using the message, c, sent by p_1, the timed intruders were able to send the message c to the participant p_2.

For another example, consider the following Bundle, where timed intruder ti uses his key $k \in K_P$ and the messages c_1 and c_2 to compose the message $enc(\{c_1, c_2\}, k)$ to p_3:

$$\langle p_1, +c_1\rangle @tt_1 \qquad\qquad\qquad\qquad \langle p_2, +c_2\rangle @tt_2$$
$$\langle ti, -c_1, +c_1\rangle @(tt_3, tt_3') \qquad\qquad \langle ti, -c_2, +c_2\rangle @(tt_4, tt_4')$$
$$\langle ti, +k\rangle @tt_6 \qquad \langle ti, -c_1, -c_2, +\{c_1, c_2\}\rangle @(tt_5, tt_5', tt_5'')$$
$$\langle ti, -k, -\{c_1, c_2\}, +enc(\{c_1, c_2\}, k)\rangle @(tt_7, tt_7', tt_7'') \longrightarrow \langle p_3, -enc(\{c_1, c_2\}, k)\rangle @tt_8.$$

The corresponding bundle restricted to the participants p_1, p_2 and p_3 is:

$$\langle p_1, +c_1\rangle @tt_1 \longrightarrow \langle p_3, -enc(\{c_1, c_2\}, k)\rangle @tt_8 \longleftarrow \langle p_2, +c_2\rangle @tt_2$$

It captures the fact that the messages sent by p_1 and p_2 are used to generate the message received by p_3 without explicitly showing how intruders manipulated these messages.

Notice that unlike bundles, a receive node in a restricted bundle may have multiple incoming edges, reflecting the possibility of processing by multiple intruders.

The next two lemmas follow directly from the definition of Bundles and restricted Bundles.

Lemma 1. *Let* $p = n \leadsto_1 n_1 \leadsto_2 n_2 \leadsto_3 \cdots \leadsto_{j-1} n_j \leadsto_j n'$ *be a path from* n *in* $\mathcal{P}(n', \mathcal{B})$ *to* n'*, where* $\leadsto_i$ *is either* $\rightarrow$ *or* $\Rightarrow$ *for* $1 \leq i \leq j$*. Then* p *is necessarily of the form:*

$$\langle p, snd \rangle @tt \rightarrow \langle ti_1, s_1 \rangle @tt_1 \leadsto_2 \langle ti_2, s_2 \rangle @tt_2 \leadsto_2 \cdots \leadsto_{j-1} \langle ti_j, s_j \rangle @tt_j \rightarrow \langle p', rcv \rangle @tt'$$

where snd *is a message send* (+m) *or a timed message send* (+m # tc)*, rcv is a message receive* (−m) *or a timed message receive* (−m # tc)*, and for* $1 \leq i \leq j$*,* $\langle ti_i, s_i \rangle$ *are timed intruder strands.*

Lemma 2. *Let* $\mathcal{T}(\mathcal{B}, td)$ *be the Time Constraint Set of* $\mathcal{B}$ *for a given Network Topology* td*. Let* p *be a path in* $\mathcal{B}$ *as described in Lemma 1 of the form:*

$$\langle p, snd \rangle @tt \rightarrow \langle ti_1, s_1 \rangle @tt_1 \leadsto_1 \langle ti_2, s_2 \rangle @tt_2 \leadsto_2 \cdots \leadsto_{j-1} \langle ti_j, s_j \rangle @tt_j \rightarrow \langle p', rcv \rangle @tt'$$

Then any satisfying model of $\mathcal{T}(\mathcal{B}, td)$ *will also satisfy the constraint:*

$$tt' \geq tt + td(p, ti_1) + td(ti_1, ti_2) + \cdots + td(ti_{j-1}, ti_j) + td(ti_j, p').$$

The following specifies the equivalence of two Bundles.

Definition 9. *Let* $\mathcal{P}$ *be a set of participants and* $\mathcal{I}, \mathcal{I}'$ *be two possibly equal sets of Timed Intruders. Let* $td_1 = td_{\mathcal{P}} \uplus td_{\mathcal{I}}$ *and* $td_2 = td_{\mathcal{P}} \uplus td_{\mathcal{I}'}$ *be Network Topologies. Then we say that a Timed Bundle* $\mathcal{B}_1$ *over* td_1 *is equivalent to a Timed Bundle* $\mathcal{B}_2$ *over* td_2*, written* $\mathcal{B}_1 \cong_{td_1}^{td_2} \mathcal{B}_2$*, if their Bundles restricted to* $\mathcal{P}$ *are (syntactically) identical, i.e.,* $\mathcal{B}_1^{\mathcal{P}} = \mathcal{B}_2^{\mathcal{P}}$*.*[2]

Intuitively, the condition $\mathcal{B}_1^{\mathcal{P}} = \mathcal{B}_2^{\mathcal{P}}$ specifies that for the honest participants the two Bundles are equivalent, although they may have different timed intruders in different locations manipulating messages in different ways. Thus, if such a $\mathcal{B}_1$ constitutes an attack, then $\mathcal{B}_2$ also constitutes an attack.

Timed Intruder Completeness Problem:

Let $\mathcal{P} = \{p_1, \ldots, p_n\}$ be a set of participants and $\mathcal{I} = \{ti_1, \ldots, ti_m\}$ be a set of timed intruders. Let $td_{\mathcal{P}}$ be a Network Topology of the participants. Is there a subset $\mathcal{I}' \subseteq \mathcal{I}$ and $td_{\mathcal{I}'}$ such that for any $td_{\mathcal{I}}$ and any Bundle $\mathcal{B}_1$ over $td_1 = td_{\mathcal{P}} \uplus td_{\mathcal{I}}$, there is a Bundle $\mathcal{B}_2$ over $td_2 = td_{\mathcal{P}} \uplus td_{\mathcal{I}'}$ such that $\mathcal{B}_1 \cong_{td_1}^{td_2} \mathcal{B}_2$?

In other words, given a particular scenario with $\mathcal{P}$ participants and a Network Topology for these participants $td_{\mathcal{P}}$, is there a Network Topology $td_{\mathcal{I}}'$ involving a collection of Timed Intruders $\mathcal{I}'$ that can be used to carry out the same observable events for any other Network Topology $td_{\mathcal{I}}$ with a possibly larger number of Timed Intruders?

If such an $\mathcal{I}'$ and $td_{\mathcal{I}'}$ exists then an automated verification tool does not have to guess how many timed intruders there are, and where they are located, but simply can use $\mathcal{I}'$ and $td_{\mathcal{I}'}$.

---

[2] It is possible to relax this definition so that they are identical modulo time variable names, but this is not needed here.

4.1 Completeness Proof

We are given a set of participants $\mathcal{P} = \{p_1, \ldots, p_n\}$, a set of Timed Intruders $\mathcal{I} = \{ti_1, \ldots, ti_m\}$, and a Network Topology $td_\mathcal{P}$ specifying the time messages take to travel between participants.

A Solution for the Timed Intruder Completeness Problem: For our solution, we assume that there are as many timed intruders as participants. If this is not the case, we can safely add more dummy timed intruders. We associate with each participant p_i one Timed Intruder ti_{p_i}. Thus:

$$\mathcal{I}' = \{ti_{p_1}, \ldots, ti_{p_n}\}.$$

Moreover, we assume that the time a message takes to travel between p_i to ti_i is 0 (or negligible). Moreover, the time for a message to travel between two Timed Intruders ti_{p_i} and ti_{p_j} is the same as the time it takes to travel between their corresponding participants p_i and p_j. Thus:

$$\begin{aligned}
td_{\mathcal{I}'}(p_i, ti_{p_i}) = td_{\mathcal{I}'}(ti_{p_i}, p_i) = 0 &\qquad \text{for all } p_i \in \mathcal{P}; \\
td_{\mathcal{I}'}(ti_{p_i}, ti_{p_j}) = td_\mathcal{P}(p_i, p_j) &\qquad \text{for all } p_i, p_j \in \mathcal{P}.
\end{aligned}$$

The Timed Intruders in $\mathcal{I}'$ collude in the following form: whenever a Timed Intruder t_{p_i} learns a message m sent by p_i, it broadcasts this message m to the remaining Timed Intruders in $\mathcal{I}' \setminus \{ti_{p_i}\}$. For example, the Strand for when p_1 sends a message is then as follows:

$$\langle p_1, +m\rangle @ tt_1 \longrightarrow \langle ti_{p_1}, -m, +m\rangle @ (tt_1', tt_1')$$

$$\langle ti_{p_2}, -m, +m\rangle @ (tt_2, tt_2) \quad \langle ti_{p_3}, -m, +m\rangle @ (tt_3, tt_3) \quad \cdots \quad \langle ti_{p_n}, -m, +m\rangle @ (tt_n, tt_n)$$

Notice that the message m reaches to a Timed Intruder ti_{p_i} at time tt_i which is subject to the Time Constraints $tt_i \geq tt_1' + td_\mathcal{P}(p_1, p_i)$ and $tt_1' \geq tt_1 + td(p_1, ti_{p_1})$, which reduces to $tt_1' \geq tt_1$ as $td(p_1, ti_{p_1}) = 0$. Thus, $tt_i \geq tt_1 + td_\mathcal{P}(p_1, p_i)$. Moreover, if the Timed Intruder ti_{p_i} forwards this message to the participant p_i, then this message will be received at a time $tt_i' \geq tt_1 + td_\mathcal{P}(p_1, p_i)$, that is, as if the message had traveled directly from p_1 to p_i without passing through intruders ti_{p_1} and ti_{p_i}

Proof. We will now show that the $\mathcal{I}'$ and $td_{\mathcal{I}'}$ defined above provide a solution for the Timed Intruder Completeness Problem. For this, assume given a $td_\mathcal{I}$ and a Bundle $\mathcal{B}_1$ over $td_1 = td_\mathcal{P} \uplus td_\mathcal{I}$.

We will construct a Bundle $\mathcal{B}_2$ over $td_2 = td_\mathcal{P} \uplus td_{\mathcal{I}'}$ such that $\mathcal{B}_1 \cong_{td_1}^{td_2} \mathcal{B}_2$. We do so by transforming $\mathcal{B}_1$ into $\mathcal{B}_2$.

Let the following be a sub-graph of $\mathcal{B}_1$ restricted to $\mathcal{P}$:

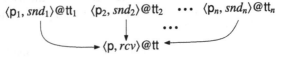

where for all $1 \leq i \leq n$, snd_i is a Message Output $(+m_i)$ or a Timed Message Output $(+m_i \# tc)$, rcv is a Message Input $(-m)$ or a Timed Message Input $(-m \# tc)$.

Let p be an arbitrary path from node $\langle p_i, snd_i \rangle @tt_i$ to $\langle p, rcv \rangle @tt$ path in $\mathcal{B}_1$. From Lemma 1, p has the shape:

$$\langle p_i, snd_i \rangle @tt_i \rightarrow \langle ti_1, s_1 \rangle @tt_1 \leadsto_1 \langle ti_2, s_2 \rangle @tt_2 \leadsto_2 \cdots \leadsto_{j-1} \langle ti_j, s_j \rangle @tt_j \rightarrow \langle p', rcv \rangle @tt$$

Moreover, from Lemma 2, any model satisfying $\mathcal{B}_1$ will also satisfy the constraint:

$$tt \geq tt_i + td(p_i, ti_1) + td(ti_1, ti_2) + \cdots + td(ti_{j-1}, ti_j) + td(ti_j, p). \quad (2)$$

Given our assumption on the Network Topology (Eq. 1), we also have that

$$td(p_i, p) \leq td(p, ti_1) + td(ti_1, ti_2) + \cdots + td(ti_{j-1}, ti_j) + td(ti_j, p)$$

That is, the time it takes to travel directly from p_i to p is less than or equal to the time it takes to travel from p_i to p via the timed intruders $ti_1, \ldots, ti_j$.

From our solution, we obtain for the sub-graph shown above the following subgraph where all the messages $m_1, \ldots, m_n$ are broadcast to all Timed Intruders including the Timed Intruder ti_p:

$$\langle p_1, +snd_1 \rangle @tt_1 \qquad \cdots \qquad \langle p_n, +snd_n \rangle @tt_n$$
$$\downarrow \qquad\qquad\qquad\qquad\qquad \downarrow$$
$$\langle ti_{p_1}, -m_1, +m_1 \rangle @(tt'_1, tt'_1) \qquad \cdots \qquad \langle ti_{p_n}, -m_n, +m_n \rangle @(tt'_n, tt'_n)$$
$$\downarrow \qquad\qquad\qquad\qquad\qquad \downarrow$$
$$\langle ti_p, -m_1, +m_1 \rangle @(tt''_1, tt''_1) \qquad \cdots \qquad \langle ti_p, -m_n, +m_n \rangle @(tt''_n, tt''_n)$$

where the intruder ti_p receives the messages $m_1, \ldots, m_n$. Notice that for $1 \leq i \leq n$, we have that $tt''_i \geq tt_i + td(p_i, p)$. At this point the intruder ti_p has all the information he needs to compose the message m. Moreover, he can do so without losing time. Thus he is able to deliver the message m to p at time tt satisfying the constraints:

$$tt \geq tt_1 + td(p_1, p) \quad tt \geq tt_2 + td(p_2, p) \quad \cdots \quad tt \geq tt_n + td(p_n, p). \quad (3)$$

As any model of the Time Constraints Set of $\mathcal{B}_1$ satisfies Eq. 2, the same assignment for $tt_1, \ldots, tt_n, tt$ will also satisfy the time constraints in Eq. 3. Moreover, if any of $snd_1, \ldots, snd_n$ is a Timed Output $(p_i, +m_i \# tc_i)$ or rcv is a Timed Input $(p, -m \# tc)$ the same assignment will also satisfy tc_i and tc because protocol participant strands and timed intruder strands do not share time variable (Time Variable Disjointness Assumption).

By repeating this procedure for each sub-graph in $\mathcal{B}_1$ restricted to $\mathcal{P}$ as shown above, we are able to construct $\mathcal{B}_2$ using $td_{\mathcal{I}'}$ where the only timed intruder strands are those of the intruders $\mathcal{I}'$ leading to the following result.

Theorem 1. *Let $\mathcal{P}$ be participant names and $\mathcal{I}$ be Timed Intruders, such that $|\mathcal{I}| \geq |\mathcal{P}|$. Let $\mathcal{I}'$ and $td_{\mathcal{I}'}$ be as described above. Then $\mathcal{I}'$ and $td_{\mathcal{I}'}$ solve the Timed Intruder Completeness Problem.*

Remark 2. It should be possible to extend our completeness result for cases with different transmission channels (See Remark 1). For this, our solution would assume that the intruders communicate with the fastest transmission speed available. This is enough to prove Eq. 2 without relying on Eq. 1. We leave a more careful analysis to future work.

Remark 3. Our solution of placing a timed intruder close to each participant might be unrealistic for some scenarios, *e.g.*, when a participant, A, is guaranteed to be alone due to some physical barrier which ensures that intruders are at least d units away. We speculate that by instead of placing a single intruder for A, we would need n intruders, where n is the number of participants. Each intruder would be placed d units away from A in the direction of each other participant. This should be enough to prove a corresponding completeness theorem. We leave this interesting problem to future work.

5   Examples and Preliminary Experimental Results

We illustrate with some examples that our solution is able to identify attacks on CPSP. We are using the terminology of attacks described in [10].

External Distance Fraud. Assume two honest participants p_1 (Verifier) and p_2 (Prover). They exchange some information, normally to authenticate p_2, for example [24], using a standard Needham-Schroeder-Lowe protocol session [17], and then carry-out a distance bounding protocol session. The following Timed Strand captures the attack where the intruder ti_{p_1} fools player p_1 that p_2 is closer than he actually is by completing the distance bounding challenge:

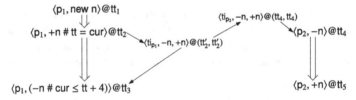

Notice that the timed intruder ti_{p_1} is able to complete the distance bounding session as he is very close to the verifier p_1. This is captured by the Time Constraint Set of this Bundle. Moreover, here we assume that they exchange a nonce, but if we allow equational theories specifying, for example xor operations $\oplus$ as done in [13], a similar Timed Bundle would be obtained.

Attack-in-Between-Ticks. The In-Between-Ticks attack [15] is an instance of a Lone Distance Fraud attack [10], where the prover is dishonest but is not colluding with other Timed Intruders. This attack exploits the fact that real verifiers are running on a processor with a slow clock speed. When the verifier receives the response from the prover, he is only able to record the time of receival in the following clock cycle. This is captured by using the Time Constraint $(\text{floor}(\text{cur}) + 1)$ as illustrated by the following Timed Strand:

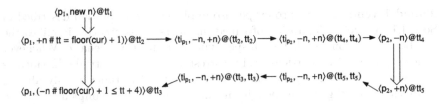

It is possible to show that the Time Constraint Set of this Timed Strand, $\mathcal{T}$, is satisifiable although the distance between p_1 and p_2 is greater than the distance bound 4. That is, it is possible to show that the set $\mathcal{T} \cup \{td(p_1, p_2) > 4, td(p_2, p_1) > 4\}$ is satisfiable.

Distance Hijacking. In our technical report [21], we show the Timed Bundle with the Distance Hijacking attack described in [24] on the protocol that combines the traditional Needham-Schroeder-Lowe protocol and a distance bounding session.

5.1 Prototype Implementation

We developed a prototype implementation, which can be found at [22], of this strategy in a version of Maude [8] integrated with the SMT solver CVC4 [2]. Our preliminary results seem quite promising.

In addition to symbolic time constraints we implemented a symbolic constraint solver in order to tackle the state-space explosion due to the fact that a timed intruder can generate an unbounded number of messages. It works along the same lines as in usual implementations of such constraint solvers used by tools assuming the standard Dolev-Yao intruder by not instantiating messages generated by the intruder, but rather using symbolic constraints.

Our prototype used and implements mechanisms for the main contributions of this paper:

- **Network Topology as a Constraint Set:** While here we assume that the Network Topology is given by a function td which completely determines the time messages take to travel between agents, our implementation allows the user to specify the Network Topology as a set of constraints. For example, the constraint $td(p_1, p_2) > 4$ specifies the set of Network Topologies where the time it takes for a message to travel from p_1 to p_2 is greater than 4. This reduces even further the decision choices needed when specifying some scenario as one does not need to consider grounded Network Topologies.
- **Time Variables and Time Constraints:** As described here, we use time variables and keep track of the Time Constraints of the constructed Timed Strand, which is initially empty. Whenever a command in our protocol language is executed, we add the corresponding constraint to the set of constraints following Definition 5. We then call the SMT solver to check whether the set of constraints is satisfiable. If it is not, then search on this branch of the search tree is aborted.

- **Timed Intruders:** Our prototype also implements the solution described in Sect. 4.1 for the configuration of timed intruders. This greatly simplifies the number of decisions needed when specifying a verification scenario. Whenever a message is sent by a participant, his corresponding timed intruder broadcasts this message to all other Timed Intruders. A timed intruder is only able to learn such a message when enough time has elapsed. This is implemented also using the SMT solver and adding appropriate time constraints.

Table 1 summarizes some preliminary experimental results.

Table 1. Preliminary experimental results

Scenario	Size of protocols	No of states	Search time
External Distance Fraud	5	12	31ms
Attack-in-Between-Ticks	5	70	55ms
Simplified Paywave	14	3224	8s
Paywave	22	20807	78s
NSL + Distance Bounding ⋆	15	86	108ms

The External Distance Fraud and Attack-in-Between-Ticks are as described above. The number of states traversed is quite small for finding these. The distance bounding protocol scheme is used by many other protocols, such as the protocol described in [24] (NSL + Distance Bounding) and the lack of its use leads to an attack on the Paywave protocol [6]. We implemented these to check how our tool scales to larger protocols. We implemented a simplified version of the Paywave protocol omitting some of the steps taken and only concentrating on the core part of the protocol. Our tool was able to find the attack in 8s traversing around 3.2k states. Finally, we implemented the whole Paywave protocol and our tool was also able to find the attack, but now in 78s traversing 20.8k states.

The use of the SMT solver was essential to reduce the number of states. However, it seems that it is possible to reduce the overhead caused by each call of the SMT solver.

We also experimented with protocols that fall outside of our language fragment. The NSL + Distance Bounding protocol described in [24] with a small modification carries out a standard Needham-Schroeder-Lowe protocol session, followed by a distance bounding protocol using xor. Since our tool does not support yet equational theories, a subject for future work, we modeled the distance bounding session with a pair. Our tool was able to find a terrorist attack in 108 ms traversing 86 states. This attack was not reported in [24] as they did not assume that intruders are close to the participants.

Finally, we also obtained preliminary results on using the tool for checking whether there is a privacy attack on a protocol [7]. In order to check for such an attack, we need to enumerate all possible executions. (The formal definitions are out of the scope of this paper.) In order to have an idea of how big this set of executions is, we implemented the protocol used for RFID in European passports. The total number of states was only 10 states. This is a promising result for extending this work to check for properties that rely on observational equivalence [5].

6   Related and Future Work

Meadows *et al.* [19] and Pavlovic and Meadows in [23] propose and use a logic called Protocol Derivation Logic (PDL) to formalize and prove the safety of a number of cyber-physical protocols. In particular, they specify the assumptions and protocol executions in the form of axioms, specifying the allowed order of events that can happen, and show that safety properties are implied by the axiomatization used. They do not formalize an intruder model. Another difference between their work and ours is that their PDL specification is not an executable specification.

Another approach similar to [19], in the sense that it uses a theorem proving approach, is given by Basin *et al.* [3]. They formalize an intruder model that is similar to ours in Isabelle, and also formalize some cyber-physical security protocols. They then prove the correctness of these protocols under some specific conditions and also identify attacks when some conditions are not satisfied. Their work has been a source of inspiration for our intruder model specified in Sect. 3. However, they do not propose or investigate the Timed Intruder Completeness Problem.

Chothia *et al.* [6] investigate empirically the execution times of commands of CPSP which are carried out by limited resource devices and then, based on these measurements, they propose the inclusion of a distance bounding session to mitigate relay attacks. They proved the security of CPSP by modeling the protocol in different phases. As we illustrate in Example 2, our language allows the inclusion of the measurements themselves. We leave a more detailed analysis to future work.

Cheval and Cortier [5] propose a way to prove the observational equivalence with time by reducing it to the observational equivalence based on the length of inputs. They are able to automatically show that RFID protocols used by passports suffer a privacy attack. Their approach is, therefore, different as they do not investigate the Timed Intruder Completeness Problem. Also it is not clear whether from their language one can capture attacks such as the Attack-in-Between Ticks which exploits the time constraints of the verifier. Finally, from our initial experiments with the Passport RFID protocol, we believe that it is also feasible to check for privacy attacks given the very low number of states encountered by our tool. This is left for future work.

Corin *et al.* [9] propose using timed automata to model check security protocols taking into account retransmission and error states of security protocols. This is an early contribution on the analysis of timing aspects of security protocols which did not consider CPSP nor the completeness of timed intruders.

Finally, Malladi *et al.* [18] formalize distance bounding protocols in strand spaces. They then construct an automated tool for protocol verification using a constraint solver to verify a number of examples. There are some similarities between their goals and the goal we want to achieve, namely, the automated verification of CPSP and in the use of SMT solvers to do so. However, there are some important differences. Firstly, we formalize and provide a solution to the Timed Intruder Completeness Problem and, secondly, our language seems to have more expressive features, *e.g.*, our time constraints.

The definition of restricted bundle to characterize executions from the protocol participants perspective is inspired by the notions of skeleton and shape in strand space based protocol analysis [11,12].

Arnaud *et al.* [1] propose a model for specifying and reasoning about secured routing protocols where nodes communicate in a direct way with their neighbors. It seems possible to represent our network model using time constraints as they do and not only reason about the routing of packets, but also the time when these arrive, which is important for cyber-physical systems where agents use some routing protocol to communicate. We leave this to future work.

We are currently investigating methods to control even further the state space explosion, for example, using more elaborate symbolic constraint systems for messages and investigating how to support backward Narrowing as in Maude-NPA [14]. Moreover, we are extending our implementation to support message signatures with equational theories using the library available in Maude [13]. Finally, we are investigating definitions of observational equivalence which involve time and that can be implemented using SMT-solvers.

Acknowledgments. We thank the anonymous reviewers for their valuable comments and observations. Talcott was partially supported by NSF grant CNS-1318848 and ONR grant N00014-15-1-2202. Nigam and Talcott were partially supported by Capes Science without Borders grant 88881.030357/2013-01. Nigam was partially supported by Capes and CNPq.

References

1. Arnaud, M., Cortier, V., Delaune, S.: Modeling, verifying ad hoc routing protocols. Inf. Comput. **238**, 30–67 (2014). Special Issue on Security and Rewriting Techniques
2. Barrett, C., Conway, C.L., Deters, M., Hadarean, L., Jovanović, D., King, T., Reynolds, A., Tinelli, C.: CVC4. In: Gopalakrishnan, G., Qadeer, S. (eds.) CAV 2011. LNCS, vol. 6806, pp. 171–177. Springer, Heidelberg (2011)
3. Basin, D.A., Capkun, S., Schaller, P., Schmidt, B.: Formal reasoning about physical properties of security protocols. ACM Trans. Inf. Syst. Secur. **14**(2), 16 (2011)
4. Cervesato, I.: Data access specification and the most powerful symbolic attacker in MSR. In: Okada, M., Babu, C.S., Scedrov, A., Tokuda, H. (eds.) ISSS 2002. LNCS, vol. 2609, pp. 384–416. Springer, Heidelberg (2003)
5. Cheval, V., Cortier, V.: Timing attacks in security protocols: symbolic framework and proof techniques. In: Focardi, R., Myers, A. (eds.) POST 2015. LNCS, vol. 9036, pp. 280–299. Springer, Heidelberg (2015)

6. Chothia, T., Garcia, F.D., de Ruiter, J., van den Breekel, J., Thompson, M.: Relay cost bounding for contactless EMV payments. In: Böhme, R., Okamoto, T. (eds.) FC 2015. LNCS, vol. 8975, pp. 189–206. Springer, Heidelberg (2015)

7. Chothia, T., Smirnov, V.: A traceability attack against e-passports. In: Sion, R. (ed.) FC 2010. LNCS, vol. 6052, pp. 20–34. Springer, Heidelberg (2010)

8. Clavel, M., Durán, F., Eker, S., Lincoln, P., Martí-Oliet, N., Meseguer, J., Talcott, C.: All About Maude: A High-Performance Logical Framework. Springer, Heidelberg (2007)

9. Corin, R., Etalle, S., Hartel, P.H., Mader, A.: Timed model checking of security protocols. In: FMSE. ACM (2004)

10. Cremers, C.J.F., Rasmussen, K.B., Schmidt, B., Capkun, S.: Distance hijacking attacks on distance bounding protocols. In: IEEE Symposium on Security and Privacy, SP (2012)

11. Doghmi, S.F., Guttman, J.D., Thayer, F.J.: Searching for shapes in cryptographic protocols. In: Grumberg, O., Huth, M. (eds.) TACAS 2007. LNCS, vol. 4424, pp. 523–537. Springer, Heidelberg (2007)

12. Doghmi, S.F., Guttman, J.D., Thayer, F.J.: Skeletons, homomorphisms, shapes, characterizing protocol executions. In: Mathematical Foundations of Program Semantics (2007)

13. Durán, F., Eker, S., Escobar, S., Martí-Oliet, N., Meseguer, J., Talcott, C.: Built-in variant generation and unification, and their applications in Maude 2.7. In: Olivetti, N., Tiwari, A. (eds.) IJCAR 2016. LNCS, vol. 9706, pp. 183–192. Springer, Heidelberg (2016). doi:10.1007/978-3-319-40229-1_13

14. Escobar, S., Meadows, C.A., Meseguer, J.: Maude-NPA, cryptographic protocol analysis modulo equational properties. In: Aldini, A., Barthe, G., Gorrieri, R. (eds.) FOSAD 2007/2008/2009. LNCS, vol. 5705, pp. 1–50. Springer, Heidelberg (2009)

15. Kanovich, M., Kirigin, T.B., Nigam, V., Scedrov, A., Talcott, C.: Discrete vs. dense times in the analysis of cyber-physical security protocols. In: Focardi, R., Myers, A. (eds.) POST 2015. LNCS, vol. 9036, pp. 259–279. Springer, Heidelberg (2015)

16. Kanovich, M.I., Kirigin, T.B., Nigam, V., Scedrov, A., Talcott, C.L.: Towards timed models for cyber-physical security protocols. Available in Nigam's homepage (2014)

17. Lowe, G.: Breaking and fixing the Needham-Schroeder public-key protocol using FDR. In: Margaria, T., Steffen, B. (eds.) TACAS 1996. LNCS, vol. 1055, pp. 147–166. Springer, Heidelberg (1996)

18. Malladi, S., Bruhadeshwar, B., Kothapalli, K.: Automatic analysis of distance bounding protocols. CoRR, abs/1003.5383 (2010)

19. Meadows, C., Poovendran, R., Pavlovic, D., Chang, L., Syverson, P.F.: Distance bounding protocols, authentication logic analysis and collusion attacks. In: Poovendran, R., Roy, S., Wang, C. (eds.) Secure Localization and Time Synchronization for Wireless Sensor and Ad Hoc Networks. Advances in Information Security, vol. 30, pp. 279–298. Springer, New York (2007)

20. Millen, J.K.: A necessarily parallel attack. In: Workshop on Formal Methods and Security Protocols (1999)

21. Nigam, V., Talcott, C., Urquiza, A.A.: Towards the automated verification of cyber-physical security protocols, Bounding the number of timed intruders. CoRR, abs/1605.08563 (2016)

22. Nigam, V., Talcott, C., Urquiza, A.A.: https://github.com/SRI-CSL/VCPublic. git (2016)

23. Pavlovic, D., Meadows, C.: Deriving ephemeral authentication using channel axioms. In: Security Protocols, Workshop, pp. 240–261 (2009)

24. Santiago, S., Escobar, S., Meadows, C.A., Meseguer, J.: Effective sequential protocol composition in Maude-NPA. CoRR, abs/1603.00087 (2016)
25. Thayer, F.J., Herzog, J.C., Guttman, J.D.: Strand spaces: proving security protocols correct. J. Comput. Secur. **7**(1), 191–230 (1999)

Safeguarding Structural Controllability in Cyber-Physical Control Systems

Cristina Alcaraz[✉] and Javier Lopez

Department of Computer Science, University of Malaga,
Campus de Teatinos s/n, 29071 Malaga, Spain
{alcaraz,jlm}@lcc.uma.es

Abstract. Automatic restoration of control wireless networks based on dynamic cyber-physical systems has become a hot topic in recent years, since most of their elements tend to have serious vulnerabilities that may be exploited by attackers. In fact, any exploitation may rapidly extend to the entire control network due to its problem of non-locality, where control properties of a system and its *structural controllability* can disintegrate over time. Unfortunately, automated self-healing processes may become costly procedures in which the reliability of the strategies and the time-critical of any recovery of the control can become key factors to re-establish the control properties in due time. This operational need is precisely the aim of this paper, in which four *reachability-based recovery* strategies from a theoretical point of view are proposed so as to find the best option/s in terms of optimization, robustness and complexity. To do this, new definitions related to structural controllability in relation to the type of distribution of the network and its control load capacity are given in this paper, resulting in an interesting practical study.

Keywords: Structural controllability · Control systems · Cyber-physical systems · Restoration · Self-healing

1 Introduction

As control systems continue to grow both in size and complexity [1] by adapting the new cyber-physical systems (CPSs) for the automation of operations, the protection of such networks from external or unforeseen forces becomes an essential issue. Namely, operational efficiency has an important role to play in the monitoring and management of many of our critical infrastructures (CIs) such as industrial automation applications or power grids. Unfortunately such functionality today is highly susceptible to threats and/or changes. Many of these changes come from vulnerabilities or incompatibilities of the cyber-physical control elements, which tend to incorporate and connect computation elements with existing physical components [2,3] through multiple types of communication technologies like, for example, wireless [4]. However, the exploitation of these vulnerabilities is also intertwined with the nature of the threats, which may

© Springer International Publishing Switzerland 2016
I. Askoxylakis et al. (Eds.): ESORICS 2016, Part II, LNCS 9879, pp. 471–489, 2016.
DOI: 10.1007/978-3-319-45741-3_24

sometimes cause a minor or even, major impact on the performance, security and safety of the underlying infrastructures [5].

In these circumstances it is easy to understand that preventive measures related to resilience and fault-tolerance have to be properly addressed in critical environments [6], regardless of the fact that some measures can become quite difficult to implement [7,8]. For example, the mere act of helping restore large and complex control distributions to their natural state in time, might provoke serious complexities that may subsequently affect the overall performance of the system. So it becomes crucial to research how to design optimized recovery mechanisms that can 'automatically' establish connectivity of control from anywhere and at any time. However, the implementation of large control networks can also be quite costly from a research point of view. This means that the modeling and simulation of the challenge (taking into account the network topology and the nature of its distribution), have to be done through *graph theory*.

Within the literature some authors have already tried to address restoration topics through graph theory. For example, Nakayama *et al.* base their research on tie-set notions, associated with graphical-theoretical tree structures so as to implement a ring-based solution against link failures [9]. A variant of this solution is the rapid spanning tree protocol (RSTP), an evolution of the spanning tree protocol (STP), to manage traffic loops and broadcast congestion in mesh topologies [10]. Tree-like structures are also applied to group and activate, through a nice tree decomposition, backup instances of driver nodes in charge of delivering control signals to the rest of nodes of the network [11], or to build edge-redundant networks to activate backup links [11–13]. Médard *et al.* in [12] support their approach on two trees so that the removing of any resource leaves each destination connected to one of the directed trees; whereas Quattrociocchi *et al.* in [13] center their study on modeling a routing protocol based on the maximum spanning tree and on the online activation of fixed redundant links. Likewise, Wang *et al.* apply the redundancy concept in the controllability field by applying transitivity of control routes, taking into account a control robustness index with reliance on the number of driver nodes [14]. Wang *et al.* in [15] and Ding *et al.* in [16] also propose optimizing the robustness of controllability by adding a minimum number of strategic links within the network.

However, more research on dynamic preservation of control structural properties for critical environments is still required since most of these approaches are composed of static structures for the recovery, and/or are centered on the restoration of general-purpose networks. Indeed, the vast majority of the critical control systems follow particular topological structures of the type power-law $y \propto x^\alpha$, [17], whose structures tend to produce small sub-networks similar to current control substations. Moreover, this research shortfall also forces us to think that it is necessary to propose specific restoration strategies that help the underlying system (i) maintain its control properties at all times and (ii) survive in crisis situations. So, four restoration strategies for *structural controllability* are presented in this paper. They are based on the automatic activation of redundant edges so as to exhibit the optimal scenario, and on the dynamic reachability of nodes through relink techniques together with a further set of parameters described throughout this paper. To complement this study, analyses on which of these approaches are the most suitable for critical contexts with heavy dependence on CPSs are also presented, thereby complying with optimization aspects.

In order to clarify some theoretical concepts introduced in the following sections and their relationships with respect to the main goals and contributions of this paper, topics related to structural controllability and power dominance are described here. The concept of structural controllability was introduced by Lin in 1974 [18] so as to model the controllability and its control capacity through graphical representations, where the control is generally associated with a subset of nodes with the maximum capacity of dominance. This subset of nodes, also known as driver nodes and denoted here as N_D, has to be selected according to a predefined method based on the type of context and the general structure of its networks; in our case, attending to power-law control networks. A suitable method is, for example, the POWER DOMINATING SET (PDS) problem defined by Haynes *et al.* in [19] rather than the traditional maximum matching method. Through PDS it is possible to obtain the set of N_D in charge of managing the control of the entire or a supart of the network, whose concept was originally designed as a variant of the well-studied problem of domination and motivated in part by the structure of electric power networks and their monitoring networks [19]. Therefore these two concepts, structural controllability and PDS, constitute the theoretical basis of our research, and the goal now is to provide a redundancy-based restoration layer with the possibility of reaching linear complexities in optimal restoration scenarios.

The remainder of this paper is structured as follows: Sect. 2 outlines preliminary concepts concerning dynamic control networks, in addition to detailing the initial assumptions and the threat model. Section 3 presents the four recovery strategies together with their redundancy principles, which are theoretically developed and discussed in Sect. 4. Finally, Sect. 5 concludes the paper and presents future work.

2   Dynamic Control: Preliminary

Let a directed weighted $\mathcal{G}_w(V, E)$ graph represent the construction of a control system composed of V control nodes corresponding to cyber-physical elements, and E communication links. Through $\mathcal{G}_w(V, E)$, it is possible to characterize dynamic control networks capable of accepting the existence of *loops* and *weighted edges* to plot control loads related to controllability. In the real-world, many of these variables traverse specific links that help control devices (or driver nodes), such as remote terminal units or gateways in charge of managing sensor or actuator states, to be reached. This in turn recreates a decentralized system where the main control exclusively depends on a dominant subset of elemental nodes and links. Concretely, these links contain the maximum capacity to conduct the main traffic[1] between two points, also defined here as the *control load capacity* (CLC).

To represent this capacity it is necessary to work with a weighted decentralized system containing information about the edge betweeness centrality (EBC) [5]. EBC is an indicator that corresponds to the sum of the fraction of the shortest paths that pass through a given edge, such that, edges with the highest centrality participate in a large number of shortest paths. The result is a weighted matrix related to $\mathscr{G}_w(V, E)$ whose weights are computed as follows:

$$E_{BC}(e) = \sum_{s,t \in V} \frac{\delta(s,t \mid e)}{\delta(s,t)} \tag{1}$$

where $\delta(s,t)$ denotes the number of shortest (s,t)-paths and $\delta(s,t \mid e)$ the number of paths passing through the edge e. Hence, CLC in control theory corresponds to the traditional weighted interaction strength matrix $\mathbf{A}$ [5] supported by the linear time-invariant (LTI) dynamical system introduced by Kalman in [20]:

$$\dot{x}(t) = \mathbf{A}x(t) + \mathbf{B}u(t), \qquad x(t_0) = x_0 \tag{2}$$

From this equation, $\dot{x}(t)$ comprises the vector $(x_1(t), \ldots, x_n(t))^T$ containing the current state of n nodes at time t; $\mathbf{A}$, the network topology with the interaction strength $(n \times n)$; and $\mathbf{B}$ an *input* matrix $(n \times m, m \leq n)$ holding the set of driver nodes, controlled by a time-dependent *input vector* $u(t) = (u_1(t), \ldots, u_m(t))$ responsible for forcing the system to reach a desired configuration state. The system in Eq. 2 is *controllable* if and only if rank$[\mathbf{B}, \mathbf{AB}, \mathbf{A}^2\mathbf{B}, \ldots, \mathbf{A}^{n-1}\mathbf{B}] = n$ (Kalman's rank criterion). However, whilst the computation of this equation seems to be straightforward, for large and heterogeneous networks like CPSs embedded in control systems where the number of nodes grows exponentially (e.g., sensors, actuators, smart meters, remote units or hand-led interfaces), it becomes extremely expensive and problematic. So the problem associated with maintaining weights in $\mathbf{A}$ and the exponential growth of nodes leads to a new control theory known as structural controllability [18], which is described in more detail below.

2.1   Structural Controllability and its CLC

Structural controllability refers to a graphical-theoretical interpretation of the style $\mathscr{G}_w(\mathbf{A}, \mathbf{B}) = (V, E)$ where $\mathbf{A}$ and $\mathbf{B}$ contain non-zero weights, such that $V = V_\mathbf{A} \cup V_\mathbf{B}$ comprises the set of vertices and $E = E_\mathbf{A} \cup E_\mathbf{B}$ the set of edges. In this representation, $V_\mathbf{B}$, analogous to $u(t)$ in Eq. 2, embraces all those nodes with the capacity to inject control signals throughout the entire network, which is composed of different control load capacities, $l_{i,j}$, for each edge $e_{i,j}$ in E (i.e., $l_{i,j}$ is part of the concept of CLC).

---

[1] Note that we do not consider in this study either the type of traffic or the content of messages, only those concepts that help define mechanisms of restoration.

As indicated above, there are two main approaches that obtain the minimum, but not the only set of driver nodes associated with V_B: the maximum matching and the PDS. In graph theory, the former aims to obtain N_D (unmatched nodes) by identifying those nodes that do not share input vertices [21]. Although the concept has been proven multiple times [5,14,15], we primarily focus on the PDS problem by offering the necessary means to exemplify, through graph theory, structures similar to real power grids and their monitoring systems, and whose concept corresponds to an extension of the DOMINATING SET (DS). From the original formulation of the PDS, given by Haynes *et al.* in [19], the problem was later simplified into two fundamental observation rules by Kneis *et al.* in [22]. These two rules, substantiated on the 'dominance' concept, are as follows:

OR1 *A vertex in N_D observes itself and all its neighbors*, complying with DS.
OR2 *If an observed vertex v of degree $d^+ \geq 2$ is adjacent to $d-1$ observed vertices, the remaining un-observed vertex becomes observed as well.* This also implies that **OR1** $\subseteq$ **OR2** given that the subset of nodes that comply with **OR1** becomes part of the set of nodes that complies with **OR2**.

Both rules and their susceptibility to threats have also been analyzed in recent publications [1,23], and for different types of graphs under the restriction of degree and specific graph structures (circle, planar, split, and partial k-tree graphs as well as grid and blocks). However, and as previously mentioned, we are not interested in applying the concept of PDS in general distributions. Rather our interest lies in applying the PDS problem in power-law networks since most of the topologies of CIs follow similar structures to $y \propto x^\alpha$ [17].

The pursuit of all these methods and their application as a whole results in a complex control structure supported by E_{BC} to establish control loads. The handling of anomalous loads is done through the definition given by Nie *et al.* in [5], in which the capacity of a node, $l_{i,j}$, is always bounded to *"the maximum load that the edge, $e_{i,j}$, can operate"*. In normal situations, $l_{i,j}$, has to be related to the initial capacity, denoted here as $L^0_{i,j}$ $(n \times n)$, and depending on the type of activity within the network and the overloading of the links, the initial state of the network may significantly vary over time. Therefore, the load capacity has to be managed each time by verifying that $l_{i,j}$ does not exceed *maximum CLC* [5]:

$$H_{i,j} = (1 + \alpha) \times L^0_{i,j} \tag{3}$$

of size $n \times n$, where α comprises a tolerance indicator with value $\alpha > 0$ and $L^{t=0}_{i,j} \leq L^{t>0}_{i,j} \leq H_{i,j}$. Under these conditions, any topological impact may force the system not only to redistribute its control loads, but also its shortest paths, thereby affecting, sooner or later, the network diameter. This could also trigger a *cascading effect* when the permitted thresholds, retained in $H_{i,j}$, are clearly surpassed. Given this and its importance for control contexts, the following section provides a set of initial assumptions required for dynamic control restoration together with the threat model.

2.2   Initial Assumptions and the Adversarial Model

Apart from cyclicity between nodes, the existence of $l_{i,j}$ in each $e_{i,j}$ and $l_{i,j} \leq H_{i,j}$, the two observation rules (**OR1, OR2**) introduced in the previous section must not be violated at any moment. In relation to this, the number of driver nodes should not increase significantly during the life cycle of the network, maintaining, as much as possible, its spatial complexity. This also means that no protection approach should hamper the control processes and the responsiveness degree of the system, while still providing the necessary means to self-heal the control in time, with a reasonable computational cost.

For the analysis, the adversary model follows a weak model in which adversaries are able to access the general structure of the graph, its topology and the location of the current driver nodes, despite the random nature of N_D. We also assume that their mobility within the network and their performances remain reduced to a random subset of nodes, such that $\delta \leq \frac{|V|}{2}$, where their actions are focused on availability and integrity of assets, composed of random (launch random actions on an arbitrary set of nodes) or targeted attacks (specific actions on particular nodes).

Within the random category, four attacks are highlighted:

– **[R1]** isolate a selective set of nodes by removing all their edges (e.g., jamming);
– **[R2]** arbitrarily choose some nodes and remove a few, but not all, of their edges (e.g., obstacles, congestion);
– **[R3]** randomly insert a limited set of nodes whose links are causally created; and
– **[R4]** arbitrarily add new edges within the network.

In real scenarios, there also exists the possibility of finding mobile automation contexts in which nodes do not necessarily have to be compromised. They may, for example, (i) leave a network by themselves (henceforth denoted as **[Lv]**) by simply removing all their connections, or (ii) join the network, by themselves, by increasing the number of members and links. To tackle these two new situations, we consider the definition of **[R1]** but without applying preventive measures to avoid the re-connection, and **[R3]** to engage the new joining.

With respect to the targeted class, four kinds of attacks can be identified:

– **[T1]** isolate those nodes with the highest degree, i.e., the hubs;
– **[T2]** isolate the node with the highest strength within the network, equivalent to the node with the highest CLC $- max(\sum_{i \in E}(E_{EB}(v, i) + E_{EB}(i, v)))$; and
– **[T3]** remove an arbitrary set of δ links with the highest peaks of centrality.

3   Four Reachability-Based Strategies

Reachability of assets and their maintenance can be achieved through four types of reconnection approaches, the strategies of which aim to find redundant pathways, for each disconnected vertex $v_i \in V$. For the relink, the approaches force the system to first identify those most prominent $\{n_{d_1}, \ldots, n_{d_n}\} \in N_D$, such that:

STG1 Select one "brother" n_d located in the surrounding area, such that $(n_d, v_i) \notin E$, but there exists a common node $v_j \in E$ where $(v_j, n_d) \in E$ and $(v_j, v_i) \in E$, and it may serve as a possible candidate to establish a new redundant relationship $(n_d, v_i) \in E$. Note that the selection of prominent nodes is restricted to the redundancy principles described below.

STG2 Choose one "father" n_d with the capacity for reconnecting $(n_d, v_i) \in E$.

STG3 Take one "grandfather" n_d located to 2-hops with the ability to relink v_i.

STG4 Select one "remote" n_d situated at n-hops with the possibility of relinking v_i in crisis situation.

If we observe Fig. 1, it is possible to see that the first three scenarios (**STG**x ($x = \{1, 2, 3\}$)) establish a protection on a local level, whereas **STG4** addresses the protection for a remote level in which the selection of outstanding driver nodes relies on the minimum diameter, using for this the traditional *breadth-first search* (BFS) method. Each link represents the control load capacity between two points, $l_{i,j}$; and when a node has different paths (e.g., x, y, z) to transmit a critical message until reaching j, then it is necessary to choose the path with the highest load capacity: $max\{l_{i,x}, l_{i,y}, l_{i,z}\}$. For the mapping of secondary routes, it is also necessary to redesign the **OR1** and **OR2** algorithms specified in [1], not only to select the best driver candidates but also to introduce, from the initial stage (the commissioning phase), redundant pathways. This modification involves:

- expanding the *DS* selection scheme (**OR1** included in [1]) by adding redundant links; and

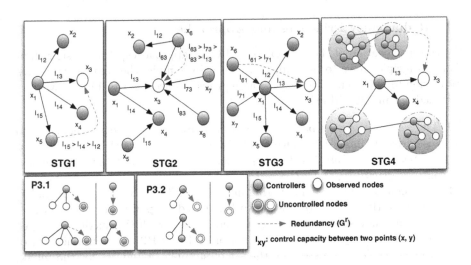

Fig. 1. Restoration scenarios **STG**x ($x = \{1, 2, 3, 4\}$) and redundancy principles **P3.1** and **P3.2**

– extending the approach **OR2** from [1] so as to avoid breaking the second observation rule due to the existence of new links.

Given this, the next section specifies the new approaches of **OR1** and **OR2**, since they constitute the foundation of the new restoration strategies.

Algorithm 3.1. REDUNDANCY PRINCIPLES $(\mathscr{G}_w(V, E), \mathscr{G}_w^r(V, E'), DS, N_D^{P1}, v_i)$

---

output (N_D^{P2})
local $candidate, O_nd, DS_{nd}, N_D^{P2} \leftarrow \varnothing;$

while $(N_D^{P1} \neq \varnothing)$

$\quad\quad\begin{cases} candidate \leftarrow Randomly\ select\ one\ candidate \in N_D^{P1}; \\ DS_{nd} \leftarrow (\text{CHILDREN}^a(candidate, \mathscr{G}_w(V, E)) \cap DS; \\ O_{nd} \leftarrow (\text{CHILDREN}(candidate, \mathscr{G}_w(V, E)) \setminus DS_{nd}; \\ \text{comment: } \textbf{P3.1}\ (\text{see Section 3.1}); \end{cases}$

do $\quad\begin{cases} \textbf{if } (v_i \in DS)\ \textbf{and}\ restriction\ given\ in\ \textbf{P3.1} \\ \quad\textbf{then } \begin{cases} DS_{nd} \leftarrow (\text{CHILDREN}(\mathscr{G}_w^r(V, E), candidate)) \cap DS; \\ O_{nd} \leftarrow (\text{CHILDREN}(\mathscr{G}_w^r(V, E), candidate)) \setminus DS_{nd}; \\ \textbf{if } restriction\ given\ in\ \textbf{P3.1} \\ \quad\textbf{then } \{N_D^{P2} \leftarrow N_D^{P2} \cup candidate; \end{cases} \\ \text{comment: } \textbf{P3.2}\ (\text{see Section 3.1}); \\ \textbf{else } \begin{cases} \textbf{if } (v_i \notin DS)\ \textbf{and}\ restriction\ given\ in\ \textbf{P3.2} \\ \quad\textbf{then } \begin{cases} DS_{nd} \leftarrow (\text{CHILDREN}(\mathscr{G}_w^r(V, E), candidate)) \cap DS; \\ O_{nd} \leftarrow (\text{CHILDREN}(\mathscr{G}_w^r(V, E), candidate)) \setminus DS_{nd}; \\ \textbf{if } restriction\ given\ in\ \textbf{P3.1} \\ \quad\textbf{then } \{N_D^{P2} \leftarrow N_D^{P2} \cup candidate; \end{cases} \end{cases} \\ N_D^{P1} \leftarrow N_D^{P1} \setminus candidate; \end{cases}$

return (N_D^{P2})

---

a CHILDREN: returns the children of a given node v_i, such that $\forall v_j \in V, (v_i, v_j) \in E$.

3.1 Redundancy Principles and Approaches

For the specification of the new **OR1** and **OR2** approaches, three basic redundancy principles have to be defined, which help remodel the control structures in relation to redundant pathways. These principles are described as follows and sketched out in Algorithm 3.1:

P1 The selection of new paths is conditioned by all those edges belonging to those driver nodes $\in DS$ (since **OR1** $\subseteq$ **OR2** – cf. Sect. 2.1) with the highest edge betweeness centrality $E_{BC}(v)$ – i.e., those nodes containing the highest control capacity $l_{i,j}$.

P2 Any relink should be done, taking into account the properties of the underlying network. As the control network is based on power law distributions, the redundancy should be subject to those nodes with the maximum degree in order to comply with the power notion. **P1** and **P2** result in a new set of driver nodes N_D^{P1} representing the set of suitable candidates for the relink, capable of ensuring the greatest control transference in perturbed scenarios.

P3 The selection of driver nodes has to be limited to **OR2** (cf. Sect. 2.1), in which the type of node to be relinked has to be considered (see Fig. 1):

P3.1 If the unobserved node is part of DS, then it is necessary to find a driver node $n_d \in N_D^{P1}$ that does not infringe **OR2**, such that: ($|O_{nd}| \geq 2$ and $|DS_{nd}| \geq 0$) or ($|O_{nd}| = 0$ and $|DS_{nd}| \geq 0$), where O_{nd} denotes the set of observed nodes controlled by an n_d, and DS_{nd} represents the set of driver nodes controlled by an $n_d \in DS$.

P3.2 If the unobserved node is not part of DS, then it is necessary to find a driver node $n_d \in N_D^{P1}$ such that ($|O_{nd}| \geq 1$ and $|DS_{nd}| \geq 0$) or ($|O_{nd}| = 0$ and $|DS_{nd}| = 0$).

The result of **P3** is a new set of driver nodes N_D^{P2}, such that $N_D^{P1} \subseteq N_D^{P2}$. To satisfy these principles and to obtain the maximum CLC (i.e., $H_{i,j}$ in Eq. 3) that $\mathscr{G}_w$ can support at any given moment, a second graph $\mathscr{G}_w^r(V, E')$ of the same size as $\mathscr{G}_w$ is required. $\mathscr{G}_w^r$ comprises all the redundant links from the commissioning phase such that $|E'| \geq |E|$, and through this graph it is possible to map the entire system and compute $H_{i,j}$, whereas $L_{i,j}^{t \geq 0}$ provides information of $\mathscr{G}_w$ at each state $t \geq 0$. The update of $\mathscr{G}_w^r$ will depend on the optimization of the restoration mechanisms, which are described in detail below.

3.2 OR1 and OR2 Based on Redundant Pathways

The reconstruction of **OR1** and **OR2** presupposes considering the four restoration strategies laid out in Sect. 3 and the redundancy principles specified in Sect. 3.1, leading to Algorithms 3.2 and 3.4. Both extend the rudimentary versions defined in [1] so as to include redundant links in E' from the commissioning phase, and protect the most critical control pathways over time. The identification of these routes is done through Algorithm 3.3, which is responsible for extracting the most prominent driver nodes from N_D^{P1} and N_D^{P2}.

Algorithm 3.2. OR1_{v2} [a] $(\mathscr{G}_w(V, E), \mathscr{G}_w^r(V, E'), STG, Lv$ [b]$)$

---

local $DS, relink \leftarrow \varnothing, N \leftarrow V$;
output $(\mathscr{G}_w(V, E), \mathscr{G}_w^r(V, E), DS)$

$DS \leftarrow \text{OR1}(\mathscr{G}_w(V, E));$ **comment:** Procedure **OR1** included in [1];
while $(N \neq \varnothing)$

$\text{do} \begin{cases} \textit{Randomly choose one } v_i \in N; \\ \{\mathscr{G}_w(V, E), \mathscr{G}_w^r(V, E')\} \leftarrow \text{STGs } (STG, \mathscr{G}_w(V, E), \mathscr{G}_w^r(V, E'), \\ DS, v_i, Lv); \\ \textbf{if } v_i \in DS \\ \quad \textbf{then } N \leftarrow N \setminus \{v_i\}; \\ \textbf{else} \begin{cases} \textbf{if } relink \neq \varnothing \\ \quad \textbf{then } DS \leftarrow DS \cup v_i; \\ \quad \textbf{else } N \leftarrow N \setminus \{v_i\}; \end{cases} \end{cases}$

return $(\mathscr{G}_w(V, E), \mathscr{G}_w^r(V, E), DS)$

---

[a] OR1_{v2}, a redesigned version from the original OR1 specified in [1].

[b] Lv represents the set of those nodes that leave (by themselves) a determined network.

Algorithm 3.3. STGs $(STG, \mathscr{G}_w(V, E), \mathscr{G}_w^r(V, E'), DS, v_i, relink, Lv)$

---

output $(\mathscr{G}_w(V, E), \mathscr{G}_w^r(V, E'))$
local $fathers, brothers, grandfathers, O_{nd}, DS_{nd}, N_D^{P1}, N_D^{P2}, candidate;$

comment: P1 and **P2** (see Section 3.1);
if $STG \neq$ **STG4**

$\textbf{then} \left\{ \textbf{do} \left\{ \begin{array}{l} fathers \leftarrow ((\text{FATHERS}(\mathscr{G}_w(V, E), v_i) \setminus Lv) \cap DS \\ \textbf{while } (fathers \neq \varnothing) \\ \left\lceil \textbf{if } STG \neq \textbf{STG2} \right. \\ \quad \textbf{then} \left\{ \begin{array}{l} \textbf{if } STG = \textbf{STG1} \\ \quad \textbf{then} \begin{cases} brothers \leftarrow ((\text{CHILDREN}(\mathscr{G}_w(V, E), \\ \quad fathers(i)) \setminus Lv) \cap DS \\ N_D^{P1} \leftarrow N_D^{P1} \cup \text{MAXI EBC}^{*a}(\mathscr{G}_w(V, E), \\ \quad fathers(i), brothers); \end{cases} \\ \quad \textbf{else} \begin{cases} grandfathers \leftarrow ((\text{FATHER}^b(\mathscr{G}_w(V, E), \\ \quad fathers(i)) \setminus Lv) \cap DS \\ N_D^{P1} \leftarrow N_D^{P1} \cup \text{MAX EBC}^*(\mathscr{G}_w(V, E), \\ \quad fathers(i), grandfathers); \end{cases} \\ fathers \leftarrow fathers \setminus fathers(i); \end{array} \right. \\ \textbf{if } STG = \textbf{STG2} \\ \quad \textbf{then } N_D^{P1} \leftarrow \text{MAX EBC}^*(\mathscr{G}_w(V, E), fathers, v_i); \end{array} \right. \right.$
$\quad \textbf{else } \{N_D^{P1} \leftarrow \text{MINIMUM DIAMETER WITH EBC}^{*c}(\mathscr{G}_w(V, E), DS);$
comment: P3 (see Section 3.1);
$N_D^{P2} \leftarrow \text{REDUNDANCY PRINCIPLES}(\mathscr{G}_w(V, E), \mathscr{G}_w^r(V, E'), DS, N_D^{P1}, v_i);$
if $N_D^{P2} \neq \varnothing$
$\quad \textbf{then} \begin{cases} candidate \leftarrow Randomly\ select\ one\ candidate \in N_D^{P2}; \\ \mathscr{G}_w^r(V, E) \leftarrow \text{UPDATE NETW}^d(\mathscr{G}_w^r(V, E'), candidate, v_i); \end{cases}$
return $(\mathscr{G}_w(V, E), \mathscr{G}_w^r(V, E'))$

---

[a] MAX EBC*: returns N_D with the maximum E_{BC} included in $\mathscr{G}_w(V, E)$ **(P1)** and the maximum dominance **(P2)**.

[b] FATHERS: set of fathers nodes f_j that comprises a determined node v_i / $\forall f_j$ $(f_j, v_i) \in E$.

[c] MINIMUM DIAMETER WITH EBC*: returns N_D with the min. diameter and the max. EBC*.

[d] UPDATE NETW: relinks the candidate to node v_i / (candidate, node) $\in E$.

The second observation rule **OR2** in Algorithm 3.4 has to verify until twice the fulfillment of the dominance. The first round is applied in $\mathscr{G}_w$ and the second one in its extended version $\mathscr{G}_w^r$. In this way, any activation of redundant pathways in $\mathscr{G}_w$ at a state t, will prevent the appearance of one or several n_d of degree $d^+ \geq 2$ adjacent to $d-1$ observed vertices, which could infringe **OR2** (cf. Sect. 2.1). This double exploration is crucial to providing a complete enough control structure at each life state t of the system.

As part of this analysis, we provide a brief study of computational complexity, evaluating the upper bound for the new versions of **OR1** and **OR2** together with their restoration scenarios **STGx** ($x = \{1, 2, 3, 4\}$). For simplicity, we denote $\mid V \mid = n$, $\mid E \mid = e$, $\mid \textbf{N}_D \mid = nd$, where we assume that $nd \approx n$ in the worst case. Concretely, Algorithms 3.2 and 3.4 are quite dependent on the complexity of the traditional algorithms **OR1** and **OR2**, also analyzed in [11] with an overhead of $O(n^2)$, and on the complexity of Algorithm 3.3 and the type of restoration scenario. For **STGx** ($x = \{1, 2, 3\}$), Algorithm 3.3 has to explore, for each node $\in V$, the existence of a father, brother or grandfather driver with the highest CLC in $\mathscr{G}_w$ **(P1)** and the highest degree **(P2)**; both entailing a cost of $O(n + e + n + e) = O(e + n) = O(n)$ – the process of verifying **P1** and**P2** is encompassed in a unique function denoted here as EBC*. **STG4** becomes analogous to **STG**x ($x = \{1, 2, 3\}$) but with the difference that it needs to explore those $n_d \in N_D$ with the minimum diameter. As we apply the BFS method (well-known to be $O(n+e)$) to obtain the minimal N_D with the minimum diameter in $\mathscr{G}_w$, the cost of obtaining N_D^{P1}, considering EBC* in this first stage, is $O(n + e + e + n) = O(n)$.

Algorithm 3.4. OR2$_{v2}$ ^{a} $(\mathscr{G}_w(V, E), \mathscr{G}_w^r(V, E'), STG, Lv)$

---

local DS, N_D
output $(\mathscr{G}_w(V, E), \mathscr{G}_w^r(V, E), N_D)$

$\{\mathscr{G}_w(V, E), \mathscr{G}_w^r(V, E'), DS\} \leftarrow$ **OR1**$(\mathscr{G}_w(V, E), \mathscr{G}_w^r(V, E'), STG, Lv)$;
comment: Procedure **OR2** included in [1] with an overhead of $O(n^2)$ [11];

$N_D \leftarrow$ **OR2**$(\mathscr{G}_w(V, E), DS)$;
comment: In the following, the algorithm considers $\mathscr{G}_w^r(V, E')$ and **OR2**;

$i \leftarrow 1$;
while $i \leq | N_D |$
do $\begin{cases} Choose\ vertex\ w \in N_D\ with\ degree\ d \geq 2; \\ N \leftarrow \text{CHILDREN}(\mathscr{G}_w^r(V, E), w); \\ \textbf{if}\ (d - 1\ vertices\ \in N\ \textbf{and}\ (\exists\ a\ vertex\ w_1 \in U\ where\ w_1 \in N) \\ \quad \textbf{then}\ \begin{cases} N_D \leftarrow N_D \cup \{w_1\}; U \leftarrow U \setminus \{w_1\}; i \leftarrow 1; \\ \textbf{else}\ i \leftarrow i + 1; \end{cases} \end{cases}$
return $(\mathscr{G}_w(V, E), \mathscr{G}_w^r(V, E'), N_D)$

---

^{a} OR1$_{v2}$, a redesigned version from the original OR2 specified in [1].

Once N_D^{P1} has been computed, Algorithm 3.1 has to be executed to extract N_D^{P2}. Assuming that $| N_D^{P1} | \approx nd$ in the worst case, the verification of **OR2** in $\mathscr{G}_w$ and $\mathscr{G}_w^r$ for each descendant driver node in N_D^{P1} becomes $O(n^2)$. Note that the costs implicit in *assignment* and *if* instructions tend to $O(1)$, and the same occurs with the updating of $\mathscr{G}_w$ and $\mathscr{G}_w^r$ since the insertion of new links does not involve an additional cost to Algorithm 3.3. As a result, the cost of computing Algorithm 3.3 becomes $O(n + n^2) = O(n^2)$. With all this information in hand, the cost of computing the new version of **OR1** is of at least $O(n \times n^2) = O(n^3)$ in the commissioning phase; whereas the new version **OR2** implies $O(n^3)$ by computing Algorithm 3.2, $O(kn^2)$ (**OR2** of [1]) and $O(kn^2)$ by processing the second rule in $\mathscr{G}_w^r$) (also stated in [11]), resulting in an overhead of $O(n^3 + kn^2 + kn^2) = O(n^3)$. Unfortunately, the computational cost of the new dominance versions (**OR1**, **OR2**) is higher than the traditional versions, but this increase is only applicable in the initial phase, when the redundant control is being configured. With respect to spatial complexities, it is worth noting that the spatial cost is heavily dependent on each **STG**x ($x = \{1, 2, 3, 4\}$). In the case of **STG2**, the cost may be similar to the cost required by the traditional **OR1** and **OR2** since the redundancy is exclusively concentrated on the father drivers. In contrast, the spatial cost in **STG**x ($x = \{1, 3, 4\}$) may significantly rise depending on the selection of external driver nodes (brothers, grandfathers or remote nodes) and its penalty in **OR2** (see Algorithm 3.4).

4 Analysis and Discussion

Let Lv be the set of leaving nodes belonging to **[Lv]** (cf. Sect. 2.1); A_e the set of active links in $\mathscr{G}_w(V, E)$ such that $A_e \subseteq E'$; and F_{nd} the set of father drivers that observe a determined vertex in V. Algorithm 4.1 combines the functional features of the four restoration strategies described in the previous section.

Algorithm 4.1. Dynamic Recovery $(\mathscr{G}_w(V, E), \mathscr{G}_w^r(V, E'), N_D, Lv, A_e,$
$STG)$

---

local $v_i, F_{nd}, found, candidates, fathers$
output $(\mathscr{G}_w(V, E), \mathscr{G}_w^r(V, E'), N_D)$

for $v_i \leftarrow 1$ to $|V|$
do
$\quad F_{nd} \leftarrow$ Fathers$(\mathscr{G}_w(V, E), v_i) \cap N_D$;
$\quad$if $(F_{nd} = \varnothing)$ and $(v_i \notin Lv)$
$\qquad$comment: Optimal solution;

$\qquad found \leftarrow$ false ;
$\qquad fathers \leftarrow$ Fathers$(\mathscr{G}_w^r(V, E), v_i) \cap N_D$;
$\qquad$while $fathers \neq \varnothing)$ and not $found$
$\qquad\quad$do $\{$ Randomly choose a vertex candidate $\in fathers$;
$\qquad\qquad\quad$ if $(candidate \notin A_e)$
$\qquad\qquad\qquad$ then $found \leftarrow$ true ;
$\qquad$if $found$
then
$\qquad\quad$then $\{\mathscr{G}_w^r(V, E) \leftarrow$ Update Netw $(\mathscr{G}_w^r(V, E), candidate, v_i)$;
$\qquad\qquad\quad A_e \leftarrow A_e \cup \{candidate\}$;
$\qquad$comment: Sub-optimal sol. - **STG4** in Algorithm 3.3;

$\qquad\quad N_D^{P1} \leftarrow$ Min. Diameter with EBC*$(\mathscr{G}_w(V, E), N_D \setminus Lv)$;
$\qquad\quad N_D^{P2} \leftarrow$ Red. Principles$(\mathscr{G}_w(V, E), \mathscr{G}_w^r(V, E'), DS, N_D^{P1}, v_i)$;
$\qquad\quad$if $N_D^{P2} \neq \varnothing$
$\qquad$else $\{$
$\qquad\qquad\quad$then $\{$ candidate $\leftarrow$ Randomly select one $n_d \in N_D^{P2}$;
$\qquad\qquad\qquad \mathscr{G}_w^r(V, E) \leftarrow$ Update Netw $(\mathscr{G}_w^r(V, E),$
$\qquad\qquad\qquad candidate, v_i)$;
$\qquad\qquad\qquad \mathscr{G}_w(V, E) \leftarrow$ New EBC$^a(\mathscr{G}_w(V, E))$;
$\qquad\qquad\qquad A_e \leftarrow A_e \cup \{candidate\}; found \leftarrow$ true ;
$\qquad\quad$if not $found$
$\qquad\qquad$then $\{$ comment: Non-optimal solution;
$\qquad\qquad\qquad N_D \leftarrow N_D \cup \{v_i\}$;
$\qquad\qquad$else $\{\{\mathscr{G}_w(V, E), \mathscr{G}_w^r(V, E')\} \leftarrow$ STGs $(STG, \mathscr{G}_w(V, E),$
$\qquad\qquad\qquad \mathscr{G}_w^r(V, E'), N_D, v_i, Lv)$;
return $(\mathscr{G}_w(V, E), \mathscr{G}_w^r(V, E'), N_D)$

---

^{a} New EBC: re-compute Eq. 1 to update the control load capacities retained in $\mathscr{G}_w(V, E)$.

The heuristic (i.e., Algorithm 4.1) is based on three main restoration blocks, categorized according to:

- *Optimal* solution, capable of reestablishing the control by automatically activating an $e_{i,j} \in E'$. As the link activation is practically straightforward, the computational cost in performing this part of the algorithm is $O(n)$.
- *Sub-optimal* solution, with the ability to: (i) dynamically find an $n_d \in N_D$ with the minimum diameter in $\mathscr{G}_w$ and the maximum EBC* that ensures coverage of the unobserved node; and (ii) search a redundant pathway (dependent

on **STG**x ($x = \{1, 2, 3, 4\}$)) that guarantees a secondary way to the unobserved node in the near future. This dynamic search of prominent driver nodes follows the principles **P1**, **P2** and **P3**. If none of these principles are achieved, then Algorithm 4.1 looks at the possibility of offering at least a non-optimal solution. The computational overhead, at this point, becomes important since it not only contemplates the charge required in EBC* ($O(n)$) but also the charge necessary to verify **P3.1** or **P3.2** (Algorithm 3.1, $O(n^2)$), the upgrading of loads in $\mathscr{G}_w(V, E)$ after reparation with a further cost of $O(n^2 log(n))$ [24], and the updating of $\mathscr{G}_w(V, E)$ and A_e. That is, $O(n + n^2 + n^2 log(n)) = O(n^2 log(n))$.

- *Non-optimal* solution, to the contrary, deals with transforming any unobserved node to an observed node by including it as part of the N_D. In this way, the node is able to observe itself and comply with at least the first observation rule, **OR1**. Note that this option is also closely related to **[R3]**, when new nodes need to be joined to the network, or the previous options are not reached properly. In either of these two circumstances, the spatial complexity proportionally grows according to the number of unobserved nodes, tearing up the desirable conditions described in Sect. 2.2.

The correctness proof of the restoration problem is solved when the following requirements are satisfied: (1) the algorithm that restores, ensures controllability without violating the control structural properties (*restoration*); (2) the algorithm is able to properly finish in a finite time (*termination*); and (3) the algorithm is able to terminate and provide control at any moment (*validity*).

For the former requirement, if a node v_i is not observed by an $n_d \in N_D$ in a state t, then the control at that moment is not guaranteed. But if there exists (either at local or at remote) a redundant link in $E' \in \mathscr{G}_w^r(V, E')$ created from the commissioning phase, such that $(n_{d_2}, v_i) \in E'$ and $n_{d_2} \in N_D$, then this link is activated complying with **OR1** and **OR2** via Algorithms 3.2 and 3.4. Otherwise, Algorithm 4.1 finds an n_{d_2} with the minimum diameter and EBC* (i.e., **P1** and **P2**) such that $(n_{d_2}, v_i) \in E'$ and it ensures **OR2** (**P3**) by Algorithm 3.1, further complying with **OR1** by having found a suitable driver node n_{d_2} capable of observing itself and all its neighbors. In the case that it is unable to find an appropriate candidate, Algorithm 4.1 is forced to convert the unobserved v_i to a driver node to obey at least **OR1** such that **OR1** $\subseteq$ **OR2**. This way of modeling the network repair means that the structural controllability is maintained at all times where all the nodes are observed by one or several driver nodes $\in N_D$ or by itself if it is an n_d.

Through induction we show the termination of the algorithm, where we first define the initial and final conditions, and the base cases. The precondition adds that $\mathscr{G}_w$ is threatened by one or several (targeted or random) attacks (cf. Sect. 2.2), probably leaving some nodes in $\mathscr{G}_w$ without observation ($F_{nd} = \oslash$); whereas the post-condition certifies that the network is fully observed ($F_{nd} \neq \oslash$) where **OR1** and **OR2** are fulfilled. As for the base cases:

Case 1: $\forall$ nodes in V, $F_{nd} \neq \oslash$ after perturbation. In this case the loop of Algorithm 4.1 is completely processed where all the nodes are covered by a driver node in N_D.

Case 2: $\forall$ nodes processed in V, $\exists$ one $v_i \in V$ such that $F_{nd} = \oslash$ after perturbation. In these circumstances, three scenarios must be distinguished for v_i:

- Optimal solution: $\exists$ a father $n_d \in fathers$ such that $(n_d, v_i) \in E'$. In this case, the conditions, **P1**, **P2** and **P3** are met from the commissioning phase onward.

- Sub-optimal solution: $\mathscr{G}_w^r(V, E')$ does not cover v_i through an edge in E', so it is necessary to explore the existence of one or several candidates $\{n_{d_1}, n_{d_2}, \ldots, n_{d_n}\}$ with: (i) the minimum diameter and EBC*, and (ii) with the capability to relink v_i complying with **P3**.
  If these candidates exist, then $N_D^{P1} \neq 0$ and Algorithm 3.1 verifies the existence of an $n_d \in N_D^{P1}$ that suffices **P3.1** or **P3.2** depending on v_i. If in addition this n_d exists, then $N_D^{P2} \neq \oslash$ guaranteeing the relink. Otherwise, the algorithm enters the non-optimal solution.

- Non-optimal solution: if there is no suitable redundant link in E' or $N_D^{P2} = \oslash$, then N_D is updated by adding v_i as driver node; i.e.: $N_D \longleftarrow N_D \cup \{v_i\}$.

In the first two cases, the network is updated through a new link and in such a way that $\forall$ nodes in V, $F_{nd} \neq \oslash$, satisfying the post-condition. For the second case, N_D is actualized and **OR1** is finally met where **OR1** $\subseteq$ **OR2**.

Induction: if we assume that we are in step k ($k \geq 1$) of the loop where $\exists$ several nodes $\{v_1, v_2, \ldots, v_n\}$ in V with $F_{nd} = \oslash$, we can observe that for these nodes, three possible cases can arise as stated in Case 2. At the end of Algorithm 3.1 with $k = |V|$, the set $F_{nd} \neq \oslash$ for all the nodes in V, once again satisfies the post-condition. This also states that the latter requirement (the validity) is also satisfied since Algorithm 4.1 finishes and ensures that the two observation rules are provided at all times.

4.1   Experimental Results and Discussion

In order to show the practical validity of Algorithm 4.1 for small ($\sim$100–500 nodes), medium ($\sim$500–1000 nodes) and large ($\sim$1000–1500 nodes) networks, a case study written in Matlab is presented in this section. The experiments have been planned to perturb a random number of nodes ($\delta \leq \frac{|V|}{2}$) belonging to pure power-law distributions. Specifically, our research focuses on the Power-Law Out-Degree (PLOD) [25] with a low connectivity probability of $\alpha = 0.1$ for illustrating realistic scenarios, where we evaluate: (1) the spatial overhead invested in N_D, and (2) the effects caused after δ disturbances such as the cascading effect and the optimization of **STG**x ($x = \{1, 2, 3, 4\}$).

Figure 2 shows the spatial cost invested by the new versions **OR1** (DS) and **OR2**. To understand this, it is necessary to observe the value associated with N_D^{bef} (the state of N_D before repair) with respect to the N_D^{orig} given in [1],

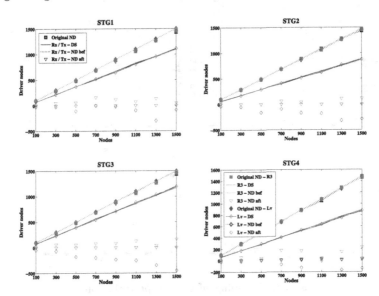

Fig. 2. Spatial complexity before and after perturbation and restoration

as well as the increase of N_D^{aft} after repair. The results indicate that the cardinality of the new N_D^{bef} regarding $|N_D^{orig}|$ is insignificant, regardless of the increase of DS for **STG**x ($x = \{1,3\}$). Namely, the difference between $|N_D^{aft}|$ and $|N_D^{bef}|$ after repair becomes relevant when the threat is related to [**Lv**] or [**R3**], since the controllability properties are infringed and the network in general needs a new assignation of driver nodes (a concept also supported by the analysis in Sect. 4).

In relation to this research, Fig. 3 illustrates the effect of the threats carried out in the respective recovery scenarios, where we observe that the joining of δ members ([**R3**]), the insertion of δ edges ([**R4**]), and the isolation of the node with the highest degree (the hubs, [**T1**]) and the highest strength ([**T2**]) are the most devastating threats. The effect becomes more notable in those scenarios in which the redundant control is located in the surrounds (**STG**x ($x = \{1,2,3\}$)), reaching a fall of 60–80% of the entire network for [**R3**] and [**R4**]. This also means that **STG4** can become more resilient to topological changes. Moreover, these results certainly ratify the findings in [13,21], where it is concluded that power-law networks are in general quite sensitive to threats related to degree sequence.

Figures 4 and 5, in contrast, simplify the simulation results with respect to the optimization of strategies **STG**x ($x = \{1,2,3,4\}$). From these two figures it is possible to appreciate how the system, depending on the degradation of the structural controllability properties after a threat, is able to drive one (non-optimal, suboptimal or optimal) strategy or another. In addition, as the number of attacks can be high in a round ($\delta \leq \frac{|V|}{2}$), the degradation of the structural controllability can drastically change. If the majority of surrounding links are

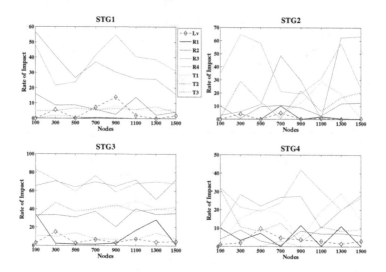

Fig. 3. Cascading effect after perturbation

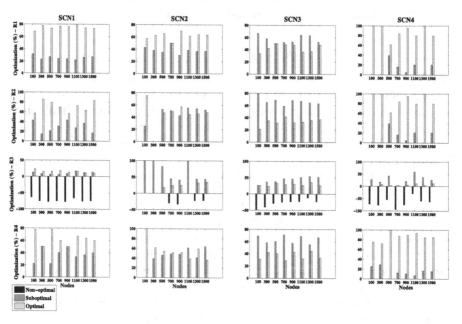

Fig. 4. Optimization of **STG**x ($x = \{1, 2, 3, 4\}$) considering random attacks

lost, the recovery should then depend on the less optimal strategies. But even so, it is also possible to note from the figures that **STG4** followed by **STG1** are the best strategies for self-healing with reduced restoration costs ($O(n)$) for the majority of simulated cases, whereas the worst scenario is **STG3** in

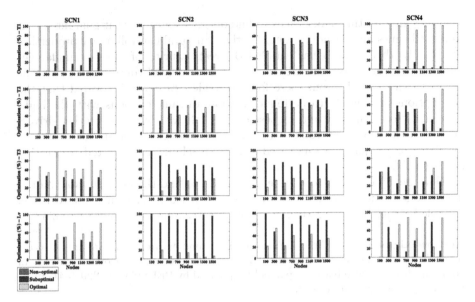

Fig. 5. Optimization of **STG**x ($x = \{1, 2, 3, 4\}$) considering targeted attacks and [**Lv**]

which the rate of optimization is mainly bounded to the sub-optimal solution. However, **STG**x ($x = \{1, 4\}$) is quite susceptible to new integrations where the non-optimal rate reaches more than 50 %, as opposed to the outcome of **STG2**. In these conditions, we determine that critical wireless environments should primarily be subject to relink procedures based on **STG4**. But even so, we also believe that the combined option **STG**x ($x = \{1, 4\}$) would be the best option to guarantee protection at both local and remote level, without discarding the possibility of adapting **STG2** to facilitate the integration of new members within a given network. However, this hypothesis requires evaluating the trade-off between safety and maintenance costs [26, 27] when one or several redundancy strategies are established for each node within the network. So this study will be part of our future work.

5   Conclusions and Future Work

Modernized control systems based on CPSs for dynamic automation of operations tend to suffer from (slight or grave) perturbations or frequent changes due to the mobile and sensitive nature of the wireless communications. In this context, the inherent non-locality problem of the control networks is a matter of utmost importance. Automated and reliable self-healing solutions have to be considered as an integral part of network designs. However, most current solutions lack efficient strategies that ensure an acceptable repair cost and responsiveness in time [11], complicating the provision of effective solutions for critical environments. For this reason, four reachability-based restoration strategies have been presented in this paper, so as to find optimal solutions that guarantee control at all times and without damaging the structural controllability properties. Specifically, this research has entailed the restructuring of the two fundamental dominance rules given in [22] to allow redundancy of control links, either at local or remote level. From these four strategies, we have discovered that the best options are mainly to be found in those distant locations with the highest control load capacity and highest degree, followed by those brother drivers located in the nearest surrounding area. Both strategies offer optimal solutions for the great majority of simulated studies, reaching the expected restoration costs $(O(n))$.

Now, our intention is to broaden the study to find the most suitable redundancy combinations considering the lessons learned here, trying not to lose a suitable balance between installation and maintenance costs, and safety [26,27].

Acknowledgment. The first author receives funding from the *Ramón y Cajal* research programme financed by the Ministerio de Economía y Competitividad. In addition, this work also has been partially supported by PERSIST (TIN2013-41739-R) financed by the same Ministerio.

References

1. Alcaraz, C., Miciolino, E.E., Wolthusen, S.: Structural controllability of networks for non-interactive adversarial vertex removal. In: Luiijf, E., Hartel, P. (eds.) CRITIS 2013. LNCS, vol. 8328, pp. 120–132. Springer, Heidelberg (2013)
2. Alcaraz, C., Zeadally, S.: Critical control system protection in the 21st century: threats and solutions. IEEE Comput. **46**, 74–83 (2013)
3. Pasqualetti, F., Dorfler, F., Bullo, F.: Attack detection and identification in cyber-physical systems. IEEE Trans. Autom. Control **58**(11), 2715–2729 (2013)
4. Sridhar, S., Hahn, A., Govindarasu, M.: Cyber-physical system security for the electric power grid. Proc. IEEE **100**(1), 210–224 (2012)
5. Nie, S., Wang, X., Zhang, H., Li, Q., Wang, B.: Robustness of controllability for networks based on edge-attack. PLoS ONE **9**(2), 1–8 (2014)
6. Alcaraz, C., Lopez, J.: Wide-area situational awareness for critical infrastructure protection. IEEE Comput. **46**(4), 30–37 (2013)
7. Sanjay, B., Sanjeev, S., Ishita, T.: A detailed review of fault-tolerance techniques in distributed system. Int. J. Internet Distrib. Comput. Syst. **1**(1), 33–39 (2012)
8. Treaster, M.: A survey of fault-tolerance and fault-recovery techniques in parallel systems. ACM Computing Research Repository, CoRR 501002, pp. 1–11 (2005)
9. Nakayama, K., Shinomiya, N., Watanabe, H.: An autonomous distributed control method for link failure based on tie-set graph theory. IEEE Trans. Circuits Syst. I Regul. Pap. **59**(11), 2727–2737 (2012)
10. Marchese, M., Mongelli, M.: Simple protocol enhancements of rapid spanning tree protocol over ring topologies. Comput. Netw. **56**(4), 1131–1151 (2012)
11. Alcaraz, C., Wolthusen, S.: Recovery of structural controllability for control systems. In: Butts, J., Shenoi, S. (eds.) Critical Infrastructure Protection. IFIP AICT, vol. 441, pp. 47–63. Springer, Heidelberg (2014)
12. Médard, M., Finn, S.G., Barry, R.A.: Redundant trees for preplanned recovery in arbitrary vertex-redundant or edge-redundant graphs. IEEE/ACM Trans. Netw. **7**(5), 641–652 (1999)

13. Quattrociocchi, W., Caldarelli, G., Scala, A.: Self-healing networks: redundancy and structure. PLoS ONE **9**(2), e87986 (2014)
14. Wang, B., Gao, L., Gao, Y., Deng, Y.: Maintain the structural controllability under malicious attacks on directed networks. EPL (Europhys. Lett.) **101**(5), 58003 (2013)
15. Wang, W.-X., Ni, X., Lai, Y.-C., Celso, G.: Optimizing controllability of complex networks by minimum structural perturbations. Phys. Rev. E **85**, 026115 (2012)
16. Ding, J., Lu, Y.-Z., Chu, J.: Recovering the controllability of complex networks. In: 9th World Congress The International Federation of Automatic Control (IFAC), pp. 10894–10901 (2014)
17. Pagani, G.A., Aiello, M.: The power grid as a complex network: a survey. Physica A **392**(11), 2688–2700 (2013)
18. Lin, C.-T.: Structural controllability. IEEE Trans. Autom. Control **19**(3), 201–208 (1974)
19. Haynes, T., Hedetniemi, S.M., Hedetniemi, S.T., Henning, M.A.: Domination in graphs applied to electric power networks. SIAM J. Discrete Math. **15**(4), 519–529 (2002)
20. Kalman, R.E.: Mathematical description of linear dynamical systems. J. Soc. Ind. Appl. Math. Control Ser. A **1**, 152–192 (1963)
21. Liu, Y., Slotine, J.-J., Barabási, A.-L.: Controllability of complex networks. Nature **473**, 167–173 (2011)
22. Kneis, J., Mölle, D., Richter, S.: Parameterized power domination complexity. Inf. Process. Lett. **98**(4), 145–149 (2006)
23. Guo, J., Niedermeier, R., Raible, D.: Improved algorithms and complexity results for power domination in graphs. Algorithmica **52**(2), 177–202 (2008)
24. Robinson, E.: Complex graph algorithms. In: Graph Algorithm in the Language of Linear Algebra, Chap. 6, pp. 59–85. SIAM (2011)
25. Palmer, C., Steffan, J.: Generating network topologies that obey power laws. In: Global Telecommunications Conference, GLOBECOM 2000, vol. 1, pp. 434–438 (2000)
26. Alcaraz, C., Zeadally, S.: Critical infrastructure protection: requirements and challenges for the 21st century. Int. J. Crit. Infrastruct. Protection (IJCIP) **8**, 53–66 (2015)
27. Alcaraz, C., Lopez, J.: Analysis of requirements for critical control systems. Int. J. Crit. Infrastruct. Protection (IJCIP) **5**(137–145), 2012 (2012)

Attacks

The Beauty or The Beast? Attacking Rate Limits of the Xen Hypervisor

Johanna Ullrich[✉] and Edgar Weippl

SBA Research, Vienna, Austria
{JUllrich,EWeippl}@sba-research.org

Abstract. Rate limits, i.e., throttling network bandwidth, are considered to be means of protection; and guarantee fair bandwidth distribution among virtual machines that reside on the same *Xen* hypervisor. In the absence of rate limits, a single virtual machine would be able to (unintentionally or maliciously) exhaust all resources, and cause a denial-of-service for its neighbors.

In this paper, we show that rate limits snap back and become attack vectors themselves. Our analysis highlights that *Xen*'s rate limiting throttles only outbound traffic, and is further prone to burst transmissions making virtual machines that are rate limited vulnerable to externally-launched attacks. In particular, we propose two attacks: Our side channel allows to infer all configuration parameters that are related to rate limiting functionality; while our denial-of-service attack causes up to 88.3 % packet drops, or up to 13.8 s of packet delay.

1 Introduction

Cloud computing is here to stay; and has become an all-embracing solution for numerous challenges in information technology: Defending against cyber attacks, countries back up their "digital monuments" in clouds [1]; clouds support censorship evasion [2]; clouds accommodate power-restrained mobile devices with computing [3]; automotive clouds connect a vehicle's sensors and actuators with other vehicles or external control entities for safer and more comfortable driving [4]; and also healthcare applications are hosted in the cloud [5]. Its total market is worth more than 100 billion US dollars [6]; and recently, even the conservative banking sector is jumping on the bandwagon [7,8].

A key technology in cloud computing is virtualization as provided by the *Xen* hypervisor [9] that enables multiple virtual instances to share a physical server [10]; but at the same time, resource sharing provides opportunity for adversarial virtual machines to launch attacks against its neighbors. For example, side channels exploiting shared hard disks [11] or network capabilities [12] allow to check for co-residency of two virtual machines; data might be leaked from one virtual instance to another via covert channels exploiting CPU load [13] or cache misses [14]; an instance might free up resources for itself when tricking the neighbor into another resource's limit [15]; and shared network interfaces allow to infer a neighbor's networking behavior [16,17]. Mitigation follows two principal

© Springer International Publishing Switzerland 2016
I. Askoxylakis et al. (Eds.): ESORICS 2016, Part II, LNCS 9879, pp. 493–511, 2016.
DOI: 10.1007/978-3-319-45741-3_25

directions: On the one hand, dedicated hardware eliminates mutual dependencies and thus the threat of co-residency, but contradicts cloud computing's premise of resource sharing. On the other hand, isolation reduces the impact of a virtual machine's behavior on its neighbors despite resource sharing. With respect to networking, rate limits are introduced as means of isolation in order to throttle a virtual machine's maximum amount of traffic per time interval. This approach is considered to guarantee fair distribution of bandwidth among virtual instances and mitigates denial-of-service of neighbors in case a single instance (accidentally or maliciously) requests all bandwidth. The *Xen* hypervisor provides such a rate limiting functionality [18].

The introduction of a countermeasure should raise the question whether it does not form a new attack vector itself. Throttling network traffic however seems to be such a universal approach that its implementation into the *Xen* hypervisor is barely scrutinized. Solely, [19] investigates rate limiting's quality of isolation; [20] analyzes rate limiting with respect to bandwidth utilization. The paper at hand overcomes this gap and examines the impact of *Xen*'s rate limiting functionality on security. Our analysis reveals that rate limits might protect from co-residency threats, but allow (yet unknown) attacks that are directed against the rate limited virtual machine itself. In particular, we propose a side channel and a denial-of-service attack. The side channel reveals *Xen*'s configuration parameters that are related to the rate limiting functionality, while the denial-of-service attack causes up to 88.3 % of packet loss or up to 13.8s of delay in benign connections. Our results emphasize that *Xen*'s rate limiting snaps back, and revision should be considered.

The remainder of the paper is structured as follows: Sect. 2 provides details on *Xen*'s networking in general and its rate limit functionality in particular, whereas Sect. 3 analyzes this mechanism with respect to security. Section 4 presents our side channel revealing configuration parameters and respective measurement results; Sect. 5 presents three flavors of our denial-of-service attacks and discusses them with respect to their impact on benign connections. It is followed by related work in Sect. 6. Overall results are discussed Sect. 7. Section 8 concludes.

2   Background

This section first provides a general overview on Xen's networking architecture. Its rate limiting functionality however throttles only a virtual machine's outbound traffic; thus, we describe a virtual machine's outbound traffic path in a second step. Finally, we focus on the credit-based algorithm eventually throttling a machine's traffic.

General Networking Architecture: The Xen hypervisor follows the approach of paravirtualization; it provides device abstractions to its virtual machines – in terms of Xen virtual machines are called *domains* – so that all sensitive instruction like those for device I/O are redirected over the hypervisor. Paravirtualizing hypervisors do not need specific hardware capabilities; but require modifications

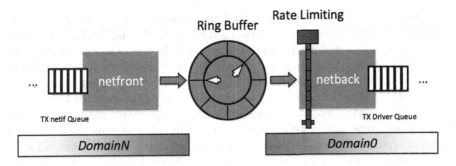

Fig. 1. Xen's outbound traffic path

of the operating systems running in the virtual machines [9]. With respect to Xen, the hypervisor in the narrower sense is responsible for CPU scheduling, memory management and interrupt forwarding. The remainder tasks are delegated to *domain0* – a privileged virtual machine with the right to access physical I/O devices and to interact with other (non-privileged) domains. Abstract networking devices consist of two distinct parts: (1) *netfront* devices are provided to non-privileged domains replacing classic network interfaces; (2) its counterpart *netback* resides in *domain0*, multiplexes packets from multiple *netfront* devices and forwards them to the physical network interface card as in standard Linux operating systems [19,21].

Outbound Traffic Path: Packets originating from non-privileged virtual machines (*domainN*) have to pass *domain0* on their way to the physical network; the respective handover path is depicted in Fig. 1. Therefore, Xen provides descriptor rings, i.e., ring buffers, as central points of communication. The ring does not directly contain data; this data is rather stored in buffers that are indirectly referenced via the ring descriptors. Packets pass this path in the following manner. First, packets are enqueued in the virtual machine's network interface TX queue. Then, netfront forwards these packets from the TX queue to the ring buffer, and notifies netback. Netback – being within *domain0* and thus having access to physical drivers – hands them over to the physical network interface card's driver queue and removes them from the ring buffer. Beyond, netback is the place of rate limiting. If a respective virtual machine exceeds its assigned bandwidth quota, netback refrains from taking further packets from the ring buffer and discontinues forwarding for some time. As items are not removed from the ring anymore, the buffer becomes full. As soon as a virtual machine's netfront detects this, it signalizes this fact to the upper networking layers by means of a flag. Packets pending in the ring buffer have to wait for further processing until the next bandwidth quota is received.

Rate Limiting: Rate limiting throttles a virtual machine's bandwidth – however, it confines outbound traffic only – and is configured by means of two parameters [18]. The parameter *rate* defines the respective bandwidth limit in MB/s, while *time window* defines the replenish interval of the rate limiting algorithm. Its default value is 50 ms. Looking behind the scenes, the algorithm is credit-based[1]. With every packet forwarded from the ring buffer, the respective packet size is subtracted from the remaining credit. In case of lacking credits, two alternatives remain: (1) immediate replenishment of credits and continuation of transmission, or (2) discontinuation and waiting for replenishment of credits at a later point in time. Immediate replenishment is only possible if the last replenishment happened at least the time defined by the parameter *time window* ago. In the alternative case, a timer is set to the time of next replenishment, and packet transmission is rescheduled as soon as credits are regained. According to the parameters *rate r* and *time window t*, the credit bytes per interval c calculates to $c = r \cdot t$, and the total amount of available credit is limited to this number. This implies that accumulating unused credits for later transmission is impossible. There is a single exception if c remains below 128 kB, i.e., rates of less than 2.5 MB/s at the default time window, as then jumbo packets might seize up the interface. In such a case, credit accumulation up to 128 kB is allowed.

3 Security Analysis

In this section, we perform a manual security analysis of the Xen's rate limit functionality. This analysis reveals distinct characteristics that may serve as attack surface; we describe these characteristics, highlight their implication on security and discuss them with respect to cloud computing. Finally, we provide a high-level overview of our attacks that exploit the found characteristics.

(1) Unidirectional Bandwidth Limits: Xen allows to restrict a virtual machine's outbound bandwidth, but inbound remains unlimited without any chance for change. In consequence, the transmission paths are asymmetric. In principle, asymmetry in bandwidth is a known phenomena, e.g., *Asymmetric digital subscriber line* (ADSL), but Xen's asymmetry appears to contradict its application in cloud services as highlighted by the following analogy. ADSL's asymmetry is concordant with its application in consumer broad-band connections. Consumers typically request more downstream than upstream bandwidth, and thus favoring the first direction (at the expense of the latter) is reasonable. Cloud instances predominantly require higher outbound than inbound bandwidth, e.g., when used as application, web or streaming servers. Xen however performs precisely the opposite and limit's the more utilized outbound direction[2].

Bandwidth is not only unequally distributed, but also differs by magnitudes as in consequence inbound traffic is only limited by the underlying hardware. Outbound bandwidth in public clouds starts from 12.5 MB/s for small cloud instances; assuming a 10-Gigabit physical network in the data center, maximum inbound outperforms maximum outbound bandwidth by a factor up to 100.

---

[1] Kernel 3.16.0, /net/xen-netback/netback.c.

[2] Cloud providers like Rackspace (see https://www.rackspace.com/cloud/servers) or Amazon EC2 (see https://aws.amazon.com/en/ec2/pricing/) typically do not even charge inbound traffic.

(2) Susceptibility to Burst Transmissions: Xen's algorithm is prone to burst transmissions. A virtual machine transmitting high amounts of traffic shoots its wad at the begin of a time slot, and has to wait for new credits then. At the time of replenishment, further packets might already wait for transmission and cause another burst consuming all credits. In consequence, packets experience latencies when pausing for the next slot; however, these latencies are only experienced by outbound traffic due to the unidirectional bandwidth limitation. In case the outbound traffic exceeds the configured bandwidth for a longer period of time, packets might even be dropped: Packets remain in the ring buffer as a result of credit shortage. As a consequence, netfront cannot forward packets to the ring descriptor anymore and causes a growing backlog in the virtual machines TX queue. If the number of packets becomes larger than this queue's size, packets are dropped. By default, time window is set to 50 ms; according to the documentation *"a good balance between latency and throughput and in most cases will not require changing"* [18]. This implies that the credit-based algorithm is rather coarse-grained as time slots in the virtual machine's traffic are of the same order of magnitude as round trip times, and the bursts are externally observable.

Attacks Exploiting Rate Limiting: We found two attacks exploiting these characteristics – a side channel revealing Xen configuration parameters that are related to its rate limit functionality, and a denial-of-service attack causing significant delays and packets drops in benign connections to third parties. We provide a high-level overview on these attacks, before addressing them in more detail in Sects. 4 and 5.

1. **Side Channel:** Pushing a virtual machine into its outbound traffic limits, leads to burst transmissions that can be observed. By measuring time between two bursts, it is possible to infer the parameter *time window* t; by summing up the bytes of a burst, an adversary is able to infer the amount of credits c per interval, and subsequently also calculate the *rate* r.
2. **Denial-of-Service Attack:** An adversary might force a virtual machine to spend all its credits; in consequence, a virtual machine has not enough credits left in order to serve benign requests. Respective responses are significantly delayed as they have to wait for credit replenishment, or dropped due to full buffers. This denial-of-service attack is insofar remarkably as it exhausts outbound bandwidth in comparison to ordinary bandwidth exhaustion attacks exhausting inbound bandwidth.

4   Side Channel

If a virtual machine requires more bandwidth than assigned, its traffic becomes bursty due to Xen's credit-based rate limit algorithm. An adversary might exploit this behavior to determine a virtual machine's configuration parameters *time window* t and *rate* r by means of the following side channel. The adversary

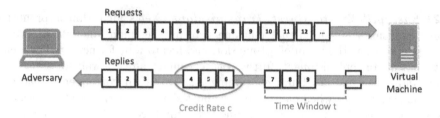

Fig. 2. Side channel attack scenario

sends a high number of legitimate requests to the virtual machine. The latter replies according to the chosen protocol; however, the sum of all replies exceeds the assigned bandwidth and outbound traffic becomes bursty as depicted in Fig. 2. The time interval between two bursts is equivalent to the configured *time window t*, as the virtual machine receives credits for further transmission immediately after the timer expires. Summing up the size of all packets within a burst allows to determine the victim's *credit rate c*. Finally, the adversary is able to calculate the victim's assigned bandwidth (parameter *rate*) $r = c/t$. The side channel is advantageously protocol independent. The only stringent objective is that the virtual machine reliably replies; thus, a wide variety of protocols are worth considering, e.g., ICMP, DNS, etc. The more outbound traffic, the better; the larger the amplification between outbound and inbound traffic, the better; both facilitate to reach the assigned rate limit for outbound traffic.

We evaluated this side channel in our experiments[3]. The virtual machine was limited to 5 MB/s at the default time window of 50 ms. Checking the configuration with *iperf*[4], we measured 4.7 MB/s from the virtual machine to the adversary (throttled outbound traffic), and 117.3 MB/s in the other direction (unthrottled inbound traffic). Attacking the virtual machine, the adversary sent 16 ICMP Echo Request of 1458 bytes, waiting a millisecond before sending the next 16 ICMP Echo Requests causing up to 22.2 MB/s of inbound traffic for the virtual machine. In total, the attack runs for 1000 of such cycles sending in total 16000 Echo Requests. Repeating this attack ten times, we inferred the configuration parameter from the measurements according to the following approaches:

– **Time Window:** The begin of a time window is indicated by a packet following a (larger than usual) pause. Thus, we extracted all packets following a pause of at least 5 ms, and measured the time window between these first packets of subsequent bursts. Rounding off to whole milliseconds, we took the most frequent candidate of all test runs.

---

[3] For our experiments, we use Xen version 4.4.1 (on Debian 8.2) on an Intel i5-750. On the hypervisor, two virtual machines run Debian 7.9; each guest is pinned to a separate CPU, *domain0* runs on the remaining two CPUs. The two virtual instances were rate limited and bridged via the hypervisor. The adversary ran Debian 8.2 on an Lenovo X200 laptop. The hypervisor and the adversary's laptop were connected via a 1 Gbit/s network switch.

[4] https://iperf.fr/.

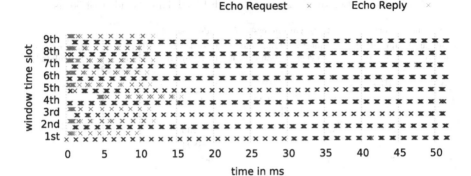

Fig. 3. Side channel measurement results using ICMP

- **Credit Rate:** In the previous step, the first packets of bursts have already been determined; the credit rate is now calculated by summing up the size of all packets from this first packet of the burst to the last one. The last packet of the burst is the one right before the first packet of the next burst. Again, the most frequent candidate is taken from all candidates.

This way, we inferred a *time window* t of 52 ms, and a *credit rate* c of 249,318 bytes; the resulting bandwidth r is thus 4.8 MB/s. Figure 3 depicts a network trace of the side channel from the adversary's point of view; for reasons of simplicity, the graph is already slotted in time intervals of 52 ms. While the adversary sends requests in regular intervals, the virtual machines replies predominantly at the begin of a time slot. Afterwards, it remains silent due to lacking further credits. One can also see in the figure that the number of sent replies is high at the begin of a time slot; this is an indicator that all waiting replies are sent at once immediately after credit replenishment. The side channel was measured with different configurations of the virtual machine. First, we altered the bandwidth keeping the time window at the default configuration of 50 ms; results are provided in Table 1. Then, we modified the time window at a fixed bandwidth of 5 MB/s; results are provided in Table 2. The first line of Table 1, and the second line of Table 2 represents the results of the measurement that has been described above.

Our results show that the measured time window is slightly longer than the configured time window. Taking a look into Xen's source code, the time window is strictly speaking the time period for the timer; this additional time of mostly 2 ms might be caused by credit replenishment, packet forwarding, etc. that is necessary after the timer expires. Actual bandwidth appears to be below the configuration parameter; however, our side channel appears to reflect *iperf* measurements well. Measurements for 30 MB/s at 50 ms of Table 1 shows an increased time window; however, evaluation shows two almost equally frequent candidates – 56 ms and 48 ms – both equally distant from the expected 52 ms. Similarly, measurements for 5 MB/s at 20 ms (peaks at 16 ms and 24 ms) as well

Table 1. Bandwidth Measurements with Fixed Time Window of 50 ms

Xen configuration		Attack parameters		Side channel		
Configured bandwidth	iperf (Outbound)	Requests per cycle	Inbound bandwidth	Credit rate c (Measured)	Time window t (Measured)	Rate r (Calculated)
MB/s	MB/s		MB/s	B	ms	MB/s
5	4.7	16	23.3	249318	52	4.8
10	9.4	32	46.7	498636	52	9.6
20	18.9	32	46.7	998730	52	19.2
30	27.8	48	70.0	1498824	56	26.8
40	37.0	60	87.5	1998918	52	38.4

Table 2. Time Window Measurements with Fixed Bandwidth of 5 MB/s

Xen configuration		Attack parameters		Side channel		
Configured time window	iperf (Outbound)	Requests per cycle	Inbound bandwidth	Credit rate c (Measured)	Time window t (Measured)	Rate r (Calculated)
ms	MB/s		MB/s	B	ms	MB/s
70	4.8	16	23.3	349920	72	4.8
50	4.7	16	23.3	249318	52	4.8
30	4.6	16	23.3	148716	32	4.6
20	4.9	16	23.3	100602	24	4.2
10	4.1	16	23.3	49572	8	6.2

as 5 MB/s at 10 ms (peaks at 8 ms and 16 ms) of Table 2 show two such peaks. For the latter however the lower peaks has slightly more candidates. The reason for less quality of the latter two results might be the rather small *time window t*. Pauses before first packets of a burst become shorter with decreasing time windows; thus, our algorithm looking for 5 ms pauses might struggle to detect begin packets at such low time windows accurately. This might be overcome by looking for shorter pauses.

5   Denial-of-Service

Traffic exceeding the rate limit has to wait for a free time slot in the future; beyond, if the backlog of waiting packets becomes too much, buffers become full and packets are dropped. Deliberately filling the buffers, an adversary might exploit this behavior in order to perform a denial-of-service attack causing significant packet delays or even drops of benign traffic.

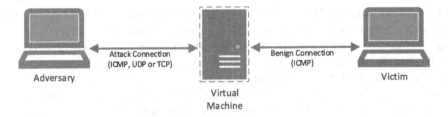

Fig. 4. Denial-of-service attack scenario

For evaluation, we extended the measurement setup by an additional host representing the victim[5] as depicted in Fig. 4. The victim had a benign connection to the virtual machine; we decided to probe the virtual machine with ICMP Echo Requests at an interval of 10 ms. In total, these requests (and potentially received replies) require a maximum bandwidth of 19.6 kB/s which is negligible in comparison to the attack traffic. For the adversary, we tested three alternatives for causing the backlog – by means of ICMP Echo Requests, UDP-based traffic amplification and TCP acceleration as described in the following paragraphs.

ICMP Echo Requests: As with the side channel, the adversary sends multiple Echo Requests and pauses afterwards for 1 ms repeating both actions in a loop. Echo Requests however bear the drawback of being non-amplifying, i.e., the virtual machine's (maximum) outbound traffic is of the same amount as the inbound traffic from the adversary.

UDP-Based Traffic Amplification: A virtual machine might host a service that answers with replies that exceed the requests in size and thus amplifies inbound traffic. An adversary sending numerous such requests is able to trigger more outbound traffic than with ICMP. Susceptible protocols are predominantly UDP-based, e.g., NTP, DNS, SSDP or BitTorrent, and bandwidth amplification factors reach up to 4670.0 [22][6]. For our evaluation, we scripted a simple UDP server that responded with a bandwidth amplification factor of 100. The server ran on the virtual machine; our adversary sent respective UDP requests in the same manner as the ICMP Requests – sending a certain number of UDP requests before pausing for 1 ms repeating both actions in a loop.

---

[5] The victim ran Ubuntu 14.4 LTS on a Lenovo X60 laptop. The virtual machines were rate limited to 5 MB/s at the default window time of 50 ms.

[6] [22] investigated amplifying protocols with respect to reflective denial-of-service. Such attacks require source address spoofing in order to redirect replies to the victim – a prerequisite that is not necessary for our denial-of-service attack. This implies that (1) there are even more protocols than described in this paper that are susceptible to our attack and (2) ingress filtering does not prevent our attack.

TCP Acceleration: TCP connections, e.g., when serving a HTTP request, are frequently asymmetric with respect to transmitted payload; a server is sending amounts of data while the client almost exclusively acknowledges receipt with a couple of bytes. TCP is a reliable protocol, adjust its speed according to given network capabilities and thus does not automatically lead into a denial-of-service attack; but an adversary might intentionally accelerate a TCP connection by means of optimistic acknowledgments [23]. Such optimistic acknowledgments are sent prior the receipt of the respective segment, lead the server to believe in higher available bandwidth and make the server send at a higher speed than normally. For our evaluation, we installed an Apache[7] server on the virtual machine providing a 100 MB file for download. For the adversary, we re-implemented this attack with respect to current TCP implementations as congestion control has significantly changed over the last decade and ran the attack when downloading the previously mentioned file.

Results for ICMP and UDP-Based Attacks: Results for the ICMP-based attacks are found in Table 3; results for the UDP-based attack with traffic amplification in Table 4[8]. Inbound bandwidth refers to the traffic that is sent from the adversary to the virtual machine, while the potential outbound bandwidth refers to the bandwidth that would be caused in the reverse direction in the absence of rate limits. The remaining three columns show the average delay of replies to the victim's Echo Requests, the observed maximum delay as well as the relative amount of dropped replies. In both tables, the first line represents the latter values in the absence of an attack for reasons of comparison.

The results highlight the following: (1) All attacks significantly increase the delays by two orders of magnitudes. (2) The higher the ICMP bandwidth, the more packet drops. The average delay however appears to decrease at higher attack bandwidths; and might be an artifact of increased drop rates as less replies were received by the victim and were taken into account for average delay calculation. The maximum delay of *icmp16* might be higher than the remainder for the same reason. (3) UDP-based attacks do not cause any packets drops; average and maximum delay are higher than in the ICMP-based attacks, and appear to be independent of the attack bandwidth. The reason might be that the virtual machine favors ICMP traffic over UDP, and thus drops attack traffic rather than the victim's. However, amplification allows the adversary to reduce the amount of sent traffic in order to gain the same potential outbound bandwidth at the virtual machine; for example, attack *icmp16* leads to the same potential outbound bandwidth as *udp4*. Figure 5 depicts a test run of the ICMP-based attack, Fig. 6 of the UDP-based attack. Both figures show the increased round-trip times of the victim; the first figure further shows packet drops.

Results for TCP-Based Attack: The results of our TCP attack are found in Table 5. In comparison to ICMP- or UDP-based attacks, delays are much higher.

---

[7] https://httpd.apache.org/.

[8] As in the side channel, the results are based on ten test runs each.

Table 3. Denial-of-service attack with ICMP echo requests

ID	Adversary			Victim		
	Requests per cycle	Inbound bandwidth	Potential outbound band-width	Average delay	Maximum delay	Dropped replies
		MB/s	MB/s	ms	ms	%
noattack				0.221	0.491	0
icmp16	16	23.3	23.3	14.3	65.7	67.5
icmp32	32	46.7	46.7	23.6	49.3	85.6
icmp48	48	70.0	70.0	21.8	51.5	83.6
icmp60	60	87.5	87.5	16.7	52.8	88.3

Table 4. Denial-of-service attack with UDP-based traffic amplification

ID	Adversary			Victim		
	Requests per cycle	Inbound bandwidth	Potential outbound band-width	Average delay	Maximum delay	Dropped replies
		MB/s	MB/s	ms	ms	%
noattack				0.221	0.491	0
udp4	4	0.2	23.2	23.0	53.3	0
udp8	8	0.5	46.4	22.9	53.5	0
udp12	12	0.7	69.6	22.7	53.4	0
udp15	15	0.9	87.0	23.6	53.7	0

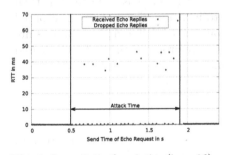

Fig. 5. Impact on the victim (icmp16)

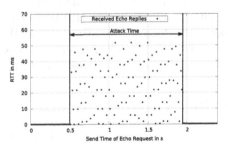

Fig. 6. Impact on the victim (udp4)

The average delay is 1625.8 ms, the maximum delay even 13791 ms, i.e., almost 14s. Packet drops are however below the ICMP-based attack: 33.2 %.

Figure 7 shows the sequence numbers of sent TCP acknowledgments and received TCP payload from the adversary's perspective. While the first increases

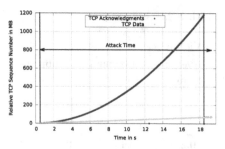
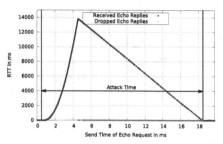

Fig. 7. Relative sequence numbers (tcp)

Fig. 8. Impact on the victim (tcp)

Table 5. Denial-of-service attack with TCP

ID	Adversary			Victim		
	Requests per cycle	Inbound bandwidth	Potential outbound bandwidth	Average delay	Maximum delay	Dropped replies
		MB/s	MB/s	ms	ms	%
noattack				0.221	0.491	0
tcp		0.01	65.8	1625.8	13791.6	33.2

exponentially to maximize the virtual machine's congestion window, the latter increases only in a linear manner. This linear increase is caused by the rate limit of 5 MB/s, and provides a first evidence that the virtual machine operates at its networking limits. Moreover, enlarged sections of this figure would clearly depict the bursty transmission and the underlying 50 ms intervals (but were omitted due to space constraints). Figure 8 shows the attack's impact on the victim's round-trip times: Right at the start, round-trip times are as expected less than a millisecond; then, round-trip times start to increase. The maximum recorded delay is 13,791.6 ms. In a third phase, the buffers are full and Echo Replies are dropped at a large-scale. As numerous packets are dropped, the buffer is released and round-trip times decrease back to normal.

6   Related Work

Our research is based on three foundations. First, we summarize related work on Xen's network rate limits in general. Then, we discuss known side channels as well as denial-of-service attacks in cloud computing; by now, no approach exploited a hypervisor's rate limit functionality.

Rate Limit Functionality: Related work on Xen's rate limit for networking is rather scarce, and must not be mistaken for (the more frequently discussed) rate limits with respect to CPU scheduling, e.g., [24–26].

Adamczyk et al. [19] investigate rate limits' quality of isolation, i.e., protection against malicious neighbor virtual machines. The authors infer that performance isolation is moderate in case of applied rate limits. Nevertheless, the authors propose round robin for more fairness among co-resident tenants. Mei et al. [20] analyze rate limits with respect to bandwidth utilization, and considers Xen's rate limiting to be *static* as a virtual machine cannot provide spare tokens to neighbors. The authors propose a new bandwidth allocation algorithm that dynamically provides bandwidth based on current and past bandwidth consumption. While this algorithm definitely increases bandwidth allocation, an actively networking virtual machine would increase its assigned bandwidth with time, and lead to starving neighbors. Summarizing, the impact of rate limits on security of the throttled virtual machine themselves has never been raised.

Side Channels: Numerous side channels in cloud computing exploit network timing. Bowers et al. [27] measure file access times to extract data's hardware spread in order to check a cloud provider's hardware redundancy, Benson et al. [28] measure file access times in order to determine the geographic location of files. Multiple side channels check for co-residency, i.e., whether two virtual machines reside on the same physical server: Ristenpart et al. [11] exploit round-trip times, Bates et al. [16,17] packet arrival rates and Herzberg et al. [12] latencies when downloading a file.

Beyond, side channels enabling to spy on neighbors are available. Kadloor et al. [29,30] measure round-trip times in order to infer a neighbor's traffic amount. Bates et al. [16,17] observe a distinct TCP throughput ratio therefore. Herzberg et al. [12] propose address deanonmyization, i.e., discovery of private IP addresses, by exploiting again latencies in file downloads, and further infer the number of intermediate hops by finding the minimal TTL in order to gain a successful connection.

Denial-of-Service Attacks: Alarifi et al. [31] present an attack that forces a virtual instance to migrate to another physical host. This behavior is triggered by co-resident virtual machines riding a workload wave. Ficco et al. [32] propose an attack that stealthily increases resource use (by means of XML-based denial-of-service attack) in order to remain undetected. The authors aim to harm the victim economically as the increased resource use is charged by the provider. Liu et al. [33] discuss under-provision of network links in data centers, e.g., that uplink capacity remains typically smaller than the total subnet bandwidth. An adversary might spot such bottlenecks in clouds and strike it in a concerted action of multiple virtual machines.

Shea et al. [34,35] analyze the impact of TCP SYN floods on virtualized environments and infer that virtualization overhead negatively impacts a host's vulnerability to denial-of-service attacks. Ferriman et al. [36] analyze the impact of denial-of-service attacks on Google App Engine and saw an increased rendering time for a test application. Chonka et al. [37] perform XML-based attacks in order to evaluate their service-oriented traceback architecture. Beyond, distributed denial-of-service attacks striking software-defined networks are known [38].

Our attacks differ with respect to three attributes from the available approaches: (1) Our side channel does not only reveal a victim's network bandwidth, but rather extracts the (more accurate) parameters *credit rate* and *time window* of the applied rate limiting. (2) Both – our side channels as well as the denial-of-service attack – are the very first that exploit the asymmetric behavior of Xen's rate limiting and its susceptibility to burst transmissions in order to gain information about the victim or negatively impact the latter's availability. (3) In contrast to side channels from related work measuring network bandwidth, the adversary neither has to control the measured virtual instance nor be co-resident to the victim instance; the latter holds for the denial-of-service attack, too.

7   Discussion

Throttling network bandwidth hinders a virtual machine from claiming all available resources and cutting off supply to neighbor machines. Such rate limits have always been considered as means of security against denial-of-service attacks, but not as an attack vector themselves. Notwithstanding, our work conveys by the example of the popular Xen hypervisor that (1) configuration parameters of rate limits are easily gained through a side channel and that (2) novel denial-of-service attacks exploiting (allegedly protective) rate limits are feasible. In comparison to traditional bandwidth consumption attacks, our denial-of-service attack shows a peculiarity with respect to the point of consumption. A traditional denial-of-service attack jams the virtual machine's *inbound* link, exploiting rate limiting functionality as shown in the paper at hand causes jam on the *outbound* link. In the first case, a virtual machine would not receive any further traffic and might suspect irregularities on the network. In the latter case, it would still obtain requests and would be (mostly) unaware that responses are stuck in the hypervisor. Digging its own grave, it would even answer incoming requests strengthening the attack. Xen's unilateral bandwidth limits (not throttling inbound traffic) is an additional blessing as requests from the adversary are reliably forwarded to the victim. This means that there is in principle no need for traffic amplification; but admittedly, the attack is more likely to succeed with some sort of traffic amplification, e.g., when striking over the Internet with much lower bandwidth.

Our side channel allows to infer all configuration parameters of Xen's rate limits – the rate and the window time. These parameters are sensitive insofar as they allow a more detailed look on network characteristics than conventional means of bandwidth measuring, and serve various attacks. On the one hand, this enables an adversary to plan an attack, e.g., our denial-of-service-attack, more accurately. Further, an adversary once knowing these parameters of a virtual machine would be able to glean the latter's networking behavior; but also benign customers might use the side channel to check compliance of the configuration with their service contract. On the other hand, the side channel may also serve as a way to identify the underlying hypervisor of a virtual machine as Xen. By now, however, it remains unclear whether burst transmissions are just an issue of Xen, or also applicable to other hypervisors and container solutions.

In dependence on the outcome, burst transmissions themselves would imply the use of Xen; otherwise, fingerprinting would have to focus on more subtle differences in bursts among different hypervisors; we plan respective investigations for future work. Beyond, the side channel has potential to be developed further into a covert channel. A limitation is however given by network jitter as an adversary depends on clear distinction between subsequent time slots. This limitation however is only valid for the side channel, not for the denial-of-service attack.

Our denial-of-service attack causes latencies of almost 14s, and packet drops of up to 88.3%. Service degradation is generally undesired, for example, it decreases interactivity [39]; but there are also scenarios beyond the obvious that we would like to highlight. First, virtual machines are remotely synchronized by means of a synchronization protocol like Network Time Protocol (NTP) for purposes of time measurements [40, 41]. However, the synchronization algorithm easily looses its stability in case of variable path delays [42], and these delays are heavily increased for a certain period before going back to normal by our attack; further, synchronization is prone to path asymmetry [42], and this asymmetry is also exacerbated by our attack. Synchronization errors are already in the milliseconds in presence of moderate CPU load [41], and will become significantly worse in presence of our attack making accurate time measurements in the clouds a nightmare. Second, temporal lensing was lately introduced as a way of attacking [43]; thereby an adversary performs a reflective denial-of-service attack that concentrates into a single (short, but high-bandwidth) pulse striking the victim. This is achieved by using reflectors with different attack path latencies, i.e., requesting reflectors with long paths before those with shorter ones, with the goal that all replies reach the victim simultaneously. The more reflectors with higher latencies are found, the more the adversary is able to funnel. The longest path latency found by the authors was 800 ms. In case such a reflector resided on a virtual machine, its responses could be delayed up to almost 14s by hitting this virtual machine with our TCP attack. This approach would significantly increase temporal lensing's power of impact by providing seamlessly controllable reflectors.

Finally, our results provide a further explanation to cloud phenomena: [44] measured TCP and UDP performance in the *Amazon EC2* cloud that is known to use the Xen hypervisor, and identified regular bandwidth drops[9]. They seem to occur roughly every 50 ms, and might be a consequence of rate limits. This observation might further be an indicator that rate limits were (and possibly still are) deployed at this major cloud provider; but Rackspace – another public cloud provider also using Xen – might also throttle virtual machines this way as they claim that only outbound traffic is limited [45]. Parenthetically, public cloud providers charge only outbound traffic while inbound remains free. This implies that our denial-of-service attack does not only impact a virtual machine's availability, but also costs the owner actual money and could be used to economically harm somebody.

---

[9] See Fig. 5 in [44].

In consequence, mitigation is of utter importance; however, none of the following suggestions fully prevents our attacks. (1) Throttling inbound traffic as well would only prevent non-amplifying attacks, but might negatively impact a host's availability. However, providers could choose to apply such limits only in the presence of an attack – provided that adequate detection mechanisms are prevalent. (2) A modification of the credit-based scheduler enabling short spikes (by spending previously saved credits) would increase the effort to overwhelm rate limits and buffers for the adversary. (3) Decreasing the *time window* t makes our side channel more prone to jitter (and thus prevent it) as the time slots cannot be clearly distinguished anymore, but would have a negative impact on performance. Alternatively, the algorithm might be modified in order to be less deterministic, e.g., by randomizing the time window.

8   Conclusion

Rate limits are known to guarantee fair bandwidth distribution and to prevent denial-of-service attacks among virtual machines on the same *Xen* hypervisor; but our work shows that rate limits themselves become a vector for externally-launched attacks. The underlying reasons are *Xens* unidirectional rate limits throttling outbound traffic only, and its susceptibility to burst transmissions. In the paper at hand, we propose two distinct attacks exploiting rate limits. Our side channel reveals configuration parameters that are related to rate limit functionality; our denial-of-service attack causes up to 13.8s of packet delay or up to 88.3 % packet drops. Beyond ordinary service degradation, these latencies may heavily destabilize time synchronization in clouds due to increased path asymmetry and path variability; but may also strengthen temporal lensing attacks due to providing reflectors with controllable path latency. There is indication that popular cloud providers like *Amazon EC2* or *Rackspace* are using *Xen*'s rate limits; thus, a large number of hosts remains conceivably vulnerable.

Acknowledgments. The authors thank Peter Wurzinger, and Adrian Dabrowski for many fruitful discussions; Rob Sherwood for sharing the original implementation of optimistic acknowledging and David Lobmaier for reimplementing it with respect to current TCP implementations. Further, the authors are grateful to our reviewers for their comments, especially on the aspect of mitigation.

This research was funded by P 842485 and COMET K1, both FFG - Austrian Research Promotion Agency.

References

1. With an eye on Russia, Estonia seeks security in cloud computing, December 2015. http://www.firstpost.com/business/with-an-eye-on-russia-estonia-seeks-security-in-cloud-computing-2535650.html
2. Dou, E., Barr, A.: U.S. Cloud Providers Face Backlash From China's Censors, March 2015. http://www.wsj.com/articles/u-s-cloud-providers-face-backlash-from-chinas-censors-1426541126

3. Khan, A., Othman, M., Madani, S., Khan, S.: A survey of mobile cloud computing application models. IEEE Commun. Surv. Tutorials **16**(1), 393–413 (2014)
4. Ericsson, Connected Vehicle Cloud Under The Hood
5. Gilpin, L.: How The Cloud Is Revolutionizing Healthcare, December 2015. http://www.forbes.com/sites/lyndseygilpin/2015/12/01/how-the-cloud-is-revolutionizing-healthcare/
6. Departement of Commerce, 2015 Top Markets Report Cloud Computing - A Market Assessment Tool for U.S. Exporterts (2015)
7. FCA paves the way for cloud computing in UK financial services, November 2015. http://www.out-law.com/en/articles/2015/november/fca-paves-the-way-for-cloud-computing-in-uk-financial-services/
8. Finnegan, M.: How Tesco Bank has adopted AWS cloud as 'business as usual' in eight months, November 2015. http://www.computerworlduk.com/cloud-computing/how-tesco-bank-has-adopted-aws-cloud-as-business-as-usual-in-eight-months-3629767/
9. Barham, P., Dragovic, B., Fraser, K., Hand, S., Harris, T., Ho, A., Neugebauer, R., Pratt, I., Warfield, A.: Xen and the art of virtualization. In: Proceedings of the Nineteenth ACM Symposium on Operating Systems Principles, SOSP 2003, pp. 164–177 (2003)
10. Mather, T., Kumaraswamy, S., Latif, S.: Cloud security and privacy: an enterprise perspective on risks and compliance. O'Reilly Media Inc., Sebastopol (2009)
11. Ristenpart, T., Tromer, E., Shacham, H., Savage, S.: Hey, you, get off of my cloud: exploring information leakage in third-party compute clouds. In: 16th ACM Conference on Computer and Communications Security, pp. 199–212 (2009)
12. Herzberg, A., Shulman, H., Ullrich, J., Weippl, E.: Cloudoscopy: services discovery and topology mapping. In: ACM Cloud Computing Security Workshop, pp. 113–122 (2013)
13. Okamura, K., Oyama, Y.: Load-based covert channels between Xen virtual machines. In: Proceedings of the 2010 ACM Symposium on Applied Computing, pp. 173–180 (2010)
14. Xu, Y., Bailey, M., Jahanian, F., Joshi, K., Hiltunen, M., Schlichting, R.: An exploration of l2 cache covert channels in virtualized environments. In: Proceedings of the 2011 ACM Workshop on Cloud Computing Security Workshop, pp. 29–40 (2011)
15. Varadarajan, V., Kooburat, T., Farley, B., Ristenpart, T., Swift, M.M.: Resource-freeing attacks: improve your cloud performance (at your neighbor's expense). In: ACM Conference on Computer and Communications Security, pp. 281–292 (2012)
16. Bates, A., Mood, B., Pletcher, J., Pruse, H., Valafar, M., Butler, K.: Detecting co-residency with active traffic analysis techniques. In: ACM Cloud Computing Security Workshop, pp. 1–12 (2012)
17. Bates, A., Mood, B., Pletcher, J., Pruse, H., Valafar, M., Butler, K.: On detecting co-resident cloud instances using network flow watermarking techniques. Int. J. Inf. Secur. **13**(2), 171–189 (2014)
18. redhat, 33.10.Limit network bandwidth for a Xen guest (2016). https://access.redhat.com/documentation/en-US/Red_Hat_Enterprise_Linux/5/html/Virtualization/sect-Virtualization-Tips_and_tricks-Limit_network_bandwidth_for_a_Xen_guest.html
19. Adamczyk, B., Chydzinski, A.: On the performance isolation across virtual network adapters in Xen. In: Proceedings of the 2nd International Conference Cloud Comput. GRIDs Virtual, CLOUD COMPUTING 2011, pp. 222–227 (2011)

20. Mei, L., Lv, X.: Optimization of network bandwidth allocation in Xen. In: 2015 IEEE 17th International Conference on High Performance Computing and Communications (HPCC), 2015 IEEE 7th International Symposium on Cyberspace Safety and Security (CSS), 2015 IEEE 12th International Conferen on Embedded Software and Systems (ICESS), pp. 1558–1566, August 2015

21. Li, C., Xi, S., Lu, C., Gill, C.D., Guerin, R.: Prioritizing soft real-time network traffic in virtualized hosts based on Xen. In: 21st IEEE Real-Time and Embedded Technology and Applications Symposium, pp. 145–156, April 2015

22. Rossow, C.: Amplification hell: revisiting network protocols for DDoS abuse. In: Network and Distributed System Security Symposium (NDSS) (2014)

23. Sherwood, R., Bhattacharjee, B., Braud, R.: Misbehaving TCP receivers can cause internet-wide congestion collapse. In: Proceedings of the 12th ACM Conference on Computer and Communications Security (CCS), pp. 383–392 (2005)

24. Xu, Y., Musgrave, Z., Noble, B., Bailey, M.: Bobtail: avoiding long tails in the cloud. In: Presented as Part of the 10th USENIX Symposium on Networked Systems Design and Implementation (NSDI 2013), pp. 329–341 (2013)

25. Xu, Y., Bailey, M., Noble, B., Jahanian, F.: Small is better: avoiding latency traps in virtualized data centers. In: Proceedings of the 4th Annual Symposium on Cloud Computing, SOCC 2013 (2013)

26. Varadarajan, V., Ristenpart, T., Swift, M.: Scheduler-based defenses against Cross-VM side-channels. In: 23rd USENIX Security Symposium (USENIX Security 2014), pp. 687–702, August 2014

27. Bowers, K.D., van Dijk, M., Juels, A., Oprea, A., Rivest, R.L.: How to tell if your cloud files are vulnerable to drive crashes. In: 18th ACM Conference on Computer and Communications Security, pp. 501–514 (2011)

28. Benson, K., Dowsley, R., Shacham, H.: Do you know where your cloud files are? In: 3rd ACM Cloud Computing Security Workshop, pp. 73–82 (2011)

29. Kadloor, S., Gong, X., Kiyavash, N., Tezcan, T., Borisov, N.: Low-cost side channel remote traffic analysis attack in packet networks. In: IEEE International Conference on Communications (ICC), pp. 1–5, May 2010

30. Kadloor, S., Kiyavash, N., Venkitasubramaniam, P.: Mitigating timing based information leakage in shared schedulers. In: IEEE INFOCOM, pp. 1044–1052 (2012)

31. Alarifi, S., Wolthusen, S.D.: Robust coordination of cloud-internal denial of service attacks. In: 2013 Third International Conference on Cloud and Green Computing (CGC), pp. 135–142, September 2013

32. Ficco, M., Rak, M.: Stealthy denial of service strategy in cloud computing. IEEE Trans. Cloud Comput. 3(1), 80–94 (2015)

33. Liu, H.: A new form of DOS attack in a cloud and its avoidance mechanism. In: Proceedings of the 2010 ACM Workshop on Cloud Computing Security Workshop, CCSW 2010, pp. 65–76 (2010)

34. Shea, R., Liu, J.: Understanding the impact of denial of service attacks on virtual machines. In: Proceedings of the 2012 IEEE 20th International Workshop on Quality of Service, IWQoS 2012, pp. 27:1–27:9 (2012)

35. Shea, R., Liu, J.: Performance of virtual machines under networked denial of service attacks: experiments and analysis. IEEE Syst. J. 7(2), 335–345 (2013)

36. Ferriman, B., Hamed, T., Mahmoud, Q.H.: Storming the cloud: a look at denial of service in the Google App Engine. In: 2015 International Conference on Computing, Networking and Communications (ICNC), pp. 363–368, February 2015

37. Chonka, A., Xiang, Y., Zhou, W., Bonti, A.: Cloud security defence to protect cloud computing against HTTP-DoS and XMLAQ2DoS attacks. J. Netw. Comput. Appl. 34(4), 1097–1107 (2011)

38. Yan, Q., Yu, F.R.: Distributed denial of service attacks in software-defined networking with cloud computing. IEEE Commun. Mag. **53**(4), 52–59 (2015)
39. Sanaei, Z., Abolfazli, S., Gani, A., Buyya, R.: Heterogeneity in mobile cloud computing: Taxonomy and open challenges. IEEE Commun. Surv. Tutorials **16**(1), 369–392 (2014)
40. Lampe, U., Kieselmann, M., Miede, A., Zöller, S., Steinmetz, R.: A tale of millis and nanos: time measurements in virtual and physical machines. In: Lau, K.-K., Lamersdorf, W., Pimentel, E. (eds.) ESOCC 2013. LNCS, vol. 8135, pp. 172–179. Springer, Heidelberg (2013)
41. Broomhead, T., Cremean, L., Ridoux, J., Veitch, D.: Virtualize everything but time. In: USENIX Symposium on Operating Systems Design and Implementation (OSDI 2010) (2010)
42. Ullmann, M., Vogeler, M.: Delay attacks: implication on NTP and PTP time synchronization. In: 2009 International Symposium on Precision Clock Synchronization for Measurement, Control and Communication, October 2009
43. Rasti, R., Murthy, M., Weaver, N., Paxson, V.: Temporal lensing and its application in pulsing denial-of-service attacks. In: 2015 IEEE Symposium on Security and Privacy, pp. 187–198, May 2015
44. Wang, G., Ng, T.S.E.: The impact of virtualization on network performance of amazon EC2 data center. In: INFOCOM, 2010 Proceedings IEEE, pp. 1–9, March 2010
45. Rackspace, Pricing (2016). https://www.rackspace.com/cloud/servers/pricing

Autocomplete Injection Attack

Nethanel Gelernter[1,2,3]([⊠]) and Amir Herzberg[2,3]

[1] Cyberpion, Givat Shmuel, Israel
`nethanel.gelernter@gmail.com`
[2] College of Management Academic Studies, Rishon LeZion, Israel
[3] Bar Ilan University, Ramat Gan, Israel

Abstract. Autocomplete, a well-known feature in popular search engines, offers suggestions for search terms before the user has even completed typing their query. We present the *autocomplete injection attack* and its potential exploits. In this attack, a cross-site attacker injects terms into the autocomplete suggestions offered by a web-service to a victim user. The most popular web search engines are vulnerable to the attack, as well as other websites.

Autocomplete injection can be exploited in multiple ways, including *phishing, framing, illegitimate content-promotion* and sometimes *persistent cross-site scripting attacks*. We evaluated the effectiveness of the attack with several experiments. Our results show the potential impact of the autocomplete injection attacks.

Keywords: Web-security · Phishing · Cross-site attacks · Usable security · Autocomplete injection attack · Cross-site framing · Blackhat SEO · Cross site scripting · Persistent XSS · CSRF

1 Introduction

Web-services invest considerable efforts to improve their user experience. More specifically, services are often *personalized* using information collected about each user, including the history of previous interactions. *Autocomplete mechanisms* are one of the personalization methods most widely-used by web-services to ease the entry of search terms. As the user types the first few letters of a query, the autocomplete mechanism offers several suggestions for the complete query. The user can either avoid typing the rest of the term by choosing one of the suggestions or type additional letters, which will prompt updated suggestions. Autocomplete suggestions allow users to choose long terms while decreasing the number of keystrokes [3,27]. This serves to improve the user experience, especially for users with disabilities (for whom it was originally designed).

We show that the autocomplete mechanism can also be *abused* by a rogue website visited by the user, allowing multiple attacks on those who have an active 'session' in one of several popular websites. Based on this new type of 'cross-site' attack, we tested for - and found - autocomplete vulnerabilities in five sites: the

© Springer International Publishing Switzerland 2016
I. Askoxylakis et al. (Eds.): ESORICS 2016, Part II, LNCS 9879, pp. 512–530, 2016.
DOI: 10.1007/978-3-319-45741-3_26

three most-popular search-engines: *Google, Yahoo!* and *Bing*, and the three most popular websites (Google, Facebook and Youtube) [2].

This paper shows how it is possible to manipulate the autocomplete suggestions, and demonstrates and evaluates this possibility on Google, Yahoo! and Bing. Our results show that it is possible to control the first autocomplete suggestion that will be offered by these websites to the victim, for almost every prefix she types. We refer to this manipulation as the *autocomplete injection attack*.

Autocomplete injections can be exploited in different ways to benefit the attacker and harm the user. We present four ways in which autocomplete injections can be exploited by attackers: *phishing, framing, illegitimate content-promotion*, and *persistent cross-site scripting attacks*. We discuss each of these exploits in a dedicated section, and briefly introduce them below.

Phishing Attacks (Sect. 3). In phishing attacks, the victim is tricked into visiting a malicious 'imposter' website that mimics a legitimate site [12]. Tricking the user into visiting the imposter site is a critical part of the attack. In most phishing attacks, this is done by the user clicking on a link from a phishing email, website, or ad [23]. However, this 'direct' approach has disadvantages, most notably, the victim accesses the imposter page as a result of an external event (e.g., email or ad), and not as a result of the user's own agenda; this may make the user more alert upon visiting the phishing site, especially when the user is aware of the threat of phishing attacks. The autocomplete injection attack allows launching sophisticated phishing attack; that attack tricks the user into visiting a malicious page by clicking on a result in her favorite search engine.

Illegitimate 'Black-Hat' Content Promotion (Sect. 4). The autocomplete injection attack can be used to promote content. So far, the methods to promote content include the use of ads and public-relations methods, or Search-Engine Optimization (SEO) techniques, including illegitimate *blackhat-SEO* methods. The goal is to cause search engines to return the website as one of their top results, increasing the likelihood of access by users. Content promotion via autocomplete injection is significantly easier, and complementary: the promotion occurs via the autocomplete suggestions for related terms. Note that autocomplete-injection-based content promotion does not require users to search for a particular term, and can work with many or most search queries. This is somewhat similar to the *search poisoning* blackhat-SEO technique [21].

Cross-site Framing Attacks (Sect. 5). The personalization of autocomplete features causes different people to get different suggestions. This fact is known to many web-users. An attacker that is able to control these autocomplete suggestions can mislead the environment of the user, such as spouse, family, and colleagues, into believing the user was surfing sinister content or to draw incorrect conclusions about her interests. Such attacks are a variant of *cross-site framing attacks* [8]. For example, it is possible to plant autocomplete suggestions that will give indications that a married user is interested in dating services, and even in a particular type of dating services (e.g., with specific sexual orientation). In this paper, we evaluated even more severe framing attacks, in which the attacker plants pedophile-related terms in the autocomplete suggestions of her victims.

Persistent Cross-Site Scripting (Sect. 6). The autocomplete injection attack allows a rogue website, to manipulate a popular web-service into sending users attacker-controlled autocomplete suggestions. If the attacker can include a script as part of the autocomplete string, this may allow a *Persistent Cross-Site Scripting attack* [16]. We found that Yahoo! is vulnerable to such an attack and demonstrate how an attacker can manipulate the autocomplete suggestions of Yahoo! such that for every typed letter, the malicious script of the attacker will run.

1.1   Contributions

Our main contribution is the introduction of the autocomplete injection attack. We demonstrate how the attack can be used for four different purposes: phishing, framing, illegitimate content-promotion, and persistent cross-site scripting attacks. We evaluated the applicability of these attacks on highly popular sites (Google, Yahoo!, Bing, Facebook and Youtube), and found that all are vulnerable, allowing phishing, framing, and illegitimate content-promotion. We further found that the autocomplete-injection attack on Yahoo! allows persistent cross-site scripting.

We hope that the publication of this paper will urge websites, including the very popular ones we tested, to protect their users against this threat. We informed all websites of the vulnerability.

Ethics. This research involved several IRB-approved experiments to measure the effectiveness of different autocomplete attacks on users. Ethics was a major issue in the planning of all these experiments, which were designed to avoid causing damage to users and web-services. We describe the relevant ethical considerations for every experiment. We informed all the websites about this vulnerability, giving them sufficient time to address it. Indeed, Yahoo! blocked the cross-site scripting vulnerability posed by the autocomplete injection attack.

1.2   Related Work

Phishing. The idea of tempting the victim into naturally contacting the attacker was presented by Irani et al. in the context of social networks [14]. In their reverse social engineering attack, the attacker tricks the user into creating the initial contact with the attacker, without using classical spear phishing techniques [23] that are often detected by users with some security background.

Illegitimate Content Promotion and Search Engine Optimizations (SEO). Current research on illegitimate content promotion focuses on 'blackhat-SEO' techniques [6,21]. Xing et al. [29] presented an SEO attack based on polluting the search history of users, causing the search engine to offer them different results. We are not aware of previous proposals to promote content or websites by abusing the autocomplete mechanism.

Cross-Site Framing Attacks. Framing attacks in the cross-site adversary model were presented recently [8]. However, unlike most attacks noted [8], injected autocomplete suggestions are likely to be noticed by individuals who can see the victim's display, such as family and co-employees. This can cause severe damage without requiring additional intervention by the attacker (e.g., contacting police and reporting about someone).

2   Adversary Model and Autocomplete-Injection Attack

This section briefly explains the adversary model in this work (Sect. 2.1) and reviews the technical aspects of injecting autocomplete suggestions into websites (Sect. 2.2). The applications of these manipulations are discussed and analyzed in the following sections.

2.1   The Cross-Site Adversary Model

Cross-site attacks require only a modest capability from the attacker: controlling a 'rogue' web-page visited by the victim user. A cross-site attack sends the victim user a web-page, often containing a script that causes the victim's browser to issue requests to some *target* web-service; such requests are often referred to as *cross-site requests*. Cross-site requests are essential to the use of the web and generally used for legitimate purposes. In particular, search-engines and other popular sites use cross-site requests to allow third-party sites to perform search queries. Cross-site requests are also used by well-known web attacks, such as cross-site scripting (XSS) [16], cross-site request forgery (CSRF) [28], cross-site search [9] and clickjacking [25].

Luring random or specific victims into visiting a rogue website is considered an easy task, e.g., using phishing emails, ads, and social-engineering techniques [7,14,15].

To manipulate the autocomplete suggestions offered by a target website, the victim who visits the rogue website must be logged into that website from the same browser. Several well-known techniques allow a cross-site attacker to efficiently detect such cross-site login [4,9,17].

2.2   Injecting Autocomplete Suggestions

A website allows cross-site requests, if it serves requests that were sent from another domain as though they were issued (legitimately) by the client currently authenticated to the website. Many web-services and search engines allow cross-site search requests (queries). Namely, websites can send search requests to one of the popular search engines to which the current user (victim) is logged in; the search engines will treat this search request as if it was sent by the victim.

Search engines maintain logs of the searches done by each of their users. These logs are used to personalize services given to the users by the search engines. One use of the search history logs is to offer personalized autocomplete suggestions. Under the assumption that users tend to search for the same terms again and again, search engines offer terms from the search history log as autocomplete suggestions. We denote such autocomplete suggestions as *history-based* autocomplete suggestions. History-based autocomplete suggestions usually appear first, before *general* autocomplete suggestions, which are based on local and global trends.

The autocomplete injection attack exploits the ability to add entries to the search history logs by sending cross-site search request and the fact that websites present history-based autocomplete suggestions.

The attacker sends a cross-site search request with a query and causes the search engine to add that query to the history log. Later, when the user types a prefix of the injected query, she will see the query as an autocomplete suggestion.

2.3   Autocomplete Injection in Popular Websites

Our work focuses on search engines, and in particular on Google, Yahoo! and Bing, the most popular search engines in the US [2]. The same techniques can be applied to other websites such as Facebook and YouTube.

Figure 1 illustrates the way autocomplete suggestions are presented to the user by the three search engines. It is possible to see the differences between the search engines in both the number of history-based autocomplete suggestions and whether history-based suggestions visually differ from the general autocomplete suggestions.

Other differences between the search engines relate to content filtering and the number of cross-site requests required to plant a term. Google is the only search engine that filters out content related to pornography, violence, hate

Fig. 1. Autocomplete suggestions as presented by the Google, Yahoo! and Bing search engines in US. Injected suggestions appear as history-based autocomplete suggestions.

Table 1. Differences between the three most popular search engines [2] with regarding to history-based autocomplete suggestions as presented to their users

	Maximal number	Colored differently	Filtering	Number of searches to be added
Google	2	$\checkmark$	$\checkmark$	1–3
Yahoo!	2	$\checkmark$	X	1
Bing	8	X	X	1

speech, and illegal and dangerous objects [10]. This fact is relevant mainly for the framing attacks using autocomplete injection and discussed in Sect. 5.1. Google also differs from the other search engines in the number of cross-site search requests required for a term to appear as an autocomplete suggestion. We created a webpage that sent cross-site search requests for a list of 14 terms. These terms included meaningful and meaningless terms, and other types of terms that are being injected during the attacks described in this paper. The page sent only a single request for each of the terms, and we checked whether the term appears as autocomplete suggestion or not. In both Yahoo! and Bing, all the autocomplete suggestions were presented immediately, but in Google some of them did not appear. Hence, we repeated the test on 10 active Google accounts when 2 and 3 requests are sent. After sending 2 cross-site search requests for each term, the term appeared in 95 % of the cases. *All* the terms appeared after sending 3 cross-site search requests. Table 1 summarizes the differences between the search engines.

3 Phishing

The ability to manipulate the autocomplete suggestions seems ideal for phishing attacks. Theoretically, the attacker simply plants autocomplete suggestions that mislead the search engine to offer the phishing website instead of the original one. A user that relies on the injected autocomplete suggestion will get the phishing website in her search results.

Although the idea seems simple, in practice it is not easy to manipulate the search engine to offer incorrect results for terms that are related to popular websites. In this section we describe the challenge of the attacker and offer two techniques that can be used to launch a successful phishing attack using autocomplete injection. At the end of the section, we present the results of an experiment we conducted to evaluate these techniques.

3.1 The Challenge

When users search a popular page they usually type the name of the website or the name of the organization associated with the website. Even if the user incorrectly spells a popular term, the search engines usually offer results that are based on the correctly-spelled term. Similarly, combining terms that are strongly related to a (popular) website with the name of another website will yield search results that are related to the original website. For example, if an attacker concatenates the name of a phishing website to the name of some bank in an autocomplete suggestion and the user searches this suggestion, the search engines will return entries from the bank website and the phishing website will not appear in the first entries.

This poses a challenge to the attacker; the attacker has to find autocomplete suggestions that will satisfy the following conditions:

1. Relevant for the search so the user will select them.
2. Yield search results without the real website appearing at the top.
3. Yield search results with the phishing website at the top of the list.

3.2   Phishing Autocomplete Suggestions

We describe two techniques to create autocomplete suggestions that satisfy the three requirements of the phishing challenge. The first uses advanced search operators and the second relies on homographs.

Advanced Search Operators. Although most of the users rely on the simple search, search engines also support advanced search operators. The attacker can use some of these operators to abuse the search results.

The first operator is the *not* operator, usually denoted by the minus sign (-). Attaching the *not* operator to a term means searching for results that do not contain that term. The attacker can abuse the *not* operator in terms that contain more than a single word. For example, for a term such as *bank Somebank* that can be searched also as *bank-Somebank*, the attacker can inject the autocomplete suggestion *bank -Somebank <bait>*. This will cause a search for results *without* the name of the bank, *Somebank*, and *with* the terms *bank* and *<bait>*. Here, *<bait>* is a search-term that is bound to cause the phishing-website (e.g., its domain name *phishingsite.com*) to be the top result.

Another operator that can be used for this purpose is the *site/inurl* operator. This operator specifies the site/url of the results. By concatenating this operator after relevant search terms to specify that the results must come from the phishing website, the attacker ensures that the results will be only from the phishing website.

Homographic Autocomplete Attacks. Another direction is to use homographs. A homograph is one of two or more characters, or sequences of characters, with shapes that either appear identical or cannot be differentiated by quick visual inspection. Homographs are usually used to deceive users in classical phishing attacks [1,13,22]. For example: replacing the English letter *o* (code 006 F in Unicode) in "Bank *of* America" with the Cyrillic small letter "o" (code 043E in Unicode). A search for this simple homograph in Google brings the real result for Bank of America only in the eighth entry. By replacing also the two appearances of the English letter a in the word "america" (autocomplete suggestions always appear in small letters) with the Cyrillic letter "a" (code 0430 in Unicode), the attacker gets a homograph that will yield search results without the real website of Bank of America.

Once the attacker has a homograph that yields search results without the real website, the attacker needs to create a phishing website that will appear in the first results for that homograph. This is not considered a hard task, because the homograph used by the attacker is not a common search term.

When choosing the homograph, it is preferable to replace several characters. Otherwise, the search engines might refer to the term as a typo and, and due to the similarity to a popular real term, will present the results for that term. However, to increase the exposure of the autocomplete suggestion, it is better to replace characters toward the end of the term, such that the homograph and the real term share a prefix that is as long as possible.

3.3   Evaluation

To evaluate the autocomplete injection attack for phishing purposes, we designed a one-minute usability experiment. The experiment evaluated both the techniques described in Sect. 3.2.

Experiment 1: Bank Phishing

Goal: Check whether users will choose injected autocomplete suggestions that will lead to phishy search results for each of the techniques described in Sect. 3.2. Also check whether they will follow the phishy search results to the phishing website.

Methodology and Ethics: The experiment was carried out with 100 volunteer undergraduate students in a security course and with employees working in a security firm. The participants agreed to participate and did the experiment on their computers. To avoid 'contaminating' their real accounts, the experiment used a dedicated search page, which used the autocomplete suggestions and search results of Bing, by presenting Bing's results in an iframe[1]. We added to this page the "injected" autocomplete suggestions.

To analyze the phishing results, we created a page with search results for the phishing terms and loaded this page as the search results when the user clicked on the phishing autocomplete suggestions. This was the alternative for buying a phishing domain, creating a real phishing website and promoting it in search engines.

Process: We chose one of the three largest banks in our country, and instructed the users to find its website using our search engine and to open the website in a new window and then to press on a button to finish the experiment. For each participant, we only saved whether the person used the phishing or legitimate

---

[1] Yahoo! and Google prevent presentation of search results in iframes.

autocomplete suggestions or none at all, and whether they clicked on the phishing website. The experiment was completed once the user clicked on the phishing website or when she opened the real website in a new window and clicked on the finish button.

Phishing Details: For the phishing website, we chose a name that is similar to the name of a real bank. For half the participants we used the advanced search operators as described in Sect. 3.2 (the *AO* group). For the other participants we used a homograph in which we replaced two English letters with two Cyrillic letters as described in Sect. 3.2 (the *HG* group). The phishy autocomplete suggestions for both the AO and HG groups yielded a page where the first search result points to the phishing website. However, for each autocomplete suggestion s', a homograph of s, in the HG group, this page also contained a question that appears by Bing for such searches: "Do you mean s"? We found that for these particular autocomplete suggestions, both Yahoo! and Bing prompt this question but Google does not. We also asked the users to report any unusual or suspicious behavior they noticed.

Results: We observed that using homographs is much more effective than using advanced search operators. Users from the AO group almost completely avoided the phishing autocomplete results; only two of them searched for the injected phishing autocomplete suggestions, and both users also followed the results to the phishing website. The explanation we got for the lack of use in the autocomplete suggestion was that the phishy suggestions that rely on advanced search operators did not reflect the exact search the users planned to submit. In the HG group, 26 % of the users used the homograph autocomplete suggestion. However, only 20 % clicked on the phishing website. The other 6 % simply clicked on the question raised by the search engine ("Do you mean ...?") and got new search results without any phishing website. Figure 2 depicts the results.

Our most important observation is that *no user reported* a suspected phishing attack. Although users probably noticed the unusual autocomplete suggestions, mainly in the AO group, none of them linked this anomaly with a phishing attack. This means the attacker can launch the attack on a large scale without being

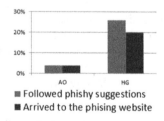

Fig. 2. Users who clicked on injected phishy autocomplete suggestions and users that followed the phishy suggestions and clicked on the phishing website in the search results. The results separate users who were tricked using advanced search operators (AO) and users who were tricked using homographs (HG).

worried about detection. Moreover, the autocomplete-injection attack allows an attacker to exploit a random visit to his rogue website, and manipulate the user ('Alice') into accessing the phishing website later on, when Alice *initiates* a visit to her bank. These are significant advantages compared to classical spear phishing attacks [23]. Specifically, it is far more likely that Alice will 'fall for' a phishing site, when Alice initiates the visit to the bank [14].

Although only 20 % of the users were phished in the experiment, the results indicate that autocomplete injection can be used for effective phishing attacks. The autocomplete injection attack is effective only against users who rely on autocomplete suggestions. When it comes to users who relied on autocomplete suggestions, the homograph variant of the attack achieved a 76 % success rate.

4   Illegitimate (Black-Hat) Content-Promotion

Companies and organizations spend large amounts of money to promote products, slogans, and other content, using advertising and PR campaigns. Hacktivists and 'black-hat organizations', may use illegitimate mechanisms to promote content; these tend to be more effective or less expensive. For example, these may be used to promote illegal or illegitimate content, which may be banned by legitimate advertising and PR providers. In this section we explore the potential abuse of the autocomplete injection attack to perform *illegitimate content promotion*, delivering messages and slogans to website visitors. The content may include malicious content such as the promotion of malware websites, or be part of phishing campaigns, complementing the mechanisms described in Sect. 3.

The attack allows a website, visited by a user, to add a desired string to the autocomplete suggestions offered by popular search engines/sites. This string could be a slogan or other text used to 'promote' some product or idea. It may also be a 'negative text', e.g., discrediting a competitor. Because such goals could be attractive to many attackers, the ease with which a website can launch the autocomplete injection attack makes it a real risk.

This section evaluates the promotion of a slogan using the autocomplete injection attack. Slogans have considerable marketing value, and organizations invest considerable effort and funds to promote and advertise them. Autocomplete-injection even allows the slogan/phrase to appear for users typing relevant terms, for highly-effective targeted advertising. A company can inject slogans and advertisements in the autocomplete suggestions of its website visitors and influence their searches in external search engines. For example, assume a company wants to promote the Doritos® chips brand. The autocomplete-injection can display a relevant slogan, such as the fabricated slogan 'America likes Doritos' (as we used in Experiment 2) arbitrarily or when the user types relevant words and phrases, e.g., *snack*.

Experiment 2: Promoting a Slogan

Goal: Validate that injected autocomplete terms are noticed by users. Evaluate their impact on users and their potential for exposing users to a slogan using the fabricated slogan 'America likes Doritos'.

Methodology and Ethics: The experiment was carried out with 95 volunteer undergraduate students who signed a consent form, and used their own computers to simulate reality. To avoid (unintentional) bias by participants and/or staff, the experiment was 'double blinded', i.e., users were assigned randomly to one of three sets (no injection, or one of two injection modes described below), without awareness of either user or staff. To avoid injecting suggestions to the accounts of the users, we used a search page we built as described in Experiment 1.

Process: Users were instructed to use our search form to send the search queries of their choice. Users accessed a webpage with instructions to run searches during five minutes using the provided search form. Each user was randomly (and blindly) assigned to one of three groups: *None, Letters* and *Terms*. For *Letters* users, we inserted autocomplete strings consisting of each letter in the alphabet concatenated with the slogan, and also each letter repeated (e.g., *aa*). For *Terms* users, for each alphabet letter we chose a popular search term T beginning with this letter, and concatenated the slogan to T in two ways: "T : slogan" and "T - slogan". For *None* users, nothing was injected[2]. After five minutes of search, we redirected the user to a form with a single question: *What does America like?*. There were five possible answers: (1) Fries. (2) Waffles. (3) Kinder. (4) Doritos. (5) I don't know.

Results: As can be seen in Fig. 3, users in both of the 'autocomplete-injection' groups were far more likely to select the answer corresponding to the slogan, compared to users in the control group ('none'). While the number of users is not sufficient for this study to be conclusive, it gives a good indication that users notice autocomplete injections and are influenced by them. These results also show that people notice injected autocomplete suggestions, even in short free searches. This means autocomplete-injection may be effective as a way to 'frame' an innocent victim user, by presenting suspect autocomplete suggestions in the victim's computer; see next section.

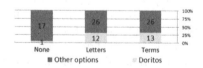

Fig. 3. Participants' answers to the question "What does America like?" in each of the modes

---

[2] The probability of getting each of the *Letter* and the *Terms* modes was twice the probability of getting the *None* mode.

5   Framing Attacks

This section evaluates the effectiveness of framing attack using autocomplete injection and the damage that such an attack can cause. By planting autocomplete suggestions, the attacker can create a false impression about the victim. For example, autocomplete suggestions that are related to dating sites indicate that the user is interested in finding dates. In cases where the user already has a spouse, such autocomplete suggestions might create relationship issues if observed by someone else.

We investigate the likelihood that a casual user will notice *and* take action, when faced with (fake) autocomplete phrases; these phrases were chosen to create an impression of searches for pedophile contents. This is significant, since autocomplete phrases are automatically offered to any user of the browser. Even casual users, using somebody else's computer and with no intent to snoop, may be exposed to them. This is in contrast to other methods of computer framing [8], which are generally unlikely to be viewed by a casual user. For example, Google requires users to re-authenticate before presenting their search history (and only a snoopy visitor would even try to look up the search history).

The findings of Experiment 2 show that users often notice the injected autocomplete suggestions. However, the fact that users notice autocomplete phrases does not necessarily imply that this can be *noticeable* framing evidence. First of all, users may not deduce from observing the autocomplete phrases that there are implications regarding the user of the computer. More significantly, even if they do, they may not feel the need or confidence to report this. This *bystander* phenomenon, where eyewitnesses fail to report crimes, has been reported and studied in many social-science studies and experiments [11,19].

We therefore conducted Experiment 3 to evaluate the potential abuse of the autocomplete mechanism, as noticeable framing (false) evidence. We focused on autocomplete phrases that seem to indicate searches for pedophilia sites and related activities. Section 5.1 describes how to circumvent Google filtering for inappropriate autocomplete suggestions.

Experiment 3: Bystander and Pedophilia-Autocomplete

Ethical Restrictions and Pilot Experiment: This experiment involved ethical challenges. Clearly, it would not be ethical to inject such phrases into the computers of subjects. In fact, the first author performed such an experiment on his own Google account, by authenticating to the framed account in his home PC, which is also used by his spouse. It took one day until the author was confronted with an upset spouse and had to explain and show that this was just an experiment. For this reason, all further experiments were performed in our lab. Another challenge is the fact that users must see the framing autocomplete suggestions in a natural way and hence must not know the real purpose of the experiment. We explained to the users what we expected them to do and asked for their consent; we only disclosed the real purpose of the experiment toward the very end. Participants were paid and allowed to leave the experiment at any given time without forfeiting the payment. At the end of the experiment, we explained the real purpose of the experiment and repeated our request for their permission to use the collected information.

Experiment Design: To achieve the most realistic and reliable results possible, the experiment was designed to emulate a typical workplace situation, searching for terms using Google. After signing consent forms, participants were asked to run 25 web-searches on a computer, supposedly as part of a user experience study. At the outset of the experiment, the computer dedicated to the experiment was found inoperative. This was an excuse to have the participants use a laptop belonging to a contractor, Vic, who worked in the lab and was currently away. Essentially, Vic represents the victim, 'framed' to be suspected of pedophilia. We explained that Vic was away, so we would use his laptop to substitute for the regular experiment computer. We made a phone call to Vic, but he did not respond, so we used the laptop anyway. Supposedly this was the approved, standard practice in our lab.

During the searches, users could see that Vic was 'logged on' to his Google account. In reality, 'Vic's' laptop was configured for the experiment, equipped with a video (camera) and a screen-recording application. It was also injected with pedophilia-related autocomplete phrases. Since Google filters most pedophilia terms, we used homographic variants or 'typos' such as *childp ornography* (see Subsect. 5.1), which we had no difficulty injecting.

Participants were instructed to search for 25 phrases using Google; the phrases were played from an audio file. The phrases included questions like "what is my IP" and "how to find the median", websites like Youtube and Facebook, movies-related search terms, and more. Half of the search phrases had a common prefix with some of the framing autocomplete phrases; we also had many benign autocomplete phrases, to avoid over-visibility.

After searching for the 25 audio-played phrases, participants were asked to run arbitrary searches for 2 more minutes. Participants answered a few statistical questions and were given a paper and envelop for anonymous feedback to be read only by the professor responsible for the lab. This was selected as a comfortable mechanism for them to raise any concerns. To make sure participants did not plan to raise their concerns before leaving, we paid them at this point and allowed them to leave, then asked them to return for two more questions, the first being: *Did you notice any bothersome thing during the experiment?*. If the answer was yes, we asked the participant to write it down. Finally, we explained the real goals of the experiment to the participants, and asked their discretion and their agreement for us to use their results (all agreed). We also asked whether the participants saw any pedophile-related phrases. Participants who reported noticing were asked whether they reported it, and if not, why.

Participants: We recruited 25 participants, all students (ages: 18–38), via ads. We did not include computer science students, since they were expected to have a higher awareness of the autocomplete mechanism. Four students were disqualified after not meeting our minimal threshold of proficiency in English. The complexity of the experiment process prevented us from conducting the experiment on a larger group of participants. Due to the experiment's design, we had to perform the experiment on each participant separately, such that no single participant could observe the experiment of another participant.

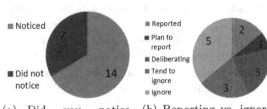

(a) Did you notice pedophile-related autocomplete suggestions?

(b) Reporting vs. ignoring the framing attack.

Fig. 4. Framing experiment results

Results and Analysis (see Fig. 4): As shown in Fig. 4(a), two-thirds (14) of the 21 qualified participants, reported that they noticed the pedophilia content. Five of them reported this only when asked explicitly about signs of pedophilia, in the very last question. Even without these 5, 9 (43%) reported pedophilia content without being asked about it specifically.

We did not have the resources to run a control group without injection, and the number of participants is not sufficient to draw significant conclusions. However, this seems to provide testimony further to Experiment 2, that users notice and are impacted by the autocomplete phrases. Note that in Experiment 2, only about a third of the responders selected the injected slogan (see Fig. 3), possibly because in Experiment 2, the participants were asked to search for whatever they want; they might not have searched for terms with a long prefix of an injected autocomplete suggestion.

Out of the 14 participants that acknowledged noticing pedophilia content, 2 (14%) used the feedback form to write elaborate complaints to the professor. They explained the pedophilia-phrases and their implications, and demanded immediate and conclusive action, offering to contact authorities themselves otherwise. Of the remaining 14 that reported noticing pedophilia content, 4 reported that they planned to report or considered reporting. Although it may seem that only a small percentage of participants reported, or even planned/considered reporting, the percentage is, in fact, surprisingly high, compared to the 15–25% reported in most previous studies of the bystander effect, e.g., [11,19].

Our analysis of the recorded behavior of the participants and correlated screen contents offers insight into the reasons seven participants failed to notice the framing pieces of evidence. Apparently the reasons are technical and not very relevant to the use of autocomplete injections and red-flag framing evidence. For example, one of them typed very quickly, such that autocomplete suggestions were almost irrelevant for him (e.g., due to their latency). Most of the others could be seen in the video looking primarily at the keyboard and/or to be on the verge of disqualified for poor English.

5.1 Circumventing Autocomplete Excluded-Phrases

Because Google is the most popular search engine, we used a framed Google account to evaluate framing attacks (Experiment 3). Our focus on injecting pedophilia-related phrases raised a challenge. Unlike the other two search engines, Yahoo! and Bing, Google filters pedophilia-related and certain other 'problematic' terms, like pornography, violence, hate speech, illegal and dangerous objects, and terms that are frequently used to find content that violates copyright [10]. Therefore, an attacker who wishes to use Google for framing must circumvent this filtering.

In spite of Google's filters, it is still possible to inject search queries related to these subjects using simple homographs (see Sect. 3.2). We were able to inject inappropriate autocomplete suggestions using basic homographs, for example: *pornography*, where the first *o* is the Cyrillic small letter "о" (code 043E in Unicode). Another direction is to use minor typos, e.g., *childp ornography*, or adding, dropping, or duplicating letters.

6   Stored Cross-Site Scripting (XSS)

The injection of data controlled by an attacker to a website might result in a cross-site scripting (XSS) attack [16]. The same origin policy (SOP) [24] restricts websites from running scripts that will affect websites with a different origin. The XSS attack circumvents SOP by injecting a malicious script into the attacked page. Once the malicious script is running from the attacked page, it is allowed to access pages and to perform actions in the domain of the attacked page[3].

XSS attacks can be classified into three categories: DOM-based, reflected, and stored attacks. In DOM-based XSS [20], the malicious code is injected in the client side. Stored (persistent) and reflected (non-persistent) are two types of XSS attack in which the server itself returns a page with malicious script. In reflected XSS, the malicious script is reflected from the request, usually from the URL, and hence, it usually requires accessing a malicious link. In stored XSS, the attacker injects the malicious script to the server, and the server embeds this script in some HTTP responses it returns. Among the three types of XSS, stored XSS is considered the most severe. It is harder to detect by browsers, and it requires minimal interaction from the user.

The autocomplete suggestions injected by the attacker are stored by the server and are used later when the user is typing search queries. Therefore, if the attacker injects an autocomplete suggestion that contains malicious script and the server does not filter or sanitize them, the website is vulnerable to a stored XSS attack. The malicious script will be triggered when the user types some prefix of the autocomplete suggestion in which the malicious script was included.

To launch an effective XSS attack, the attacker will want to increase the probability that the malicious script will be run and decrease the user interaction required for the attack. The autocomplete injection allows an attacker to plant the malicious script in a manner that will trigger it for any letter typed in the search box. For every possible character, the attacker can plant an autocomplete

---

[3] Countermeasures like content security policy (CSP) [26] can mitigate XSS attacks, but are beyond the scope of this paper.

suggestion that is the concatenation of the character and the malicious script. In this way, the website will present the victim with an autocomplete suggestion that will trigger the malicious script execution upon typing every single letter in the search box.

Among the five web-services we tested, we found that only Yahoo! is vulnerable to the autocomplete injection XSS attack. We injected a script into Yahoo!'s autocomplete within the *onerror* attribute of an *img* HTML tag with a bad *src* attribute. We found that when the user moves the cursor over the autocomplete dialog, possibly with the keyboard when moving down toward other autocomplete suggestions, the malicious script is automatically executed. Such a cross-site scripting attack can be abused in many ways, e.g., to take-over the account. The attack exploits a combination of two vulnerabilities. The first is the lack of input sanitation, which allows cross-site scripting but requires the user to search for a script that will attack herself. The second vulnerability is the autocomplete-suggestions based on cross-site historical searches.

The combination of autocomplete injection attack with this innocuous XSS, results in a severe XSS vulnerability that can be exploited easily by an attacker.

7   Defenses

Web-services that offer autocomplete mechanisms should defend against the autocomplete injection attack. Autocomplete injection attacks are based on sending cross-site search requests, i.e., search requests initiated by a third-party rogue website; these requests are regarded by the web-service as searches performed by the current user (identified by cookie). A simple solution is to use CSRF defenses (see below), and prevent cross-site search requests. If cross-site search requests are considered useful and should be permitted, the websites should not take these searches into account as part of the 'history' of searches by the user. In particular, they should not let these searches influence the history-based autocomplete suggestions.

Web-services can detect most cross-site requests by inspecting the Referer or Origin HTTP request headers. However, these headers are not always sent, often due to filtering by client-tools for privacy; this could foil reliance on these headers to detect cross-site requests. As a solution, web-services can simply ignore searches that do not contain Referer or Origin headers, when determining the history-based autocomplete suggestions.

Alternatively, web-services can use other cross-site request forgery (CSRF) countermeasures. (See Overview [28]). The most popular active defense taken by a website is anti-CSRF tokens. In this basic defense against CSRF, an unpredictable token is sent with a request from the web-service, and is then validated by the server. Because the attacker cannot forge a token, she cannot send a request from another site that will pass the validation on the web-service side. Other CSRF countermeasures are discussed in [5,18,30].

Several of the most effective autocomplete injection attacks make use of *homographs*. Web-services can easily detect potential homographic attacks.

We believe that there will be no noticeable overhead in performance or loss-of-usability, due to blocking such homographic search strings (at least from the log of search strings).

Unfortunately, our experience shows that some web-service operators are reluctant to fix autocomplete-injection vulnerabilities. This motivates the development and use of client-side defenses. In particular, we recommend that, by default, browsers block cross-site requests that are suspected of being homographic attacks. Similar to web-services, we believe browsers can also detect such attacks with no noticeable 'costs', in terms of performance or usability. More advanced client-side defenses against CSRF attacks may also be applicable, e.g., [5].

8   Conclusions

Popular web-services offer autocomplete suggestions based on the history of user search strings; this saves users the effort of repeating a previous search. Additionally, web-services often allow cross-site queries, i.e., queries initiated by third-party sites, as long as the queries do not result in 'change of state'. More specifically, cross-site search-requests are allowed by many web-services, since they are considered 'harmless'.

Our experiments show that several attacks are feasible by exploiting the combination of the autocomplete mechanism, based on previous search strings, and the use of cross-site search requests. Specifically, we demonstrate how this facilitates autocomplete-based phishing, framing, illegitimate content-promoting and, at least in Yahoo!, persistent cross-site scripting. We propose both browser-based and web-server-based defenses against the autocomplete injection attack. We hope this paper will call attention to the problem and help address this potential vulnerability. It is also our goal to raise awareness regarding the general risk of permitting 'seemingly harmless' cross-site requests.

Acknowledgments. This work was supported by grant 1354/11 from the Israeli Science Foundation (ISF), and by grants from the Israeli Ministry of Science, Technology and Space.

References

1. Helou, A.J., Scott, T.: Multilingual web sites: Internationalized Domain Name homograph attacks. In: 12th IEEE International Symposium on Web Systems Evolution (WSE), pp. 89–92. IEEE (2010)
2. Alexa.Top Sites in United States, April 2016. http://www.alexa.com/topsites/countries/US
3. Anson, D., Moist, P., Przywara, M., Wells, H., Saylor, H., Maxime, H.: The effects of word completion and word prediction on typing rates using on-screen keyboards. Assistive Technol. **18**(2), 146–154 (2006)
4. Bortz, A., Boneh, D.: Exposing private information by timing web applications. In : Proceedings of the 16th International Conference on World Wide Web, pp. 621–628. ACM (2007)

5. Czeskis, A., Moshchuk, A., Kohno, T., Wang, H.J.: Lightweight server support for browser-based CSRF protection. In: Proceedings of the 22nd International Conference on World Wide Web, pp. 273–284 (2013)
6. Dover, D., Dafforn, E.: Search Engine Optimization (SEO) Secrets. Wiley Publishing (2011)
7. Ferguson, A.J.: Fostering e-mail security awareness: the west point carronade. EDUCASE Quarterly (2005)
8. Gelernter, N., Grinstein, Y., Herzberg, A.: Cross-site framing attacks. In: Proceedings of the 31st Annual Computer Security Applications Conference, pp. 161–170. ACM (2015)
9. Gelernter, N., Herzberg, A.: Cross-site search attacks. In: Proceedings of the 22nd ACM Conference on Computer and Communications Security, CCS 2015, pp. 1394–1405 (2015)
10. Google. Google Search Autocomplete (2014). https://support.google.com/websearch/answer/106230?hl=en
11. Greenberg, M.S., Wilson, C.E., Ruback, R.B., Mills, M.K.: Social and emotional determinants of victim crime reporting. Soc. Psychol. Q. **42**, 364–372 (1979)
12. Herzberg, A., Jbara, A.: Security and identification indicators for browsers against spoofing, phishing attacks. ACM Trans. Internet Techn. **8**(4), 16:1–16:36 (2008)
13. Holgers, T., Watson, D.E., Gribble, S.D.: Cutting through the confusion: a measurement study of homograph attacks. In: USENIX Annual Technical Conference, General Track, pp. 261–266 (2006)
14. Irani, D., Balduzzi, M., Balzarotti, D., Kirda, E., Pu, C.: Reverse social engineering attacks in online social networks. In: Holz, T., Bos, H. (eds.) DIMVA 2011. LNCS, vol. 6739, pp. 55–74. Springer, Heidelberg (2011)
15. Jagatic, T.N., Johnson, N.A., Jakobsson, M., Menczer, F.: Social phishing. Commun. ACM **50**(10), 94–100 (2007)
16. Manico, J., Williams, J., Mattatall, N.: Cross site scripting prevention cheat sheet, March 2016. https://www.owasp.org/index.php/XSS_(Cross_Site_Scripting)_Prevention_Cheat_Sheet
17. Grossman, J.: I know what websites you are logged-in to (Login-Detection via CSRF) (2009). http://blog.whitehatsec.com/i-know-what-websites-you-are-logged-in-to-login-detection-via-csrf/
18. Jovanovic, N., Kirda, E., Kruegel, C.: Preventing cross site request forgery attacks. In: Securecomm and Workshops, pp. 1–10. IEEE (2006)
19. Kidd, R.F.: Crime reporting. Criminology **17**(3), 380–394 (1979)
20. Klein, A.: DOM Based Cross Site Scripting or XSS of the Third Kind. Technical report, July 2005. http://www.webappsec.org/projects/articles/071105.shtml
21. Lu, L., Perdisci, R., Lee, W.: Surf: detecting and measuring search poisoning. In: Proceedings of the 18th ACM Conference on Computer and Communications Security, pp. 467–476. ACM (2011)
22. Milletary, J., CERT Coordination Center: Technical Trends in Phishing Attacks (2005). Accessed 1 Dec 2007
23. Parmar, B.: Protecting against spear-phishing. Comput. Fraud Secur. **2012**(1), 8–11 (2012)
24. Ruderman, J.: Same origin policy for javascript (2001). https://developer.mozilla.org/En/Same_origin_policy_for_JavaScript
25. Rydstedt, G., Bursztein, E., Boneh, D., Jackson, C.: Busting frame busting: a study of clickjacking vulnerabilities at popular sites. In: IEEE Oakland Web 2.0 Security and Privacy (W2SP), pp. 1–13 (2010)

26. Stamm, S., Sterne, B., Markham, G.: Reining in the web with content security policy. In: Rappa, M., Jones, P., Freire, J., Chakrabarti, S. (eds.) Proceedings of the International Conference on World Wide Web, pp. 921–930. ACM (2010)

27. Tam, C., Wells, D.: Evaluating the benefits of displaying word prediction lists on a personal digital assistant at the keyboard level. Assistive Technol. **21**(3), 105–114 (2009)

28. The Open Web Application Security Project. Cross-Site Request Forgery (2010). https://www.owasp.org/index.php/Cross-Site_Request_Forgery_(CSRF)

29. Xing, X., Meng, W. , Doozan, D., Snoeren, A.C., Feamster, N., Lee, W.: Take this personally: attacks on personalized services. In: Proceedings of the 22nd USENIX Conference on Security, pp. 671–686. USENIX Association (2013)

30. Zhou, M., Bisht, P., Venkatakrishnan, V.N.: Strengthening XSRF defenses for legacy web applications using whitebox analysis and transformation. In: Mathuria, A., Jha, S. (eds.) ICISS 2010. LNCS, vol. 6503, pp. 96–110. Springer, Heidelberg (2010)

Breaking into the KeyStore: A Practical Forgery Attack Against Android KeyStore

Mohamed Sabt[1,2(✉)] and Jacques Traorè[1]

[1] Orange Labs, 42 Rue des Coutures, 14066 Caen, France
{mohamed.sabt,jacques.traore}@orange.com
[2] Sorbonne Universités, Université de technologie de Compiègne Heudiasyc,
Centre de recherche Royallieu, 60203 Compiègne, France

Abstract. We analyze the security of Android KeyStore, a system service whose purpose is to shield users credentials and cryptographic keys. The KeyStore protects the integrity and the confidentiality of keys by using a particular encryption scheme. Our main results are twofold. First, we formally prove that the used encryption scheme does not provide integrity, which means that an attacker is able to undetectably modify the stored keys. Second, we exploit this flaw to define a forgery attack breaching the security guaranteed by the KeyStore. In particular, our attack allows a malicious application to make mobile apps to unwittingly perform secure protocols using weak keys. The threat is concrete: the attacker goes undetected while compromising the security of users. Our findings highlight an important fact: intuition often goes wrong when security is concerned. Unfortunately, system designers still tend to choose cryptographic schemes not for their proved security but for their apparent simplicity. We show, once again, that this is not a good choice, since it usually results in severe consequences for the whole underlying system.

Keywords: Android KeyStore · Authenticated encryption · Integrity

1 Introduction

Smartphones are used in an ever-growing variety of use-cases, including highly-sensitive tasks. Third party applications often need to generate and use some sensitive data, such as authentication credentials and cryptographic keys. Unfortunately, no strong protection is guaranteed for these highly valuable data, which might attract powerful attackers motivated by economic gain. This lack has hindered the adoption of smartphones in certain areas in which the use of cryptographic keys is crucial. The development of smartphone market spurs mobile system designers to reinvent their security features. Starting from Android 4.3, aka Jelly Bean, official support for app-specific secrets storage has been provided by a newly introduced component, called *Android KeyStore*.

The Android KeyStore is an Android system service that allows applications to generate, use and store their cryptographic keys. Once inside the KeyStore,

© Springer International Publishing Switzerland 2016
I. Askoxylakis et al. (Eds.): ESORICS 2016, Part II, LNCS 9879, pp. 531–548, 2016.
DOI: 10.1007/978-3-319-45741-3_27

keys can no longer be extracted. They can be used for cryptographic operations without ever leaving the KeyStore.

Multiple implementations exist for the KeyStore. The default one, provided by Google, does all key-related operations using the OpenSSL library. It protects the integrity and the confidentiality of its keys by storing them in encrypted form using authenticated encryption (AE). For some reason, the scheme in use is particular and does not follow any standardized or provably secure construction. Its idea is simple: the message (representing the stored key) is appended to its MD5 hash value before encrypting it with CBC (cipher block chaining) mode. Henceforth, we call this AE scheme *Hash-then-CBC-Encrypt*.

At the first look, Hash-then-CBC-Encrypt is a lightweight mode that has many advantages over other popular AE schemes. It is more efficient than those based on the generic composition approach [6], since the message is needed not to be processed twice. In addition, it is much simpler to implement compared to others. Therefore, it might seem to be the most fitting scheme to implement inside mobile devices for the protection of users keys.

1.1   Our Contribution

In this paper, we show that the use of non-provably secure cryptographic schemes in complex architectures could cause severe consequences. We start by proving that the AE scheme **Hash-then-CBC-Encrypt** does not provide authenticity **regardless of the used hash function**. To this end, we show that it does not satisfy two notions of integrity: integrity of ciphertext (INT-CTXT) and ciphertext unforgeability (CUF-CPA). Then, we present a selective forgery attack where an adversary exploits this weakness to substantially reduce the length of the symmetric keys protected by the KeyStore.

We illustrate this security flaw by defining an attack scenario in which an application entrusts the KeyStore with its symmetric key. Our attack lulls users into a false sense of security by silently transforming, for instance, 256-bit HMAC keys into 32-bit ones. This allows a malicious third party that controls the network to break any secure protocol based on these weak keys. Such an attack might constitute a real threat, since it could happen undetected. At the writing of this paper, our attack affects the latest Android build (android-6.0.1_r22).

Our work brings to light an interesting fact: security in modern systems still does not withstand a simple cryptanalysis. Astonishingly, recently, the KeyStore has been significantly enhanced by new features without reviewing its security correctness. We show that, once again, security by feature-enhancing is disappointedly misleading. Moreover, it is really tempting for system designers to use ad hoc cryptographic schemes due to their straightforwardness and flexibility to meet special needs. The particularity of our work is that we use advanced security notions, such as indistinguishability, in order to compromise a system like Android. Our attack demonstrates that any theoretical weakness concerning the security of a cryptographic scheme could be utilized to break the whole system. We thus show that the scope of these notions extends beyond theory. We advocate the shift onto *provably secure cryptography* in order to prevent potential vulnerabilities that will be hard to find inside a complex system.

1.2 Related Work

KeyStore Security. Encryption in mobile devices is increasingly becoming a topic of utmost importance. Teufl et al. have thoroughly analyzed the encryption components of Android in [24]. This concerns both full disk encryption and credential storage. Authors provide a descriptive study of the two systems. However, no cryptanalysis of the presented cryptographic schemes is given. Works in [9,17] highlight the severity of physical attacks, such as cold boot, against Android's disk encryption. The primary limitation of these attacks is that they require a physical access to the targeted mobile devices.

As for secure credential storage, authors in [25] show that app developers tend to implement their own mechanisms to store credentials. They underline the prevalence of flawed solutions by designing a tool capable of automatically identifying and retrieving app credentials. Developers are thus urged to use the security services proposed by the Android system itself, that is KeyStore. The different flavors, software-based and hardware-based, of the KeyStore are subjected to close scrutiny in [8]. The investigation involves how an adversary is able to compromise the different access controls to the stored keys. However, the study assumes that all the cryptographic algorithms were properly defined and implemented, which is proved not to be true in [10]. Hay et al. exploit a buffer overflow vulnerability that permits the execution of an arbitrary code inside the keystore process. To the best of our knowledge, we present the first cryptanalysis-based attack against the KeyStore. In addition, our attack has the advantages to be software-only and remotely executable.

Authenticated Encryption. Authenticated encryption is a symmetric encryption scheme that protects data confidentiality and integrity. Integrity (authenticity) means that no adversary is able to produce new valid ciphertexts. This entails that encrypted data cannot be undetectably modified. Recently, the design of AE primitives has renewed interest, not least because of the currently running CAESAR competition [7]. The security notions of AE were formalized in the early 2000s in [5,11]. Generic composition [6] is the most popular approach for numerous security protocols, such as SSH,TLS and IPsec. This approach is about combining a confidentiality-providing encryption scheme together with a message authentication code (MAC). Nevertheless, the pursuit of more efficiency than that offered by these two-pass schemes has motivated the construction of dedicated AE designs, such as the Galois Counter Mode (GCM) [14].

It turns out that designers do not only strive for efficiency, but also for implementation simplicity. Therefore, authenticity obtained from *Encryption-with-Redundancy* (EwR) has long been attractive. In such a paradigm, encryption consists of computing some public function h over the message M to get a checksum $\sigma = h(M)$. Then, $M||\sigma$ is encrypted and returned. As for decryption, the ciphertext is decrypted to get $M||\sigma$ and then the equality $\sigma = h(M)$ is verified. Several of these schemes have been partially or fully broken [15,16]. A generic attack attributed to Wagner on a large class of CBC-Encryption-with-Redundancy is described in [20]. An and Bellare in [1] formally prove that this AE scheme does not guarantee security regardless of how the checksum is computed.

Some might argue that Hash-then-Encrypt (HtE) is just a special case of EwR, where the checksum function h is a hash function. However, we argue that this is not true. Indeed, the checksum is appended at the end of the message $(M||\sigma)$ in EwR, while the hash value is appended at the beginning of the message $(\sigma||M)$ in HtE. Thus, generic attacks against EwR, Wagner's for instance, are easier to apply than those against HtE. This is due to the fact that the former typically requires to remove the last block of ciphertexts, and for many schemes, the decryption of the first blocks does not depend on the last ones (e.g. CBC and CTR). Moreover, the proof of Bellare only shows that EwR does not offer a sufficient condition for security even if the underlying base encryption is secure. A similar result related to MAC-then-Encrypt (MtE) is given in [6]. In order to avoid misinterpretation, we emphasize that these results only imply that such constructions are not *generically* secure: the soundness of the underlying primitives does not constitute a sufficient condition to guarantee security. Indeed, the proof consists of providing a counterexample, i.e. a particular MtE scheme that it is not IND-CCA although its encryption and MAC algorithms are secure. The proof is applicable only for special IND-CPA encryption schemes whose ciphertexts can be modified without changing their corresponding plaintexts, which is clearly not the case for CBC and CTR modes. We note that the results of [6] do not mean that all MtE schemes are inherently broken. A body of results (e.g. [18]) has proved the security of several schemes following this construction.

In this paper, we give the first proof that HtE for both CBC and CTR modes, indeed, does not guarantee integrity. In addition, the proof that we provide is not a mere existential forgery or a theoretical distinguishing attack. Unlike related work, we provide a practical attack that could be exploited to compromise the Android KeyStore. The threat is concrete: the broken HtE in CBC mode (Hash-then-CBC-Encrypt) is the cryptographic scheme that is used to safeguard the stored keys in Android mobile devices.

1.3   Responsible Disclosure

We communicated our findings to Google in January 2016. The Android security team has acknowledged the attack presented in this paper and confirmed that the broken encryption scheme is planned for removal.

1.4   Paper Outline

The rest of the paper is structured as follows: Sect. 2 reviews some classical definitions and notations. In Sect. 3, we provide two proofs that Hash-then-CBC-Encrypt does not provide integrity. Section 4 describes some technical details about the Android KeyStore. We present our attack scenario in Sect. 5. Section 6 provides some discussion and specific recommendations related to the identified vulnerability.

2   Definitions

A message is a string. A string is a member of $\{0,1\}^*$. The concatenation of strings X and Y is denoted $X||Y$ or simply XY. For a string X, its length is represented by $|X|$. A *block cipher* is a function $E : \text{Key} \times \{0,1\}^n \longrightarrow \{0,1\}^n$, where Key is a finite nonempty set and $E_k(.) = E(k,.)$ is a permutation, hence invertible, on $\{0,1\}^n$. The number n is called the *block length*. We use the notation $\mathbf{A}^{\mathcal{O}}$ to denote the fact that the algorithm $\mathbf{A}$ can make queries to the function $\mathcal{O}$. Hereafter, we say that the *adversary* $\mathbf{A}$ has access to the *oracle* $\mathcal{O}$. If f is a randomized (resp., deterministic) algorithm, then $y \xleftarrow{R} f(x)$ (resp., $y \leftarrow f(x)$) denotes the process of running f on input x and assigning the result to y.

SYMMETRIC ENCRYPTION SCHEMES. Following Bellare et al. in [4], a *symmetric encryption scheme* $\mathcal{SE}$ is given by three algorithms $(\mathcal{K}, \mathcal{E}, \mathcal{D})$, where (1) the *key generation algorithm*, $\mathcal{K}$, takes a security parameter $k \in \mathbb{N}$ and returns a key K. We write $\mathsf{K} \xleftarrow{R} \mathcal{K}(k)$; (2) the *encryption algorithm*, $\mathcal{E}$, takes a key K and a plaintext M to produce a ciphertext C. We write $C \xleftarrow{R} \mathcal{E}_k(M)$; and (3) the *decryption algorithm*, $\mathcal{D}$, takes a key K and a ciphertext C to return either the corresponding plaintext M or a special symbol $\perp$ to indicate that the ciphertext is invalid. We require that $\mathcal{D}_k(\mathcal{E}_k(M)) = M$ for all M and K.

SECRECY OF A SYMMETRIC ENCRYPTION SCHEME. The security of symmetric encryption schemes is usually classified from the point of view of their goals and attack models. The classical goal of secure encryption is to protect the confidentiality of messages, which could be defined by various concepts [23].

The most used one is *indistinguishability* (IND) that is formalized as follows [4]: given a symmetric encryption $\mathcal{SE} = (\mathcal{K}, \mathcal{E}, \mathcal{D})$ and a ciphertext of one of two plaintexts, no adversary can distinguish which one was encrypted. IND can be expressed as an experiment. Let $\mathcal{E}_k(\mathcal{LR}(.,.,b))$ be a *left-or-right* oracle where $b \in \{0,1\}$: the oracle takes two messages of equal length as input, m_0 and m_1, and returns $C \leftarrow \mathcal{E}_k(m_b)$. The adversary submits queries of the form (m_0, m_1), where $|m_0| = |m_1|$, to the oracle, and must guess which message was encrypted. If all adversaries cannot succeed with probability better than a random guess, then $\mathcal{SE}$ is called *IND-ATK secure*, where *ATK* represents the attack model.

The standard attack models are as follows: (1) The *chosen plaintext attack* (CPA) in which an adversary has access to the encryption oracle $\mathcal{E}_k(\mathcal{LR}(.,.,b))$, so that she can choose a set of plaintexts and obtain the corresponding ciphertexts; (2) the *chosen ciphertext attack* (CCA) in which an adversary has access, besides the encryption oracle, to the decryption oracle $\mathcal{D}_k(.)$, so that she can choose a set of ciphertexts and obtain their plaintexts.

Definition 1 *(Indistinguishability of a Symmetric Encryption Scheme).* Let $\mathcal{SE} = (\mathcal{K}, \mathcal{E}, \mathcal{D})$ be a symmetric encryption scheme. Let A be a polynomial-time adversary. For $b \in \{0,1\}$ and $k \in \mathbb{N}$, consider the following experiments:

Experiment $Exp_{\mathcal{SE},A_{cpa}}^{ind-cpa-b}(k)$

1: $K \xleftarrow{R} \mathcal{K}(k)$
2: $x \longleftarrow A_{cpa}^{\mathcal{E}_k(\mathcal{LR}(.,.,b))}$
3: **return** x

Experiment $Exp_{\mathcal{SE},A_{cca}}^{ind-cca-b}(k)$

1: $K \xleftarrow{R} \mathcal{K}(k)$
2: $x \longleftarrow A_{cca}^{\mathcal{E}_k(\mathcal{LR}(.,.,b)), \mathcal{D}_k}$
3: **return** x

The adversary A is prohibited from querying $\mathcal{D}_k(.)$ on a ciphertext C output by the encryption oracle. For $atk \in \{cpa, cca\}$, the advantage of the adversary is defined as follows:

$$Adv_{\mathcal{SE}}^{ind-atk}(k) = Pr[Exp_{\mathcal{SE},A}^{ind-atk-1} = 1] - Pr[Exp_{\mathcal{SE},A}^{ind-atk-0} = 1]$$

The scheme $\mathcal{SE}$ is *secure* if the advantage of any adversary is negligible.

THE CIPHER BLOCK CHAINING (CBC) MODE. Encryption with a raw block cipher is not used in practice. Instead, several modes of operation exist. Here, we only consider the CBC mode.

Definition 2 *(The CBC Encryption Scheme).* Let $E_k :$ Key $\times \{0,1\}^l \longrightarrow \{0,1\}^l$ be a block cipher and let E_k^{-1} be its inverse. Let $\text{CBC}[E_k] = (\mathcal{K}, \mathcal{E}, \mathcal{D})$ be its associated CBC encryption scheme. Given a message $M = m_1||...||m_n \in \{0,1\}^{ln}$, the encryption and the decryption algorithms are defined as follows:

CBC Encryption $\mathcal{E}_k^{\text{CBC}}(M)$

1: Parse M as $m_1||...||m_n$
2: $c_0 \xleftarrow{R} \{0,1\}^l$
3: **for** $i = 1...n$ **do**
4:     $c_i \longleftarrow E_k(c_{i-1} \oplus m_i)$
5: **end for**
6: **return** $c_0||c_1||...||c_n$

CBC Decryption $\mathcal{D}_k^{\text{CBC}}(C)$

1: Parse C as $c_0||c_1||...||c_n$
2: **for** $i = 1...n$ **do**
3:     $m_i \longleftarrow E_k^{-1}(c_i) \oplus c_{i-1}$
4: **end for**
5: **return** $m_1||...||m_n$

Two points should be noted in the definition. First, the random IV is denoted c_0 in order to highlight that the IV is included along with the ciphertext. Second, we make the simplifying assumption that $\mathcal{D}_k^{\text{CBC}}(.)$ never returns the error message $\perp$. It takes any ciphertext as input, and always returns some string.

3 Hash-Then-CBC-Encrypt Does Not Provide Integrity

In this section, we start by reviewing the different concepts of integrity which our proof relies on. We then provide a formal definition of Hash-then-CBC-Encrypt. We end by proving that this scheme is not secure.

3.1 Integrity of a Symmetric Encryption Scheme

In the context of symmetric encryption, integrity (or authenticity) means that only valid parties possessing the secret key K are able to produce a valid ciphertext; i.e. whose decryption does not give $\perp$. Symmetric encryption schemes in general do not protect the integrity of messages. For example, the CBC mode does not provide integrity, since it never returns $\perp$. The IND-CPA secure schemes that also provide integrity are called authenticated encryption schemes.

Throughout this paper, we consider two notions of integrity: integrity of ciphertext (INT-CTXT) [6] and ciphertext unforgeability (CUF-CPA) [12]. Both notions require that no adversary be able to produce a valid ciphertext which the encryption oracle had never produced before. However, contrary to INT-CTXT, the adversary in CUF-CPA has no access to the decryption oracle and outputs only one attempted forgery. Despite of their similarity, these two notions are defined to accomplish different goals. Indeed, INT-CTXT is a strong measure for security, while CUF-CPA is a strong one for the effectiveness of the potential attacks. Thus, proving that a symmetric scheme does not achieve neither INT-CTXT nor CUF-CPA entails two consequences: (1) the scheme does not provide high security and therefore it should not be used by scheme designers; and (2) the found attack is very damaging due to its readily implementation in practice.

Definition 3 *(Integrity of an Authenticated Encryption Scheme).* Let $\mathcal{SE} = (\mathcal{K}, \mathcal{E}, \mathcal{D})$ be a symmetric encryption scheme. Let A be a polynomial-time adversary. Let S be the list of all ciphertexts generated by the adversary queries to $\mathcal{E}_k(.)$. For $k \in \mathbb{N}$, the following experiments are defined:

Experiment $Exp_{\mathcal{SE}, A_{ctxt}}^{int\text{-}ctxt}(k)$	**Experiment** $Exp_{\mathcal{SE}, A_{\text{-}cpa}}^{cuf\text{-}cpa}(k)$
1: $\mathsf{K} \xleftarrow{R} \mathcal{K}(k)$	1: $\mathsf{K} \xleftarrow{R} \mathcal{K}(k)$
2: **if** $C \leftarrow A_{ctxt}^{\mathcal{E}_k(.), \mathcal{D}_k(.)}$ such that	2: $C \longleftarrow A_{cuf\text{-}cpa}^{\mathcal{E}_k(.)}$
$\quad \mathcal{D}_k(C) \neq \perp$ and $C \notin \mathsf{S}$ **then**	3: **if** $\mathcal{D}_k(C) \neq \perp$ and $C \notin \mathsf{S}$ **then**
3: $\quad\quad$ **return 1**	4: $\quad\quad$ **return 1**
4: **else**	5: **else**
5: $\quad\quad$ **return 0**	6: $\quad\quad$ **return 0**
6: **end if**	7: **end if**

For both experiments, the adversary's advantage is defined to be:

$$Adv_{\mathcal{SE}, A}^{int}(k) = Pr[Exp_{\mathcal{SE}, A}^{int} = 1]$$

The scheme $\mathcal{SE}$ is *INT-CTXT secure* (or *CUF-CPA secure*) if the corresponding advantage is negligible for any adversary.

3.2 Hash-then-CBC-Encrypt

Conceptually, Hash-then-CBC-Encrypt in its general setting is an authenticated encryption scheme obtained from the association of any given hash function with any given CBC encryption algorithm.

Construction 1 *(Hash-then-CBC-Encrypt (hCBC)).* Let $CBC[E_k] = (\mathcal{K}, \mathcal{E}, \mathcal{D})$ be an IND-CPA CBC encryption scheme, where E_k is a block cipher of block length l. Let h be a hash function. Without loss of generality, we suppose that the output length of h is l bits (otherwise, padding is needed). For $M \in \{0,1\}^{ln}$, we define the composite Hash-then-CBC-Encrypt $hCBC = (h, \mathcal{K}, \mathcal{E}', \mathcal{D}')$ as follows:

Encryption $\mathcal{E}'_k(M)$	**Decryption** $\mathcal{D}'_k(C)$
1: $\sigma \longleftarrow h(M)$	1: Parse $\mathcal{D}^{CBC}_k(C)$ as $\sigma' \| M$
2: $C \longleftarrow \mathcal{E}^{CBC}_k(\sigma \| M)$	2: if $\sigma' \neq h(M)$ then
3: return C	3: return $\perp$
	4: end if
	5: return M

3.3   Hash-then-CBC-Encrypt is not INT-CTXT

Here, we provide an indirect proof that $hCBC$ is not secure against INT-CTXT. For this, we use the relations among notions that are defined in [6]. In particular, we use a derived one: if an AE scheme is IND-CPA and not IND-CCA, then it is not INT-CTXT (**IND-CPA** $\wedge$ **¬IND-CCA** $\Rightarrow$ **¬INT-CTXT**), which is easily obtained from **IND-CPA** $\wedge$ **INT-CTXT** $\Rightarrow$ **IND-CCA**. Therefore, our proof is composed of two parts: firstly we prove that $hCBC$ is IND-CPA and secondly we prove that it is not IND-CCA.

Proposition 1 *Hash-then-CBC-Encrypt is IND-CPA secure.*

The proof is based on a standard reduction argument, and the understanding of the rest of the paper does not depend on it. We leave it for [22].

Proposition 2 *Hash-then-CBC-Encrypt is not IND-CCA secure.*

Proof Let A be an IND-CCA adversary for $hCBC = (h, \mathcal{K}, \mathcal{E}, \mathcal{D})$. Its algorithm is shown below.

Algorithm. $A^{\mathcal{E}_k(\mathcal{LR}(.,.,b)), \mathcal{D}_k}_{cca}$

1: Let m_0 and m_1 be two messages	7: $x \longleftarrow \mathcal{D}_k(C')$
2: $m'_0 \longleftarrow h(m_0) \| m_0$	8: if $x \neq \perp$ then
3: $m'_1 \longleftarrow h(m_0) \| m_1$	9: return 0
4: $C \longleftarrow \mathcal{E}_k(\mathcal{LR}(m'_0, m'_1, b))$	10: else
5: Parse C as $c_0 \| c_1 \| c_2 \| c_3$	11: return 1
6: $C' \longleftarrow c_1 \| c_2 \| c_3$	12: end if

We claim that the previous adversary succeeds whether $b = 0$ or $b = 1$. Therefore, $Adv^{ind-cca}_{hCBC}(A) = 1$, and as a result, $hCBC$ is not CCA-secure. Recall that the oracle $\mathcal{E}_k(\mathcal{LR}(.,.,b))$ returns the ciphertext of one of the two submitted messages. Thus, we have $C = \mathcal{E}_k(m'_b = h(m_0) \| m_b)$. Applying $hCBC$, C can be written as $\mathcal{E}^{CBC}_k(h(h(m_0) \| m_b) \| h(m_0) \| m_b)$, which is composed as follows:

$$C = c_0 \| \overbrace{E_k(c_0 \oplus h(h(m_0) \| m_b))}^{c_1} \| \overbrace{E_k(c_1 \oplus h(m_0))}^{c_2} \| \overbrace{E_k(c_2 \oplus m_b)}^{c_3}$$

We see that for C', c_0 is removed and c_1 becomes the new initial value. Considering the new IV, the CBC decryption algorithm performed over C' returns the rest of the plaintext $h(m_0)||m_b$. Therefore, $\mathcal{D}_k(C')$ outputs m_0 when $b = 0$, $\perp$ otherwise (unless $h(m_0) = h(m_1)$), which concludes our proof.

3.4 Hash-then-CBC-Encrypt is not CUF-CPA

As a matter of fact, we have already proved that hCBC is not CUF-CPA. Indeed, following [19], if a scheme is not INT-CTXT, then consequently, it is not CUF-CPA. Nevertheless, our goal here is to explicitly provide a selective forgery upon which our attack scenario against the KeyStore is built. We note that the presented attack is quite powerful: the adversary succeeds in forging a valid ciphertext for any message M after only one query to the encryption oracle.

Proof Let A be a CUF-CPA adversary for hCBC $= (h, \mathcal{K}, \mathcal{E}, \mathcal{D})$. We will show that A can forge a valid ciphertext for any $M \in \{0,1\}^{ln}$.

Algorithm. $A_{\text{cuf-cpa}}^{\mathcal{E}_k}(M)$

1: $M' \longleftarrow h(M)||M$	4: $C' \longleftarrow c_1||c_2||...||c_{n+2}$
2: $C \longleftarrow \mathcal{E}_k(M')$	5: **return** C'
3: Parse C as $c_0||c_1||c_2||...||c_{n+2}$	

As mentioned in Definition 3, the adversary A wins if the output ciphertext C' is both new and valid. Trivially, C' has never been produced by the encryption oracle $\mathcal{E}_k(.)$ before, and thus it is new. In addition, we argue that the oracle $\mathcal{D}_k(.)$ on C' will not return $\perp$. Indeed, using the same arguments given in Proposition 2, C' could be written as $\mathcal{E}_k^{\text{CBC}}(h(M)||M)$. Thus, $\mathcal{D}_k(C') = M(\neq \perp)$.

4 The Android KeyStore

The Android KeyStore is a high-level service that enables applications to store their credentials. The original credential store was created in Android 1.6 and was limited to store VPN and Wi-Fi EAP credentials. Back then, only the operating system, and not user applications, could access the stored keys and certificates. It is worth mentioning that hereafter all the implementation details that we provide concern the KeyStore of the build *android-6.0.1_r22*, which is the latest version of Android at the writing of this paper.

As illustrated in Fig. 1, the KeyStore is comprised of three layers: *Public APIs*, *Keystore service*, and *Keymaster*. The security of keys is primarily ensured by the *Keymaster* which is designed to protect keys from extraction. This implies that it is the only component that has a direct access to keys material, and therefore keys are represented differently outside Keymaster: alias (name) in *Public APIs* and key handlers in *Keystore service*.

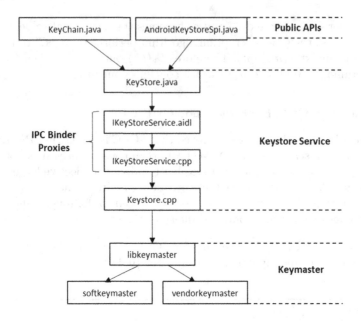

Fig. 1. Android KeyStore Architecture

Generally speaking, the key handler is an opaque object that identifies a keymaster-protected key. Key handlers are implementation-dependent. We only consider the default software-only keymaster provided by Google. By inspecting its implementation that is found in `keymaster_openssl.cpp`, we see that the key handler is just an encoded version of the corresponding key. Encoding is achieved by concatenating a header of describing meta data to the key. The header includes: a 4-byte constant value for software keys, a 4-byte key type, and a 4-byte big endian integer for key length. Thus, the default key handler is written as follows: `Soft_Key_Magic` || `Key_Type` || `Key_Length` || `Key`.

Our target in this paper is the stored keys on mobile device. Therefore, in what follows, we focus solely on the secure mechanism performed by the *Keystore service* for storing keys (or more precisely key handlers).

4.1   Keystore Service

Similar to other services, the Keystore service spans two layers in the Android architecture: the Java world (application framework) and the native world (system service). Based on the Binder, its different components, *KeyStore.java* and *Keystore.cpp*, communicate via the Binder proxy *IKeyStoreService*.

The implementation [2] of the Keystore reveals how the blobs of key handlers are stored on mobile device. A key handler blob (binary large object) contains a serialized version of the key handler. The keystore saves its files in */data/misc/keystore*, where there is one directory for each user. Each directory includes files that have the following content:

- A single master key. The Keystore service is initialized by generating a 128-bit master key using the internal entropy source *dev/urandom*. The master key is then encrypted by a 128-bit AES key derived from the screen passcode. The encrypted keymaster is stored in the .*masterkey* file.
- Key handler blobs related to user's applications. Each file contains a header of meta data as well as the encryption of the key handler using Hash-then-CBC-Encrypt. The content of the file is written as follows:

$$\texttt{meta data} \parallel \mathcal{E}^{\mathrm{CBC[AES]}}_{master\_key}(\texttt{MD5(key handler)} \parallel \texttt{key handler})$$

We note that the KeyStore applies $h\mathrm{CBC} = (\texttt{MD5}, \mathcal{K}, \mathcal{E}^{\mathrm{CBC}}_{\mathrm{AES}}, \mathcal{D}^{\mathrm{CBC}}_{\mathrm{AES}})$ to protect key handlers. Therefore, the adversary defined in Sect. 3.4 is able to maliciously forge new key handlers given valid ones. However, this attack fails in practice when performed against the Keystore service because the produced key handlers would yield errors while being decoded. We recall that key handlers have a special encoding format that is specified by the keymaster. In the next Section, we adapt our forgery attack so that an adversary could fabricate a valid key handler which the keymaster successfully parses to its related key.

5   Attacking the Android KeyStore

5.1   Technical Background

As mentioned previously, our target is the secure storage of keys. As a result, among all other operations provided by the KeyStore, only those involving the encryption of the stored keys will be relevant to us. This includes two operations: *key generation* and *key import*.

The KeyStore is designed to work not only with its own keys, but with those generated by a third party system. This implies that all keys, generated or imported, must follow a special format when being serialized. For instance, the keymaster requires formatting keys before wrapping them inside key handlers. The file `keymaster_defs.h` shows that there are three categories of formats:

```
typedef enum {
    KM_KEY_FORMAT_X509 = 0,   /* for public key export */
    KM_KEY_FORMAT_PKCS8 = 1,  /* for asymmetric key pair import */
    KM_KEY_FORMAT_RAW  = 3,   /* for symmetric key import */
} keymaster_key_format_t;
```

We notice that standard formats (i.e. X.509 and PKCS#8) are used for key-pairs, while no format is provided for symmetric keys. Thus, the exact bytes comprising a symmetric key are encapsulated inside the stored key handler. This is due to the fact that their support is quite recent. Indeed, until lately, the KeyStore was limited to asymmetric key-pairs (e.g. RSA, DSA and EC).

This lack of formatting makes the adversary task easier. Indeed, it is hard to fabricate a ciphertext that is both valid and properly formatted. Consequently, the current version of our attack is limited to applications using symmetric keys.

5.2   Threat Model

The adversary's goal is to undetectably undermine the security of the applications relying on symmetric keys for their security. For this purpose, we assume that the adversary installs some malware on the mobile device. This malware is capable of importing keys inside the KeyStore, since any installed application does have this capability. In addition, the malware is supposed to be granted the read-write permission on the KeyStore directory (i.e. */data/misc/keystore*).

Furthermore, the malware is executed inside a mobile device with protective tools. First, the mobile system detects any malware trying to connect to a remote server. Second, the mobile system imposes the use of a strong screen passcode. This helps to avoid exhaustive attacks, since the master key of the KeyStore is derived from this passcode. Third, the system prohibits the KeyStore from storing short or obviously non-random keys. Thus, the adversary cannot perform the trivial attack consisting of generating the same key for all applications or generating a different key for each application and communicating it to a server. In both cases, the attack would be detected. We insist that these assumptions are highly plausible in corporate environments where companies enforce the security of their employees mobile devices.

Finally, the adversary controls all communications with the mobile, and thus can intercept and tamper with any exchanged message. Besides, it is assumed that any proved cryptographic mechanism is secure unless weak keys are used.

To sum up, in order to succeed her attack, the adversary should silently "break into" the KeyStore to shorten, and hence weaken, the stored keys which the targeted applications would blindly continue using.

5.3   The Forgery Attack

The purpose of the forgery attack is that given a ciphertext of a symmetric key, the adversary can fabricate another ciphertext that decrypts to a shorter key. As already stated, the KeyStore protects keys by encrypting their key handlers with hCBC. Thus, keys protection, involving their confidentiality and integrity, is done using a variant of hCBC which we call *encode-then-hCBC* (*eh*CBC).

Informally, *eh*CBC is an AE scheme where messages are encoded before hCBC-encrypting them. To be more precise, let *eh*CBC $= (\mathcal{K}', \mathcal{E}', \mathcal{D}')$ be an encoded version of hCBC $= (h, \mathcal{K}, \mathcal{E}, \mathcal{D})$. Then, for all message M, the next relation holds: $\mathcal{E}'(M) = \mathcal{E}(\texttt{Length}(M)\|M)$. In what follows, we adapt the CUF-CPA adversary of hCBC in order to compromise *eh*CBC.

Let M be an arbitrary weak symmetric key, and let **A** be an attacker that can import keys of its choice to the KeyStore. For the sake of clarity, we omit the constant values in the header of the key handler, and so only the key_length is kept. Therefore, the import function corresponds to the *eh*CBC-encryption operation ($\mathcal{E}'_k$). It is worth mentioning that this simplifying assumption does not alter the logic of the attack. **A** wins if it can produce a valid *eh*CBC-ciphertext of M. However, conforming to our threat model (Sect. 5.2), the attacker cannot import M directly. To this end, **A** executes the algorithm below:

Algorithm. $A_{\text{malicious}}^{\text{import}}(M)$

1: $M' \longleftarrow \text{Len}(M) \,\|\, M$
2: $M'' \longleftarrow \text{MD5}(M') \,\|\, M'$
3: $C \longleftarrow \mathcal{E}'_k(\text{padding} \,\|\, M'')$
so that $\text{Len}(.)\|\text{padding}$ is l-block

4: Parse C as $c_0\|c_1\|c_2\|C'$
5: $C'' \longleftarrow c_2 \,\|\, C'$
6: **return** C''

Following the same arguments provided in Sects. 3.3 and 3.4, we can see that $\mathcal{D}_k^{eh\text{CBC}}(C'')$ outputs M, which means that **A** achieves its goal. Though, it is important to notice that the attacker owes part of its success to the absence of verification of sound key lengths. Indeed, considering all the technical details that we provided, the length in bytes of the imported key ($\text{padding}\|M''$) is always greater than 32, since it is constructed of at least two AES blocks (i.e. $\text{MD5}(.)$ and $\text{Len}(.)\|\text{padding}$). For instance, if **A** selects 4-byte M (or key), it calls the import function on a key of length 36 bytes. We recall that AES keys cannot be longer than 32 bytes. Fortunately (for the attacker), no checking is done by import, and consequently the attack ends successfully.

We underline that the interest of the above attack is twofold. First, it can be abused by some malware to breach the KeyStore security even in a well-protected mobile system. Second, we prove that encoding does not improve the security of hCBC unlike for many other AE schemes. We believe that this result is of independent importance regardless of the introduced attack scenario.

5.4   The Undetected Malware

We illustrate the fallout of our forgery against the KeyStore by a complete attack scenario. We emphasize that the severity of protecting highly sensitive data, like keys, by a broken cryptographic scheme is not limited to the suggested scenario.

In our scenario, the intent of the attacker is to maliciously modify all the exchanged messages between an app and a remote server even if they are protected by proved cryptography. This is possible thanks to some malware installed on the mobile and which soundlessly weakens the keys of the KeyStore. This attacker represents a new kind of threat, since she can go undetected while compromising the security of users including those hiding behind secure protocols.

Actors. We define five actors to describe the plot of the attack: (1) a *security manager* who enforces the security of the mobile system. In particular, the KeyStore refuses to store weak (i.e. short) keys. Additionally, the system would detect any malware trying to communicate with its accomplice server; (2) a *victim* who uses the said mobile to perform some services requiring to protect their critical transactions. The corresponding cryptographic keys are managed by the KeyStore; (3) a *remote server* related to the running services and to which the critical transactions are sent; (4) a *malicious application* viciously shortening the keys of other applications; and (5) a *colluding party* that is able to intercept and alter any exchanged message on the network.

Attack Workflow. We suppose that the attacker has already convinced the victim in some way to install the malicious application on her device. The attack scenario is structured into three phases: provisioning, lulling and attacking.

Provisioning phase. The malicious application runs in background and executes the algorithm described in Sect. 5.3. Thus, it craftily generates several symmetric keys of length $32 + x$ bytes. Then, it imports these keys into the KeyStore which accepts them for two reasons: they are seemingly strong and no verification is done concerning their abnormal length. Afterward, it cuts them down into keys of length x bytes. Here, we take x to be 4, so that keys are small enough to allow a swift brute-force attack. For the sake of completeness, we precise that once the keys are trimmed, their meta data are required to be padded with some dummy data. This is because the files containing the keys must remain of constant size. For brevity, we omit the technical details related to this balancing operation.

Lulling phase. In this phase, an application on the victim's device asks the KeyStore to generate a key with *alias* as its name. The malicious application, snooping on the KeyStore, notes this alias as well as the UID of the caller application. As soon as the key is generated and its associated file is created, the malicious application modifies the name of one of its keys in such a way that the renamed key is believed to belong to the targeted application. Some might argue that this operation is delicate, since the malicious application is assumed to continuously supervise the KeyStore activities. Nevertheless, we argue that no special privilege is required. Indeed, it can be done with quite ease by monitoring the content of the KeyStore folder. This is due to the fact that the key's alias and the creating application's UID could be guessed from the key file name.

Attacking phase. Now, the user is carrying out some operations that involve transmitting sensitive messages to a server. The application handling such operations needs to protect the integrity of these messages. Therefore, it asks the KeyStore to generate an HMAC tag over each message. The KeyStore returns a tag unwittingly generated with the weak key. Concatenated to their tag, the messages are then intercepted by the colluding party while being sent to the server. The latter performs an exhaustive search to find the secret key used to generate the HMAC tag. Since the search space being explored is shrunk, the brute-force search ends quite fast. The colluding party then modifies the content of some messages (e.g. the total amount of a payment transaction), and recomputes a valid tag for them before forwarding the new messages to the server. In this way, the attacker effortlessly breaks into victims who think that they are safe with primitives, HMAC for example, which are believed to be secure.

5.5   The Hidden Assumption

The malicious application is supposed to have read/write permissions to the folder `/data/misc/keystore`. Nevertheless, in practice, the Android system restricts access to this folder: only the *keystore* user is allowed to see or modify its contents. Thus, the success of our attack depends on how likely the malicious application is to bypass the access control mechanisms of Android. This requires one of these two extra abilities: (1) executing an arbitrary code inside the keystore process by either code injection or code reuse; and (2) obtaining root or kernel-level privileges. Some might argue that once such abilities have been gained the presented attack in Sect. 5.4 could be realized otherwise. Here, we present three possible scenarios and we discuss how our attack is more effective.

The Trivial Scenario. With a root privilege, we need not bother mutating key blobs. Instead, we can simply recover the master key from the keystore memory in order to decrypt/re-encrypt any keystore file. This scenario is not as straightforward as it seems to be. Indeed, it involves a program to parse the memory. The problem is that the keystore has been regularly updated recently, so its memory layout has been continuously changing. Therefore, this program may require to be different depending on the installed Android version. In addition, it should be constantly maintained to keep on with any further update. We note that the format of the keystore files has not changed since Android 4.3. Involving only basic I/O file operations, our attack is much simpler and more portable.

The Big-Brother Function. The malicious application and her colluding party agree on a function $\mathcal{B}$ to generate keys that could be quickly guessed. Unable to communicate, otherwise the subversion will be detected, the function $\mathcal{B}$ is embedded into the malicious application. It is easy to see that this attack ends successfully following our threat model. However, we claim that our attack is more practical because it satisfies two additional properties: (1) *stateless*: the adversary (i.e. colluding party) needs not to store data related to the victim (i.e. the mobile device) so as to win; and (2) *size-oblivious*: the complexity of the attack does not increase with the number of the targeted users. In contrast, the other attack cannot be both stateless and size-oblivious. Indeed, the function $\mathcal{B}$ outputs a new key for each device. Keys shall seem to be strong, otherwise they will be rejected. The more the attacker targets new devices, the bigger the keys search space becomes. Avoiding this increase in time of execution involves the parameterization of the function $\mathcal{B}$ for each user. For instance, $\mathcal{B}$ might be seeded with the device IMEI (International Mobile station Equipment Identity). Hence, the attack becomes size-oblivious, but stateful. Statelessness is important in our context due to its relevance to stronger undetectability.

Man in the KeyStore. The scenario supposes that all calls to the KeyStore are intercepted at runtime by the malicious application. Subverted values are returned for any intercepted call, including all cryptographic operations. Surely, this attack is powerful, but we argue that it is more limited than ours. Firstly, actively proxying all calls might be resource-consuming, i.e. slowing down the mobile or shortening its battery life, which makes the attack quite detectable. Secondly, the Keystore service is based on the Binder architecture, and thus intercepting calls requires an attack of type *Man in the Binder* (MitB). However, a success MitB [3] necessitates deep insight on how Binder works, consequently it is version-dependent and more complicated than just reading/writing files.

6 Discussion and Recommendations

An important aspect of any forgery is what it implies in practice. Here, we have demonstrated how a theoretical weakness could be exploited to undermine the security of a real-world system, namely Android. In addition, the defined attack is attractive to implement, since it is simple and not demanding in term of resources. We insist that this scenario is just an example: a wholly new class of threat could be built from our forgery attack.

Furthermore, it is worth noting that the attack of Sect. 5 is conceived to be applicable only against software-only implementations of KeyStore. We admit that it does not directly impact hardware-based implementations which exist on some mobile devices. Indeed, our scenario involves forging keys by forging key handlers. Hardware-backed implementations, such as those based on Trusted Execution Environment (TEE) [21], encrypt their keys with AE schemes to produce their key handlers. Therefore, the integrity of keys is protected by two means: the Keystore service and the TEE. In our scenario, an attacker can still forge a valid key handler that is sent to the Keymaster (i.e., TEE). The TEE in its turn will detect the forgery when it decodes the forged key handler, which means that the attack does not succeed. However, we can imagine other possible vectors of attack. For example, an attacker might perform a fuzzy attack by generating valid key handlers and send them to the TEE. A malformed key handler might allow the attacker to carry out, for instance, a stack overflow attack.

Finally, we believe that even if some may argue that our attack is difficult to mount, there is value in identifying these types of design flaws. Corporate-issued devices or state-level malware could easily execute the described attack in order to gain undetectable long-term access to device communications.

Recommendations. Having thus presented our main results, we are now on a position to make specific recommendations. We recall that any countermeasure intended to fix a deployed system must not cause intrusive changes that affect the entire architecture of this system. Fortunately, the KeyStore design is modular enough to allow modifying the scheme hCBC without involving the rest.

The quickest solution would be to keep the *hash-then-encrypt* paradigm and use it with another encryption mode. The Counter (CTR) mode is often perceived as being advantageous to other modes. However, we prove that the scheme *Hash-then-CTR-Encrypt* does not provide integrity either. The full proof is given in [22]. We could have proposed other encryption modes, however the lack of obvious attacks cannot be taken as evidence of the soundness of a scheme. Instead, it would be better to switch to proved AE encryption schemes. At first glance, the simplest solution to make would seem to be Encrypt-then-MAC (EtM). Unfortunately, the 'generic composition' approach does not suit systems like Android. In fact, efficiency is important for mobile devices. EtM might incur some overhead while computing ciphertexts. Moreover, it might be hard to implement because of manually managing two different cryptographic primitives.

Thus, we might believe that mobile designers should just go and pick up one of the AE one-pass dedicated schemes. It turns out that choosing a proper scheme is a great hassle for system designers. Let us discuss two popular ones:OCB (Offset Codebook Mode) [13] and GCM (Galois Counter Mode) [14]. OCB is a fast, secure and easy to implement AE encryption scheme. However, Rogaway, its inventer, holds a patent on it, and therefore it is not free to use. As for GCM, it is also fast and secure, but it involves hard mathematical concepts. As a result, most system designers feel unable to go through and implement GCM. We suspect that the absence of trusted implementations while defining the first KeyStore architecture might have been the reason of using hCBC. Today, GCM is being increasingly supported by free libraries, such as OpenSSL. Hence, we recommend to replace hCBC by GCM in the Android KeyStore.

It is worth reiterating that proved cryptography is the way to go. A key lesson from this paper is that cryptographers and system designers must work closely together. Bridging the gap that separates these communities will be essential for keeping future systems secure.

Acknowledgments. We would like to thank Mohammed Achemlal, Marc Girault and Olivier Sanders for valuable discussions.

References

1. An, J.H., Bellare, M.: Does encryption with redundancy provide authenticity? In: Pfitzmann, B. (ed.) EUROCRYPT 2001. LNCS, vol. 2045, pp. 512–528. Springer, Heidelberg (2001)

2. Android: Keystore implementation. https://android.googlesource.com/platform/system/security/+/master/keystore/keystore.cpp

3. Artenstein, N., Revivo, I.: Man in the Binder: He who controls IPC, controls the droid (2014). www.blackhat.com/docs/eu-14/materials/eu-14-Artenstein-Man-In-The-Binder-He-Who-Controls-IPC-Controls-The-Droid-wp.pdf

4. Bellare, M., Desai, A., Jokipii, E., Rogaway, P.: A concrete security treatment of symmetric encryption. In: Proceedings of the 38th Annual Symposium on Foundations of Computer Science, FOCS 1997, pp. 394–405. IEEE (1997)

5. Bellare, M., Namprempre, C.: Authenticated encryption: relations among notions and analysis of the generic composition paradigm. In: Okamoto, T. (ed.) ASIACRYPT 2000. LNCS, vol. 1976, p. 531. Springer, Heidelberg (2000)

6. Bellare, M., Namprempre, C.: Authenticated encryption: relations among notions and analysis of the generic composition paradigm. J. Cryptology **21**(4), 469–491 (2008)

7. Bernstein, D.J.: CAESAR: Competition for Authenticated Encryption, December 2015. http://competitions.cr.yp.to/caesar.html

8. Cooijmans, T., de Ruiter, J., Poll, E.: Analysis of secure key storage solutions on android. In: Proceedings of the 4th ACM Workshop on Security and Privacy in Smartphones & Mobile Devices, SPSM 2014, pp. 11–20. ACM (2014)

9. Götzfried, J., Müller, T.: Analysing android's full disk encryption feature. J. Wireless Mobile Netw. Ubiquitous Comput. Dependable Appl. (JoWUA) **5**(1), 84–100 (2014)

10. Hay, R., Dayan, A.: Android keystore stack buffer overflow - CVE-2014-3100 (2014)

11. Katz, J., Yung, M.: Unforgeable encryption and chosen ciphertext secure modes of operation. In: Schneier, B. (ed.) FSE 2000. LNCS, vol. 1978, p. 284. Springer, Heidelberg (2001)

12. Krawczyk, H.: The order of encryption and authentication for protecting communications (or: how secure is SSL?). In: Kilian, J. (ed.) CRYPTO 2001. LNCS, vol. 2139, p. 310. Springer, Heidelberg (2001)

13. Krovetz, T., Rogaway, P.: The software performance of authenticated-encryption modes. In: Joux, A. (ed.) FSE 2011. LNCS, vol. 6733, pp. 306–327. Springer, Heidelberg (2011)

14. McGrew, D.A., Viega, J.: Flexible and efficient message authentication in hardware and software. Manuscript (2003)

15. Mitchell, C.J.: Analysing the IOBC authenticated encryption mode. In: Boyd, C., Simpson, L. (eds.) ACISP. LNCS, vol. 7959, pp. 1–12. Springer, Heidelberg (2013)

16. Mitchell, C.J.: Cryptanalysis of two variants of PCBC mode when used for message integrity. In: Boyd, C., González Nieto, J.M. (eds.) ACISP 2005. LNCS, vol. 3574, pp. 560–571. Springer, Heidelberg (2005)

17. Müller, T., Spreitzenbarth, M.: FROST: forensic recovery of scrambled telephones. In: Jacobson, M., Locasto, M., Mohassel, P., Safavi-Naini, R. (eds.) ACNS 2013. LNCS, vol. 7954, pp. 373–388. Springer, Heidelberg (2013)

18. Namprempre, C., Rogaway, P., Shrimpton, T.: Reconsidering generic composition. In: Nguyen, P.Q., Oswald, E. (eds.) EUROCRYPT 2014. LNCS, vol. 8441, pp. 257–274. Springer, Heidelberg (2014)

19. Paterson, K.G., Watson, G.J.: Authenticated-encryption with padding: a formal security treatment. In: Naccache, D. (ed.) Cryphtography and Security: From Theory to Applications. LNCS, vol. 6805, pp. 83–107. Springer, Heidelberg (2012)

20. Preneel, B.: Cryptographic primitives for information authentication - state of the art. In: Preneel, B., Rijmen, V. (eds.) State of the Art in Applied Cryptography. LNCS, vol. 1528, p. 49. Springer, Heidelberg (1998)

21. Sabt, M., Achemlal, M., Bouabdallah, A.: Trusted execution environment: what it is, and what it is not. In: Trustcom/BigDataSE/ISPA, vol. 1, pp. 57–64 (2015)

22. Sabt, M., Traoré, J.: Breaking into the keystore: a practical forgery attack against android keystore. Cryptology ePrint Archive, Report 2016/677 (2016)

23. Shafi, G., Micali, S.: Probabilistic encryption. J. Comput. Syst. Sci. **28**(2), 270–299 (1984)

24. Teufl, P., Fitzek, A.G., Hein, D., Marsalek, A., Oprisnik, A., Zefferer, T.: Android encryption systems. In: Privacy & Security in Mobile Systems (2014)

25. Zhou, Y., Wu, L., Wang, Z., Jiang, X.: Harvesting developer credentials in android apps. In: Proceedings of the 8th ACM Conference on Security & Privacy in Wireless and Mobile Networks, WiSec 2015, pp. 23:1–23:12. ACM, New York (2015)

Attribute-Based Cryptography

Traceable CP-ABE with Short Ciphertexts: How to Catch People Selling Decryption Devices on eBay Efficiently

Jianting Ning[1], Zhenfu Cao[2(✉)], Xiaolei Dong[2(✉)], Junqing Gong[1], and Jie Chen[2(✉)]

[1] Department of Computer Science and Engineering, Shanghai Jiao Tong University, Shanghai 200240, China
jtning@sjtu.edu.cn, gongjunqing@126.com
[2] Shanghai Key Lab for Trustworthy Computing, East China Normal University, Shanghai 200062, China
{zfcao,dongxiaolei}@sei.ecnu.edu.cn, S080001@e.ntu.edu.sg

Abstract. Ciphertext-policy attribute-based encryption (CP-ABE) is a highly promising solution for cloud computing, which has been widely applied to provide fine-grained access control in cloud storage services recently. However, for CP-ABE based cloud storage systems, if a decryption device appears on eBay described and advertised to be able to decrypt any ciphertexts with policies satisfied by an attribute set or even with a specific access policy only, no one can trace the malicious user(s) who built such a decryption device using their private key(s). This has been known as a major obstacle to deploying CP-ABE systems in real-world commercial applications. Due to the one-to-many encryption mechanism of CP-ABE, the same decryption privilege is shared by multiple users who have the same attributes. It is difficult to identity the malicious user(s) who built such a decryption device. To track people selling decryption devices on eBay efficiently, in this paper, we develop a new methodology for constructing traitor tracing functionality, and present the first black-box traceable CP-ABE (BT-CP-ABE) with short ciphertexts which are independent of the number of users $\mathcal{N}$. The black-box traceability is *public*, *fully collusion-resistant*, and adaptively traceable against both *key-like decryption black-box* and *policy-specific decryption black-box*.

Our construction combines the conventional CP-ABE with Anonymous Hierarchical Identity-Based Encryption (A-HIBE) in a novel way, which is the first to construct the (underlying) traitor tracing system from A-HIBE. The resulting ciphertexts are independent of $\mathcal{N}$ while the private keys are linear in $\mathcal{N}$, which partially answers an open problem posed by Boneh and Waters [CCS 2006]. We believe this work is a constructive step towards efficient traitor tracing system with short ciphertexts and private keys. In particular, we believe that following the route of this work, any progress in A-HIBE (i.e., with shorter ciphertexts and private keys) may result in some progress in BT-CP-ABE and finally give a satisfactory solution to this open problem.

© Springer International Publishing Switzerland 2016
I. Askoxylakis et al. (Eds.): ESORICS 2016, Part II, LNCS 9879, pp. 551–569, 2016.
DOI: 10.1007/978-3-319-45741-3_28

Keywords: Attribute-Based Encryption · Black-box traceability · Anonymous Hierarchical Identity-Based Encryption · Short ciphertexts

1 Introduction

Traditional public key encryption enables a user to share her/his sensitive data with others in a private manner. The access capability of the shared data is all or nothing. That is, if given the private key, one can get the entire access capability to the shared data; otherwise, nothing will be revealed. The traditional way is useful for applications where the user knows specifically who will get access to the shared data. However, in many cases, a user may want to share her/his data with multiple potential and authorized receivers. Ciphertext-Policy Attribute-Based Encryption (CP-ABE, [7]) is introduced to fulfill the above requirement, which enables fine-grained access control over encrypted data. In particular, CP-ABE provides a scalable way of encrypting data such that the data owner defines the attribute sets that the data consumer needs to possess in order to decrypt the ciphertext. As a sophisticated one-to-many encryption mechanism, CP-ABE has been widely applied to provide fine-grained access control for commercial applications, especially for cloud computing.

However, there exists an important and practicality issue that hinders the wide utilization of CP-ABE to date. In particular, a ciphertext can be decrypted by multiple users whose attributes satisfy the access structure of this ciphertxt. In other words, the decryption privilege is shared by multiple users who have the same attributes and not associated with individuals. As a result, malicious users may deliberately leak their decryption keys or some decryption privilege in the form of a decryption black-box/device to others for profits.

Consider a CP-ABE based commercial application (such as cloud storage service), if a decryption device which is described and advertised as a decryption black-box function is being sold on eBay for financial gain at a lower price, due to the nature of CP-ABE, no one can track the malicious user(s) who built such a decryption device using their secret key(s). In practice, such decryption black-box could be quite useful and deemed to be very attractive to potential buyers with their lower prices, and the resulting financial gain could be a big incentive for malicious users to build and sell such a decryption black-box online with little risk of getting caught.

The problem, as described above, is the one of the main obstacles to deploying CP-ABE systems in real-world commercial applications [4]. To address this problem, we need to add the *traceability* property to the conventional CP-ABE. According to the evidence of trace procedure, there are roughly two flavors of traceability. The first one is *white-box traceability*, given a well-formed decryption key, a tracing algorithm can identify the malicious user who leaks the key. The second one is *black-box traceability*, given a decryption black-box/device, a tracing algorithm can identify the malicious user(s) who built the device using their secret key(s). Intuitively, black-box traceability is stronger than white-box traceability. This paper investigates the black-box traceability.

Furthermore, there are two types of decryption black-boxes/devices [15,17] in general. A *key-like decryption black-box* behaves as a decryption key associated with an attribute set. A *policy-specific decryption black-box* is associated with an access policy and can decrypt ciphertexts with this access policy. These two types of decryption black-boxes reflect different practical scenarios. Policy-specific decryption black-box has weaker decryption capacity than key-like decryption black-box, and tracing it is deemed to be more difficult. In fact, Liu *et al.* [17] proved that, for CP-ABE, traceability against policy-specific decryption black-box implies traceability against key-like decryption black-box, and it is sufficient to investigate traceability against policy-specific decryption black-box. In the rest of the paper, we focus on the traceability against policy-specific decryption black-box.

The problem of building a black-box traceable CP-ABE has recently been studied in [15]. However, as we will review that an efficient (i.e., with short ciphertexts) and expressive CP-ABE supporting adaptive traceability against both key-like and policy-specific decryption black-boxes is yet to be built: the ciphertexts in [15] grow sub-linearly in the number of users $\mathcal{N}$ in the system. Technically, they adopted a traitor tracing method similar to [2,3,6] and indices for users are arranged in an $\sqrt{\mathcal{N}} \times \sqrt{\mathcal{N}}$ matrix. The resulting ciphertexts are sub-linear in $\mathcal{N}$, which is the most efficient level to date. In addition, they only achieved selective traceability against policy-specific decryption black-box.

1.1   Our Results

In this paper, we propose a new CP-ABE with high expressiveness (i.e., supporting any monotonic access structures) and full security (i.e., provably secure against adaptive adversaries in the standard model) as [15] as well as following features:

High efficiency: The ciphertexts are independent of the number of users $\mathcal{N}$ in the system rather than sub-linear in $\mathcal{N}$ (i.e. $\sqrt{\mathcal{N}}$) in [15] (which is the most efficient one so far), the public parameters are shorter than that of [15], while the private keys are linear in $\mathcal{N}$. We note that, in practice, since the ciphertexts are generated and transferred more frequently than secret keys, the ciphertext size has greater impact on overall system performance and the user experience. We emphasize that reducing ciphertext size is more significant. It is desirable to obtain a black-box traceable CP-ABE with short ciphertexts which are independent of $\mathcal{N}$.

Public, fully collusion-resistance, adaptive traceability: It achieves fully collusion-resistant adaptive traceability against policy-specific decryption black-box, that is, it can track at least one of the malicious users even if there are an arbitrary number of malicious users colluding by pulling all of their decryption keys together when building a policy-specific decryption black-box. The tracing algorithm needs no secrets and can be run by anyone.

Table 1. Comparison with other related work[a]

	Traceability	CS	PubKS	PriKS	Fully Secure
[12]	×	$2l + 3$	$|\mathcal{U}| + 4$	$|S| + 3$	$\checkmark$
[16]	White-box	$2l + 3$	$|\mathcal{U}| + 4$	$|S| + 4$	$\checkmark$
[18]	White-box	$3l + 3$	7	$2|S| + 4$	×
[15]	Black-box 1	$2l + 17\sqrt{\mathcal{N}}$	$|\mathcal{U}| + 3 + 4\sqrt{\mathcal{N}}$	$|S| + 4$	$\checkmark$
Ours	Black-box 2	$2l + 5$	$|\mathcal{U}| + 8 + \mathcal{N}$	$|S| + 6 + \mathcal{O}(\mathcal{N})$	$\checkmark$

[a]CS, PubKS, PriKS represent the ciphertext size, the public key size, the private key size respectively. Let l be the size of an access policy, $|\mathcal{U}|$ the size of the attribute universe, $|S|$ the size of the attribute set of a private key, $|I|$ the number of attributes in a private key that satisfies a ciphertext's access policy, $\mathcal{N}$ the number of users in the system. Black-box 1 means that it is public, fully collusion-resistant, adaptively traceable against key-like black-box, but only selectively traceable against policy-specific black-box. Black-box 2 means that it is public, fully collusion-resistant, adaptively traceable against both key-like and policy-specific black-boxes.

To the best of our knowledge, this is the first CP-ABE that simultaneously supports all these features. Table 1 gives the comparison between our work and some other related work.

1.2 Our Techniques

Following the routes of [2,3,6,15], to construct a black-box traceable CP-ABE with adaptive traceability against policy-specific decryption black-box (BT-CP-ABE for short), instead of building one from scratch, we first define a simpler primitive named Enhanced CP-ABE, then we extend it to BT-CP-ABE. An Enhanced CP-ABE can be extended to BT-CP-ABE provided that it is message-hiding and index-hiding secure.

However, taking a traitor tracing method similar to [2,3,6,15] (i.e., encode each user as an entry in a matrix and partition the ciphertexts) to construct an Enhanced CP-ABE, the resulting ciphertexts are sub-linear in the number of users $\mathcal{N}$ in the system, which is the most efficient level to date. To go beyond the sub-linear barrier, in this paper, we put forward a novel method to construct a message-hiding and index-hiding secure Enhanced CP-ABE where the ciphertexts are independent of $\mathcal{N}$. The inspiration for our construction comes from the notion of Anonymous Hierarchical Identity-Based Encryption (A-HIBE), which is an extension of Identity-Based Encryption (IBE) allowing high level users to delegate their key generation ability to the low level users. More concretely, we begin with a conventional CP-ABE [12] and an A-HIBE [24] with constant size ciphertexts (which is based on [10,25]), and obtain a message-hiding and index-hiding secure Enhanced CP-ABE with hierarchical key delegation and anonymous (short) ciphertexts via a novel combination. We construct the tracing part of our system from A-HIBE by utilizing its key delegation and anonymity properties. Note that simply combine the tracing part (i.e. the A-HIBE part) and the CP-ABE part only provide weak traceability. Consider two users n_i (with attribute set S_{n_i} and index n_i) and n'_i (with attribute set $S_{n'_i}$ and index n'_i) collude to make a decryption black-box $\mathcal{D}$ with only S_{n_i} satisfies an access policy $\mathbb{A}$ (i.e. $S_{n'_i}$ does not satisfy $\mathbb{A}$). $\mathcal{D}$ uses user n_i's key (the part corresponding to S_{n_i}) to decrypt the ciphertext associated with $\mathbb{A}$ from the underlying CP-ABE system and user n'_i's key (the part corresponding to index n'_i) to decrypt the ciphertext from the underlying tracing system. As a result, user n'_i is identified to be malicious, but $S_{n'_i}$ does not satisfy $\mathbb{A}$. To achieve strong traceability, we use a randomly chosen "binder term" to bind the CP-ABE part and the A-HIBE part in a user's private key together, and set the private key such that it is used in both CP-ABE part and the A-HIBE part (i.e. the tracing part) in the ciphertext simultaneously.

Specifically, let $\mathcal{N}$ be the number of users in the system, and each user is assigned and identified by a unique index n_i for $n_i \in \{1, 2, ..., \mathcal{N}\}$. The index of a user n_i is encoded into her/his private key by generating her/his private key $sk_{n_i,S}$ according to her/his attribute set S and a sub-identity $ID_{n_i} = (ID_1, ID_2, ..., ID_{\mathcal{N}+1-n_i})$. Due to the key delegation property of the underlying A-HIBE, a user n_i can generate the decryption key $sk_{n_{i'},S}$ provided that $n_i > n_{i'}$. The $\mathbf{Encrypt}_E(pp, \mathbb{A}, n_j, m)$ algorithm is defined similar to conventional CP-ABE except for taking one more parameter $n_j \in \{1, ..., \mathcal{N} + 1\}$, and the encrypted message m can be recovered using a decryption key $sk_{n_i,S}$ provided that S satisfies the access policy $\mathbb{A}$ and $n_i \geq n_j$.

The message-hiding security of Enhanced CP-ABE is a typical semantic security and is based on the underlying CP-ABE security and A-HIBE security against adaptive adversaries, except that each key is identified by a unique index. The index-hiding security of Enhanced CP-ABE roughly follows from the anonymity of the underlying A-HIBE.

1.3 Related Work

Sahai and Waters first introduced the notion of Fuzzy Identity-Based Encryption in [23]. Goyal et al. [7] later formalized two notions of ABE: CP-ABE and KP-ABE. Subsequently, lots of constructions of CP-ABE and KP-ABE systems were proposed [1,5,13,26]. And a series of work has been done for ABE as the following directions: new proof techniques to obtain adaptive security [1,10,13], secure outsourcing computation [8,14,21] and decentralizing trust by setting multiple authorities [11,22].

Katz et al. [9] introduced the notion of traceability in the context of predicate encryption. They added traceability to any inner-product predicate encryption with additional overhead linear in the number of users $\mathcal{N}$. Liu et al. [15] later proposed a black-box traceability CP-ABE system at the expense of sub-linear (i.e. $\sqrt{\mathcal{N}}$) overhead. Recently, Ning et al. [18–20] proposed practical CP-ABE systems with white-box traceability. However, there exists no efficient black-box traceable CP-ABE with short ciphertexts which are independent of $\mathcal{N}$.

1.4   Future Work

Our work raises the following open problems: (1) Can we reduce the sizes of the public parameters, private keys, ciphertexts to a constant simultaneously? (2) Can we further improve the system flexibility, say allowing unlimited number of users in the system, without sacrificing short ciphertexts, public parameters and private keys?

We note that progress on either problem would likely require improving on the A-HIBE and CP-ABE: for the first problem, reducing the public parameters, private keys and ciphertexts to a constant is a long-standing open problem; for the second problem, an unbounded A-HIBE and compact CP-ABE with short ciphertexts, public parameters and private keys are desirable which is also a long-standing open problem.

1.5   Organization

Section 2 introduces the background. Section 3 gives the definition of BT-CP-ABE and its security model. Section 4 gives the definition of Enhanced CP-ABE, its security model and the transformation from Enhanced CP-ABE to BT-CP-ABE. Section 5 presents the construction of our Enhanced CP-ABE as well as the security proof. Finally, Sect. 6 presents a briefly conclusion.

2   Background

We define $[l] = \{1, 2, ..., l\}$ and $[l_1, l_2] = \{l_1, l_1 + 1, ..., l_2\}$, where l, l_1, l_2 are positive integers. Let $\mathcal{N}$ be the number of users in the system, each user is assigned and identified by a unique index $n_i \in [\mathcal{N}]$.

Access Structure. Let U denote the attribute universe. A collection $\mathbb{A} \subseteq 2^U$ of non-empty sets of attributes is an access structure on U. The sets in $\mathbb{A}$ are called the authorized sets, and the sets not in $\mathbb{A}$ are called the unauthorized sets. A collection $\mathbb{A} \subseteq 2^U$ is called monotone if $\forall B, C \in \mathbb{A} : if\ B \in \mathbb{A}$ and $B \subseteq C$, then $C \in \mathbb{A}$.

Linear Secret-Sharing Schemes (LSSS). Let U denote the attribute universe. A secret-sharing scheme $\prod$ with domain of secrets $\mathbb{Z}_p$ realizing access structure on U in called linear (over $\mathbb{Z}_p$) if (1) The shares of a secret $s \in \mathbb{Z}_p$ for each attribute form a vector over $\mathbb{Z}_p$; (2) For each access structure $\mathbb{A}$ on U, there exists a matrix M with l rows and n columns called the share-generating matrix. For $i = 1, ..., l$, we define a function ρ labels row i of M with attribute $\rho(i)$ from the attribute universe U. When we consider the column vector $\overrightarrow{v} = (s, r_2, ..., r_n)^{\perp}$, where $r_2, ..., r_n \in \mathbb{Z}_p$ are randomly chosen. Then $M \overrightarrow{v}$ is the vector of l shares of the secret s according to $\prod$. The share $(M \overrightarrow{v})_j$ "belongs" to attribute $\rho(j)$, where $j \in [l]$.

Composite Order Bilinear Groups. We let $\mathcal{G}$ denote a group generator, which takes a security parameter λ and outputs a description of a bilinear group G. Define the output of $\mathcal{G}$ as $(p_1, p_2, p_3, p_4, G, G_T, e)$, where p_1, p_2, p_3, p_4 are distinct primes, G, G_T are cyclic groups of order $N = p_1 p_2 p_3 p_4$, and $e : G^2 \to G_T$ is a map such that: (1) Bilinearity: $\forall u, v \in G$ and $a, b \in \mathbb{Z}_p$, we have $e(u^a, v^b) = e(u, v)^{ab}$; (2) Non-degeneracy: $\exists g \in G$ such that $e(g, g)$ has order N in G_T.

Complexity Assumptions. The message-hiding security of our Enhanced CP-ABE in $Game_{MH_1}^E$ will rely on four assumptions (the Assumption 1, the General Subgroup Decision Assumption, the 3-Party Diffie-Hellman Assumption in a Subgroup, and the Source Group q-Parallel BDHE Assumption in a subgroup) which are used in [12] to achieve full security of their CP-ABE system, excepting that we extend them to four subgroups (i.e. $N = p_1 p_2 p_3 p_4$) and give one more subgroup generator g_4 to the distinguisher D. The message-hiding security of our Enhanced CP-ABE in $Game_{MH_{N+1}}^E$ will rely on three assumptions (the General Subgroup Decision Assumption, the Assumptions 5 and 6) which are used in [24] to achieve full security of their HIBE system. Assumption 7 will be used to prove the index-hiding security of our Enhanced CP-ABE in $Game_{IH}^E$, which is used in [24] to achieve the anonymity of their HIBE system.

Assumption 1. [12] *Given a group generator $\mathcal{G}$, define the following distribution:* $\mathbb{G} = (N = p_1 p_2 p_3 p_4, G, G_T, e) \xleftarrow{R} \mathcal{G}, \alpha, s \xleftarrow{R} \mathbb{Z}_N, g_1 \xleftarrow{R} G_{p_1}, g_2, X_2, Y_2 \xleftarrow{R} G_{p_2}, g_3 \xleftarrow{R} G_{p_3}, g_4 \xleftarrow{R} G_{p_4}, D = (\mathbb{G}, g_1, g_2, g_3, g_4, g_1^\alpha X_2, g_1^s Y_2), T_0 = e(g_1, g_1)^{\alpha s}, T_1 \xleftarrow{R} G_T.$

An algorithm $\mathcal{A}$'s advantage in breaking this assumption is: $Adv_{\mathcal{G},\mathcal{A}}^1(\lambda) = |\Pr[\mathcal{A}(D, T_0) = 1] - \Pr[\mathcal{A}(D, T_1) = 1]|$. We say that $\mathcal{G}$ satisfies Assumption 1 if $Adv_{\mathcal{G},\mathcal{A}}^1(\lambda)$ is a negligible function of λ for any PPT algorithm $\mathcal{A}$.

Assumption 2. *(The General Subgroup Decision Assumption):* [12] *Given a group generator $\mathcal{G}$ and a collection of non-empty subsets of $\{1, 2, 3, 4\}$ $Z_0, Z_1, ..., Z_k$ where each Z_i for $i \geq 2$ satisfies either $Z_0 \cap Z_i = \phi = Z_1 \cap Z_i$ or $Z_0 \cap Z_i \neq \phi \neq Z_1 \cap Z_i$. Define the following distribution:* $\mathbb{G} = (N = p_1 p_2 p_3 p_4, G, G_T, e) \xleftarrow{R} \mathcal{G}, g_{Z_2} \xleftarrow{R} G_{Z_2}, ..., g_{Z_k} \xleftarrow{R} G_{Z_k}, D = (\mathbb{G}, g_{Z_2}, ..., g_{Z_k}), T_0 \xleftarrow{R} G_{Z_0}, T_1 \xleftarrow{R} G_{Z_1}.$

Fixing the collection of sets $Z_0, Z_1, ..., Z_k$, the advantage of an algorithm $\mathcal{A}$ in breaking this assumption is: $Adv_{\mathcal{G},\mathcal{A}}^{SD}(\lambda) = |\Pr[\mathcal{A}(D, T_0) = 1] - \Pr[\mathcal{A}(D, T_1) = 1]|$. We say that $\mathcal{G}$ satisfies the General Subgroup Decision Assumption if $Adv_{\mathcal{G},\mathcal{A}}^{SD}(\lambda)$ is a negligible function of λ for any PPT algorithm $\mathcal{A}$ and any suitable collection of subsets $Z_0, Z_1, ..., Z_k$.

Assumption 3. *(The 3-Party Diffie-Hellman Assumption in a Subgroup):* [12] *Given a group generator $\mathcal{G}$, define the following distribution:* $\mathbb{G} = (N = p_1 p_2 p_3 p_4, G, G_T, e) \xleftarrow{R} \mathcal{G}, x, y, z \xleftarrow{R} \mathbb{Z}_N, g_1 \xleftarrow{R} G_{p_1}, g_2 \xleftarrow{R} G_{p_2}, g_3 \xleftarrow{R} G_{p_3}, g_4 \xleftarrow{R} G_{p_4}, D = (\mathbb{G}, g_1, g_2, g_3, g_4, g_2^x, g_2^y, g_2^z), T_0 = g_2^{xyz}, T_1 \xleftarrow{R} G_{p_2}.$

An algorithm $\mathcal{A}$'s advantage in breaking this assumption is: $Adv_{\mathcal{G},\mathcal{A}}^{3DH}(\lambda) = |\Pr[\mathcal{A}(D, T_0) = 1] - \Pr[\mathcal{A}(D, T_1) = 1]|$. We say that $\mathcal{G}$ satisfies the 3-Party Diffie-Hellman Assumption in a Subgroup if $Adv_{\mathcal{G},\mathcal{A}}^{3DH}(\lambda)$ is a negligible function of λ for any PPT algorithm $\mathcal{A}$.

Assumption 4. *(The Source Group q-Parallel BDHE Assumption in a Subgroup):* [12] *Given a group generator $\mathcal{G}$ and a positive integer q, define the following distribution:* $\mathbb{G} = (N = p_1p_2p_3p_4, G, G_T, e) \xleftarrow{R} \mathcal{G}, c, d, f, b_1, ..., b_q \xleftarrow{R} \mathbb{Z}_N,$
$g_1 \xleftarrow{R} G_{p_1}, g_2 \xleftarrow{R} G_{p_2}, g_3 \xleftarrow{R} G_{p_3}, g_4 \xleftarrow{R} G_{p_4}, D = (\mathbb{G}, g_1, g_2, g_3, g_4, g_2^f, g_2^{df}, g_2^c, g_2^{c^2},$
$..., g_2^{c^q}, g_2^{c^{q+2}}, ..., g_2^{c^{2q}}, g_2^{c^i/b_j} \ \forall i \in [2q]\backslash\{q+1\}, j \in [q], g_2^{dfb_j} \ \forall j \in [q], g_2^{dfc^ib_{j'}/b_j} \ \forall i \in$
$[q], j, j' \in [q] \ s.t. \ j \neq j'), T_0 = g_2^{dc^{q+1}}, T_1 \xleftarrow{R} G_{p_2}.$

An algorithm $\mathcal{A}$'s advantage in breaking this assumption is: $Adv_{\mathcal{G},\mathcal{A}}^q(\lambda) = |\Pr[\mathcal{A}(D, T_0) = 1] - \Pr[\mathcal{A}(D, T_1) = 1]|$. We say that $\mathcal{G}$ satisfies the Source Group q-Parallel BDHE Assumption in a Subgroup if $Adv_{\mathcal{G},\mathcal{A}}^q(\lambda)$ is a negligible function of λ for any PPT algorithm $\mathcal{A}$.

Assumption 5. [24] *Given a group generator $\mathcal{G}$, define the following distribution:* $\mathbb{G} = (N = p_1p_2p_3p_4, G, G_T, e) \xleftarrow{R} \mathcal{G}, X_1 \xleftarrow{R} G_{p_1}, Y_2 \xleftarrow{R} G_{p_2}, X_3, Y_3, Y_3' \xleftarrow{R}$
$G_{p_3}, X_4 \xleftarrow{R} G_{p_4}, D \leftarrow (\mathbb{G}, X_1, Y_2Y_3, X_3, X_4), T_0 \xleftarrow{R} Y_2Y_3', T_1 \xleftarrow{R} G_{p_2p_3}.$

An algorithm $\mathcal{A}$'s advantage in breaking this assumption is: $Adv_{\mathcal{G},\mathcal{A}}^5(\lambda) = |\Pr[\mathcal{A}(D, T_0) = 1] - \Pr[\mathcal{A}(D, T_1) = 1]|$. We say that $\mathcal{G}$ satisfies Assumption 5 if $Adv_{\mathcal{G},\mathcal{A}}^5(\lambda)$ is a negligible function of λ for any PPT algorithm $\mathcal{A}$.

Assumption 6. [24] *Given a group generator $\mathcal{G}$, define the following distribution:* $\mathbb{G} = (N = p_1p_2p_3p_4, G, G_T, e) \xleftarrow{R} \mathcal{G}, g, X_1, Y_1 \xleftarrow{R} G_{p_1}, X_2, Y_2, Z_2 \xleftarrow{R}$
$G_{p_2}, X_3, Z_3 \xleftarrow{R} G_{p_3}, X_4 \xleftarrow{R} G_{p_4}, D = (\mathbb{G}, g, X_1X_2, X_3, Y_1Y_2, Z_2Z_3, X_4), T_0 = e(X_1, Y_1), T_1 \xleftarrow{R} G_T.$

An algorithm $\mathcal{A}$'s advantage in breaking this assumption is: $Adv_{\mathcal{G},\mathcal{A}}^6(\lambda) = |\Pr[\mathcal{A}(D, T_0) = 1] - \Pr[\mathcal{A}(D, T_1) = 1]|$. We say that $\mathcal{G}$ satisfies Assumption 6 if $Adv_{\mathcal{G},\mathcal{A}}^6(\lambda)$ is a negligible function of λ for any PPT algorithm $\mathcal{A}$.

Assumption 7. [24] *Given a group generator $\mathcal{G}$, define the following distribution:* $\mathbb{G} = (N = p_1p_2p_3p_4, G, G_T, e) \xleftarrow{R} \mathcal{G}, X_1, Y_1, W_1 \xleftarrow{R} G_{p_1}, Y_2, Z_2, W_2, W_2'$
$\xleftarrow{R} G_{p_2}, Z_3 \xleftarrow{R} G_{p_3}, X_4, Z_4, W_4, W_4' \xleftarrow{R} G_{p_4}, D \leftarrow (\mathbb{G}, X_1X_4, Y_1Y_2,$
$Z_2, Z_3, Z_4, W_1W_2W_4), T_0 = W_1W_2'W_4', T_1 \xleftarrow{R} G_{p_1p_2p_4}.$

An algorithm $\mathcal{A}$'s advantage in breaking this assumption is: $Adv_{\mathcal{G},\mathcal{A}}^7(\lambda) = |\Pr[\mathcal{A}(D, T_0) = 1] - \Pr[\mathcal{A}(D, T_1) = 1]|$. We say that $\mathcal{G}$ satisfies Assumption 7 if $Adv_{\mathcal{G},\mathcal{A}}^7(\lambda)$ is a negligible function of λ for any PPT algorithm $\mathcal{A}$.

3   Black-box Traceable CP-ABE

3.1   Definition

A black-box traceable CP-ABE (BT-CP-ABE) system is a CP-ABE system where a decryption black-box can be traced to the corresponding malicious users who built it. We extend the conventional (non-traceable) CP-ABE by assigning and identifying users with unique indices, and adding a **Trace** algorithm to it. In particular, following the notation of the CP-ABE system introduced in [12], a BT-CP-ABE system consists of five algorithms as follows:

- **Setup**$(\lambda, \mathcal{U}, \mathcal{N}) \rightarrow (pp, msk)$. The algorithm takes a security parameter λ, the attribute universe description $\mathcal{U}$ and the number of users $\mathcal{N}$ in the system. It outputs the public parameters pp and a master secret key msk.
- **KeyGen**$(pp, msk, S) \rightarrow sk_{n_i,S}$. The algorithm takes the public parameters pp, the master secret key msk and a set of attributes S. It outputs a private key $sk_{n_i,S}$, which is assigned and identified by a unique index $n_i \in \{1, ..., \mathcal{N}\}$. And we assume that S is implicitly included in $sk_{n_i,S}$.
- **Encrypt**$(pp, \mathbb{A}, m) \rightarrow ct$. The algorithm takes the public parameters pp, an access structure $\mathbb{A}$ over the universe of attributes and a message m. It outputs a ciphertext ct. We assume that $\mathbb{A}$ is implicitly included in ct.
- **Decrypt**$(pp, sk_{n_i,S}, ct) \rightarrow m$ or $\perp$. The algorithm takes the public parameters pp, a secret key $sk_{n_i,S}$, and a ciphertext ct. If S satisfies ct's access policy, the algorithm outputs the message m. Otherwise, it outputs $\perp$.
- **Trace**$^{\mathcal{D}}(pp, \mathbb{A}_{\mathcal{D}}, \epsilon) \rightarrow \mathbb{N}_T$: The tracing algorithm takes the public parameters pp, an access policy $\mathbb{A}_{\mathcal{D}}$ and a probability value (lower-bound) ϵ^1. It is an oracle algorithm interacts with a policy-specific decryption black-box $\mathcal{D}$. It runs in time polynomial in 1^λ and $1/\epsilon$, and outputs an index set $\mathbb{N}_T \subseteq \{1, ..., \mathcal{N}\}$ of malicious user(s). Note that in our setting, we treat $\mathcal{D}$ as a probabilistic circuit that takes as input a ciphertext ct and returns a message m or $\perp$. And such a decryption black-box does not need to be perfect, we only require it to decrypt successfully with non-negligible probability.

3.2 Message-Hiding Security

The message-hiding security is a typical semantic security similar to that of conventional CP-ABE system [12], excepting every key query is companied with a unique index. Similar to [15], to capture the security that an adversary can choose keys to corrupt adaptively, we allow an adversary to specify the index (which is originally assigned by the **KeyGen** algorithm) to a decryption key when he makes a key query. Note that to guarantee that each user/key can be identified by an index uniquely, an adversary can adaptively ask for a decryption key corresponding to (n_i, S_{n_i}) for $i \in \{1, ..., q\}$, where $n_i \in \{1, ..., \mathcal{N}\}, q \leq \mathcal{N}$. Also note that for any two pairs (n_i, S_{n_i}) and (n_j, S_{n_j}) where $n_i \neq n_j$ for $\forall i \neq j, i, j \in \{1, ..., q\}$, we do not require $S_{n_i} \neq S_{n_j}$.

The message-hiding security is described by a security game $Game_{MH}$ between an adversary $\mathcal{A}$ and a challenger $\mathcal{C}$. The phases of the game are as follows:

---

1 Note that ϵ is the lower-bound of a policy-specific decryption black-box's decryption ability, and it has to be polynomially related to the security parameter.

- **Setup:** C runs **Setup**$(\lambda, \mathcal{U}, \mathcal{N})$ and sends pp to $\mathcal{A}$.
- **Query Phase 1:** For $i = 1$ to q_1, $\mathcal{A}$ adaptively submits (n_i, S_{n_i}), and C responds with $sk_{n_i, S_{n_i}}$.
- **Challenge:** $\mathcal{A}$ submits two equal length messages m_0, m_1 and an access policy $\mathbb{A}^*$. $\mathbb{A}^*$ cannot be satisfied by any of the queried $S_{n_1}, ..., S_{n_{q_1}}$. C flips a random coin $\beta \in \{0, 1\}$ and gives an encryption of m_β under $\mathbb{A}^*$ to $\mathcal{A}$.
- **Query Phase 2:** For $i = q_1 + 1$ to q, $\mathcal{A}$ adaptively submits (n_i, S_{n_i}) with the restriction that none of these queried attribute sets satisfy $\mathbb{A}^*$, and C responds with $sk_{n_i, S_{n_i}}$.
- **Guess:** $\mathcal{A}$ outputs a guess $\beta' \in \{0, 1\}$ for β.

$\mathcal{A}$'s advantage is defined as $Adv = \Pr[\beta' = \beta] - \frac{1}{2}$ in $Game_{MH}$.

Definition 1. *A $\mathcal{N}$-user BT-CP-ABE system is adaptively message-hiding secure if there exists no probabilistic polynomial-time (PPT) adversary has a non-negligible advantage in the above security game.*

Selective message-hiding security is defined by adding an initialization phase where the adversary must declare the access policy $\mathbb{A}^*$ before seeing the public parameters pp.

3.3   Black-box Traceability

The black-box traceability definition is described by a security game $Game_{BT}$ between an adversary $\mathcal{A}$ and a challenger C. The phases of the game are as follows:

- **Setup:** C runs **Setup**$(\lambda, \mathcal{U}, \mathcal{N})$ and sends pp to $\mathcal{A}$.
- **Key Query:** For $i = 1$ to q, $\mathcal{A}$ adaptively submits (n_i, S_{n_i}), and C responds with $sk_{n_i, S_{n_i}}$.
- **(Policy-Specific) Decryption Black-box Generation:** $\mathcal{A}$ outputs a decryption black-box $\mathcal{D}$ associated with an access policy $\mathbb{A}_{\mathcal{D}}$ and a probability value ϵ.
- **Trace:** C runs **Trace**$^{\mathcal{D}}(pp, \mathbb{A}_{\mathcal{D}}, \epsilon)$ to get an index set $\mathbb{N}_T \subseteq \{1, ..., \mathcal{N}\}$ of malicious user(s).

Let $\mathbb{N}_{\mathcal{D}} = \{n_i | 1 \leq i \leq q\}$ be the index set of corrupted keys. We say $\mathcal{A}$ wins the above game if the following conditions hold:

(1) $\mathcal{D}$ generated by $\mathcal{A}$ is a useful policy-specific decryption black-box. That is, it holds that $\Pr[\mathcal{D}(\mathbf{Encrypt}(pp, \mathbb{A}_{\mathcal{D}}, m)) = m] \geq \epsilon$, where the probability is taken over the random coins of $\mathcal{D}$ and the random choices of message m.
(2) S_{n_i} does not satisfy $\mathbb{A}_{\mathcal{D}}$ for $\forall n_i \in \mathbb{N}_T$, or $\mathbb{N}_T \not\subseteq \mathbb{N}_{\mathcal{D}}$, or $\mathbb{N}_T = \emptyset$.

Definition 2. *A $\mathcal{N}$-user BT-CP-ABE system is adaptively traceable against policy-specific decryption black-box if there exists no PPT adversary has a non-negligible advantage in the above game.*

Selective black-box traceability is defined by adding an initialization phase where the adversary must declare the access policy $\mathbb{A}_{\mathcal{D}}$ before seeing the public parameters pp.

Note that as of [2,3,6,9,15], in this paper, we are modeling a stateless (resettable) decryption black-box.

4   Enhanced CP-ABE

Following the routes of [2,3,6,15], instead of constructing BT-CP-ABE directly, We define a simpler primitive named Enhanced CP-ABE (EnCP-ABE for short) and its security notion first, then we show that BT-CP-ABE can be transformed from EnCP-ABE.

4.1   Definition

An EnCP-ABE system consists of the following five algorithms.

- **Setup**$_E(\lambda, \mathcal{U}, \mathcal{N}) \rightarrow (pp, msk)$. The algorithm takes a security parameter λ, the attribute universe description $\mathcal{U}$ and the numbers of users $\mathcal{N}$ in the system. It outputs the public parameters pp and a master secret key msk.
- **KeyGen**$_E(pp, msk, S) \rightarrow sk_{n_i,S}$. The algorithm takes the public parameters pp, the master secret key msk and a set of attributes S. It outputs a private key $sk_{n_i,S}$, which is assigned and identified by a unique index $n_i \in [\mathcal{N}]$.
- **KeyDel**$_E(pp, sk_{n_i,S}) \rightarrow sk_{n'_i,S}$ $_{s.t. \ n_i \in [2,\mathcal{N}], n'_i \in [\mathcal{N}], n'_i < n_i}$ [2]. The algorithm takes the public parameters pp and a secret key $sk_{n_i,S}$. It outputs a secret key $sk_{n'_i,S}$ corresponding to the attribute set S and index n'_i subject to $n'_i < n_i$.
- **Encrypt**$_E(pp, \mathbb{A}, n_j, m) \rightarrow ct$. The algorithm takes the public parameters pp, an access structure $\mathbb{A}$ over the universe of attributes, an index $n_j \in [\mathcal{N} + 1]$ and a message m. It outputs a ciphertext ct.
- **Decrypt**$_E(pp, sk_{n_i,S}, ct) \rightarrow m$ or $\perp$. The algorithm takes the public parameters pp, a secret key $sk_{n_i,S}$, and a ciphertext ct encrypted with index n_j. If S satisfies ct's access policy and $n_i \geq n_j$, the algorithm outputs the message m. Otherwise, it output $\perp$.

Note that if we always set n_j of the **Encrypt**$_E(pp, \mathbb{A}, n_j, m)$ algorithm equal to 1, the functions of EnCP-ABE are identical to that of BT-CP-ABE.

4.2   Message-Hiding Security

The message-hiding security is described by a security game between an adversary $\mathcal{A}$ and a challenger $\mathcal{C}$. The phases of the game are as follows:

---

[2] This key delegation algorithm is a weak one than that of [24]. We remove the key re-randomization operation since it will only be invoked by the **Decrypt** algorithm.

- **Setup:** $\mathcal{C}$ runs $\mathbf{Setup}_E(\lambda, \mathcal{U}, \mathcal{N})$ and sends pp to $\mathcal{A}$.
- **Query Phase 1:** For $i = 1$ to q_1, $\mathcal{A}$ adaptively submits (n_i, S_{n_i}), and $\mathcal{C}$ responds with $sk_{n_i, S_{n_i}}$.
- **Challenge:** $\mathcal{A}$ submits two equal length messages m_0, m_1 and an access policy $\mathbb{A}^*$. $\mathcal{C}$ flips a random coin $\beta \in \{0, 1\}$ and gives $ct \leftarrow \mathbf{Encrypt}_E(pp, \mathbb{A}^*, n_j, m_\beta)$ to $\mathcal{A}$.
- **Query Phase 2:** For $i = q_1 + 1$ to q, $\mathcal{A}$ adaptively submits (n_i, S_{n_i}), and $\mathcal{C}$ responds with $sk_{n_i, S_{n_i}}$.
- **Guess:** $\mathcal{A}$ outputs a guess $\beta' \in \{0, 1\}$ for β.

We define game $Game_{MH_1}^E$ as follows. We let $\mathcal{C}$ give $ct \leftarrow \mathbf{Encrypt}_E(pp, \mathbb{A}^*, 1, m_\beta)$ to $\mathcal{A}$ during the **Challenge** phase. And $\mathcal{A}$ wins the game if $\beta' = \beta$ with the restriction that none of the queried attribute sets $S_{n_1}, ..., S_{n_q}$ satisfy $\mathbb{A}^*$. $\mathcal{A}$'s advantage is defined to be $Adv_1 = \Pr[\beta' = \beta] - \frac{1}{2}$ in this game.

And we define game $Game_{MH_{\mathcal{N}+1}}^E$ as follows. We let $\mathcal{C}$ give $ct \leftarrow \mathbf{Encrypt}_E(pp, \mathbb{A}^*, \mathcal{N} + 1, m_\beta)$ to $\mathcal{A}$ during the **Challenge** phase. And $\mathcal{A}$ wins the game if $\beta' = \beta$. $\mathcal{A}$'s advantage is defined to be $Adv_{\mathcal{N}+1} = \Pr[\beta' = \beta] - \frac{1}{2}$ in this game.

Definition 3. *A $\mathcal{N}$-user Enhanced CP-ABE system is adaptively message-hiding secure if there exists no PPT adversary has a non-negligible advantage in the security game $Game_{MH_1}^E$ and $Game_{MH_{\mathcal{N}+1}}^E$.*

4.3 Index-Hiding Security

Similar to [15,17], the index-hiding security against policy-specific decryption black-box is to guarantee that there has no adversary can distinguish between $\mathbf{Encrypt}_E(pp, \mathbb{A}^*, n_j, m)$ and $\mathbf{Encrypt}_E(pp, \mathbb{A}^*, n_j + 1, m)$ for any access policy $\mathbb{A}^*$ without a secret key $sk_{n_j, S_{n_j}}$, where S_{n_j} satisfies $\mathbb{A}^*$. It is described by a security game $Game_{IH}^E$ between an adversary $\mathcal{A}$ and a challenger $\mathcal{C}$. The game takes as input a parameter $n_j \in [\mathcal{N}]$ which is given to both $\mathcal{A}$ and $\mathcal{C}$. The phases of the game are as follows:

- **Setup:** $\mathcal{C}$ runs $\mathbf{Setup}_E(\lambda, \mathcal{U}, \mathcal{N})$ and sends pp to $\mathcal{A}$.
- **Key Query:** For $i = 1$ to q, $\mathcal{A}$ adaptively submits (n_i, S_{n_i}), and $\mathcal{C}$ responds with $sk_{n_i, S_{n_i}}$.
- **Challenge:** $\mathcal{A}$ submits a message m and an access policy $\mathbb{A}^*$. $\mathcal{C}$ flips a random bit $\beta \in \{0, 1\}$ and gives $ct \leftarrow \mathbf{Encrypt}_E(pp, \mathbb{A}^*, n_j + \beta, m)$ to $\mathcal{A}$.
- **Guess:** $\mathcal{A}$ outputs a guess $\beta' \in \{0, 1\}$ for β.

We define $\mathcal{A}$ wins the game if $\beta' = \beta$ with the restriction that none of the queried pairs $\{(n_1, S_{n_1}), ..., (n_q, S_{n_q})\}$ satisfy $(S_{n_i}\ satisfies\ \mathbb{A}^*) \wedge (n_i = n_j)$ for any $i \in [q]$. $\mathcal{A}$'s advantage is defined as $Adv_{n_j} = \Pr[\beta' = \beta] - \frac{1}{2}$ in this game.

Definition 4. *A $\mathcal{N}$-user Enhanced CP-ABE system is adaptively index-hiding secure against policy-specific decryption black-box if there exists no PPT adversary has a non-negligible advantage Adv_{n_j} for any $n_j \in [\mathcal{N}]$ in $Game_{IH}^E$.*

4.4 Transform from EnCP-ABE to BT-CP-ABE

Following the routes of [2,3,6,15], we show that a BT-CP-ABE can be transformed from an EnCP-ABE with message-hiding and index-hiding security. We denote an EnCP-ABE as Γ_e, then a BT-CP-ABE can be transformed from Γ_e by the following three steps:

(1) Let EnCP-ABE be message-hiding secure and index-hiding secure.
(2) Set the parameter n_j of $\mathbf{Encrypt}_E(pp, \mathbb{A}, n_j, m)$ equal to 1, i.e.,
   $\mathbf{Encrypt}_E(pp, \mathbb{A}, n_j, m) = \mathbf{Encrypt}_E(pp, \mathbb{A}, 1, m)$.
(3) Add a **Trace** algorithm to Γ_e defined as follows.

- **Trace**$^{\mathcal{D}}(pp, \mathbb{A}_{\mathcal{D}}, \epsilon) \to \mathbb{N}_T \subseteq [\mathcal{N}]$: The tracing algorithm takes the public parameters pp, an access policy $\mathbb{A}_{\mathcal{D}}$ and a probability value ϵ. Given a decryption black-box $\mathcal{D}$ associated with the access policy $\mathbb{A}_{\mathcal{D}}$, it works as follows:
  1. For $n = 1$ to $\mathcal{N} + 1$, do as follows:
    (1) Repeat the following steps $8\lambda(\mathcal{N}/\epsilon)^2$ times: First, randomly sample message m from the message space. Then, let $ct \leftarrow$ $\mathbf{Encrypt}_E(pp, \mathbb{A}_{\mathcal{D}}, n, m)$. Next, Call oracle $\mathcal{D}$ on input ct and compare the output of $\mathcal{D}$ with m;
    (2) Let f_n be the fraction of times that $\mathcal{D}$ decrypted the ciphertexts correctly.
  2. Let $\mathbb{N}_T$ be the set of all $n \in [\mathcal{N}]$ for which $f_n - f_{n+1} \ge \epsilon/(4\mathcal{N})$.
  3. Output the set $\mathbb{N}_T$ as the malicious users.

We denote Γ_{bt} as the modified Γ_e after the above transformation.

Theorem 1. *If Γ_e is adaptively (resp. selectively) message-hiding secure and adaptively (resp. selectively) index-hiding secure against policy-specific decryption black-box, then Γ_{bt} is a BT-CP-ABE with adaptive (resp. selective) traceability against policy-specific decryption black-box.*

Proof. The proof is nearly identical to that of Theorem 1 in [15], replacing "$S_{n_i} \supseteq S_{\mathcal{D}}$" with "$S_{n_i}$ *satisfies* $\mathbb{A}_{\mathcal{D}}$".

5 An Efficient Enhanced CP-ABE

5.1 Construction

- **Setup**$_E(\lambda, \mathcal{U}, \mathcal{N}) \to (pp, msk)$. The algorithm chooses a bilinear group G of order $N = p_1 p_2 p_3 p_4$ (four distinct primes). It randomly chooses α, a, k, $\{b_i\}_{i \in \mathcal{U}}$, f, h, $\{u_i\}_{i \in [0, \mathcal{N}]} \in \mathbb{Z}_N$, $g \in G_{p_1}, Y_3 \in G_{p_3}$ and $Y_4, R_{g,4}, R_{a,4}, R_{k,4}$, $\{R_{b_i,4}\}_{i \in \mathcal{U}}, R_{f,4}, R_{h,4}, \{R_{u_i,4}\}_{i \in [0, \mathcal{N}]} \in G_{p_4}$. It then sets $G = gR_{g,4}, A = g^a R_{a,4}, K = g^k R_{k,4}, F = g^f R_{f,4}, H = g^h R_{h,4}, \{U_i = g^{u_i} R_{u_i,4}\}_{i \in [0, \mathcal{N}]}, \{B_i = g^{b_i} R_{b_i,4}\}_{i \in \mathcal{U}}$ and $E = e(g, g)^\alpha$. The public parameter pp is

$$(N, G, A, K, E, \{B_i\}_{i \in \mathcal{U}}, F, H, \{U_i\}_{i \in [0, \mathcal{N}]}, Y_4)$$

and the master secret key msk is

$$(g, g^\alpha, g^a, g^k, \{g^{b_i}\}_{i \in \mathcal{U}}, g^f, g^h, \{g^{u_i}\}_{i \in [0, \mathcal{N}]}, Y_3).$$

- **KeyGen$_E$**$(pp, msk, S) \rightarrow sk_{n_i}$. For a user with index $n_i \in [\mathcal{N}]$, the algorithm represents n_i in its unary-style form (i.e., $1^{\mathcal{N}+2-n_i})^3$. It randomly chooses $t, c, \delta, t_0, t_1 \in \mathbb{Z}_N, R, R', R'', R_3, R_3', R_3'', \{R_i\}_{i \in [\mathcal{N}+2-n_i, \mathcal{N}]}$ $s.t.$ $n_i \geq 2$, $\{R_i'\}_{i \in S} \in G_{p_3}$. The secret key sk_{n_i} is

$$\begin{pmatrix} K_1 = g^\alpha g^{at} g^{kc} g^\delta R, K_2 = g^c R', K_3 = g^t R'', \\ \{K_i' = (g^{b_i})^t R_i'\}_{i \in S}, \\ K_4 = g^{t_1} R_3, K_5 = g^\delta g^{ft_0} (g^h \Pi_{i=0}^{\mathcal{N}+1-n_i} g^{u_i})^{t_1} R_3', \\ K_6 = g^{t_0} R_3'', \{T_i = (g^{u_i})^{t_1} R_i\}_{i \in [\mathcal{N}+2-n_i, \mathcal{N}]} \ s.t. \ n_i \geq 2 \end{pmatrix}.$$

- **KeyDel$_E$**$(sk_{n_i}, pp) \rightarrow sk_{n_i'} \ _{s.t. \ n_i \in [2, \mathcal{N}], n_i' \in [\mathcal{N}], n_i' < n_i}$. Given a secret key sk_{n_i}, the algorithm creates a secret key $sk_{n_i'}$ subject to $n_i' < n_i$, where $n_i \in [2, \mathcal{N}], n_i' \in [\mathcal{N}]$. Without loss of generality, the algorithm generates $sk_{n_i'}$ for $n_i' = n_i - 1$ as follows.
  (1) It parses sk_{n_i} as $(\tilde{K}_1, \tilde{K}_2, \tilde{K}_3, \tilde{K}_4, \tilde{K}_5, \tilde{K}_6, \{\tilde{K}_i'\}_{i \in S}, \{\tilde{T}_i\}_{i \in [\mathcal{N}+2-n_i, \mathcal{N}]} \ s.t. \ n_i \geq 2)$.
  (2) It takes the following (weak) delegation step to generate $sk_{n_i'}$ for $n_i' = n_i - 1$. It sets

$$\begin{pmatrix} K_1 = \tilde{K}_1, K_2 = \tilde{K}_2, \\ \{K_i' = \tilde{K}_i'\}_{i \in S}, \\ K_4 = \tilde{K}_4, K_5 = \tilde{K}_5 \tilde{T}_{\mathcal{N}+2-n_i}, \\ K_6 = \tilde{K}_6, \{T_i = \tilde{T}_i\}_{i \in [\mathcal{N}+3-n_i, \mathcal{N}]} \ s.t. \ n_i \geq 3 \end{pmatrix}.$$

It returns $sk_{n_i'} = (K_1, K_2, K_3, K_4, K_5, K_6, \{K_i'\}_{i \in S}, \{T_i\}_{i \in [\mathcal{N}+2-n_i', \mathcal{N}]} \ s.t. \ n_i' \geq 2)$.

We note that, the algorithm will only be invoked by the decryption algorithm, we focus on the decryption ability. The distribution of the secret key does not matter in our case. A user with sk_{n_i} who can delegate all the secret keys $sk_{n_i'}$ subject to $n_i' < n_i$ is deemed to have all the decryption abilities corresponding to $sk_{n_i'}$ for all $n_i' < n_i$.

- **Encrypt$_E$**$(pp, (M, \rho), n_j, m) \rightarrow ct$. M is an $l \times n$ matrix and ρ is a map from each row M_j of M to an attribute $\rho(i) \in \mathcal{U}$. The algorithm represents n_j in its unary-style form (i.e., $1^{\mathcal{N}+2-n_j}$). It then randomly chooses a random vector $\boldsymbol{y} = (s, y_2, ..., y_n)$, where s is the random secret to be shared. For each row M_j of M, it randomly chooses $r_j \in \mathbb{Z}_N$. Then it randomly chooses $R_{4,1}, R_{4,2}, R_{4,3}, R_{4,4}, \{R_{j,1,4}, R_{j,2,4}\}_{j \in [l]} \in G_{p_4}$. The ciphertext ct is

$$\begin{pmatrix} C_0 = m \cdot E^s, C_1 = G^s R_{4,1}, C_2 = K^s R_{4,2}, \\ \{C_{j,1} = A^{M_j \boldsymbol{y}} B_{\rho(j)}^{-r_j} R_{j,1,4}, C_{j,2} = G^{r_j} R_{j,2,4}\}_{j \in [l]}, \\ C_3 = (H \cdot \Pi_{i=0}^{\mathcal{N}+1-n_j} U_i)^s R_{4,3}, C_4 = F^s R_{4,4} \end{pmatrix}.$$

---

[3] For each index $n_i \in [\mathcal{N}]$, instead of picking a sub-identity $ID_{n_i} = (ID_0, ID_1, ID_2, ..., ID_{\mathcal{N}+1-n_i})$ from a random pseudo identity $ID = (ID_0, ID_1, ID_2, ..., ID_{\mathcal{N}}) \in \mathbb{Z}_N^{\mathcal{N}+1}$, we represents n_i in a unary-style form similar to the unary representation, i.e., $1^{\mathcal{N}+2-n_i}$. Concretely, we may view our unary-style representation as a special form of the pseudo identity in the paper, i.e., we actually set $ID_0 = ID_1 = \cdots = ID_{\mathcal{N}} = 1$.

– $\mathbf{Decrypt}_E(pp, sk_{n_i}, ct) \rightarrow m$ or $\perp$. Assume ct is encrypted with index n_j. If $n_i > n_j$, the algorithm calls $\mathbf{KeyDel}_E(sk_{n_i}, pp)$ algorithm and gets the secret key sk_{n_j}. If S does not satisfy (A, ρ), the algorithm outputs $\perp$. Otherwise, it computes the constants $\omega_j \in \mathbb{Z}_N$ such that $\sum_{\rho(j) \in S} \omega_j A_j = (1, 0, ..., 0)$. It then computes:

$$\frac{e(K_1, C_1)e(K_4, C_3)e(K_6, C_4)(e(K_2, C_2)e(K_5, C_1))^{-1}}{\prod_{\rho(j) \in S}(e(K_3, C_{j,1})e(K'_{\rho(j)}, C_{j,2}))^{\omega_j}} = e(g, g)^{\alpha s}.$$

Then m can be recovered as $C_0/e(g, g)^{\alpha s}$. Note that the decryption works if and only if S satisfies the access policy of ct and $n_i \geq n_j$.

5.2 Message-Hiding Security in $Game_{MH_1}^E$

Theorem 2. *If Assumption 1, the General Subgroup Decision Assumption, the 3-Party Diffie-Hellman Assumption in a Subgroup, the Source Group q-Parallel BDHE Assumption in a Subgroup hold, no PPT adversary can achieve a non-negligible advantage in winning $Game_{MH_1}^E$.*

Due to space, we refer the reader to Appendix A for the proof of this theorem.

5.3 Message-Hiding Security in $Game_{MH_{\mathcal{N}+1}}^E$

Theorem 3. *If the General Subgroup Decision Assumption, Assumptions 5 and 6 hold, no PPT adversary can achieve a non-negligible advantage in winning $Game_{MH_{\mathcal{N}+1}}^E$.*

Due to space, we refer the reader to Appendix B for the proof of this theorem.

5.4 Index-Hiding Security

Theorem 4. *If the General Subgroup Decision Assumption, the 3-Party Diffie-Hellman Assumption in a Subgroup, the Source Group q-Parallel BDHE Assumption in a Subgroup, Assumptions 5, 6 and 7 hold, no PPT adversary can achieve a non-negligible advantage in winning $Game_{IH}^E$.*

Due to space, we refer the reader to Appendix C for the proof of this theorem.

6 Conclusions

In this paper, we proposed an efficient traceable CP-ABE supporting public fully collusion-resistant black-box traceability and high expressiveness. The system is proved fully secure and adaptively traceable against both key-like and policy-specific decryption black-boxes in the standard model. Compared with the most efficient black-box traceable CP-ABE currently available with high expressiveness and full security, ciphertexts in the proposed system are independent of the number of users $\mathcal{N}$ in the system, rather than sub-linear in $\mathcal{N}$, while the public parameters and private keys are linear in $\mathcal{N}$. These make our proposed system more suitable and more practical for commercial applications. We thought our new methodology of realizing traitor tracing functionality may serve as the first step towards more practical solution to BT-CP-ABE.

Acknowledgments. This work is supported in part by the National Natural Science Foundation of China (Grant No. 6163000206, 61373154, 61371083, 61472142 and 61411146001), in part by the Prioritized Development Projects through the Specialized Research Fund for the Doctoral Program of Higher Education of China (Grant No. 20130073130004), in part by Shanghai High-tech field project (Grant No. 16511101400), and in part by Science and Technology Commission of Shanghai Municipality (Grant No. 14YF1404200).

A Proof of Theorem 2

Proof Overview. Roughly speaking, the message-hiding security of our EnCP-ABE in the sense of $Game_{MH_1}^E$ is guaranteed by the IND-CPA security of the CP-ABE system in [12]. Hence the proof of this theorem mainly follows the proof of IND-CPA in [12]. For simplicity, here we prove this theorem by reducing the message-hiding of our EnCP-ABE in $Game_{MH_1}^E$ to the IND-CPA security of the CP-ABE system in [12]. Due to space, complete proof will be given in the full paper.

B Proof of Theorem 3

Proof Overview. Roughly speaking, the message hiding of our EnCP-ABE in the sense of $Game_{MH_{\mathcal{N}+1}}^E$ is guaranteed by the IND-CPA of the HIBE system in [24]. The proof of this theorem also follows that of [24]. For simplicity, here we prove this theorem by reducing the message-hiding of our EnCP-ABE in $Game_{MH_{\mathcal{N}+1}}^E$ to the IND-CPA security of the HIBE system in [24]. Due to space, complete proof will be given in the full paper.

C Proof of Theorem 4

We prove the theorem by considering two cases separately. Let $\bar{n}_j$ be the parameter which is given to both the adversary $\mathcal{A}$ and the challenger defined in $Game_{IH}^E$. $\mathcal{A}$ will eventually behave in one of two different ways in $Game_{IH}^E$:

Case 1: In Key Query phase, each query (n_i, S_{n_i}) submitted by $\mathcal{A}$ satisfies $n_i \neq \bar{n}_j$. It will not violate the restriction in the model even when $S_{n_i} \in \mathbb{A}^*$.

Case 2: In Key Query phase, $\mathcal{A}$ will submit an query (n_i, S_{n_i}) such that $(n_i = \bar{n}_j)$. The restriction in the security model implies that $S_{n_i} \notin \mathbb{A}^*$.

We prove our EnCP-ABE is index-hiding in both cases in the following Theorems 5 and 6 respectively. Since our classification above is complete, combining them together immediately concludes the proof of Theorem 4.

Proof of Case 1

Theorem 5. *If the General Subgroup Decision Assumption, Assumptions 5, 6 and 7 hold, no PPT adversary can achieve a non-negligible advantage in winning $Game_{IH}^E$ in Case 1.*

Proof Overview. Basically, the case-1 index-hiding of our Enhanced CP-ABE in the sense of $Game_{IH}^E$ is almost the same to that of [24]. Due to space, complete proof will be given in the full paper.

Proof of Case 2. From high-level point of view, the index-hiding in the second case relies on both the CP-ABE part and the A-HIBE part. For query with $n_i \neq \bar{n}_j$, we may deal with the key in a similar way as the proof of case 1. The main challenge is how to deal with the query with $n_i = \bar{n}_j$ in which case the above technique fails. Fortunately, our construction allows us to borrow the security from the CP-ABE part using the restriction that attribute set S_{n_i} must not satisfy the challenge policy $\mathbb{A}^*$. We prove the following theorem.

Theorem 6. *If the General Subgroup Decision Assumption, the 3-Party Diffie-Hellman Assumption in a Subgroup, the Source Group q-Parallel BDHE Assumption in a Subgroup, Assumptions 5 and 7 hold, no PPT adversary can achieve a non-negligible advantage in winning $Game_{IH}^E$ in Case 2.*

Proof Overview. We prove the theorem via a hybrid argument over a sequence of games similar to those used for proving index-hiding in case 1. Due to space, complete proof will be given in the full paper.

References

1. Attrapadung, N.: Dual system encryption via doubly selective security: framework, fully secure functional encryption for regular languages, and more. In: Nguyen, P.Q., Oswald, E. (eds.) EUROCRYPT 2014. LNCS, vol. 8441, pp. 557–577. Springer, Heidelberg (2014)
2. Boneh, D., Sahai, A., Waters, B.: Fully collusion resistant traitor tracing with short ciphertexts and private keys. In: Vaudenay, S. (ed.) EUROCRYPT 2006. LNCS, vol. 4004, pp. 573–592. Springer, Heidelberg (2006)
3. Boneh, D., Waters, B.: A fully collusion resistant broadcast, trace, and revoke system. In: Proceedings of the 13th ACM Conference on Computer and Communications Security, pp. 211–220. ACM (2006)
4. Cao, Z.: New trends of information security - how to change people's life style? Sci. China Inf. Sci. 59(5), 050106:1–050106:3 (2016)
5. Chen, J., Gay, R., Wee, H.: Improved dual system ABE in prime-order groups via predicate encodings. In: Oswald, E., Fischlin, M. (eds.) EUROCRYPT 2015. LNCS, vol. 9057, pp. 595–624. Springer, Heidelberg (2015)
6. Garg, S., Kumarasubramanian, A., Sahai, A., Waters, B.: Building efficient fully collusion-resilient traitor tracing and revocation schemes. In: Proceedings of the 17th ACM Conference on Computer and Communications Security, pp. 121–130. ACM (2010)

7. Goyal, V., Pandey, O., Sahai, A., Waters, B.: Attribute-based encryption for fine-grained access control of encrypted data. In: Proceedings of the 13th ACM Conference on Computer and Communications Security, pp. 89–98. ACM (2006)

8. Green, M., Hohenberger, S., Waters, B.: Outsourcing the decryption of ABE ciphertexts. In: USENIX Security Symposium, p. 3 (2011)

9. Katz, J., Schröder, D.: Tracing insider attacks in the context of predicate encryption schemes. In: ACITA (2011)

10. Lewko, A., Waters, B.: New techniques for dual system encryption and fully secure HIBE with short ciphertexts. In: Micciancio, D. (ed.) TCC 2010. LNCS, vol. 5978, pp. 455–479. Springer, Heidelberg (2010)

11. Lewko, A., Waters, B.: Decentralizing attribute-based encryption. In: Paterson, K.G. (ed.) EUROCRYPT 2011. LNCS, vol. 6632, pp. 568–588. Springer, Heidelberg (2011)

12. Lewko, A., Waters, B.: New proof methods for attribute-based encryption: achieving full security through selective techniques. In: Safavi-Naini, R., Canetti, R. (eds.) CRYPTO 2012. LNCS, vol. 7417, pp. 180–198. Springer, Heidelberg (2012)

13. Lewko, A., Waters, B.: New proof methods for attribute-based encryption: achieving full security through selective techniques. In: Safavi-Naini, R., Canetti, R. (eds.) CRYPTO 2012. LNCS, vol. 7417, pp. 180–198. Springer, Heidelberg (2012)

14. Li, J., Lin, X., Zhang, Y., Han, J.: KSF-OABE: outsourced attribute-based encryption with keyword search function for cloud storage. IEEE Trans. Serv. Comput. **PP**(99) (2016). doi:10.1109/TSC.2016.2542813

15. Liu, Z., Cao, Z., Wong, D.S.: Blackbox traceable CP-ABE: how to catch people leaking their keys by selling decryption devices on ebay. In: Proceedings of the ACM SIGSAC Conference on Computer & Communications Security, pp. 475–486. ACM (2013)

16. Liu, Z., Cao, Z., Wong, D.S.: White-box traceable ciphertext-policy attribute-based encryption supporting any monotone access structures. IEEE Trans. Inf. Foren. Secur. **8**(1), 76–88 (2013)

17. Liu, Z., Cao, Z., Wong, D.S.: Traceable CP-ABE: how to trace decryption devices found in the wild. IEEE Trans. Inf. Foren. Secur. **10**(1), 55–68 (2015)

18. Ning, J., Cao, Z., Dong, X., Wei, L., Lin, X.: Large universe ciphertext-policy attribute-based encryption with white-box traceability. In: Kutyłowski, M., Vaidya, J. (eds.) ESORICS 2014, Part II. LNCS, vol. 8713, pp. 55–72. Springer, Heidelberg (2014)

19. Ning, J., Dong, X., Cao, Z., Wei, L.: Accountable authority ciphertext-policy attribute-based encryption with white-box traceability and public auditing in the cloud. In: Computer Security–ESORICS 2015, pp. 270–289. Springer (2015)

20. Ning, J., Dong, X., Cao, Z., Wei, L., Lin, X.: White-box traceable ciphertext-policy attribute-based encryption supporting flexible attributes. IEEE Trans. Inf. Foren. Secur. **10**(6), 1274–1288 (2015)

21. Parno, B., Raykova, M., Vaikuntanathan, V.: How to Delegate and verify in public: verifiable computation from attribute-based encryption. In: Cramer, R. (ed.) TCC 2012. LNCS, vol. 7194, pp. 422–439. Springer, Heidelberg (2012)

22. Qian, H., Li, J., Zhang, Y.: Privacy-preserving decentralized ciphertext-policy attribute-based encryption with fully hidden access structure. In: Qing, S., Zhou, J., Liu, D. (eds.) ICICS 2013. LNCS, vol. 8233, pp. 363–372. Springer, Heidelberg (2013)

23. Sahai, A., Waters, B.: Fuzzy identity-based encryption. In: Cramer, R. (ed.) EUROCRYPT 2005. LNCS, vol. 3494, pp. 457–473. Springer, Heidelberg (2005)

24. Seo, J.H., Cheon, J.H.: Fully secure anonymous hierarchical identity-based encryption with constant size ciphertexts. IACR Cryptology ePrint Archive, 2011:21 (2011)
25. Seo, J.H., Kobayashi, T., Ohkubo, M., Suzuki, K.: Anonymous hierarchical identity-based encryption with constant size ciphertexts. In: Jarecki, S., Tsudik, G. (eds.) PKC 2009. LNCS, vol. 5443, pp. 215–234. Springer, Heidelberg (2009)
26. Waters, B.: Ciphertext-policy attribute-based encryption: an expressive, efficient, and provably secure realization. In: Catalano, D., Fazio, N., Gennaro, R., Nicolosi, A. (eds.) PKC 2011. LNCS, vol. 6571, pp. 53–70. Springer, Heidelberg (2011)

Server-Aided Revocable Attribute-Based Encryption

Hui Cui[1(✉)], Robert H. Deng[1], Yingjiu Li[1], and Baodong Qin[2]

[1] School of Information Systems, Secure Mobile Centre,
Singapore Management University, Singapore, Singapore
{hcui,robertdeng,yjli}@smu.edu.sg
[2] School of Computer Science and Technology,
Southwest University of Science and Technology, Mianyang, China
qinbaodong@swust.edu.cn

Abstract. As a one-to-many public key encryption system, attribute-based encryption (ABE) enables scalable access control over encrypted data in cloud storage services. However, efficient user revocation has been a very challenging problem in ABE. To address this issue, Boldyreva, Goyal and Kumar [5] introduced a revocation method by combining the binary tree data structure with fuzzy identity-based encryption, in which a key generation center (KGC) periodically broadcasts key update information to all data users over a public channel. The Boldyreva-Goyal-Kumar approach reduces the size of key updates from linear to logarithm in the number of users, and it has been widely used in subsequent revocable ABE systems; however, it requires each data user to keep a private key of logarithmic size and all non-revoked data users to periodically update decryption keys for each new time period. To further optimize user revocation in ABE, in this paper, we propose a notion called server-aided revocable ABE (SR-ABE), in which almost all workloads of data users incurred by user revocation are delegated to an untrusted server and each data user only needs to store a key of constant size. We then define a security model for SR-ABE, and present a concrete SR-ABE scheme secure under this model. Interestingly, due to the key embedding gadget employed in the construction of SR-ABE, our SR-ABE scheme does not require any secure channels for key transmission, and also enjoys an additional property in the decryption phase, where a data user only needs to perform one exponentiation computation to decrypt a ciphertext.

Keywords: Revocation · Attribute-based encryption · Server-aided

1 Introduction

Attribute-based encryption (ABE) [22] is a promising solution to preserve data privacy in scenarios where data users are identified by their attributes (or credentials) and data owners want to share their data stored in the cloud with data users

© Springer International Publishing Switzerland 2016
I. Askoxylakis et al. (Eds.): ESORICS 2016, Part II, LNCS 9879, pp. 570–587, 2016.
DOI: 10.1007/978-3-319-45741-3_29

whose attributes satisfy a certain access structure (or policy). In a ciphertext-policy ABE (CP-ABE) system, a trusted key generation center (KGC) issues a private key for every data user corresponding to his/her attribute set, and each data owner specifies an access policy over an attribute set to an encrypted message[1]. A data user is able to decrypt a ciphertext if the attribute set associated with his/her private key satisfies the access policy ascribed to the ciphertext.

Since an ABE system may involve a large number of data users, efficient user revocation, due to either private key compromises or user resignations, has been regarded as a very important and challenging problem. Boldyreva, Goyal and Kumar [5] put forth an efficient revocation method by combining the fuzzy identity-based encryption (IBE) scheme [22] with the binary tree data structure [18], where the KGC issues a long-term private key to each data user and publicly broadcasts key updates at the beginning of each time period, but only non-revoked data users can generate decryption keys from their long-term private keys and the key updates to decrypt the newly created ciphertexts. The revocable ABE schemes in [1,5,9,21] following the Boldyreva-Goyal-Kumar approach mitigate the KGC's communication overhead incurred in the key update process, but they fail to reduce the workloads of data users since every data user is required to keep a private key of logarithmic size and all non-revoked data users need to periodically update decryption keys to decrypt newly encrypted data. Regarding this crux, Qin et al. [19] proposed a solution in identity-based encryption, called server-aided revocable identity-based encryption (SR-IBE), where almost all workloads on data users are delegated to a untrusted server who manages data users' public keys and key updates sent by the KGC periodically, and each data user keeps just one private key of constant size (i.e., $O(1)$) and are not required to communicate with either the KGC or the untrusted server during the key update phase. However, this problem has not caught sufficient attention in the attribute-based setting.

1.1   Our Contributions

Motivated by SR-IBE in [19], we put forth a notion called server-aided revocable ABE (SR-ABE) to accomplish efficient and secure user revocation in ABE. The architecture of an SR-ABE scheme is depicted in Fig. 1 under the scenario of cloud storage [24]. The architecture consists of four types of entities: a KGC, data owners, data users and an untrusted server[2]. Note that the untrusted server could be operated by anyone, including the cloud storage system. The KGC possesses a master private key, and publishes its public parameter. When a new data user,

---

[1] There are two complimentary forms of ABE: CP-ABE and key-policy ABE (KP-ABE). In a KP-ABE system, the situation is reversed in that a private key is associated with an access policy and a ciphertext is associated with a set of attributes. In the rest of the paper, unless otherwise specified, we will focus on CP-ABE.

[2] The server is untrusted in the sense that it honestly follows the protocol, but does not hold any secret information (i.e., it may collude with data users), and all operations done by the server can be performed by anyone, including data users (i.e., any dishonest behaviour from the server can be easily detected).

say Alice, joins the system, she first generates a public and private user-key pair by herself. She keeps the private user-key to herself and sends the public user-key (along with a proof showing that she knows the corresponding private user-key) to the KGC, which, based on Alice's public user-key and attributes, generates a public attribute-key for Alice and sends it to the untrusted server. Also, the KGC periodically generates key updates for all non-revoked data users and publicly transmits them to the untrusted server. The same as that in the standard CP-ABE, to upload a message in the current time period to the cloud, a data owner encrypts the message over an access structure and a time period using the system public parameter, and outsources the resulting ciphertext to the cloud. To decrypt a ciphertext, a data user forwards the ciphertext to the untrusted server. If the data user is not revoked and his/her set of attributes satisfies the access structure ascribed to the ciphertext, the untrusted server is able to generate a transformation key from his/her public attribute-key and the key update information, with which the server can partially decrypt the ciphertext. This partially decrypted ciphertext can be fully decrypted by the data user using his/her private user-key. Notice that SR-ABE only requires all data users to contact the KGC during the user registration phase, while operations caused by user revocation are completely handled by the untrusted server and are totally transparent to the data users.

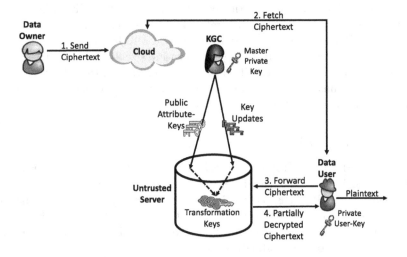

Fig. 1. System architecture of server-aided revocable attribute-based encryption.

The key challenge in constructing an SR-ABE scheme is how to enable the untrusted server to assist decryption while without knowing the underlying plaintext. In an IBE system, each user has a unique identity and every ciphertext is exclusively designated to one recipient. Therefore, in the SR-IBE scheme presented in [19], after the server partially decrypts a ciphertext for a data user, the user can obtain the underlying plaintext using his/her identity-based private key. However, in an ABE scheme, the same attributes could be shared among multiple users, so if using the master private key splitting methodology in [19] in an SR-ABE scheme, given the partial decryption of a ciphertext by the untrusted server, a data user would be able to fully decrypt the partially decrypted ciphertext, regardless of the data user being revoked or not, as long as his/her set of attributes satisfies the access structure in the ciphertext. To conquer this challenge, we equip each data user with a pair of self-generated public and private user-keys[3] (i.e., it does not require a secure channel for key transmission), and then trickly embed the public user-key into the public attribute-key generated by the KGC. As a result, the untrusted server can still partially decrypt ciphertexts for non-revoked users, but every partially decrypted ciphertext is bound with a public user-key, which can only be decrypted by the user possessing the corresponding private user-key.

We define a security model for SR-ABE, which formalizes the possible realistic threats and takes into account all adversarial capabilities of the standard ABE security notion. The adversary is able to learn private user-keys and public attribute-keys of data users with attributes of its choice. The adversary should not be able to learn any partial information about the message encrypted for the challenge access structure. In addition, we consider the adversary having access to periodic key updates, transformation keys for different time periods and being able to revoke users of its choice. The adversary should also not be able to learn any partial information about the messages encrypted for any revoked data user whose attributes satisfy the challenge access structure when the encryption is done after the time of revocation.

Then we present a concrete SR-ABE construction for this model based on the large universe CP-ABE scheme in the prime-order groups presented by Rouselakis and Waters [20]. For the sake of building the SR-ABE scheme, we resort to the technique in [23] and the binary tree data structure [18], and combine them with the Rouselakis-Waters CP-ABE scheme [20]. In our SR-ABE scheme, components corresponding to each attribute in a transformation key follow the form of the second level private key of the HIBE scheme [6]. A technique similar to that in [23] is used to generate the public attribute-keys and key updates, where the master private key of the KGC is randomly divided into two parts and each part is respectively bound to the public attribute-keys and key updates. Also, to reduce the size of key updates from linear to logarithmic in the number of data users, the binary tree data structure in [18] is used. We present the full details of the construction in Sect. 4. It is worth noticing that though SR-ABE is derived from SR-IBE, due to the gadget we employ in the public attribute-key generation algorithm, our SR-ABE construction enjoys two additional advantages that the SR-IBE scheme in [19] does not have: (1) there is no need of secure channels for the distribution of private keys, since they are generated by each data user

---

[3] This user-key pair can also be generated and securely sent to the data user by the KGC as that in [19], but this requires a secure channel between the data user and the KGC for key distribution.

himself/herself; (2) in the decryption phase, each privileged data user only needs to perform one exponentiation computation and no pairing computation.

Since the Rouselakis-Waters CP-ABE scheme [20] is selectively secure, where the adversary has to commit the challenge access structure in advance, our SR-ABE scheme which is constructed based on [20] is also selectively secure. Note that the techniques can be applied to fully secure ABE schemes (e.g., [21]) to obtain fully secure server-aided ABE schemes.

In a nutshell, our contributions in this paper can be summarized as follows.

- We first propose a notion called server-aided revocable attribute-based encryption (SR-ABE), in which almost all data users' workloads incurred in key update phase are delegated to an untrusted server and each data user only needs to keep a private user-key of constant size for decryption.
- We define a security model for SR-ABE which considers all possible adversarial behaviours that could be executed by an adversary in the real world.
- Due to the gadget employed in the construction of SR-ABE, our SR-ABE scheme does not require any secure channels for key transmission, and enjoys an additional property in the decryption phase, where a data user only needs to perform one exponentiation computation to decrypt a ciphertext.

1.2 Related Work

Revocable IBE. Boneh and Franklin [8] suggested to renew users' private keys periodically to achieve user revocation in IBE, but this requires all users to regularly contact the KGC over secure channels, regardless of whether their keys have been exposed. That is, the size of key updates is linear in the number of non-revoked users (i.e., $O(N - R)$, where N is the number of all users and R is the number of revoked users). Hanaoka et al. [11] presented a method for users to periodically renew their private keys without interacting with the KGC, where the KGC publicly posts the key update information; however, each user needs to possess a tamper-resistant hardware device, making the solution rather cumbersome. Boldyreva, Goyal and Kumar [5] presented an efficient revocable IBE scheme to reduce the size of key updates from linear to logarithmic (i.e., $O(R \log(\frac{N}{R}))$) and remove the secure channels required during key updates, but all non-revoked users still need to periodically update their private keys for decryption. There are also revocable IBE schemes with a third party [3,7,10,14, 16,17,19], where a semi-trusted[4] or untrusted third party is required to hold the shares of all users' private keys and help them decrypt. Once a user is revoked, the third party stops decrypting (or is disallowed to decrypt) for the user.

Revocable ABE. Two kinds of user revocation mechanisms have been proposed for revocable ABE [1,9]: direct and indirect revocation. In direct revocation, data owners directly specify the revocation list when encrypting [2,12,15]. In addition, Yang et al. [26] proposed a revocable ABE scheme by giving the direct

---

[4] In this paper, unless otherwise specified, "semi-trusted" means that the party is disallowed to collude with data users.

revocation capability to a semi-trusted server who shares the decryption ability with data users, and will terminate decryption operations for revoked users. In indirect revocation, the KGC indirectly disables revoked users through a key update process. Boldyreva, Goyal and Kumar [5] proposed a revocable KP-ABE scheme following the indirect revocation approach, Attrapadung and Imai [1] gave a hybrid revocable KP-ABE system which allows a data owner to select either direct or indirect revocation when encrypting a message, Sahai, Seyalioglu and Waters [21] provided a generic way to achieve indirect revocation in ABE schemes, and Cui and Deng [9] gave two revocable ABE schemes in the setting where the KGC'role is split across multiple KGCs.

Note that direct revocation can be done immediately without key updates, but it requires all data owners to keep a current revocation list. This makes the system impurely attribute-based, since data owners in the attribute-based setting create a ciphertext based solely on attributes without caring each data user's status. In this paper, we focus on ABE with indirect revocation.

1.3 Organization

The remainder of this paper is organized as follows. In Sect. 2, we briefly review the notions and definitions relevant to this paper. In Sect. 3, we describe the framework of our SR-ABE, and then present its security model. In Sect. 4, we give a concrete construction of SR-ABE, prove its security, and compare it with previous revocable ABE schemes. We conclude the paper in Sect. 5.

2 Preliminaries

In this section, we review the basic cryptographic definitions that are to be used in this paper.

2.1 Bilinear Pairings and Complexity Assumptions

Let G be a group of order p generated from g, and p be a prime number. We define $\hat{e} : G \times G \to G_1$ to be a bilinear map if it has the following properties [8].

- Bilinear: for all $g \in G$, and $a, b \in Z_p^*$, we have $\hat{e}(g^a, g^b) = \hat{e}(g, g)^{ab}$.
- Non-degenerate: $\hat{e}(g, g) \neq 1$.

We say that G is a bilinear group if the group operation in G is efficiently computable and there exists a group G_1 and an efficiently computable bilinear map $\hat{e} : G \times G \to G_1$ as above.

Decisional $(q-1)$ Assumption [20]. The decisional $(q-1)$ problem is that for any probabilistic polynomial-time algorithm, given $\overrightarrow{y} =$

$$
\begin{aligned}
&g, g^{\mu}, g^{1/a}, \\
&g^{a^i}, g^{b_j}, g^{\mu b_j}, g^{a^i b_j}, g^{a^i/b_j^2} \ \forall \ (i,j) \in [q,q], \\
&g^{a^i/b_j} && \forall \ (i,j) \in [2q,q] \text{ with } i \neq q+1, \\
&g^{a^i b_j/b_{j'}^2} && \forall \ (i,j,j') \in [2q,q,q] \text{ with } j \neq j', \\
&g^{\mu a^i b_j/b_{j'}}, g^{\mu a^i b_j/b_{j'}^2} && \forall \ (i,j,j') \in [q,q,q] \text{ with } j \neq j',
\end{aligned}
$$

it is difficult to distinguish $(\overrightarrow{y}, \hat{e}(g,g)^{a^{q+1}\mu})$ from $(\overrightarrow{y}, Z)$, where $g \in G$, $Z \in G_1$, $a, \mu, b_1, ..., b_q \in Z_p^*$ are chosen independently and uniformly at random.

2.2 Access Structures and Linear Secret Sharing

Definition 1 (Access Structure) [13,25]. *Let $\{P_1, ..., P_n\}$ be a set of parties. A collection $\mathbb{A} \subseteq 2^{\{P_1,...,P_n\}}$ is monotone if $\forall B, C :$ if $B \in \mathbb{A}$ and $B \subseteq C$, then $C \subseteq \mathbb{A}$. A monotone access structure is a monotone collection $\mathbb{A}$ of nonempty subsets of $\{P_1, ..., P_n\}$, i.e., $\mathbb{A} \subseteq 2^{\{P_1,...,P_n\}} \setminus \{\emptyset\}$. The sets in $\mathbb{A}$ are called authorized sets, and the sets not in $\mathbb{A}$ are called unauthorized sets.*

Definition 2 (Linear Secret Sharing Schemes (LSSS)) [13,25]. *Let P be a set of parties. Let $\mathbb{M}$ be a matrix of size $l \times n$. Let $\rho : \{1, ..., l\} \to P$ be a function that maps a row to a party for labeling. A secret sharing scheme Π over a set of parties P is a linear secret-sharing scheme over Z_p if*

1. The shares for each party form a vector over Z_p.
2. There exists a matrix $\mathbb{M}$ with l rows and n columns, called the share-generating matrix, for Π. For $x = 1, ..., l$, the x-th row of matrix $\mathbb{M}$ is labelled by a party $\rho(i)$, where $\rho : \{1, ..., l\} \to P$ is a function that maps a row to a party for labelling. Considering that the column vector $\overrightarrow{v} = (\mu, r_2, ..., r_n)$, where $\mu \in Z_p$ is the secret to be shared and $r_2, ..., r_n \in Z_p$ are randomly chosen, then $\mathbb{M}\overrightarrow{v}$ is the vector of l shares of the secret μ according to Π. The share $(\mathbb{M}\overrightarrow{v})_i$ belongs to party $\rho(i)$.

It has been noted in [13] that every LSSS also enjoys the linear reconstruction property. Suppose that Π is an LSSS for an access structure $\mathbb{A}$. Let $\mathbf{A}$ be an authorized set, and define $I \subseteq \{1, ..., l\}$ as $I = \{i | \rho(i) \in \mathbf{A}\}$. Then the vector $(1, 0, ..., 0)$ is in the span of rows of matrix $\mathbb{M}$ indexed by I, and there exist constants $\{w_i \in Z_p\}_{i \in I}$ such that, for any valid shares $\{v_i\}$ of a secret μ according to Π, we have $\sum_{i \in I} w_i v_i = \mu$. These constants $\{w_i\}$ can be found in polynomial time with respect to the size of the share-generating matrix $\mathbb{M}$ [4].

On the other hand, for an unauthorized set $\mathbf{A}'$, no such constants $\{w_i\}$ exist. Moreover, in this case it is also true that if $I' = \{i | \rho(i) \in \mathbf{A}'\}$, there exists a vector $\overrightarrow{w}$ such that its first component w_1 is any non-zero element in Z_p and $< \mathbb{M}_i, \overrightarrow{w} > = 0$ for all $i \in I'$, where $\mathbb{M}_i$ is the i-th row of $\mathbb{M}$ [20].

Boolean Formulas [13]. Access policies can also be described in terms of monotonic boolean formulas. LSSS access structures are more general, and can be derived from representations as boolean formulas. There are standard techniques to convert any monotonic boolean formula into a corresponding LSSS matrix. The boolean formula can be represented as an access tree, where the interior nodes are AND and OR gates, and the leaf nodes correspond to attributes. The number of rows in the corresponding LSSS matrix will be the same as the number of leaf nodes in the access tree.

2.3   Binary Tree

We recall the definition about binary tree described in [5,19]. Denote BT by a binary tree with N leaves corresponding to N users. Let **root** be the root node of the tree BT. If θ is a leaf node, then Path(θ) denotes the set of nodes on the path from θ to **root**, which includes both θ and **root**. If θ is a non-leaf node, then θ_l, θ_r denote left and right child of θ. Assume that nodes in the tree are uniquely encoded as strings, and the tree is defined by all of its node descriptions. The algorithm KUNodes is used to compute the minimal set of nodes for which key update needs to be published so that only the non-revoked users at a time period t are able to decrypt the ciphertexts. This algorithm takes a binary tree BT, a revocation list rl and a time period t as the input, and outputs a set of nodes which is the minimal set of nodes in BT such that none of the nodes in rl with corresponding time period before or at t (users revoked at or before t) have any ancestor (or, themselves) in the set, and all other leaf nodes (corresponding to non-revoked users) have exactly one ancestor (or, themselves) in the set. We give a pictorial depiction on how the KUNodes algorithm works in Fig. 2, where it firstly marks all the ancestors of the revoked nodes as revoked, and then it outputs all the non-revoked children of revoked nodes. Below is a

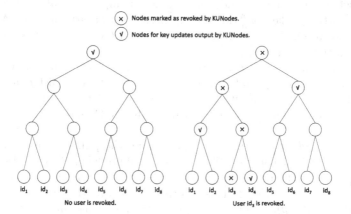

Fig. 2. A pictorial description about how the KUNodes algorithm works.

formal definition of the KUNodes algorithm.

KUNodes(BT, rl, t)
$\quad X, Y \leftarrow \emptyset.$
$\quad \forall\ (\theta_i, t_i) \in rl$, if $t_i \leq t$, then add Path(θ_i) to X.
$\quad \forall\ x \in X$, if $x_l \notin X$, then add x_l to Y; if $x_r \notin X$, then add x_r to Y.
$\quad$ If $Y = \emptyset$, then add **root** to Y.
$\quad$ Return Y.

3   Framework and Security Model

In this section, we describe the framework and security definition of SR-ABE.

3.1   Framework

An SR-ABE scheme involves four types of entities: a key generation center (KGC), data owners, data users and a untrusted server, and consists of nine algorithms given below. We assume that the server keeps a list of tuples (identity, attribute set, public attribute-key), i.e., $(id, \mathbf{A}, pk_{id}^{\mathbf{A}})$.

- Setup(1^λ) $\to$ (par, msk, rl, st). Taking a security parameter λ as the input, this algorithm outputs the public parameter par, the master private key msk, an initially empty revocation list rl and a state st. This algorithm is run by the KGC.
- UserKG(par, id) $\to$ (sk_{id}, pk_{id}). Taking the public parameter par and an identity as the input, this algorithm outputs a public and private user-key pair (sk_{id}, pk_{id}). This algorithm is run by each data user.
- PubKG(par, msk, id, pk_{id}, $\mathbf{A}$, st) $\to$ ($pk_{id}^{\mathbf{A}}$, st). Taking the public parameter par, the master private key msk, an identity id with a public user-key pk_{id} and a set of attributes $\mathbf{A}$, and a state st as the input, this algorithm outputs a public attribute-key $pk_{id}^{\mathbf{A}}$ for user id possessing an attribute set $\mathbf{A}$ and an updated state st. This algorithm is run by the KGC, and ($pk_{id}^{\mathbf{A}}$, st) is sent to the untrusted server.
- TKeyUp(par, msk, t, rl, st) $\to$ (tku_t, st). Taking the public parameter par, the master private key msk, a time period t, a revocation list rl and a state st as the input, this algorithm outputs a key update message tku_t and an updated state st. This algorithm is run by the KGC, and (tku_t, st) is sent to the server.
- TranKG(par, id, $pk_{id}^{\mathbf{A}}$, tku_t) $\to$ $tk_{id,t}$. Taking the public parameter par, an identity id with the corresponding public attribute-key $pk_{id}^{\mathbf{A}}$ and a key update message tku_t as the input, this algorithm outputs a transformation key $tk_{id,t}$ for user id in time period t. This algorithm is run by the server.
- Encrypt(par, $(\mathbb{M}, \rho)$, t, M) $\to$ CT. Taking the public parameter par, an access structure $(\mathbb{M}, \rho)$, a time period t and a message M as the input, this algorithm outputs a ciphertext CT. This algorithm is run by each data owner, and CT will be stored in the cloud.

- Transform(par, id, $\mathbf{A}$, $tk_{id,t}$, CT) → CT$'$/⊥. Taking the public parameter par, an identity id with the corresponding transformation key $tk_{id,t}$ and a ciphertext CT as the input, this algorithm outputs either a partially decrypted ciphertext CT$'$ when the attributes $\mathbf{A}$ associated with the transformation key $tk_{id,t}$ satisfies the access structure of the ciphertext CT or ⊥ indicating the failure of the transformation. This algorithm is run by the server. After the partial decryption, CT$'$ is sent to the data user id.
- Decrypt(par, id, sk_{id}, CT$'$) → M/⊥. Taking the public parameter par, an identity id with a private user-key sk_{id} and a transformed ciphertext CT$'$ as the input, this algorithm outputs a message M or a failure symbol ⊥. This algorithm is run by a data user id.
- Revoke(id, t, rl, st) → rl. Taking an identity id to be revoked, a time period t, a revocation list rl and a state st, this algorithm outputs an updated revocation list rl. This algorithm is run by the KGC.

The correctness of an SR-ABE scheme requires that for any security parameter λ and any message M, if the data user id is not revoked at time period t, and if all parties follow the described algorithms as above, we have Decrypt(par, sk_{id}, CT$'$) = M.

3.2 Security Model

Below we describe the security definition of indistinguishability under chosen plaintext attacks (IND-CPA security) for SR-ABE between an adversary algorithm $\mathcal{A}$ and a challenger algorithm $\mathcal{B}$.

- Setup. Algorithm $\mathcal{B}$ runs the setup algorithm, and gives the public parameter par to algorithm $\mathcal{A}$, and keeps the master private key msk, an initially empty revocation list rl and a state st.
- Phase 1. Algorithm $\mathcal{A}$ adaptively issues a sequence of following queries to algorithm $\mathcal{B}$.
  - Private-User-Key oracle. Algorithm $\mathcal{A}$ issues a private user-key query on an identity id. Algorithm $\mathcal{B}$ returns sk_{id} by running UserKG(par, id).
    Note that once algorithm $\mathcal{B}$ runs UserKG(par, id), it adds (id, pk_{id}, sk_{id}) to a list so that the same (sk_{id}, pk_{id}) is used for all queries on id.
  - Public-Attribute-Key oracle. Algorithm $\mathcal{A}$ issues a public attribute-key query on an identity id and an attribute set $\mathbf{A}$. Algorithm $\mathcal{B}$ returns $pk_{id}^{\mathbf{A}}$ by running UserKG(par, id) (if id has not been issued to the Private-User-Key oracle), PubKG(par, msk, id, pk_{id}, $\mathbf{A}$, st).
  - Transformation-Key-Update oracle. Algorithm $\mathcal{A}$ issues a key update query on a time period t. Algorithm $\mathcal{B}$ runs TKeyUp(par, msk, t, rl, st) and returns tku_t.
  - Transformation-Key oracle. Algorithm $\mathcal{A}$ issues a transformation key query on a time period t and an identity id with an attribute set $\mathbf{A}$. Algorithm $\mathcal{B}$ returns $tk_{id,t}$ by running UserKG(par, id) (if id has not been issued to the Private-User-Key oracle), PubKG(par, msk, id, pk_{id}, $\mathbf{A}$, st), TKeyUp(par,

msk, t, rl, st), TranKG(par, id, $pk_{id}^{\mathbf{A}}$, tku_t). Note that this oracle cannot be queried on a time period t before a transformation key update oracle has been queried on t.

- Revocation oracle. Algorithm $\mathcal{A}$ issues a revocation query on an identity id and a time period t. Algorithm $\mathcal{B}$ runs Revoke(id, t, rl, st) and outputs an updated revocation list rl.Note that a time period t on which a transformation key update query has been issued cannot be issued to this oracle.

- Challenge. Algorithm $\mathcal{A}$ outputs two messages M_0^*, M_1^* of the same size, an access structure $(\mathbb{M}^*, \rho^*)$ and a time period t^* satisfying the following constraints.
  1. Case 1: if (1) an identity id^* has been queried to the Private-User-Key oracle, and (2) $(\mathbb{M}^*, \rho^*)$ can be satisfied by a query on $(id^*, \mathbf{A}^*)$ issued to the Public-Attribute-Key oracle, then (1) the revocation oracle must be queried on (id^*, t) on $t = t^*$ or any t occurs before t^*, and (2) the Transformation-Key oracle cannot be queried on (id^*, t^*).
  2. Case 2: if an identity id^* whose attribute set $\mathbf{A}^*$ can be satisfied by the challenge access structure $(\mathbb{M}^*, \rho^*)$ is not revoked at or before t^*, then id^* should not be previously queried to the Private-User-Key oracle.
  Algorithm $\mathcal{B}$ randomly chooses $\gamma \in \{0, 1\}$, and forwards the challenge ciphertext CT^* to algorithm $\mathcal{A}$ by running Encrypt(par, $(\mathbb{M}^*, \rho^*)$, t^*, M_γ^*).
- Phase 2. Algorithm $\mathcal{A}$ continues issuing queries to algorithm $\mathcal{B}$ as in Phase 1, following the restrictions defined in the Challenge phase.
- Guess. Algorithm $\mathcal{A}$ makes a guess γ' for γ, and it wins the game if $\gamma' = \gamma$.

The advantage of algorithm $\mathcal{A}$ in this game is defined as $\Pr[\gamma = \gamma'] - 1/2$. An SR-ABE scheme is IND-CPA secure if any probabilistic polynomial time (PPT) adversary has at most a negligible advantage in the security parameter λ. In addition, an SR-ABE scheme is said to be selectively IND-CPA secure if an Init stage is added before the Setup phase where algorithm $\mathcal{A}$ commits to the challenge access structure $(\mathbb{M}^*, \rho^*)$ (and the challenge time period t^*) which it attempts to attack.

Remark. Seo and Emura [23] defined a security model to prevent a realistic threat called decryption key exposure attacks such that no information of the plaintext is revealed from a ciphertext even if all (short-term) decryption keys of a "different time period" are exposed, which the revocable ABE schemes in [1,5,9,21] following the Boldyreva-Goyal-Kumar technique cannot resist[5]. To cover such attacks in our IND-CPA security model, different from those previous security notions [1,5,9,21] in revocable ABE, the adversary in our CP-ABE definition is given access to an additional Transformation-Key oracle, since the decryption key generated by a data user in a normal ABE scheme is now created by the server and renamed as transformation key in our SR-ABE scheme.

---

[5] This does not contradict with the security proofs of these schemes, because such attacks are excluded from their security models.

4   Server-Aided Revocable Attribute-Based Encryption

In this section, we present a construction of SR-ABE, and analyze its security.

4.1   Construction

Assume that both the attribute space and the time space are Z_p, and the message space is G_1. The proposed SR-ABE scheme, which is based on the CP-ABE scheme in [20], consists of the following algorithms.

- Setup. This algorithm takes a security parameter λ as the input. It randomly chooses a group G of prime order p with $g \in G$ being the corresponding generator, and defines a bilinear map $\hat{e} : G \times G \to G_1$. Additionally, it randomly chooses u, h, u_0, h_0, w, $v \in G$, $\alpha \in Z_p$. Let rl be an empty list storing revoked users and BT be a binary tree with at least N leaf nodes. Define two functions F_1 and F_2 to map any element y in Z_p to an element in G by $F_1(y) = u^y h$ and $F_2(y) = u_0{}^y h_0$. The public parameter is $par = (g, w, v, u, h, u_0, h_0, \hat{e}(g,g)^\alpha)$ along with rl and st, where st is a state which is set to be BT. The master private key is $msk = \alpha$.
- UserKG. This algorithm takes the public parameter par and an identity id as the input. It randomly chooses $\beta \in Z_p$, and outputs a private and public user-key pair $(sk_{id}, pk_{id}) = (\beta_{id}, g^{\beta_{id}})$ for user id.
- PubKG. This algorithm takes the public parameter par, the master private key msk, an identity id with a public key pk_{id} and an attribute set **A**, and a state st as the input. Let A_1, ..., A_k be the elements of **A**. It firstly chooses an undefined leaf node θ from the binary tree BT, and stores id in this node. Then, for each node $x \in \text{Path}(\theta)$, it runs as follows.
  1. It fetches g_x from the node x. If x has not been defined, it randomly chooses $g_x \in G$, computes $g'_x = pk_{id}{}^\alpha / g_x$, and stores g_x in the node x.
  2. It randomly chooses $r_x, r_{x,1}, ..., r_{x,k} \in Z_p$, and computes

$$P_{x,1} = g'_x \cdot w^{r_x}, \quad P_{x,2} = g^{r_x}, \quad P_{x,3}^{(i)} = g^{r_{x,i}}, \quad P_{x,4}^{(i)} = F_1(A_i)^{r_{x,i}} \cdot v^{-r_x}.$$

  3. It outputs $pk_{id}^{\mathbf{A}} = \{x, P_{x,1}, P_{x,2}, P_{x,3}^{(i)}, P_{x,4}^{(i)}\}_{x \in \text{Path}(\theta), i \in [1,k]}$ as the public attribute-key and an updated state st.
- TKeyUp. This algorithm takes the public parameter par, the master private key msk, a time period t, a revocation list rl and a state st as the input. For all $x \in \text{KUNodes}(\text{BT}, rl, t)$, it fetches g_x (note that g_x is always predefined in the PubKG algorithm) from the node x. It then randomly chooses $s_x \in Z_p$, and outputs the transformation key update information $tku_t = \{x, Q_{x,1}, Q_{x,2}\}_{x \in \text{KUNodes}(\text{BT}, rl, t)}$ where $Q_{x,1} = g_x \cdot F_2(t)^{s_x}$, $Q_{x,2} = g^{s_x}$.
- TranKG. This algorithm takes the public parameter par, an identity id with a public attribute-key $pk_{id}^{\mathbf{A}}$ and the transformation key update information tku_t as the input. Denote I as $\text{Path}(\theta)$, J as $\text{KUNodes}(\text{BT}, rl, t)$. It parses $pk_{id}^{\mathbf{A}}$ as $\{x, P_{x,1}, P_{x,2}, P_{x,3}^{(i)}, P_{x,4}^{(i)}\}_{x \in I, i \in [1,k]}$, tku_t as $\{x, Q_{x,1}, Q_{x,2}\}_{x \in J}$ for some set of

nodes I, J. If $I \cap J = \emptyset$, it returns $\perp$. Otherwise, for any node $x \in I \cap J$, it randomly chooses $r'_x, r'_{x,1}, ..., r'_{x,k}, s'_x \in Z_p$, and computes

$$tk_1 = P_{x,1} \cdot Q_{x,1} \cdot w^{r'_x} \cdot F_2(t)^{s'_x} = pk_{id}{}^{\alpha} \cdot w^{r_x + r'_x} \cdot F_2(t)^{s_x + s'_x},$$

$$tk_2 = P_{x,2} \cdot g^{r'_x} = g^{r_x + r'_x}, \quad tk_3^{(i)} = P_{x,3}^{(i)} \cdot g^{r'_{x,i}} = g^{r_{x,i} + r'_{x,i}},$$

$$tk_4^{(i)} = P_{x,4}^{(i)} \cdot F_1(A_i)^{r'_{x,i}} \cdot v^{-r'_x} = F_1(A_i)^{r_{x,i} + r'_{x,i}} \cdot v^{-(r_x + r'_x)},$$

$$tk_5 = Q_{x,2} \cdot g^{s'_x} = g^{s_x + s'_x}.$$

It outputs the transformation key $tk_{id,t} = (tk_1, tk_2, \{tk_3^{(i)}, tk_4^{(i)}\}_{i \in [1,k]}, tk_5)$.
- Encrypt. This algorithm takes the public parameter par, an LSSS access structure $(\mathbb{M}, \rho)$, a time period t and a message M as the input. Let $\mathbb{M}$ be a $l \times n$ matrix. It randomly chooses a vector $\vec{v} = (\mu, y_2, ..., y_n)^{\perp} \in Z_p^n$. These values will be used to share the encryption exponent μ. For $i = 1$ to l, it calculates $v_i = \mathbb{M}_i \cdot \vec{v}$ where $\mathbb{M}_i$ is the i-th row of $\mathbb{M}$. In addition, it randomly chooses $\mu_1, ..., \mu_l \in Z_p$, and outputs the ciphertext $CT = ((\mathbb{M}, \rho), t, C_0, C_1, \{C_2^{(i)}, C_3^{(i)}, C_4^{(i)}\}_{i \in [1,l]}, C_5)$ where

$$C_0 = \hat{e}(g,g)^{\alpha\mu} \cdot M, \quad C_1 = g^{\mu}, \quad C_2^{(i)} = w^{v_i} \cdot v^{\mu_i},$$
$$C_3^{(i)} = F_1(A_i)^{-\mu_i}, \quad C_4^{(i)} = g^{\mu_i}, \quad C_5 = F_2(t)^{\mu}.$$

- Transform. This algorithm takes the public parameter par, an identity id with a transformation key $tk_{id,t}$ over an attribute set $\mathbf{A}$ and a time period t and a ciphertext CT over an access structure $(\mathbb{M}, \rho)$ and the same time period t as the input. Suppose that $\mathbf{A}$ satisfies the access structure $(\mathbb{M}, \rho)$. Let I be defined as $I = \{i : \rho(i) \in \mathbf{A}\}$. Denote by $\{w_i \in Z_p\}_{i \in I}$ a set of constants such that if $\{v_i\}$ are valid shares of any secret μ according to $\mathbb{M}$, then $\sum_{i \in I} w_i v_i = \mu$. It parses CT, and outputs the transformed ciphertext $CT' = (C'_0, C_0)$ where

$$C'_0 = \frac{\prod_{i \in I} \left(\hat{e}(C_2^{(i)}, tk_2)\hat{e}(C_3^{(i)}, tk_3^{(i)})\hat{e}(C_4^{(i)}, tk_4^{(i)})\right)^{w_i} \hat{e}(C_5, tk_5)}{\hat{e}(C_1, tk_1)} = \frac{1}{\hat{e}(g, pk_{id}{}^{\alpha})^{\mu}}.$$

- Decrypt. This algorithm takes the public parameter par, an identity id with a private user-key sk_{id} and a transformed ciphertext CT' as the input. It outputs the message M as $M = (C'_0)^{1/\beta} \cdot C_0$.
- Revoke. This algorithm takes an identity id, a time period t, a revocation list rl and a state st as the input. For all the nodes x associated with identity id, it adds (x, t) to rl, and outputs the updated rl.

Notes and Comments. In the above scheme, g'_x in the PubKG algorithm can also be set as $g^{\alpha + \beta_{id}}/g_x$ such that the KGC runs the UserKG algorithm as follows. For each id, the KGC randomly chooses $\beta_{id}, r, r_1, ..., r_k \in Z_p$, and outputs a private user-key $sk_{id} = \{K_1, K_2, K_3^{(i)}, K_4^{(i)}\}_{i \in [1,k]}$, where

$$K_1 = g^{\beta_{id}} \cdot w^r, \quad K_2 = g^r, \quad K_3^{(i)} = g^{r_i}, \quad K_4^{(i)} = F_1(A_i)^{r_i} \cdot v^{-r}.$$

However, this requires a secure channel between the KGC and each data user for key transmission. In addition, the KGC possesses all secrets of data users. Lastly, since this key structure follows that in the basic Rouselakis-Waters CP-ABE scheme [20], each data user's computational cost in decryption could not be mitigated, and their storage sizes of private keys are linear to the numbers of the attributes entitled to them.

Remark. Note that the techniques applied in our SR-ABE construction can be used to realize other cryptographic primitives.

- Server-aided revocable KP-ABE. Since our SR-ABE construction uses the same binary tree data structure as in the revocable KP-ABE scheme [1], it is not difficult to see that the technique of having an untrusted server to facilitate computation used in our construction can be applied in a straightforward manner to realize server-aided revocable KP-ABE.
- Server-aided revocable IBE with efficient decryption. In our SR-ABE scheme, we embed a public user-key into the attribute-key such that the server is only able to partially decrypt a ciphertext, and leaves the partially decrypted ciphertext to user for fully decryption using her private user-key. Such a gadget can be easily adopted in the SR-IBE scheme in [19] to reduce data users' decryption costs and remove secure channels for key distribution.

4.2 Security

Theorem 1. *Under the decisional* $(q-1)$ *problem, our SR-ABE scheme is selectively IND-CPA secure.*

Proof. The proof is divided into two cases. In Case 1, it is assumed that an identity id^* whose attribute set $\mathbf{A}^*$ satisfying the challenge access structure $(\mathbb{M}^*, \rho^*)$ is revoked at or before the challenge time period t^*. In Case 2, it is assumed that an identity id^* whose attribute set $\mathbf{A}^*$ satisfying the challenge access structure $(\mathbb{M}^*, \rho^*)$ is not revoked at or before the challenge time period t^*. Briefly speaking, the adversary is allowed to issue a private user-key query on id^* in Case 1, while this query is prohibited in Case 2. We detail the proof in the full version of this paper[6]. $\qquad\qquad\square$

4.3 Comparison

To our knowledge, in addition to our work in this paper, [1,5,21,26] are also revocable ABE schemes from bilinear pairings (excluding dual vector pairing spaces [21]) in the prime-order groups. Recall that our goal in this paper is to achieve indirect user revocation in a CP-ABE system by delegating data users' workloads to an untrusted server such that the KGC indirectly accomplishes user revocation by stopping updating the keys for revoked data users. In [5], a KP-ABE scheme with indirect revocation is proposed where the KGC enables user

---

[6] Please contact the authors for it.

Table 1. Comparison between our SR-ABE scheme and existing revocable ABE (R-ABE) schemes from standard bilinear pairings in the prime-order groups.

	R-ABE in [5]	R-ABE in [1]	R-ABE in [26]	R-ABE in [21]	Our SR-ABE
Revocation Mode	Indirect	Indirect & Direct	Direct	Indirect	Indirect
Type of ABE	KP-ABE	KP-ABE	CP-ABE	KP-ABE & CP-ABE	CP-ABE
Server	–	–	Semi-trust	–	Untrust
Key Exposure Resistance	No	No	–	No	Yes
Security	Selective	Selective	Selective	Selective	Selective
Secure Channel	Yes	Yes	Yes	Yes	No
Size of Key Updates	$O(R\log(\frac{N}{R}))$	$O(R\log(\frac{N}{R}))$	–	$O(R\log(\frac{N}{R}))$	$O(R\log(\frac{N}{R}))$
Size of Key Stored by Data User	$O(l\log N)$	$O(l\log N)$	$O(1)$	$O(l\log N)$ & $O(k\log N)$	$O(1)$
Computation Cost in Decrypt	$\geq 2(E+P)$	$\geq 3E+4P$	E	$\geq E+P$	E

revocation by stopping posting key update information for revoked data users, thereby forcing revoked data users to be unable to update their decryption keys. A hybrid revocable KP-ABE system is given in [1], which allows a data owner to select either direct or indirect revocation mode when encrypting a message. In [26], a revocable ABE scheme is put forth by giving the direct revocation capability to a semi-trusted server, where the server shares part of the decryption capability of the data users and stops the decryption operation for any revoked data users. A generic way to realize ABE supporting dynamic credentials is provided in [21], where the KGC indirectly accomplishes revocation by stopping updating the keys for revoked data users.

Table 1 compares our SR-ABE scheme with revocable ABE schemes under prime-order groups in [1,5,21,26]. Let N be the number of all data users, R be the number of revoked data users, l be the number of attributes presented in an access structure, and k be the size of the attribute set associated with an attribute-key. Also, let "−" denote not-applicable, "E" denote exponentiation operation, and "P" denote pairing operation, respectively. It is straightforward to see from Table 1 that the schemes in [1,5,21] require secure channels between the KGC and every data user for key transmission, and every data user to keep a private key of which the size is determined by their attributes and the associated nodes in the predefined binary tree. While the scheme in [26] does not require every data user to store a key of large size but requires a secure channel between the KGC and the semi-trusted server, and is subject to collusion attacks between the semi-trusted server and revoked data users. Clearly, our SR-ABE scheme has an edge over previous solutions in that it does not require any secure channels between the system participants, and is secure against collusion attacks between the untrusted server and revoked data users. Also, our SR-ABE scheme achieves desirable efficiency in decryption run by data users, which only requires one exponentiation operation.

5 Conclusions

In this paper, we introduced a notion called server-aided revocable attribute-based encryption (SR-ABE) to achieve efficient user revocation in attribute-based encryption (ABE). We formally defined the (selective) IND-CPA security for SR-ABE, proposed a concrete construction of SR-ABE in terms of ciphertext-policy attribute-based encryption (CP-ABE), and then proved that the proposed SR-ABE scheme is selectively IND-CPA secure. Compared with the previous revocable ABE schemes, our SR-ABE scheme has three salient advantages. First, our SR-ABE scheme delegates almost all computational overheads of data users resulted in key updates to an untrusted server. Second, instead of storing a private key, of which the size is logarithmic to the number of data users, by each data user as in most of the existing revocable ABE schemes, each data user in our SR-ABE scheme only needs to keep a private key of one group element. Third, in our SR-ABE scheme, most of the computational cost in decryption is delegated to the untrusted server, and a data user is only required to perform one exponentiation operation to decrypt a ciphertext. Besides constructing server-aided revocable CP-ABE schemes, the same techniques introduced in this paper can be easily applied to build server-aided revocable key-policy ABE schemes and IBE schemes.

Acknowledgments. This research work is supported by the Singapore National Research Foundation under the NCR Award No. NRF2014NCR-NCR001-012, the National Natural Science Foundation of China under the Grant No. 61502400 and the Foundation of Sichuan Educational Committee under the Grant No. 16ZB0140.

References

1. Attrapadung, N., Imai, H.: Attribute-based encryption supporting direct/indirect revocation modes. In: Parker, M.G. (ed.) Cryptography and Coding 2009. LNCS, vol. 5921, pp. 278–300. Springer, Heidelberg (2009)
2. Attrapadung, N., Imai, H.: Conjunctive broadcast and attribute-based encryption. In: Shacham, H., Waters, B. (eds.) Pairing 2009. LNCS, vol. 5671, pp. 248–265. Springer, Heidelberg (2009)
3. Baek, J., Zheng, Y.: Identity-based threshold decryption. In: Bao, F., Deng, R., Zhou, J. (eds.) PKC 2004. LNCS, vol. 2947, pp. 262–276. Springer, Heidelberg (2004)

4. Beimel, A.: Secure schemes for secret sharing and key distribution. Ph.D. thesis, Israel Institute of Technology, June 1996
5. Boldyreva, A., Goyal, V., Kumar, V.: Identity-based encryption with efficient revocation. In: Proceedings of the ACM Conference on Computer and Communications Security, CCS 2008, Alexandria, Virginia, USA, 27–31 October 2008, pp. 417–426. ACM (2008)
6. Boneh, D., Boyen, X.: Efficient selective identity-based encryption without random oracles. J. Cryptology **24**(4), 659–693 (2011)
7. Boneh, D., Ding, X., Tsudik, G., Wong, C.: A method for fast revocation of pub-lickey certificates and security capabilities. In: 10th USENIX Security Symposium, 13–17 August 2001, Washington, D.C., USA. USENIX (2001)
8. Boneh, D., Franklin, M.: Identity-based encryption from the weil pairing. In: Kilian, J. (ed.) CRYPTO 2001. LNCS, vol. 2139, p. 213. Springer, Heidelberg (2001)
9. Cui, H., Deng, R.H.: Revocable and decentralized attribute-based encryption. Comput. J. doi:10.1093/comjnl/bxw007
10. Ding, X., Tsudik, G.: Simple identity-based cryptography with mediated RSA. In: Joye, M. (ed.) CT-RSA 2003. LNCS, vol. 2612, pp. 193–210. Springer, Heidelberg (2003)
11. Hanaoka, Y., Hanaoka, G., Shikata, J., Imai, H.: Identity-based hierarchical strongly key-insulated encryption and its application. In: Roy, B. (ed.) ASI-ACRYPT 2005. LNCS, vol. 3788, pp. 495–514. Springer, Heidelberg (2005)
12. Horváth, M.: Attribute-based encryption optimized for cloud computing. In: Italiano, G.F., Margaria-Steffen, T., Pokorný, J., Quisquater, J.-J., Wattenhofer, R. (eds.) SOFSEM 2015-Testing. LNCS, vol. 8939, pp. 566–577. Springer, Heidelberg (2015)
13. Lewko, A., Waters, B.: Decentralizing attribute-based encryption. In: Paterson, K.G. (ed.) EUROCRYPT 2011. LNCS, vol. 6632, pp. 568–588. Springer, Heidelberg (2011)
14. Li, J., Li, J., Chen, X., Jia, C., Lou, W.: Identity-based encryption with outsourced revocation in cloud computing. IEEE Trans. Comput. **64**(2), 425–437 (2015)
15. Li, Q., Xiong, H., Zhang, F.: Broadcast revocation scheme in composite-order bilinear group and its application to attribute-based encryption. IJSN **8**(1), 1–12 (2013)
16. Liang, K., Liu, J.K., Wong, D.S., Susilo, W.: An efficient cloud-based revocable identity-based proxy re-encryption scheme for public clouds data sharing. In: Kutyłowski, M., Vaidya, J. (eds.) ICAIS 2014, Part I. LNCS, vol. 8712, pp. 257–272. Springer, Heidelberg (2014)
17. Libert, B., Quisquater, J.: Efficient revocation and threshold pairing based cryptosystems. In: Proceedings of the Twenty-Second ACM Symposium on Principles of Distributed Computing, PODC 2003, Boston, Massachusetts, USA, 13–16 July 2003, pp. 163–171. ACM (2003)
18. Naor, D., Naor, M., Lotspiech, J.: Revocation and tracing schemes for stateless receivers. In: Kilian, J. (ed.) CRYPTO 2001. LNCS, vol. 2139, p. 41. Springer, Heidelberg (2001)
19. Qin, B., Deng, R.H., Li, Y., Liu, S.: Server-aided revocable identity-based encryption. In: Pernul, G., Y A Ryan, P., Weippl, E. (eds.) ESORICS. LNCS, vol. 9326, pp. 286–304. Springer, Heidelberg (2015). doi:10.1007/978-3-319-24174-6_15
20. Rouselakis, Y., Waters, B.: Practical constructions and new proof methods for large universe attribute-based encryption. In: ACM SIGSAC Conference on Computer and Communications Security, CCS 2013, Berlin, Germany, 4–8 November 2013, pp. 463–474. ACM (2013)

21. Sahai, A., Seyalioglu, H., Waters, B.: Dynamic credentials and ciphertext delegation for attribute-based encryption. In: Safavi-Naini, R., Canetti, R. (eds.) CRYPTO 2012. LNCS, vol. 7417, pp. 199–217. Springer, Heidelberg (2012)

22. Sahai, A., Waters, B.: Fuzzy identity-based encryption. In: Cramer, R. (ed.) EUROCRYPT 2005. LNCS, vol. 3494, pp. 457–473. Springer, Heidelberg (2005)

23. Seo, J.H., Emura, K.: Revocable identity-based encryption revisited: security model and construction. In: Kurosawa, K., Hanaoka, G. (eds.) PKC 2013. LNCS, vol. 7778, pp. 216–234. Springer, Heidelberg (2013)

24. Wan, Z., Liu, J., Deng, R.H.: HASBE: a hierarchical attribute-based solution for flexible and scalable access control in cloud computing. IEEE Trans. Inf. Forensics Secur. **7**(2), 743–754 (2012)

25. Waters, B.: Ciphertext-policy attribute-based encryption: an expressive, efficient, and provably secure realization. In: Catalano, D., Fazio, N., Gennaro, R., Nicolosi, A. (eds.) PKC 2011. LNCS, vol. 6571, pp. 53–70. Springer, Heidelberg (2011)

26. Yang, Y., Ding, X., Lu, H., Wan, Z., Zhou, J.: Achieving revocable fine-grained cryptographic access control over cloud data. In: Desmedt, Y. (ed.) ISC 2013. LNCS, vol. 7807, pp. 293–308. Springer, Heidelberg (2015). doi:10.1007/978-3-319-27659-5_21

Online/Offline Public-Index Predicate Encryption for Fine-Grained Mobile Access Control

Weiran Liu[1,2], Jianwei Liu[1], Qianhong Wu[1,3,4], Bo Qin[5(✉)], and Kaitai Liang[6]

[1] School of Electronic and Information Engineering, Beihang University, No. 37,
XueYuan Road, Haidian District, Beijing 100191, China
liuweiran900217@gmail.com, {liujianwei,qianhong.wu}@buaa.edu.cn
[2] State Key Laboratory of Integrated Services Networks,
Xidian University, Xi'an 710071, China
[3] State Key Laboratory of Cryptology, P.O. Box 5159, Beijing 100878, China
[4] State Key Laboratory of Information Security,
Institute of Information Engineering, Chinese Academy of Sciences,
Beijing 100093, China
[5] Key Laboratory of Data Engineering and Knowledge Engineering,
Ministry of Education, School of Information, Renmin University of China,
No. 59, ZhongGuanCun Avenue, Haidian District, Beijing 100872, China
bo.qin@ruc.edu.cn
[6] Department of Computer Science, Aalto University,
Konemiehentie 2, 01250 Espoo, Finland
kaitai.liang@aalto.fi

Abstract. Public-Index Predicate Encryption (PIPE) allows users to encrypt according to boolean predicates defined on arbitrary attributes. The expensive algebraic operations are the major efficiency obstacle for PIPE to be applied to mobile clouds. This paper proposes a general Online/Offline PIPE (OO-PIPE) framework to address this issue. First, we propose a generic transformation from a Large Universe PIPE (LU-PIPE) secure against chosen plaintext attack (CPA) to OO-PIPE in the same security model. The challenge is to generate ciphertext without the knowledge of the associated ciphertext attributes in the offline phase. We address the challenge by identifying an interesting *attribute-malleability* property in many LU-PIPE schemes. The property allows an encryptor to efficiently malleate a ciphertext associated with one ciphertext attribute to any assigned ciphertext attribute. Second, we design a generic transformation from CPA-secure LU-PIPE to OO-PIPE secure against adaptively chosen ciphertext attack (CCA2), assuming the underlying LU-PIPE has *attribute-malleability* and *public-verifiability* properties. The main obstacle here is that the online/offline mechanism endogenously implies forgery in the sense that a pre-computed ciphertext must be able to be efficiently malleated to the resulting ciphertext associated with a different ciphertext attribute and a plaintext, while any efficient valid ciphertext forgery is forbidden in CCA2 security. We circumvent

© Springer International Publishing Switzerland 2016
I. Askoxylakis et al. (Eds.): ESORICS 2016, Part II, LNCS 9879, pp. 588–605, 2016.
DOI: 10.1007/978-3-319-45741-3_30

this obstacle by employing a universally collision resistant Chameleon hash, namely, only the original encryptor can malleate the ciphertext to associate with different attributes and provide a hash collision of the ciphertext components.

1 Introduction

Mobile cloud computing becomes more and more attracting in cloud-assisted networks. However, security risks of mobile computing may hinder its wide applications. Since data are outsourced to the cloud, it is required that data must be stored securely, while allowing legal access for authenticated users. Traditional encryption techniques supporting limited access control are not seamlessly applicable to mobile cloud computing. Public-Index Predicate Encryption (PIPE) is an emerging asymmetric encryption allowing fine-grained access control over encrypted data. In a PIPE system, the access control policy is described by a predicate. A ciphertext is associated with a ciphertext attribute, and a secret key is assigned to a key attribute. One can decrypt if and only if the ciphertext attribute specified in the ciphertext matches the key attribute in his/her secret key according to the pre-defined predicate.

PIPE is a general cryptographic concept capturing a wide range of cryptographic primitives, including Identity-Based Encryption (IBE) [5,34], Revocation Encryption (RE) [23], Attribute-Based Encryption (ABE) [33] in Key-Policy settings [15] and in Ciphertext-Policy settings [2]. PIPE is classified into two categories: Small Universe PIPE (SU-PIPE) and Large Universe PIPE (LU-PIPE). In SU-PIPE, the size of attribute is polynomially bounded in security parameter [9,12,15], which poses constraints in practice. LU-PIPE does not suffer from this constraint and its attribute space can be exponentially large [25,31,32]. This desirable feature makes many instances of LU-PIPE, e.g., (H)IBE [19,20], ABE [39], become attractive to secure mobile cloud computing.

There are still hindrances for LU-PIPE to be widely deployed in mobile cloud computing. Most LU-PIPE schemes require time-consuming algebraic operations and encryption time grows with the number of ciphertext attributes. This may limit their efficiency. When the encryption is run on a mobile device, it may raise poor user experience with long latency and meanwhile, exhaust the battery quickly. Moreover, since LU-PIPE is usually suggested to secure data stored on untrusted but powerful servers, a strong security level, i.e., CCA2 security, is necessary for holding against powerful active attackers. Note that CCA2-secure LU-PIPE is less efficient than its CPA-secure counterpart. This further deteriorates the resource consumption and user experience.

Online/offline encryption may mitigate the efficiency problem. The encryption is split into offline and online phases. In the offline phase, an encryptor conducts the majority of the computation task on a high-end computer or when battery recharge before knowing the ciphertext attributes. In the online phase, the encryptor needs only few computations to fulfill the encryption when knowing the corresponding ciphertext attributes. In this way, it is feasible to implement LU-PIPE on resource-limited mobile devices with desirable user experience.

Several online/offline PIPE (OO-PIPE) schemes have been designed in an *ad hoc* way [10,17,18,27,29]. It is desirable to investigate generic OO-PIPE transformation from LU-PIPE. Theoretically, such a work allows a better understanding on LU-PIPE and online/offline mechanism. Practically, it enables one to instantly obtain OO-PIPE with better security and/or efficiency whenever an advantageous LU-PIPE scheme is available.

1.1 Our Contributions

We aim at proposing a framework for constructing OO-PIPE with CCA2 security. Our contribution includes the following aspects.

We start by identifying a useful property, i.e., *attribute-malleability* consisting of *private malleability* and *public malleability*, of many LU-PIPE schemes. The *private malleability* allows an encryptor to malleate a ciphertext associated with one ciphertext attribute to a ciphertext associated with any given ciphertext attribute at a very low cost. In contrast, the *public malleability* states that even through others may malleate a ciphertext associated with one ciphertext attribute to a ciphertext associated with some other ciphertext attribute, they cannot know (the key of) any matching key attribute.

We propose a generic CPA-secure OO-PIPE construction from attribute-malleable CPA-secure LU-PIPE. With *private malleability*, an encryptor prepares a ciphertext under a randomly chosen ciphertext attribute in the offline phase, and then replaces it with the target ciphertext attribute in the online phase. With *public malleability*, we show that the security of the resulting OO-PIPE can be tightly reduced to the CPA security of the underlying LU-PIPE.

We next propose a generic CCA2-secure OO-PIPE construction from any CPA-secure attribute-malleable LU-PIPE with *public-verifiability*. The *public-verifiability* states that there exists a public verification mechanism to verify whether the ciphertext has been honestly generated. This property enables one to establish a built-in LU-PIPE ciphertext validation check mechanism. We further exploit universally collision resistant Chameleon hash for ciphertext validation so that an encryptor can replace the randomly encrypted ciphertext attribute in the offline phase with the target ciphertext attribute in the online phase, while an attacker cannot make such malleation.

Technically, our constructions offer a novel application of Chameleon hash in encryption systems. Chameleon hash was previously used in (online/offline) signature applications [35]. It has been recently used as a security proof tool in constructing CCA2-secure KP-ABE [28]. We strengthen regular Chameleon hash with universal collision resistance and propose a generic universally collision resistant Chameleon hash from a regular Chameleon hash and a standard cryptographic hash. Our work illustrates the unique value of Chameleon hash in online/offline encryption cryptosystems, in contrast to its previous use in online/offline signatures.

1.2   Related Work

LU-PIPE. The simplest LU-PIPE is IBE that was theoretically introduced by Shamir [34] and practically constructed by Boneh and Franklin [5]. In 2005, Sahai and Waters [33] proposed Fuzzy IBE with a more expressive predicate. The concept of ABE, a versatile type of LU-PIPE, was also introduced in their work. Subsequently, two types of ABE, i.e., KP-ABE and CP-ABE, were respectively proposed by Goyal et al. [15] and Bethencourt et al. [2]. These schemes are proven secure in the selective security model. Fully secure ABE constructions were provided by Okamoto et al. [30,31] and Lewko et al. [26]. They follow the dual system encryption methodology due to Waters [36] and Lewko et al. [24] to achieve fully security. Another kind of typical LU-PIPE systems, i.e., Revocation Encryption (RE), was introduced by Lewko, Sahai and Waters [23] in the selective and fully security model.

CCA2-Secure LU-PIPE. Many researches have devoted their efforts to the constructions of CCA2-secure LU-PIPE schemes. The Canetti-Halevi-Katz approach [8] is widely used for the CCA2 security transformation at the cost of one-time signatures. Their approach was first applied for converting CPA-secure IBE to CCA2-secure PKE, and converting CPA-secure Hierarchical IBE (HIBE) to CCA2-secure IBE. It was later used to obtain CCA2-secure KP-ABE from CPA-secure KP-ABE by Goyal et al. [15], and CCA2-secure CP-ABE from CPA-secure CP-ABE by Cheung et al. [2]. Yamada et al. [37] generalized this approach and introduced a generic framework to transform CPA-secure ABE to CCA2-secure ABE. Yamada et al. [38] further extended this approach into PE settings and showed that any CPA-secure PE scheme could be converted into a CCA2-secure one assuming that the underlying PE scheme is verifiable, i.e., all legitimate receivers of a ciphertext can obtain the same message upon decryption. All the above CCA2-secure PE constructions need one-time signatures. Boyen et al. [7] introduced a shrink approach to obtain CCA2-secure PKE from CPA-secure IBE using standard collision resistant hash functions, by exploiting the specific ciphertext structure of the underlying schemes [4]. Recently, Liu et al. [28] refined this technique in KP-ABE and proposed a direct CCA2-secure KP-ABE scheme from the Rouselakis-Waters KP-ABE [32].

OO-PIPE. Online/offline cryptosystems were first proposed by Even et al. [11]. The goal of design is to have a very short response time after a pre-processing phase in which all expensive operations are pre-computed. They instantiated this technique in the context of digital signatures. The signing process is divided into online and offline phases. Most of the computation work is done in the offline phase without knowledge of the message to be signed. Once the message to be signed is given, the resulting signature can be quickly obtained in the online phase. Shamir and Tauman [35] showed how to use Chameleon hash functions to transform any digital signature scheme to an online/offline signature scheme. In the online phase, one only needs to find a Chameleon hash collision, which usually only requires several modular multiplications [22]. Guo et al. [17] considered online/offline variants of the Boneh-Boyen IBE [3] and the Gentry

IBE [14], followed by the work of Liu *et al.* [27]. Subsequently, online/offline HIBE [29] and online/offline Identity-Based Key Encapsulation [10] were proposed. Hohenberger and Waters [18] proposed CPA-secure online/offline ABE schemes based on the Rouselakis-Waters ABE [32]. Most of the existing CCA2-secure OO-PIPE schemes employ the Canetti-Halevi-Katz approach [17,29] with the help of one-time signatures. Chow *et al.* [10] presented a generic transformation to get CCA2-secure OO-IBE from any OO-IBE in the key encapsulation mechanism. Their transformation, inspired by the technique from Fujisaki and Okamoto [13], is actually very efficient, although one needs to model the output of the hash function as a random oracle.

2 Preliminaries

We write $[a, b]$ to denote the set $\{a, a+1, \cdots, b\}$ containing consecutive integers, and $[a]$ as shorthand for $[1, a]$ if there is no ambiguity. For a set S, we use $|S|$ to denote the number of elements in S. We use $s_1, s_2, \cdots, s_n \overset{R}{\leftarrow} S$ for $n \in \mathbb{N}$ to represent that $s_i \overset{R}{\leftarrow} S$ for each $i \in [n]$.

For a randomized algorithm A, we denote $y \leftarrow \mathsf{A}(x; R)$ as the process of running the algorithm A on input x with randomness R to output y, where R is sampled from the space $\mathcal{R}_{\mathsf{A}}$, i.e., $R \overset{R}{\leftarrow} \mathcal{R}_{\mathsf{A}}$. We interchangeably use the notations $y \leftarrow \mathsf{A}(x)$ and $y \leftarrow \mathsf{A}(x; R)$, depending on whether we need emphasis on the randomness. We denote $S[\mathsf{A}(x)]$ as the range space of A with the input x.

2.1 Definition of LU-PIPE

We follow the LU-PIPE definition given by Yamada *et al.* [38]. We work in the Key Encapsulation Mechanism (KEM) setting, where the ciphertext hides a symmetric session key *key* for encryption of regular digital contents. Let $U = \{0, 1\}^*$ be an attribute space and $P_n = \{K_n \times E_n \rightarrow \{0, 1\} | n \in \mathbb{N}\}$ be a large universe predicate family, where n denotes the dimension of the predicate P_n. Let K_n denote the "key attribute" space and E_n denote the "ciphertext attribute" space over U. A Large Universe Public-Index Predicate KEM (LU-PIP-KEM) for P_n consists of four polynomial time algorithms:

$(msk, pp) \leftarrow \mathsf{Setup}(\lambda, n)$. Take as inputs a security parameter $\lambda \in \mathbb{N}$ and a dimension n of the predicate P_n. It outputs a master secret key msk and a public parameter pp.

$sk_x \leftarrow \mathsf{KeyGen}(pp, msk, x)$. Take as inputs the public parameter pp, the master secret key msk, and a key attribute $x \in K_n$. It outputs a secret key sk_x associated with the key attribute x.

$(key, ct_y) \leftarrow \mathsf{Encrypt}(pp, y; R_y)$. Take as inputs the public parameter pp and a ciphertext attribute $y \in E_n$. It outputs a session key *key* and a ciphertext ct_y associated with the ciphertext attribute y under the randomness R_y.

$key \leftarrow$ Decrypt(pp, ct_y, y, sk_x, x). Take as inputs the public parameter pp, a ciphertext ct_y associated with the ciphertext attribute $y \in E_n$, and a secret key sk_x associated with the key attribute $x \in K_n$. It outputs the session key key.

A LU-PIP-KEM scheme is correct if for all $(msk, pp) \leftarrow$ Setup(λ, n), all $sk_x \leftarrow$ KeyGen(pp, msk, x) with $x \in K_n$, and all $(key, ct_y) \leftarrow$ Encrypt(pp, y, R_y) with $y \in E_n$, it holds that if $P_n(x, y) = 1$, then Decrypt$(pp, ct_y, y, sk_x, x) = key$; else if $P_n(x, y) = 0$, then Decrypt$(pp, ct_y, y, sk_x, x) = \perp$.

The chosen plaintext security in LU-PIP-KEM is defined through a game played between an adversary $\mathcal{A}$ and a challenger $\mathcal{C}$. Both of them take the security parameter λ and the dimension n of the predicate as input.

Setup. $\mathcal{C}$ runs Setup to generate and give the public parameter pp to $\mathcal{A}$.

Phase 1. $\mathcal{A}$ adaptively submits secret key queries for the key attribute $x \in K_n$. $\mathcal{C}$ generates a secret key sk_x for x and returns it to $\mathcal{A}$.

Challenge. $\mathcal{A}$ outputs a challenge ciphertext attribute $y^* \in E_n$ on which it wishes to be challenged. The challenge ciphertext attribute y^* must satisfy that $P_n(x, y^*) = 0$ for any x that $\mathcal{A}$ has already queried for the secret key sk_x. $\mathcal{C}$ runs Encrypt(pp, y^*) to obtain (key^*, ct^*). Then, it flips a random coin $b \in \{0, 1\}$. If $b = 0$, $\mathcal{C}$ returns (key^*, ct^*) to $\mathcal{A}$. If $b = 1$, it selects a random session key key_R^* and returns (key_R^*, ct^*).

Phase 2. Phase 1 is repeated with a restriction that $\mathcal{A}$ cannot submit secret key queries for $x \in K_n$ with $P_n(x, y^*) = 1$.

Guess. Finally, $\mathcal{A}$ outputs a guess $b' \in \{0, 1\}$ and wins in the game if $b = b'$.

The advantage of $\mathcal{A}$ in attacking the LU-PIP-KEM system with security parameter λ is defined as $Adv_{\mathcal{A}}^{\text{LU-PIP-KEM}}(\lambda) = \left| \Pr[b' = b] - \frac{1}{2} \right|$.

Definition 1. *A LU-PIP-KEM system is CPA-secure if for any polynomial time adversary $\mathcal{A}$, the advantage of winning the above game is a negligible function ϵ in λ, i.e., $Adv_{\mathcal{A}}^{LU\text{-}PIP\text{-}KEM}(\lambda) < \epsilon$.*

A weaker security notion called selective security can be defined in the above game with an extra **Init** phase in which $\mathcal{A}$ must commit to the challenge ciphertext attribute $y^* \in E_n$ before **Setup**.

We next review the notion of *OR-compatibility* for a predicate. A predicate P_n is said to have *OR-compatibility* if for two ciphertext attributes, the predicate is able to capture the presence of one *or* the other. This property was first introduced by Yamada et al. [38]. They commented that *OR-compatibility* is commonly achieved in many concrete LU-PIPE schemes [2,15,21].

Definition 2. *A predicate $P_n = \{K_n \times E_n \to \{0, 1\} | n \in \mathbb{N}\}$ is said to have OR-compatibility if for all $d \in \mathbb{N}$, there exists a map $OR : E_n \times E_d \to E_{n+d}$ and two attribute extension maps $EN : K_n \to K_{n+d}$, $ED : K_d \to K_{n+d}$ such that for all $x_1 \in K_n$, $x_2 \in K_d$, $y_1 \in E_n$, $y_2 \in E_d$,*

$$P_{n+d}(EN(x_1), OR(y_1, y_2)) = P_n(x_1, y_1),$$
$$P_{n+d}(ED(x_2), OR(y_1, y_2)) = P_d(x_2, y_2).$$

2.2   Definition of Public-Verifiability

We review the *public-verifiability* of a LU-PIP-KEM scheme. This property was first defined in the IBE setting [16] and then be extended to FE settings by Yamada *et al.* [37]. Intuitively, a LU-PIP-KEM has *public-verifiability* if there exists a public verification mechanism to verify whether a given ciphertext is honestly generated. As remarked by Abdalla *et al.* [1], any encryption schemes with *public-verifiability* cannot be anonymous (or known as Private Index Predicate Encryption [6]). Hence, *public-verifiability* can only be achieved in PIPE, which is also the focus of this paper.

To define *public-verifiability*, we introduce a polynomial time algorithm Verify.

0 or $1 \leftarrow$ Verify(pp, ct_y, y). Take as inputs the public parameter pp and a ciphertext $ct_y \in \{0, 1\}^*$ under a ciphertext attribute $y \in E_n$. It outputs 0 or 1.

Verify needs to satisfy that for all $(key, ct_y) \in S[\mathsf{Encrypt}(pp, y, R_y)]$, it holds that Verify$(pp, ct_y, y) = 1$, while for all $(key, ct_y) \notin S[\mathsf{Encrypt}(pp, y, R_y)]$, it must have that Verify$(pp, ct_y, y) = 0$ except with a negligible probability.

Definition 3. *A LU-PIP-KEM scheme is said to have public-verifiability if there exists an algorithm* Verify *in the LU-PIP-KEM scheme satisfying the completeness requirement defined above.*

3   Modelling OO-PIPE

We formally define OO-PIPE in the KEM setting. An OO-PIP-KEM scheme consists of five polynomial time algorithms OO.Setup, OO.KeyGen, OO.OffEncrypt, OO.OnEncrypt and OO.Decrypt. The definitions of OO.Setup and OO.KeyGen are identical to those of LU-PIP-KEM systems shown in Sect. 2.1. The others are defined as follows.

$ict \leftarrow$ OO.OffEncrypt(pp). Only take as input the public parameter pp and outputs an intermediate ciphertext ict.

$(key, ct_y) \leftarrow$ OO.OnEncrypt(pp, y, ict). Take as inputs the public parameter pp, a target ciphertext attribute $y \in E_n$, and an intermediate ciphertext ict. It outputs a session key key and a ciphertext ct_y associated with y.

$key \leftarrow$ OO.Decrypt(pp, ct_y, y, sk_x, x). Take as inputs the public parameter pp, a ciphertext ct_y associated with the ciphertext attribute $y \in E_n$, and a secret key sk_x associated with the key attribute $x \in K_n$. It outputs the session key key.

The correctness requires that for all $(msk, pp) \leftarrow$ OO.Setup(λ, n), all $x \in K_n$, all $sk_x \leftarrow$ OO.KeyGen(pp, msk, x), all $ict \leftarrow$ OO.OffEncrypt(pp), all $y \in E_n$, and all $(key, ct_y) \leftarrow$ OO.OnEncrypt(pp, y, ict), if $P_n(x, y) = 1$, then we have that

OO.Decrypt$(pp, ct_y, y, sk_x, x) = key$; else if $P_n(x, y) = 0$, then we have that
OO.Decrypt$(pp, ct_y, y, sk_x, x) = \perp$ except with a negligible probability.

We next define chosen ciphertext security in OO-PIP-KEM. The security model is similarly defined through a game played between an adversary $\mathcal{A}$ and a challenger $\mathcal{C}$, both of which are given the parameter λ and the dimension n of the predicate as inputs.

Setup. $\mathcal{C}$ runs OO.Setup to generate public parameter pp and sends it to $\mathcal{A}$.

Phase 1. $\mathcal{A}$ adaptively issues queries:

– **Secret Key Query.** $\mathcal{A}$ submits a key attribute $x \in K_n$ to $\mathcal{C}$. $\mathcal{C}$ generates and gives a secret key sk_x for x to $\mathcal{A}$.
– **Decryption Query.** $\mathcal{A}$ submits a ciphertext ct_y with ciphertext attribute $y \in E_n$ to $\mathcal{C}$. $\mathcal{C}$ constructs a key attribute $x \in K_n$ with $P_n(x, y) = 1$, and runs OO.KeyGen(pp, msk, x) to generate a secret key sk_x. It then runs OO.Decrypt(pp, ct_y, y, sk_x, x) and returns the decryption result to $\mathcal{A}$.

Challenge. $\mathcal{A}$ outputs a challenge ciphertext attribute $y^* \in E_n$ on which it wishes to be challenged. The challenge ciphertext attribute y^* must satisfy that $P_n(x, y^*) = 0$ for any x that $\mathcal{A}$ queried for the secret key sk_x. $\mathcal{C}$ generates a session key key^* and a ciphertext ct^* under the challenge attribute y^*. Then, it flips a random coin $b \in \{0, 1\}$. If $b = 0$, $\mathcal{C}$ returns (key^*, ct^*) to $\mathcal{A}$. Otherwise, it randomly selects a session key key_R^* and returns (key_R^*, ct^*) to $\mathcal{A}$.

Phase 2. $\mathcal{A}$ further adaptively issues the following two kinds of queries:

– **Secret Key Query** for key attributes $x \in K_n$ satisfying $P_n(x, y^*) = 0$.
– **Decryption Query** for the ciphertext ct_y with a constraint that $ct_y \neq ct^*$.

$\mathcal{C}$ responds the same as in **Phase 1**.

Guess. Finally, $\mathcal{A}$ outputs a guess $b' \in \{0, 1\}$ and wins in the game if $b = b'$.

The advantage of $\mathcal{A}$ who issues q_S secret key queries and q_D decryption queries in attacking the OO-PIP-KEM system with security parameter λ is defined as $Adv_{\mathcal{A}, q_S, q_D}^{OO\text{-}PIP\text{-}KEM}(\lambda) = \left| \Pr[b' = b] - \frac{1}{2} \right|$.

Definition 4. *An OO-PIP-KEM system is CCA2-secure if for any polynomial time adversary $\mathcal{A}$ who makes a total of q_S secret key queries and q_D decryption queries, the advantage of winning the security game defined above is at most negligible function ϵ in λ, i.e., $Adv_{\mathcal{A}, q_S, q_D}^{OO\text{-}PIP\text{-}KEM}(\lambda) < \epsilon$.*

The CPA security for OO-PIP-KEM system can also be defined as in the preceding game, with a constraint that $\mathcal{A}$ is not allowed to issue decryption queries in **Phase 1** and **Phase 2**.

Definition 5. *An OO-PIP-KEM system is CPA-secure if for any polynomial time adversary $\mathcal{A}$ who makes a total of q_S secret key queries and no decryption query, the advantage of winning the security game defined above is at most negligible function ϵ in λ, i.e., $Adv_{\mathcal{A}, q_S, 0}^{OO\text{-}PIP\text{-}KEM}(\lambda) < \epsilon$.*

Similar to LU-PIP-KEM, the selective security of an OO-PIP-KEM system can be defined in the above game by adding an **Init** phase before **Setup** phase. $\mathcal{A}$ must decide the challenge ciphertext attribute $y^* \in E_n$ in the **Init** phase.

4   CPA-secure OO-PIP-KEM from LU-PIP-KEM

The major challenge in constructing OO-PIP-KEM is that in the offline phase, the encryptor cannot know the ciphertext attribute that a ciphertext will be associated with. We manage to overcome this challenge by identifying a useful property, i.e., *attribute-malleability*, in many LU-PIPE schemes. Coarsely speaking, a LU-PIP-KEM scheme has *attribute-malleability* if an encryptor can malleate a ciphertext ct_{ori} associated with an original ciphertext attribute y_{ori} to a new ciphertext ct_{new} associated with a new ciphertext attribute y_{new} with the same session key key. The ones who have the secret key sk_x with key attribute x satisfying $P(x, y_{new}) = 1$ can also correctly decrypt ct_{new} to recover key.

The *attribute-malleability* enables an encryptor to prepare the ciphertext without knowing the associated ciphertext attribute. In the offline phase, the encryptor randomly chooses a ciphertext attribute y_{ori}, and encapsulates a session key key under that ciphertext attribute to generate a ciphertext ct_{ori}. When the target ciphertext attribute y is available to the encryptor in the online phase, he malleates the ciphertext ct_{ori} with the ciphertext attribute y_{ori} to a target ciphertext ct_y associated with the given ciphertext attribute y with the same session key key. In decryption, the receiver who has the secret key sk_x with the key attribute x satisfying $P(x, y) = 1$ can decrypt the ciphertext ct_y and recover the session key key.

4.1   Definition of Attribute-Malleability

We first introduce three polynomial time algorithms, PriMalleate, PubMalleate, Combine in LU-PIP-KEM, and their necessary properties.

$y_{mall} \leftarrow$ PriMalleate$(y_{ori}, y_{new}, R_{ori})$. Take as inputs the original ciphertext attribute $y_{ori} \in E_n$, a new ciphertext attribute y_{new}, and the randomness R_{ori} used to run $(key, ct_{ori}) \leftarrow$ Encrypt$(pp, y_{ori}; R_{ori})$. It outputs a malleated ciphertext attribute $y_{mall} \in E_n$.

$\widetilde{ct}_{ori} \leftarrow$ PubMalleate$(pp, \widetilde{ct}_{new}, \widetilde{y}_{mall})$. Take as inputs the public parameter pp, a ciphertext $\widetilde{ct}_{new}$ associated with the new ciphertext attribute y_{new}, and a malleated ciphertext attribute $\widetilde{y}_{mall} \in E_n$. It outputs a ciphertext $\widetilde{ct}_{ori} \in E_n$.

$ct_{new} \leftarrow$ Combine(pp, ct_{ori}, y_{mall}). Take as inputs the public parameter pp, a ciphertext ct_{ori} associated with the ciphertext attribute y_{ori}, and the malleated ciphertext attribute y_{mall}. It outputs a ciphertext ct_{new} associated with the given ciphertext attribute y_{new}.

These algorithms need to meet the following requirements.

- *Private Malleability.* For all $(key, ct_{ori}) \leftarrow \mathsf{Encrypt}(pp, y_{ori}; R_{ori})$ with a randomly chosen ciphertext attribute $y_{ori} \xleftarrow{R} E_n$ and all ciphertext attribute $y_{new} \in E_n$, if y_{mall} is output by $y_{mall} \leftarrow \mathsf{PriMalleate}(y_{ori}, y_{new}, R_{ori})$, and ct_{new} is generated as $ct_{new} \leftarrow \mathsf{Combine}(pp, ct_{ori}, y_{mall})$, then we have $(key, ct_{new}) = \mathsf{Encrypt}(pp, y_{new}; R_{ori})$.
- *Public Malleability.* For all $(key, \widetilde{ct}_{new}) \leftarrow \mathsf{Encrypt}(pp, y_{new}; R_{new})$ with a ciphertext attribute $y_{new} \in E_n$ and randomly chosen $\widetilde{y}_{mall} \xleftarrow{R} E_n$, if $\widetilde{ct}_{ori} \leftarrow \mathsf{PubMalleate}(pp, \widetilde{ct}_{new}, \widetilde{y}_{mall})$, then $(key, \widetilde{ct}_{ori}) = \mathsf{Encrypt}(pp, \widetilde{y}_{ori}; R_{new})$. Also, $\widetilde{ct}_{new} = \mathsf{Combine}(pp, \widetilde{ct}_{ori}, \widetilde{y}_{mall})$.
- *Efficiency.* Running $y_{mall} \leftarrow \mathsf{PriMalleate}(y_{ori}, y_{new}, R_{ori})$ for all $y_{ori}, y_{new} \in E_n$ is more efficient than running $(key, ct_{new}) \leftarrow \mathsf{Encrypt}(pp, y_{new}; R_{new})$.

Definition 6. *We say a LU-PIP-KEM scheme has attribute-malleability if there exist polynomial time algorithms PriMalleate, PubMalleate and Combine satisfying private malleability, public malleability and efficiency defined above.*

4.2 Generic Transformation

We now describe our transformation. Let $\Pi' = (\mathsf{Setup}, \mathsf{KeyGen}, \mathsf{Encrypt}, \mathsf{Decrypt})$ be a CPA-secure LU-PIP-KEM scheme for predicate P_n over the attribute universe $U = \{0,1\}^*$ that has *attribute-malleability* defined in Definition 6. We can construct a CPA-secure OO-PIP-KEM scheme $\Pi = (\mathsf{OO.Setup}, \mathsf{OO.KeyGen}, \mathsf{OO.OffEncrypt}, \mathsf{OO.OnEncrypt}, \mathsf{OO.Decrypt})$ for the same predicate P_n as follows.

$\mathsf{OO.Setup}(\lambda, n)$. The setup algorithm imply invokes $(msk, pp) \leftarrow \mathsf{Setup}(\lambda, n)$ and outputs the master secret key and the public parameter as (msk, pp).

$\mathsf{OO.KeyGen}(pp, msk, x)$. Given a key attribute $x \in K_n$, the key generation algorithm simply calls $sk_x \leftarrow \mathsf{KeyGen}(pp, msk, x)$ and outputs the secret key sk_x.

$\mathsf{OO.OffEncrypt}(pp)$. The offline encryption algorithm will generate a ciphertext under a randomly chosen ciphertext attribute and treat it as an intermediate ciphertext. In detail, it randomly chooses $y_{ori} \xleftarrow{R} E_n$. Then, it runs $(key, ct_{ori}) \leftarrow \mathsf{Encrypt}(pp, y_{ori}; R_{ori})$ with randomly chosen randomness R_{ori} to obtain a session key and a ciphertext associated with the original ciphertext attribute y_{ori}. The intermediate ciphertext is $ict = (key, y_{ori}, ct_{ori}, R_{ori})$.

$\mathsf{OO.OnEncrypt}(pp, y, ict)$. When knowing the target ciphertext attribute $y \in E_n$, the online encryption algorithm first runs $y_{mall} \leftarrow \mathsf{PriMalleate}(y_{ori}, y, R_{ori})$ to obtain a malleated ciphertext attribute $y_{mall} \in E_n$. The session key key is unchange. The ciphertext associated with the ciphertext attribute y is $ct_y = (ct_{ori}, y_{mall})$. Note that the online encryption procedure only involves operations for running algorithm PriMalleate.

$\mathsf{OO.Decrypt}(pp, ct_y, y, sk_x, x)$. If $P_n(x, y) = 0$, then the key attribute x does not satisfy the predicate P_n for the ciphertext attribute y and the decryption algorithm simply outputs $\perp$. Otherwise, it first parses ct_y as (ct_{ori}, y_{mall}). Then, it runs $ct_y \leftarrow \mathsf{Combine}(pp, ct_{ori}, y_{mall})$ and gets a ciphertext ct_y associated with the ciphertext attribute y. It runs $key \leftarrow \mathsf{Decrypt}(pp, ct_y, y, sk_x, x)$ to recover the session key key.

Correctness. Due to the *private malleability*, for the session key and the ciphertext generated by calling $(key, ct_{ori}) \leftarrow \mathsf{Encrypt}(pp, y_{ori}; R_{ori})$ in $\mathsf{OO.OffEncrypt}$ with the randomly chosen $y_{ori} \overset{R}{\leftarrow} E_n$ and for $y_{mall} \leftarrow \mathsf{PriMalleate}(y_{ori}, y, R_{ori})$, we get a LU-PIP-KEM ciphertext associated with the ciphertext attribute y by running $ct_y \leftarrow \mathsf{Combine}(pp, ct_{ori}, y_{mall})$ in the decryption algorithm. Therefore, if a secret key associated with key attribute $x \in K_n$ satisfies $P_n(x, y) = 1$, then the decryption algorithm can correctly recover the session key by running $key \leftarrow \mathsf{Decrypt}(pp, ct_y, y, sk_x, x)$.

Performance. Only operations for running $\mathsf{PriMalleate}$ are required in the online encryption procedure, whereas in the original LU-PIP-KEM, the encryption procedure involves running algorithm $\mathsf{Encrypt}$. With the *efficiency* requirement, for all $y_{new} \in E_n$, running $\mathsf{PriMalleate}$ is more efficient than running $\mathsf{Encrypt}$. Therefore, the efficiency of the online encryption procedure is improved.

4.3   Security Analysis

The CPA security of our OO-PIP-KEM relies on the CPA security of the underlying LU-PIP-KEM. The major obstacle in the security proof is how to convert the challenge LU-PIP-KEM ciphertext into a challenge OO-PIP-KEM ciphertext in the **Challenge** phase. We overcome this obstacle by exploiting the *public malleability* implied by *attribute-malleability*.

When obtaining the challenge LU-PIP-KEM session key $\widetilde{key}^*$ and ciphertext $\widetilde{ct}^*$ associated with the challenge ciphertext attribute y^* from the LU-PIP-KEM challenger, we randomly choose a malleated ciphertext attribute $\widetilde{y}^*_{mall} \in E_n$ and calls $\widetilde{ct}^*_{ori} \leftarrow \mathsf{PubMalleate}(pp, \widetilde{ct}^*, \widetilde{y}^*_{mall})$ to obtain a ciphertext $\widetilde{ct}^*_{ori}$. We then construct the challenge OO-PIP-KEM ciphertext as $ct^* = (\widetilde{ct}^*_{ori}, \widetilde{y}^*_{mall})$.

- Since $\widetilde{ct}^*_{ori} \leftarrow \mathsf{Encrypt}(pp, \widetilde{y}^*_{ori})$, $\widetilde{ct}^*_{ori}$ is a LU-PIP-KEM ciphertext.
- Since $\widetilde{ct}^* = \mathsf{Combine}(pp, \widetilde{ct}^*_{ori}, \widetilde{y}^*_{mall})$, $\widetilde{ct}^*$ is associated with y^*.

Therefore, ct^* is a well-formed challenge OO-PIP-KEM ciphertext for the ciphertext attribute y^* due to the *public malleability*. In this way, the challenge ciphertext simulation in the **Challenge** phase goes through. The formal proof is shown in the full version of the paper.

Theorem 1. *If the underlying LU-PIP-KEM for predicate P_n is CPA-secure and attribute-malleable, then the proposed OO-PIP-KEM scheme is CPA-secure for the same predicate P_n.*

5   CCA2-secure OO-PIP-KEM from LU-PIP-KEM

5.1   Universally Collision Resistant Chameleon Hash Function

Collision Resistant Chameleon Hash. A Chameleon hash [22] has a hash key chk and a trapdoor td. Anyone knowing the hash key chk can efficiently compute the hash value for any given input. There also exists an efficient algorithm for the holder of the trapdoor td to find collisions for every given input. However, it is impossible for others unaware of td to compute collisions for any given input, except with a negligible probability.

A Chameleon hash function [22] family CH with hash value space $\mathcal{H}$ consists of three polynomial time algorithms CHGen, CHash and Coll defined as follows.

$(chk, td) \leftarrow$ CHGen(λ). Take the security parameter $\lambda \in \mathbb{N}$ as input, and outputs a Chameleon hash key/trapdoor pair (chk, td).

$H \leftarrow$ CHash(chk, m, r). Take as inputs the Chameleon hash key chk, a message m, and an auxiliary random parameter r. It outputs the hash value $H \in \mathcal{H}$ for the given message m.

$r' \leftarrow$ Coll(td, m, r, m'). Take as inputs the Chameleon hash trapdoor td, a message m with its auxiliary random parameter r for previously calculating the hash value H, and another message $m' \neq m$. It outputs another auxiliary random parameter r' such that

$$CHash(chk, m, r) = CHash(chk, m', r') = H$$

A Chameleon hash function should satisfy the *collision resistance* requirement, i.e., given the Chameleon hash key chk as input, no efficient algorithm can find two pairs $(m, r) \neq (m', r')$ such that CHash$(chk, m, r) =$ CHash(chk, m', r') except with a negligible probability.

Universally Collision Resistant Chameleon Hash. Our construction exploits Chameleon hash with universal collision resistance. A Chameleon hash function family is *universal collision resistant* if even though the attacker is allowed to choose the Chameleon hash key chk, it remains hard to find a hash collision for any given input. Roughly speaking, the hash value H can be only computed using the fixed Chameleon hash key chk.

We denote such a Chameleon hash family as UCH consisting of algorithms UCHGen, UCHash, UColl. Formally, UCH is universally collision resistant if, given only a description of the Chameleon hash function family, no efficient algorithm can find two tuples $(chk, m, r) \neq (chk', m', r')$ such that UCHash$(chk, m, r) =$ UCHash(chk', m', r') except with a negligible probability.

Generic Construction of UCH. We can construct *universally collision resistant* Chameleon hash functions based on any regular Chameleon hash and a standard cryptographic hash Hash $: \{0, 1\}^* \rightarrow \mathcal{H}$. The construction is as follows.

UCHGen(λ). The hash key/trapdoor pair is $(chk, td) \leftarrow$ CHGen(λ).

UCHash(chk, m, r). The hash value is $H =$ Hash$($CHash$(chk, m, r)\|chk)$.

UColl(td, m, r, m'). Directly output $r' \leftarrow$ Coll(td, m, r, m').

One with the trapdoor td can still find collisions for any given input since

$$H = UCHash(chk, m, r) = Hash(CHash(chk, m, r)\|chk)$$
$$= Hash(CHash(chk, m', r')\|chk) = UCHash(chk, m', r')$$

Without td, any polynomial time algorithm cannot find two tuples $(chk, m, r) \neq (chk', m', r')$ with $H = \mathsf{UCHash}(chk, m, r) = \mathsf{UCHash}(chk', m', r')$. Otherwise,

$$\mathsf{UCHash}(chk, m, r) = \mathsf{Hash}(\mathsf{CHash}(chk, m, r)\|chk)$$
$$= \mathsf{UCHash}(chk', m', r') = \mathsf{Hash}(\mathsf{CHash}(chk', m', r')\|chk')$$

which implies that we find a collision for either Hash or CH, contradicting to their security notion.

5.2   Basic Idea

The *public-verifiability* in LU-PIPE allows a ciphertext verification mechanism, i.e., testing whether the ciphertext is honestly generated with the assigned ciphertext attribute. We can leverage such a built-in verification mechanism to construct OO-PIPE with CCA2 security. Precisely, we add an on-the-fly verification attribute y_v in the ciphertext. We split the attribute universe U into two parts: one is the regular attribute universe $\mathcal{U}$, and another is the verification attribute universe $\mathcal{V}$ for the verification attributes. The verification attribute $y_v \in \mathcal{V}$ is only used for ciphertext verification. In encryption, the encryptor hashes the components of a ciphertext, and treats the result as the ciphertext attribute y_v to encrypt again. In the decryption procedure, the receiver computes the hash result again, and verifies whether the ciphertext is encrypted under the assigned ciphertext attribute, and under the hash ciphertext attribute y_v using the ciphertext verification mechanism.

Similar built-in verification has been used by Boyen *et al.* [7]. However, one may encounter an obstacle when directly employing their technique. The online/offline mechanism implies ciphertext forgery in the sense that a ciphertext with an ciphertext attribute can be efficiently malleated to a target ciphertext with a genuine ciphertext attribute, while any efficient ciphertext forgery must be prevented in CCA2 security. A plausible solution is to follow the technique proposed by Liu *et al.* [28] by replacing the regular hash to a Chameleon hash function. With the help of hash collision algorithm Coll in the Chameleon hash function, it is possible to malleate the ciphertext with an ciphertext attribute to a target ciphertext with the genuine ciphertext attribute, while remaining the verification terms unchange. However, for invoking hash collision algorithm, all encryptors must know the trapdoor of the target Chameleon hash key bounded in the public parameter, which obviously implies security problem.

To circumvent this obstacle, we use a "dynamic" universally collision resistant Chameleon hash to replace the regular Chameleon hash for each ciphertext. In offline encryption, the encryptor generates a Chameleon hash key/trapdoor pair (chk, td), chooses a random ciphertext attribute y_{ori}, and calculates the intermediate ciphertext components for y_{ori} and the temporary hash value y_v. When learning the genuine ciphertext attribute in the online phase, the encryptor replaces the random ciphertext attribute with the genuine one, while leveraging UCHash with the trapdoor td to remain y_v unchange. The cost is an additional Chameleon hash key chk in the ciphertext. In the online phase, the encryptor will run UColl, which is efficient in some Chameleon hash instantiations based on discrete log [22]. In this way, the online encryption cost keeps low.

5.3   Generic Transformation

Let Π' be a CPA-secure LU-PIP-KEM scheme consisting of four algorithms Setup, KeyGen, Encrypt, Decrypt for predicate P_n over the attribute universe $U = \{0,1\}^*$. Suppose that the predicate P_n has *OR-compatibility* defined in Definition 2, Π' has *attribute-malleability* defined in Definition 6, and Π' has *public-verifiability* defined in Definition 3. We below construct a CCA2-secure OO-PIP-KEM scheme Π including the algorithms CCA.Setup, CCA.KeyGen, CCA.OffEncrypt, CCA.OnEncrypt, CCA.Decrypt for the same predicate P_n over the regular attribute universe $\mathcal{U}$ and the verification attribute universe $\mathcal{V}$ with $|\mathcal{U}| = |\mathcal{V}|$, $\mathcal{U} \cap \mathcal{V} = \emptyset$ and $\mathcal{U} \cup \mathcal{V} = U$.

CCA.Setup(λ, n). The setup algorithm runs $(msk, pp) \leftarrow$ Setup$(\lambda, n+d)$. Then, it chooses a secure UCH function UCH $: \{0,1\}^* \rightarrow E_d$ with an auxiliary parameter universe $\mathcal{R}$. The system restricts that E_d is over $\mathcal{V}$. The master secret key is msk. The public parameter is published as $(pp, \mathsf{UCH}, \mathcal{R})$.

CCA.KeyGen(pp, msk, x). Given the key attribute $x \in K_n$, the algorithm first extends x to $EN(x) \in K_{n+d}$ using the map EN. Then, it runs $sk_{EN(x)} \leftarrow$ KeyGen$(pp, msk, EN(x))$ and outputs the secret key $sk_x = sk_{EN(x)}$.

CCA.OffEncrypt(pp). The offline encryption algorithm first randomly chooses an original ciphertext attribute $y_{ori} \xleftarrow{R} E_n$. Then, it runs $(chk, td) \leftarrow$ UCHGen(λ). It next picks a random $r' \xleftarrow{R} \mathcal{R}$, and calculates an on-the-fly verification attribute $y_v = $ UCHash (chk, y_{ori}, r'). It uses map OR to obtain the ciphertext attribute $OR(y_{ori}, y_v) \in E_{n+d}$ and runs $(key, ct_{ori}) \leftarrow$ Encrypt$(pp, OR(y_{ori}, y_v); R_{ori})$ with randomness R_{ori} to generate the session key and the ciphertext. The intermediate ciphertext is $ict = (key, y_{ori}, y_v, ct_{ori}, R_{ori}, chk, td, r')$.

CCA.OnEncrypt(pp, y, ict). Once the target ciphertext attribute $y \in E_n$ is available, the online encryption algorithm extends the ciphertext attribute $y \in E_n$ to $OR(y, y_v)$ and obtains a malleated ciphertext attribute $y_{mall} \in E_{n+d}$ by running $y_{mall} \leftarrow$ PriMalleate$(OR(y_{ori}, y_v), OR(y, y_v), R_{ori})$. It next runs $r \leftarrow$ UColl$(td, y_{ori}, r', ct_{ori}\|y_{mall})$. The session key is key, while the ciphertext ct_y associated with the ciphertext attribute y is $ct_y = (ct_{ori}, y_{mall}, chk, r)$. Note that the online encryption algorithm only needs invocations of PriMalleate and UColl.

CCA.Decrypt(pp, ct_y, y, sk_x, x). The decryption algorithm recovers the on-the-fly verification attribute $y_v = $ UCHash $(chk, ct_{ori}\|y_{mall}, r)$. Then, it runs $ct_y \leftarrow$ Combine(pp, ct_{ori}, y_{mall}) to rebuild the ciphertext ct_y with the ciphertext attribute $OR(y, y_v)$. One can verify whether the ciphertext is legitimate by testing

$$\mathsf{Verify}\,(pp, ct_y, OR(y, y_v)) \stackrel{?}{=} 1$$

The property of Chameleon hash ensures $y_v = \mathsf{UCHash}\,(chk, ct_{ori}\|y_{mall}, r) = \mathsf{UCHash}\,(chk, y_{ori}, r')$ and the on-the-fly verification attribute remains the same in the online encryption procedure. If Verify outputs 0, the ciphertext is invalid and the decryption algorithm simply outputs $\perp$. Otherwise, the decryption algorithm runs $key \leftarrow \mathsf{Decrypt}(pp, ct_y, OR(y, y_v), sk_x, EN(x))$ to recover key.

Correctness. If the ciphertext ct_y is honestly generated by the encryptor with the ciphertext attribute y, then $(key, ct_y) = \mathsf{Encrypt}(pp, OR(y, y_v))$ for $ct_y \leftarrow \mathsf{Combine}(pp, ct_{ori}, y_{mall})$, where y_v can be correctly obtained by invoking $y_v = \mathsf{UCHash}\,(chk, ct_{ori}\|y_{mall}, r)$. Hence, we have that $\mathsf{Verify}(pp, ct_y, OR(y, y_v)) = 1$. The decryption can be done using $sk_x = sk_{EN(x)}$ for $P_{n+d}\,(EN(x), OR(y, y_v)) = P_n(x, y) = 1$. The session key can be correctly recovered with

$$key = \mathsf{Decrypt}(pp, ct_y, OR(y, y_v), sk_x, EN(x)).$$

Performance. Comparing with OO-PIP-KEM, operations for running UColl are additionally required in the online encryption of our CCA2-secure OO-PIP-KEM construction. By properly applying Chameleon hash functions with rather efficient algorithm Coll [22], and by our construction shown in Sect. 5.1, UColl is also efficient. Therefore, the online encryption algorithm remains efficient. The additional communication cost is the extra ciphertext components chk, r, both of which have constant size in all existing Chameleon hash instantiations.

5.4   Security Analysis

Our OO-PIP-KEM is CCA2-secure if the underlying LU-PIP-KEM is CPA-secure. The obstacle in the CCA2 security proof is how to respond the decryption queries for ciphertexts associated with the challenge ciphertext attributes y^*.

We overcome this obstacle by using the extended key attribute $x_d \in K_d$ and the extended verification attribute $y_v \in E_d$. In the **Challenge** phase, the challenge attribute for the LU-PIP-KEM challenger is extended to $OR(y^*, y_v^*)$. When the adversary issues a decryption query for a ciphertext ct_y associated with a ciphertext attribute $OR(y^*, y_v)$, where y_v is its verification ciphertext attribute corresponding to ct_y, we first run Verify to check the validity of the ciphertext. The *public-verifiability* ensures that Verify outputs 1 if and only if the ciphertext is honestly generated. Then, we construct a key attribute $x_v \in E_d$ such that $P(x_v, y_v) = 1$, and issues the secret key associated with $ED(x_v) \in K_{n+d}$ to the LU-PIP-KEM challenger. On one hand, the *OR-compatibility* ensures $P_{n+d}(ED(x_v), OR(y^*, y_v)) = P_d(x_v, y_v)$ so that we can use this secret key to decrypt the ciphertext. On the other hand, the universal collision resistance of UCH implies $y_v \neq y_v^*$ except with a negligible probability. Hence, we have $P(ED(x_v), OR(y^*, y_v^*)) = P_d(x_v, y_v^*) = 0$, and the secret key query is valid to the LU-PIP-KEM challenger. The decryption query is perfectly responded.

The universal collision resistance of UCH is crucial for the security proof. Although chk^* in the challenge ciphertext is chosen by the encryptor, and y_v^* is generated honestly, if the Chameleon hash only hash collision resistance property, it is possible for the adversary to replace chk^* to others of its choice, while remaining y_v^* unchange. In detail, if the Chameleon hash is only collision resistant, after obtaining the challenge ciphertext $ct^* = (\widetilde{ct}_{ori}^*, \widetilde{y}_{mall}^*, chk^*, r^*)$, the adversary can replace chk^* with a hash key $chk'_\mathcal{A}$ of its own choice, for which it knows its trapdoor $td'_\mathcal{A}$ in order to construct a ciphertext $ct' = (\widetilde{ct}'_{ori}, \widetilde{y}'_{mall}, chk'_\mathcal{A}, r'_\mathcal{A})$, where $(chk^*, r^*) \neq (chk'_\mathcal{A}, r'_\mathcal{A})$ but $y'_v = y_v^*$. In this case, the decryption oracle would be stuck. The universal collision resistance of the Chameleon hash family prevents the adversary from such attacks since the hash key chk^* is fixed into the hash value and can be verified by the decryption oracle. The formal security proof is shown in the full version of the paper.

Theorem 2. *The proposed OO-PIP-KEM is CCA2-secure if the underlying CPA-secure LU-PIP-KEM has the properties of attribute-malleability, public-verifiability and OR-compatibility.*

6   Instantiations

Our OO-PIP-KEM transformations can apply to existing LU-PIPE schemes, including OO-IBE schemes proposed by Guo *et al.* [17], and OO-ABE schemes proposed by Hohenberger and Waters [18]. In addition, one can illustratively instantiate a new OO-PIP-KEM scheme by applying our transformation to a LU-PIP-KEM scheme. In 2010, Lewko, Sahai and Waters proposed a revocation encryption (RE) scheme [23]. The ciphertext is associated with an identity set of revoked users. Users who are not in the revoked set can decrypt. It can be shown that their RE satisfies *attribute-malleability* and *public-verifiability*. Hence, one can obtain an OO-RE scheme in the KEM setting by following our generic transformation.

7   Conclusion

We provided a general framework for constructing CCA2-secure OO-PIPE. We proposed a generic transformation from attribute-malleable LU-PIP-KEM to OO-PIP-KEM with CPA security. We further transformed CPA-secure LU-PIP-KEM to CCA2-secure OO-PIP-KEM at the cost of a Chameleon hash, assuming the underlying LU-PIP-KEM has *attribute-malleability* and *public-verifiability*.

Acknowledgement. This paper is supported by the Natural Science Foundation of China through projects 61370190, 61272501, 61402029, 61472429, 61202465 and 61532021, by the Guangxi natural science foundation through project 2013GXNSFBB053005. K. Liang is supported by privacy-aware retrieval and modelling of genomic data (No. 13283250), the Academy of Finland.

References

1. Abdalla, M., et al.: Searchable encryption revisited: consistency properties, relation to anonymous IBE, and extensions. In: Shoup, V. (ed.) CRYPTO 2005. LNCS, vol. 3621, pp. 205–222. Springer, Heidelberg (2005)

2. Bethencourt, J., Sahai, A., Waters, B.: Ciphertext-policy attribute-based encryption. In: S&P 2007, pp. 321–334 (2007)
3. Boneh, D., Boyen, X.: Efficient selective-ID secure identity-based encryption without random oracles. In: Cachin, C., Camenisch, J.L. (eds.) EUROCRYPT 2004. LNCS, vol. 3027, pp. 223–238. Springer, Heidelberg (2004)
4. Boneh, D., Boyen, X., Goh, E.-J.: Hierarchical identity based encryption with constant size ciphertext. In: Cramer, R. (ed.) EUROCRYPT 2005. LNCS, vol. 3494, pp. 440–456. Springer, Heidelberg (2005)
5. Boneh, D., Franklin, M.: Identity-based encryption from the weil pairing. In: Kilian, J. (ed.) CRYPTO 2001. LNCS, vol. 2139, pp. 213–229. Springer, Heidelberg (2001)
6. Boneh, D., Sahai, A., Waters, B.: Functional encryption: definitions and challenges. In: Ishai, Y. (ed.) TCC 2011. LNCS, vol. 6597, pp. 253–273. Springer, Heidelberg (2011)
7. Boyen, X., Mei, Q., Waters, B.: Direct chosen ciphertext security from identity-based techniques. In: CCS 2005, pp. 320–329. ACM (2005)
8. Canetti, R., Halevi, S., Katz, J.: Chosen-ciphertext security from identity-based encryption. In: Cachin, C., Camenisch, J.L. (eds.) EUROCRYPT 2004. LNCS, vol. 3027, pp. 207–222. Springer, Heidelberg (2004)
9. Cheung, L., Newport, C.: Provably secure ciphertext policy abe. In: CCS 2007, pp. 456–465. ACM (2007)
10. Chow, S.S.M., Liu, J.K., Zhou, J.: Identity-based online/offline key encapsulation and encryption. In: Cheung, B.S.N., Hui, L.C.K., Sandhu, R.S., Wong, D.S. (eds.) ASIACCS 2011, pp. 52–60. ACM (2011)
11. Even, S., Goldreich, O., Micali, S.: On-line/off-line digital signatures. In: Brassard, G. (ed.) CRYPTO 1989. LNCS, vol. 435, pp. 263–275. Springer, Heidelberg (1990)
12. Fiat, A., Naor, M.: Broadcast encryption. In: Stinson, D.R. (ed.) CRYPTO 1993. LNCS, vol. 773, pp. 480–491. Springer, Heidelberg (1994)
13. Fujisaki, E., Okamoto, T.: Secure integration of asymmetric and symmetric encryption schemes. In: Wiener, M. (ed.) CRYPTO 1999. LNCS, vol. 1666, pp. 537–554. Springer, Heidelberg (1999)
14. Gentry, C.: Practical identity-based encryption without random oracles. In: Vaudenay, S. (ed.) EUROCRYPT 2006. LNCS, vol. 4004, pp. 445–464. Springer, Heidelberg (2006)
15. Goyal, V., Pandey, O., Sahai, A., Waters, B.: Attribute-based encryption for fine-grained access control of encrypted data. In: CCS 2006, pp. 89–98. ACM (2006)
16. Green, M., Hohenberger, S.: Blind identity-based encryption and simulatable oblivious transfer. In: Kurosawa, K. (ed.) ASIACRYPT 2007. LNCS, vol. 4833, pp. 265–282. Springer, Heidelberg (2007)
17. Guo, F., Mu, Y., Chen, Z.: Identity-based online/offline encryption. In: Tsudik, G. (ed.) FC 2008. LNCS, vol. 5143, pp. 247–261. Springer, Heidelberg (2008)
18. Hohenberger, S., Waters, B.: Online/offline attribute-based encryption. In: Krawczyk, H. (ed.) PKC 2014. LNCS, vol. 8383, pp. 293–310. Springer, Heidelberg (2014)
19. Huan, J., Yang, Y., Huang, X., Yuen, T.H., Li, J., Cao, J.: Accountable mobile e-commerce scheme via identity-based plaintext-checkable encryption. Inf. Sci. 345, 143–155 (2016)
20. Huang, X., Liu, J.K., Tang, S., Xiang, Y., Liang, K., Xu, L., Zhou, J.: Cost-effective authentic and anonymous data sharing with forward security. IEEE Trans. Comput. 64(4), 971–983 (2015)
21. Katz, J., Sahai, A., Waters, B.: Predicate encryption supporting disjunctions, polynomial equations, and inner products. In: Smart, N.P. (ed.) EUROCRYPT 2008. LNCS, vol. 4965, pp. 146–162. Springer, Heidelberg (2008)

22. Krawczyk, H., Rabin, T.: Chameleon signatures. In: NDSS 2000. The Internet Society (2000)

23. Lewko, A., Sahai, A., Waters, B.: Revocation systems with very small private keys. In: S&P 2010, pp. 273–285. IEEE (2010)

24. Lewko, A., Waters, B.: New techniques for dual system encryption and fully secure HIBE with short ciphertexts. In: Micciancio, D. (ed.) TCC 2010. LNCS, vol. 5978, pp. 455–479. Springer, Heidelberg (2010)

25. Lewko, A., Waters, B.: Decentralizing attribute-based encryption. In: Paterson, K.G. (ed.) EUROCRYPT 2011. LNCS, vol. 6632, pp. 568–588. Springer, Heidelberg (2011)

26. Lewko, A., Waters, B.: New proof methods for attribute-based encryption: achieving full security through selective techniques. In: Safavi-Naini, R., Canetti, R. (eds.) CRYPTO 2012. LNCS, vol. 7417, pp. 180–198. Springer, Heidelberg (2012)

27. Liu, J.K., Zhou, J.: An efficient identity-based online/offline encryption scheme. In: Abdalla, M., Pointcheval, D., Fouque, P.-A., Vergnaud, D. (eds.) ACNS 2009. LNCS, vol. 5536, pp. 156–167. Springer, Heidelberg (2009)

28. Liu, W., Liu, J., Wu, Q., Qin, B., Zhou, Y.: Practical direct chosen ciphertext secure key-policy attribute-based encryption with public ciphertext test. In: Kutyłowski, M., Vaidya, J. (eds.) ICAIS 2014, Part II. LNCS, vol. 8713, pp. 91–108. Springer, Heidelberg (2014)

29. Liu, Z., Xu, L., Chen, Z., Mu, Y., Guo, F.: Hierarchical identity-based online/offline encryption. In: ICYCS 2008, pp. 2115–2119. IEEE (2008)

30. Okamoto, T., Takashima, K.: Fully secure functional encryption with general relations from the decisional linear assumption. In: Rabin, T. (ed.) CRYPTO 2010. LNCS, vol. 6223, pp. 191–208. Springer, Heidelberg (2010)

31. Okamoto, T., Takashima, K.: Fully secure unbounded inner-product and attribute-based encryption. In: Wang, X., Sako, K. (eds.) ASIACRYPT 2012. LNCS, vol. 7658, pp. 349–366. Springer, Heidelberg (2012)

32. Rouselakis, Y., Waters, B.: Practical constructions and new proof methods for large universe attribute-based encryption. In: CCS 2013, pp. 463–474. ACM (2013)

33. Sahai, A., Waters, B.: Fuzzy identity-based encryption. In: Cramer, R. (ed.) EUROCRYPT 2005. LNCS, vol. 3494, pp. 457–473. Springer, Heidelberg (2005)

34. Shamir, A.: Identity-based cryptosystems and signature schemes. In: Blakely, G.R., Chaum, D. (eds.) CRYPTO 1984. LNCS, vol. 196, pp. 47–53. Springer, Heidelberg (1985)

35. Shamir, A., Tauman, Y.: Improved online/offline signature schemes. In: Kilian, J. (ed.) CRYPTO 2001. LNCS, vol. 2139, pp. 355–367. Springer, Heidelberg (2001)

36. Waters, B.: Dual system encryption: realizing fully secure IBE and HIBE under simple assumptions. In: Halevi, S. (ed.) CRYPTO 2009. LNCS, vol. 5677, pp. 619–636. Springer, Heidelberg (2009)

37. Yamada, S., Attrapadung, N., Hanaoka, G., Kunihiro, N.: Generic constructions for chosen-ciphertext secure attribute based encryption. In: Catalano, D., Fazio, N., Gennaro, R., Nicolosi, A. (eds.) PKC 2011. LNCS, vol. 6571, pp. 71–89. Springer, Heidelberg (2011)

38. Yamada, S., Attrapadung, N., Santoso, B., Schuldt, J.C.N., Hanaoka, G., Kunihiro, N.: Verifiable predicate encryption and applications to CCA security and anonymous predicate authentication. In: Fischlin, M., Buchmann, J., Manulis, M. (eds.) PKC 2012. LNCS, vol. 7293, pp. 243–261. Springer, Heidelberg (2012)

39. Yeh, L., Huang, J.: Pbs: a portable billing scheme with fine-grained access control for service-oriented vehicular networks. IEEE Trans. Mob. Comput. **13**(11), 2606–2619 (2014)

Author Index

Printed in the United States
by Bookmasters

Printed in the United States
By Bookmasters